The Routledge Reviewer's Guide to Mixed Methods Analysis

The Routledge Reviewer's Guide to Mixed Methods Analysis is a groundbreaking edited book – the first devoted solely to mixed methods research analyses, or mixed analyses. Each of the 30 seminal chapters, authored by internationally renowned scholars, provides a simple and practical introduction to a method of mixed analysis.

Each chapter demonstrates "how to conduct the analysis" in easy-to-understand language. Many of the chapters present new topics that have never been written before, and all chapters offer cutting-edge approaches to analysis. The book contains the following four sections: Part I Quantitative Approaches to Qualitative Data (e.g., factor analysis of text, multidimensional scaling of qualitative data); Part II Qualitative Approaches to Quantitative Data (e.g., qualitizing data, mixed methodological discourse analysis); Part III "Inherently" Mixed Analysis Approaches (e.g., qualitative comparative analysis, mixed methods social network analysis, social media analytics as mixed analysis, GIS as mixed analysis); and Part IV Use of Software for Mixed Data Analysis (e.g., QDA Miner, WordStat, MAXQDA, NVivo, SPSS).

The audience for this book includes (a) researchers, evaluators, and practitioners who conduct a variety of research projects and who are interested in using innovative analyses that will allow them to extract more from their data; (b) academics, including faculty who would use this book in their scholarship, as well as in their graduate-level courses, and graduate students who need access to a comprehensive set of mixed analysis tools for their dissertations/theses and other research assignments and projects; and (c) computer-assisted data analysis software developers who are seeking additional mixed analyses to include within their software programs.

Anthony J. Onwuegbuzie holds the following positions: Senior Research Associate, Faculty of Education, University of Cambridge, England; Distinguished Visiting Professor, Department of Educational Leadership and Management/Department of Educational Psychology, University of Johannesburg, Johannesburg, South Africa; Honorary Professor, University of South Africa; Visiting Senior Scholar, St. John's University, New York; and Honorary Recognised Supervisor (Online), School of Histories, Languages and Cultures, University of Liverpool. He writes extensively on qualitative, quantitative, and mixed methodological topics. With an h-index of 100, he has had published more than 500 works, including more than 350 journal articles, 60 book chapters, and six books. He has delivered more than 1,000 presentations, 250 methodological workshops, and 60 keynote addresses worldwide.

R. Burke Johnson (PhD, University of Georgia, Research, Evaluation, Measurement, and Statistics Program) is a Professor in the Department of Counseling and Instructional Sciences, University of South Alabama. He has graduate degrees in methodology, psychology, sociology, and public policy, which give him a multidisciplinary perspective on research methodology. He is coauthor/coeditor of nine books.

The Routledge Reviewer's Guide to Mixed Methods Analysis

Edited by

ANTHONY J. ONWUEGBUZIE

R. BURKE JOHNSON

Routledge
Taylor & Francis Group
NEW YORK AND LONDON

First published 2021
by Routledge
52 Vanderbilt Avenue, New York, NY 10017

and by Routledge
2 Park Square, Milton Park, Abingdon, Oxon, OX14 4RN

Routledge is an imprint of the Taylor & Francis Group, an informa business

© 2021 Taylor & Francis

The right of Anthony J. Onwuegbuzie and R. Burke Johnson to be identified as the author of the editorial material, and of the authors for their individual chapters, has been asserted in accordance with sections 77 and 78 of the Copyright, Designs and Patents Act 1988.

With the exception of Chapter 24, no part of this book may be reprinted or reproduced or utilised in any form or by any electronic, mechanical, or other means, now known or hereafter invented, including photocopying and recording, or in any information storage or retrieval system, without permission in writing from the publishers.

Chapter 24 of this book is available for free in PDF format as Open Access from the individual product page at www.routledge.com. It has been made available under a Creative Commons Attribution-Non Commercial-No Derivatives 4.0 license

Trademark notice: Product or corporate names may be trademarks or registered trademarks, and are used only for identification and explanation without intent to infringe.

Library of Congress Cataloging-in-Publication Data
Names: Onwuegbuzie, Anthony J., 1962- editor. | Johnson, R. Burke, editor.
Title: The Routledge reviewer's guide to mixed methods analysis / edited by
Anthony J. Onwuegbuzie and R. Burke Johnson.
Description: New York, NY : Routledge, 2021. | Includes bibliographical
references and index. | Identifiers: LCCN 2020044070 (print) | LCCN 2020044071 (ebook) | ISBN
9781138305267 (hardback) | ISBN 9781138305274 (paperback) | ISBN 9780203729434 (ebook)
Subjects: LCSH: Mixed methods research. | Social sciences–Methodology.
Classification: LCC H62 .R685 2021 (print) | LCC H62 (ebook) | DDC 300.72/1–dc23
LC record available at https://lccn.loc.gov/2020044070

ISBN: 978-1-138-30526-7 (hbk)
ISBN: 978-1-138-30527-4 (pbk)
ISBN: 978-0-203-72943-4 (ebk)

DOI: 10.4324/9780203729434

Typeset in Times
by KnowledgeWorks Global Ltd.

Contents

List of Figures and Tables vii
List of Contributors xiii

1. Mapping the Emerging Landscape of Mixed Analysis 1
   Anthony J. Onwuegbuzie and R. Burke Johnson

Part I Quantitative Approaches to Qualitative Data

2. **Exploratory Factor Analysis of Text** 25
   James Van Haneghan

3. **Correspondence Analysis of Qualitative Data** 37
   Wendy B. Dickinson

4. **Multidimensional Scaling of Qualitative Data** 45
   Ahmet Suerdem

5. **Cluster Analysis for Mixed Methods Research** 57
   Normand Péladeau

6. **Chi-Square Automatic Interaction Detection Analysis of Qualitative Data** 69
   Kathleen M. T. Collins

7. **Multiple Linear Regression Analysis with Qualitative Data that Have Been Quantitized** 77
   Kyle Cox, Richard Lambert, and John H. Hitchcock

8. **Structural Equation Modeling with Qualitative Data that Have Been Quantitized** 89
   David Newman and Shannon Constantinides

9. **Hierarchical Linear Modeling with Qualitative Data that Have Been Quantitized** 99
   John H. Hitchcock, Richard Lambert, and T. Scott Holcomb

10. **Bayesian Analyses with Qualitative Data** 109
    Prathiba Natesan Batley

11. **Item Response Theory Integrating Qualitative Data** 117
    Vanessa Scherman and Linda Liebenberg

12. **Diachronic Analysis of Qualitative Data** 125
    M. Teresa Anguera, Mariona Portell, Antonio Hernández-Mendo, Pedro Sánchez-Algarra, and Gudberg K. Jonsson

Part II Qualitative Approaches to Quantitative Data

13. **Qualitizing Data** 141
    Anthony J. Onwuegbuzie and Nancy L. Leech

14. **Coding Techniques for Quantitative and Mixed Data** 151
    Johnny Saldaña

15. Mixed Methodological Discourse Analysis 161
    Zsuzsanna Géring

Part III "Inherently" Mixed Analysis Approaches

16. Ethnographic Decision Models with Qualitative Data: A Thoroughly Mixed Method 173
    Gery W. Ryan and H. Russell Bernard

17. Qualitative Comparative Analysis (QCA): An Integrative Approach Suited for Diverse Mixed Methods and Multimethod Research Strategies 185
    Benoît Rihoux, Priscilla Álamos-Concha, and Bojana Lobe

18. Q Methodology as Mixed Analysis 199
    Susan Ramlo

19. Social Network Analysis as Mixed Analysis 209
    Dominik E. Froehlich and Jasperina Brouwer

20. Social Media Analytics as Mixed Analysis 219
    Tom Liam Lynch and Hannah R. Gerber

21. Geographic Information Systems as Mixed Analysis 227
    Nigel G. Fielding and Joan M. Verd

22. Nonverbal Communication Analysis as Mixed Analysis 239
    Anthony J. Onwuegbuzie and Sandra Schamroth Abrams

23. Development of a Joint Display as a Mixed Analysis 259
    Michael D. Fetters and Timothy C. Guetterman

24. The Case Comparison Table: A Joint Display for Constructing and Sorting Simple Tables as Mixed Analysis 277
    Judith Schoonenboom and R. Burke Johnson

Part IV Use of Software for Mixed Analysis

25. Mixing Beyond Mixed Methods: QDA Miner, SimStat, and WordStat 291
    Normand Péladeau

26. Using MAXQDA for Mixed Methods Research 305
    Udo Kuckartz and Stefan Rädiker

27. Introduction to Dedoose for Mixed Analysis 319
    Eli Lieber, Michelle Salmona, and Dan Kaczynski

28. Introduction to ATLAS.ti for Mixed Analysis 331
    Brigitte Smit

29. Using NVivo for Mixed Methods Research 343
    Pat Bazeley

30. Introduction to SPSS for Mixed Analysis 355
    Nancy L. Leech

Index 377

List of Figures and Tables

Figures

Figure 1.1	The non-crossover mixed analysis process	4
Figure 2.1	The Wordstat 7 dictionaries page	30
Figure 2.2	Screenshot of options page in Wordstat 7	31
Figure 2.3	Topic modeling screen in Wordstat 7.	31
Figure 2.4	Keywords associated with topics highlighted and shown within context	32
Figure 2.5	Percentage of comments on TRAT and IRAT process in STEM and non-STEM classes	32
Figure 2.6	Percentage of comments surrounding understanding of correct and incorrect answers.	33
Figure 3.1	Parents in prison: Caregiver by gender of incarcerated parent	40
Figure 4.1	Geometrical representation of the idea of distance	47
Figure 4.2	Initial parameters	48
Figure 4.3	Diagnostics for model fit	49
Figure 4.4	Comparing Torgerson with random configurations: Final fit	50
Figure 4.5	INDSCAL results for the media framing of AI	53
Figure 5.1	Dendrogram showing average linkage between words in political speeches	60
Figure 5.2	Illustration of three agglomeration rules	60
Figure 5.3	Silhouette for a six-cluster solution	62
Figure 5.4	Silhouette analysis of 239 participants clustered in 20 groups	63
Figure 5.5	Dendrogram of 81 statements on research in alphabetization	64
Figure 5.6	Silhouette index by number of clusters	65
Figure 5.7	Number of misclassified items by number of clusters	65
Figure 6.1	Themes evolving from undergraduates' perceptions of characteristics of effective college teachers	72
Figure 6.2	Segmentation of student-centered theme as a function of the emergent themes	73
Figure 6.3	Segmentation of ethnicity as a function of the demographic variables	73
Figure 8.1	Path analysis	91
Figure 8.2	Graphical representation of a CFA model	92
Figure 8.3	Latent variable structural equation model	92
Figure 8.4	Latent growth model	92
Figure 10.1	Three distributions with the same mean and standard deviation	110
Figure 10.2	Plot showing the number of problem behaviours for Sam	112
Figure 10.3	Posterior density plot of the rate ratio effect size for problem behaviours	113
Figure 11.1	Item-person map	121
Figure 12.1	Relationships between focal behavior and conditioned behaviors in each quadrant	131
Figure 12.2	The lower part of this figure shows a simple real-time behavior record	131

Figure 12.3	Structure extracted from the lag sequential analysis realized in its basic form by manual calculation	132
Figure 12.4	Graphical representation of the vectors	133
Figure 12.5	Number of individual patterns detected in Question 1	134
Figure 12.6	Pattern found in the Repeaters group concerning Question 1 and 2	134
Figure 13.1	Contrasting 1 + 1 = 3 partial integration and 1 + 1 = 1 full integration in mixed methods research	142
Figure 13.2	Keyword co-occurrence map of responses to the following question	146
Figure 14.1	An Excel spreadsheet of quantitative and qualitative data for the "Lifelong Impact" study	157
Figure 16.1	Decision to recycle cans (ethnographic sample, N = 70)	177
Figure 16.2	Decision to recycle cans—simplified model (ethnographic sample, N = 70)	179
Figure 16.3	Decision to recycle cans (national sample, N = 386)	180
Figure 17.1	Mixed data-informed QCA strategy	187
Figure 17.2	Case-informed QCA strategy	187
Figure 17.3	In-depth case-informed QCA strategy	189
Figure 17.4	QCA-causal process tracing strategy	190
Figure 17.5	QCA-statistical strategy	191
Figure 18.1	Sorting grid used in the views of factor analysis in Q study based on the grid in Ramlo (2019)	202
Figure 19.1	Egocentric and sociocentric networks	210
Figure 19.2	Example of using the concentric circles method for qualitative data collection	212
Figure 21.1	Location and boundaries of the Parc dels Tres Turons in relation to the city districts of Barcelona	232
Figure 21.2	Amendments to the boundaries of the park and the expropriation of houses met in 2009 with regard to the General Metropolitan Plan of 1976	233
Figure 21.3	Adjustment sequence between different options in the urban reordering of the Parc dels Tres Turons	233
Figure 22.1	Dimensions of the Nonverbal Communication Analysis model	241
Figure 22.2	Correspondence analysis of the ten categories of communication vagueness	250
Figure 23.1	Procedural diagram of the convergent mixed methods design of the ADAPT-IT project	263
Figure 23.2	Excerpt from the ADAPT-IT project	263
Figure 23.3	First draft of the ADAPT-IT joint display format	264
Figure 23.4	Box plots based on the responses	266
Figure 23.5	The second iteration of the ADAPT-IT joint display using box plots	267
Figure 23.6	The third iteration of the ADAPT-IT joint display using intuitive restructuring	268
Figure 23.7	The fourth iteration of the ADAPT-IT joint display using color/shading	269
Figure 23.8	The fifth iteration of the ADAPT-IT joint display using labelling	270
Figure 23.9	A meta-joint display figure of three joint displays	271
Figure 23.10	A joint display figure of clinical trial expert opinions	272
Figure 23.11	A joint display figure using progressive grayscale shading	272
Figure 24.1	Heuristic for the analysis of case comparison tables	281
Figure 24.2	Heuristic for the analysis of case comparison tables, applied to Example 1	282
Figure 25.1	QDA Miner main interface	292
Figure 25.2	QDA Miner Timeline feature	295

List of Figures and Tables ix

Figure 25.3	Graphic tools for co-occurrence analysis	297
Figure 25.4	WordStat topic modeling feature	298
Figure 25.5	Deviation table for four candidates of the 2008 U.S. presidential election	299
Figure 25.6	Use of "protest" words versus "riot" words by media	302
Figure 26.1	Points of integration in convergent design (highlighted with circles)	306
Figure 26.2	MAXQDA's Import ribbon tab	307
Figure 26.3	Different qualitative data types in MAXDQA's "Document System" window	308
Figure 26.4	MAQDA's Data Editor for quantitative data	309
Figure 26.5	Results table of crosstab "Employment Status * Region"	310
Figure 26.6	Results table of anova "life satisfaction index * age group"	310
Figure 26.7	MAXQDA's Mixed Methods ribbon tab	311
Figure 26.8	Writing thematic summaries for integrative analysis	312
Figure 26.9	Case map as a joint display for "Case James K"	313
Figure 26.10	Joint display of summaries and variable values	314
Figure 26.11	Schematic structure of the "QUAL Themes by QUAN Groups" display	315
Figure 26.12	Schematic structure of the "number of coded segments for quantitative groups" display (Crosstab)	315
Figure 26.13	Selection dialog for the joint display "Statistics by Qualitative Groups"	316
Figure 26.14	Joint display "Statistics by Qualitative Groups" (Typology Table)	316
Figure 27.1	Building a web of connections	321
Figure 27.2	Primary aspects and connections in a Dedoose project database	323
Figure 27.3	Illustration of navigation from visualization to underlying qualitative content	326
Figure 27.4	Example of excerpt filtering by code weight values	327
Figure 27.5	Snapshot of analysis workspace with descriptor by descriptor by code chart active	328
Figure 28.1	Geo document: University of Pretoria	334
Figure 28.2	An example of a word list from ATLAS.ti 8	336
Figure 28.3	An example of a word cloud from ATLAS.ti 8	337
Figure 28.4	A network of a theme from the literature	339
Figure 29.1	Concept map to show theory of change	345
Figure 29.2	Import options, allowing mixed data types	345
Figure 29.3	Navigation pane, showing data management tools	346
Figure 29.4	Using see also links to connect reflections with source material	347
Figure 29.5	Code retrieval for complementary analysis	348
Figure 29.6	Matrix showing contribution of different sources on topic of physical activity	349
Figure 29.7	Wellbeing for older women—preliminary concept map	350
Figure 29.8	Cross-case analysis using a framework matrix	350
Figure 29.9	Using the Crosstab tool to compare comments	351
Figure 29.10	A case by variable table derived from transformed qualitative coding	352
Figure 29.11	Part of a similarity matrix showing frequency with which pairs of nodes intersect	352
Figure 29.12	Correspondence analysis biplot	353

Figure 29.13	Wellbeing nodes clustered, based on the similarity of words coded into those nodes	353
Figure 30.1	Steps for using SPSS with data from a mixed methods research study	358
Figure 30.2	G*power calculation for Chi-square/Phi test	369
Figure 30.3	A section of the Excel spreadsheet used for classical content analysis	370
Figure 30.4	The Excel spreadsheet edited for importing to SPSS	370
Figure 30.5	Recoding in SPSS	371
Figure 30.6	The data in SPSS	371
Figure 30.7	Visual display of a section of the data split by rural or not rural	372
Figure 30.8	Phi output from SPSS	372
Figure 30.9	Crossover display of results	373

Tables

Table 1.1	Examples of Analytic Techniques, Methods and Approaches	6
Table 1.2	Example of Frequency-Based Inter-Respondent Matrix U	7
Table 1.3	Example of Incident-Based Inter-Respondent Matrix	8
Table 1.4	Example of Intensity-Based Inter-Respondent Matrix	8
Table 2.1	Results of the Factor Analysis of the Benefits of Team-Based Learning Documents	32
Table 3.1	Comprehension + Extension = Mixed Methods Approach	41
Table 3.2	Software Resources for Creating CA Displays	41
Table 7.1	Association Between Family Poverty Percentages and Key Informant Ratings of Implementation Challenges	83
Table 7.2	Model estimated NSLP Percentage by Percentage of Students of Color	84
Table 8.1	Structural Equation Modeling Techniques	90
Table 8.2	SEM Symbols	90
Table 8.3	Key SEM Terms	90
Table 8.4	Checklist of General Technical Points to Consider	94
Table 8.5	CFA Goodness of Fit Indices and Suggested Criteria of Fit	94
Table 9.1	Checklist of General Technical Points to Consider	102
Table 9.2	Association between Quantitative Indicators of Implementation Fidelity and Key Informant Ratings of Implementation Challenges	105
Table 10.1	Descriptives of Posteriors of Parameter Estimates for Sam's Problem Behaviours	112
Table 12.1	Example of Dimensions	127
Table 12.2	Tabular Structure Prepared to Obtain the Code Matrix	128
Table 12.3	Simulated Example of a Record	128
Table 12.4	Profile of the Vectors of each Quadrant	130
Table 12.5	Code Matrix Corresponding to the Systematic Record	132
Table 12.6	Simple and Matching Frequencies	132
Table 12.7	Z Values Obtained Through the HOISAN Program	133
Table 12.8	Length and Angle Parameters	133

List of Figures and Tables xi

Table 12.9	Resources to Learn HOISAN Software	135
Table 13.1	Crossover Display of the Sentiment Analysis Findings	147
Table 15.1	Summary of the Three DA-Approaches	162
Table 16.1	Reasons for Recycling or not Recycling from 21 Informants	176
Table 16.2	Questions Asked in the Recycling Study	178
Table 16.3	Verbatim Justifications for 33 Recycling Choices from Ethnographic Sample	181
Table 17.1	Five Main Strategies for Inserting QCA in Mixed Methods and Multimethod Research	186
Table 18.1	Factor Array with Xs Indicating Association with a Single Factor	203
Table 18.2	Statements that Distinguish Factor 1 from the Other Factors	204
Table 18.3	Statements that Distinguish Factor 2 from the Other Factors	205
Table 22.1	Nonverbal Communication Data: Emotions × Participants	247
Table 22.2	Participant Observations	248
Table 23.1	Checkbox of Considerations	260
Table 23.2	Purpose, Data Sources, Description of the Source, and Outcome of Data	263
Table 24.1	Reconstructed Simple Case Comparison Table	278
Table 24.2	Reconstructed Simple Case Comparison Table	279
Table 26.1	MAXQDA's Tools for the Analysis of Qualitative Data	309
Table 26.2	Template for the Planning of a Qualitative Follow-up	317
Table 27.1	The Basics	322
Table 27.2	Moving on with Dedoose	322
Table 27.3	Advanced Features	323
Table 30.1	A Sample of Mixed Analyses Available to Conduct with SPSS	357
Table 30.2	SPSS Menus for Mixed Analyses	374

List of Contributors

Sandra Schamroth Abrams, PhD, is Professor in the School of Education at St. John's University, New York. Abrams is author/editor of over 70 works, including eight books and six special issues. Abrams serves on multiple editorial boards and is an Associate Editor for the *International Journal of Multiple Research Approaches* and a founding co-editor of the Gaming Ecologies and Pedagogies book series (Brill). Along with Tony Onwuegbuzie, Abrams is co-author of *An Integrated Mixed Methods Approach to Nonverbal Communication Data: A Practical Guide to Collection and Analysis in Online and Offline Spaces* (Routledge).

Priscilla Álamos-Concha is senior research fellow in comparative management at the Nijmegen School of Management (Radboud University, The Netherlands). Her expertise in social research methods such as Qualitative Comparative Analysis (QCA), Process-Tracing, and concept formation, led her to be part of a Trans-Atlantic Platform funded project on why and how social innovation projects carried out in and around multinational companies address inequality in interaction with civil society and government stakeholders. Her substantive research interests comprise among others social innovation scalability, organizational change, social movements and research methods. She is also part of the management team of a global network (www.compasss.org).

M. Teresa Anguera is Emeritus Professor of Methodology of the Behavioral Sciences at the University of Barcelona (Spain). She holds degrees in Psychology and Law, and a Doctorate in Psychology. Since 1972, she has taught various methodological subjects. Her lines of research are observational methodology, mixed methods, and program evaluation. She has coordinated 12 competitive research projects and made numerous publications in journals, books, proceedings, and presentations in international conferences, with more than 16,000 citations, and h-index of 62. She has carried out research stays in Chile, Colombia, USA, Mexico and Portugal. She has directed/co-directed 59 Doctoral Theses already defended.

Prathiba Natesan Batley is a methodologist and statistician who specializes in developing methodological solutions to address real world data problems such as small sample cases, non-normality, dependence of observations, etc. which are generally antithetical to commonly used parametric techniques. She has worked with large data problems that involve latent variable and multilevel modelling, as well as with small data problems such as single case experimental designs. Her interdisciplinary collaborations span across many fields such as medicine, education, geography, marketing, psychology, architecture, library sciences, and management. Recently, she has been developing Bayesian methodologies for single-case designs and mixed methods analyses.

Pat Bazeley is Director of Research Support P/L and Adjunct Professor in the Translational Research and Social Innovation Centre at Western Sydney University. Pat has provided research training and project consulting to academics, students and practitioners across Australia and internationally. Her publications include books, chapters, and articles on qualitative and mixed methods research, with a focus on data analysis and use of software for management and analysis of data. She serves on the Editorial Board of the *Journal of Mixed Methods Research* and was 2015–16 President of the Mixed Methods International Research Association.

H. Russell Bernard is director of the Institute for Social Science Research at Arizona State University and Professor emeritus of anthropology of the University of Florida. His work in network analysis includes helping develop the network scale-up method for estimating the size of uncountable populations and his work in linguistics includes helping indigenous peoples publish books in their ancestral languages. Bernard is the founder and editor of *Field Methods* and is the author or co-author of several texts on research methods. Bernard is the recipient of the Franz Boas Award from the American Anthropological Association and is a member of the U.S. National Academy of Sciences.

Jasperina Brouwer is employed as assistant professor at the Department Educational Sciences at the University of Groningen, The Netherlands. She has expertise in social networks, in particular longitudinal social network analysis. In her work, she combines quantitative with qualitative approaches. She is interested in social capital and small group or team processes in higher education and at the workplace.

Kathleen M. T. Collins, PhD, is a professor in the Department of Curriculum and Instruction at the University of Arkansas at Fayetteville. To date, she has presented more than 100 research papers at international, national, and regional conferences, and she has published more than 80 research articles, book chapters, and encyclopedia chapters. Dr. Collins teaches graduate-level online and face-to-face courses in mixed research. Over the years, she has served as editorial board member and reviewer for international and national refereed journals. Presently, she is past-president of the Mixed Methods International Research Association.

Shannon Constantinides, PhD, MSN, NP-C, FNP, is a sports medicine specialist and Director of Research at the Colorado Center of Orthopedic Excellence in Colorado Springs, CO. In her current role, she is leading research studying surgical practices and outcomes during the Covid-19 pandemic. She received her PhD from Florida Atlantic University, where she focused on the use of applied statistics to study population health and healthcare delivery systems. Dr. Constantinides has publications related to nursing, philosophy, and statistics. She routinely speaks at medical conferences on the topic of "statistics for clinicians."

Kyle Cox is an assistant professor of educational research, measurement, and evaluation at University of North Carolina at Charlotte where he teaches graduate level statistics and research methods courses. His research focuses on improving the feasibility of multilevel studies through design improvements and analytic advancements. This work is particularly applicable in educational research as the methods accommodate the hierarchical structures and complex theories present in educational settings. Specifically, Kyle has investigated statistical power in experimental multilevel mediation and moderation studies and is interested in improving the estimation of multilevel structural equation models when sample sizes are limited.

Wendy B. Dickinson, PhD, provides expertise as an external evaluator for federal granting agencies including National Science Foundation, National Aeronautics and Space Administration, the United States Department of Education, and as Faculty Consultant to Educational Testing Service (AP Statistics). Research interests include data analytics and programming (SAS Global Forum: 2019, 2020) and data visualization (Mixed Methods International Research Association (Trinidad and Tobago: 2019; Japan: 2020)). Artwork exhibitions include Aqua Miami (2015) and Spectrum Miami (2018, 2019). Dr. Dickinson serves as an Editorial Board Member for *International Journal of Multiple Research Approaches* (2019–present).

Michael D. Fetters, MD, MPH, MA, serves as Professor of Family Medicine, Director of the Mixed Methods Program, and Director of the Japanese Family Health Program at the University of Michigan. He is Co-Editor in Chief of the *Journal of Mixed Methods Research* and co-edited a Special Issue on conducting research in primary care in *Family Medicine and Community Health* (2019). His research focuses on cultural influences on medical decision making, health services research, and qualitative and mixed methods research methodology. He authored the book *The Mixed Methods Research Workbook—Activities for Designing, Implementing, and Publishing Projects* (Sage, 2020).

Nigel G. Fielding, BA (Sussex) MA (Kent) PhD (LSE), is Emeritus Professor of Sociology at the University of Surrey, a Fellow of the Academy of Social Sciences, and a member of the Community of Experts of the European Science Foundation. His interests in research methodology include mixed methods, socio-spatial methods, qualitative software, interview methods, field observation, and digitally-mediated fieldwork. Nigel has authored/edited 27 books, many in research methodology, including the *Handbook of Online Research Methods* (Sage, 2018 (second edition), with Grant Blank and Ray Lee).

Dominik E. Froehlich is postdoctoral researcher at the Department of Education and senior lecturer at the Centre for Teacher Education at the University of Vienna. His research focuses on mixed-methods research, social network analysis, mixed-methods social network analysis, informal learning, and innovation.

Hannah R. Gerber, PhD, is an Associate Professor at Sam Houston State University and an Honorary Professor at the University of South Africa. Gerber is currently the President of the International Council for Educational Media. With multiple research awards, including the Divergent Award for Excellence in 21st Century Literacies Research and a two-time recipient of the College of Education Faculty Excellence in Research Award, she has over 80 published works, including five books. Gerber is an Associate Editor for the *International Journal of Multiple Research Approaches* and a founding co-editor of the Gaming Ecologies and Pedagogies book series (Brill).

Zsuzsanna Géring is the director of Future of Higher Education Research Centre at Budapest Business School, Hungary. She received her PhD in Sociology in 2015. Her PhD dissertation gained 'Highly Commended' qualification at Emerald/EFMD Outstanding Doctoral Research Awards in 2018. Her main research relates to corporate social responsibility, organizational communication, and the future of higher education. She is an expert in mixed methodological research designs with a special interest in textual analysis such as content and discourse analysis. Her most recent research has been on a large corpus of higher education institutions' online texts, applying mixed methodological discourse analysis.

Timothy C. Guetterman, PhD, is an applied research methodologist, Assistant Professor, and Associate Director of the Mixed Methods Program at the University of Michigan. His methodological interest is in advancing rigorous methods of quantitative, qualitative, and mixed methods research, particularly strategies for integrating and intersecting qualitative and quantitative research. Funded by the National Institutes of Health (NIH), his applied research investigates informatics technology to improve health communication. Tim is also actively engaged developing research methods capacity through foundation grants and the NIH Mixed Methods Research Training Program for the Health Sciences.

James P. Van Haneghan is professor in the Instructional Design and Development Program at the University of South Alabama where he teaches research methods and learning theory. His scholarly interests surround learning in STEM fields, program evaluation, assessment and motivation. His PhD is in Applied Developmental Psychology from the University of Maryland Baltimore County. Prior to working at the University of South Alabama, he was part of the Educational Psychology program at Northern Illinois University and did postdoctoral work at George Peabody College of Vanderbilt University.

Antonio Hernández-Mendo is a Full Professor at Malaga University and coordinator of the Official Master's Degree in Physical Activity and Sport Research. He has published 265 articles, 14 books and 80 chapters. He has 19 patents.

He has directed 29 doctoral theses. He has given 115 conferences. He is Director of the journal *Cuadernos de Psicología del Deporte*, Guest Associate Editor for *Frontiers and Sustainability* and editor of the *Journal of Sports Psychology*. He is Vice President of the Ibero-American Society of Sports Psychology. He has collaborated with Olympic athletes, sports teams and soccer teams.

John H. Hitchcock, PhD (University at Albany, State University of New York), is a Principal Research Associate at Westat. He specializes in mixed methods evaluations, particularly those used to understand interventions designed to support students with special learning needs. Dr. Hitchcock has served as a co-principal investigator on several randomized controlled trials and research syntheses. He has, to date, co-authored 60+ works on advancing mixed methods research and other topics. Hitchcock has served as an associate editor or board member for *School Psychology Review* since 2011 and he is co-editor in chief of the *International Journal of Multiple Research Approaches*.

T. Scott Holcomb is a doctoral student in the Educational Research, Measurement, and Evaluation program within the College of Education at the University of North Carolina at Charlotte. He works as a graduate research assistant for the *Center for Educational Measurement and Evaluation* at UNC-Charlotte. Prior to beginning his doctoral studies, he was a classroom teacher and interventionist in North Carolina and South Carolina elementary schools. His research interests include assessment, interrater reliability, school accountability, and educational measurement topics.

R. Burke Johnson (PhD, University of Georgia) is a Professor in the Department of Counseling and Instructional Sciences, University of South Alabama. He has graduate degrees in educational research, psychology, sociology, and public policy which give him a multidisciplinary perspective on research methodology. His most recent journal articles address (a) causation in MM research, (b) dialectical pluralism, (c) how to construct an MM research design, (d) MM-grounded theory, and (e) unpacking the philosophy of pragmatism. He is coauthor/coeditor of nine books, including this recent book on MM research: *Integrating Quantitative and Qualitative Approaches in the Social and Behavioral Sciences* (Tashakkori, Johnson, and Teddlie).

Gudberg K. Jonsson, PhD, is a Research Scientist at the Human Behavior Laboratory, University of Iceland. He has been involved in various international research projects related to movement science, cognition and communication, especially concerning the form and structure of human interaction/communication. He also coordinates an international university research network called MASI (Methodology for the Analysis of Social Interaction). His work includes number of publications in books and journals and presentations at international conferences. His academic background is in psychology, methodology and human ethology and he conducted his studies at the University of Iceland, University of Paris and University of Aberdeen.

Dan Kaczynski is a qualitative and mixed methods researcher who is associated with universities in Australia and the United States. He is a professor in the Faculty of Education at the University of Canberra providing supervisory support for doctoral candidates. In addition, he is a senior research fellow with the Institute for Mixed Methods Research and professor emeritus at Central Michigan University. Dan's research interests include technological innovations in qualitative and mixed methods data analysis in the social sciences. He has over 20 years' program evaluation experience and extensive grants experience as principal investigator with over $35 million in awards.

Dr. Udo Kuckartz is a Professor Emeritus of Methods of Social Research in Education at the Philipps-Universität Marburg, Germany. His research focuses on qualitative and quantitative methods, mixed methods and visualization of social science research data. He has published more than 20 textbooks in German, English, Spanish, Chinese, and Japanese, among others *Qualitative Text Analysis: A Guide to Methods, Practice and Using Software* and *Analyzing Qualitative Data with MAXQDA: Text, Audio, and Video*.

Richard Lambert, PhD, EdS, is a Professor in the Department of Educational Leadership in the Cato College of Education at the University of North Carolina at Charlotte, Director of the *Center for Educational Measurement and Evaluation,* and editor of the *Journal of Applied Educational Policy Research*. His research interests include formative assessment for young children, applied statistics, and teacher stress and coping. He has recently served as principal investigator for a grant from the North Carolina Office of Early Learning where he and colleagues are investigating the validity of a kindergarten entry assessment.

Nancy L. Leech, PhD, is a professor at the University of Colorado Denver. Her area of research is promoting new developments and better understandings in applied qualitative, quantitative, and mixed methodologies. To date, she has published more than 90 articles in refereed journals, over 20 book chapters, and is co-author of three books: *SPSS for Basic Statistics: Use and Interpretation*; *SPSS for Intermediate Statistics: Use and Interpretation*; and *Research Methods in Applied Settings: An Integrated Approach to Design and Analysis*, all published by Taylor and Francis. Dr. Leech has made more than 100 presentations at regional, national, and international conferences.

Eli Lieber is an Associate Research Psychologist at UCLA where he has spent over 20 years focused on the advancement of thinking about and strategically implementing qualitative and mixed methods approaches in social science research. Trained as a quantitative psychologist, he soon embraced the complementary value of qualitative methods and recognized the challenges to conducting efficient and collaborative mixed methods research. As president of Dedoose.com and vice president of the Institute for Mixed Methods Research, he works to develop and promote the appropriate and informed use of technologies to enhance the effectiveness of mixed methods research across the social sciences.

Linda Liebenberg, PhD, is a researcher and evaluator with a core interest in children and youth with complex needs, and the communities they live in. Her work explores the promotion of positive youth development and mental health through civic engagement and community development. As a key component of this work, Linda reflects critically on how best to conduct research and evaluations with children and their communities, including participatory image-based methods; sophisticated longitudinal quantitative designs; and the design of measurement instruments used with children and youth. Linda has presented internationally and published extensively on these topics of research and youth.

Bojana Lobe is an Assistant Professor at the Faculty of Social Sciences, University of Ljubljana (UL), where she teaches a number of methodological courses. Her research interests include online qualitative research methods, integration of qualitative and quantitative methods online, qualitative comparative analysis, researching children's experiences and digital technologies. She has authored a book Integration of Online Research Methods. She is a member of the research programme Social Science Methodology, Statistics and Informatics at UL. Dr. Lobe is a member of the editorial board of *International Journal of Multiple Research Approaches*.

Tom Liam Lynch is Director of Education Policy at the Center for New York City Affairs at The New School and Editor-in-Chief of the website InsideSchools. A former educational technology professor, English teacher, and school district official for the New York City Department of Education, Lynch has written dozens of articles and presented the world over on educational technologies, online learning, school reform, new literacies, and K–12 computer science.

David Newman, PhD, is an Associate Professor and biostatistician/research methodologist at Christine E. Lynn College of Nursing, Florida Atlantic University. He is also one of six faculty assigned to the Biostatistician Core at FAU. This core helps to support research across the university. Dr. Newman has more than 70 scholarly publications (journal articles and textbook chapters). In addition to teaching advanced statistics and research methodology classes in the PhD and DNP programs, he is the principal investigator or co-investigator on multiple National Institutes of Health grants as well as other federal, state, and foundation funded grants.

Anthony J. Onwuegbuzie is a Senior Research Associate at the University of Cambridge. Further, he is a Distinguished Visiting Professor at the University of Johannesburg; an Honorary Professor at the University of South Africa; a Visiting Senior Scholar, St. John's University, New York; and an Honorary Recognised Supervisor (Online), University of Liverpool. He writes extensively on qualitative, quantitative, and mixed methodological topics. With an h-index of 100, he has had published more than 500 works, including more than 350 journal articles, 60 book chapters, and six books. He has delivered more than 1,000 presentations, 250 methodological workshops, and 60 keynote addresses worldwide.

Normand Péladeau is the president and CEO of Provalis Research, a software company based in Montreal. Normand Péladeau has a doctorate degree in psychology and more than 35 years of experience as a social science researcher and as a consultant in research methodology for large corporations, governmental agencies, and international organization. Dr. Péladeau has trained thousands of people in text analysis techniques in a wide range of applications, such as business intelligence, market research, urban planning, aviation safety, media analysis, survey research, and international crime analysis.

Mariona Portell is Associate Professor in the Department of Psychobiology and Methodology of Health Sciences at the Autonomous University of Barcelona (Spain). Her research interests include research design and program evaluation, systematic observation and research methods for studying everyday life, and risk prevention and health promotion. Her work includes a number of relevant publications in books, journals and proceedings and presentations at international conferences. She has led research projects about teaching of research methods (teaching innovation). Since 2010, she is a member of the international research team on observational methodology and mixed methods led by Professor M. Teresa Anguera.

Dr. Stefan Rädiker is a consultant and trainer for research methods and evaluation. He holds a degree in educational sciences and his research focuses on the computer-assisted analysis of qualitative and mixed methods data with the analysis software MAXQDA. He has published more than seven textbooks in German, English, Spanish and Chinese, among others *Analyzing Qualitative Data with MAXQDA: Text, Audio, and Video* and *Focused Analysis of Qualitative Interviews with MAXQDA: Step by Step* (both with Udo Kuckartz).

Susan Ramlo is a physicist and education researcher recognized as an international expert of Q methodology. Susan has held various leadership positions within the international Q research society, International Society for the Scientific Study of Subjectivity. She has a YouTube channel dedicated to assisting researchers interested in Q methodology (Sue-Z Q). Ramlo is currently an independent researcher in Northeast Ohio, USA. Previously she spent 26 years at The University of Akron as a Professor of General Technology – Physics. Prior to becoming an academic 26 years ago, Ramlo worked as an industrial physicist in the radiation detection industry.

Benoît Rihoux is full professor in comparative politics at the University of Louvain (UCLouvain, Belgium), where he chairs the Centre for political science and comparative politics (CESPOL). His substantive research interests comprise among others political parties, political behavior, organizational change, social movements, gender and politics, and professional ethics. He plays a leading role in the development of configurational comparative methods and QCA (Qualitative Comparative Analysis), co-ordinates a global network (www.compasss.org) in that field and has published multiple related

List of Contributors

pieces including a reference textbook (Sage 2009; with Charles Ragin). He is also joint Academic convenor of the ECPR Methods School.

Gery W. Ryan is a professor in Health Systems Science at the Kaiser Permanente Bernard J. Tyson School of Medicine. Before joining Kaiser Permanente, he was a Senior Behavioral Scientist at the RAND Corporation and served as Assistant Dean of Academics at the Pardee RAND Graduate School in Policy Analysis. Trained as a medical anthropologist and methodologist, his research spans mental and physical health and includes work on HIV/AIDS, homelessness, depression, serious mental illness, childhood illnesses, obesity, social networks, human trafficking and complementary and alternative medicine. He has also spent extensive time in Africa, Latin America, and the Middle East addressing health and education-related problems. As a methodologist and evaluator, he specializes in the integration of qualitative and quantitative methodologies; designing, implementing and assessing complex system interventions; and quality-improvement projects. Dr. Ryan has taught graduate courses and mentored clinical researchers in advanced ethnographic methods; run qualitative workshops sponsored by NSF, NIH, CDC and WHO; and co-authored a comprehensive textbook on text analysis.

Johnny Saldaña is Professor Emeritus from Arizona State University's School of Film, Dance, and Theatre. He is the author of *Longitudinal Qualitative Research: Analyzing Change through Time*, *Fundamentals of Qualitative Research*, *The Coding Manual for Qualitative Researchers*, *Thinking Qualitatively: Methods of Mind*, *Ethnotheatre: Research from Page to Stage*, *Writing Qualitatively: The Selected Works of Johnny Saldaña*, co-author with the late Miles and Huberman for *Qualitative Data Analysis: A Methods Sourcebook*, and co-author with Matt Omasta for *Qualitative Research: Analyzing Life*. Saldaña's qualitative methods works have been cited and referenced in more than 18,000 research studies conducted in over 130 countries.

Michelle Salmona is President of the Institute for Mixed Methods Research and an international consultant in: program evaluation; research design; and mixed-methods and qualitative data analysis using data applications. Michelle is also an Adjunct Professor at the University of Canberra, Australia, specializing in qualitative and mixed methods research. As a project management professional and a senior fellow of the Higher Education Academy, UK, her research focus is to better understand how to support doctoral success through strengthening the research process and build data-driven decision-making capacity through technological innovation.

Pedro Sánchez-Algarra, PhD, is Emeritus Professor of Statistics at the University of Barcelona (Spain). He has a degree in Physical Sciences, Educational Sciences, and Economics. Since 1974 he has taught multiple subjects in Statistics, Algebra, Analysis, and Multivariate Analysis. His current lines of research are located in Mathematical Statistics and in Applications of Statistics in Social Sciences (analysis of variance, regression analysis, discriminant analysis, cluster analysis), and more specifically in observational studies. His work includes relevant publications in books and journals and presentations at international conferences. Currently is participating in consolidated and financed projects led by M. Teresa Anguera.

Vanessa Scherman been working at the University of South Africa since 2015, previously being employed at the University of Pretoria. Her fields of expertise are psychometrics as well as school effectiveness research, specifically related to psychosocial support and socio-emotional learning in schools. Previously as part of her work on school effectiveness studies, she worked extensively on the adaptation and implementation of monitoring frameworks as well as exploring the influence of relationships within the school context on the achievement of learners. She has collaborated with National and Provincial Departments of Education. She has served on national and international committees such as the UMALUSI Accreditation Committee, Psychological Society in South Africa Research Methodology Division and Chair of Governance of the Mixed Methods International Research Association.

Judith Schoonenboom holds the chair for empirical pedagogy at the University of Vienna, Austria. She has wide experience in designing and evaluating innovations in education. Judith specializes in mixed methods research in education, with a focus on mixed methods design and the foundations of mixed methods research. Since 2014, she has held around 20 invited workshops on mixed methods research design. In the academic year 2020–2021, Judith is the President of the Mixed Methods International Research Association (MMIRA). She co-organized the 2018 MMIRA global conference in Vienna. Judith is associate editor of the Journal of Mixed Methods Research.

Brigitte Smit (PhD, MEd Cum Laude, Bed (Hons), BA(Ed), University of Pretoria) is currently an Assistant Adjunct Professor at the University of Alberta, Canada and a Visiting Professor at the University of Johannesburg. Brigitte is a twice National Research Foundation Rated Researcher, a Senior Accredited Professional Trainer of ATLAS.ti, and former Research Professor in Educational Leadership and Management, at the University of South Africa. Her research focuses on qualitative research methodology, female leadership and relational ethics. She serves as a co-editor of the *International Journal of Multiple Research Approaches*, and as editor (Africa) for the *International Journal of Qualitative Methods*.

Ahmet Suerdem is currently a research advisor at Istanbul Bilgi University and is a Senior Academic visitor at LSE Psychological and Behavioural Sciences department. He has received his Educational Sciences doctorate from Paris 8 University. He was a Post-Doc fellow at Paris 5, Social Anthropology department and Visiting Research Fellow at the UCLA and UCI, Marketing departments. His areas of expertise include science in society, text mining, social network analysis, multivariate statistical analysis, and bridging qualitative and quantitative research methods. He is an expert in many statistical and qualitative data analysis software and coding tools such as R and Python.

Joan M. Verd is Associate Professor in the Department of Sociology at the Autonomous University of Barcelona (UAB). He holds BAs in Political Science and Sociology (1994) and Economics and Business Studies (1996) and a PhD in Sociology (2002). He is director of the Sociological Research Centre on Everyday Life and Work (QUIT) since 2013 and a member of the Institute for Labour Studies (IET) since its foundation in 2011. His research interests focus on Sociology of Labour (social capital and employment, youth and the labour market) and Research Methods (social network analysis, mixed methods, computer assisted qualitative data analysis).

1

Mapping the Emerging Landscape of Mixed Analysis

Anthony J. Onwuegbuzie and R. Burke Johnson

1 Definition of Mixed Analysis

Data analysis in mixed methods research—more commonly known as *mixed methods analysis*, or, more simply, as *mixed analysis*—is considered by many, if not most, beginning researchers and emergent researchers to be the most difficult step of the mixed methods research process. Even many experienced researchers find this step to be challenging. This challenge stems from the fact that mixed analysis typically necessitates competence in conducting both quantitative data analyses and qualitative data analyses. Quantitative data analyses include the fields of *frequentist parametric statistical analysis* (i.e., involving statistical inference wherein the assumption of the analyst is that sample data come from a population that can be adequately modeled by a probability distribution that has a fixed set of parameters; e.g., Field, 2018; Geisser, 2006), *frequentist nonparametric statistical analysis* (i.e., involving statistical inference wherein the assumption of the analyst is that sample data come from a population that can be adequately modeled by a probability distribution in which the set of parameters is not fixed; e.g., Gibbons, 1993; Hollander, Wolfe, & Chicken, 2014; Leech & Onwuegbuzie, 2019; Noether, 2012; Siegel, 1956), *Bayesian statistical analysis* (i.e., involving the use of Bayes's theorem to update the probability for a hypothesis as more evidence or information becomes available; e.g., Gelman et al., 2013; Gill, 2014; Lynch, 2007; see Chapter 10, this volume), *fiducial inference analysis* (i.e., involving making probabilistic statements about values of unknown parameters; based on the distribution of population values about which the inference is to be made; see, for e.g., Cui & Hannig, 2019), and *randomization tests/permutation tests/exact tests* (i.e., a testing method that not only is nonparametric/distribution free but also produces tests that are *exact*, inasmuch as it has exactly the significance level that the analyst desires, regardless of size of the sample; Howell, 2017), as well as *psychometric analyses* (e.g., Rasch analysis [e.g., Andrich, 1988; Bond & Fox, 2015], item response theory [e.g., Baker, 2001; Hambleton, Swaminathan, & Rogers, 1991; see also Chapter 11, this volume]). Qualitative data analyses include qualitative analysis approaches (i.e., whole systems of data analyses that typically originated from a specific qualitative research methodology/theoretical framework; e.g., constant comparison analysis that emanated from grounded theory; cf. Glaser, 1965; Glaser & Strauss, 1967), qualitative analysis methods (i.e., data analyses that represent part of an approach or system; e.g., Miles and Huberman's [1994] array of within-case analyses and cross-case analyses; see also Miles, Huberman, and Saldaña [2020]), and qualitative analysis techniques (i.e., data analyses that represent a single step, or procedure, in the qualitative data analysis process; e.g., Saldaña's (2016) 33 coding strategies).

Onwuegbuzie, Leech, and Collins (2011) made the following observation:

> a mixed research study might involve any one of the 58 classes of quantitative data analysis approaches and any one of the 60 qualitative data analysis approaches/techniques [that they identified]. Thus, if a researcher were to utilize only one quantitative analysis technique and one qualitative analysis technique within what can be termed as a mixed analysis framework, he/she would have at least 3,480 (i.e., 58 × 60) combinations of quantitative and qualitative analysis techniques from which to choose. This number of combination increases exponentially when classes of nonparametric quantitative analyses and classes of Bayesian analyses are included. Further, the number of combinations increases exponentially for mixed research studies in which at least two quantitative data analysis approaches/techniques and/or at least two qualitative data analysis techniques are used. (pp. 6–7)

Although, as can be seen, there are numerous ways of conducting quantitative analysis of quantitative data (*quantitative monoanalysis*) and qualitative analysis of qualitative data (*qualitative monoanalysis*), many of these analyses can be learned by taking graduate-level quantitative research courses (e.g., statistics, measurement) and qualitative research courses, as well as workshops, webinars, and the like. Further, numerous textbooks, journal articles, websites, YouTube videos, and the like are available that explain at least some of these analyses. Therefore, (beginning) researchers have numerous avenues for learning how to conduct an array of quantitative and qualitative analyses. However, albeit being an important component, mixing or integrating findings stemming from the quantitative monoanalysis and qualitative monoanalysis is not the only way of conducing a mixed analysis. Indeed, this form of mixed analysis represents the most basic form.

As conceptualized by Onwuegbuzie and Combs (2010),

> Mixed analysis involves the use of both quantitative and qualitative analytical techniques within the same framework, which is guided either a priori, a posteriori, or iteratively (representing analytical decisions that occur both prior to the study and during the study). It might be based on one of the existing mixed methods research paradigms (e.g., pragmatism, transformative-emancipatory) such that it meets one of more of the following rationales/purposes: triangulation, complementarity, development, initiation, and expansion. Mixed analyses involve the analysis of one or both data types (i.e., quantitative data *or* qualitative data; or quantitative data *and* qualitative data), which occur either concurrently (i.e., in no chronological order), or sequentially in two phases (in which the qualitative analysis phase precedes the quantitative analysis phase or vice versa, and findings from the initial analysis phase inform the subsequent phase) or more than two phases (i.e., iteratively). The analysis strands might not interact until the data interpretation stage yielding a basic parallel mixed analysis, although more complex forms of parallel mixed analysis can be used, in which interaction takes place in a limited way before the data interpretation phase. The mixed analysis can be designed based, wherein it is directly linked to the mixed methods design (e.g., sequential mixed analysis techniques used for sequential mixed methods designs). Alternatively, the mixed analysis can be phase based, in which the mixed analysis takes place in one or more phases (e.g., data transformation). In mixed analyses, either the qualitative or quantitative analysis strands might be given priority or approximately equal priority as a result of a priori decisions (i.e., determined at the research conceptualization phase) or decisions that emerge during the course of the study (i.e., a posteriori or iterative decisions). The mixed analysis could represent case-oriented, variable-oriented, and process/experience-oriented analyses. The mixed analysis is guided by an attempt to analyze data in a way that yields at least one of five types of generalizations (i.e., external statistical generalizations, internal statistical generalizations, analytical generalizations, case-to-case transfer, naturalistic generalization). At its most integrated form, the mixed analysis might involve some form of cross-over analysis, wherein one or more analysis types associated with one tradition (e.g., qualitative analysis) are used to analyze data associated with a different tradition (e.g., quantitative data). (pp. 425–426)

Of most importance for this book is the last sentence, namely, that "At its most integrated form, the mixed analysis might involve some form of cross-over analysis, wherein one or more analysis types associated with one tradition (e.g., qualitative analysis) are used to analyze data associated with a different tradition (e.g., quantitative data)" (p. 426)—which Onwuegbuzie and Combs (2010) refer to as a *cross-over mixed analysis*, hereafter referred to as *crossover mixed analysis*.

Now, with respect to mixed analysis, we have four basic formulae:

Mixed analysis = non-crossover mixed analysis + crossover mixed analysis (1)

Non-crossover mixed analysis = quantitative analysis of quantitative data + qualitative analysis of qualitative data (2)

Quantitative monoanalysis = quantitative analysis of quantitative data (3)

Qualitative monoanalysis = qualitative analysis of qualitative data (4)

Crossover mixed analysis = (quantitative analysis of qualitative data) ∪ (qualitative analysis of quantitative data) ∪ (quantitative analysis of quantitative data + qualitative data) ∪ (qualitative analysis of quantitative data + qualitative data) ∪ (qualitative analysis ∪ quantitative analysis of multidata) (5)

where in, using set theory notation, ∪ is the Union of all five sets of parenthetical elements in Equation 5 (i.e., it contains any of the following combination of parenthetical elements in Equation 5: Parenthetical Element 1; Parenthetical Element 2; Parenthetical Element 3; Parenthetical Element 4; Parenthetical Element 5; Parenthetical Elements 1 and 2; Parenthetical Elements 1 and 3;……. Parenthetical Elements 1, 2, 3, 4, and 5); and wherein *multidata* (in Parenthetical Element 5)—a term coined by Onwuegbuzie, Gerber, and Abrams (2017, p. 28)—denotes qualitative data and quantitative data that cannot be separated (i.e., both data types co-exist), such as spirituality (i.e., noös) data, which "includes a sense of 'being present with' and empathy…, [that] is not as easily defined, qualified, or quantified"; McLafferty, Slate, & Onwuegbuzie, 2010, p. 58). Equation 1 means that *all* mixed *analyses* will involve some combination of non-crossover mixed analysis and crossover mixed analysis. Specifically, (a) some mixed analyses involve the exclusive use of non-crossover mixed analysis (cf. Equations 2–4)—which currently is the norm; (b) some mixed analyses involve the exclusive use of crossover mixed analysis (cf. Equation 5); and (c) the remaining mixed analyses involve *both* non-crossover mixed analysis and crossover mixed analysis in some combination (cf. Equation 1). As stated previously, there are numerous quantitative- (e.g., statistics, measurement) and qualitative-based research textbooks and other resources to help researchers conduct non-crossover (or traditional) form of mixed analyses (i.e., Point a; cf. Equations 2–4). However, the other two forms of mixed analyses (i.e., Points b and c) are important for the continued advancement of "truly" mixed analysis and they necessitate guidance in how to conduct crossover mixed analyses. Unfortunately, such guidance is lacking in the literature for this emerging component of mixed analysis. To this end, crossover mixed analysis occupies a central part throughout this book. In fact, virtually every chapter in this book involves, at least to some degree, some form of *crossover mixed analysis*. *A primary purpose of this book is to show the importance of multiple kinds of crossover analyses for mixed methods research and beyond.* As such, we believe that our book represents a seminal book because it is the first book devoted to mixed analysis in general and to crossover mixed analyses in particular.

2 When Use of Mixed Analysis is Appropriate in Mixed Methods Research

Mixed analysis in general and crossover analysis in particular are appropriate in virtually every mixed methods research study. In fact, possibly the only situation in mixed methods research wherein no form of mixed analysis or crossover analysis is appropriate is when

- Both quantitative data and qualitative data are collected, analyzed, and interpreted *independently*. In other words, the quantitative data are quantitatively analyzed and interpreted separately, whereas the qualitative data are qualitatively analyzed and interpreted separately;
- Once both the quantitative component(s) and the qualitative component(s) have been completed, they are often published as separate studies via different outlets;
- If the qualitative and quantitative components are published in the same article, they are presented in different sections with minimal integration (e.g., a Quantitative Results section, followed by a Qualitative Results section, followed by a Quantitative Discussion section, followed by a Qualitative Discussion section; a Quantitative Results section followed by a Quantitative Discussion section, followed by a Qualitative Results section, followed by a Qualitative Discussion section; a Quantitative Results and Discussion section combined, followed by a Qualitative Results and Discussion section combined);
- If the quantitative research component(s) and qualitative research component(s) occur in a parallel manner. Some authors (e.g., Onwuegbuzie & Leech, 2004) refer to this independence as representing a *parallel mixed methods analysis*.

These parallel mixed methods research analyses lead to the quantitative analysis and qualitative analysis not interacting with each other in a meaningful way (although the results might later be integrated)—yielding to what Onwuegbuzie and Combs (2010) referred to as "non-cross-over mixed analyses" (p. 423) or non-crossover analyses (i.e., involving *solely* the quantitative analysis of quantitative data and the qualitative analysis of qualitative data), wherein the mixed analysis process emphasizes pure or traditional qualitative analysis and pure or traditional quantitative analysis. This is an important approach, but a goal of crossover analysis is to motivate us to move beyond a minimalist approach to mixed analysis, and to transition the field into a mixed world where analyses fit the mixed nature of much of the world in which we live. In short, non-crossover mixed analyses represent a lower form of integration than do crossover mixed analyses. As a general rule, we reject what Johnson, Onwuegbuzie, de Waal, Stefurak, and Hildebrand (2017) criticized as a binary "either/or logic" (p. 260) and, instead, recommend the use of a "both-and" logic and the "logic of synthesis/integration" (Johnson, Russo, & Schoonenboom, 2019, p. 143) that is preferred and applied by many mixed methods researchers.

For most other situations in mixed methods research, at the very least, some form of mixed analysis is appropriate, and, in many instances, crossover analysis is an important consideration. In fact, using Onwuegbuzie and Hitchcock's (2020) notion of the decomposition of the non-crossover mixed analysis process (see Figure 1.1), a mixed analysis is used whenever the mixed methods researcher wants to produce what are known as meta-inferences, which includes inferences stemming from both the qualitative and quantitative findings being combined into a coherent whole (Tashakkori & Teddlie, 1998). Figure 1.1 shows that, in situations wherein both quantitative data and qualitative data are collected, meta-inferences can be yielded via a *horizontal mixed analysis* process or a *vertical mixed analysis* process. A *horizontal* mixed analysis process involves a quantitative monoanalysis that yields quantitative findings and a qualitative monoanalysis that yields qualitative findings; however, these quantitative findings and qualitative findings do not interact with each other in any way until the data interpretation phase. The word *horizontal* is appropriate here because this word denotes being side by side or parallel. In contrast, although a *vertical* mixed analysis process also involves a quantitative monoanalysis that yields quantitative findings and a qualitative monoanalysis that yields qualitative findings, these quantitative and qualitative findings interact to some degree during the mixed analysis process. The word *vertical* is used here to denote intersection. For example, a quantitative analysis of a set of examination responses may lead to scores that are used to determine which interview responses are analyzed qualitatively. As such, a major distinction between a vertical mixed analysis process and a horizontal mixed analysis process is that whereas a horizontal mixed analysis process exclusively involves concurrent mixed analyses (or interactive analysis) wherein the quantitative monoanalysis and the qualitative monoanalysis occur independently, in a vertical mixed analysis process, the quantitative monoanalysis and the qualitative monoanalysis typically involve sequential mixed analyses because the emergent quantitative findings and qualitative findings depend on each other to some degree. That is, one or more strands of quantitative findings help to inform one or more strands of qualitative findings to some degree, or vice versa, or is the case of what Li, Marquart, and Zercher (2000) called *cross-tracks analysis* that is characterized by the quantitative monoanalyses and qualitative monoanalyses oscillating continually between both data sets throughout various stages of the mixed analysis process. Therefore, as can be seen, mixed methods researchers have numerous and wide-ranging possibilities for conducting non-crossover mixed analyses alone. In the next and subsequent sections, we focus on crossover mixed analyses because they provide the highest form of integration—hence the focus of our book.

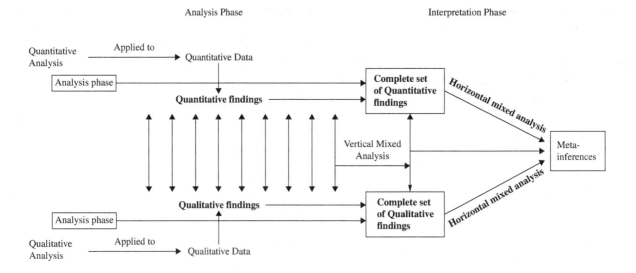

FIGURE 1.1 The non-crossover mixed analysis process decomposed into the vertical mixed analysis (i.e., minimal interaction) process and the horizontal mixed analysis (i.e., full[er] interaction) process.

Adapted from Onwuegbuzie and Hitchcock (2021).

Note: This figure shows that, in situations wherein both quantitative data and qualitative data are collected, meta-inferences can be yielded via a *horizontal* mixed analysis process or a *vertical* mixed analysis process. A horizontal mixed analysis process involves a quantitative monoanalysis (i.e., quantitative analysis of quantitative data) that yields quantitative findings and a qualitative monoanalysis (i.e., qualitative analysis of qualitative data) that yields qualitative findings; however, these quantitative findings and qualitative findings do not interact with each other in any way until the data interpretation phase. The word horizontal is appropriate here because this word denotes being parallel. In contrast, although a vertical mixed analysis process also involves a quantitative monoanalysis that yields quantitative findings and a qualitative monoanalysis that yields qualitative findings, these quantitative and qualitative findings interact to some degree (as represented by the series of vertical lines) during the mixed analysis process. The word vertical is appropriate here because this word denotes intersection.

3 Technical Outline of Mixed Analysis for Mixed Methods Research

Hitchcock and Onwuegbuzie (2020) developed what they called a crossover analysis framework (CAF), which, as they stated, "represents a potentially important advancement to mixed methods analyses because using crossover analyses can support advanced and multi-layered inquiry into social phenomena" (p. 64). An important aspect of their CAF entails distinguishing among analytical *approaches*, *methods*, and *techniques*. According to these authors, *approaches* are data analyses—specifically *macroanalyses*—that represent whole systems in quantitative research, qualitative research, and mixed methods research that can be intermingled. For example, with respect to quantitative research, approaches represent broad systems of analyses that include descriptive analyses, exploratory analyses, measurement, and inferential analyses. In qualitative research, as noted previously, constant comparison analysis (Glaser, 1965) is directly associated with grounded theory (Glaser & Strauss, 1967); similarly, interpretative phenomenological analysis (IPA; Larkin, Watts, & Clifton, 2006; Reid, Flowers, & Larkin, 2005; Smith, 1996, 2011; Smith, Flowers, & Larkin, 2009; Todorova, 2011) emanates from interpretive phenomenological research (Van Manen, 1990). In the context of mixed methods research, analytic approaches refer to broad analytic systems such as concurrent mixed analyses (i.e., quantitative and qualitative analyses being conducted independently but with interpretations stemming from each set of analyses yielding meta-inferences) and sequential mixed analyses (i.e., mixing of quantitative and qualitative analyses in chronological order such that they are dependent on each other), as well as, of course, crossover mixed analyses (i.e., which, as mentioned previously, involves using one or more analysis types associated with one tradition [e.g., quantitative analysis] to analyze data representing a different tradition [e.g., qualitative data]; Onwuegbuzie & Combs, 2010).

In contrast, analytical *methods* is the next level in Hitchcock and Onwuegbuzie's (2020) CAF hierarchy. Specifically, analytical methods are data analyses—specifically *mesoanalyses*—that represent part of an approach (or system). In quantitative research, measuring central tendency, measuring dispersion/variability, measuring position, measuring distribution shape, and utilizing analyses that are part of the general linear model (e.g., independent samples t test, analysis of variance, multiple regression, canonical correlation analysis) all represent types of statistical methods. In qualitative research, analytical methods include Miles and Huberman's (1994) array of within-case analyses and cross-case analyses (see also Miles et al., 2020). In mixed methods research, analytic methods include methods such as quantitizing (i.e., one data type—specifically, qualitative data—converted into numerical codes that can be analyzed statistically; Miles & Huberman, 1994; Sandelowski, Voils, & Knafl, 2009; Tashakkori & Teddlie, 1998) and qualitizing (i.e., one data type—specifically, numerical data—transformed into narrative data that can be analyzed qualitatively; Onwuegbuzie & Leech, 2019; Tashakkori & Teddlie, 1998; see also Chapter 13 of this volume).

Finally, by analytic *techniques*, which are *microanalyses*, Hitchcock and Onwuegbuzie (2020) refer to the specific procedures that represent a single component in the data analysis process. In quantitative research, analytic techniques include the calculation of a mean, median, mode, standard deviation, percentile rank, and so on. As explained by Hitchcock and Onwuegbuzie, one or more quantitative analysis techniques and methods usually are vital elements of a quantitative data analysis approach. As an example, calculation of a mean and standard deviation (i.e., techniques) are essential components of an independent samples *t* test (i.e., method), which, in turn, are part of the array of inferential analyses (i.e., approach). In qualitative research, techniques include Saldaña's (2016) 33 coding strategies (e.g., values coding, wherein codes that comprise attitudes, values, and beliefs, are applied to examine a participant's perspective or worldview). Accordingly, one or more qualitative analysis techniques and methods can be used alongside any qualitative data analysis approach without affecting the integrity of the underlying approach. For example, values coding can be used as part of an IPA without preventing the qualitative researcher from claiming that an IPA was conducted. On the other hand, if any one qualitative data analysis approach (i.e., whole systems; e.g., constant comparison analysis) was used as part of another qualitative data analysis approach (e.g., IPA), then the integrity of the IPA approach would be compromised, at least to some degree.

In the context of mixed methods research, analytic techniques include frequency analysis of themes (Onwuegbuzie & Teddlie, 2003; Sandelowski et al., 2009). Typically, one or more mixed analysis techniques and methods are essential components of a mixed analysis approach. For example, the mixed analysis technique of frequency analysis of themes (i.e., representing a quantitizing method) could be a component of a sequential mixed analysis approach (i.e., wherein the quantitative analysis component[s] and the qualitative analysis component[s] are dependent in some manner, with one component[s] preceding, and hence informing to some degree, the other component[s] within the mixed analysis process), a concurrent mixed analysis approach (i.e., wherein the quantitative analysis component[s] and the qualitative analysis component[s] are independent of one another, regardless of when these components take place within the mixed analysis process), or another mixed analysis approach. Therefore, as concluded by Hitchcock and Onwuegbuzie (2020), "in qualitative, quantitative, and mixed research, with respect to data analysis, techniques are nested within methods, which, in turn, are nested within approaches" (p. 66).

Table 1.1 presents Hitchcock and Onwuegbuzie's (2020) crossover matrix that has been adapted for this book. This table, which incorporates all the non-software mixed analysis chapters (i.e., Chapters 2–24), represents a 3 (i.e., level of analysis: analytic technique vs. analytic method vs. analytic approach) x 3 (i.e., level of complexity: non-complex vs. intermediate vs. complex) x 3 (i.e., tradition: quantitative vs. qualitative vs. mixed methods) matrix. The rows of this table illustrate the nesting nature (i.e., level of analysis) of crossover analyses, wherein, for example, in the first row of Table 1.1, with regard to quantitative analyses, the *mean* is nested within a *t* test, which, in turn, in nested within *univariate analyses*. In contrast, the columns of Table 1.1 illustrate the level of complexity: with respect to quantitative analytic techniques, the *mean* is less complex than is a *standard deviation* (which comprises a mean), which, in turn, is less complex than is a *skewness/kurtosis coefficient* (which comprises both a mean and standard deviation); with regard to quantitative analytic techniques, *in vivo coding* is less complex (because it is closest to the original data) than is *values coding* (which involves applying codes consisting of three elements, namely, value, attitude, belief, to examine a participant's perspectives or worldviews), which, in turn, is less complex than is *causation coding* (which involves analyzing causality by identifying causes, outcome, and links between the text) because identifying causation is a more complex tasks. As can be seen in Table 1.1, in addition to level of analysis, level of complexity, and tradition, inherent in this matrix is the notion of degree of integration, which is the degree that qualitative and quantitative analytical assumptions are combined. The more that these assumptions are combined, the more likely that the overall analysis will represent some form of crossover mixed analysis (Hitchcock & Onwuegbuzie, 2020). According to Hitchcock and Onwuegbuzie (2020),

> consideration of techniques, methods, and approaches; their overall complexity; and how they interact can inform the conceptualization and innovation of crossover analysis approaches. This is because when conceptualizing an approach, there are several components to consider, and it can help specify these components when attempting to develop a clear roadmap, which, in turn, can lay out steps that analysts might want to be aware of when planning and conducting their mixed methods research studies and associated analytic plans. Mapping out component steps might further inform future mixed analysis innovations. (p. 66)

Dimensions of Crossover Mixed Analyses

Crossover mixed analyses can be framed as being *quantitative-dominant*, *qualitative-dominant*, or *equal-status* (Onwuegbuzie & Combs, 2010; Onwuegbuzie & Hitchcock, 2015). When conducting quantitative-dominant crossover mixed analyses, analysts may adopt a postpositivist stance, while, at the same time, operate under the belief that the inclusion of qualitative data and analysis can help address the research question(s) more comprehensively. Contrastingly, when conducting qualitative-dominant crossover mixed analyses, analysts may adopt any stance associated with the qualitative research tradition (e.g., constructivist stance, critical theorist stance, participatory stance) with respect to the research process in general and the analysis process in particular, while, at the same time, operate under the belief that the addition of quantitative data and analysis can help them address the research question(s) to a greater extent.

TABLE 1.1

Examples of Analytic Techniques, Methods and Approaches across Degree of Complexity

	Analytic Techniques[a] (a microanalysis/ component step in the data analysis process)	*Analytic Methods* (a mesoanalysis [i.e., middle-level] that is part of an approach)	*Analytic Approaches* (a macroanalysis; a broad system of analyses)
Non-complex (few analytic actions required, generally low-inference, descriptive goals)	Quantitative: calculation of a mean Qualitative: in vivo (i.e., verbatim) coding Mixed: frequency analysis of themes	*Quantitative*: *t* tests, measuring distribution of shape *Qualitative*: event listing for a within-case display; critical incidence chart *Mixed*: single quantitizing; single qualitizing (see Chapter 13, this volume)	*Quantitative*: descriptive analyses; univariate analyses *Qualitative*: word count *Mixed*: parallel analysis
Intermediate complexity (multiple analytic actions required, relational/predictive goals)	*Quantitative*: standard deviation; correlation coefficient *Qualitative*: values coding *Mixed*: modal profile information; coding techniques for quantitative data (see Chapter 14, this volume)	*Quantitative*: analysis of variance (ANOVA) *Qualitative*: cross-case display; contrast table in a cross-case display *Mixed*: multi-quantitizing; multi-qualitizing (see Chapter 13, this volume); joint display for constructing and sorting simple tables as mixed analysis (see Chapter 23, this volume); joint display as mixed analysis (see Chapter 24, this volume);	*Quantitative:* Univariate analyses *Qualitative:* Constant comparison analysis *Mixed:* Sequential analysis; Concurrent analysis
Complex (multiple analytic actions required, highly inferential in nature)	*Quantitative*: skewness and kurtosis calculations *Qualitative*: causation coding *Mixed*: holistic profile information	*Quantitative*: Hierarchical Linear Modeling *Qualitative*: Use of a poem in a within-case display; causal network; decision modeling *Mixed*: fully integrated quantitizing; fully integrated qualitizing (see Chapter 13, this volume); correspondence analysis of themes (see Chapter 3, this volume); exploratory factor analysis of themes (see Chapter 2, this volume); multidimensional scaling of qualitative data (see Chapter 4, this volume); cluster analysis of qualitative data (see Chapter 5, this volume); chi-square automatic interaction detection of qualitative data (see Chapter 6, this volume); multiple linear regression with qualitative data (see Chapter 7, this volume); structural equation modeling with qualitative data (see Chapter 8, this volume); hierarchical linear modeling with qualitative data (see Chapter 9, this volume); qualitative comparative analysis (see Chapter 17, this volume)	*Quantitative*: Multilevel analyses; Bayesian analysis *Qualitative*: Interpretive phenomenological analysis *Mixed*: Crossover mixed analyses; Fully integrated mixed analysis (see Chapter 10, this volume); item response theory with qualitative data (see Chapter 11, this volume); diachronic analysis of qualitative data (see Chapter 12, this volume); mixed methodological discourse analysis (see Chapter 15, this volume); ethnographic decision models with qualitative data (see Chapter 16, this volume); Q Methodology as mixed analysis (see Chapter 18, this volume); social network analysis as mixed analysis (see Chapter 19, this volume); social media analytics as mixed analysis (see Chapter 20, this volume); geographic information systems as mixed analysis (see Chapter 21, this volume); nonverbal communication analysis as mixed analysis (see Chapter 22, this volume)

[a] Recall that a technique, in this framework, is conceptualized as a step in an analytic process (hence, we also use the phrase *microanalysis*). The result of a technique typically will require one or more additional reference points for enhanced meaning making. For example, suppose one calculates the standard deviation of the physical weight of some group of people, this information by itself would normally be difficult to interpret without another reference point, such as a mean (or another standard deviation). Methods (i.e., middle or *mesoanalyses*) require several components or steps—that is, integrated sets of techniques. Finally, approaches (or *macroanalyses*) are broad analytic systems and might incorporate several methods and/or techniques.

Adapted from Hitchcock and Onwuegbuzie, 2020, p. 67.

Finally, analysts conducting equal-status crossover mixed analyses believe that using both qualitative and quantitative data analysis can optimally address the underlying research question(s). As a result, these analysts would need to adopt a flexible research philosophical stance that embraces a diversity of approaches and a both-and logic (Johnson et al., 2019), such as dialectical pluralism (Johnson, 2012, 2017; Tucker, Johnson, Onwuegbuzie, & Icenogle, 2020) and critical dialectical pluralism (Onwuegbuzie & Frels, 2013). As concluded by Hitchcock and Onwuegbuzie (2020),

> This approach to analysis, of course, would require philosophical clarity (i.e., "the degree that the researcher is aware of and articulates her/his philosophical proclivities in terms of philosophical assumptions and stances in relation to all components, claims, actions, and uses in a mixed research study"; Collins, Onwuegbuzie, & Johnson, 2012, p. 855). A lack of such clarity could lead to an analyst to adopt poor analytical practices such as by ignoring assumptions associated with qualitative and quantitative analyses. (p. 73)

That crossover mixed analyses can be framed as being quantitative-dominant, qualitative-dominant, or equal-status has intuitive appeal because it means that crossover mixed analyses not only are accessible to mixed methods researchers, but also they can be conducted by quantitative researchers and qualitative researchers. In particular, quantitative researchers likely would gravitate towards quantitative-dominant crossover mixed analyses, whereas qualitative researchers likely would have greater proclivity towards qualitative-dominant crossover mixed analyses. As such, the first three parts of this book are based on these types of crossover mixed analyses. Specifically, Part I contains quantitative-dominant crossover mixed analyses, Part II contains qualitative-dominant crossover mixed analyses, and Part III contains equal-status crossover mixed analyses.

Quantitizing as a Core Crossover Mixed Analysis

One of two popularized methods of crossover mixed analyses is what is referred to in the mixed methods research community as *quantitizing*. Traditionally, quantitizing has been defined as the process of transforming qualitative data into numerical codes that can, in turn, be subjected to statistical analyses (Miles & Huberman, 1994; Sandelowski et al., 2009; Tashakkori & Teddlie, 1998). (For an expanded definition of quantitizing, see Onwuegbuzie & Hitchcock, 2020; see also the discussion of quantitizing in Chapter 7 of this volume.) As conceptualized by Onwuegbuzie and Hitchcock (2020), the quantitizing process can be broadly categorized as descriptive-based quantitizing, exploratory-based quantitizing, measurement-based quantitizing, or inferential-based quantitizing. Each of these concepts will be outlined in the following sections.

Descriptive-based Quantitizing

As the phrase suggests, descriptive-based quantitizing involves the use of descriptive analyses. Broadly speaking, descriptive analyses involve the following four measures: *measures of central tendency*, *measures of variation/dispersion*, *measures of position/relative standing*, and *measures of distributional shape*. In particular, central tendency is a descriptive summary of a dataset using a single value that reflects the center of the data distribution. Measures of central tendency include mean, median, and mode. For example, a mixed methods researcher might decide to develop what Onwuegbuzie (2003) referred to as an *inter-respondent matrix* (see also Onwuegbuzie & Teddlie, 2003) of themes, in which each emergent theme is quantitized such that the number of times that each participant made a statement during an interview that was classified under that theme was tallied. This process would yield an inter-respondent matrix of themes (i.e., participant x theme matrix), which consists only of frequency counts. The term "inter-respondent" was used by Onwuegbuzie (2003) to denote the fact that by going down a theme column, one can see differences among the respondents (i.e., animal [if it is alive; e.g., human respondent], vegetable [if it grows; e.g., plants], or mineral [if it is not alive, does not grow, and comes from the ground; e.g., asbestos]). From this matrix, the mean frequency of each theme can be computed, which serve as manifest effect sizes (i.e., effect sizes that pertain to observable content; Onwuegbuzie, 2003).

As outlined by Onwuegbuzie and Hitchcock (2020), Table 1.2 provides an example of a *frequency-based inter-respondent*

TABLE 1.2

Example of Frequency-Based Inter-Respondent Matrix Used to Conduct a Mixed Analysis from Interview Responses

Pseudonym	Theme 1	Theme 2	Theme 3	Theme 4	Theme 5	Total	Mean
Halle	5	3	4	0	6	18	3.60
Kadeem	8	4	4	1	5	22	4.40
Sandra	3	7	1	3	3	17	3.40
Nadia	6	3	0	7	3	19	3.80
Peter	2	9	5	8	0	24	4.80
Augustine	7	6	8	4	0	25	5.00
Total	31	32	22	23	17	125	20.83
Mean	5.17	5.33	3.67	3.83	2.83	25.00	4.17
Median	5.50	5.00	4.00	3.50	3.00	20.50	4.10
Standard Deviation	2.32	2.42	2.88	3.19	2.48	3.31	0.66

matrix used to conduct a mixed analysis from six sets of interview responses. For example, it can be seen from Table 1.2 that Halle's interview responses were coded five times under Theme 1 and six times under Theme 5. Reporting frequency counts via inter-respondent matrices is one way to produce what Onwuegbuzie (2003) referred to as *effect sizes* in qualitative research, providing more information than the use of words like "few," "many," "most," and even "all." It should be noted that the assumption underlying the creation of this matrix is that the more times a theme is coded across the participants, the more important it is. Of course, this is not always the case, and so an assessment of the context should occur before making this assumption. For example, the appropriateness of the assumption that there is a positive association between frequency of occurrence and importance varies by factors such as the uniqueness of the event, experience, phenomenon, or the like, underlying the theme (e.g., the more unique the event/experience/phenomenon/etc., the less the assumption is justified) and the number of participants (e.g., the smaller the sample size, the more the use of frequency data might distort the findings; the larger the sample size, the more justified it is for frequency data to be used to make generalizations to the sample as a whole, and even beyond the sample, in the case of big[ger] data). (For more discussion of assumptions, see Onwuegbuzie & Hitchcock, 2020.) Now, assuming that it is appropriate to quantitize the themes in this current example, the last two rows of Table 1.2 reveal that Theme 2 is the most prevalent theme. Also, the frequency-based, inter-respondent matrix can be used to determine, for example, which participant contributed the most to the thematic development. The last two columns reveal that this participant was Augustine.

As described by Onwuegbuzie and Hitchcock (2020), Table 1.3 provides an example of an *incident-based inter-respondent matrix* used to conduct a mixed analysis of open-ended survey responses from 933 participants. Here, each emergent theme is quantitized such that if a participant made one or more statements during an interview that was classified under that theme, then a score of "1" is given to the theme for that response; otherwise, a score of "0" is given. This dichotomization process will yield an inter-respondent matrix of themes (i.e., participant x theme matrix), which consists only of 0s and 1s. By calculating the frequency of each theme from the inter-respondent matrix, the prevalence rate of each theme can be computed. These frequencies also serve as manifest effect sizes, which as described by Onwuegbuzie (2003), are effect sizes that refer to content that is observable, such as counts

TABLE 1.3

Example of Incident-Based Inter-Respondent Matrix Used to Conduct a Mixed Analysis from Survey Responses

ID	Theme 1	Theme 2	Theme 3	Theme 4	Theme 5	Theme 6
001	1	1	0	0	0	1
002	0	1	0	1	0	0
003	0	1	1	0	0	1
.....	.	.	.	.		
.....	.	.	.	.		
933	1	1	0	0	1	0

TABLE 1.4

Example of Intensity-Based Inter-Respondent Matrix Used to Conduct a Mixed Analysis from Survey Responses Using a 5-Point Rating Scale

ID	Theme 1	Theme 2	Theme 3	Theme 4	Theme 5	Theme 6
001	1	2	1	4	5	4
002	1	1	2	2	3	4
003	3	4	5	5	1	2
.....	.	.	.	.		
.....	.	.	.	.		
612	4	2	2	1	2	3

of significant statements (e.g., words, phrases, sentences, paragraphs, pages) and observations that underlie emergent themes.

As explained by Onwuegbuzie and Hitchcock (2020), Table 1.4 provides an example of *intensity-based inter-respondent matrix* used to conduct a mixed analysis from 612 sets of survey responses via a 5-point rating scale. Here, the analyst would attempt to use a trustworthy coding scheme for assessing the intensity of the event, experience, phenomenon, or the like, underlying each theme using a rating scale (i.e., a set of x categories that have been developed to elicit information about a quantitative or a qualitative attribute, wherein the respondent selects the number [from 1 to x] that is considered to reflect her/his attitude or opinion) or Likert-format scale (i.e., a symmetric agree-disagree scale [i.e., containing the same number of "agree" and "disagree" options] wherein each participant responds to a series of statements [not questions] by specifying her/his level of agreement or disagreement). Strategies to verify the coding scheme include interviewing participants to have them member check the accuracy of the analyst's statements and ratings (Onwuegbuzie & Hitchcock, 2020), assessing intra-coder and/or inter-coder agreement (Onwuegbuzie & Hitchcock, 2020), and debriefing the analyst (Collins, Onwuegbuzie, Johnson, & Frels, 2013; Frels & Onwuegbuzie, 2012; Onwuegbuzie, Leech, & Collins, 2008). Alternatively, mixed methods researchers can seek to extract these ratings directly from the participants during the initial interview, as each event/experience/phenomenon/and so forth is being described.

Whatever type of inter-respondent matrix is created, as can be seen, these matrices can be used to undertake descriptive-based quantitizing. This descriptive-based quantitizing can serve as the *end goal* of the quantitizing process. However, such matrices can be used to produce more complex mixed analyses—which is the focus of Part I of this book, namely, the section entitled, "Quantitative Approaches to Qualitative Data"—which is represented by frequentist parametric statistical analyses (i.e., Chapters 1–5, 7–9, 12), a frequentist non-parametric statistical analysis (i.e., Chapter 6), a Bayesian statistical analysis (i.e., Chapter 10), and a psychometric analysis (i.e., Chapter 11).

Exploratory-based Quantitizing

Exploratory-based quantitizing involves the quantitizing of qualitative data for the purpose of identifying group membership. Here, the grouping could be participants or variables (e.g., themes, words). The following four chapters in Part I can be classified as exploratory-based quantitizing: Chapter 2: Exploratory Factor Analysis of Text; Chapter 3: Correspondence Analysis of Qualitative Data; Chapter 4: Multidimensional Scaling of Qualitative Data; and Chapter 5: Cluster Analysis for Mixed Methods Research. What these four chapters have in common is the non-testing of hypotheses.

In Chapter 2, the author (Jim Van Haneghan) excellently discusses the analysis method of an exploratory factor analysis of text, which, as he states, is more commonly referred to as factor analysis topic modelling (FATM). For this analysis, the inter-respondent matrix takes the form of a case unit (e.g., document, sentence, paragraph) x word frequencies data matrix, or a word frequency correlation matrix. Specifically, the software program WordStat (i.e., Topic Extraction feature) facilitates conduct of a principal components analysis with a varimax rotation, from which components or factors (i.e., topics) are extracted that, via the varimax rotation (see Gorsuch, 1983) of the components, are independent of each other within the texts.

In Chapter 3, the author (Wendy Dickinson) outlines very effectively the correspondence analysis of qualitative data. In the context of mixed analysis, the correspondence analysis involves the analysis of an inter-respondent matrix that takes the form of a case unit (e.g., participant) x code/theme frequencies data matrix. Specifically, this analysis creates a two-dimensional visual display that shows the relationship among the participants with respect to the codes/themes, the relationship among the codes/themes, and the relationship between the participants and the themes. Extensions to correspondence analysis include multiple correspondence analysis, which displays associations in more than two dimensions that involve multiple qualitative variables; and discriminant correspondence analysis (i.e., barycentric discriminant analysis), which is the equivalent of discriminant analysis for qualitative data. Interestingly, both QDA Miner and WordStat—two software programs highlighted in Chapter 25—facilitate the use of correspondence analysis of codes/themes.

In Chapter 4, the author (Ahmet Suerdem) describes very interestingly the multidimensional scaling of qualitative data. This analytical method involves the analysis of an inter-respondent matrix that is based on the co-occurrences of words or content categories. More specifically, this matrix takes the form of a distance matrix, which is a square matrix (i.e., two-dimensional representation) that contains the distances, taken pairwise, between the elements of a set. This analysis facilitates identification of the similarity between documents or cases, with QDA Miner and WordStat being among the software with which this analysis can be conducted.

In Chapter 5, the author (Normand Péladeau) describes very interestingly the cluster analysis of qualitative data. For this analysis, the inter-respondent matrix takes the form of a similarity matrix (e.g., word co-occurrence matrix), which can be subjected to hierarchical clustering, the process of which can be represented in a form of a tree graph, called a dendrogram, in which lines are successively drawn to connect items (e.g., words) as they are merged. This dendrogram displays the arrangement of the clusters produced by the analysis. Consistent with qualitizing, a structured narrative may be built around each grouping of codes/themes. QDA Miner has a cluster extraction feature in which similar responses are grouped and displayed alongside each other, thereby allowing analysts to code them by clusters rather than individually.

In the spirit of mixed analysis, cluster analysis can be used to analyze qualitative data that have been quantitized or quantitative data (i.e., for the purpose of qualitizing). In addition to hierarchical clustering—which is most useful when the goal is to cluster a small number (less than a few hundred) of objects, other clustering procedures that can be used include *twostep clustering*, which facilitates the creation of clusters based on both qualitative (i.e., categorical) and quantitative (i.e., continuous) variables and can accommodate a large number of objects; and *k means clustering*, which is appropriate to use when the analyst wants to assign cases (e.g., participants, variables) to a fixed number of groups (clusters) whose characteristics are not yet known but are based on a set of specified variables and is most useful for a large number (i.e., thousands) of cases.

Measurement-based Quantitizing

Measurement-based quantitizing involves the quantitizing of qualitative data for the purpose of instrument development or construct validation (cf. Onwuegbuzie, Bustamante, & Nelson, 2010). Confirmatory factor analysis is a common way to test whether the underlying data generated by an instrument fit a hypothesized measurement model. Although the use of qualitative data as part of the confirmatory factor analysis process has logical appeal, as of the time of writing, this notion has not been advanced. And unfortunately, the present book does not contain a chapter on the topic of confirmatory factor analysis of qualitative data. However, Chapter 11 contains an excellent discussion by the authors (Vanessa Scherman and Linda Liebenberg) of the integration of qualitative data when using item response theory in general and Rasch analysis in particular. For this analysis, the inter-respondent matrix takes the form of a person x item matrix that is analyzed.

Inferential-based Quantitizing

Inferential-based quantitizing involves the quantitizing of qualitative data for the purpose of estimation or prediction. The following six chapters discuss some aspect of estimation/prediction: Chapter 6: Chi-Square Automatic Interaction Detection Analysis of Qualitative Data; Chapter 7: Multiple Linear Regression Analysis with Qualitative Data that have been Quantitized; Chapter 8: Structural Equation Modeling with Qualitative Data that Have Been Quantitized; Chapter 9: Hierarchical Linear Modeling with Qualitative Data that have been Quantitized; Chapter 10: Bayesian Analyses with Qualitative Data; and Chapter 12: Diachronic Analysis of Qualitative Data. In Chapter 6, the author (Kathleen M. T. Collins) convincingly shows how nonparametric analysis approaches can be applied to qualitative data within a mixed analysis process. This author uses what is called a chi-square automatic interaction detection (CHAID) analysis to analyze qualitative data that have been quantitized. CHAID is a decision tree technique, involving adjusted significance testing (e.g., Bonferroni adjustment) that is based on an inter-respondent matrix that includes quantitized (e.g., dichotomous) data. These quantitized variables can serve as the independent and/or dependent variables in the CHAID model (cf. Onwuegbuzie & Collins, 2010). As demonstrated by the author of this chapter, an appeal of CHAID analysis is that it produces outputs that are highly visual and easy to interpret.

Chapters 7, 8, and 9 represent a trilogy of chapters inasmuch as they directly refer to each other, and two of these chapters (i.e., Chapters 7 and 9) have two authors in common. All three excellent chapters involve the analysis of some form of inter-respondent matrix. For example, in Chapter 7, the authors (Kyle Cox, Richard Lambert, and John H. Hitchcock) described what they refer to as a theme matrix for conducting multiple linear regression analysis with qualitative data (cf. Newman, Onwuegbuzie, & Hitchcock, 2015). In Chapter 8, the authors (David Newman and Shannon Constantinides) describe how the inter-respondent matrix takes the form of a covariance matrix, whereas in Chapter 9, although not explicitly stated by the authors (John H. Hitchcock, Richard Lambert, and T. Scott Holcomb), the inter-respondent matrix is represented by a structured covariance matrix. For all three sets of analyses, the underlying matrix incorporates one or more columns of qualitative data that have been quantitized.

Representing an alternative to both frequentist parametric statistical analysis (e.g., multiple linear regression, structural equation modeling, hierarchical linear modeling) and frequentist nonparametric statistical analysis (i.e., CHAID), in Chapter 10, the author (Prathiba Natesan Batley) provides an intriguing discussion of Bayesian analyses with qualitative data. The notion of Bayesian analysis as a mixed analysis approach only recently has been championed by Onwuegbuzie, Hitchcock, Natesan, and Newman (2018). And in Chapter 10, the author extends this discussion. As an example, as described in detail by Onwuegbuzie, Hitchcock, et al. (2018), the author discussed the combination of meta-analysis (i.e., involving the combining or aggregating of quantitative findings from the extant literature in order to integrate the findings; Glass, 1976) and meta-synthesis (i.e., involving the integration of qualitative findings from the extant literature for the hermeneutic purpose of theory development aimed at understanding and explaining phenomena; Sandelowski & Barroso, 2003; Stern & Harris, 1985), which yields a mixed methods-based synthesis known as Bayesian meta-analysis that has been utilized by only three sets of researchers to date (cf. Crandell, Voils, Chang, & Sandelowski, 2011; Roberts, Dixon-Woods, Fitzpatrick, Abrams, & Jones, 2002; Voils et al., 2009). Bayesian meta-analysis involves the analysis of an inter-respondent matrix that takes the form of a matrix that summarizes the coding of the themes extracted from both the qualitative and quantitative research studies, wherein each theme is quantitized across all of these studies.

In Chapter 12—the final chapter in Part I—the authors (M. Teresa Anguera, Mariona Portell, Antonio Hernández-Mendo, Pedro Sánchez-Algarra, and Gudberg K. Jonsson) excellently discuss diachronic analysis of qualitative data. In contrast to synchronic analysis, diachronic analysis—which includes lag sequential analysis, polar coordinate analysis, and t-pattern analysis—is the study of change in a phenomenon (e.g., a code) over a period of time. As described by the authors, for diachronic analysis, the inter-respondent matrix is represented by a code matrix that contains qualitative data—which is essential for the process of quantitizing—but, at the same time, allows for its subsequent quantitative treatment. According to the authors, the ensuing code matrix emerges by assigning each of the observation units to the respective code. Interestingly, an array of data modalities such as drawings, photographs, and sounds can be incorporated into the code matrix, for which computer software programs (e.g., HOISAN, LINCE, GSEQ5, THEME Edu) have been developed to facilitate their analyses.

Qualitizing as a Core Crossover Mixed Analysis

The second of two popularized methods of crossover mixed analyses is what are referred to in the mixed methods research community as *qualitizing*. Traditionally, qualitizing is the process of transforming numerical data into narrative form, and then, these narrative data can be subjected to qualitative analyses (Tashakkori & Teddlie, 1998). (For an expanded definition of qualitizing, see Onwuegbuzie & Leech, 2019; see also Chapter 13 of this volume.) As conceptualized by Onwuegbuzie and Leech (2019), as is the case for quantitizing, the qualitizing process operates at different levels. In particular, qualitizing can take the form of *single qualitizing*, *multi-qualitizing*, and *fully integrated qualitizing*. In Chapter 13, the authors (Anthony J. Onwuegbuzie and Nancy L. Leech) discuss Onwuegbuzie and Leech's (2019) expanded definition of qualitizing that includes these three levels of qualitizing.

The difference among these three forms of qualitizing relate to the quantity and quality of the qualitizing process. Specifically, as the term suggests, single qualitizing involves a single phase of qualitizing quantitative data. In the groundbreaking Chapter 14, Johnny Saldaña provides numerous examples of single qualitizing of quantitative data, such as qualitative process coding, descriptive coding, structural coding, magnitude coding, and evaluation coding. Although not mentioned by the author, an example of multi-qualitizing would be the use of two or more of these qualitizing techniques within the analytical process. Regardless, as with all chapters in this book, there is no doubt that Chapter 14 will make an important contribution to the literature.

Fully integrated qualitizing refers to both quantitative data and qualitative data as well as qualitive analysis and quantitative analysis being used to inform the qualitizing process. In Chapter 15, which is the final chapter in Part II, the author (Zsuzsanna Géring) introduces what she calls a mixed methodological discourse analysis. Because discourse analysis represents multiple traditions (e.g., linguistic approach, discursive psychology, critical linguistics/critical discourse analysis), it represents a whole system of data analyses that is always an iterative process. As such, as described by the author, mixed methodological discourse analysis relies on the collection of qualitative and quantitative data and the use of qualitative and quantitative analysis, including narrative thematic analysis with quantitizing and sometimes qualitizing of measurement data to provide more meaningful findings. Hence, it relies, on traditional qualitative and quantitative analysis as well as crossover analysis.

Inherently Mixed Crossover Analyses

As a recap, Part I of this book contains 11 chapters that are devoted to quantitative-dominant crossover mixed analyses and Part II of this book contains three chapters that are devoted to qualitative-dominant crossover mixed analyses. In Part III, there are nine chapters dedicated that naturally represent (approximately) equal-status crossover mixed analyses. These analyses are classified as being inherently mixed because, optimally, they involve the substantive collection, analysis, and interpretation of both quantitative and qualitative data.

In Chapter 16, the authors (Gery W. Ryan and H. Russell Bernard) excellently discuss ethnographic decision models with qualitative data. According to these authors, ethnographic decision models (EDMs) stem from a rigorous mixed methods research approach that leads to the prediction of episodic behaviors, such as choosing whether or not to wear a mask/face covering during the current COVID-19 pandemic or deciding whether or not to read this *The Routledge Reviewer's Guide to Mixed Methods Analysis* book. These models are informed by a deep understanding of the cultural context that underlies people's decisions. In Phase 1, EDM researchers use semi-structured interviews to collect qualitative data on people's decision-making process and then use qualitative methods to identify decision criteria (Qualitative Phase). In Phase 2, the researchers develop and administer a survey instrument to collect data on people's actual choices and the antecedents of these choices (Quantitative Phase). In Phase 3, the survey data are used to build an ethnographically grounded decision model that predicts or explains the decision outcomes, either via case-to-case transfer (Qualitative Phase) or via machine learning (Quantitative Phase). Interestingly, machine learning (see some discussion in Chapters 8, 20, 22, 25), which is a data analytics technique, at least in part (e.g., Natural language processing), involves a quantitative analysis (i.e., using algorithms) of qualitative outcomes, which yields crossover mixed analyses. In Phase 4, the researchers test the accuracy of the model by assessing its predictability on a new sample (Quantitative Phase) and by testing its content validity (Qualitative Phase). Interestingly, crossover analysis can be used to assess both predictability and content validity (see Onwuegbuzie et al., 2010).

In Chapter 17, the authors (Benoît Rihoux, Priscilla Álamos-Concha, and Bojana Lobe) excellently frame qualitative comparative analysis (QCA; Ragin, 1987) as both a mixed methods research and multimethod research approach. According to these authors, QCA represents an inherently mixed approach, being based on both qualitative (i.e., case-oriented) and quantitative (i.e., mathematical) methods (Blanchard, Rihoux, & Álamos-Concha, 2017). Moreover, QCA concerns obtaining case-based evidence, rather than examining relationships among "variables," as in most quantitative research. It looks at the logical connections of what are called, in quantitative research, single levels of variables. It connects specific sequences of *levels* of variables, rather than looking at how "variables are related." It uses Boolean operators and set theory to identify approximations to "necessary" and/or "sufficient" conditions for outcomes of interest (e.g., voting for a particular presidential candidate, deciding to drop out of college). According to the authors, QCA is a data analysis method, as opposed to a data collection method. These authors provide several applications of QCA in mixed methods research. An additional one that was not mentioned by the authors is the use of QCA to analyze findings from the extant literature (Onwuegbuzie & Weinbaum, 2017). In particular, when qualitative findings are converted to a truth table (i.e., a mathematical table used in logic), then a crossover mixed analysis ensues.

In Chapter 18, the author (Susan Ramlo) excellently demonstrates how Q methodology is inherently mixed. Q methodology is a complete methodology (i.e., broad system) for studying subjectivity (Brown, 1980, 2008). As stated by the author, Q methodology includes the process of collecting conversations and/or dialogue, factor analysis, correlation, and interpretation; therefore, it involves an interplay between quantitative and qualitative methods. The author provides some applications of Q methodology in mixed methods research. Excitingly, an additional application that was not mentioned by the authors is the use of Q Methodology as part of the literature review process (Onwuegbuzie & Frels, 2015).

In Chapter 19, the authors (Dominik Froehlich and Jasperina Brouwer) convincingly discuss social network analysis (SNA) as an inherently mixed analysis. Although SNA was traditionally viewed as a "quantitative method," researchers, such as Froehlich and Brouwer, are attempting to increase its power by producing *mixed* versions of SNA. Mixed methods SNA relies on the collection of qualitative and quantitative data (via interviews, observations, and questionnaires) to understand social interaction-and-networking, including its subjective/intersubjective meaning to participants or actors in the world. Results are depicted visually as well as via descriptive and explanatory text. In the last decade, there has been a significant increase in the intersection of mixed methods research with SNA (cf. Edwards, 2010; Hollstein, 2011; Onwuegbuzie, 2020), also known as mixed methods research SNA or MMSNA (Froehlich, Rehm, & Rienties, 2020). MMSNA has a lot of potential for crossover mixed analysis. For example, in using MMSNA to examine the role of knowing and valuing other people's expertise in accelerating information exchange, Carbonell et al. (2020) collected qualitative data, which, subsequently, they quantitized using a coding schema. Notwithstanding, MMSNA is still in its early stages of development. Therefore, Chapter 19 is particularly timely. For example, Onwuegbuzie (2020) advocated

> the simultaneous collection of quantitative and qualitative data (e.g., for name generating), for example, via surveys that contain both open-ended and closed-ended items. Then, the qualitative data could be quantitized via what is referred to as an adjacency matrix, wherein ties between actors are recorded as present (1) or absent (0). This would allow both the quantitative data and quantitized data to be placed in the same matrix, which then could be analyzed using SNA software like UCINET. (p. 255)

In Chapter 20, the authors (Tom Liam Lynch and Hannah R. Gerber) excellently outline social media analytics as mixed analysis. Digital research methods are increasingly being used to conduct research in the 21st century. However, most of the literature in this area either tends to be field-specific or to lean either toward method or theory without an intentional intersection of the two (Gerber, Lynch, & Onwuegbuzie, in press). Therefore, this chapter also is very timely because it weaves these elements together. Central to this chapter is the notion of unique theoretical principles referred to as an ontological imperative (Lynch & Gerber, 2018). According to the ontological imperative, researchers must understand the very nature of digital data and methods if they are to maximize their use in research.

In Chapter 21, the authors (Nigel G. Fielding and Joan M. Verd) excellently build the case for geographic information systems (GIS) as mixed analysis. In the last decade, a few authors have framed GIS as representing a mixed methods approach (Fielding & Cisneros-Puebla, 2009; Frels, Frels, & Onwuegbuzie, 2011). Encouragingly, as the authors note, aided by GIS, geographers recently have started utilizing mixed methods approaches to inform their works. The current chapter should help provide much-needed guidance for conducting mixed analysis in the context of GIS for geographers whom the authors call *closet* mixed methodologists, as well as for mixed methods researchers who wish to venture into the important world of GIS.

In Chapter 22, the authors (Anthony J. Onwuegbuzie and Sandra Schamroth Abrams), building on the work of Onwuegbuzie and Abrams (in press), provide a discussion of an analysis that rarely takes place in a comprehensive manner in quantitative, qualitative, or mixed methods research using thick data (Denham & Onwuegbuzie, 2013), namely, what is termed as a nonverbal communication (NVC) analysis (Onwuegbuzie & Abrams, in press). The current authors show how both qualitative researchers and quantitative researchers can conduct NVC analysis as a mixed analysis without having to reframe their studies as mixed methods research studies.

The last two chapters of Part III deal with the topic of joint displays, which is a way of analyzing and presenting mixed analysis findings that is becoming more popularized. As explained by Onwuegbuzie and Hwang (2019a), joint displays are a special case of crossover displays (i.e., displays that are created after some form of crossover analysis [e.g., quantitizing, qualitizing] has taken place), involving the presentation of *both* qualitative and quantitative findings (Fetters, Curry, & Creswell, 2013; Guetterman, Creswell, & Kuckartz, 2015; Guetterman, Fetters, Curry, & Creswell, 2015), and involving "using tables or figures that combine and display both quantitative and qualitative data together" (Johnson, Grove, & Clarke, 2019, p. 301). Interestingly, the use of visual displays is not only positively linked to readability, writing quality, and communication clarity (Onwuegbuzie & Hwang, 2019b) but also it is a predictor of the quality of a (mixed methods) manuscript, with manuscripts containing one or more visual displays being 2.04 (95% confidence interval = 1.33, 3.12) times less likely to be rejected for publication by the editor than are manuscripts that do not contain any visual displays (Onwuegbuzie & Hwang, 2019a).

Specifically, in Chapter 23, the authors (Michael D. Fetters and Timothy C. Guetterman) excellently demonstrate the development of a joint display as a mixed analysis. These authors provide an expanded definition of a joint display as being a form of *analysis* rather than just presentation of results. Further, they provided 14 considerations for constructing a joint display for mixed analyses. Finally, in Chapter 24, the authors (Judith Schoonenboom and R. Burke Johnson) introduce a specific type of joint display table, namely, the case comparison table, and show how it is used iteratively for mixed analysis. They define a case comparison table as a simple table, wherein each row contains information on one case of the research study (e.g., student, group) and the columns represent qualitative and quantitative characteristics of interest. The data are collected and extracted from qualitative data sources (e.g., in-depth interview data) and quantitative data sources (e.g., structured questionnaire data). The data in the columns are systematically sorted (one at a time) as the analyst interrogates the data to produce increasingly informative research results. This chapter nicely completes Part II of our book.

Use of Software for Mixed Analysis

Part IV, entitled, "Use of Software for Mixed Analysis," is the last part of our book. This exciting section contains six excellent chapters describing eight different computer-assisted data analysis software. Specifically, Chapter 25, authored by Normand Péladeau, introduces the following three software programs for facilitating mixed analyses: *QDA Miner* (i.e., qualitative analysis features for the coding and analysis of qualitative text data and images such as coding-and-retrieval, memoing, reporting, and teamwork features), *WordStat* (i.e., content analysis and text mining module), and *SimStat* (i.e., a general statistical software for the analysis of numerical and categorical data). Beyond its excellent content, what is particularly noteworthy about this chapter is that its author is the developer of all three software programs.

Chapter 26, authored by Udo Kuckartz and Stefan Rädiker, introduces the software program, MAXQDA, as a mixed analysis tool. The authors describe MAXQDA as a software package for the analysis of qualitative and mixed data. According to the authors, MAXQDA allows users to analyze both types of data, qualitative and quantitative, separately and integratively. Beyond its excellent content, like the previous chapter, the fact that the authors of this software program are its developers is noteworthy.

Chapter 27, authored by Eli Lieber, Michelle Salmona, and Dan Kaczynski, introduces the software program, Dedoose, as a mixed analysis tool. Dedoose is a cloud-based Research and Evaluation Data Application (REDA). Being web-based, Dedoose facilitates collaboration, wherein members of a research/evaluation team can work together on a project simultaneously in real time from any location by building a database that all can analyze when needed during a research study. Like the two software chapters before it, a particular strength of this chapter is that it is authored by a lead author who contributed to the development of Dedoose, a second author with more than 15 years of experience as a trainer in the use of Dedoose, and a third author who is known for advancing technological innovations in qualitative and mixed methods data analysis in the social sciences.

Chapter 28, authored by Brigitte Smit, introduces the software program, ATLAS.ti, as a mixed analysis tool. ATLAS.ti is a software program for the data analysis of large bodies of textual, graphical, audio, and video data. As stated by the author, to date, little has been written on the use of ATLAS.ti for mixed methods research in general and mixed analysis in particular. Therefore, this chapter is extremely timely. A particular strength of this chapter is that it is authored by a qualitative research methodologist who is an ATLAS.ti-accredited senior professional trainer.

Chapter 29, authored by Pat Bazeley, introduces the software program, NVivo, as a mixed analysis tool. NVivo has been designed to support analysis of qualitative and mixed methods data. This software program facilitates the combining of demographic and numeric variables with their text data, as well as the conversion of qualitative coding to quantitative variables. Like its predecessors, a notable feature of this software chapter is that, for the last two decades, its author has been providing research training and consulting to internationally based academics, graduate students, and practitioners from a wide range of disciplines and settings in how to make sense of qualitative, quantitative, and mixed methods data and in using computer programs for management and analysis of data in order for researchers to move beyond simple descriptive/thematic analyses of rich data to understand more complex phenomena and "relationships" in the data (sometimes called stage-two analysis).

Chapter 30, the final chapter in Part IV and in this book, authored by Nancy L. Leech, introduces SPSS as a mixed analysis tool. Originally designed as a statistical software program, as outlined by the author, SPSS can be utilized for integrating qualitative and quantitative data in mixed methods research studies. A distinguishing feature of this chapter is that its author has co-authored several books on SPSS, with two of these books already in their fifth edition at the time of writing.

Summary of Technical Outline of Mixed Analysis for Mixed Methods Research

As can be seen, our book contains 29 cutting-edge chapters across four sections. These sections are centered on quantitative-dominant crossover mixed analyses, qualitative-dominant crossover mixed analyses, equal-status crossover mixed analyses, and software programs for conducting mixed analyses. In all of these chapters, the authors provide some original discussion that, indubitably, will make an important contribution to the mixed methods research literature. As can be seen, the final section, Part IV, contains the leading qualitative and mixed methods software authored either by the developers themselves or by a longstanding educator/trainer of the software (e.g., via courses, workshops, books).

4 Empirical Demonstration of Mixed Analysis

In this section, we demonstrate how a researcher can design a study for which many of the mixed analyses discussed in this book can be conducted. This ongoing study, conducted by Ojo and Onwuegbuzie (in press), is a follow-up to the study conducted by Ojo and Onwuegbuzie (2020) to examine the perceptions and attitudes of students regarding online learning in an era of disruption of the COVID-19 pandemic. The first study (i.e., Ojo & Onwuegbuzie, 2020), involving 4,419 Wits University students, led to an array of crossover mixed analysis approaches, some of which are described in Chapter 13. The current study, which is ongoing (i.e., Ojo & Onwuegbuzie, in press), focuses on faculty and examines the perceptions, attitudes, and experiences of students regarding teaching and scholarship conducted online in an era of disruption of the COVID-19 pandemic. (Both of these studies are currently being replicated in several countries in Africa [e.g. Africa, Nigeria, Namibia, Zambia], in the United States [e.g., New York], in Canada, in South America [e.g., Brazil], and in the Caribbean.)

At the time of writing, an online survey has been sent to more than 5,000 faculty at a large university in South Africa. (A response rate of 20% would yield a sample of more than 1,000 faculty members, which would allow the researchers to conduct an array of analyses.) The survey instrument, which has been developed specifically for this multi-mixed methods (i.e., involving the partial integration of multiple methods research approaches and mixed methods research approaches) and meta-methods (i.e., involving the full[er] integration of multiple methods research approaches and mixed methods research approaches) research study, contains four parts: (a) Section I: demographic information; (b) Section II: a 5-point, Likert-format scale (1 = Strongly Disagree, 2 = Disagree, 3 = Neutral, 4 = Agree, and 5 = Strongly Agree) measuring academic staff perceptions of readiness and motivation for online teaching, postgraduate supervision, and assessments (i.e., Scale 1); (c) Section IIII: a 5-point Likert-format scale (1 = Strongly Disagree, 2 = Disagree, 3 = Neutral, 4 = Agree, and 5 = Strongly Agree) measuring academic staff research in the context of the COVID-19 pandemic (i.e., Scale 2); (d) Section IV: a 5-point, Likert-format scale (1 = Strongly Disagree, 2 = Disagree, 3 = Neutral, 4 = Agree, and 5 = Strongly Agree) assessing the general health of South African academics to online teaching, postgraduate supervision, and assessment during the disruption caused by the COVID-19 pandemic; and (e) Section V: containing the following six open-ended items relating to their reflections on the current era of disruption: (i) "To what extent do you consider your current home situation suitable and adaptable to do your work as an academic?" (i.e., Item 1); (ii) "What personal challenges do you have that could hinder your ability to successfully function effectively online?" (i.e., Item 2); (iii) "How have you managed with your postgraduate supervision role since the lockdown started and the University moved to teaching online?" (i.e., Item 3); (iv) "In what ways have you managed your postgraduate supervision role?" (i.e., Item 4); (v) "How has the current situation impacted on your research productivity as an academic?" (i.e., Item 5); and (vi) "Please provide any general comment that you think might be useful to share" (i.e., Item 6). For the purpose of this demonstration, and keeping in mind the amount of data that will be generated by this survey instrument, we will limit our current discussion only to the demographic information (i.e., Section 1), academic staff perception of readiness and motivation for online teaching, postgraduate supervision, and assessments (i.e., Scale 1), and the open-ended Item 1 (i.e., "To what extent do you consider your current home situation suitable and adaptable to do your work as an academic?"). Based on these items, here are some of the research questions that we intend to address and analyses by research phase that we intend to conduct:

Quantitative Phase

- Research Question 1: What are the characteristics of the sample?
  - Analysis: Descriptive analyses
    - Measures of central tendency (e.g., median age, mean years of faculty experience)
    - Frequency distribution (e.g., gender composition, ethnic/racial composition)
- Research Question 2: What is the hierarchical structure of a measure of academic staff perceptions of readiness and motivation for online teaching, postgraduate supervision, and assessments?
  - Principal components analysis
    - Eigenvalue-greater-than-one rule; scree test; parallel analysis
    - Orthogonal rotation (i.e., varimax); Oblique rotation (i.e., direct oblimin rotation with a delta value of zero)
  - Exploratory factor analysis
  - Bayesian exploratory factor analysis
  - Item response theory (IRT) modeling
- Research Question 3: Based on the hierarchical structure (see Research Question 1), what demographic variables predict academic staff perceptions of readiness and motivation for online teaching, postgraduate supervision, and assessments?
  - Analysis of variance (Independent variable [IV]: each select categorical variable with more than two levels; Dependent variable [DV]: total perception scale scores only OR select perception subscale scores)
  - Independent samples *t* test (IV: each select dichotomous variable; DV: total perception scale scores only OR select perception subscale scores)
  - Multiple analysis of variance (IV: all select categorical variables with two or more levels; DV: two or more perception subscale scores)
  - Discriminant analysis (IV: two or more perception subscale scores; DV: each select categorical variable with two or more levels)
  - Logistic regression (IV: two or more perception subscale scores; DV: each select categorical variable with two or more levels)
  - Canonical correlation analysis (IV: all select categorical variables with two levels and continuous variables; DV: two or more perception subscale scores)
  - Structural equation modeling (assessing measurement model [i.e., perception scale] and the path model; DV: two or more perception subscale scores)
  - Hierarchical linear modeling (IV: Level 1: faculty member [e.g., quantitized themes, demographic variables]; Level 2: home city of faculty [other Level-2 variables can be extracted as secondary data, such as poverty index for each province]; DV: total perception scale scores only OR select perception subscale scores); (To justify city as a Level 2-variable, at least 30 of the 74 cities across 9 provinces in South Africa should be represented by at least 30 participant faculty members; cf. Bell, Morgan, Schoeneberger, Kromrey, & Ferron, 2014; Hox, 1998; Maas & Hox, 2004, 2005; Moineddin, Matheson, & Glazier, 2007.)

Qualitative and Mixed Analysis Phase

- Research Question 4: To what extent do faculty members consider their current home situations suitable and adaptable for them to conduct their work as an academic?
  - Topic modeling (i.e., a text-mining tool for identifying hidden semantic structures within a body of text) via a factor analysis to extract the main themes from the responses to the open-ended (i.e., qualitative) question (WordStat 8.0.29). See Chapters 2 and 25.
  - Descriptive-based quantitizing: Quantitize themes emerging from topic modeling to yield an inter-respondent matrix.
  - Exploratory-based quantitizing: Exploratory factor analysis and principal components analysis of quantitized themes (after converting the ensuing matrix of correlations between themes to a matrix of tetrachoric correlation coefficients; cf. Onwuegbuzie et al., 2007) to determine the hierarchical structure of these themes (see Anderson et al., 2012; Combs & Onwuegbuzie, 2010; Onwuegbuzie, 2003; Onwuegbuzie & Combs, 2011; Onwuegbuzie & Teddlie, 2003; Onwuegbuzie et al., 2007).
  - Descriptive-based quantitizing: Sentiment analysis (i.e., involving the use of text analysis, natural language processing, computational linguistics, and the like, systematically to identify, to extract, to quantify, and to examine affective dispositions and subjective information) based on themes in the inter-respondent matrix. For each theme, and for each faculty participant, record a "1" if the theme represents a positive sentiment and a "0" if the theme represents a negative sentiment; or record a "1" if the theme represents a positive sentiment, a "0" if the theme represents

a neutral sentiment or simultaneously represents a positive and negative sentiment, and a "-1" if the theme represents a negative sentiment (cf. Ojo & Onwuegbuzie, 2020; also see Chapter 25).
- Inferential-based quantitizing: Sentiment codes correlated with demographic variables to determine the subgroups that are most likely to provide negative sentiments.
- Descriptive-based quantitizing: Aggregate quantitized themes in the inter-respondent matrix by South African province (a total of 9 provinces); 1 column for each province in the inter-respondent matrix).
- Exploratory-based quantitizing: Correspondence analysis of aggregated themes (from inter-respondent matrix) as a function of South African province to determine (a) the relationship among the provinces of faculty perceptions, (b) the relationship among the themes, and (c) the relationship between the themes and the provinces. See Chapter 3.
- Exploratory-based quantitizing: 2-D and 3-D multidimensional scaling on co-occurrences of words or content categories relating faculty perceptions. See Chapters 4 and 25.
- Exploratory-based quantitizing: Hierarchical clustering used to explore the similarity among the provinces with respect to themes extracted from the topic modeling. See Chapters 5 and 25.
- Inferential-based quantitizing: Chi-square automatic interaction detection analysis to determine which of the quantitized (i.e., binarized) themes extracted from the topic modeling is related to a categorized (e.g., high vs. medium vs. low) quantitative perception scale scores or select categorized subscale scores from the quantitative phase. See Chapters 6 and 30.
- Inferential-based quantitizing: Multiple linear regression analysis to examine the extent to which the quantitized (i.e., binarized) themes extracted from the topic modeling (with or without select demographic variables) predicts quantitative perception scale scores or select subscale scores from the quantitative phase. See Chapters 7 and 30.
- Inferential-based quantitizing: Structural equation modeling of involving the quantitized (i.e., binarized) themes extracted from the topic modeling, the quantitative perception scale/subscale scores, and demographic variables. See Chapter 8.
- Inferential-based quantitizing: Hierarchical linear modeling (IV: Level 1: faculty member [e.g., quantitized themes, demographic variables]; Level 2: home city of faculty [other Level 2 variables can be extracted as secondary data, such as poverty index for each province]; DV: total perception scale scores only OR select perception subscale scores). See Chapter 9.

- Inferential-based quantitizing: Bayesian linear regression analysis to examine the extent to which the quantitized (i.e., binarized) themes extracted from the topic modeling (with or without select demographic variables) predicts quantitative perception scale scores or select subscale scores from the quantitative phase. See Chapters 10 and 30.
- Multi-quantitizing: Twostep cluster analysis of quantitized themes in the inter-respondent matrix to determine the number of clusters (i.e., profiles) underlying the open-ended responses. Then, a series of chi-square analyses of these clusters with respect to the categorical demographic variables (e.g., gender) and a series of independent samples t test with regard to the continuous demographic variables to determine how these clusters differed. These analyses would yield comparative narrative profiles (i.e., *qualitizing* based on both *quantitative data* and *qualitative data*). See Chapters 13 and 30.
- Quantitizing and qualitizing: Qualitative comparative analysis by creating a truth table involving the quantitized (i.e., binarized) themes extracted from the topic modeling and a categorized (e.g., high vs. medium vs. low) quantitative perception scale scores or select categorized subscale scores from the quantitative phase. See Chapter 17.
- Exploratory-based quantitizing and qualitizing: Social network analysis of faculty perceptions (VOSviewer 1.6.14; Van Eck & Waltman, 2014, 2017). See Chapters 19 and 20.
- Exploratory-based quantitizing and qualitizing: Using the city and state/province (or post code) information extracted from the online survey to convert to longitude and latitude data. Then, using the longitude and latitude data to map both the themes extracted from the topic modeling and the quantitative perception scale scores and subscale scores from the quantitative phase, alongside other secondary data (e.g., poverty index). See Chapter 21.
- Quantitizing and qualitizing: Conducting a nonverbal communication analysis of the open-ended responses, for example, by analyzing emojis, bitmojis, and other images or symbols used by the faculty participants. See Chapter 22.
- Quantitizing and qualitizing: Developing one or more case comparison tables wherein the provinces serve as the cases. See Chapter 23.
- Quantitizing and qualitizing: Developing one or more joint displays that include both qualitative data (e.g., themes extracted from open-ended responses) and quantitative data (e.g., quantitative perception scale scores and subscale scores; demographic information). See Chapter 24.

Therefore, as can be seen, of the 23 sets of mixed analysis approaches described in the 23 chapters of Parts I–III, the ongoing study (i.e., Ojo & Onwuegbuzie, in press) has the potential to utilize 17 of them. Only the following six mixed analyses likely cannot be incorporated for the present study: item response theory integrating qualitative data (Chapter 11), diachronic analysis of qualitative data (Chapter 12), coding techniques for quantitative and mixed data (Chapter 14), mixed methodological discourse analysis (Chapter 15), ethnographic decision models with qualitative data (Chapter 16), and Q methodology with qualitative data (Chapter 18). These analyses would not be possible without going beyond Ojo and Onwuegbuzie's (in press) online survey by collecting more data (e.g., collecting Q-sort data for a Q methodology mixed analysis). Nevertheless, this example shows that by being creative in the analysis process, for almost any given mixed methods study, researchers have many options for conducting mixed analysis in general and crossover mixed analyses in particular.

5 Suggested Applications of Mixed Analysis

Onwuegbuzie and Hitchcock (2019) recently called for an extension of mixed methods research wherein mixed methods research is combined with multiple methods research to yield even richer and more rigorous studies. In particular, these authors introduced the concept of *multi-mixed methods research approaches* and *meta-methods research approaches*. According to these authors, multi-mixed methods research approaches involve the partial integration of multiple methods research approaches and mixed methods research approaches, whereas meta-methods study approaches involve the full[er] integration of multiple methods research approaches and mixed methods research approaches. Ojo and Onwuegbuzie's (2020) study, mentioned earlier, provides an example of both a *multi-mixed methods research approach* and *meta-methods research approach*, as indicated by the title of their empirical study. Like this study, the ongoing study (i.e., Ojo & Onwuegbuzie, in press) described in the previous section showed how using multiple mixed analysis approaches allows the researcher to answer increasingly complex and complicated research questions. For example, by combining a general linear model-based mixed analysis approach (e.g., multiple linear regression of qualitative data) with both a diachronic analysis-based crossover mixed analysis approach and a GIS-based crossover mixed analysis approach, the analyst will be incorporating time, place, and space into the mixed analyses. Therefore, we encourage researchers to be as creative as possible when designing their crossover mixed analysis approaches.

6 Strengths and Limitations of Mixed Analysis

An important limitation to the use of mixed analyses in general and crossover mixed analyses in particular stems from the lack of methodological guidance in the extant literature on these topics. However, by including 29 chapters, it is hoped that this book represents a giant leap in an appropriate direction. Notwithstanding, we encourage authors of mixed methods research works to focus some of their authorship efforts to providing a discussion of the topic of (crossover) mixed analyses.

Another limitation associated with the use of (crossover) mixed analyses is the additional resources needed. These resources include intellectual, financial, and time resources needed to incorporate a more in-depth analysis. One way of reducing these demands is via collaboration. Interestingly, Onwuegbuzie, Wilcox, et al. (2018) documented that the degree of collaboration for mixed methods research journal articles lies between 66.7% (for articles published in the *International Journal of Multiple Research Approaches* [*IJMRA*]: 2007–2014) and 71.2% (for articles published in the *Journal of Mixed Methods Research* [*JMMR*]: 2007–2014), with the mean number of authors for *JMMR* being statistically significantly higher than is the rate for quantitative research journals and qualitative research journals. So, clearly, collaboration is the norm among mixed methods researchers. Therefore, we encourage researchers, especially inexperienced researchers, whenever possible, to collaborate whenever they plan to conduct (crossover) mixed analyses. In fact, most researchers—even experienced mixed methods researchers—could benefit from collaboration because few researchers are adept in both quantitative analysis and qualitative analysis to negotiate a crossover mixed analysis alone.

In terms of the conduct of crossover mixed analyses, researchers need to be cognizant of the fact that there might be times when the use of crossover mixed analyses is not justified. Onwuegbuzie and Johnson (in press) referred to the threat to legitimation that crossover mixed analyses pose as providing a threat to crossover analysis legitimation. Broadly speaking, crossover mixed analysis legitimation is the extent to which using a crossover mixed analysis yields findings and, subsequently, meta-inferences that are credible, trustworthy, dependable, transferable, and/or confirmable. Crossover analysis legitimation includes conversion legitimation, mixed analysis assumption legitimation, sequential mixed analysis legitimation, and mixed analysis commensurability approximation legitimation. As conceptualized by Onwuegbuzie and Johnson (2006), *conversion legitimation* is the extent to which the quantitizing and/or qualitizing yields quality meta-inferences. As such, this represents more of an issue pertaining to external credibility. That is, conversion legitimation represents an external credibility issue because it "pertains to the confirmability and transferability of findings and conclusions" (Onwuegbuzie & Leech, 2007, p. 235), bearing in mind that meta-inferences represent generalizations (i.e., meaning-making) that stem from the underlying set of findings.

In contrast, *mixed analysis assumption legitimation* refers to the extent that the assumptions relating to the quantitative analysis and/or the qualitative analysis have been met (Onwuegbuzie & Johnson, in press). For example, in order to justify use of an exploratory factor analysis/principal components analysis of themes that have been quantitized within an inter-respondent matrix, all assumptions regarding the exploratory factor analysis/principal components analysis should be met, with the most important assumption being normality. Now because the quantitizing of themes yields categorical data in general and typically yields dichotomous data, when the inter-respondent matrix of themes is converted to a matrix of bivariate associations among the themes, these bivariate associations are not appropriate to use for an exploratory factor analysis/principal components analysis because of the violation of the bivariate normality assumption. Instead, this matrix of bivariate associations should be converted to a matrix of tetrachoric correlation coefficients because the latter is based on the assumption that for each manifest dichotomous variable, there is a normally distributed latent continuous variable with zero mean and unit variance (Onwuegbuzie et al., 2007). That is, tetrachoric correlation coefficients are appropriate to use when one is determining the relationship between two (artificial) dichotomous variables. If, instead, a matrix of tetrachoric correlation coefficients from the original correlations is used, then this would affect positively the validity of the solution extracted via the exploratory factor analysis/principal components analysis. Another important assumption associated with an exploratory factor analysis/principal components analysis is the participant-to-variable ratio. Now, a minimum participant-to-variable ratio of 10 participants per variable has been suggested by some factor analysts (Cattell, 1978; Everitt, 1975; Gorsuch, 1983; Hatcher, 1994; Onwuegbuzie & Daniel, 2003), and even a participant-to-variable ratio of 20 participants per variable has been suggested by Hair, Anderson, Tatham, and Black (1995) and MacCallum, Widaman, Preacher, and Hong (2001). Further, the recommended minimum sample size for exploratory factor analysis/principal components analysis has ranged between 150 and 250 that Hogarty, Hines, Kromrey, Ferron, and Mumford (2005) identified from an array of textbooks and research articles. Therefore, failure to follow the normality assumption, sample size assumptions, and other assumptions would threaten analysis assumption legitimation. A sample size of, say, less than 50 (Comrey & Lee, 1992) likely would yield unstable results, unless the data are *well conditioned*, characterized by high communality, small number of factors, *and* a large number of themes (de Winter, Dodou, & Wieringa, 2009), or a technique called maximum likelihood regularized exploratory factor analysis is used (Jung & Takane, 2008), which can yield stable factor-loading estimates for very small sample sizes (often in the order of tens) (Jung & Lee, 2011). Therefore, mixed analysis assumption legitimation represents an internal credibility issue because it refers to the "truth value, applicability, consistency, neutrality, dependability, and/or credibility of interpretations and conclusions within the underlying setting or group" (Onwuegbuzie & Leech, 2007, p. 234). As such, when planning their mixed analysis designs, researchers should be aware of the pertinent analysis assumptions.

Sequential mixed analysis legitimation refers to (a) the degree to which the mixed analyses appropriately build on earlier qualitative and/or quantitative *analyses* and (b) the extent to which the meta-inferences could be affected by reversing the sequence of the mixed analyses (Onwuegbuzie & Johnson, in press). This legitimation threat is different than Onwuegbuzie and Johnson's (2006) sequential legitimation threat, which is the extent to which the researchers appropriately build on effects and findings from earlier qualitative and quantitative *phases* and has minimized the potential problem wherein the meta-inferences could be affected by reversing the sequence of the quantitative and qualitative *phases* [emphasis added], which, for example, is not a threat in concurrent mixed methods research designs. In contrast, sequential mixed *analysis* legitimation also is a threat in concurrent mixed methods research designs because such designs do not prevent sequential mixed analyses from taking place. Sequential mixed analysis legitimation is an external credibility issue because a particular mixed analysis sequence could yield quality meta-inferences, but nonetheless, meta-inferences that are different than if another mixed analysis sequence had been used. Consequently, when meaning making, researchers should reflect on the role that the mixed analysis sequence might have played in the meta-inferencing process.

Mixed analysis commensurability approximation legitimation refers to the extent to which the ensuing meta-inferences reflect quantitative analyses and qualitative analyses that reflect a similar level of analytic competence and rigor. For example, if either the quantitative analysis phase(s) or qualitative analysis phase(s) reflects an under-analysis (i.e., overly simplistic analysis) of the data, then the level of interaction between findings stemming from the quantitative analyses and qualitative analyses might not be optimal, thereby adversely reflecting the quality of meta-inferences. Mixed analysis commensurability approximation legitimation is an internal credibility issue because it refers to the richness of the findings themselves. Therefore, we encourage researchers to select their teams carefully such that for every intended analysis in the mixed analysis process, there is at least one competent researcher on the team to conduct the analyses. In fact, we suggest that crossover analysis approaches are most enhanced via a team-based approach (Baim-Lance, Onwuegbuzie, & Wisdom, 2020) that incorporates one of the following three collaborative models: (a) a team of researchers consisting of at least one researcher who is competent in an array of quantitative data analysis approaches and at least one researcher who is competent in an array of qualitative research approaches; (b) a team of researchers that consists of researchers with minimum competency in conducting an array of both quantitative and qualitative data analysis approaches, alongside a specialized set of competencies in conducting one of these two analysis approaches—what Teddlie and Tashakkori (2003) referred to as "the minimum competency model" (p. 45); or (c) a team that contains not only some researchers with minimum competency in conducting both quantitative and qualitative data analysis approaches but also includes at least one researcher who

> is competent at conducting mixed research (e.g., a mixed researcher) who can serve the triple role as a process person (who strives for "philosophical clarity and [recognizes that] the perspectives and values and standards of the relevant com-munities of practice play continuous, holistic, and synergistic roles in the legitimation process" [Collins, Onwuegbuzie, & Johnson, 2012, p. 854]), a translator (who explains the methods used to members of the research team who are not proficient with that tradition), and a negotiator (who identifies and negotiates contradictions, paradoxes, and tensions that emerge when findings from the qualitative and quantitative phases are compared and contrasted). (Collins et al., 2013, p. 278)

In any case, despite these limitations, conducting crossover mixed analyses has logical and practical appeal because it promotes a more comprehensive and interactive approach to analyzing data in mixed methods research. Indeed, we believe that conducting crossover mixed analyses is consistent with the notion of *active mixed analyses*, wherein crossover mixed analyses promote active meaning-making endeavors. Thus, crossover mixed analyses have significant potential for transforming the mixed analysis process, going far beyond the traditional practice in mixed methods research of only conducting quantitative monoanalysis coupled with qualitative monoanalysis. Moreover, by increasing the level of integration during the mixed analysis process, crossover mixed analyses can help mixed methods researchers fulfill the hermeneutic circle, as an iterative circle of understanding (Warren, 2002).

In advancing crossover mixed analyses in our book, we are promoting an alternative epistemological model of analyzing data in mixed methods research studies, as well as quantitative research studies and qualitative research studies. However, it should be noted that we are not advocating that crossover analyses *replace* non-crossover analyses. In fact, many crossover analyses involve some form of monoanalysis. For example, quantitizing (which, as a reminder, involves the quantitative analysis of qualitative data) often follows the qualitative analysis of qualitative data (i.e., monoanalysis) as a first step—for instance, using constant comparison analysis of interview data to identify themes (i.e., qualitative analysis of qualitative data), which then are binarized (e.g., before being situated within an inter-respondent matrix for additional analyses). Therefore, for the most part, crossover analyses *do not replace* non-crossover analyses; if anything, they *add* to non-crossover analyses, thereby enabling researchers to get more out of their data.

We believe that by conducting crossover mixed analyses, the ensuing findings can provide richer information that can enhance understanding (i.e., increasing Verstehen; Dilthey, 1961; Martin, 2000; Outhwaite, 1975; Weber & Shils, 1949) of the underlying phenomenon, thereby helping to address important research questions about our rich and complex social world. Notwithstanding, we recognize that this alternative model of mixed analysis adds a layer of complexity to the data analysis process; yet, we believe that this is offset by the fact that this method of analyzing data encourages the researcher to dig deeper into the corpus of data. Thus, by conducting crossover mixed analyses, new forms of knowledge and understanding occur. We are hopeful that, after reading this book, mixed analyses in general and crossover mixed analyses in particular provide a concrete, systematic, progressive, and interactive methodology for shifting mixed analyses from just a simple and linear process (i.e., quantitative monoanalysis + qualitative monoanalysis) to a dynamic, integrated, and engaging mixed analysis process, affording pathways for helping mixed methods researchers conduct mixed analyses that get more out of their data.

7 Resources for Learning More About Mixed Analysis

Some discussion of mixed analyses are available as YouTube videos, as follows:

youtube.com/watch?v=YnUMpJ0gmLU
www.youtube.com/watch?v=3D8A7fm4S9g

Also, here are links to two useful YouTube Videos on joint displays:

www.youtube.com/watch?v=U6KvCN-7ZKM&t=134s
www.youtube.com/watch?v=jnJe0Vo2vVM

Further, there are several YouTube videos presented by software developers and trainers/educators.

However, the best resources for learning about mixed analysis can be obtained by reading (and studying) every chapter in this book, examining the resources provided at the end of each chapter, and identifying and reading empirical research articles that use the mixed analyses covered in this book (and any additional mixed analyses not seen in this book). Finally, we recommend that readers download as many versions of the free-trial qualitative and mixed methods software programs (which are often 30 days in length) at a time when they can familiarize themselves with these software programs, as well as view/read the tutorials and manuals, and register for the (free) webinars that the software developers offer.

REFERENCES

Anderson, M. T., Ingram, J. M., Buford, B. J., Rosli, R., Bledsoe, M. L., & Onwuegbuzie, A. J. (2012). Doctoral students' perceptions of characteristics of effective college teachers: A mixed analysis. *International Journal of Doctoral Studies*, 7, 279–309. Retrieved from http://ijds.org/Volume7/IJDSv7p279-309Anderson0360.pdf

Andrich, D. (1988). *Rasch models for measurement*. Thousand Oaks, CA: Sage.

Baim-Lance, A., Onwuegbuzie, A. J., & Wisdom, J. (2020). Project management principles for optimizing publication productivity of mixed methods studies. *The Qualitative Report*, 25, 646–661. Retrieved from https://nsuworks.nova.edu/tqr/vol25/iss3/6

Baker, F. B. (2001). *The basic of item response theory* (2nd ed.). Retrieved from http://ericae.net/

Bell, B. A., Morgan, G. B., Schoeneberger, J. A., Kromrey, J. D., & Ferron, J. M. (2014). How low can you go? An investigation of the influence of sample size and model complexity on point and interval estimates in two-level linear models. *Methodology*, 10, 1–11. doi:10.1027/1614-2241/a000062

Blanchard, P., Rihoux, B., & Álamos-Concha, P. (2017). Comprehensively mapping political science methods: An instructors' survey. *International Journal of Social Research Methodology*, 20, 209–224. doi:10.1080/1364557 9.2015.1129128

Bond, T. G., & Fox, C. M. (2015). *Applying the Rasch model: Fundamental measurement in the human sciences* (3rd ed). London, England: Lawrence Erlbaum Associates.

Brown, S. R. (1980). *Political subjectivity: Applications of Q methodology in political science*. New Haven, CT: Yale University Press.

Brown, S. R. (2008). Q methodology. In L. M. Given (Ed.), *The SAGE encyclopedia of qualitative research methods* (pp. 700–704). Thousand Oaks, CA: Sage.

Carbonell, K. B., Marcum, C., Könings, K. D., Stassen, P. M., Segers, M., & van Merriënboer, J. (2020). The role of knowing and valuing others' expertise in accelerating information exchange, In D. Froehlich, M. Rehm, & B. Rienties (Eds.), *Mixed methods approaches to social network analysis* (pp. 189–205). London, England: Routledge.

Cattell, R. B. (1978). *The scientific use of factor analysis in behavioral and life sciences*. New York, NY: Plenum.

Collins, K. M. T., Onwuegbuzie, A. J., & Johnson, R. B. (2012). Securing a place at the table: A review and extension of legitimation criteria for the conduct of mixed research. *American Behavioral Scientist, 56*, 849–865. doi:10.1177/0002764211433799

Collins, K. M. T., Onwuegbuzie, A. J., Johnson, R. B., & Frels, R. K. (2013). Practice note: Using debriefing interviews to promote authenticity and transparency in mixed research. *International Journal of Multiple Research Approaches, 7*, 271–283. doi:10.5172/mra.2013.7.2.271

Combs, J. P., & Onwuegbuzie, A. J. (2010). Describing and illustrating data analysis in mixed research. *International Journal of Education, 2*(2), EX, 1–23. Retrieved from www.macrothink.org/journal/index.php/ije/article/viewFile/526/392

Comrey, A. L., & Lee, H. B. (1992). *A first course in factor analysis* (2nd ed.). Hillsdale, NJ: Erlbaum.

Crandell, J. L., Voils, C.I., Chang, Y., & Sandelowski, M. (2011). Bayesian data augmentation methods for the synthesis of qualitative and quantitative research findings. *Quality & Quantity, 45*, 653–669. doi:10.1007/s11135-010-9375-z

Cui, Y., & Hannig, J. (2019, September). Nonparametric generalized fiducial inference for survival functions under censoring. *Biometrika, 106*, 501–518. doi:10.1093/biomet/asz016

de Winter, J. C. F., Dodou, D., & Wieringa, P. A. (2009). Exploratory factor analysis with small sample sizes. *Multivariate Behavioral Research*, 147–181. doi:10.1080/00273170902794206

Denham, M. A., & Onwuegbuzie, A. J. (2013). Beyond words: Using nonverbal communication data in research to enhance thick description and interpretation. *International Journal of Qualitative Methods, 12*, 670–696. doi:10.1177/160940691301200137

Dilthey, W. (1961). *Patterns and meanings in history* (H. P. Ruckman, Trans.). New York, NY: Harper & Row.

Edwards, G. (2010). *Mixed-method approaches to social network analysis*. Southampton, England: ESRC National Centre for Research Methods.

Everitt, B. S. (1975). Multivariate analysis: The need for data, and other problems. *British Journal of Psychiatry, 126*, 237–240. doi:10.1192/bjp.126.3.237

Fetters, M. D., Curry, L. A., & Creswell, J. W. (2013). Achieving integration in mixed methods designs. Principles and practice. *Health Services Research, 48*, 2134–2156. doi:10.1111/1475-6773.12117

Field, A. (2018). *Discovering statistics: Using SPSS for Windows* (5th ed.). London, England: Sage.

Fielding, N., & Cisneros-Puebla, C. (2009). CAQDAS-GIS convergence: Towards a new integrated mixed method research practice? *Journal of Mixed Methods Research, 3*, 349–370. doi:10.1177/1558689809344973

Frels, J. G., Frels, R. K., & Onwuegbuzie, A. J. (2011). Geographic information systems: A mixed methods spatial approach in business and management research and beyond. *International Journal of Multiple Research Approaches, 5*, 367–386. doi:10.5172/mra.2011.5.3.367

Frels, R. K., & Onwuegbuzie, A. J. (2012). Interviewing the interpretive researcher: An impressionist tale. *The Qualitative Report, 17*(Art. 60), 1–27. Retrieved from www.nova.edu/ssss/QR/QR17/frels.pdf

Froehlich, D., Rehm, M., & Rienties, B. (Eds.). (2020). *Mixed methods approaches to social network analysis*. London, England: Routledge.

Geisser, S. (2006). *Modes of parametric statistical inference*. New York, NY: John Wiley & Sons.

Gelman, A., Carlin, J. B., Stern, H. S., Dunson, D. B., Vehtari, A., & Rubin, D. B. (2013). *Bayesian data analysis* (3rd ed.). Boca Raton, FL: Chapman & Hall.

Gerber, H. G., Lynch, T. L., & Onwuegbuzie, A. J. (in press). *Making big data small: Designing integrated digital approaches for social science research*. Thousand Oaks, CA: Sage.

Gibbons, J. D. (1993). *Nonparametric measures of association* (Sage University Paper series on Quantitative Applications in the Social Sciences, series no. 07B091). Newbury Park, CA: Sage.

Gill, J. (2014). *Bayesian methods: A social and behavioral sciences approach* (3rd ed.). Boca Raton, FL: Chapman & Hall.

Glaser, B. G. (1965). The constant comparative method of qualitative analysis. *Social Problems, 12*, 436–445. doi:10.1525/sp.1965.12.4.03a00070

Glaser, B. G., & Strauss, A. L. (1967). *The discovery of grounded theory: Strategies for qualitative research*. Chicago, IL: Aldine.

Glass, G. (1976). Primary, secondary, and meta-analysis of research. *Educational Researcher, 5*(10), 3–8. doi:10.3102/0013189X005010003

Gorsuch, R. L. (1983). *Factor analysis* (2nd ed.). Hillsdale, NJ: Lawrence Erlbaum Associates.

Guetterman, T., Creswell, J. W., & Kuckartz, U. (2015). Using joint displays and MAXQDA software to represent the results of mixed methods research. In M. T. McCrudden, G. Schraw, & C. W. Buckendahl (Eds.), *Use of visual displays in research and testing* (pp. 145–175). Charlotte, NC: Information Age Publishing.

Guetterman, T. C., Fetters, M. D., & Creswell, J. W. (2015). Integrating quantitative and qualitative results in health science mixed methods research through joint displays. *Annals of Family Medicine, 13*, 554–561. doi:10.1370/afm.1865

Hair, J. F. J., Anderson, R. E., Tatham, R. L., & Black, W. C. (1995). *Multivariate data analysis* (4th ed.). Saddle River, NJ: Prentice Hall.

Hambleton R. K., Swaminathan, H., & Rogers, H. J. (1991). *Fundamentals of item response theory*. Newbury Park, CA: Sage.

Hatcher, L. (1994). *A step-by-step approach to using the SAS® system for factor analysis and structural equation modeling*. Cary, N.C.: SAS Institute, Inc.

Hitchcock, J. H., & Onwuegbuzie, A. J. (2020). Developing mixed methods crossover analysis approaches. *Journal of Mixed Methods Research, 14*, 63–83. doi:10.1177/1558689819841782

Hogarty, K. Y., Hines, C. V., Kromrey, J. D., Ferron, J. M., & Mumford, K. R. (2005). The quality of factor solutions in exploratory factor analysis: The influence of sample size, communality, and overdetermination. *Educational and Psychological Measurement, 65*, 202–226. doi:10.1177/0013164404267287

Hollander, M., Wolfe, D. A., & Chicken, E. (2014). *Nonparametric statistical methods* (3rd ed.). Hoboken, NJ: John Wiley & Sons.

Hollstein, B. (2011). *Qualitative approaches to social reality: The search for meaning.* In J. Scott & P. J. Carrington (Eds.), *The Sage handbook of social network analysis* (pp. 404–416). London, England: Sage.

Hox, J. J. (1998). Multilevel modeling: When and why. In I. Balderjahn, R. Mathar, & M. Schader (Eds.), *Classification, data analysis, and data highways* (pp. 147–154). New York, NY: Springer.

Howell, D. C. (2017). *Fundamental statistics for the behavioral sciences* (9th ed.). Boston, MA: Cengage Learning.

Johnson, R. B. (2012). Dialectical pluralism and mixed research. *American Behavioral Scientist, 56*, 751–754. doi:10.1177/0002764212442494

Johnson, R. B., Onwuegbuzie, A. J., de Waal, C., Stefurak, T., & Hildebrand, D. (2017). Unpacking pragmatism for mixed methods research: The philosophies of Peirce, James, Dewey, and Rorty. In D. Wyse, N. Selwyn, E. Smith, & L. E. Suter (Eds.), *The BERA/SAGE Handbook of Educational Research* (pp. 259–279). London, England: Sage.

Johnson, R. B. (2017). Dialectical pluralism: A metaparadigm whose time has come. *Journal of Mixed Methods Research, 11*(2), 156–173. doi:10.1177/1558689815607692

Johnson, R. B., Russo, F., & Schoonenboom, J. (2019). Causation in mixed methods research: The meeting of philosophy, science, and practice. *Journal of Mixed Methods Research, 13*, 143–162 doi:10.1177/1558689817719610

Jung, S., & Lee, S. (2011). Exploratory factor analysis for small samples. *Behavioral Research Methods, 43*, 701–709. doi10.3758/s13428-011-0077-9

Jung, S., & Takane, Y. (2008). Regularized exploratory factor analysis. In K. Shigemasu, A. Okada, T. Imaizumi, & T. Hoshino (Eds.), *New trends in psychometrics* (pp. 141–149). Tokyo, Japan: University Academic Press.

Larkin, M., Watts, S., & Clifton, E. (2006). Giving voice and making sense in interpretative phenomenological analysis. *Qualitative Research in Psychology, 3*, 102–120. doi:10.1191/1478088706qp062oa

Leech, N. L., & Onwuegbuzie, A. J. (2019). A call for greater use of nonparametric statistics. *Research in the Schools, 26*(2), xiii–xxvi.

Li, S., Marquart, J. M., & Zercher, C. (2000). Conceptual issues and analytical strategies in mixed-method studies of preschool inclusion. *Journal of Early Intervention, 23*, 116–132. doi:10.1177/105381510002300206

Lynch, S. M. (2007). *Introduction to applied Bayesian statistics and estimation for social scientists.* New York, NY: Springer.

Lynch, T. L., & Gerber, H. R. (2018). The ontological imperative when researching in the digital age. *International Journal of Multiple Research Approaches, 10*, 112–123. doi:10.29034/ijmra.v10n1a7

Maas, C. J. M., & Hox, J. J. (2004). Robustness issues in multilevel regression analysis. *Statistica Neerlandica, 58*, 127–137. doi:10.1046/j.0039-0402.2003.00252.x

Maas, C. J. M., & Hox, J. J. (2005). Sufficient sample sizes for multilevel modeling. *Methodology, 1*, 86–92. doi:10.1027/1614-2241.1.3.86

MacCallum, R. C., Widaman, K. F., Preacher, K. J., & Hong, S. (2001). Sample size in factor analysis: The role of model error. *Multivariate Behavioral Research36*, 611–637. doi:10.1207/S15327906MBR3604_06

Martin, M. (2000). *Verstehen: The uses of understanding in social science.* New Brunswick, NJ: Transaction.

McLafferty, C. L., Slate, J. R., & Onwuegbuzie, A. J. (2010). Transcending the quantitative–qualitative divide with mixed methods: A multidimensional framework for understanding congruence, coherence, and completeness in the study of values. *Counseling and Values, 55*(1), 46–62. doi:10.1002/j.2161-007X.2010.tb00021.x

Miles, M., & Huberman, A. M. (1994). *Qualitative data analysis: An expanded sourcebook* (2nd ed.). Thousand Oaks, CA: Sage.

Miles, M., Huberman, A. M., & Saldaňa, J. (2020). *Qualitative data analysis: A methods sourcebook* (4th ed.). Thousand Oaks, CA: Sage.

Moineddin, R., Matheson, F. I., & Glazier, R. H. (2007). A simulation study of sample size for multilevel logistic regression models. *BMS Medical Research Methodology, 7*, 1–10. doi:10.1186/1471-2288-7-34

Newman, I., Onwuegbuzie, A. J., & Hitchcock, J. H. (2015). Using the general linear model to facilitate the full integration of qualitative and quantitative analysis: The potential to improve prediction and theory building and testing. *General Linear Model Journal, 41*(1), 12–28. Retrieved from www.glmj.org/archives/articles/Newman_v41n1.pdf

Noether, G. E. (2012). *Introduction to statistics: The nonparametric way.* New York, NY: Springer-Verlag.

Ojo, E. O., & Onwuegbuzie, A. J. (2020). University life in an era of disruption of COVID-19: A meta-methods and multimixed methods research study of perceptions and attitudes of South African students. *International Journal of Multiple Research Approaches, 12*(3), 4–19. doi:10.29034/ijmra.v12n1editorial2.

Ojo, E. O., & Onwuegbuzie, A. J. (in press). Faculty life in an era of disruption of COVID-19: A meta-methods and multimixed methods research study of perceptions, attitudes, and experiences of South African faculty regarding teaching and scholarship conducted online. *International Journal of Multiple Research Approaches.*

Onwuegbuzie, A. J. (2003). Effect sizes in qualitative research: A prolegomenon. *Quality & Quantity: International Journal of Methodology, 37*, 393–409. doi:10.1023/A:1027379223537

Onwuegbuzie, A. J. (2020). The PRICE of Mixed Methods Social Network Analysis (MMSNA): Towards an ethical process for MMSNA. In D. Froehlich, M. Rehm, & B. Rienties (Eds.), *Mixed methods approaches to social network analysis* (pp. 245–262). London, England: Routledge.

Onwuegbuzie, A. J., & Abrams, S. S. (in press). *An integrated mixed methods approach to nonverbal communication data: A practical guide to collection and analysis in online and offline spaces.* New York, NY: Routledge.

Onwuegbuzie, A. J., Bustamante, R. M., & Nelson, J. A. (2010). Mixed research as a tool for developing quantitative instruments. *Journal of Mixed Methods Research, 4*, 56–78. doi:10.1177/1558689809355805

Onwuegbuzie, A. J., & Collins, K. M. T. (2010). An innovative method for stress and coping researchers for analyzing themes in mixed research: Introducing chi-square automatic interaction detection (CHAID). In G. S. Gates, W. H. Gmelch, & M. Wolverton (Series Eds.) & K. M. T. Collins, A. J. Onwuegbuzie, & Q. G. Jiao (Vol. Eds.), *Toward a broader understanding of stress and coping: Mixed methods approaches* (pp. 287–301). The Research on Stress and Coping in Education Series (Vol. 5). Charlotte, NC: Information Age Publishing.

Onwuegbuzie, A. J., & Combs, J. P. (2010). Emergent data analysis techniques in mixed methods research: A synthesis. In A. Tashakkori & C. Teddlie (Eds.), *Handbook of mixed methods in social and behavioral research* (2nd ed., pp. 397–430). Thousand Oaks, CA: Sage.

Onwuegbuzie, A. J., & Combs, J. P. (2011). Data analysis in mixed research: A primer. *International Journal of Education*, 3(1): E13. Retrieved from www.macrothink.org/journal/index.php/ije/article/view/618/550

Onwuegbuzie, A. J., & Daniel, L. G. (2003, February 12). Typology of analytical and interpretational errors in quantitative and qualitative educational research. *Current Issues in Education*, 6(2). Retrieved from https://cie.asu.edu/ojs/index.php/cieatasu/article/view/1609/651

Onwuegbuzie, A. J., & Frels, R. K. (2013). Introduction: Towards a new research philosophy for addressing social justice issues: Critical dialectical pluralism 1.0. *International Journal of Multiple Research Approaches*, 7, 9–26. doi:10.5172/mra.2013.7.1.9

Onwuegbuzie, A. J., & Frels, R. K. (2015). Using Q methodology in the literature review process: A mixed research approach. *Journal of Educational Issues*, 1, 90–109. doi:10.5296/jei.v1i2.8396. Retrieved from www.macrothink.org/journal/index.php/jei/article/view/8396/6991

Onwuegbuzie, A. J., Gerber, H. R., & Abrams, S. S. (2017). Mixed methods research. *The International Encyclopedia of Communication Research Methods*, 1–33. doi:10.1002/9781118901731.iecrm0156

Onwuegbuzie, A. J., & Hitchcock, J. H. (2015). Advanced mixed analysis approaches. In S. N. Hesse-Biber & R. B. Johnson (Eds.), *Oxford handbook of multimethod and mixed methods research*. New York, NY: Oxford.

Onwuegbuzie, A. J., & Hitchcock, J. H. (2019). Using mathematical formulae as proof for integrating mixed methods research and multiple methods research approaches: A call for multimixed methods and meta-methods in a mixed research 2.0 era. *International Journal of Multiple Research Approaches*, 11, 213–234. doi:10.29034/ijmra.v11n3editorial2

Onwuegbuzie, A. J., & Hitchcock, J. H. (2020). On qualitizing revisited. Unpublished manuscript, University of Cambridge

Onwuegbuzie, A. J., Hitchcock, J. H., Natesan, P., & Newman, I. (2018). Using fully integrated Bayesian thinking to address the 1 + 1 = 1 integration challenge. *International Journal of Multiple Research Approaches*, 10, 666–678. doi:10.29034/ijmra.v10n1a43

Onwuegbuzie, A. J., & Hwang, E. (2019a). Frequency in the use of visual displays and its predictability of the editor's decision of manuscripts submitted to *Research in the Schools*? *Research in the Schools*, 26(1), i–x.

Onwuegbuzie, A. J., & Hwang, E. (2019b). Writing style, readability, and communication vagueness as a predictor of the use of visual displays among manuscripts submitted to *Research in the Schools*. *Research in the Schools*, 26(2), i–xii.

Onwuegbuzie, A. J., & Johnson, R. B. (2006). The validity issue in mixed research. *Research in the Schools*, 13(1), 48–63.

Onwuegbuzie, A. J., & Johnson, R. B. (in press). Legitimation in a mixed research 2.0 era. *International Journal of Multiple Research Approaches*.

Onwuegbuzie, A. J., & Leech, N. L. (2004). Enhancing the interpretation of "significant" findings: The role of mixed methods research. *The Qualitative Report*, 9, 770–792. Retrieved from https://nsuworks.nova.edu/tqr/vol9/iss4/10/Onwuegbuzie.pdf

Onwuegbuzie, A. J., & Leech, N. L. (2007). Validity and qualitative research: An oxymoron? *Quality & Quantity: International Journal of Methodology*, 41, 233–249. doi:10.1007/s11135-006-9000-3

Onwuegbuzie, A. J., & Leech, N. L. (2019). On qualitizing. *International Journal of Multiple Research Approaches*, 11, 98–131. doi:10.29034/ijmra.v11n2editorial2

Onwuegbuzie, A. J., Leech, N. L., & Collins, K. M. T. (2008). Interviewing the interpretive researcher: A method for addressing the crises of representation, legitimation, and praxis. *International Journal of Qualitative Methods*, 7(4), 1–17.

Onwuegbuzie, A. J., Leech, N. L., & Collins, K. M. T. (2011). Toward a new era for conducting mixed analyses: The role of quantitative dominant and qualitative dominant crossover mixed analyses. In M. Williams & W. P. Vogt (Eds.), *The Sage handbook of innovation in social research methods* (pp. 353–384). Thousand Oaks, CA: Sage.

Onwuegbuzie, A. J., & Teddlie, C. (2003). A framework for analyzing data in mixed methods research. In A. Tashakkori & C. Teddlie (Eds.), *Handbook of mixed methods in social and behavioral research* (pp. 351–383). Thousand Oaks, CA: Sage.

Onwuegbuzie, A. J., & Weinbaum, R. (2017). A framework for using qualitative comparative analysis for the review of the literature. *The Qualitative Report*, 22, 359–372. Retrieved from http://nsuworks.nova.edu/tqr/vol22/iss2/1

Onwuegbuzie, A. J., Wilcox, R., Gonzales, V., Hoisington, S., Lambert, J., Jordan, J., Aleisa, M., Benge, C. L., Wachsmann, M. S., & Valle, R. (2018). Collaboration patterns among mixed researchers: A multidisciplinary examination. *International Journal of Multiple Research Approaches*, 10, 437–457. doi:10.29034/ijmra.v10n1a30

Onwuegbuzie, A. J., Witcher, A. E., Collins, K. M. T., Filer, J. D., Wiedmaier, C. D., & Moore, C. W. (2007). Students' perceptions of characteristics of effective college teachers: A validity study of a teaching evaluation form using a mixed-methods analysis. *American Educational Research Journal*, 44, 113–160. doi:10.3102/0002831206298169

Outhwaite, W. (1975). *Understanding social life: The method called Verstehen*. London, England: George Allen & Unwin.

Ragin, C. C. (1987). *The comparative method: Moving beyond qualitative and quantitative strategies*. Berkeley, CA: University of California Press.

Reid, K., Flowers, P., & Larkin, M. (2005). Exploring lived experience: An introduction to interpretative phenomenological analysis. *The Psychologist*, 18, 20–23.

Roberts, K., Dixon–Woods, M., Fitzpatrick, R., Abrams, K., & Jones, D. R. (2002). Factors affecting uptake of childhood immunisation: An example of Bayesian synthesis of qualitative and quantitative evidence. *Lancet, 360*, 1596–1599. doi:10.1016/S0140-6736(02)11560-1

Saldaña, J. (2016). *The coding manual for qualitative researchers* (3rd ed.). London, England: Sage.

Sandelowski, M., & Barroso, J. (2003). Creating metasummaries of qualitative findings. *Nursing Research, 52*, 226–233. doi:10.1097/00006199–200307000–00004

Sandelowski, M., Voils, C. I., & Knafl, G. (2009). On quantitizing. *Journal of Mixed Methods Research, 3*, 208–222. doi:10.1177/1558689809334210

Siegel, S. (1956). *Nonparametric statistics for the behavioral sciences*. New York, NY: McGraw-Hill.

Smith, J. A. (1996). Beyond the divide between cognition and discourse: Using interpretative phenomenological analysis in health psychology. *Psychology & Health, 11*, 261–271. doi:10.1080/08870449608400256

Smith, J. A. (2011). Evaluating the contribution of interpretative phenomenological analysis. *Health Psychology Review, 5*, 9–27. doi:10.1080/17437199.2010.510659

Smith, J. A., Flowers, P., & Larkin, M. (2009). *Interpretative phenomenological analysis: Theory, method, and research*. Los Angeles, CA: Sage.

Stern, P., & Harris, C. (1985). Women's health and the self-care paradox: A model to guide self-care readiness—clash between the client and nurse. *Health Care for Women International, 6*, 151–163. doi:10.1080/07399338509515689

Tashakkori, A., & Teddlie, C. (1998). *Mixed methodology: Combining qualitative and quantitative approaches*. Applied Social Research Methods Series (Vol. 46). Thousand Oaks, CA: Sage.

Teddlie, C., & Tashakkori, A. (2003). Major issues and controversies in the use of mixed methods in the social and behavioral sciences. In A. Tashakkori & C. Teddlie (Eds.), *Handbook of mixed methods in social and behavioral research* (pp. 3–50). Thousand Oaks, CA: Sage.

Todorova, I. (2011). Explorations with interpretative phenomenological analysis in different socio-cultural contexts. *Health Psychology Review, 5*, 34–38. doi:10.1080/17437199.2010.520115

Tucker, S., Johnson, R. B., Onwuegbuzie, A. J., & Icenogle, M. L. (2020). Conducting mixed methods research: Using dialectical pluralism and social psychological strategies. In P. Leavy (Ed.), *Oxford handbook of qualitative research methods* (2nd ed., pp. 836–875). Oxford, England, Oxford University Press.

Van Eck, N. J., & Waltman. L. (2014). Visualizing bibliometric networks. In Y. Ding, R. Rousseau, & D. Wolfram (Eds.), *Measuring scholarly impact: Methods and practice* (pp. 285–320). Dordrecht, Netherlands: Springer.

Van Eck, N. J., & Waltman, L. (2017). Citation-based clustering of publications using CitNetExplorer and VOSviewer. *Scientometrics, 111*, 1053–1070. doi:10.1007/s11192-017-2300-7

Van Manen, M. (1990). *Researching lived experience: Human science for an action sensitive pedagogy*. Albany, NY: State University of New York Press.

Voils, C., Hassselblad, V., Crandell, J., Chang, Y., Lee, E., & Sandelowski, M. (2009). A Bayesian method for the synthesis of evidence from qualitative and quantitative reports: The example of antiretroviral medication adherence. *Journal of Health Services Research and Policy, 14*, 226–233. doi:10.1258/jhsrp.2009.008186

Warren, C. A. B. (2002). Qualitative interviewing. In J. Gubrium & J. Holstein (Eds.), *Handbook of interview research: Context and method* (pp. 83–101). Thousand Oaks, CA: Sage.

Weber, M., & Shils, E. (1949). *Max Weber on the methodology of the social sciences*. Glencoe, Ill: Free Press.

Part I

Quantitative Approaches to Qualitative Data

2

Exploratory Factor Analysis of Text

James Van Haneghan

Acknowledgements

The author would like to thank Normand Péladeau for providing some of the background sources for this technique. The author would also like to thank Melissa Dean for her formatting and editing help.

Exploratory Factor Analysis of Text

Historically, the analysis of text has been examined through two approaches. One approach has involved the content analysis of large numbers of texts to explore both quantitative and qualitative aspects of the text (Bernard & Ryan, 2000; Krippendorf, 2013; Ryan & Bernard, 2000). Over the years, content analyses have been helped by the emergence of computer software for carrying out these types of analyses. As far back as the 1960s, Borko (1965) and Iker and Harway (1965) produced software to analyze text quantitatively. The other approach has been the primarily qualitative (e.g., line-by-line) analysis of transcripts and other written documents to discover their meaning. The search for meaning often involves in-depth analysis of documents searching for themes that help the researcher gain theoretical and/or practical insight into the problem, program, policy, or other issue. Ryan and Bernard (2000) provided a variety of methods for finding themes in text. At the end of their discussion, they state:

> We do not want to minimize the profound intellectual differences in the epistemological positions of positivists and interpretivists. We think, however, that when researchers can move easily and cheaply between qualitative and quantitative data collection and analysis, the distinctions between the two epistemological positions will become of less practical importance. That is, as researchers recognize the full array of tools at their disposal, and as these tools become easier to use, the pragmatics of research will lessen the distinction between qualitative and quantitative data and analysis. (p. 792)

Yet, a third stream of text analysis, spurred on by the digital revolution, brought to fruition the potential noted by Ryan and Bernard (2000). Electronic texts and media make it possible to easily consider thousands of documents at a time. Text data mining associated with computer and information systems (e.g., Blei, Carin, & Dunson, 2010; Pang & Lee, 2008) has become popular. New methods that use machine learning techniques to find insights from large sets of text data have been developed (Blei, Ng, Jordan, & Lafferty, 2003).

In the rapid development of new ideas, old ideas that showed potential can sometimes be overlooked. The factor analysis of text data (Borko, 1965; Iker & Harway, 1965) was found to be useful in identifying topics from sets of text data. Yet, this work has sometimes been forgotten (see Iker, 1975), has been used sparingly (e.g., Onwuegbuzie, 2003), and, until recently, not compared with newer techniques (Péladeau & Davoodi, 2018). One text analytics package that realizes Ryan and Bernard's (2000) vision of a quick and efficient tool for text analysis is QDA Miner and WordStat (Provalis Research, 2014). It includes factor analysis in its set of tools for extracting topics from text. In this chapter, we explore this latest instantiation of this tool for carrying out factor analysis of text data.

1 Definition of Factor Analysis for Mixed Methods Research

In the world of quantitative research, exploratory factor analysis is a technique for extracting, from a set of observed variables, a small number of factors that represent constructs or latent variables. Linear combinations of the observed variables (*weighted sums*) are created that maximize the shared variability among the variables through the solution of an eigen equation. On a simple level, the number of factors chosen and their interpretation are determined by two elements of the output: the amount of variability accounted for in the data set as indicated by the eigenvalues (the bigger the better) and the correlations of the observed variables to the factors (*factor loadings*). The goal is to create a simple structure (Gorsuch, 1983) wherein a small set of factors explain the data and each factor is defined such that observed variables only *load* on one factor. This process of simplifying the structure is further helped through the rotation of the factors. The axes along which the factors are found are rotated such that the variables are more likely to load on only one factor. There are volumes of advice on how to conduct an exploratory factor analysis and there are also structural equation programs that can do confirmatory factor analysis as well. Ultimately, the goal is either to reduce the complexity of data such that a few underlying mathematically constructed variables can be used to explain a data set with a large number of variables in it (as is typically done in exploratory factor analysis), or to confirm the existence of underlying constructs that can explain the data (as in confirmatory factor analysis). The former goal is usually accomplished through principal components analysis. The latter is accomplished through principal factors and other approaches that focus on only the shared variance in the data set and are more concerned with the generalizability of the constructs than just the specific data set at hand (see Gorsuch, 1983 and Tabachnick & Fidell, 2013 for more discussion). In this chapter, the instantiation of the technique in analyzing text uses the principal components approach.

Factor analysis in the context of mixed methods research (MMR) is a technique for creating a smaller number of factors out of a large corpus of text units. Because the most recent instantiation of factor analysis of text data has come in conjunction with the development of techniques with similar goals in computer science, the vocabulary associated with the technique when applied to text data changes. The term factor analysis topic modelling (FATM) is used rather than factor analysis. Factors are described as topics or themes. The goal is to capture topics by examining the correlations of frequencies of words within text units. Just like in traditional factor analysis, the number of factors (topics) is chosen based on the size of eigenvalues. Also, just like in traditional factor analysis, the meaning of the topics depends on which words (variables) load onto the topic. These topics then can be used in a variety of ways. The topics could serve as a basis for coding text units and reduce the labor associated with analyzing large bodies of text data. The text units that contain the topics modelled could be used to go back and further examine the text qualitatively or through other techniques (e.g., phrases could be extracted from the text). The topics also could serve as a basis for creating a dictionary of terms that could be applied quantitatively to the data to capture sentiments towards a product, service, or program (Pang & Lee, 2008).

As noted earlier, data miners out of computer information systems introduced, or reintroduced (see Iker, 1974; Péladeau & Davoodi, 2018), the concept of topic modelling. The concept of FATM involves the extraction of topics out of text words or phrases that co-occur with each other. A word frequency by case data matrix is used to extract the topics. Factor analysis, specifically, principal components analysis with a varimax rotation, is one approach that has been used in the past and been instantiated in the WordStat analysis tool from QDA Miner. The principal components analysis creates components or factors (topics). The varimax rotation (see Gorsuch, 1983) of the components helps simplify the structure of the factors such that the variance of the loadings within factors is maximized so that variables (i.e., words) tend to load on only a few factors (i.e., topics). In essence, the technique helps researchers to extract topics that are somewhat independent of one another within the texts.

Although the FATM technique involves the use of the mathematics of one form of factor analysis, the approach can focus largely on describing a single data set rather than searching for underlying constructs that can be generalized across samples. Because of that, some concerns that would arise in conducting a factor analysis in the other contexts (e.g., replicating the structure in another sample) are not necessarily considered in the context of text analysis. Although there might be an interest in the generalizability of the analysis to other text corpuses, in many cases, the concern is only the meaning of the text at hand. Further, whereas in the world of quantitative research the factor structure is sometimes an end in itself, in WordStat, it is just one of several tools for extracting topics from the data. For example, WordStat includes cluster analysis tools and tools for extracting phrases from the text corpus (see Péladeau, this volume).

2 When Factor Analysis Topic Modeling is Appropriate in MMR

As stated previously, in the world of quantitative research, factor-analytic techniques are carried out to reduce large quantities of measured variables into smaller more digestible underlying constructs (Gorsuch, 1983). Shift to the world of text data collected in the context of a mixed methods research study. Imagine a survey data set with both quantitative ratings and open-ended responses from more than 10,000 cases. Even if each text response is just one sentence long, that is 10,000 data points to explore. Assuming coding took one minute per sentence that would take approximately 167 hours to code. This also assumes that coders generate reliable coding, which requires taking more time to collect evidence of reliability. Imagine large corporations who constantly get reviews that can number in the millions per month. Even with an army of employees, the reading of a large corpus of texts is fraught with potential problems due the limited processing capacity of the human information processing system.

FATM involves extracting out of text words that co-occur with each other. For example, if I were to carry out a text analysis of popular press articles on the Common Core State Standards Initiative (CCSSI) in K-12 education, I might find that sets of words that surround tests and assessment would often occur together. If one were to review the texts in which those words appeared, it is likely the researcher would find that there is a coherent set of themes surrounding assessment controversies and the CCSSI. Although coherent topics might emerge from FATM, care needs to be taken to make sure that the topics' meanings are consistent and that artefactual topics do not appear. Filtering out portions of a search with more precise keyword searches and prepping the documents before conducting the analysis can help, but sometimes they can be semantically ambiguous. For example, take the word "assessment." It could have something do with testing (e.g., "The assessment used to evaluate the Common Core is flawed"), or could mean something different (e.g., "Governor Jones' assessment of the Common Core was not positive").

FATM can be used to identify clusters of words that can be used to create meaningful topics that help researchers understand text meaning by giving them a basis for summarizing the data. Just as in traditional exploratory factor analysis, the researcher names factors from the statistical patterns of loadings extracted from the data. Also, just as exploratory factor analysis of quantitative measures is an imperfect process, FATM for topic extraction is also an imperfect process. The polysemy of text data, as noted earlier, makes preparing text data for factor analysis important. The old "garbage in garbage out" adage holds for these kinds of analyses.

Chakrabarti and Frye (2017) report three challenges in their field of demography that the use of FATM can overcome. One is the excess of data. Large compendiums of text data can be enormously difficult and time consuming to analyze. As noted earlier, even a single text box from a survey can be quite challenging to analyze if there are 10,000 cases.

Second, they note that data from qualitative analyses are often difficult to connect to external variables. For example, they note that when researchers are coding text, their linkage of the themes to external variables (e.g., gender) is often confounded by the presence of those variables in the manually coded text. As they note, the presence of something that is mentioned by one member of a group in one text, colors the finding of that theme and connects it to that group, even when the theme might be idiosyncratic to that case rather than typical of the group. Additionally, the linkage to external variables is often difficult to undertake when there is a large compendium of data to analyze. So, they argue that another benefit from this quantitative analysis of text data is that it allows for connections to external variables more easily. QDA Miner and WordStat (Provalis Research, 2014), the software used to demonstrate FATM here, can easily connect text themes to variables. For example, in its most current form as of this writing (Version 5), surveys from Qualtrics or Survey Monkey can be downloaded into the software. Thus, themes from text analysis can be easily linked to variables from surveys.

Third, Chakrabarti and Frye (2017) address the transparency of text analysis. Many interpretations can come out of a qualitative analysis of text. The basis for those interpretations can sometimes be difficult to make transparent. Although still requiring a number of decisions that make for some potentially different outcomes (e.g., how the text is edited, what words are excluded, whether stemming or lemmatization is carried out), the nature of those decisions can be more transparent and publicly documentable. Thus, there is the potential for more transparency in such analyses that cannot be found in more intuitively based coding of text.

So, situations where the researcher is interested in analyzing large quantities of text and has an interest in linking those topics to external variables are good candidates for factor analysis. When there are small amounts of data, traditional types of qualitative analyses might be sufficient to identity topics and FATM might not be mathematically plausible. FATM might also not be the best choice when philosophical or paradigmatic objections concerning its legitimacy are raised (Bergman, 2010). The decontextualized nature of the approach might be a barrier to collaboration with some qualitative researchers in a mixed methods research study. On the other hand, there is no reason why qualitatively oriented researchers could not argue or question topics extracted from the FATM analysis. They could also examine the topics to see whether their line-by-line extraction of themes made sense or adequately captured all the text had to offer. There are statistical regularities in the co-occurrence of words in language, and those statistical regularities are one set of indicators of meaning. It would be difficult for even the most ardent qualitative researcher to ignore the potential meaning that FATM presents.

Further, topic modelling might serve as a bridge to engage quantitative researchers in more qualitative analysis. If researchers can get past the incompatibility concerns of quantitative and qualitative methods (Howe, 1988), the dialectic around similarities and differences between the quantitatively and qualitatively derived themes can provide a nexus for getting a firmer grasp on underlying concepts in the data. Topic modelling combined with the traditional qualitative approach might provide a way for researchers to validate the thematic analysis. Similarities in the themes that arise from traditional inductive coding and FATM could validate both processes (see Baumer, Mimno, Guha, Quan, & Gay, 2017, for a similar argument). Further, FATM could be used even though it was not an end in and of itself. For example, it could serve as a basis for developing a coding system that could then be examined using more traditional approaches. It could be used after the traditional approach was applied to examine whether there were any themes that were missing using a traditional approach. The limited nature of our human information processing system and the epistemological and ontological understandings of researchers introduce bias in what is considered a valid analysis of text. Hence, using both quantitative and qualitative approaches to analyzing text data can help provide multiple views that could increase the credibility of the data across paradigms (Johnson, 2017).

FATM also can be used to create category or content dictionaries (Bernard & Ryan, 2000; Ryan & Bernard, 2000, 2003) that define beliefs, attitudes, sentiments towards something, knowledge of something, and so on that can be applied to new text data sets. FATM can iteratively be examined in conjunction with other textual analyses (e.g., cluster analyses or extraction of phrases) to help build a corpus of words that are associated with particular meanings. For example, there are several sentiment analysis dictionaries that have been developed (Rice & Zorn, 2013), and there are dictionaries like LIWC (Tausczik & Pennebaker, 2010) that have been used to analyze text in relation to affective and other psychological constructs.

Themes from FATM could be used to create quantitative scales. For example, a series of open-ended topics could be turned into quantitative survey items. Thus, the topics could have a heuristic purpose as well as serving as an end in and of itself. Overall, the technique is flexible and could be used both as an endpoint for identifying themes, a technique for generating themes and connecting them with variables, a validation tool for traditional kinds of analysis, or even as a source for quantitative items once the topics have been generated from the text base.

Note that FATM is not the only approach to topic modeling. Latent Dirichlet Allocation (LDA; Blei et al., 2003) is another approach that is quite popular. LDA involves the use of joint probabilities of words to help generate topics. However, Péladeau and Davoodi (2018) report data that purport to show that topics extracted from FATM are judged as being more coherent and sensible than are topics derived from LDA. Thus, there is evidence that the FATM approach can be at least as useful as LDA, if not better, in extracting topics.

3 Technical Outline of Factor Analysis Topic Modeling for MMR

In what follows is a basic set of steps for carrying out FATM. The example analysis was carried out in WordStat 7 (Provalis Research, 2014). Subsequent to the write up of this analysis, Wordstat 8 (Provalis Research, 2018) was released. The analysis carried out here can still be carried out in Wordstat 8, but there is an additional topic modeling approach: Nonnegative Matrix Factorization (NMF). Wordstat documentation (Provalis Research, 2018) suggests that the NMF approach can handle larger data sets, but that the results will generally be similar. Additionally, the output contains coherence statistics that represent the average correlation of the words included as part of the topic. Regardless of the approach taken, WordStat provides not only the FATM algorithm, but also the tools to prepare the data for analysis. The analysis carried out here uses the principal components analysis with a varimax rotation to extract components approach as the basis for thematic topics.

WordStat provides a user-friendly approach to conducting the analysis; however, other programs that facilitate factor analysis could potentially be used to do everything except label the factors. All that is needed is a case unit (document, sentence, paragraph, or whatever is used as the case unit) by word frequencies matrix of data or a word frequency correlation matrix for the FATM to be conducted (Iker, 1974, 1975). The analysis itself is fairly simple to carry out. What takes most of the work is preparing the data. WordStat provides the tools for this data preparation. As will be seen later, the process is an imperfect one and, ultimately, the decisions made by researchers to exclude words (common words, words that appear in most documents, names or other proper nouns, words that are artefacts of the document structure—e.g., a question asked or a label like "abstract") or to transform the words (e.g., fix misspellings, lemmatization or stemming of words) can have a significant impact on the process.

The example data set presented in this chapter comes from course evaluation data from courses that had used the Team Based Learning (TBL) approach (Michaelsen, Knight, & Fink, 2002) and included two open-ended questions asking about benefits and challenges to the approach. In this example, we will focus on the 2,235 responses to the benefits question. The students were asked, "What the most beneficial aspect of TBL?"

There are five basic steps for carrying out the analysis. The first step is to prepare the text for processing. The second step involves extracting the topics, and the third involves examining the topics for sensibility. The fourth step involves making revisions to the topics extracted, or perhaps changing the inclusion criteria for the words analyzed and carrying out the analysis again. The fifth and final step is to make use of the results in conjunction with qualitative coding, quantitative variables, or other approaches to FATM (e.g., cluster analysis, phrase extraction). The last step will depend upon the nature of the study and could even involve turning the topics into a dictionary to be used to quantitatively analyze the data or future sets of data. Each of these steps is discussed in more detail in the following sections.

Step 1: Data Preparation

The first step in the process is data preparation and is crucial in determining whether meaningful topics will be extracted. One issue that requires some thought is the nature of the text data itself. For example, although researchers have the ability to parse their own data as they work through the process of transcribing interviews, external data sources can sometimes have artefacts in them that need to be addressed or might be difficult to parse. For example, when downloading Reference Information System (RIS) files (i.e., interchangeable reference manager files), the text has to be cleaned to exclude words like "abstract" that will show up in every item.

Further, it is important to make sure one has only the relevant documents. For example, one could conduct FATM from a list of references downloaded from a literature search to a reference manager file. Careful consideration of the chosen Boolean logic to choose references would be important. For example, if one uses a key word or even subject term like "intelligence," there are several different areas of interest that we label intelligence. There is intelligence relating to human intelligence, there is artificial intelligence that will call up literature in computer science (mostly), and there is intelligence relating to espionage information. If one is interested in research themes in human intelligence and does not want to include the other meanings of intelligence, careful upfront work to exclude these abstracts needs to be undertaken.

What these examples suggest is that knowing what you have, what you want to exclude, and formatting will make the process quicker and avoid the need to delete some topics and/or reiterate the process because the results were not relevant. Thus, both choosing and preparing the text data are important to the process.

An additional concern is whether there are enough cases to conduct the factor analysis of the text data. There are no clear cut points for number of cases for implementing the technique. A larger number of units is better than a smaller number in general, especially if one wants more stable results, but if the factors are used in conjunction with other ways of extracting themes and the focus is on the document set at hand, then sample size is not as much of a concern as interpretability. Additionally, concerns about normality and other issues that relate to finding the factors and exact loadings of words are less of a concern. The exact size of loadings is not the issue, only the themes suggested by the loadings of certain words on a factor.

Another case consideration is the unit of analysis. WordStat uses three different units. The results could be different depending upon the unit. The unit could be a sentence, a paragraph, or even a whole document. The choice of unit depends on the nature of the documents and their length. For example, in the case we will consider here, sentence makes sense as a unit because in making comments, some students might have multiple ideas to get across.

Having considered whether there are enough cases and the unit to examine, the next step is to consider what words to include in the analysis and which ones to exclude. Further, the question of whether to use stemming or lemmatization to reduce different forms of the same word needs to be considered. Lemmatization refers to removing inflections from words so that the base form is used and variations in endings (e.g., -tion, -ed, -s, -ing) can be seen as one. Stemming is the general process of using root words or strings within words to capture similar word meanings. Readers wishing a more detailed discussion can find it in the literature (e.g., Tellez et al., 2017) and in the WordStat 7 manual (Provalis Research, 2014). Wordstat has automatic lemmatization available in several languages (English, French, Spanish, Swedish, German, Norwegian, Italian and others) and users should contact Provalis if they need support for other languages. Although reducing the words down to core forms can make the analysis more efficient, it is not without its downsides. For example, plural or different verb tense forms might be important in conveying different meanings. In considering words to exclude, WordStat has an exclusion list of common words that do not convey unique meanings.

A useful way to determine whether such issues exist is to analyze the frequencies of words and extract phrases from the data. These preliminary analyses will provide hints about words or phrases that might be excluded. The frequency option in WordStat involves the use of a selected set of parameters to display the frequencies of words potentially meaningful for the analysis. Parameters set by the user can eliminate very rare words and activation of an exclusion dictionary eliminates very common words that while very frequent do not provide insight into the topic (e.g., the word "the"). The results of the frequency conducted can be perused to examine whether there are misspellings as well as proper names (what WordStat labels *known entities*) that might be excluded from the analysis. Misspellings can be changed in the document or they can be substituted for in the analysis by simply right clicking on the item. Known entities can be removed, and substitutions for acronyms or abbreviations can be employed. Additionally, misspellings, acronyms, or specialized terms can be substituted for in the texts. For example, TBL is short for Team-based Learning, and so when someone mentions either one, he or she is referring to the same thing. Likewise, the data set used as an example here mentions IRAT, IRATS, TRAT, and TRATS. IRAT and TRAT stand for individual and team readiness assessment tests, respectively. Plural or singular, the concept is the same, so TRAT or IRAT can be substituted for plural forms. The 199-page WordStat 7 manual (Provalis Research, 2014) provides detailed descriptions about the types and forms of exclusion, stemming, lemmatization, correcting, and substituting. WordStat 8 extends these features for processing data. As of this writing, WordStat 8 manual has yet to be published. The WordStat help menu and numerous tutorials and webinars on the Provalis website provide updated information on data processing.

Step 2: Analysis

Once the data have been prepared, an initial activation of the factor analysis topic extraction algorithm can be conducted. The maximum number of topics extracted and the minimal size of loading that is considered meaningful are designated (usually around 0.30). With the release of WordStat 8, the program can run either a principal components analysis with a varimax rotation or the NMF approach. Both approaches produce a list of topics labelled via an algorithm and the words that load on that topic.

Step 3: Examining the Topics for Sensibility

These topics can be examined and then decisions made about their sensibility. One easy way to make initial decisions about the topics is to take advantage of WordStat's ability to click to see the full text associated with each topic extracted. The researcher can go back and forth between the text and topics to deem them meaningful, not meaningful, duplicative, or in need of further investigation.

Step 4: Revise Topics as Needed

Just like traditional exploratory factor analysis, the examination of the results might lead one to combine factors, remove artefactual factors (e.g., the questions stem noted previously—if it did not get excluded earlier), exclude more words, and possibly rerun the analysis with a leaner data set. After satisfaction with the set of topics, several different directions can be taken by the researcher. The direction depends on the research purpose and questions.

Step 5: Use the Topics as Directed by the Research Purpose and Questions

This approach to topic extraction can be used within the context of many different types of studies, so that the decisions about what to do with the topics is linked to the research design. For example, there are several ways the topics could be used for thematic analyses of text. The topics could be used to describe the major themes of the data set if the researcher believed that the topics were representative and made sense. A researcher could then turn the topics into codes in the data (QDA Miner and WordStat can facilitate this) that could be examined further in relation to other variables in the data. For instance, we might examine how the comments about the benefits of TBL vary by class level, prior experience with TBL or some other variable using correspondence analysis or multidimensional scaling. Also, if we used the topics as codes in the data, we not only see what the potential major themes are, but by using QDA Miner to view cases without coding, an analysis of atypical cases could take place.

Another possible use might be to compare the topics generated from the analysis with topics that are generated by traditional inductive qualitative coding. For example, the data we will show here were previously coded. The topics extracted quantitatively were compared to the topics that were generated from inductive human coding. The consistency or inconsistency in the themes and topics could provide a basis for validation or further examination of the texts.

The analysis can be taken in multiple directions and its usefulness depends on the research questions asked. If looking for broad themes from large set of cases, it can be useful, but careful screening for artefactual topics is necessary. Filtering cases and running separate analyses to compare groups might also be useful. For example, when comparing news stories, one could look at the different topics extracted by conservative versus liberal news organizations. Further, one may cross themes with quantitative results serving as a basis for a joint display(s) of data. For example, in a research study of an educational program widely implemented, successful students might yield different topics or themes than do unsuccessful ones.

4 Empirical Demonstration of Factor Analysis of Text Data for MMR

In our example, a set of responses to a question on student evaluations concerning the "benefits" of TBL was analyzed. The responses were generally a sentence or two and were cleaned for spellings and formatting prior to entry as a spreadsheet into QDA Miner. Once in QDA Miner, the first task was to activate WordStat from the analysis menu. With the release of WordStat 8, it is no longer necessary to enter data in QDA Miner to access WordStat. Data can be directly entered in WordStat using the same interface as in QDA Miner. Once in WordStat, *options* for selection and exclusion and *dictionaries* for exclusion, substitution, stemming, lemmatization, and other facets of inclusion, exclusion, and transformation of the data can be made. In our example, the exclusion list dictionary was checked to address common words that did not add to the meaning of the topics that will be addressed. Exclusions were further addressed as the data were processed in Wordstat. Figure 2.1 illustrates the dictionaries page in Wordstat 7 that presents options for transformation and inclusion.

Figure 2.2 presents the options page. As can be seen in the figure, the options page has some inclusions options and also addresses how or whether to include various text elements.

After setting options, just like in any other quantitative analysis, basic frequencies for the included words should be conducted. The frequency run is usually set to limit the number of total words as well as providing upper and lower frequency bounds for choosing words. Very low frequency words (occurring less than ten times typically on smaller data sets and ideally less than 30 to 50 times on larger data sets; Provalis Research, 2014) simply do not provide much insight into the common themes. Very high frequency words that occur in almost every case unit can be less insightful as well. Often these words can be artefacts that need to be excluded. For example, the word "beneficial" occurred in a great number of the cases because students tended to respond by restating the question, "the most beneficial part of TBL is …" Thus, the word beneficial was moved to the exclusion list. Although frequency is one reason to move a word to the exclusion list, there are other reasons as well. For example, sometimes, proper nouns that indicate a person's name might not be needed. It is also useful to examine whether there are several different ways of saying the same thing. For example, students could write out the phrase "Team Based Learning" or simply use the acronym TBL. TBL was substituted for Team Based Learning.

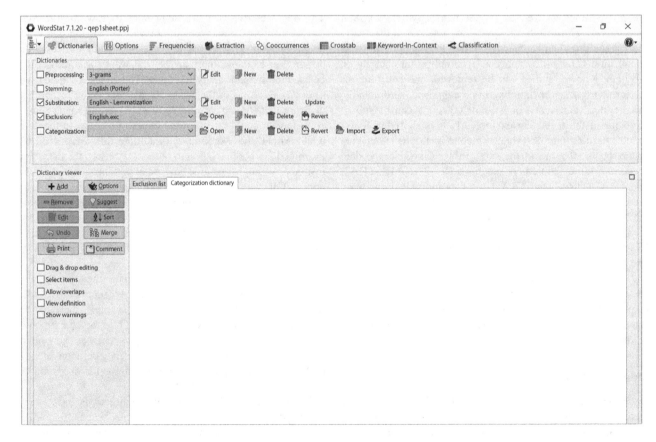

FIGURE 2.1 The Wordstat 7 dictionaries page.

Exploratory Factor Analysis of Text 31

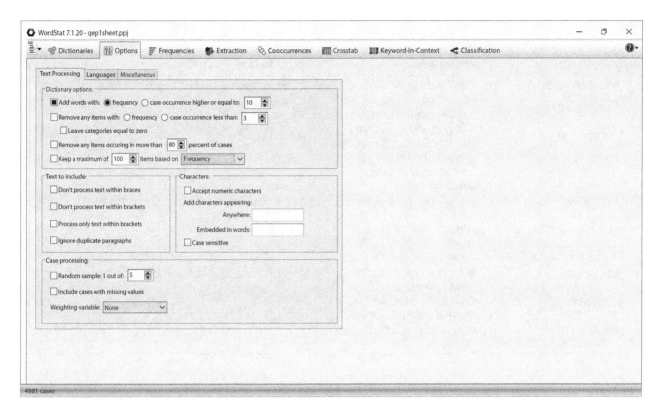

FIGURE 2.2 Screenshot of options page in Wordstat 7.

Once the data have been cleaned and transformed, the factor analysis is conducted via the *extraction* feature of WordStat. A principal components analysis with a varimax rotation is conducted on the case unit by word frequency data matrix. Just like factor analysis algorithms in other programs, decisions need to be made before conducting the analysis. Most notably, the researcher has to determine the number of factors or topics to be extracted and the minimal loading size of a word that would be seen as meaningful to a factor. As noted previously, as of this writing, there are no options for conducting different forms of factor analysis. A screen shot of the screen for using the extraction feature can be seen in Figure 2.3.

FIGURE 2.3 Topic modeling screen in Wordstat 7.

Notice the case unit is set to sentence (Segmentation: by Sentence), the number of topics (No. topics) is set to 10 and the minimum factor loading (Loading) is set to 0.30.

The results of the initial analysis are shown in Table 2.1. Note that just as in other applications of exploratory factor analysis, it is legitimate to reexamine the data, reanalyze it, or rename the factors/topics. WordStat uses an algorithm based on word frequency within topics to generate topic names. These names can be changed, and if the researcher believes that two topics are really taking about the same thing, he or she can combine those topics together.

The best way to make sense of the factors is to go back to the original text to see the keywords extracted within the context of use. A right click on a topic while it is highlighted in WordStat will bring up the texts that contain the keywords associated with the topic/factor. A perusing of those texts can help the researcher determine whether the topic makes sense, should be joined with another topic or topics, or whether topic should be given a more descriptive name. Figure 2.4 below shows the text context for the "Real World" topic. As can be seen, most of the texts suggest that the topic reflects students working on real-world problems in TBL classes.

An examination of the results from Table 1 shows that most of the topics were meaningful and they did not need to be combined (they addressed different strengths of TBL). For example, "Point of View" captured topics that addressed listening to the points of view of others in the classroom. "Real World" involved comments about working with real-world problems. The topic "skill" was one that I considered relabeling. It refers to communication, critical thinking, and social skills—what

TABLE 2.1

Results of the Factor Analysis of the Benefits of Team-Based Learning Documents

F #	Topic NAME	KEYWORDS	EIGENVALUE	VAR %	FREQ	CASES #	CASES %
1	POINT OF VIEW	VIEW; POINT	3.28	1.71	202	124	2.72
2	REAL WORLD	REAL; WORLD; LIFE; SITUATION; APPLICATION	2.17	2.09	136	72	1.58
3	SKILL	SKILL; COMMUNICATION; IMPROVE; CRITICAL; SOCIAL	1.96	2.02	250	149	3.26
4	ANSWER; CORRECT	ANSWER; CORRECT; WRONG; QUESTION; MISTAKE; DISCUSS	1.80	1.74	589	379	8.30
5	STRENGTH	STRENGTH; WEAKNESS; ENHANCE	1.75	1.66	39	27	0.59
6	SUBJECT MATTER	SUBJECT; MATTER; KNOWLEDGE	1.68	1.82	95	79	1.73
7	SOLVE A PROBLEM	PROBLEM; SOLVE	1.64	1.64	257	173	3.79
8	IRAT; TRAT	IRAT; TRAT; GRADE; SCORE; MAKE; READ	1.58	1.79	291	215	4.71
9	CONCEPT	CONCEPT; DIFFICULT; UNDERSTAND; CLARIFY	1.54	1.58	454	344	7.53
10	COMMON GOAL; TEAM-BASED LEARNING	COMMON; GOAL; LEARNING; TEAM	1.52	1.62	1154	749	16.40

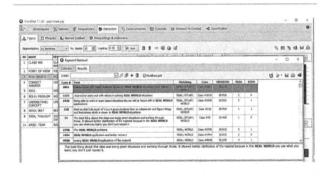

FIGURE 2.4 Keywords associated with topics highlighted and shown within context.

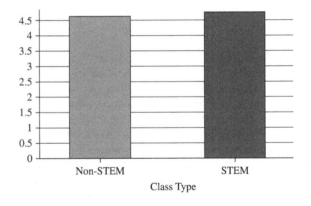

FIGURE 2.5 Percentage of comments on TRAT and IRAT process in STEM and non-STEM classes.

we typically talk about as 21st Century skills. So, perhaps I might relabel this topic as 21st Century Skills. A "right click" over a highlighted topic will pop up an option for renaming the topic. Likewise, the topic "Answer Correct" might require clarification. The topic refers to discussions about right and wrong answers that provide some insight into why something was right or wrong. So, I might change the label of this topic to something like, "Test Answer Discussions."

Once the topics have been chosen, additional analyses can be carried out. For example, one simple type of analysis might be to examine how frequently a topic is mentioned in relation to different variables in the data set. For example, one variable of interest was whether the TBL course was in a STEM (Science, Technology, Engineering, or Mathematics) domain. Below are examples of how the topics were combined with this variable. Figure 2.4 shows the percentage of comments on the IRAT and TRAT process (individual and team Readiness Assurance Tests given to assess preparation for material studied prior to the class). As can be seen in Figure 2.5, the percentage of comments about this topic is approximately the same in STEM or Non-STEM courses.

Figure 2.6 shows another example comparing STEM and non-STEM classes. As can be seen in Figure 2.6, the STEM students had a larger percentage of comments concerning the topic of discussing correct and incorrect answers to questions. These results and the results concerning the IRAT and TRAT make sense within the goals of the initiative. The readiness assurance process was one of the bigger transformations of student rituals associated with the TBL initiative. It would not be expected that students in STEM classes would be different with regard to this aspect of TBL. On the other hand, the need to consider complex constructs

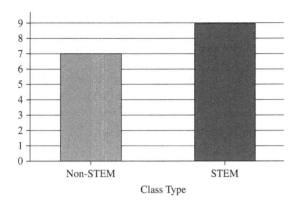

FIGURE 2.6 Percentage of comments surrounding understanding of correct and incorrect answers.

in more difficult STEM classes might suggest that students found the discussions surrounding understanding correct and incorrect answers to be beneficial more often than did students in non-STEM classes.

These two examples represent only a small sampling of the options that can be carried out once the topics have been identified. For example, the topics could be turned into codes that could be used in further qualitative or quantitative analysis of the data, or be used to set up codes for analyzing future data sets on TBL.

5 Suggested Applications of Factor Analysis of Text in MMR

Onwuegbuzie and Combs (2010) discuss factor analysis of text data as a "crossover" strategy wherein data that are typically analyzed through qualitative methods are examined quantitatively. They further suggest that crossover techniques set the stage for an analysis of the similarities and differences between findings that simultaneously approach the same data from quantitative and qualitative perspectives. FATM can also be easily used as part of a sequential design. For example, a factor analysis of text data from a survey could be used to identify topics that could be included in more in-depth interviews with individuals. It is also possible to use FATM to identify extreme or outlying cases not captured by the topics that could be then followed up with in-depth qualitative interviews or conversations. WordStat or QDA Miner could do this by identifying cases where the topics identified in the factor analysis are not coded.

On a practical level, because the technique can analyze large quantities of text data, it might encourage more quantitatively oriented researchers to include text data in large-scale studies that could open them up to more mixing of traditional quantitative designs with qualitative methods. For example, a randomized trial of a social program might include interviews with recipients that could provide insight into the processes that make the program successful. FATM could be initially carried out and, then, in-depth qualitative analyses of the text data could be undertaken to explore the topics related to program efficacy.

Not unrelated to the other uses of the technique, FATM can serve as an approach to validating the conclusions drawn by researchers. Combining qualitative and quantitative analysis of text data helps build commensurability approximation validity (Onwuegbuzie & Johnson, 2006), which involves procedures that help to integrate quantitative and qualitative approaches so that meta-inferences that combine both types of data can be more easily made. The practice of FATM requires going back and forth between identifying topics and considering their meanings. Combining that approach with qualitative analyses can help build an integrated understanding of the data that can be legitimized by researchers representing a variety of paradigms. Second, FATM can serve as a counterweight over concerns of bias that might arise in the context of typical inductive qualitative analyses. As noted earlier, Chakrabarti and Frye (2017) suggest that FATM can be used to overcome concerns about artefactually connecting themes from interviews or other texts with variables (e.g., gender). Thus, it can be used as part of a strategy to address weakness minimization validity (Onwuegbuzie & Johnson, 2006), wherein the weakness of one method (quantitative or qualitative) could be minimized by examining the result from the perspective of the other methodological approach. The potential spuriousness of a relationship found through qualitative inductive coding (a possible weakness), could be checked against a topic modeling of the text that could detect a quantitative relationship across the entire corpus of texts. It can be used to build sequential validity as well by providing the basis for moving from one phase of a study to the next. For example, the logic to support the content of an in-depth interview protocol (a qualitative data collection method) can be derived from examining the topics extracted via factor analysis (a quantitative method). Lastly, the technique can be used to support the conversion of data from quantitative to qualitative or qualitative to quantitative. Hence, it could be used as evidence to support conversion validity by providing a logical or statistical basis for converting data to different forms (Onwuegbuzie & Johnson, 2006). For example, once a set of topics emerged from the FATM, it could be argued that the topics could serve as codes to be added to any qualitative analysis of the data.

One other use of FATM that has not received a great deal of discussion, but could potentially be very powerful, concerns the generalizability of qualitative findings. The FATM technique provides a context for confirming whether themes found in a small sample of interviews or documents replicate in a larger more general sample of a population. Although qualitative studies often do not focus on such generalizability, FATM allows researchers to consider this possibility. Hence, it provides a basis for building commensurability between qualitative and quantitative results in a population. It can be used to support sample integration validity (Onwuegbuzie & Johnson, 2006)). Sample integration validity involves providing evidence that qualitative results from one sample can be legitimately connected to the results from a quantitative sample (one that may be more representative of a population). FATM has the potential to allow researchers to engage in large scale qualitative coding that can confirm findings from a small-scale qualitative study.

6 Strengths and Limitations of Factor Analysis of Text Data in MMR

The most obvious strength of the application of factor analysis to text data is that it is a quick and efficient way to find prominent themes from large quantities of text data. WordStat provides a usable interface for preparing data, factor analyzing them, and interpreting the factors. Thus, the efficiency of the method and the availability of software that can support its use can help encourage more researchers to analyze texts. Another strength relates to Chakrabarti and Frye's (2017) concern about the transparency of text coding. If one sets the same parameters and makes the same edits and substitutions to the data, the same results should be replicable with a given set of data. Yet another strength, according to Péladeau and Davoodi (2018), is that the topics generated from the factor analysis approach appear to be more sensible to human judges than do other techniques. So, there is support for the idea that this ostensibly quantitative technique can generate output that can be turned into meaningful themes. One other strength mentioned earlier is that it is a crossover technique that allows researchers to take the same data and examine it both quantitatively and qualitatively. The dialogue among researchers from different perspectives can be facilitated by such techniques which, in turn, could lead to more integrated inferences from the data.

There are limitations as well that need to be considered. First, a great deal of upfront work with text is usually required to apply the technique. If there are artefacts in the text that do not add to the meaning of the text, they can sometimes create artefactual factors that do not provide information. Although WordStat's interface reduces some of these potential issues, there is concern that some researchers will not discover artefacts in their data and produce inappropriate analyses. Also, as with any automated process that does not consider meaning, subtle differences in text meaning can be missed because words might change meaning in different contexts. Some qualitative researchers might find it difficult to accept the notion that the automated process can actually yield anything meaningful without considering the context in which the text resides. However, as noted earlier in this chapter and by others (e.g., Yu, Jannasch-Pennell, & DiGangi, 2011), the process requires more than extracting the topics. It involves exploring the original text for meaning associated with the topics, revising the topics, deleting some, and iteratively working through them to ensure that meaningful topics are derived. Another consideration has to do with the lack of a strong set of guidelines for setting analysis parameters. Further study of statistical artefacts for failures to meet assumptions concerning data distributions also need to be explored to understand their impact. Iker (1975) produced some work addressing the wide variation in the size of correlations, but little else has been undertaken to address issues related to widely varying word frequency distributions. Although the technique has been around, studies that test its limits and alternative options have not been conducted.

Ultimately, the technique will live or die based on its ability to produce meaningful sets of topics for researchers. Its implementation in multipurpose text analysis software system where it can be applied, along with other quantitative and qualitative techniques to analyze texts, might provide for more regular use—both on its own and combined with other techniques. The increased use should lead to more exploration of its properties and help to determine whether it could be a common method for use in mixed methods research studies.

7 Resources for Learning More About Text Factor Analysis

The early literature in this area provides insight into the technique (e.g., Borko, 1965; Iker, 1974, 1975; Iker & Harway, 1965). The WordStat 7 Manual (Provalis Research, 2014) also provides details on extracting topics. Finally, the Provalis Research webpage has very helpful videos for preparing and carrying out FATM. Particularly useful is the General Presentation on WordStat 8 and the Topic Extraction presentation. As noted previously, as of this writing, there is no written manual for WordStat 8; therefore, the latest information about how to use the program is found on the webpage: https://provalisresearch.com/resources/tutorials/.

REFERENCES

Baumer, E. P. S., Mimno, D., Guha, S., Quan, E., & Gay, G. K. (2017). Comparing grounded theory and topic modeling: Extreme divergence or unlikely convergence? *Journal of the Association for Information Science and Technology*, 68, 1397–1410. doi:10.1002/asi.23786

Bergman, M. (2010). Hermeneutic content analysis: Textual and audiovisual analyses within a mixed methods framework. In A. Tashakkori & C. Teddlie (Eds.), *Sage handbook of mixed methods in social and behavioral research* (2nd ed., pp. 379–396). Thousand Oaks, CA: Sage.

Bernard, H., & Ryan, G. (2000). Text analysis. In H. Bernard (Ed.), *Handbook of methods in cultural anthropology* (pp. 595–645). Lanham, MD: AltaMira. Retrieved from http://nersp.nerdc.ufl.edu/~ufruss/documents/bernard_ryan.pdf

Blei, D., Carin, L., & Dunson, D. (2010, November). Probabilistic topic models. *IEEE Signal Processing Magazine*, 27(6), 55–65. doi:10.1109/MSP.2010.938079

Blei, D. M., Ng, A. Y., Jordan, M. I., & Lafferty, J. (2003). Latent dirichlet allocation. *Journal of Machine Learning Research*, 3(4/5), 993–1022.

Borko, H. (1965). A factor analytically derived classification system for psychological reports. *Perceptual and Motor Skills*, 20, 393–406. doi:10.2466/pms.1965.20.2.393

Chakrabarti, P., & Frye, M. (2017). A mixed-methods framework for analyzing text data: Integrating computational techniques with qualitative methods in demography. *Demographic Research*, 37(November), 1351–1382. doi:10.4054/DemRes.2017.37.42

Gorsuch, R. L. (1983). *Factor analysis* (2nd ed.). Hillsdale, NJ: Lawrence Erlbaum Associates.

Howe, K. R. (1988). Against the quantitative-qualitative incompatibility thesis or dogmas die hard. *Educational Researcher*, 17(8), 10–16. doi:10.3102/0013189X017008010

Iker, H. P. (1974). An historical note on the use of word-frequency contiguities in content analysis. *Computers and the Humanities*, 8(2), 93–98. doi:10.1007/BF02530743

Iker, H. P. (1975). SELECT: A computer program to identify associationally rich words for content analysis – II. Substantive results. *Computers and the Humanities*, *9*(1), 3–12. doi:10.1007/BF02404315

Iker, H. P., & Harway, N. I. (1965). A computer approach towards the analysis of content. *Behavioral Science*, *10*, 173–182. doi:10.1002/bs.3830100209

Johnson, R. B. (2017). Dialectical pluralism: A metaparadigm whose time has come. *Journal of Mixed Methods Research*, *11*, 156–173. doi:10.1177/1558689815607692

Krippendorf. K. (2013). *Content analysis: An introduction to its methodology* (3rd ed.). Thousand Oaks, CA: Sage.

Michaelsen, L. K., Knight, A. B., & Fink, L. D. 2002. *Team-based learning: A transformative use of small groups*. Westport, CN: Praeger.

Onwuegbuzie, A. J. (2003). Effect sizes in qualitative research: A prolegomenon. *Quality & Quantity: International Journal of Methodology*, *37*, 393–409. doi:10.1023/A:1027379223537

Onwuegbuzie, A. J., & Combs, J. P. (2010). Emergent data analysis techniques in mixed methods research: A synthesis. In A. Tashakkori & C. Teddlie (Eds.), *Sage handbook of mixed methods in social and behavioral research* (2nd ed., pp. 397–430). Thousand Oaks, CA: Sage.

Onwuegbuzie, A. J., & Johnson, R. B. (2006). The validity issue in mixed research. *Research in the Schools*, *13*(1), 48–63.

Pang, P., & Lee, L. (2008). Opinion mining and sentiment analysis. *Foundations and Trends in Information Retrieval*, *2*(1–2), 1–135. doi:10.1561/1500000001

Péladeau, N., & Davoodi, E. (2018). Comparison of latent dirichlet modeling and factor analysis for topic extraction: A lesson of history. *Proceedings of the 51st Hawaii International Conference on System Sciences*, *9*, 615–623. Retrieved from https://scholarspace.manoa.hawaii.edu/bitstream/10125/49965/1/paper0078.pdf

Provalis Research. (2014). *WORDSTAT 7 User's Guide*. Montreal, QC, Canada: Provalis Research. Retrieved from https://provalisresearch.com/Documents/WordStat7.pdf

Provalis Research. (2018). *WORDSTAT 8 [Computer software]*. Montreal, QC, Canada: Provalis Research.

Rice, D. R., & Zorn, C. (2013). Corpus-based dictionaries for sentiment analysis of specialized vocabularies. *Proceedings of NDATAD*, 1–17. doi:10.1017/psrm.2019.10

Ryan, G. W., & Bernard, H. R. (2000). Data management and analysis methods. In H. Bernard (Ed.), *Handbook of qualitative research* (pp. 769–802). Lanham, MD: AltaMira.

Ryan, G. W., & Bernard, H. R. (2003). Techniques to identify themes. *Field Methods*, *15*(1), 85–109. doi:10.1177/1525822X02239569

Tabachnick, B. G., & Fidell, L.S. (2013). *Using multivariate statistics* (6th ed.). New York, NY: Pearson.

Tausczik, Y. R., & Pennebaker, J. W. (2010). The psychological meaning of words: LIWC and computerized text analysis methods. *Journal of Language and Social Psychology*, *29*(1), 24–54. doi:10.1177/0261927X09351676

Tellez, E. S., Miranda-Jiménez, S., Graff, M., Moctezuma, D., Siordia, O. S., & Villaseñor, E. A. (2017). A case study of Spanish text transformations for twitter sentiment analysis. *Expert Systems with Applications*, *81*, 457–471. doi:10.1016/j.eswa.2017.03.071

Yu, C. H., Jannasch-Pennell, A., & DiGangi, S. (2011). Compatibility between text mining and qualitative research in the perspectives of grounded theory, content analysis, and reliability. *Qualitative Report*, *16*, 730–744.

3

Correspondence Analysis of Qualitative Data

Wendy B. Dickinson

1 Definition of Correspondence Analysis

According to Beh (2004), "Correspondence analysis is a technique that represents graphically the row and column categories and allows for a comparison of their 'correspondences' or associations, at a category level" (p. 258). As Beh (2004) stated, correspondence analysis (CA) and its variations (e.g., multiple, joint, subset, and canonical CA) have been embraced and applied by researchers across multiple disciplines, particularly within the social and environmental sciences. Greenacre (2010) stated that the CA method is

> routinely applied to a table of nonnegative data to obtain a spatial map of the important dimensions in the data, where proximities between points and other geometric features of the map indicate associations between rows, between columns and between rows and columns. (p. 958)

Within the social sciences context wherein the use of CA is well-established (Greenacre, 2010a; Greenacre & Blasius, 1994; Greenacre & Hastie, 1987), CA typically is applied to a cross-tabulation, or contingency table, between two or more categorical variables, based on classifications of respondents (Greenacre, 2010a). For example, the respondents could be cross-classified according to a demographic variable such as education level, as well as the categories of response to a survey question (Greenacre, 2010a). These associations are visualized in the resulting CA spatial maps, which are a visual product of the CA analysis. This visual product (CA map) displays the dimensions in the data, with inherent proximities, to reveal variable relationships.

2 When Use of Correspondence Analysis is Most Appropriate for Mixed Methods Research

According to Beh (2004, p. 257), "over the past few decades, correspondence analysis has gained an international reputation as a powerful statistical tool for the graphical analysis of contingency tables," whereby the contingency table contains information of a discrete or categorical nature. Categorical data (i.e., frequency data and discrete data) are most often presented in tables. Scholars have created novel visualization methods specifically for categorical data, "designed to provide explanatory and confirmatory graphic displays analogous to those used readily and easily for quantitative data" (Friendly, 2000, p. 1). Although most data visualization guidance focuses on how to represent and to analyze quantitative data visually, less attention has been paid to how to display qualitative data visually (Henderson & Segal, 2013).

Qualitative approaches focus on the "why "and the "how" of complex phenomena, which are not easily portrayed with images (Henderson & Segal, 2013). Per Lincoln and Guba (1985), qualitative data sources can be differentiated into two broad categories: humans as source (e.g., interviews, observations, and nonverbal expression) and non-human sources (e.g., documents, records, and artifacts). Azzam, Evergreen, Germuth, and Kistler (2013) further described qualitative data as being broad in scope; taking the form of transcribed interviews, recorded conversations among participants, and pictures, videos, or drawings that capture events, processes, and outcomes.

As Friendly (2000) stated, "a modest revolution has been brewing in the analysis of categorical data, as graphical methods and techniques of data visualization, so commonly used for quantitative data, have begun to be developed for frequency data and discrete data" (p. 1). Categorical data display types include robust ordination plots (Hoaglin & Tukey, 1985), mosaic displays (Friendly 1999, 2000), and CA displays. Examples of how to produce categorical data displays using SAS 9.4 are presented in this work. Developing a visual exploration of the data will "help identify patterns and discern themes not readily apparent or easily accessible in the numeric format" (Dickinson, Hines, & Onwuegbuzie, 2007, p. 1).

Thus, CA is most appropriate for mixed methods research when the goal is to compare and to contrast participants on multiple qualitative characteristics such as perceptions, beliefs, and experiences. Accordingly, CA can be conducted in both qualitative research studies (transforming qualitative research studies to mixed methods research studies), and the qualitative phase(s) of mixed methods research studies. Onwuegbuzie, Dickinson, Leech and Zoran (2010) declared that CA can be utilized to map words, codes, or themes as a function of focus group participants; such a mapping occurs as a two-dimensional representation (see also, Onwuegbuzie, Dickinson, Leech, & Zoran, 2009).

Onwuegbuzie, Frels, Leech, and Collins (2011) provided an illustrative example of a transformative CA for qualitative data, utilizing metathemes that emerged from faculty interview responses and student reflexive writings. This study provided a 2-way reflection of both faculty and student perceptions of mixed research courses orientation, level of application, and level of structure. The qualitative data from the reflexive journals were *quantitized*—utilizing a coding system to assign numeric scores—as described by Onwuegbuzie and Teddlie (2003). Thus, the subsequent application of CA to qualitative data helped the researchers accomplish three overarching goals: to map and to describe the relationship among the themes; to map and to describe the relationship among the participants; and to map and to describe the relationship between the themes and the participants (Onwuegbuzie et al., 2011). Mixed methods researchers can, and must, translate across the languages and cultures of qualitative, quantitative, and mixed methods research approaches (Molina-Azorin & Fetters, 2019). Therefore, the use of CA can serve as a methodological bridge between quantitative and qualitative data analyses and approaches.

3 Technical Outline of Correspondence Analysis for Mixed Methods Research

The Value of Visual Disparity

The mosaic display (Friendly, 1999, 2000) provides a graphical process for visualizing *n*-way contingency tables, and for building models that account for the association among depicted variables (Friendly, 2000). For mosaic displays, the frequencies from a contingency table are depicted as a collection of rectangular *tiles*, with the area of each tile being proportional to the cell frequencies (Friendly, 2000). The resulting mosaic plot can be quite striking because this method provides a visual way to see the size differences among observed cell frequencies. For example, if we think of a tiled kitchen floor, it would be quite noticeable if one of the tiles was 24 x 24 inches square, and all the other tiles were only 12 x 12 inches square. This ability to create visual disparity within the graphical output is a valuable aspect and, therefore, a compelling reason to use constructed plots for categorical data display. As Eisner (2002) stated, "Imagination gives us images of the possible, that provide a platform for seeing the actual.… The image, the central term of imagination, is qualitative in character. We do indeed see with our mind's eye" (Eisner, 2002. p. 4).

The mathematical theory of CA, as developed by Benzécri (1973, 1992), is very elegant and beautiful (Choulakian, Simonetti, & Pham Gia, 2014). CA shows how data deviate from expectation (observed values vs. expected values) when the row (e.g., gender) and column (e.g., employment status) variables are independent (Dickinson & Hall, 2008).

As Wheater, Penny, Clark, Syes, and Bellis (2003) explained, simple CA creates a two-dimensional visual display of the observed data variation, which can be utilized for examination of variable relationships. Multiple CA also can display associations in more than two dimensions, based on the underlying dataset components.

CA involves a conceptual and computational examination that best explains deviations from expected values, and the resultant analysis graphically represents each row and column by a point in a configuration plot (SAS Institute, 2010). One of the first investigations of the application of contingency tables to measure association was conducted by Fisher (1940) using a cross-classification of hair and eye color of children in Scotland to determine how the two variables were associated (Beh, 2004). CA thus offers a unique hybrid approach: both mathematics and visual imagery are deployed to produce an integrated output that is stronger than either component alone. Iron and carbon combine to form steel, a much stronger alloy. CA can become that stronger alloy—the steel with which to build contemporary research structures.

Conceptual Demonstration of Correspondence Analysis in Mixed Methods Research

For some time, CA has been invoked through a dedicated SAS macro (PROC CORRESP) that gives the analyst a great deal of flexibility (Beh, 2004, p. 520). Visual communication provides immediate and direct access to information. This access is highly prized by corporate entities and, most currently, social media outlets. The author suggests that this direct immediacy is valuable to educational stakeholders as well. Wainer (2005), after analyzing the work of William Playfair (1786) and John W. Tukey (1977), described three main points of agreement regarding visual display: impact, understanding graphs, and the message that we receive from graphs.

Wainer's (2005) analysis can be compared to the analysis of artwork and, by extension, visual imagery. The first point of agreement, *impact is important,* regards the overall impression that we receive by examining a graphical display. With graphs, as with any visual image, the initial impression or observation can be a powerful, and sometimes life-changing message. To achieve this level of the *wow* factor, visual artists develop sophisticated methods to capture the eye and thus the full attention of the viewer. In the educational community context, the viewer of graphical images may exist in multiple stakeholder roles—administrator, educator, student, parent—with many other possibilities as well.

It is the author's wish to advance the graphing capabilities of CA to invoke that same type of *wow* within the educational stakeholder community. Methods used by visual artists to provoke viewer response include subject matter (individuals, groups, locations); color theory (warm colors for excitement, cool colors for calm, and reflection); composition (the overall structure of the work), and reaction, the feelings produced within the viewer while experiencing the artwork.

The second point of agreement between Playfair and Tukey, *understanding graphs is not always automatic* (Wainer, 2005), highlights the importance of providing a clear message to the viewer. A clear message imparts immediate information to the viewer. In visual display, as in contemporary artwork, this is especially crucial to the strength of the portrayed image. If a visual display contains a powerful message, but that message is hidden or obscured in some way, the narrative value of the image plummets. This is especially relevant to visual display of research results: a picture might indeed be worth a thousand words, but if those words are written in obscure language, the message will be lost. Therefore, data displays, which are used for educational decision-making, must portray a clear picture of the research results so appropriate implications can be drawn. By delivering both a visual and empirical summary of observed data, CA offers a unique and powerful way to discern patterns in categorical data.

The third point of agreement, *a graph can tell us things that might not have been seen otherwise* (Wainer, 2005), directly links the idea of mixed methods research to graphical display (cf. Dickinson, 2001b). One of the greatest strengths of mixed methods research is the *panoramic* picture it can provide. A panoramic picture portrays all angles of the subject matter—to the left, to the right, upwards, and downwards. It is this wide-angle, wide-open view that is so attractive to the viewers. By using mixed methods research with graphical displays created by CA techniques, we can create a panoramic view to share with our audience. Consequently, mixed methods research graphical displays enhance researcher understanding of social and behavioral phenomena in general, and the meaning that underlies these phenomena in particular (Onwuegbuzie & Dickinson, 2008).

The use of categorical data to conduct CA transverses multiple fields. These interdisciplinary uses include marketing (Hoffman & Franke, 1986), medicine (Wheater et al., 2003), sociology (Cabane & Clark, 2015; Greenacre, 2017; Greenacre & Pardo, 2006; Solaz & Wolff, 2015), ecology (Greenacre, 2010a, 2010b, 2013), and war (Rusch, Hofmarcher, Hatzinger, & Hornik, 2013), and thus offers a rich methodological source to help inform decision-making and to describe relationships among variables. CA can help interpret measures of association, agree/disagree responses for dichotomous survey items, and pass/fail categories for educational assessment instruments (Dickinson & Hall, 2008). Furthermore, CA can help examine qualitative data such as interview responses, focus group themes, and reflexive journal writings.

For example, U.S. Census Bureau data are collected nationwide to investigate categorical survey responses and to summarize relationships between demographic variables and associated geographical locations. This integrated use of personal data by location and demographics was previously compared to examine immigration activity across the United States (Dickinson et al., 2007). Both continuous and discrete data may be incorporated into CA models. For example, binary coding can be utilized to indicate the presence or absence of a trait. Dickinson (2001a) illustrated the use of categorical displays to indicate the presence or absence of ritual acts conducted during coming-of-age rituals. Similarly, observational data can be coded for CA inclusion and use. Friendly (1999, 2000) discussed techniques for visualizing categorical data, including both two- and three-dimensional visual representations via computer software output (notably, SAS 9.4).

Three-dimensional visual representations typically employ a multiple axes system to display data in three-dimensional space. These representations can incorporate variables of length, width, and height (projection) to create output data displays. These data displays can be constructed to summarize data in interesting and aesthetically appealing formats. Tufte (2006) presented a set of principles for aesthetics and design; these principles were further examined by Onwuegbuzie and Dickinson (2008). Graphical representation cuts across artificial boundaries of natural language, and across disciplinary boundaries "to capture phenomena as diverse as the pulse of a heart and the downturn of an economy" (Wainer & Friendly, 2018, p. 62).

Thus, CA graphical output displays can share research results in an immediate and meaningful way. It is this quality of *meaningfulness* that most strongly aligns with mixed methods research. Mixed methods researchers can facilitate discussions among researchers from diverse backgrounds and areas of expertise, by "virtue of their appreciation and general understanding of both qualitative and quantitative research" (Molina & Fetters, 2019, p. 279).

It is not enough merely to look at one type or one approach to data investigation and analysis: we must employ multiple methods or risk missing a meaningful connection or pattern within our phenomena of interest. Friendly (2000) stated that

> numerical summaries ... are designed to compress the information in the data. In contrast, the visualization approach to data analysis is designed to (a) *expose* information and structure in the data, (b) *supplement* the information from numerical summaries, and (c) *suggest* more adequate models. (p. 14)

As Friendly (2000) declared, with regard to CA, "the notation, formulae, and terms used to describe the method vary considerably" (Friendly, 2000b, p.143). For clarity, this author follows the symbolic coding notation of Greenacre (1984) and Friendly (2000).

Within SAS, by invoking the PROC CORRESP macro, different possibilities exist for graphical display (Friendly, 2000). These possibilities include asymmetric map (options PROFILE=ROW and PROFILE=COLUMN) and the symmetric map (PROFILE=BOTH). Friendly (2000, p. 144) showed a preference for the symmetric map by stating that the symmetric map "produces better graphical displays, because both sets of coordinates (rows and columns) are scaled with the same weights." Symmetric plots (mappings) simultaneously represent the row and column profiles in a common space (Kassambara, 2017).

By delivering both a visual and empirical summary of observed data, CA offers a unique and powerful way to discern patterns in categorical data. To incorporate qualitative data into a CA, researchers can treat categorical variables as numeric by coding the indicated responses (e.g., using 0 for absence and 1 for presence), as discussed by Richter (2019).

4 Suggested Applications of Correspondence Analysis in Mixed Methods Research

The aim of CA is to represent graphically the categories of a two-way or multi-way contingency table and then to determine important associations among the categories (Beh, 1999, p. 1513). For applications to mixed methods research, we look to the past for inspiration. Dr. John Snow (1813–1858), also known as the *Father of Modern Epidemiology*, is described as "a legendary figure in the history of public health, epidemiology and anesthesiology" (Frerichs, 2018, ¶ 1). Dr. Snow famously solved the riddle of the 1854 London cholera outbreak using what we would today refer to as mixed methods research techniques. Snow conducted interviews, collected mortality data, and visually plotted the resulting deaths-by-location to pinpoint the epicenter of the outbreak: the Broad Street pump. To aid in his understanding of the significance of the Broad Street Pump, as opposed to other water sources available in the area, Dr. Snow spoke directly with family members of people who had died from the cholera outbreak. Wainer (1997) stated, that of the 10 neighborhood families interviewed, five families reported traveling specifically to the Broad Street Pump because they preferred the taste of that water to other water sources. As Johnson (2006) stated, Dr. Snow had given "the death and darkness of the Broad Street outbreak a new kind of clarity" (p. 194). By combining all these methods of inquiry—quantitative mortality counts, and qualitative data obtained from oral accounts—Snow solved a multivariate, complex problem. This problem-solving aspect of mixed methods research cannot be underestimated—researchers need such techniques to investigate contemporary, complex phenomena. This enhanced ability to create meaning and to provide clarity is a valuable characteristic of mixed methods research.

5 Empirical Demonstration of Correspondence Analysis in Mixed Methods Research: Parents in Prison

Across the United States, prisons hold the parents of more than a million children (Glaze & Maruschak, 2008). Notable among the many national organizations working to improve the criminal justice system is *The Sentencing Project*. Founded in 1986, The Sentencing Project "works for a fair and effective U.S. criminal justice system by promoting reforms in sentencing policy, addressing unjust racial disparities and practices, and advocating for alternatives to incarceration" (The Sentencing Project, 2019, p. 1).

Nationally, U.S. prisons held approximately 744,200 fathers and 65,600 mothers at midyear 2007 (Glaze & Maruschak, 2008). Parents held in the nations' prisons, comprising 52% of state inmates and 63% of federal inmates, reported having an estimated 1,706,600 minor children, accounting for 2.3% of the U.S. resident population under age 18. By incorporating the prior research methodology of Glaze and Maruschak (2008), archival data were utilized from the 2004 Survey of Inmates in State and Federal Correctional Facilities to conduct a CA regarding inmates and their minor children. The Survey of Inmates in State and Federal Correctional Facilities collects multiple data points and types, including socioeconomic, demographic, and criminal history variables. Data are divided into two distinct files: numeric data and alphanumeric data from the inmate interviews. The majority of fathers in prison (88%) report that their children are living with their non-incarcerated parent, whereas mothers in prison are more likely than are their fathers to have their children living with grandparents, other relatives, or in foster care (The Sentencing Project, 2019).

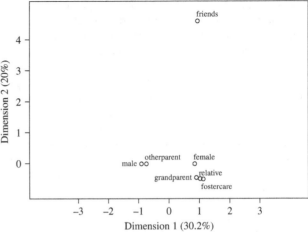

FIGURE 3.1 Parents in prison: Caregiver by gender of incarcerated parent.

The CA in the following example, Caregivers of minor children with a parent in prison, vividly displays this disparity in caregiver roles based on gender. To produce this example, SAS code was written to invoke the CA procedure. (See Appendix 1 for the complete code and documentation notes.) Variables of interest included self-reported gender, and reported percentages of minor children and their associated caregivers. Caregiver refers to the person responsible for the minor child while the parent was incarcerated. Caregiver types comprised the non-incarcerated parent, grandparents, other relative, and foster care. Responses obtained during the inmate interview process provided qualitative data regarding caregiver status for analysis. The resultant CA output includes a table of associated values (gender is the row variable, and caregiver is the column variable); and the CA graphical display, shown in Figure 3.1.

Correlation approaches provide the basis for all classical multivariate techniques (Friendly, 2002). Complex social phenomena require examination of multiple complex variables. Oftentimes, these variables are categorical in nature. Merely dichotomizing or dummy coding these variables diminishes their explanatory and predictive value. Hill (1974) has described CA as a "neglected multivariate method" (p. 340). CA utilizes contingency table analysis to detect relationships between the underlying categorical variables. For the graphical outputs, CA depicts the variable relationships in a spatial grid, with 2-dimensional representation of the row and column variables as defined by the underlying dataset.

For the CA of inmate survey data, the gender of the incarcerated parent was compared with the gender of the associated caregiver status of their minor child/children. For incarcerated female parents, the most associated caregiver was the grandparent. For incarcerated male parents, the most associated caregiver was the other parent (mother of minor child/children). By examining the resultant CA output, viewers can easily discern the striking disparities between men and women respondents, and the resultant identity and relationship of the caregivers for their minor children. Although the inmate interview process provided the qualitative responses, visualizing the information with the CA process provides a compelling summary of the inmate information.

6 Strengths and Limitations of Correspondence Analysis in Mixed Methods Research

Mixed methods research, through the appropriate combination and integration of qualitative and quantitative methods, can support useful and credible knowledge development. (Molina-Azorin & Fetters, 2019). A unique strength of CA, conducted with qualitative data that have been quantized, is the ability to generate useful information for informed decision-making and dissemination. Information vehicles or *informatives* (Clarke & Carlson, 1982; Nauta, 1970) were defined as "sets of directions that determine an idea" (Volpato, 2014, p. xxx). Table 3.1, adapted from Blasius and Greenacre (2014), displays the relationship between the mode of experience and the comprehensions and extensions of those modes. With this updated table, the author has highlighted the unique summary of comprehension and extension to provide a symbolic equation of the mixed methods research approach.

As Denzin and Lincoln (2005) stated, researchers can study phenomena analytically or holistically, organically, or culturally, and via mixed methods research. CA provides one of the strongest ways to incorporate a mixed methods research approach to the investigation of phenomena because it utilizes both numbers and images. This crossover approach enables the rich narrative of data to be conveyed in an accessible and uniquely descriptive manner. Mixed methods researchers integrate quantitative and qualitative methods to build a complete methodological *tool kit* to identify research questions, to

TABLE 3.1

Comprehension + Extension = Mixed Methods Approach

Type of Mode	Comprehension	Extension
Mode of being	Wisdom	Data
Mode of knowing	Experience	Knowledge
Summary of modal experiences	Comprehension + Extension = Mixed Methods Approach	

reframe problems, and to utilize rich evidence to understand challenges (Molina-Azorin & Fetters, 2019). CA—utilizing qualitative data which have been quantitized—can become an important member of the methodological tool kit.

Limitations of the CA approach for qualitative data would include the reminder from Azzam et al. (2013) to "ensure that the breadth and scope of the visualization does not omit important information, does not overrepresent certain data, and that the visualization accurately reflects the information contained in the data" (p. 9). Other limitations include appropriately interpreting the geometric mappings in space (Greenacre & Hastie, 1987).

7 Resources for Learning More About Correspondence Analysis

Showcased within Tukey's approach to data analysis, flexibility was an important theme (Hoaglin, 2003). CA provides contemporary researchers the flexibility to investigate both known and unknown phenomena with vivid clarity and precise visual depictions. There are several strong software applications available to support CA. Table 3.2 below provides a sampling of software resources for creating CA displays and conducting analyses.

TABLE 3.2

Software Resources for Creating CA Displays

Type of software	Resource link and comments
QDA Miner 5	https://provalisresearch.com/products/qualitative-data-analysis-software/
Quick-R	This software package offers interactive code searching in an easy-to-use platform.
	Quick-R: Correspondence Analysis: https://www.statmethods.net/advstats/ca.html This software provides packaged code for CA analysis, thus providing an accessible way to use this technique.
	How Correspondence Analysis Works (A Simple Explanation): www.displayr.com/how-correspondence-analysis-works/ This website provides an easy-to-follow explanation of the mathematics underlying CA. A template for use is also provided.
Excel	Correspondence Analysis Using Excel: www.real-statistics.com/multivariate-statistics/correspondence-analysis/correspondence-analysis-basic-concepts/
SPSS Statistics 22.0.0	www.ibm.com/support/knowledgecenter/en/SSLVMB_22.0.0/com.ibm.spss.statistics.help/spss/categories/idh_cors_model.htm
SAS	http://support.sas.com/documentation/cdl/en/imlsug/68152/HTML/default/viewer.htm#imlsug_ugmultca_sect001.htm
	"You can run the Correspondence analysis by selecting Analysis ▶ Multivariate Analysis ▶ Correspondence Analysis from the main menu. The analysis is implemented by calling the CORRESP procedure in SAS/STAT. See the documentation for the CORRESP procedure in the SAS/STAT User's Guide for additional details" (SAS Institute).
R	Nenadic, O., & Greenacre, M. (2007). Correspondence analysis in R, with two- and three-dimensional graphics: The ca package. *Journal of Statistical Software*, 20(3), 1–13. doi:10.18637/jss.v020.i03

REFERENCES

Azzam, T., Evergreen, S., Germuth, A. A., & Kistler, S. J. (2013). Data visualization and evaluation. In T. Azzam & S. Evergreen (Eds.), *Data visualization, Part 1: New directions for evaluation, 139*, 7–32.

Beh, E. J. (1999). Correspondence analysis of ranked data. *Communications in Statistics. Theory and Methods, 28*(7), 1511. doi:10.1080/03610929908832370

Beh, E. J. (2004). Simple correspondence analysis: A bibliographic review. *International Statistical Review, 72*, 257–284. doi:10.1111/j.1751-5823.2004.tb00236.x

Benzécri, J. P. (1973). *Geometric data analysis: From correspondence analysis to structured data*. New York, NY: Kluwer Academic Publishers.

Benzécri, J. (1992). *Correspondence analysis handbook [electronic resource]*. New York, NY: Marcel Dekker.

Blasius J., & Greenacre, M. (Eds.). (2014). *Visualization and verbalization of data*. Boca Raton, FL: Taylor & Francis.

Bureau of Labor Statistics (2008). *Parents in prison and their minor children*. Washington, DC: Author. Retrieved from https://www.bjs.gov/index.cfm?ty=pbdetail&iid=823.

Cabane, C., & Clark, A. (2015). Childhood sporting activities and adult labour-market outcomes. *Annals of Economics and Statistics, 119/120*, 123–148. doi:10.15609/annaeconstat2009.119-120.123

Choulakian, V., Simonetti, B., & Pham Gia, T. (2014). Some new aspects of taxicab correspondence analysis. *Statistical Methods & Applications, 23*, 401–416. doi:10.1007/s10260-014-0259-6

Clarke, H. H., & Carlson, T. (1982). Hearers and speech acts. *Language, 58*, 332–373. doi:10.1353/lan.1982.0042

Denzin, N. K., & Lincoln, Y. S. (2005). In R. E. Stake, N. K. Denzin, & Y. S. Lincoln (Eds.), *The SAGE handbook of qualitative research*. (3rd ed., pp 443–466). Thousand Oaks, CA: Sage.

Dickinson, W. B. (2001a). *Envisioning Kinaalda: Navaho magic, mystery, and myth*. Retrieved from www2.sas.com/proceedings/sugi25/25/po/25p228.pdf

Dickinson, W. B. (2001b). Visual displays for mixed methods findings. In A. Tashakkori & C. Teddlie (Eds.), *Sage handbook of mixed methods in social behavioral Research* (2nd ed., pp. 469–504). Thousand Oaks, CA: Sage.

Dickinson, W. B., & Hall, B. W. (2008). *PROC CORRESP for categorical data: Correspondence analysis (CA) for discover, display, and decision-making*. Proceedings of the SAS Global Forum 2008 Conference (Paper 227). Cary, NC: SAS Institute.

Dickinson, W. B., Hines, C. V., & Onwuegbuzie, A. J. (2007, March). *People, pattern, and place: SAS/GRAPH data display of immigration activity across the United States*. Paper presented at the annual meeting of the SAS Global Forum, Orlando, FL.

Eisner, E. W. (2002). *The arts and the creation of mind*. New Haven, CT: Yale University Press.

Fisher, R. A. (1940). The estimation of the proportion of recessives from tests carried out on a sample not wholly unrelated. *Annals of Eugenics, X*, 160–170. doi:10.1111/j.1469-1809.1940.tb02245.x

Frerichs, R. (2018). *Dr. John Snow*. Retrieved from www.ph.ucla.edu/epi/snow.html

Friendly, M. (1999). Extending mosaic display: Marginal, conditional, and partial views of categorical data. *Journal of Computational and Statistical Graphics, 8*, 373–395. doi:10.1080/10618600.1999.10474820

Friendly, M. (2000). *Visualizing categorical data*. Cary, NC: SAS Institute.

Friendly, M. (2000, April). *Visualizing categorical data: Data, stories, and pictures*. Paper 170-25. Paper presented at SAS Users Group International, Orlando, FL.

Glaze, L., & Maruschak, L. (2008). Parents in prison. *Bureau of Justice Statistics Special Reports Series*. Justice Statistics Clearinghouse: NCJ 222984.

Greenacre, M. (1984). *Theory and applications of correspondence analysis*. London, England: Academic Press.

Greenacre, M. (2010a). Canonical correspondence analysis in social science research. In H. Locarek-Junge & C. Weihs (Eds.), *Classification as a tool for research. Studies in classification, data analysis, and knowledge organization* (pp. 279–286). Berlin, Germany: Springer.

Greenacre, M. (2010b). Correspondence analysis of raw data. *Ecology, 91*, 958–963. Retrieved from www.jstor.org/stable/25661139

Greenacre, M. (2013). The contributions of rare objects in correspondence analysis. *Ecology, 94*(1), 241–249. doi:10.1890/11-1730.1

Greenacre, M. (2017). *Correspondence analysis in practice*. New York, NY: Chapman and Hall/CRC.

Greenacre, M. J., & Blasius, J. (1994). *Correspondence analysis in the social sciences: recent developments and applications*. London, England: Academic Press.

Greenacre, M., & Hastie, T. (1987). The geometric interpretation of correspondence analysis. *Journal of the American Statistical Association, 82*(398), 437–447. doi:10.1080/01621459.1987.10478446

Greenacre, M., & Pardo, R. (2006). Subset correspondence analysis: Visualization of selected response categories in a questionnaire survey. *Sociological Methods & Research, 35*, 193–218. doi:10.1177/0049124106290316

Henderson, S., & Segal, E. H. (2013). Visualizing qualitative data in evaluation research. In T. Azzam & S. Evergreen (Eds.), Data visualizations, Part 1. *New Directions for Evaluation, 139*, 53–71.

Hill, M. O. (1974). Correspondence analysis: A neglected multivariate method. *Applied Statistics, 23*, 340–354. doi:10.2307/2347127

Hoaglin, D. C., & Tukey, J. W. (1985). Checking the shape of discrete distributions. In D. C. Hoaglin, F. Mosteller, & J. W. Tukey (Eds.), *Exploring data tables, trends, and shapes* (pp. 345–416). New York, NY: John Wiley and Sons.

Hoaglin, D. C. (2003). John W. Tukey and data analysis. *Statistical Science, 18*, 311–318. doi:10.1214/ss/1076102418

Hoffman, D., & Franke, G. (1986). Correspondence analysis: Graphical representation of categorical data in marketing research. *Journal of Marketing Research, 23*, 213–227. doi:10.2307/3151480

Johnson, S. (2006). *The ghost map: The story of London's most terrifying epidemic—and how it changed science, cities, and the modern world*. New York, NY: Penguin Group.

Kassambara, A. (2017). *Practical guide to principal components methods in R*. Montpellier, France: Datanovia.

Lincoln, Y. S., & Guba, E. G. (1985). *Naturalistic inquiry*. Beverly Hills, CA: Sage.

Molina-Azorin, J. F., & Fetters, M. D. (2019). Building a better world through mixed methods research. *Journal of Mixed Methods Research, 13*, 275–281. doi:10.1177/1558689819855864

Nauta, D. (1970). *The meaning of information*. Hague, Netherlands: Mouton.

Onwuegbuzie, A. J., & Dickinson, W. B. (2008). Mixed methods analysis and information visualization: Graphical display for effective communication of research results. *The Qualitative Report, 13*, 204–225. Retrieved from https://nsuworks.nova.edu/cgi/viewcontent.cgi?article=1595&context=tqr

Onwuegbuzie, A. J., Dickinson, W. B., Leech, N. L., & Zoran, A. G. (2009). A qualitative framework for collecting and analyzing data in focus group research. *International Journal of Qualitative Methods, 8*, 1–21. doi:10.1177/160940690900800301

Onwuegbuzie, A. J., Dickinson, W. B., Leech, N. L., & Zoran, A. G. (2010). Toward more rigor in focus group research in stress and coping and beyond. In K. M. T. Collins, A. J. Onwuegbuzie, & Q. G. Jiao (Eds.), *Toward a broader understanding of stress and coping: Mixed methods approaches* (pp. 243–273). Charlotte, NC: Information Age Publishing.

Onwuegbuzie, A. J., Frels, R. K., Leech, N. L., & Collins, K. M. T. (2011). A mixed research study of pedagogical approaches and student learning in doctoral-level mixed research courses. *International Journal of Multiple Research Approaches, 5*, 169–199. doi:10.5172/mra.2011.5.2.169

Onwuegbuzie, A. J., & Teddlie, C. (2003). A framework for analyzing data in mixed methods research. In A. Tashakkori & C. Teddlie (Eds.), *Handbook of mixed methods in social and behavioral research* (pp. 351–383). Thousand Oaks, CA: Sage.

Playfair, W. (1786). *The commercial and political atlas; representing, by means of stained copper-plate charts, the exports, imports, and general trade of England, at a single view. to which are added, charts of the revenue and debts of Ireland, done in the same manner by James Corry*. London, England: Debrett, Robinson, and Sewell.

Richter, S. (2019). *Introduction to SAS for data analysis*. UNCG Quantitative Methodology Series. Greensboro, North Carolina: University of North Carolina at Greensboro. Retrieved from www.uncg.edu/mat/qms/SAS%20Workshop%20Document.pdf

Rusch, T., Hofmarcher, P., Hatzinger, R., & Hornik, K. (2013). Model trees with topic model preprocessing: An approach for data journalism illustrated with Wikileaks Afghanistan War Logs. *The Annals of Applied Statistics, 7*, 613–639. doi:10.1214/12-AOAS618

SAS Institute Inc. (2010). *Cary*, NC: Author.

Solaz, A., & Wolff, F. (2015). Intergenerational correlation of domestic work: Does gender matter? *Annals of Economics and Statistics, 117/118*, 159–184. doi:10.15609/annaeconstat2009.117-118.159

The Sentencing Project. (2019). *About us*. Washington, DC: Author. Retrieved from www.sentencingproject.org/about-us/

Tufte, E. R. (2006). *Beautiful evidence*. Cheshire, CT: Graphics Press.

Tukey, J. W. (1977). *Exploratory data analysis*. Reading, MA: Addison Wesley.

Volpato, R. (2014). Prologue: Let the data speak. In J. Blasius & M. Greenacre (Eds.), *Visualization and verbalization of data* (pp. xxvii–xlii). Boca Raton, FL: Taylor & Francis.

Wainer, H. (1997). *Visual revelations: Graphical tales of fate and deception from Napoleon Bonaparte to Ross Perot*. New York, NY: Copernicus.

Wainer, H. (2005). *Graphic discovery: A trout in the milk and other visual adventures*. Princeton, NJ: Princeton University Press

Wainer, H., & Friendly, M. (2018). Ancient visualizations. *Chance, 31*, 62–64. doi:10.1080/09332480.2018.1467645

Wheater, C. P., Penny, A. C., Clark, P., Syes, Q., & Bellis, M.A. (2003). Re-emerging syphilis: a detrended correspondence analysis of the behavior of HIV positive and negative gay men. doi:10.1186/1471-2458-3-34

Appendix 1 SAS Code to invoke CA procedure

```
*********************************
*Wendy B. Dickinson
*Parents in Prison.sas
*SAS Version 9.4
*Modified from Dickinson and Hall (2008)
*Modified from Friendly (2000)
*********************************;
*Input categorical data
*Data source: Parents in Prison
*The Sentencing Project
*********************************;
data parents;
input parent2 grandparent relative fostercare gender$;
cards;
89 13 5 4 males
37 45 23 19 females
;
title1 'Caregivers of Minor Children with a Parent in Prison';
*************************************;
*invoke Correspondence Analysis procedure
*define variables
*gender is the row variable
*caregiver is the column variable
*************************************;
proc corresp data = parents out=caregiver;
var parent2 grandparent relative fostercare ;
id gender;
proc print data = parents;
var gender;
run;
data label;
set caregiver;
xsys='2'; ysys = '2';
x = dim1;
y = dim2;
text = gender;
size = 1.5;
function = 'LABEL';
run;
```

```
*****************************************************;
*invoke SAS/Graph to create visual display of data
*use coordinate system
*define axis and axis 2
*****************************************************;
proc gplot data = parents;
plot dim1 * dim2/anno = label frame
href = 0 vref = 0 lvref = 3 lhref = 3
vaxis = axis2 haxis = axis1
vminor = 1 hminor = 1;
axis1 length = 3 in order = (-1 to 1 by .5)
label = (h=1.3 'Dimension 1');
axis2 length = 3 in order = (-1 to 1 by .5)
label = (h=1.3 a=90 r=0 'Dimension2');
symbol v=none;
run;
```

Appendix 2 Bureau of Justice Statistics

Estimated number of parents (inmates) in state and federal prisons and their associated minor children, by reported gender of inmate.

Number of Parents		Parents in state prison			Parents in federal prison		
Year	Total	Male	Female	Total	Male	Female	Total
2007	809,800	627,800	58,200	686,000	116,400	7,400	123,800
2004/b	754,900	592,300	51,800	644,100	104,200	6,600	110,800
1999	721,500	593,800	48,500	642,300	74,100	5,100	79,200
1997	649,500	544,100	42,900	587,000	58,500	4,000	62,500
1991	452,500	386,500	26,600	413,100	36,500	2,900	39,400

Number of minor children		Minor children of parents in state prison			Minor children of parents in federal prison		
Year	Total	Male	Female	Total	Male	Female	Total
2007	1,706,600	1,296,500	131,000	1,427,500	262,700	16,400	279,100
2004/b	1,590,100	1,223,700	116,600	1,340,300	235,200	14,600	249,800
1999/c	1,515,200	1,223,400	115,500	1,338,900	165,700	10,600	176,300
1997/c	1,362,900	1,121,400	102,400	1,223,800	130,800	8,300	139,100
1991/c	945,600	802,300	58,000	860,300	79,200	5,900	85,100

Table adapted from *Glaze and Maruschak (2008)*.
Report title: Parents in Prison and Their Minor Children NCJ 222984.
Data source: Survey of Inmates in State and Federal Correctional Facilities, 2004
Authors: Lauren E. Glaze and Laura M. Maruschak
Date of version: August 26, 2008

Appendix 3 Parents in Prison and their Minor Children

This report "presents data from the 2004 Survey of Inmates in State and Federal Correctional Facilities about inmates who are also parents, and their minor children. It presents the total number of children who were minors at some time during their parent's incarceration. The report describes selected background characteristics of parents in prisons, including marital status, citizenship, education, offense type, criminal history, employment, prior experiences of homelessness, drug and alcohol involvement, mental health, and physical and sexual abuse. It provides family background of inmate parents including household makeup, public assistance received by household, drug and alcohol use, and incarceration of family members. It includes information on the children's daily care, financial support, current caregivers, and frequency and type of contact with incarcerated parents" (Bureau of Justice Statistics, 2008).

Parents held in United States prisons—52% of state inmates and 63% of federal inmates—"reported having an estimated 1,706,600 minor children, accounting for 2.3% of the U.S. resident population under age 18" (Glaze & Maruschak, 2008, p. 1).

4

Multidimensional Scaling of Qualitative Data

Ahmet Suerdem

1 Definition of MDS

The concept of mental distance, or measuring the feeling of *proximity* (similarity or dissimilarity) among perceptual or conceptual stimuli (Kruskal & Wish, 1978, p. 29), is crucial to many theories in social sciences. However, measuring distance in mental space is not as straightforward as it would be in the physical space because of the subjective nature of perception. Multidimensional scaling (MDS) is a set of statistical techniques used for reducing this complexity. It is based on the transformation of the observed proximities by estimating distances among a group of real or mental *objects* to project the patterns between them upon a low-dimensional coordinate system. *Objects* might refer to products, people, colors, faces, political persuasion, or any kind of psychological or conceptual stimuli (Kruskal & Wish, 1978, pp. 23–30). Torgerson (1958), who coined the term, described MDS as a psychometric technique for understanding people's judgments of the distance between a set of stimuli. This technique has widely been used in a wide variety of disciplines, including marketing, sociology, physics, political science, and biology (Young & Hamer, 1987).

2 When Use of MDS is Appropriate in MMR (Mixed Methods Research)

Its capacities for handling both qualitative and quantitative data make MDS a very handy tool for MMR provided that appropriate data collection, preparation, and analysis methods are applied.

Data Collection and Preparation

Direct methods of data collection for MDS are based on the operationalization of subjective judgements about the proximities between the stimuli by means of rating, sorting, or rank ordering. There is a variety of such procedures differing according to the tasks performed during the administration, the sampling design, and the way of transforming raw data to proximities. *Pairwise comparisons* wherein the respondents are asked to rate the (dis)similarity of a pair of objects are widely preferred among social scientists because of the simplicity of administration. However, this method is not convenient for designs with higher number of stimuli because of its burden on the respondents. A common method for tackling this issue is using incomplete data designs wherein a random sample of pairs is selected, and the remainder is set to missing. The complete data are obtained by aggregating the individual matrices. When the number of respondents is high, such designs are found to provide highly reliable data (Spence & Domoney, 1974).

To ease the burden on the respondents, more manageable tasks such as sorting, or ranking the objects in terms of their (dis)similarities, can be preferred to pairwise comparisons. In *sorting tasks*, respondents are presented with a set of stimuli and are asked to sort them into mutually exclusive groups according to their perceived similarities. When the task finishes, the results for each respondent are arranged into an object by group co-occurrence matrix, which is then aggregated for obtaining the overall proximity matrix. The data collected by these methods are found to provide a finer grained, ordered measurement of proximity, and according to Courcoux, Qannari, Taylor, Buck, and Greenhoff (2012), they provide more robust MDS configurations. Although preparation and application of sorting tasks can be a little demanding on the side of the researcher, this can be managed by using specially designed online data collection tools such as OptimalSort (www.optimalworkshop.com).

Ranking tasks, such as *anchor stimulus method*, are less demanding both for the respondent and the researcher because less data must be compared at the same time. During this procedure, all stimuli are presented simultaneously and one of them is fixed as an anchor for comparison with the others. Then, the respondent is asked to rank order all other stimuli according to their similarity to this anchor. In the next round, another stimulus is randomly selected to take its turn as the anchor and the procedure continues in an iterative manner until all stimuli are ranked. Finally, a matrix is constructed wherein the values in the cells represent ranking of the column (comparison) stimulus compared to the row (anchor) stimulus. The drawback of this method is that it leads to conditional proximities needing special MDS procedures such as Unfolding or PREFSCAL (see Borg, Groenen, & Mair, 2018 for the details). However, if we are interested in observing preferences rather than direct proximities, this method is preferable because these procedures are based on mapping preference data (typically evaluative ratings of different persons on a set of objects) as distances between two sets of points (representing the persons and the objects).

Although both sorting and ranking tasks are efficient ways of data collection, sometimes optimizing the number of stimuli can be a problem. Lower numbers reduce the degree of measurement error but provide less precision, whereas the higher numbers provide higher precision with more measurement error. Hence, selecting the optimum number of stimuli requires a trade-off between error and precision. For a more detailed explanation of this issue and the methods for tackling it, the reader can consult Tsogo, Masson, and Bardot (2000).

Indirect Data Collection

Sometimes data are not obtained as direct comparisons but are derived from secondary data such as surveys and represented as a feature (variable) by object (case) matrix (Little, 2013). For example, respondents can be asked to rate a set of computer brands on features such as design, functionality, and performance. In such cases, proximities between two objects are calculated according to the degree of their common features (Tversky, 1977). Any relational measure such as correlations, co-occurrences, interactions, and distances can be input to MDS (Young, 2013). The decision criteria for selecting any of these measures depend on the nature of the data and the method of calculation. Of the many variants, commonly used ones are Jaccard for binary, Cramer's *V* (Chuprow) for nominal, and Euclidean for numerical data (see Bock, 2014 for a more detailed explanation of proximity calculation methods).

These methods are also applicable to qualitatively collected data such as interviews, focus groups, and observations wherein the codes can be used as substitutes for the features. Parallelly, big textual data collected from large scale archives or social media also can be used as an input for calculating the proximities indirectly wherein words represent the features. The basic idea behind these methods is that features (i.e., codes, words, concepts) with semantic similarity will tend to appear in the same documents or similar contexts (Burgess, Livesay, & Lund, 1998). Most qualitative data analysis (QDA) software provide functionalities for constructing code or word-by-document matrices, which can be exported to a spreadsheet file for further statistical analysis. Some of these software, such as QDA Miner and WordStat, also have built in functions for presenting visualization of the proximity values calculated on all included features or cases with the help of multidimensional scaling (MDS) or other statistical data reduction techniques. Despite the arguments about the inappropriateness of these techniques for conceptual instead of perceptual data (Tversky & Hutchinson, 1986), they are successfully applied for modeling the structure in semantic space (Steyvers, 2006), as will be discussed in Section 5.

Using MDS for Modeling Qualitative Data

One of the difficulties for MMR is associating the analysis and interpretation of the quantitative and the qualitative, textual data. The tools for integrating different data elements and various analysis strategies are not mature yet (Bazeley & Jackson, 2013). Although there is a vast number of statistical tools in the arsenal of quantitative researchers, not all of them are suitable for qualitative analysis. Quantitative variables are usually deductively operationalized single-dimensional scales representing pre-defined constructs (Sivesind, 1999). These variables can be modeled for statistical hypothesis testing. On the other hand, the dimensionality for qualitative variables are latent in the textual data that need to be revealed through a reading and coding process. Qualitative data are stored in unstructured textual corpora needing to be structured during the analytical process. This includes audio-visual material, which needs to be transcribed for further analysis. Automatic pattern detection techniques, such as MDS, can reduce the complexity in this process by revealing the patterns connecting the singular data pieces to the whole. These tools can inform qualitative data management and analysis by subjecting the emergent themes to an exploratory statistical analysis (Onwuegbuzie & Teddlie, 2003).

When applying statistical tools in MMR, we need to consider that knowledge generation from qualitative data is a hermeneutical process. It starts with the breaking down of whole textual corpus into smaller parts and then continues with recomposing these singular pieces into a coding frame as it would be in a puzzle. For most qualitative analysis methods, dimensionality of this frame emerges through an inductive process organizing the coded expressions according to the regularities in the contexts they occur. Despite this inductive logic, the coding act does not occur in a vacuum, but starts with relating each partial expression to a Gestalt-like whole that is greater than the sum of its parts. Coding is also a decoding process involving an attempt to discover the internal logic of the context spanning the boundaries of the expressions. Codification of partial expressions can be framed and reframed according to an emergent dimensional structure until the meaning is fixed and a plausible interpretation is reached. However, the closure of an inductive coding frame can become impossible through circular practices because interpreting and labelling any singular expression depends on its reference to the others. The complexity of this process can yield enormous cognitive overload, leading the coder to be lost in circles if the internal and external boundaries of the corpus are not clearly framed (Miles & Huberman, 1994). Statistical dimension reduction techniques such as MDS can help us to close this hermeneutical circle by providing access to code patterns and to discover their underlying dimensions.

In this vein, integrating hermeneutical understanding with dimension-reduction techniques can enable a process coined as *semiosis* by Peirce (as cited in Eco, 1987). Semiosis is not solely based on interpretation but is also an abductive analytical process defining a *code model*, a system made of signs, meanings, and coding rules. This model starts when the researcher makes inferences about the world of the text by grounding the expressions to his/her preconceptions to generate a conjectural interpretation. A theory helps to explain this interpretation by outlining the rules holding the text together. Dimension-reduction techniques can contribute to these explanations by exploring, cross-validating, or challenging this theory. They can help us to discover how code patterns fit into the whole picture so that we can modify our initial conjectures about the reading of the expressions. Hence, the hermeneutic circle closes when we reconstruct the corpus into a coherent coding frame until the conjectures about one part fit into the set of conjectures about the other parts. To sum up, it is appropriate and useful to use MDS in the quantitative analysis of qualitative data unless it is used together with hermeneutical reading and understanding through an abductive process. This technique can help us to develop a visual hermeneutics (Ihde, 1998) toolkit for identifying patterns and relationships at various levels, which subsequently can support us to see a bird's eye view of the whole corpus.

3 Technical Outline of MDS for MMR

MDS algorithms are based in Euclidian axioms reflecting our everyday experience with objects: the (shortest) distance between two points is the length of the straight line connecting them (Schiffman, Reynolds, & Young, 1981). These algorithms aim to allocate n objects in a low-dimensional Euclidean space in a way that the distances between these objects approximate the observed proximities. For a better understanding of this, let's consider mapping a set of objects onto a two-dimensional (x, y) space given their coordinates. The Euclidean distance between two objects a and b on this map can be formulated as:

$$d_{ab} = \sqrt{(x_a - x_b)^2 + (y_a - y_b)^2}.$$

The mathematics of this example is very simple: anybody who is familiar with our high school friend Pythagorean Theorem would be able to understand this: Distance between two points is equal to the length of the hypotenuse linking them in a hypothetical right triangle.

Now, let's consider the inverse of this problem: how to obtain the coordinate values of the map given the observed proximities between the objects? The principles behind classical metric MDS calculation are built on the fact that the coordinate vectors can be derived by eigenvalue decomposition of a proximity matrix. According to these principles, few eigenvalues of high value account for much of the structure in the data and the remainder represent noise. (For a more technical explanation, the reader may refer to Borg and Groenen [2005].) Accordingly, we can represent a high-dimensional coordinate space in a lower dimensional form. The calculation will generate the eigenvectors allocating the objects along the Cartesian coordinates, enabling analysts to discover the "obvious and compelling" dimensions (Torgerson, 1958, p. 254) underlying the data.

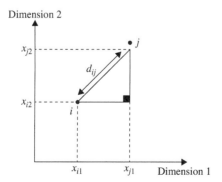

FIGURE 4.1 Geometrical representation of the idea of distance.

Iterative MDS Algorithms

Because proximity data consisting of subjective distance judgments can rarely be collected with metric precision, social sciences researchers usually prefer non-metric models transforming the ordinal data to some metric form (Borg & Groenen, 2005). The algorithms performing this operation are not confined to the eigenvalue approach but follow an iterative approach by regressing the proximities to calculated distances. Starting with an initial configuration, the algorithm iteratively transforms the proximities to estimated proximities (disparities) for calculating the configuration of the objects in the coordinates. This continues until the squared differences between the disparities and distances is minimized. These differences reflect model (mis)fit, which can be formulated with the concept of Stress:

$$Stress = \sqrt{\frac{\sum (f(x) - d)^2}{\sum d^2}}$$

Where x is a vector of proximities, f(x) is some transformation function for x, and d the point distances. The concept of Stress is akin to R^2 in regression, but it is a measure of badness-of-fit rather than goodness-of-fit. To minimize stress, we need to find an optimal configuration of points limited to a given number of dimensions.

4 Empirical Demonstration of MDS

Let's see how this works through an empirical example using a dataset that was collected by asking the respondents how they perceive the dissimilarity among 15 kinship terms (Rosenberg & Park Kim, 1975). The reader can attempt a hands-on approach by following the instructions in the link (https://asuerdem.shinyapps.io/MDS-master/). Those who are competent in R language can try package SMACOF (Mair, De Leeuw & Groenen, 2015) for more advanced applications.

Initial Parameters

For selecting the optimal MDS model, we need to make some decisions and diagnostics concerning the parameters:

Scree Plot: Deciding on the Number of Dimensions

For a given number of objects, lower dimensional models are more interpretable but produce higher Stress values. Hence, we need to make a trade-off between the interpretability and goodness of fit. Theoretically, the optimal MDS model is the one with the lowest Stress. According to the benchmarks provided by Kruskal (1964), Stress values higher than .20 indicate a bad fit, whereas Stress values lower than .10 represent a good fit. Because the value of stress is dependent on several factors, such global rules of thumb might not always be useful. For example, both an increase in the number of objects and a decrease in the dimensionality yield lower Stress values. For ordinal models, a high number of missing values and

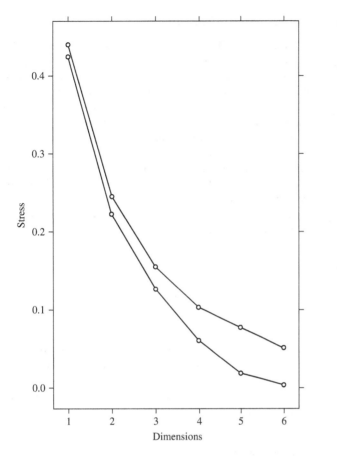
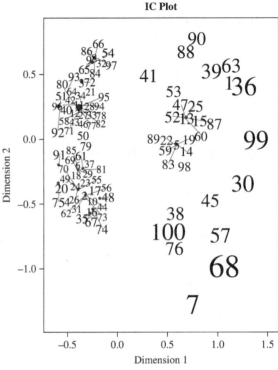

FIGURE 4.2 Initial parameters.

ties also can yield lower Stress values. Moreover, even random data contain some structure in it, decreasing Stress values with increasing dimensionality. Hence, to decide whether the structure in an *n*-dimensional model is due to random factors, we compare the model against the scree plot generated by the random data. Scree plots map the indices for meaningful Stress reduction with increasing dimensionality. According to our example, a decrease in Stress values becomes incremental for the model after three dimensions (Figure 4.2).

To proceed with the analysis, we need to make some decisions concerned with the model.

Type of MDS Transformation

As explained in section about *Iterative MDS algorithms,* MDS mathematically transforms the proximity data to calculated distance data on the assumed scale level. This can take different forms, such as ordinal, interval, ratio, or mspline (i.e., a non-negative spline function that represents a piecewise polynomial [parametric] curve), according to the level of scale. The decision criteria are dependent on the research question on hand, and the diagnostics for the model fit (see Section 4.2).

Ties

For ordinal MDS, we can break ties in a way that equal proximities need *not* be mapped into equal distances (ties = "primary") or keep the ties (ties = "secondary"). The primary approach is preferred if we think that the ties occur because of the measurement artifacts, such as not providing the respondents with enough stimuli or keeping the measurement scale range with less precision. In contrast, the secondary approach is preferred if we believe that the respondent really could not distinguish the differences between some pairs of stimuli. The primary approach leads to lower Stress. Because there is no reason to believe that ties occur because of respondents' lack of ability to distinguish between kinship figures, we can use the primary approach in our example.

Initial configurations. Stress by itself is not a reliable criterion for model choice. Ordinal models tend to provide lower Stress values, albeit with the possibility of generating uninterpretable *degenerate configurations*. Suboptimal local minima are more likely to occur in low-dimensional ordinal models, even if a global minimum is not reached (Mair et al., 2015). The initial configuration is usually something that should be explored to check the susceptibility of the data set to different initial positions. For this, most MDS algorithms use the "Torgerson" configuration obtained by the eigenvalue approach (Borg & Mair, 2017, p. 21). A complementary choice is to conduct MDS with several different random initial configurations and then select the configuration with the smallest Stress and compare the result with the Torgerson method. However, both options might not provide enough information on other local-minima solutions that could have only slightly

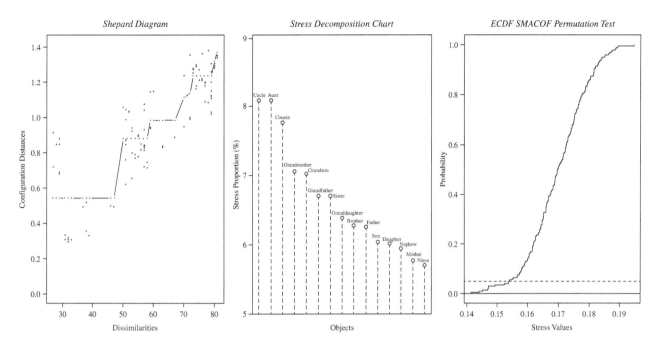

FIGURE 4.3 Diagnostics for model fit.

higher Stress values but might be theoretically better interpretable. Given the global minimum solution, it would be a good idea to check what other local-minima solutions exist, what their Stress values are, and how similar they are. In our example, there are three rather dense clusters of low Stress solutions with similar configurations on the left-hand side, and various somehow scattered solutions with higher Stress on the right-hand side of the plot (Figure 4.2). This suggests that configurations might be quite stable. We can decide on the selection of the initial by plotting an MDS solution with initial values produced by metric MDS (Torgersen) and checking its interpretability against several configurations with a reasonable Stress level.

Diagnostics for the Model Fit

Shepard Diagram

As stated previously, stress is an overall *badness-of-fit* measure. It can be artificially high or low because of outliers, non-linearity, clusters in the data, and so on. To diagnose such patterns, we need to consult the Shepard diagram, which is a scatter plot showing the dispersion between the data (proximities) and the corresponding distances around a regression line. For the ordinal data, monotonic regression line should be approximately linear with steps, with no extreme steps or curvatures. Less spread around this line implies a good fit. An important pattern that we need to check in this diagram is the existence of clearly distinct clusters with high within-correlations and low between-correlations while the overall Stress value is low. This is a rare case, but can occur if the number of objects is small ($n \leq 8$). This might imply a degenerate solution producing an uninterpretable MDS space. To remedy this, we can attempt a stronger model type (i.e., interval if the present model is ordinal) or "mspline" option and compare the solutions (see Borg & Groenen, 2005, p. 65).

The Shepard diagram in Figure 4.3 gives us an indication about how well our calculated distances for the three-dimensional model matches the original data patterns. Although there is slight scatter around it, regression curve monotonically increases (should be linearly for metric) and there are no obvious patterns.

Stress Per Point

Higher values in Stress are due to when at least one of the distances between a pair of points are being distorted on the MDS configuration. Averaging the squared errors for distances between a point and all other points can give us a Stress per point measure, which indicates how badly each individual object fits. A stress decomposition chart plots these values in a descending order according to their contribution. For our example, we can see that the worst fitting points are Uncle, Aunt, and Cousin. One possibility is that the respondents had difficulty when evaluating the dissimilarity between these kin terms and the others. For example, since Cousin is genderless, respondents might have difficulties for judging its relative position. Another possibility is that they might have used other or additional or individually different attributes when comparing these terms to what they used for the others. A simple solution might be removing them from the analysis. Another solution might be increasing the number of dimensions so that these points can move into the extra space and form new distances (Borg & Groenen, 2005, p. 69). Usually, it is a good practice to keep such points rather than eliminating them while giving them less emphasis when interpreting the MDS space.

Permutation Tests

To statistically test whether the Stress value for the observed data performs better than does the random data, we can conduct a permutation test, which shows us whether the MDS model does statistically significantly better than does a null model. Figure 4.3 shows the empirical cumulative distribution function of the permuted stress values (dotted horizontal line denotes the .05 significance threshold). The model Stress value is much below the rejection threshold; hence, the model performs statistically significantly better than does a null model based on random data.

Final MDS and Interpretation

Any configuration that passed the statistical tests might not be valid unless we can provide meaningful explanations about the patterns in the MDS space. For example, sometimes low-dimensional solutions having high Stress values might be more interpretable in terms of theory or replicability compared to higher dimensional solutions. Hence, interpretability of a solution is the essential validity test. When interpreting an MDS plot, we attempt to associate the patterns in geometric configurations of represented objects to their substantive features. To start with, we can examine points at the extreme ends of the dimensions for the distinctiveness in their content and features. Also, searching for regional groupings of points for commonalities and their directionalities can provide some insight for interpretation. Cluster analysis of proximities can help to detect such regions if used as a heuristic but not for validation purposes. We should keep in mind the fact that clusters are automatically obtained non-robust constructs while the regions are constructed through substantive thinking. This is true for the whole interpretation process. Exploration is not a theory-free act; rather, we project a given or assumed a priori knowledge onto the extracted model.

Besides using our own judgments, when we have a substantial theory about the model, we can also use some external scales to see how they correlate with the dimensions. In any case, MDS plots should not be taken for their face value. This dimension system can be arbitrarily rotated and reflected, and dimensions might be oblique. It might be a good idea to visually check for such situations and manually redraw the dimensions, regions, and so forth, without changing the point configuration.

In our example (Figure 4.4), we can see that male kins are clustered on the left and the female kins on the right hand side of Dimension 1. Alternatively, closer relatives are grouped on the lower part, whereas the far relatives on the upper part of Dimension 2. These suggest that respondents might have used *gender* as criterion for evaluating the first and *kinship degree* for the second dimension. A strong correlation between the external gender scale and the first dimension (0.97) and between the kinship degree scale and the second dimension (0.96) confirm this insight. However, the positioning of the terms does not seem to make much sense and the low correlation between the external generation scale and the third dimension (.06) does not confirm our expectation. When we carefully examine the positionings, the members of nuclear family (father; *mother, sister, brother son, daughter*) are located on the upper, the collaterals (aunt, *uncle, cousin, niece, nephew*) in the middle, and kins two generations removed from the self (*grandmother, grandfather, granddaughter and grandson*) on the lower parts of the third dimension. Apparently, this dimension points to a generation dimension that can be interpreted considering the relative position of the self to the other kin

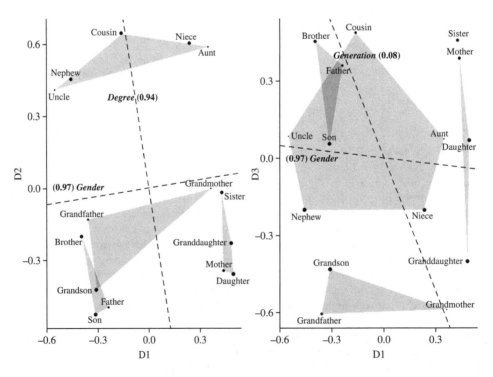

FIGURE 4.4 Comparing Torgerson with random configurations: Final fit.

members (Rosenberg & Park Kim, 1975). This example gives us an occasion to show that interpretation of MDS configurations cannot depend on general benchmarks but should be a reflexive exercise. Because we can provide sensible explanations for our interpretations, we can securely settle on this configuration, which also passed the statistical tests.

Finally, the reader should remember the following points when interpreting the MDS mapping. First, the layout of the dimensions should not be considered as fixed. We can rotate the dimensions, with right on the left or top on the bottom, but the relative positions among the items remain consistent. Second, the distance units provided in an MDS space are arbitrary. Only patterns from a bird's eye view might be reliable. Intricate details from a zoomed-in view would not make much sense because longer distances tend to be more accurate than do shorter distances on a relative scale. Last but not the least, decisions for interpreting an MDS configuration should not be limited to the position of the objects in the final mapping. These results should be interpreted in conjunction with the theory and outputs produced by the diagnostic tools.

5 Suggested Applications of MDS

Although classical MDS involves the use of a single symmetric square data matrix as an input (Kruskal, 1964; Shepard, 1962; Torgerson, 1958), modern MDS algorithms have different application types for different data shapes (Cox & Cox, 2001). These can be grouped as follows:

Multi-way MDS

For this type, each pair of objects has repeated measures coming from different replications over the same individuals or multiple raters over the same task. The dataset is arranged as an array of individual matrices that could first be averaged across individuals and then averaged once more over the two halves of the resulting complete matrix. These matrices are unconditional, meaning that they can be compared to each other. The algorithm deals with several matrices simultaneously but yields a single scaling configuration (Steyvers, 2006). Multi-way MDS is particularly useful for testing the stability of extracted dimensions.

Multi-mode MDS

Multi-mode MDS is similar to multi-way MDS; however, proximity matrices are derived from several modes representing independent experimental conditions, individuals, stimuli, and so forth. This type considers the salience of each dimension across individuals. Algorithms for modeling such data are based on the idea of "subjective metrics" (Borg & Groenen, 2005, pp. 495–518), wherein each individual matrix has a set of dimensional weights that systematically alter the aggregate stimulus space. These individual spaces are different, but they generate a common space by weighting the dimensions of the MDS model. Besides modelling the object space, subject spaces showing the positioning of the individuals along the axes according to their weights also are plotted.

MDS with Asymmetric Data

Drift vector models are applied for dealing with such data. The algorithm decomposes an asymmetric matrix into a symmetric and a skew-symmetric part. Then, it fits an MDS on the symmetric part and computes drift vectors for the skew-symmetric portion. Hence, it is possible to see how these two components are related to each other. It is limited to two dimensions only (Mair et al., 2015).

MDS with Rectangular Data

A typical case for such data might be when we have n individuals rating m stimuli. The algorithm is generally used for modelling preferential choice data, such as the unfolding models aiming to represent the ratings and the individuals on the same scale. For each individual, the corresponding scale can be folded together at the individual's point and his/her original rankings are observed (Cox & Cox, 2001, p. 165). The points representing the individuals are called ideal points, because they are the points of maximal preference in space. The closer a stimulus is to the ideal point of an individual, the stronger this individual's preference for this stimulus. The distances between an individual's ideal point and the various stimulus points represent this individual's perceived preference intensities. Metric data are generally unconditional because we can compare numbers both within and between rows. However, if the ranking information is row-conditional as in anchor stimulus method, we cannot compare the ranks given by individual i to the ranks given by individual k. Row-conditional unfolding is required in that case. Such analysis requires plenty of data (i.e., at least 15 individuals, all with different preference profiles).

An Applied Example for MMR

Now, let's see how *Multi-mode MDS* can be applied to cognitive or concept mapping, a use case that can be particularly interesting for MMR. Cognitive mapping is used for eliciting judgments about relationships between a set of concepts to visually represent how an individual or a group conceives an issue (Axelrod, 1976). It aims to create an overview of different mental models for comparing them (Carley, 1993). Cognitive mapping methods have significant potentials for MMR because of their ability in quantifying the relational patterns among symbols embedded in natural language structures and mapping them along a series of dimensions (Carley & Palmquist, 1992). Their capacity for transforming qualitative data in free textual form such as open-ended questions, interviews, focus groups, and media and social media documents into quantitative form makes them versatile tools for MMR. By mixing the strengths of automatic or manual coding-based text analysis techniques and integrating them with the use of advanced multivariate statistical methods, cognitive mapping offers great potentials for representing meaning in qualitative data. It can be inductively used for constructing coding frames and/or revisiting existing deductive coding frames, to develop follow-up interview guides or closed-ended scale items. Its ability to represent diversity and dimensionality in meaning through analysis of the entire corpus can help to reveal subgroup differences in mental structures (Trochim & Kane, 2005).

Here, I will provide an example for how cognitive mapping can be applied for representing media framings of an issue (i.e., artificial intelligence [AI]) in different cultural settings (China, US, and UK). The original study contains multiple steps mixing different procedures for qualitative and quantitative methods (Süerdem & Akkılıç, 2018). After a brief explanation of these steps, the remainder of this chapter will concentrate on how INDSCAL can be applied for mapping the significant concepts used in the AI-related news and how the media in each country weigh different dimensions in this map.

Frame mapping is a specific application of cognitive mapping to media analysis (Miller & Riechert, 2001). According to Goffman (1974), who first coined the term, a frame is a construct for defining how people organize experience. Application of framing to media analysis concerns how media emphasizes certain features while omitting the others when presenting significant events. Frames can be detected by the consistent presence or absence of certain keywords across the texts within a corpus (Entman, 1993, p. 52). Pattern-detecting techniques such as MDS are applied in frame mapping because of their strength in capturing the relationships between concepts and revealing the structure in the data based on co-occurrences of words or other relational similarities (Miller & Riechert, 2001, p. 63). With the extensive availability of online user-generated and digital media content, word co-occurrence-based similarity measures are now widely being used for automatically extracting meaningful information (i.e., structured data) from unstructured blocks of text. However, despite their convenience and reliability in processing large amounts of texts, these methods are criticized because of their inability in disambiguating the words according to their use in different contexts (Shapiro & Markoff, 1997). These methods are effective in detecting semantic similarities in words or documents but produce some validity issues when drawing inferences about the context of the concepts (Brier, De Giorgi, & Hopp, 2016). Qualitative coding through interpretive reading can help to overcome this issue but using code co-occurrences for pattern detection has its own problems.

First, qualitative coding methods are designed for an in-depth analysis of a small amount of texts and cannot handle big data produced by today's online media. Although this can be managed by a meticulous purposive sampling design, a more important challenge is achieving the reliability and validity of the coding scheme. Besides difficulties in achieving intercoder reliability, in case of non-exhaustive categorical coding or codes not corresponding to the reality of the participants, frequency counts and associative calculations might underrepresent or overrepresent the distribution of meaning in the sample (Jackson & Trochim, 2002, p. 311). Concept mapping approach offers to address these reliability and validity challenges by integrating qualitative coding with multivariate statistical methods. This approach suggests an iterative construction of meaning representation by involving the participants in the analytical process. One of the steps in the method involves MDS for modeling a set of concepts as *structured conceptualization* of an issue to facilitate an interpretation process through a group discussion.

Trochim's method is limited to a relatively small number of shorter texts generated by responses to open-ended questions. However, text corpora collating online media usually involve a huge number of documents with much more than a few paragraphs, making the application of this method very difficult, if not impossible. Brier et al. (2016) suggest using MDS together with topic modeling techniques such as Latent Dirichlet Allocation (LDA) to address this problem. This technique permits the representation of the documents in a large collection of texts as a sum of multiple topics with the topic probabilities providing an explicit representation of the corpus (Steyvers & Griffiths, 2007). The algorithm summarizes the corpus by extracting a set of manageable topics wherein each document exhibits those topics with different proportions. LDA maps words to a vector of probabilities of *latent* topics wherein words occurring in similar contexts are represented by vectors proximate to each other. Word co-occurrences infer the hidden semantic structure from a corpus of documents. Hence, when combined with interpretive reading, detected topics can help the researcher to recognize the contextual information while summarizing a large amount of unstructured textual information to a more manageable form. A word of caution though, the words in these vectors by themselves are seldom likely to be open to sensible interpretation. Annotating the contained contextual information and labeling them in a sensible manner can only be achieved by interpretive in-depth reading of the prototypical documents for each topic as it would be in qualitative analysis. Because LDA scores the documents according to the weight of each topic in its composition, we can select documents with the highest scores for a topic as a representative example for further reading. Hence, resulting topics reflecting the contextual information can be visualized by using MDS or cluster analysis to model the *structured conceptualization* as would be the case for concept mapping.

In our example, to obtain the media framing of AI for different countries, major newspapers in three countries were selected and the news containing the keyword "artificial intelligence" were retrieved to construct a corpus ($n = 2,378$, approximately 800 articles from each country). Using coherence measures as a decision criterion, we decided to settle on 25 topics. The documents with the highest scores for each topic were selected for interpreting and labelling the topic through in-depth reading. After labeling the topics, indirect data containing the topic scores by each document were used to calculate Topic by Topic proximity matrices for each country. The reader should be aware that this procedure is specific to this example. Singular Value Decomposition or other Factor Analysis methods also can be used for topic modelling instead of LDA. In particular, WordStat 8.0.28 (Provalis Research, 2020) can be used to conduct topic modeling to extract the main themes from the corpus using non-negative matrix factorization (NNMF or NMF) and factor analysis. With respect to the former, extraction can be undertaken by computing a word by word similarity matrix and then conducting a NNMF (Lee & Seung, 1999) in order to extract an appropriate number of factors. Alternatively, the QDA Miner module from the same software uses qualitative codes, instead of automatically

Multidimensional Scaling of Qualitative Data

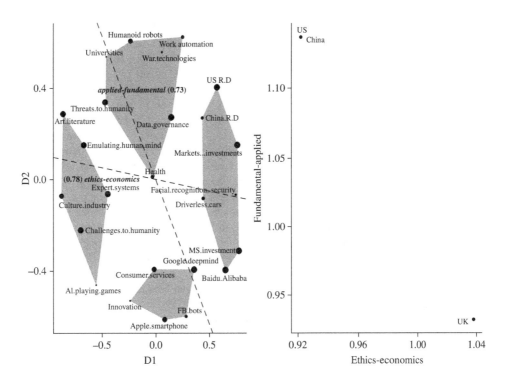

FIGURE 4.5 INDSCAL results for the media framing of AI.

generated topics, for obtaining the proximity matrices as in the case of original concept mapping. Despite these varieties in obtaining the topic proximity data, the MDS method explained in the remainder of the chapter is standard.

For mapping country differences in the media framing of AI, we used dimensional weighting model. Classical MDS calculations, as in the previous empirical example, require a square symmetric matrix. However, averaging and aggregating many sources into a single proximity matrix does no justice to the individual differences between different sources. INDSCAL was originally developed to explain the relationship between individuals' differential cognition of a set of stimuli (Carroll & Chang, 1970). It is a type of *three-way, two-mode MDS application,* which takes multiple proximity matrices having one mode for objects and one mode for subjects. As for other MDS models, it assumes that the structure of stimulus space is common for all participants. On the other hand, the model considers that the weights given to each dimension by each participant can vary. Because the output produces a configuration for individual weights reflecting the salience of each dimension for the participants, INDSCAL is an ideal tool for mapping individual differences in *structured conceptualizations.*

After applying the usual diagnostic checks, as explained in the previous section, the example model led to the selection of a three-dimensional configuration (Stress = 0.165). For ease of interpretation, only first two dimensions will be presented here. Please note that exploring initial configurations and permutation tests are not available for INDSCAL. However, these tests can be performed on a proximity matrix containing the averages of the group matrices before proceeding to INDSCAL.

When we check the patterns in the group space (Figure 4.5), we can observe a clustering of topics such as *Art-literature, Emulating human mind, Expert system,* and *Challenges to humanity* on the left-hand side of the first dimension. Topics like *Driverless cars, Markets-investments, Baidu-Alibaba, MS investment,* and so on, cluster on the right-hand side. The upper part of the map contains topics such as *humanoid robots, work automation,* and *war technologies,* whereas the lower part contains *Facebook bots, Google deep-mind, consumer services, Apple-smartphone,* and *Innovation.* To theoretically validate the interpretation of the dimensions, we identified two essential frames used in the discursive construction of science- and technology-relevant issues. Besides the well-known *fundamental-applied research* dichotomy, we recovered an *ethics-economics* dichotomy from the literature. This dichotomy is a commonly used meta-frame for contrasting *ethical values* to *economical facts* (Putnam, 2003). Before conducting the MDS, we constructed two external scales reflecting these dichotomies and ordered the topics accordingly along them. The correlation between the external *ethics-economics* and first dimension (0.78) and *applied-fundamental* scale and the second dimension (0.76) suggests that our expectations are somehow fulfilled. Clusters in the map were obtained by k-means clustering and were informative in a sense of suggesting which groups of topics have exhibited strong relationships to one another. The reader should be vigilant when interpreting clusters because they can provide only approximate information to guide our intuitive interpretation of MDS configurations. Only the presence of clusters may be commented on and not the internal relationships of points within clusters. Moreover, cluster solutions are not stable across repetitions; hence, it is possible to obtain different clusters.

When we check the configuration weights (Figure 4.5), we can see that the salience of each dimension is different for each country, implying differences in the *structural conceptualization* or media framing of AI. Although U.K. media weighs *ethics-economics* dimension more than do other countries; the United States and China weigh the *fundamental research-applied research* dimension.

6 Strengths and Limitations of MDS

A picture is worth more than a 1,000 words or numbers. MDS belongs to a family of data-reduction techniques, such as cluster analysis (CA) and factor analysis (FA), which are widely used for pattern detection and representation. The major strength of these techniques is their capacity for information visualization by reducing the dimensionality in complex data. Visualization is an important element of understanding because complex thinking processes require making holistic associations using Gestalt-like imagery. This capacity is especially valuable for analyzing qualitative data because the human mind tends first to perceive a patterned complete imagery, then to proceed to the analysis of the details. Visualization can make the complexity accessible by mapping words, numbers, and patterns between them. With the help of this map, the researcher can navigate back and forth between qualitative and quantitative analysis to explore, to develop, to test, and/or to discuss certain hypotheses for further analysis. This is explained more in detail in Section 2 of this chapter.

Despite these potentials, there are two important considerations when using data-reduction techniques for mixed methods research studies. First, we need to consider that qualitative data usually have their own sampling methods that might be incompatible with statistical analysis. Conventional quantitative methods are usually based on inferential statistics that assume a probabilistic selection of cases wherein the error rates are directly related to the sample size. Hence, the non-probabilistic nature of the qualitative data collection limits the kind of statistical procedures that might legitimately be used to generalize from a sample to the population. Hence, we can use MDS (or any other multivariate technique) in MMR only if its exploratory nature is recognized. It can be used to provide insights about previously unknown relationships but not for generalizing and testing theories about these relations. The bird's eye view of the data by itself does not allow to provide evidence for allegedly *objective* patterns. MDS provides us only with a map for navigating the complexity of the qualitative data rather than discovering a presumed hidden structure behind this. Therefore, researchers should refrain from *objectivity* claims when interpreting the MDS results. Second, increasing the integration of data-reduction techniques to QDA software automates the visual representations of qualitative data to make them available for the non-quantitative oriented researcher virtually at the touch of a button. However, naïve use of these outputs without at least examining the effects of diverse parameters applied in their production might be highly misleading. These methods are based on various assumptions about the nature of the data and their non-reflective quantification can have serious effects on the results. When the technical procedures behind these methods are overlooked, producing mindless inferences is highly probable.

Although all dimension-reduction techniques are used for uncovering hidden patterns or relationships in data, they might be competitive or complementary to each other. All these techniques involve use of a matrix of measures of associations; however, they differ in the type of data they process and how the data are presented. A major advantage of MDS over factor analysis is its ability to process both metric and non-metric data (Young, 1981). Nonmetric MDS focuses on discovering the best orthogonal dimensions describing the data, keeping as much information about point-by-point relations as possible. Although FA represents dimensions as vectors, MDS focuses more on the distances between the scaled points. Although for some research purposes, such information might merely be considered as noise, in other cases, MDS is preferable because interpreting distances between points can be more intuitive than the angles between vectors (Borg & Groenen, 2005). Furthermore, unlike FA, MDS does not depend on strict parametric assumptions such as the linearity of the data (Schiffman et al., 1981)—an advantage that yields solutions with fewer dimensions. However, this might be a disadvantage as well because decision criteria for FA modelling depends on more rigorous statistical procedures. Despite these technical details, MDS and FA are usually competitive techniques especially for analyzing indirect data. I would recommend to use them together for triangulating the results to see whether we can produce stable solutions across different methods. On the other hand, MDS and cluster analysis are complementary methods. Classical MDS literature highly recommends the mutual use of MDS and cluster analysis if the data are suitable (Arabie, Carroll, & DeSarbo, 1987; Kruskal, 1977; Shepard, 1980). However, we need to proceed with caution during this process. Because MDS provides a reduced image of the data, the groupings might be illusionary depending on the number of dimensions. Hence, it is advisable to use the original dissimilarity data instead of distances calculated by the MDS configurations when clustering the objects (Péladeau, Dagenais, & Ridde, 2017).

7 Resources for Learning More About MDS

MDS started with the simple model of Young and Householder (1938), then subsequently was elaborated by Torgerson (1958) and Gower (1966). However, because the metric assumptions of these models were found to be too restrictive, these models left their places to nonmetric algorithms during the 1960s (Guttman, 1968; Kruskal, 1964; Shepard, 1962; Young & Torgerson, 1967). MDS models started to settle during the late 1970s, and Kruskal and Wish's (1978) Multidimensional Scaling has a classical status and still is the most popular introductory text, despite being 40 years old. Other classics are Schiffman et al. (1981) and Coxon (1982). The 1970s also marked the development of individual weighting models such as INDSCAL (Carroll & Chang, 1970) and ALSCAL (Young & Lewyckyj, 1979). The reader can refer to Carroll and Arabie (1980) for a taxonomy of such models. As the MDS algorithms matured, Young and Hamer (1987) and Cox and Cox (2001) provide excellent overviews for those who wish to explore the method in more depth. Last but not the least, Borg and Groenen (2005) provide an ultimate source-gathering modern MDS theory and applications. Borg et al. (2018) condense the extensive information in this book to offer a neat and concise reference for learning MDS with software applications. A good strategy would be to start with the latter to develop a basic insight for applying different MDS methods and refer to the former for a detailed and deeper understanding of the specific algorithms. Finally, for those who are familiar with R language, SMACOF package provides a broad variety of MDS implementations (Mair et al., 2015).

REFERENCES

Arabie, P., Carroll, J. D., & DeSarbo, W. S. (1987). *Three-way scaling and clustering.* University Paper series on Quantitative Applications in the Social Sciences. Thousand Oaks, CA: Sage.

Axelrod, R. (1976), *Structure of decision: The cognitive map of political elites.* Princeton, NJ: Princeton University Press.

Bazeley, P., & Jackson, K. (2013). *Qualitative data analysis with NVivo.* Thousand Oaks, CA: Sage.

Bock, H.-H. (2014). Proximity measures. In N. Balakrishnan, T. Colton, B. Everitt, W. Piegorsch, F. Ruggeri, & J. L. Teugels (Eds.), *Wiley StatsRef: Statistics Reference Online.* doi:10.1002/9781118445112.stat06451

Borg, I., & Groenen, P. J. F. (2005). *Springer series in statistics. Modern multidimensional scaling: Theory and applications* (2nd ed.). New York, NY: Springer.

Borg, I., & Groenen, P. J. F., & Mair, P. (2018). *Applied multidimensional scaling and unfolding.* New York, NY: Springer.

Borg, I., & Mair, P. (2017). The choice of initial configurations in multidimensional scaling: Local minima, fit, and interpretability. *Austrian Journal of Statistics, 46*(2), 19–32. doi:10.17713/ajs.v46i2.561

Brier, A., De Giorgi, E., & Hopp, B. (2016). *Strategies in computer assisted text analysis.* NCRM Working Paper. Southampton, England: National Centre for Research Methods.

Burgess, C., Livesay, K., & Lund, K. (1998). Explorations in context space: Words, sentences, discourse. *Discourse Processes, 25*(2-3), 211–257. doi:10.1080/01638539809545027

Carley, K. (1993). Coding choices for textual analysis: A comparison of content analysis and map analysis. *Sociological Methodology, 23*, 75–126. doi:10.2307/271007

Carley, K., & Palmquist, M. E. (1992). Extracting, representing, and analyzing mental models. *Social Forces, 70*, 601–636. doi:10.2307/2579746

Carroll, J. D., & Arabie, P. (1980). Multidimensional scaling. In M. R. Rosenzweig & L. W. Porter (Eds.), *Annual review of psychology* (Vol. 31, pp. 607–649). Palo Alto, CA: Annual Reviews. [Also in (August, 1979) Harvard-Yale preprints in Mathematical Sociology (Vol. 14).]

Carroll, J. D., & Chang, J.-J. (1970). Analysis of individual differences in multidimensional scaling via an N-way generalization of "Eckart-Young" decomposition. *Psychometrika, 35*, 283–319. doi:10.1007/BF02310791

Courcoux, P., Qannari, E. M., Taylor, Y., Buck, D., & Greenhoff, K. (2012). Taxonomic free sorting. *Food Quality and Preference, 23*, 30–35. doi:10.1016/j.foodqual.2011.04.001

Cox, T. F., & Cox, M. A. A. (2001). *Multidimensional scaling* (2nd ed.). Boca Raton, FL: Chapman & Hall/CRC.

Coxon, A. P. M. (1982). *The user's guide to multidimensional scaling: With special reference to the MDS (X) library of computer programs.* Portsmouth, NH: Heinemann.

Eco, U. (1987). Semantics, pragmatics, and text semiotics. In J. Verschueren & M. Bertuccelli Papi (Eds.), *The pragmatic perspective* (pp. 695–714). Amsterdam, The Netherlands: John Benjamin Publishing Group.

Entman, R. M. (1993). Framing: Toward clarification of a fractured paradigm. *Journal of Communication, 43*, 51–58. doi:10.1111/j.1460-2466.1993.tb01304.x

Goffman, E. (1974). *Frame analysis: An essay in the organization of experience.* Cambridge, MA: Harvard University Press.

Gower, J. C. (1966). Some distance properties of latent root and vector methods used in multivariate analysis. *Biometrika, 53*, 325–338. doi:10.1093/biomet/53.3-4.325

Guttman, L. (1968). A general nonmetric technique for finding the smallest coordinate space for a configuration of points. *Psychometrika, 33*, 469–506. doi:10.1007/BF02290164

Ihde, D. (1998). *Expanding hermeneutics: Visualism in science.* Evanston, IL: Northwestern University Press.

Jackson, K. M., & Trochim, W. M. K. (2002). Concept mapping as an alternative approach for the analysis of open-ended survey responses. *Organizational Research Methods, 5*, 307–336. doi:10.1177/109442802237114

Kruskal, J. B. (1964). Nonmetric multidimensional scaling: A numerical method. *Psychometrika, 29*, 115–130. doi:10.1007/BF02289694

Kruskal, J. B. (1977). The relationship between multidimensional scaling and clustering. In J. V. Ryzin (Ed.), *Classification and clustering* (pp. 17–44). New York, NY: Academic Press.

Kruskal, J., & Wish, M. (1978). *Multidimensional scaling.* Newbury Park, CA: Sage.

Lee, D. D., & Seung, H. S. (1999). Learning the parts of objects by non-negative matrix factorization. *Nature, 401*, 788–791. doi:10.1038/44565

Little, T. D. (2013). *The Oxford handbook of quantitative methods.* New York, NY: Oxford University Press.

Mair, P., De Leeuw, J., & Groenen, P. J. F. (2015). *Multidimensional scaling. In R: smacof.* Technical report. Retrieved from https://cran.r-project.org/web/packages/smacof/smacof.pdf

Miles, M. B., & Huberman, A. M. (1994). *Qualitative data analysis: An expanded sourcebook* (2nd ed.). Thousand Oaks, CA: Sage.

Miller, M., & Riechert, B. P. (2001), Frame mapping: A quantitative method for analyzing for investigating issues in the public sphere. In M. West (Ed.), *Theory, method, and practice in computer content analysis* (pp. 61–75). Westport, CT: Greenwood Publishing Group

Onwuegbuzie, A. J., & Teddlie, C. (2003). A framework for analyzing data in mixed methods research. In A. Tashakkori & C. Teddlie (Eds.), *Handbook of mixed methods in social and behavioral research* (pp. 351–383). Thousand Oaks, CA: Sage.

Péladeau, N., Dagenais, C., & Ridde, V. (2017). Concept mapping internal validity: A case of misconceived mapping? *Evaluation and Program Planning, 62*, 56–63. doi:10.1016/j.evalprogplan.2017.02.005.

Provalis Research. (2020). *WordStat (Version 8.0.28) [Computer software].* Montreal, Quebec, Canada.

Putnam, H. (2003). For ethics and economics without the dichotomies. *Review of Political Economy, 15*, 395–412. doi:10.1080/09538250308432

Rosenberg, S., & Park Kim, M. (1975). The method of sorting as a data-gathering procedure in multivariate research. *Multivariate Behavioral Research, 10*, 489–502. doi:10.1207/s15327906mbr1004_7

Schiffman, S. S., Reynolds, M. L., & Young, F. W. (1981). *Introduction to multidimensional scaling: Theory, methods and applications.* New York, NY: Academic Press.

Shapiro, G., & Markoff, J. (1997). A matter of definition. In C. W. Roberts (Ed.), *Text analysis for the social sciences: Methods for drawing statistical inferences from texts and transcripts* (pp. 9–31). Hillsdale, NJ: Lawrence Erlbaum.

Shepard, R. N. (1962). The analysis of proximities: Multidimensional scaling with an unknown distance function. *Part 1. Psychometrika, 27*, 125–140. doi:10.1007/BF02289630

Shepard, R. N. (1980). Multidimensional scaling, tree-fitting, and clustering. *Science, 210*, 390–398. doi:10.1126/science.210.4468.390

Sivesind, K. H. (1999). Structured, qualitative comparison. *Quality & Quantity, 33*, 361–380. doi:10.1023/A:1004691318311

Spence, I., & Domoney, D. (1974). Single subject incomplete designs for nonmetric multidimensional scaling. *Psychometrika, 39*, 469–490. doi:10.1007/BF02291669

Steyvers, M., & Griffiths, T. (2007). Latent semantic analysis: A road to meaning. In T. Landauer, S. D. McNamara, & W. Kintsch (Eds.), *Probabilistic topic models* (pp. 427–448). Hillsdale, NJ: Laurence Erlbaum.

Steyvers, M. (2006). Multidimensional scaling. In L. Nadel (Ed.), *Encyclopedia of cognitive science* (pp. 1–5). London, England: MacMillan.

Süerdem, A., & Akkılıç, S. (2018, September). *Media representations of artificial intelligence in the UK, China and the United States.* Paper presented at Science & You conference, National Convention Center, Beijing, China.

Torgerson, W. S. (1958). *Theory and methods of scaling.* Oxford, England: Wiley.

Trochim, W., & Kane, M. (2005). Concept mapping: An introduction to structured conceptualisation in health care. *International Journal for Quality in Health Care, 17*, 187–191. doi:10.1093/intqhc/mzi038

Tsogo, L., Masson M. H., & Bardot, A. (2000). Multidimensional scaling methods for many-object sets: A review. *Multivariate Behavioral Research, 35*, 307–319. doi:10.1207/S15327906MBR3503_02

Tversky, A. (1977). Features of similarity. *Psychological Review, 84*, 327–352. doi:10.1037/0033-295X.84.4.327

Tversky, A., & Hutchinson, J. W. (1986). Nearest neighbor analysis of psychological spaces. *Psychological Review, 93*(1), 3–22. doi:10.1037/0033-295X.93.1.3

Young. F. W. (1981). *Psychometrika, 46*, 357–388. doi:10.1007/BF02293796

Young, F. W. (2013). *MDS: History, theory, and applications* (2nd ed.). New York, NY: Springer Science+Business Media.

Young, F. W., & Hamer, R. (1987). *Multidimensional scaling: History, theory, and applications.* Hillsdale, NJ: Lawrence Erlbaum.

Young, F. W., & Lewyckyj, R. (1979). *ALSCAL-4 user's guide* (2nd ed.), Chapel Hill, NC: Data Analysis and Theory Associates.

Young, F. W., & Torgerson, W. S. (1967). TORSCA, a FORTRAN IV program for Shepard-Kruskal multidimensional scaling analysis. *Behavioral Science, 12*, 498.

Young, G., & Householder, A. S. (1938). Discussion of a set of points in terms of their mutual distances. *Psychometrika, 3*, 19–22. doi:10.1007/BF02287916

5

Cluster Analysis for Mixed Methods Research

Normand Péladeau

1 Definition of Cluster Analysis

> In principle we could organize the data by grouping like with like [...] We can put all the bits of data which seem similar or related into separate piles, and then compare the bits within each pile. We may even want to divide up the items into a pile into separate 'sub-piles' if the data merits further differentiation. (Dey, 2003)

The act of comparing, grouping, and classifying is a fundamental aspect of any scientific activity. Biologists classify animals and plants into species, astronomers categorized planets and other celestial objects into classes, market researchers segment their customers into homogenous groups of persons with similar characteristics. Social workers may group multiple personal stories into a more limited set of social issues. This is also true for qualitative researchers. The above excerpt is from a book by Dey (2003) on the use of computers in qualitative analysis. The author describes how a qualitative codebook may come into life and evolve during the analysis process. It involves the act of comparing elements or objects on their attributes, grouping those that share some similarities, while separating those that differ to create homogeneous groupings. Cluster analysis is a set of statistical techniques that fundamentally attempts to achieve a similar goal and works in a very similar way but can do so on large number of objects and takes into consideration numerous attributes. For this reason, one should not be surprised to find out that it has been applied in many fields of research to provide empirical support for some ways to organize the object of study.

Cluster analysis is not a statistical method per se but a vast collection of algorithms for grouping objects based on their similarity. And contrary to many statistical methods, its main objective is not to perform any statistical testing of existing hypothesis. It belongs instead to the class of exploratory data analysis tools, and thus supports an inductive approach to the data. It can be used to identify patterns in the data that might be difficult for a human to detect, or to partition objects, often participants, into distinct groups. In this chapter, we will focus on the most commonly used clustering techniques, explain how they work, and discuss their limitations and various issues related to their use.

2 When Use of Clustering Is Appropriate for Mixed Methods Research

Many features of clustering make it a likely candidate for qualitative researchers who would like to introduce quantitative analysis techniques in their research practice. The Dey's (1993) quotation clearly shows the resemblance of clustering with the coding process. Miles and Huberman's (1994) concept of pattern coding also illustrated this practice of reducing a large number of qualitative observations into a smaller number of units. In fact, this notion of *clustering* based on similarity permeates the description of qualitative analysis methods such as inductive inquiry, thematic analysis and constant comparison methods (see Percy, Kostere, & Kostere, 2015). It is thus easy to understand why Miles and Huberman (1994) proposed statistical clustering as a means either to identify recurring patterns or to support the plausibility of patterns identified by the qualitative researcher. For them, clustering techniques allow the researcher to move to a higher level of abstraction.

We can also recognize such a process when a qualitative researcher attempts to differentiate individuals, locations, or settings according to some of their characteristics for the purpose of comparison and contrast. For example, Henry, Dymnicki, Mohatt, Allen, and Kelly (2015) used hierarchical clustering on the qualitative coding of 77 interviews of participants to training on substance abuse prevention. They were able to identify three natural groupings of community leaders who differed in their motivations for participation, an information that was later used for improving the training program.

One reason for adopting statistical clustering is that the manual comparisons, whether they are applied to participants or to qualitative codings, become more difficult as the number of attributes used for comparison or the number of elements to be partitioned increases. The inductive nature of clustering when used in an exploratory way, the common practice of subjective evaluation of topic quality, the simplicity and straightforwardness of some clustering algorithms—all those characteristics contribute to the social acceptability of this method for qualitative researchers. Finally, but not least, the fact that some forms of clustering are able to produce useful results on data sets as small as 20 (Henry et al., 2015) counters the argument that statistical techniques can only be applied on large data sets.

But we believe the usefulness of clustering for mixed methods research can go beyond the quantification of qualitative data. For example, in a quant qual sequential design, where a qualitative study is performed to achieve better understanding of the results of survey data, clustering on the responses to the quantitative survey may help identify homogeneous groups of respondents. Group membership could then be used to perform a stratified random sampling of participants for in-depth qualitative interviews, ensuring the representativeness of the small sample. When dealing with a quantity of unstructured text data that is too voluminous for qualitative coding, clustering of documents using text mining technique might also support the sampling of documents whether it is to achieve representativeness, exemplarity, or even singularity of opinions.

3 Technical Outline of Cluster Analysis for Mixed Methods Research

One attractive aspect of common clustering techniques is that their basic principles and operations are quite simple to understand and do not rely on abstract mathematical transformation or complex matrix operations. This allows us to describe in simple terms the entire process of clustering in the following way: For every object we want to organize through clustering, (a) we identify a list of features (or attributes) on which each object will be compared, (b) then we compute a similarity score for each possible pair of objects, and (c) we then use a specific strategy to group the most similar ones together to create homogeneous groups.

Quantitative researchers using cluster analysis will often refer to attributes as "variables" and objects as "cases," but clustering can be used to partition either cases or variables. In the former situation, we talk about a Q-mode analysis, while clustering variables, like a typical factor analysis, is an R-mode analysis. An example of a Q-mode clustering would be to collect qualitative and quantitative data on numerous participants, compare them on several of those variables, and cluster them into homogenous groups of participants based on how similar they are on those. Alternatively, an R-mode clustering would compare the distribution of variables (or attributes) across participants to create groupings of attributes.

The Measure of Similarity

As we can see from the aforementioned process description, an important prerequisite for performing a cluster analysis is the measurement of how similar objects are to each other. Several clustering techniques require the computation of a similarity matrix, comparing each object with all the other ones. For example, if we want to partition 25 participants into several homogeneous groups, we might need to create a matrix of 25 rows by 25 columns.

One of the simplest metrics one can imagine is the distance in the physical world. If we obtain the number of kilometers between a set of cities or calculate the distance between all data points on a two-dimensional Euclidean space, we could cluster those cities or data points based on their proximity to each other. It is important to note here that the distances are, in fact, dissimilarity measures, the higher the distance, the less similar they are. The clustering would thus tend to favor the grouping of items close to each other while clustering similarity scores would group together items with high scores. Clustering has often been presented graphically as a method to discover natural groupings of data points on a scatter plot, allowing an intuitive illustration of the clustering process. However, such distance measures are seldom encountered in social sciences. One might be tempted to apply multidimensional scaling, a technique that transforms similarity measures into Euclidian distances, and then cluster those to provide a visual representation of the obtained clusters. However, such an approach can be very problematic and often results in cluster solutions that are suboptimal compared to the clustering on the original similarity measures (see Péladeau, Dagenais, & Ridde, 2017).

A similarity measure often used for clustering and for which many researchers are familiar with is the Pearson product-moment correlation. For example, to measure similarity between two individuals on which we have obtained scores on multiple variables (e.g., scores or rating scales of a psychometric instruction, or the coding frequencies of their interviews), we could simply compute a correlation on their profiles on all those variables: the more similar their profiles are, the higher the correlation. Because variables might differ greatly on their scaling and metric types, it is recommended to standardize each variable prior to computing such a correlation. It would not make sense to merge scores on a Likert-format scale with ages measured in number of years, and annual income measured in thousands of dollars.

One property that has often been perceived as a major inconvenience of the correlation coefficient is that it is sensitive only to the shape of variations across variables and ignores differences in elevation. In other words, two individuals may be considered very similar if the level variation across variables shows a similar pattern, even if one of those individuals score systematically higher on all variables. However, there are situations where such a difference in levels may be irrelevant—for example, when comparing the consumption profiles of customers irrespective of the volume of purchases they make or when comparing the relative importance of topics mentioned in interviews irrespective of their lengths. If not only the profile but the level of each variable should be considered when assessing similarity, then metrics such as the intraclass correlation or the congruency coefficient (Lorr, 1983) should be used instead. An alternative approach would be to apply both metrics and compare the obtained cluster solutions, allowing the researcher to assess the relative contribution of each scale dimension. If the two cluster solutions are close enough, one may also conclude that there is robustness of the clustering at identifying the underlying data structure.

Another common situation consists of measuring similarity on a set of binary variables, such as when one compares cases on some properties or attributes that are either present or not, when responses consists of a series of true or false or are dichotomous such as male versus female. The aggregation of such binary results for two cases often takes the form of a 2 x 2 table representing the co-occurrence of each attribute like Table 1, where the a cell represents the total number of time specific attributes present in both cases, and d represents where attributes are absent in both cases, and the remaining two cells, *b* and *c*, consist of situations where it appears for one case but not the other.

	1	0
1	a	b
0	c	d

Another way to obtain such a co-occurrence matrix is through any type of Q-sort exercises such as in Trochim's group concept mapping technique (Kane & Trochim, 2007) in which participants are being asked to group statements into piles based on their perceived similarity. If two statements are found in a pile, it increases the value of *a*, while a pile containing one statement but not the other will increase the frequency of cell *b* or *c*. Finally, if none of the two statements appear in a specific pile, the frequency of *d* is incremented. The co-occurrence analysis of words in text mining techniques also proceeds under the same principle, assessing the strength of the relationship between two words by how often they both appear in a sample text unit, such as a sentence or a paragraph.

There are numerous association measures that may be computed on such a matrix and space limitation prevents us from presenting an exhaustive list. However, one important consideration to keep in mind is whether the common absence of an attribute should be taken into account and contributes to the assessment of similarity. We can argue that in many situations, it is preferable not to consider those common absences because they might exaggerate the level of similarity between objects. It is especially the case when the potential number of attributes is large, and their probability of occurrence is low. For example, if a hundred attributes is used to characterize plant species and a plant typically presents 10 of those, we can already presume that the total number of common absences of attributes in any comparison of two plants will be between 80 and 90 out of a hundred. In such situations, the simple fact that they share eight or nine of those attributes out of a possibility of 10 is good enough to establish a high level of similarity. Also, the fact that two words out of a vocabulary of tens of thousands of words do not appear in the same paragraph or even in the same document does not inform us in any way about their relatedness. In other situations, where most of those attributes have a high probability of occurrences, the common absence might be a distinguishing feature that can contribute to the establishment of a similarity. A good example would be the common absence of a gene or of a functioning gene in the DNA of patients suffering from the same disease. In such situations, it is the common presence that should probably be ignored.

Measures like the Jaccard coefficient, or the Dice coefficient, are frequently used and would be appropriate when common absence should be ignored. The formula for the Jaccard coefficient is:

$$\text{Jaccard} = a/(a+b+c)$$

It can be interpreted easily as the proportion of time that when either one of the two attributes appear, both of them will be present. In contrast, the Dice coefficient, also known as the Sorensen coefficient, can be computed using this formula:

$$\text{Dice} = 2a/(2a+b+c)$$

It gives more weight to matches than non-matches. It also has an intuitive interpretation as the proportion of time the two attributes appear together.

When the situation justifies the consideration of both common presences and common absences, then the simple matching coefficient should be used. Its formula is:

$$\text{Matching coefficient} = (a+d)/(a+b+c+d)$$

There are situations where the attributes to be used for computing similarity are being measured using various metrics: some may be binary variables, others may be multinomial variables or measured on a continuous scale.

Multinomial values can easily be transformed into multiple binary variables. For continuous variables, one solution would be to dichotomize them, typically by splitting them at the mean or the median value, and use a measure based on binary data. However, such a transformation, which is common in clinical research, always implies a loss in precision, often leading to inappropriate misclassification and is thus not recommended (Dawson & Weiss, 2012). A better solution would be to compute two similarity measures, one for binary variables and the other one for continuous variables and average them with proper weighting. A third solution would be to use a more complex similarity formula designed for this purpose such as Gower's general similarity measure. Once a similarity measure has been selected, the next step consists of choosing the appropriate method to group items into clusters using the chosen index. We will focus here on two broad classes of methods, hierarchical clustering and iterative partitioning.

Hierarchical Clustering Methods

The hierarchical method is one of the most common forms of clustering. It consists of starting with all objects treated as clusters containing only one element, and successively grouping the two items or the two *clusters* that are the most similar, repeating the process up until we obtain only one cluster containing every object.

This agglomeration process can be represented in a form of a tree graph, called a dendrogram, in which lines are successively drawn to connect items as they are merged (see Figure 5.1). At the beginning, represented here on the left side of the tree, all objects are independent. At the first step, we use the highest similarity score between two elements, and we connect them to create a first cluster. We then find the second-highest similarity score and connect those. As the threshold is relaxed, more and more items get connected, represented in the dendrograms by the drawing of additional connecting links. During this agglomeration process, clusters become bigger and bigger as we add increasingly dissimilar items to them, up until all elements become part of a single cluster. In the dendrogram

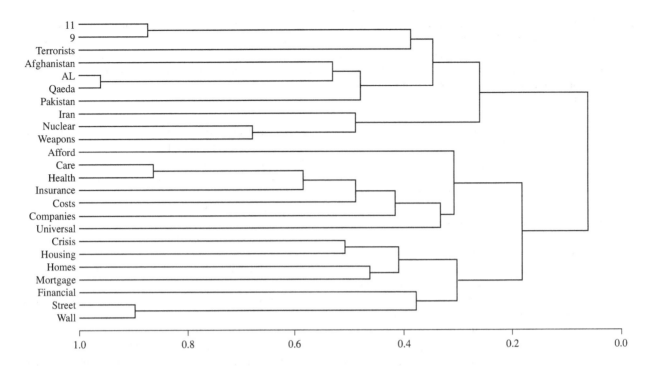

FIGURE 5.1 Dendrogram showing average linkage between words in political speeches.

presented in Figure 5.1, the lengths of leaves are proportional to the similarity measure used to group items, as it appears at the bottom. An alternative representation would be to illustrates the steps of the agglomeration process such that all steps are drawn at an equal interval. The assumption here is that if there is a structure in the data, then it should be reflected as distinct branches in the dendrograms.

The form of the tree and the clustering solution that one obtains depends not only on the similarity measure used but also on the rule that is used to decide how items are being merged.

The simplest grouping method, called *Single Linkage* (also known as nearest neighbor), consists of merging the clusters based on the two elements that are the most similar (or closer) irrespective of other elements in their respective clusters. Figure 5.2a illustrates the distance used to connect two clusters with this grouping method. Because only the higher similarity measure is being used for linking two clusters, this method has a tendency of creating elongated clusters, attaching items in close proximity of any other items already in the cluster. Although good at detecting elongated groupings, it might, however, inadvertently group elements from two separate clusters if isolated elements are located between those two homogeneous groups. When such a chaining effect occurs, it might hinder the identification of the existing data structure. On a dendrogram, chaining is often reflected by a succession of items being added to the same cluster. On the opposite, the

Complete Linkage (also known as furthest neighbor) will group two clusters to the condition that all items are similar enough. To achieve this, it uses for comparisons the smallest similarity measure or the longest distance that exists between elements in both clusters (Figure 5.2b). This method tends to create compact, spherical clusters of similar items. The *Average Linkage* lies somewhere between the two by using as a criterion to merge clusters the average distance between all elements of both clusters (Figure 5.2c). It is usually performed by computing the arithmetic mean of all similarity measures between elements in both clusters. Variation of this approach may consist of computing the distance between the centroids of those two clusters or the median distance.

The *Ward's* method is somewhat different from the previous methods, attempting to minimize the variance within a cluster rather than focusing on the distances between objects. During the agglomeration process, all successive grouping increases the size of clusters and thus, the total amount of variances within clusters. The Ward method will select the grouping that will minimize this increase.

These four methods will often give very different results when applied on the same data, yet none of these methods is intrinsically better than the others because it ultimately depends on the underlying structure of the data being analyzed. Single linkage might be better at detecting elongated clusters reflecting the presence of some continuum, whereas complete linkage or Ward's tends to create more spherical clusters.

One of the main benefits of hierarchical clustering, beside its simplicity, is the fact that it does not require one to specify in advance how many clusters to extract, presenting in a single display a sequence of partitions. An associated benefit lies in the hierarchical nature of the dendrogram that allows one to build a multilevel typology. For example, when clustering a word co-occurrence matrix, clustering can reveal at an

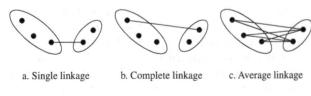

FIGURE 5.2 Illustration of three agglomeration rules.

early stage, some phrases and idioms, then later help uncover some topics, but at a later stage group those topics into broader groupings representing domains or broad themes.

One technical issue with this technique is that once an item becomes part of a cluster, it will remain in it, even if it ends up later being associated with unrelated items. The hierarchical nature prevents any correction and reassignments when the nature of the cluster shift from its original location. Such an issue can be especially present when using single linkage as the agglomeration method.

Hierarchical clustering also has some limitations related to the computational resources required when the number of items to cluster is high. For example, clustering 300 objects involves the computation of 44,700 similarity measures. Increasing this number to 1,000 necessitates the computation of almost one half a million scores. The exponential increase in computing time and in the size of the matrix to hold all these measures impose an upper limit in the number of elements that can be analyzed. The next method does not have this limitation in the number of elements to cluster.

Iterative Partitioning

A common method to group items into homogeneous groups is by partitioning them into a predefined number of clusters, either randomly or using another initialization method, and iteratively reassign items to other clusters until a homogeneous grouping is found. This method is usually undertaken by computing the centroid of each initial cluster, comparing the distance of every element to those centroids, and relocating any elements that are closer to another centroid to its associated cluster. Once all items have been assessed and, if needed, reassigned, centroids are recomputed. The steps are repeated until no further correction is possible. The most widely used iterative partitioning technique in social sciences is k-means (MacQueen, 1967). Because this technique does not require computation of the distance between all data points but only the distance of elements to a user-defined number of centroids, it can be applied to analyze much bigger data sets.

The most optimal solution would normally be obtained by testing all possible partitions and then choosing the best one. However, because the number of possible partitions, even for a limited number of elements, can be astronomical (millions and billions of possible partitions), the only realistic alternative is to attempt to approximate a solution, and iteratively adjust the partitions as described earlier using an iterative process. One critical factor that influences how close we end up to this optimal solution is the initial assignment of elements. Although it has been shown that even a purely random initial assignment might quickly converge to reasonably good partition solutions, such an approach might also result in the convergence to a local optimum that contradicts the cluster structure of the data set. Various initialization methods and corrections have been proposed to prevent such sub-optimal solutions. One interesting and easy-to-understand proposal presented by Andendelfer and Blashfield (1984) consists of randomly selecting a small number of elements to be grouped and apply a hierarchical clustering to obtain a number of groupings equivalent to the desired number of partitions, and then using the obtained centroid of those clusters as the initial centroid values. More sophisticated methods have been proposed (see Arthur & Vassilvitskii, 2007).

Choosing the Number of Clusters

An important factor that can affect the validity of the results with the partitional method, such as k-means, is the initial decision about how many clusters to extract. Although one can perform several partitionings using different values of k, it might be difficult to decide which partitioning solution is the best at representing the real structure of the data set under study. A similar issue might be raised for hierarchical clustering regarding the decision of when the agglomeration process should be stopped.

Unfortunately, the question of the number of clusters to choose is still an unsettled issue. Although there have been numerous proposals for objective criteria and data experiments to compare these (see, for e.g., Dimitriadou, Dolnicar, & Weingessel, 2002; Milligan & Cooper, 1985), no consensus yet exists as to what should be the best criteria. There does not seem to be any widespread practice among researchers using cluster analysis techniques regarding a method to select the number of clusters.

One must keep in mind that cluster analysis may be used to achieve quite different goals and that the importance of choosing a fixed number of clusters really depends on our objectives. For example, if one uses hierarchical clustering as an exploratory data analysis technique to uncover interesting patterns that will be further investigated or later submitted to hypothesis testing, then selecting the optimal number of clusters might not be such an important issue. An example of this would be an exploratory text mining analysis in which words in documents or interview transcripts are clustered to identify potential topics, as an exploratory step before a qualitative content analysis. In such situations, the criterion for choosing the appropriate number of clusters to extract or to assess the quality of various clustering solutions is often based on purely subjective criteria. Many biologists and archeologists have applied qualitative judgments by selecting solutions based on their own expert opinions, often influenced by the perceived coherence of the identified patterns or by reference to existing typologies or known categorizations. Such a subjective criterion could very well be appropriate for exploratory uses of clustering. Yet, it would be appropriate in such cases to make the various criteria in such a decision more explicit. On the other hand, if one is attempting to identify groups of participants that correspond to a valid or useful typology present in a population, or a grouping that has some predictive value, then both the choice in the number of clusters and the assessment of cluster quality becomes important.

Numerous graphical and statistical procedures have been suggested to support the decision regarding the optimal number of clusters to extract. In many cases, it involved the computation of a numerical index representing a desired cluster property for successive numbers of partitions. One then graphs the number of clusters against those numerical values to create a curved line similar to a scree plot, used in factor analysis. The task consists of identifying an elbow that indicates a sudden increase or decrease in the desired property and choose the number of clusters corresponding to the last value occurring just before a deterioration of the clustering solution as measured by the chosen index. However, this method is often prone to subjectivity when there is no sharp elbow or when two or more of them can be found. Less subjective procedures involve indices with a critical value that, when crossed, signal the correct number of clusters. Milligan and Cooper (1985) submitted 30 of these indices to simulated experiments and although they found that some perform better than others, they recognized that their results might not necessarily be consistent across alternative data structures.

One also has to keep in mind that some indices often favor specific properties of the clusters, such as their compactness (reducing the within-cluster variance), their separation (increasing the between-cluster variance), or their connectedness (assessing the closeness of an item to the nearest neighbor) and are thus not totally independent of the clustering method used. For example, an index measuring the level of connectedness might be more appropriate for a single linkage clustering, while methods combining compactness and separation might favor a complete linkage or a Ward's method.

Although a description of the various indices proposed in the literature would be lengthy and unnecessarily tedious, the silhouette method proposed by Rousseeuw (1987) possesses specific characteristics that make it suitable for an introduction to cluster analysis. The underlying computation remains relatively easy to understand and it presents itself in a graphic display that provides useful information about the relative quality of the clusters and the relationship of each element to their clusters. The silhouette plot of a cluster solution is constructed by computing for each element i a coefficient S_i using the follow formula:

$$S_i = (b_i - a_i)/max(a_i, b_i)$$

where a_i corresponds to the average distance between an element i and all other elements in its cluster, and b_i is the average distance between this element and the next closest cluster (on average). This closest cluster corresponds to the second-best choice, or the cluster to which this element would have been part of if the other elements in the cluster in which it currently belongs did not exist. The difference in distance is then computed and then divided by the largest of those two distances. Please note that if the index is a similarity score, the a_i and b_i in the numerator should be inverted. By computing this ratio, we obtain a value between −1 and +1. Positive values indicate that the item has been assigned to the appropriate cluster; the higher the value, the more likely this item is appropriately located. On the other hand, a negative value indicates that this element is likely *misclassified*, being, on average, closer to items in another cluster. Values close to zero occur for items that could very well belong to either cluster. A graphic representation of the relationship between every item and their respective cluster may then be plotted by sorting items in each cluster in descending order of this ratio and by plotting different clusters below each other. Figure 5.3 presents a silhouette for the clustering of 100 items into six clusters.

The silhouette coefficient for a cluster can be obtained by computing the average of all silhouette coefficients for every

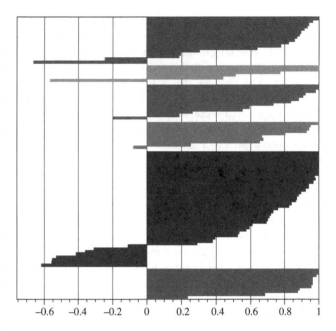

FIGURE 5.3 Silhouette for a six-cluster solution.

element in the cluster, allowing one to assess the quality of each cluster. Finally, by computing the average of silhouette coefficients of all clustered elements, we obtain a measure of the quality of the clustering solution which may then be used to select the optimal number of clusters using the elbow method presented earlier. Kaufman and Rousseeuw (1990) suggest that a silhouette with an average width of 0.5 or above is good, whereas an average width below 0.2 may indicate a lack of an underlying cluster structure.

4 Empirical Demonstration of Cluster Analysis in Mixed Methods Research

In this section, we will present two empirical examples of clustering, illustrating both an R-Type clustering wherein one attempts to group respondents based on the similarity of their profiles, and a Q-Type clustering wherein variables are clustered.

Example 1. Using Cluster Analysis for Participant Sampling

In this first example of a two-phase mixed methods study, the coding of open-ended responses of 239 survey participants will be used to select 20 participants for an in-depth interview. Although various sampling methods could have been used, such as simple random sampling or stratified random sampling on socio-demographics, the researcher attempted instead to create a sample that would represent as much as possible, various points of view. To achieve this, the qualitative coding for all five open-ended responses are merged and then transformed into numerical variables representing the frequency of each code—representing what is referred to as *quantitizing* (Miles & Huberman, 1994). A total of 62 numerical values

Cluster Analysis for Mixed Methods Research

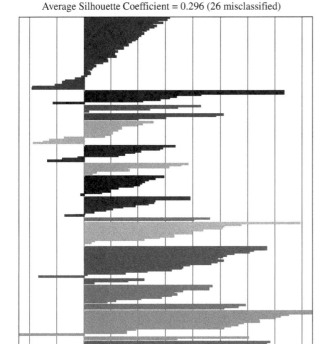

FIGURE 5.4 Silhouette analysis of 239 participants clustered in 20 groups.

for each participant is then obtained, allowing the researcher to compute a correlation matrix measuring the similarity between the coding profiles of all 239 participants. A hierarchical clustering technique is then performed on the correlation matrix in order to extract 20 clusters, corresponding to the desired number of participants for a follow-up interview. To assess the quality of the clustering, a silhouette analysis is performed (see Figure 5.4). The obtained coefficient of 0.296, although acceptable, could have been higher and the silhouette plot clearly shows that some participants may have been positioned in another grouping of participants, as can be seen with bars extending on the left side. Choosing a higher number of participants could have resulted in a lower number of misclassified participants and a higher silhouette index. However, the objective of the present study being to obtain 20 participants with heterogeneous points of view justify settling with the current solution.

From here, we could select randomly one participant per cluster, achieving a form of stratified random sampling. However, one characteristic of silhouette profiles is that items are sorted and presented in descending order of similarity with other members of the cluster. It means that by selecting the first participant in each cluster, the one represented with the longest bar at the top of the cluster, we would select the individual the most characteristic of such a cluster and the most distinct from the other group of individuals. We could say that such a selection would yield respondents archetypal of the different positions identified by the clustering process, maximizing the variability in the responses.

Example 2. Using Cluster Analysis for Identifying Topics

The previous example illustrates how clusters could be applied to segment individuals into homogeneous groups (R-mode). The next example corresponds to a Q-mode cluster analysis wherein it is the variables that are being grouped together.

To illustrate such a technique, we will use data obtained from a concept mapping study (Dagenais & Hackett, 2008). One of the objectives of concept mapping is to develop a conceptual framework to guide planning and evaluation of services (Trochim, 1989). To achieve this, eight participants in a brainstorming session were asked to generate 81 statements about research in alphabetization. Then, in order to obtain a measure of semantic similarity between statements, the same participants were asked to sort those statements in as many piles as needed based on their perceived similarity. A similarity measure was then obtained by first counting how many times two statements appear in the same pile, and then transforming the obtained co-occurrence into a Jaccard coefficient. Doing this on all possible pairs results in an 81 x 81 matrix. Although traditional concept mapping typically extracts topic by applying multidimensional scaling (MDS) and then hierarchical clustering on the Euclidian distance of the MDS plot, we have chosen instead a hierarchical clustering directly on the similarity matrix using a weighted average linkage (Péladeau et al., 2017).

Figure 5.5 displays the obtained dendrogram where length of leaves is inversely proportional to the Jaccard coefficient. If we start looking at connections from the left, we can see at the bottom, two pairs of statements with very short leaves, indicating that those items have been put in the same piles by all participants, yielding a Jaccard coefficient of 1.0. As we move to the right, we reduce the value of the similarity index needed to group items, resulting in more and more statements being clustered together. The dotted vertical line on the right allows us to delineate a solution with 15 clusters obtained when reducing the cutoff Jaccard coefficient to approximately 0.18. Reducing this criterion even further would then group Clusters #9 and #10 then, #1 and #2, #7, and #8, and so on.

To select an optimal number of clusters, we performed silhouette analyses for cluster solutions going from four clusters to 25 clusters. We then plotted, the silhouette index (Figure 5.6) as well as the number of misclassified items (Figure 5.7) for all those cluster solutions. We can see in Figure 5.6 that all cluster solutions have a silhouette index above 0.5, indicating appropriate grouping of statements. We can also notice that the index progressively decreases, reaching its lowest value for a 13-cluster solution then goes up again. However, Figure 5.7 shows that all solutions with 14 or fewer clusters contain potentially more misclassified items, whereas solutions with 15 or more have either no or only one misclassified item.

These data could very well justify choosing a cluster solution between 15 and 20; however, the objective of achieving a more parsimonious concept extraction justifies choosing a 15-cluster solution.

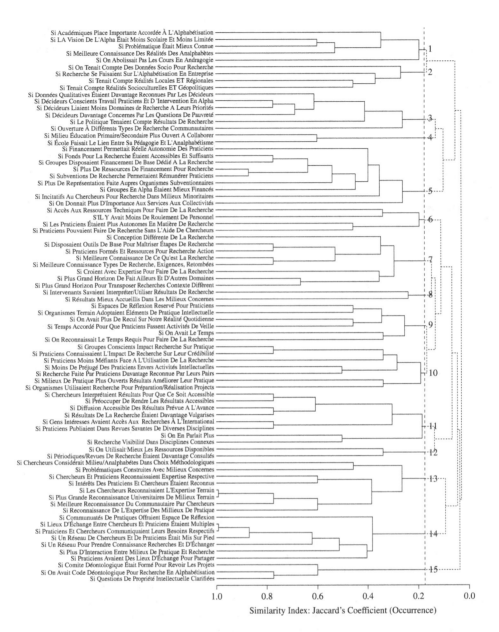

FIGURE 5.5 Dendrogram of 81 statements on research in alphabetization.

5 Suggested Applications of Cluster Analysis

Most examples of clustering analysis can be found not only in purely quantitative studies in natural sciences, but also in computer sciences and marketing. Examples of cluster analysis in qualitative or mixed methods research are scarce. The present section will review some of those applications but will also stress how clustering techniques could be used differently to support additional research activities.

We found some examples of studies with a high qualitative dominance, wherein clustering has been used to assist the interpretation of the data. In many cases, no quantitative data were ever collected, and cluster analysis was simply an intermediary step supporting the qualitative analysis of data through a provisional quantification. It thus consisted of mixed methods research solely through the process of quantifying the qual. Those studies usually fall into the two main types of applications corresponding to a Q-mode data reduction method, wherein individuals are clustered into homogeneous groups, and an R-mode type, wherein codes are clustered into smaller overarching categories. An example of a Q-mode analysis is provided by Henry et al. (2015), wherein 77 participants to a community leadership training program were interviewed. All interview transcripts were then coded, and the coding profiles of all participants were submitted to a k-means partitioning in order to extract three broad categories of community leaders. Täuscher and Laudien (2018) hand-coded documents from 100 marketplaces and performed a hierarchical cluster analysis on the qualitative research to end up with six distinctive types of marketplace business models. Macia (2015) combined socio-demographic data and coding results of 195 grievance cases extracted from 21 in-depth interviews. The score

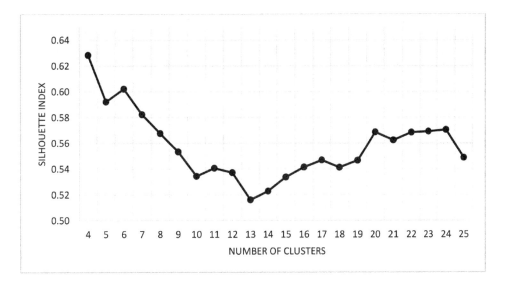

FIGURE 5.6 Silhouette index by number of clusters.

on 60 variables were then submitted to hierarchical clustering technique to group the grievance cases into seven broad categories. The author then revisited the qualitative data for each of those clusters separately in order to identify relevant elements characterizing each of them.

Clustering techniques have also been applied to group codes based on their co-occurrences within cases, typical of R-mode analysis. For example, Guest and McLellan (2003) coded interview transcripts of 35 male participants to a HIV vaccine clinical trial. The thematic analysis resulted in the extraction of 46 content-derived codes about their experience in a risk-reduction counseling service. A matrix of code co-occurrences was then submitted to a complete linkage hierarchical analysis from which three clusters of related codes were chosen. The authors then used their in-depth familiarity with the data to build a structured narrative around each grouping of codes. For these authors, "cluster analysis can help frame thematic analysis and interpretation" (p. 98), what they consider one of the most difficult parts of the interpretative process.

Clustering of coded segments can also be used to explore the possible connection between distinct dimensions. In an analysis of references to democratic system principles in Centers for Disease Control and Prevention (CDC) ethics subcommittee documents, Myers (2016) used clustering to test specific hypotheses about the co-occurrence of those principles with two other dimensions (constitutional perspective and rights vs. responsibility codes). The analysis led to the identification of key ethical issues that were then identified in the media coverage of the U.S. response to the Ebola outbreak of 2015. Cmeciu (2017) also used clustering techniques to analyze debates on genetically modified organisms (GMO) and assessed how different frame perspectives (e.g., political, health, ethics, religion) were associated with specific emotion (e.g., trust, joy, anxiety, sadness).

As exemplified earlier, clustering has also been used to assist the sampling of participants in studies adopting a sequential-explanatory design, which, as defined by Creswell, Plano Clark, Gutmann, and Hanson (2003), is "characterized by the collection and analysis of quantitative data followed

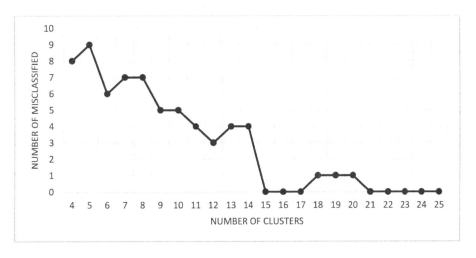

FIGURE 5.7 Number of misclassified items by number of clusters.

by the collection and analysis of qualitative data" (p. 223) for the purpose of using "qualitative results to assist in explaining and interpreting the findings of a primarily quantitative study" (p. 227). A good example of this is provided by Spillane and Hunt's (2010) study in which they obtained quantitative measures of work activities of 38 school principals in one mid-size urban school district in the south-eastern United States. A total of 20 standardized quantitative measures were used to establish a profile of leadership practices for each principal. An initial hierarchical clustering using Ward's method, followed by a k-means iterative partitioning allowed them to identify three homogeneous subgroups of principals displaying distinct leadership practices. They then proceeded to interviews of three principals, each representing one of the three patterns of practices. Another example is provided by Thøgersen-Ntoumani and Fox (2005), wherein a web survey on the physical ability and mental well-being of 312 corporate employees was followed by a hierarchical cluster analysis creating four distinct groups, and then by semi-structured interviews of 10 participants, representing at least two cases of each of these four groups.

In all these examples, clustering was performed on either collected quantitative measures or on a quantification of the manual coding of qualitative data. The clustering of text by itself represents another application of clustering that may be successfully combined with qualitative or quantitative research methods. The automatic analysis of word co-occurrence within a document, a paragraph, or a sentence for the extraction of topics or themes has a long tradition that goes back to the early sixties (Osgood, 1959) and has been applied in a wide range of disciplines. Using a pure *bag-of-words* approach, and applying clustering techniques on word co-occurrences matrices, it is possible to obtain clusters of words representing existing topics mentioned in a text collection. Using a hierarchical clustering rather than a partitioning technique has the additional advantage of providing an ordered list of topics revealing thematic structures of the text collection that can be analyzed at different levels, from specific topics to broad themes. Although not necessarily as rich in detail as qualitative analysis, themes extracted this way can achieve high correspondence with what could be identified in a qualitative thematic analysis (Baumer, Mimno, Guha, Quan, & Gay, 2017).

Based on such property, a preliminary hierarchical cluster analysis of word co-occurrence could very well represent an efficient way for a qualitative researcher to obtain a broad overview of the various topics that will be encountered during the analysis. It could even suggest a codebook structure that will accommodate the variety of themes that will be encountered, preventing the need to restructure the codebook during the qualitative analysis process. We saw before that clustering large numbers of individuals might help one obtain a small heterogenous sample of participants for a qualitative study. We could also use the same approach to sample documents when the number of text sources is too high to be analyzed qualitatively. Such sampling could be performed to achieve representativeness. It might also focus on isolated documents to identify what could more likely be minority opinions or original points of view.

Clustering text data may also provide computer assistance for the qualitative analysis of large amounts of short text responses, like open-ended responses in a survey. Such a technique was implemented in the cluster extraction feature of QDA Miner in which similar responses are grouped and presented together, allowing the researchers to code them by clusters rather than one by one.

6 Strengths and Limitations of Clustering

As we saw earlier, clustering has been considered as a suitable technique for assisting qualitative analysis (Miles & Huberman, 1994) and has several attributes that can potentially increase its acceptability for qualitative researchers. As an exploratory data analysis technique, clustering is well suited for an inductive approach to qualitative data. Its relative simplicity compared to other multivariate techniques, make it more accessible and often more transparent as to how findings are being produced. Although it can be applied on small amounts of data, its capacity to handle large datasets also offers new possibilities for combining qualitative and quantitative methods, in-depth analysis of small data samples and extensive analysis of larger data sets.

The fact that items can only belong to one cluster may be perceived as an oversimplification of some complex realities. A good example of this occurs when one performs semantic network analysis by clustering single words. Because a word often has multiple meanings or may be used in quite different contexts, forcing them into a single cluster only, sometimes results in strange amalgams of unrelated topics. Although some *fuzzy clustering* techniques do exist, allowing objects to belong to more than one cluster, those forms are not widely available in computer applications. Other multivariate techniques such as principal component analysis or factor analysis might thus be more appropriate.

Despite its long history, there is no single set of accepted rules that one can follow to select the proper distance measure, the appropriate agglomeration technique, or even to choose the optimal number of clusters. The common practice in some domains such as biology to apply strictly qualitative judgments for assessing and interpreting clustering solutions might be disconcerting for those looking for a straightforward answer. However, those more inclined to explore various facets of their data and open to experiment will appreciate the additional insights that the exploratory use of clustering might provide.

7 Resources for Learning More About Cluster Analysis

Despite having been invented almost 90 years ago, clustering continues to evolve and has become an increasingly popular multivariate method. Publications on new methodological developments are scattered throughout many journals from many fields of studies, including biology, computer science, marketing, and economics. Statistical and methodological textbooks in many of these disciplines often contain introductory chapters on cluster analysis. For those who want to further explore this technique, Andendelfer and Blashfield's (1984) book remains a good introduction and should be on top of the list for those who want a concise, yet thoughtful presentation of cluster analysis. For a more comprehensive and up-to-date overview, Everett, Landau, Leese, and Stahl (2011) present a good introduction to the method and cover more advanced topics as well as plenty of application examples.

REFERENCES

Andendelfer, M. S., & Blashfield, R. K (1984). *Cluster analysis.* Quantitative Applications in the Social Sciences. Thousand Oaks, CA: Sage.

Arthur, D., & Vassilvitskii, S. (2007). k-means++: The advantages of careful seeding. *Proceedings of the eighteenth annual ACM-SIAM symposium on Discrete algorithms.* Society for Industrial and Applied Mathematics.

Baumer, E. P. S., Mimno, D., Guha, S., Quan, E., & Gay, G. K. (2017). Comparing grounded theory and topic modeling: Extreme divergence or unlikely convergence? *Journal of the Association for Information Science and Technology, 68,* 397–1410. doi:10.1002/asi.23786

Cmeciu, C. (2017). A bottom-up discursive approach to genetically modified organism. *Journal of Media Critiques, 3*(11), 45–55. doi:10.17349/jmc117304

Creswell, J. W., Plano Clark, V. L., Gutmann, M., & Hanson, W. (2003). Advanced mixed methods research designs. In A. Tashakkori & C. Teddlie (Eds.), *Handbook of mixed methods in social and behavioral research* (pp. 209–240). Thousand Oaks, CA: Sage.

Dagenais, C., & Hackett, S. (2008). *Determinants of research use in the field of literacy: A concept mapping project.* Montreal, Canada: Unpublished manuscript. Équipe RENARD.

Dawson, N. V., & Weiss, R. (2012). Dichotomizing continuous variables in statistical analysis. *Medical Decision Making, 32,* 225–226. doi:10.1177/0272989X12437605

Dey, I. (2003). *Qualitative data analysis: A user friendly guide for social scientists.* New York, NY: Routledge.

Dimitriadou, E., Dolnicar, S., & Weingessel, A. (2002). An examination of indexes for determining the number of clusters in binary data sets. *Psychometrika, 67,* 137–160. doi:10.1007/BF02294713

Everett, B. S., Landau, S., Leese, M., & Stahl, D. (2011). *Cluster analysis.* Wiley Series in Probability and Statistics. New York, NY: John Wiley & Sons.

Guest, G., & McLellan, E. (2003). Distinguishing the trees from the forest: Applying cluster analysis to thematic qualitative data. *Field Methods, 15,* 186–201. doi:10.1177/1525822X03015002005

Henry, D., Dymnicki, A. B., Mohatt, N., Allen, J., & Kelly, J. G. (2015). Clustering methods with qualitative data: A mixed-methods approach for prevention research with small sample. *Prevention Science, 16,* 1007–1016. doi:10.1007/s11121-015-0561-z

Kane, M., & Trochim, W. M. K. (2007). *Concept mapping for planning and evaluation.* Thousand Oaks, CA: Sage.

Kaufman, L., & Rousseeuw, P. J. (1990). *Finding groups in data. An introduction to cluster analysis.* New York, NY: John Wiley & Sons.

Lorr, M. (1983). *Cluster analysis for the social sciences.* San Francisco, CA: Jossey-Bass.

MacQueen, J. B. (1967). Some methods for classification and analysis of multivariate observations. In L. M. Le Cam & J. Neyman (Eds.), *Proceedings of 5th Berkeley symposium on mathematical statistics and probability* (Vol. 1, pp. 281–297). Berkeley, CA: University of California Press.

Macia, L. (2015). Using clustering as a tool: Mixed methods in qualitative data analysis. *The Qualitative Report, 20,* 1083–1094.

Miles, M. B., & Huberman, A. M. (1994). *Qualitative data analysis: An expanded sourcebook.* Thousand Oaks, CA: Sage.

Milligan, G. W., & Cooper, M. C. (1985). An examination of procedures for determining the number of clusters in a data set. *Psychometrika, 50,* 159–179. doi:10.1007/BF02294245

Myers, N. (2016). Democracy, rights, community: Examining ethical frameworks for federal public health emergency response. *Public Integrity, 18,* 201–226. doi:10.1080/10999922.2015.1111745

Osgood, C. (1959). The representational model and relevant research methods. In I. de Sola Pool (Ed.), *Trends in content analysis* (pp. 33–88). Champaign, IL: University of Illinois Press.

Péladeau, N., Dagenais, C., & Ridde, V. (2017). Concept mapping internal validity: A case of misconceived mapping? *Evaluation and program planning, 62,* 56–63. doi:10.1016/j.evalprogplan.2017.02.005

Percy, W. H., Kostere, K., & Kostere, S. (2015). Generic qualitative research in psychology. *The Qualitative Report, 20*(2), 76–85.

Rousseeuw, P. J. (1987). Silhouettes: a graphical aid to the interpretation and validation of cluster analysis. *Journal of computational and applied mathematics, 20,* 53–65. doi:10.1016/0377-0427(87)90125-7

Spillane, J. P., & Hunt, B. R. (2010). Days of their lives: a mixed-methods, descriptive analysis of the men and women at work in the principal's office. *Journal of Curriculum Studies, 42,* 293–331. doi:10.1080/00220270903527623

Täuscher, K., & Laudien, S. M. (2018). Understanding platform business models: A mixed methods study of marketplaces. *European Management Journal, 36,* 319–329. doi:10.1016/j.emj.2017.06.005

Thøgersen-Ntoumani, C., & Fox, K. R. (2005). Physical activity and mental well-being typologies in corporate employees: A mixed methods approach. *Work & Stress, 19*(1), 50–67. doi:10.1080/02678370500084409

Trochim, W. M. K. (1989). An introduction to concept mapping for planning and evaluation. *Evaluation and Program Planning, 12*(1), 1–16. doi:10.1016/0149-7189(89)90016-5

6

Chi-Square Automatic Interaction Detection Analysis of Qualitative Data

Kathleen M. T. Collins

The premise underpinning the content of this chapter is that analysis and interpretation of qualitative data can be further expanded by researchers choosing to apply data mining techniques, namely, a decision tree algorithm called chi-square automatic interaction detection (CHAID). To structure this discussion, the first purpose is to define CHAID and to contextualize a CHAID analysis as an exemplar of data mining. Additionally, to justify the application of CHAID to the analysis of qualitative data, a juxtaposition is presented that compares the analytical activities and strengths that characterize a qualitative data analysis to the analytical activities and strengths of a CHAID data mining technique. The second purpose is to discuss when the use of CHAID is appropriate for mixed methods research (MMR). The third purpose is to outline the technical steps involved in conducting a CHAID analysis. The fourth purpose is to outline an empirical demonstration of CHAID as a form of MMR analysis. The fifth purpose is to provide applications of CHAID and to illustrate the versatility of CHAID by presenting examples of published applications of a CHAID analysis using qualitative data. The sixth purpose is to present selective examples of the strengths and limitations of CHAID. I conclude by providing recommended resources for learning more about CHAID.

1 Definition of CHAID as an Exemplar of Data Mining

The CHAID analysis is defined as a tree-based segmentation technique applicable for deriving statistically significant segments that lead to a predictive model or tree (Kass, 1980). Within this analysis, statistical algorithms are used to obtain segments that are statistically significant predictors of the dependent variable. The results are displayed as a hierarchy depicting the variables having the strongest impact on the dependent variable followed by the variables having less impact, and the results are displayed visually as classification trees (Hand, Mannila, & Smyth, 2001; Magidson, 1994). These classification trees are considered to be an effective data mining method (Song & Lu, 2015).

Data mining is the analysis of observational data, oftentimes secondary data, for the express purpose of detecting unique models, patterns, and relationships within the data that are considered valuable and informative to the stakeholder (Hand et al., 2001). Hand et al. (2001) identify observational data and secondary data as the existing data sources for data mining because these types of data, typically were collected for another purpose, and the decision to apply data mining is to add another dimension of interpretation based on pattern detection. These detected patterns then are organized into data mining models. Some examples of patterns are clusters, graphs, tree structures, linear equations, and regularly occurring patterns in a time series analysis (Hand et al., 2001).

Data Mining Process

The process of data mining comprises four steps (Hand et al., 2001). Specifically, the researcher determin[es] the nature and structure of the representation to be used"; "decid[es] how to quantify and compare how well different representations fit the data [by] choosing a 'score' function" (quotations in the original); "choos[es] an algorithmic process to optimize the score function"; "and decid[es] what principles of data management are required to implement the algorithms efficiently" (Hand et al., 2001, p. 3).

The types of representation ascertained by the application of data mining techniques fall into two distinct groups: model structure and local patterns (Hand et al., 2001). Model structure presents a global summarization of the dataset as a whole. Local patterns detail a structure focused on a subcomponent or part of the larger dataset. These models are developed for the purposes of exploration of data (exploratory data analysis), description of data (descriptive modeling), creation of a data-generation process, and development of a predictive model (Hand et al., 2001).

The steps that characterize CHAID are aligned to the four-step process defining data mining (Hand et al., 2001). Step 1 in data mining is to detect the underlying structure of the data. In a CHAID analysis, the representations are the segments that are based on the merging of categories that are homogeneous and separates categories that are heterogeneous. This merging and retention of categories are based on the statistical significance in relationship between the categorical predictor variables and the dependent variable (Magidson, 1994). Step 2 in data mining is to select a score function to optimize the quality of the fitted model. In a CHAID analysis, the score function *fits* the data by identifying the best predictors based on the variables having the lowest adjusted p value. Step 3 in data mining involves the researcher making the decision to select an algorithmic process designed to optimize the score function and to assess various models and pattern structures. In a CHAID analysis, the researcher selects one of three types of predictor variables—a decision that impacts the categorical merging algorithm (Magidson, 1994). The first type of predictor variable represents a monotonic variable that has an underlying implied order, and these variables are combined when situated adjacent to each other. Ordinal data that have an implied order are considered to be monotonic variables. The second type of predictor variable represents a free variable that does not have an underlying implicit order. Floating variables are considered monotonic, with the exception of the last category identified as an unknown or missing value. Step 4 involves the researcher determining a strategy of data management to optimize implementation of the algorithmic process detailed in Step 3.

Qualitative Research Process

Qualitative research involves the studied use and collection of a variety of empirical materials "that describe routine and problematic moments and meanings in individuals' lives ... by deploy[ing] a wide range of interpretive practices" (Denzin & Lincoln, 2011, pp. 3–4). A critical and interrelated component of this process is researchers' decisions regarding data collection and data analysis and the degree that these concomitant decisions address the research question.

The cycle of activities that characterize qualitative data analysis consists of data condensation, data display, and forming and verifying conclusions (Miles, Huberman, & Saldaña, 2014). Data condensation refers to the researcher's decisions as to what aspects of collected data to code and the formulation of meaning given to the summarization of these codes, as illustrated by the categorical label assigned to the summarization. Data display illustrates the researcher's perceptions of the best ways to exemplify the connections depicted, and it is these connections that lead to the final step of forming and verifying conclusions. Specifically, the researcher notes the "patterns, explanations, causal flows, and propositions" that characterize the analyzed data and that serve to substantiate conclusions (Miles et al., 2014, p. 13). Included in the process of qualitative data collection is determining the appropriate sampling design (i.e., sample scheme and sample size). Typically, a purposive sample scheme is the recommended strategy for sample selection in qualitative research, and the recommended sample size accompanying this decision reflects the specific design guiding the research (e.g., narrative, phenomenology, grounded theory, ethnography, case study) (Creswell, 2007). However, in practice, researchers can select random sampling designs singularly or in combination with purposive sampling designs when implementing qualitative research (Guest, Bunce, & Johnson, 2006). Implementing singularly or multiple purposive or random sampling schemes or implementing a combination of these types of schemes can provide adequate data to address complex questions (Collins, 2010; Teddlie & Yu, 2007).

Hatch (2002) described data analysis as "a systematic search for meaning, [and] it is a way to process qualitative data so that what has been learned can be communicated to others" (p. 148). As noted by Miles et al. (2014), the collected qualitative data comprise an "individual or a social process, a mechanism, or a structure at the core of events that can be captured to provide a causal description of the likely forces at work" (p. 7). However, it is the analysis and subsequent explanation of the results that provide the basis for researchers' interpretations. Researchers have multiple choices of data analysis techniques and can employ more than one type of data analysis within a single design. Some examples available to qualitative researchers are constant comparison analysis (Glaser, 1965; Glaser & Strauss, 1967); keywords-in context analysis (Fielding & Lee, 1998); domain analysis, taxonomic analysis, and componential analysis (Spradley, 1979); manifest latent analysis (Berelson, 1952); and latent analysis (Potter & Levine-Donnerstein, 1999).

Employing more than one technique leads optimally toward elevating the researcher's interpretation of the underlying meaning of the data analyzed, thereby increasing trustworthiness and rigor (Leech & Onwuegbuzie, 2007; Sechelski & Onwuegbuzie, 2019). This point is illustrated by employing data analysis triangulation for the purposes of validation based on convergence of results, complementarity leading to broader insights relative to interpreting results, and divergence based on deviation of results leading potentially to another research question to explore empirically the divergent findings (Bazeley & Kemp, 2012).

A strength of the CHAID data mining technique is that it is able to detect the underlying structure of the data (Hand et al., 2001). This strength is aligned to the premise guiding qualitative analysis that "explanations flow from an account of how differing structures produce the events that we observe" (Miles et al., 2014, p. 7), and a strength of a qualitative analysis is to discover "*meanings* people place on the events, processes, and structures of their lives" and "connecting these meanings to the *social world* around them" (Miles et al., 2014, p. 11, italics in the original).

CHAID Analysis Process

The cycle of activities that characterizes a qualitative data analysis—namely, data condensation, data display, and forming and verifying conclusions (Miles et al., 2014)—also characterizes the strengths underpinning a CHAID analysis. In a CHAID analysis, data condensation refers to the researcher's decisions as to what predictor variables and dependent variable to include in the analysis. These decisions are based on the type of model desired and the purpose that it serves in determining the underlying structure of the data, such as exploration of data (exploratory data analysis), description of data (descriptive modeling), creation of a data-generation process, and development of a predictive model (Hand et al., 2001). Data display in a CHAID analysis is addressed by the classification trees that illustrate a visual representation of the interconnections within the predictive model, leading to the final step of the analyses, which is forming and verifying the conclusions. Using CHAID to analyze qualitative data can permit the researcher to address more complex questions. Further, it can provide empirical support in the form of a model that depicts the underlying structure of the data that is not available using other forms of qualitative analyses (Hand et al., 2001; Magidson, 1994). A CHAID analysis also can add to the validity of the conclusions by providing another level of interpretive information when the researcher is formulating a theoretical explanation based on the relationship between the theoretical explanation developed from the study's finding and the analyzed data, referred to as theoretical validity (Maxwell, 1992).

2 When Use of CHAID is Appropriate for MMR

Researchers conducting a MMR analysis can implement a variety of approaches, methods, and techniques when devising and implementing the analytical phase of the study. Approaches, methods, and techniques comprise the dimensions of a crossover framework designed by Hitchcock and Onwuegbuzie (2019) to provide guidelines for researchers to "innovate yet more crossover approaches" (p. 1). Approaches are delineated into concurrent mixed analyses, whereby the qualitative and quantitative analytical phases are conducted independently, and integration of the conclusions per phase occurs at the study's conclusions. The integration of conclusions is referred to as meta-inferences (Tashakkori & Teddlie, 1998). In contrast, sequential mixed analysis involves a level of dependency between phases, whereby analysis of one phase (e.g., qualitative) informs researchers' decisions in the following phase (e.g., quantitative). Conversion mixed analyses refers to a crossover analytical process that allows researchers to collect data typically associated with one approach (e.g., qualitative) and to apply analyses associated with another approach (e.g., quantitative) (Onwuegbuzie & Combs, 2010). Methods in a MMR analysis refer to the procedural methods implemented in a conversion analysis. Qualitizing refers to a process of transforming quantitative data into a qualitative form that can be analyzed qualitatively. In contrast, quantitizing refers to the method of converting qualitative data into numerical data that can be analyzed statistically. Techniques in a MMR analysis represent a single step (or procedure) in the data analysis process that are implemented to derive conclusions based on the analyses (Hitchcock & Onwuegbuzie, 2019; Onwuegbuzie & Teddlie, 2003; Tashakkori & Teddlie, 1998). Accordingly, applying a CHAID analysis to analyze qualitative data transforms a monomethod (e.g., qualitative) study to a MMR study via a mixed analysis (i.e., quantitizing). The appropriate use of CHAID in the analysis of qualitative data leads researchers to draw conclusions and meta-inferences unlikely to occur without implementing this form of analysis. Also, implementing a CHAID analysis adds another dimension of integration at the analysis phase of the study. Integration is a critical characteristic of MMR and an important dimension of high-quality research (Collins, 2015).

3 Technical Outline of CHAID for MMR

In this technical outline, CHAID is presented as a technique for the purpose of predictive modeling, whereby prediction of a single variable's value is based on the known values of other variables (Hand et al., 2001). CHAID is a criterion-based model. The analysis comprises a categorical dependent variable consisting of a criterion of interest, a selective set of categorical predictor variables, and pre-determined parameter settings, such as alpha level, number of cases per node, and effect size to determine the stopping criterion to stop splitting into segments (Magidson, 1994). The stopping criterion is devised to avoid the splitting process developing into an overly complex decision tree, which would compromise the accuracy of the model and the generalizability of the results. Alternately, there is a procedure called exhaustive CHAID. This procedure differs slightly from the standard CHAID procedure by allowing the researcher to conduct a more in-depth merging and testing of the categorical predictor variables, thereby requiring additional computer time for the analysis. Subsequently, it is the researcher's preference to conduct a standard or exhaustive CHAID analysis based on the purpose of the analysis and the available resources (Biggs, De Ville, & Suen, 1991). The CHAID algorithm is limited to nominal or ordinal categorical predictor variables (Kass, 1980). The dependent variable is categorical, and it can be dichotomous, polytomous, trichotomous, or ordinal. However, having an ordinal-scaled dependent variable leads to a loss of statistical power (Magidson, 1994).

The CHAID analysis divides the samples into segments or subgroups based on the interactions among the predictor variables. These segments are statistically significant predictors of the dependent variable (Magidson, 1994). The analysis comprises a series of chi-square tests for independence, and the researcher applies the Bonferroni adjustment to control for Type 1 error, which occurs when the alpha level is inflated due to multiple statistical testing. The results reflect only statistically significant predictors (Magidson, 1994).

There are several steps involved in conducting a CHAID analysis. The sample comprising all cases in the study is grouped as an initial segment (Magidson, 1994). Next, the initial segment is partitioned into segments based on the lowest statistically significant Bonferroni adjusted p value associated with attaining results of a statistically significant chi-square test. This step is referred to as pre-pruning, which involves removing statistically non-significant predictor variables. In a CHAID analysis, the researcher assumes that a minimum of two predictor variables will interact. Subsequently, these interactions will permit the researcher to determine the most significant predictors among the number of possible interactions, thereby generating a parsimonious interpretation of complex interactions (Magidson, 1994). It is this combination of predictor variables that defines the segment, and each segment is assigned a probability. These probabilities are ranked in accordance to the degree that they predict the dependent variable (Van Diepen & Franses, 2006). Subsequently, the best predictor variable is the variable having the lowest Bonferonni-adjusted p value. The CHAID analyst merges categories that are homogeneous relative to the dependent variable, and the analyst also will retain the heterogeneous categories (Van Diepen & Franses, 2006). Sample size impacts the minimum sample size per node. Subsequently, the larger the sample size, the larger number of cases required per node. To address sampling variability within the data, the CHAID analysis involves splitting a predictor only if the split produces a statistically significant difference in the distribution of the dependent variable, and there can be multiple splits (Van Diepen & Franses, 2006).

Results of a CHAID analysis are presented in the format of classification tree models. These models comprise nodes and branches. Nodes consist of varying types (Song & Lu, 2015). A root node is referred to as a decision node because it represents a choice leading to the subdivision of the set into two or more mutually exclusive subsets. An internal node is referred to as a chance node because it represents one of the possible choices occurring in the tree structure when the connection occurs between parent node and child node (Song & Lu, 2015). In this context, parent node represents the results occurring when the target variable is split into two or more categories, and the child node represents the independent variables located below the parent node and, subsequently, is the cumulative results of decisions occurring using statistical algorithms (Song & Lu, 2015). The terminal nodes are the last category of the analysis, and they represent the predictor variables that have the strongest impact on the dependent variable and they are followed by the variables having the least impact (Magidson, 1994). Branches represent the chance outcomes occurring due to the statistically significant relationship between the root node and the internal node (Song & Lu, 2015). The result of the analysis is a classification tree that comprises a hierarchy of branches (Song & Lu, 2015). A CHAID analysis provides classification accuracy, specifying the proportion of cases classified correctly; and a risk estimate, specifying the proportion of cases classified incorrectly (Magidson, 1994). The resulting model is mutually exclusive and exhaustive (Magidson, 1994). The researcher can choose to cross-validate the results by splitting randomly the sample into two samples—consisting of the initial sample and a holdout sample for a cross-validation analysis (Magidson, 1994).

4 Empirical Demonstration of CHAID for MMR

To demonstrate the CHAID process, I implemented a CHAID analysis. The qualitative data analyzed in this example were collected to assess undergraduates' perceptions of effective college teaching. The sample consisted of 593 undergraduate students. The ages of the undergraduates ranged from 18 to 57 ($M = 21.78$, $SD = 5.37$). These undergraduates identified and ranked between three and six characteristics of effective college teaching, and they were asked to include an explanatory definition of each characteristic. Constant comparison analysis was used to analyze undergraduates' responses (Glaser, 1965; Glaser & Strauss, 1967). The results of this analysis led to the formulation of nine themes. Figure 6.1 presents the nine themes used in the analysis.

To prepare the data for the CHAID analysis, undergraduates' responses were dichotomized to reflect two types of scores. When an undergraduate's response pertaining to a characteristic was categorized under a particular theme, a score of "1" was given to denote endorsement of that theme, and when the undergraduate's response was not categorized under that theme, a score of "0" was given. This produced two inter-respondent matrices comprising either 1s or 0s (Onwuegbuzie & Teddlie, 2003). The software used to conduct the CHAID analysis was the Answer Tree add-on module of SPSS version 16. The algorithm used in this analysis was the CHAID algorithm (Kass, 1980). The analysis was conducted to examine the relationship between the scores of the nine themes and the following demographic variables: age of the undergraduate, grade point average, gender, and ethnicity. Bonferroni adjustment was implemented within the analysis. CHAID is a forward stepwise regression method. Because the order of entry of the predictor variables impacts the segmentation in the CHAID analysis, the predictor variables were entered simultaneously.

CHAID Analysis 1

In this analysis, the nine themes were the dependent variables, and the four demographic variables were the predictor variables. Figure 6.2 illustrates the segmentation of

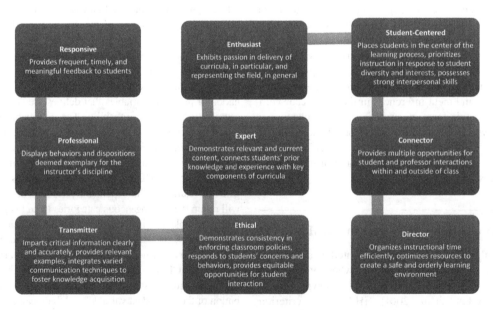

FIGURE 6.1 Themes evolving from undergraduates' perceptions of characteristics of effective college teachers.

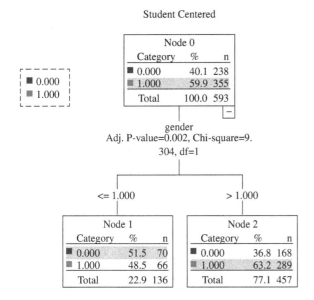

FIGURE 6.2 Segmentation of student-centered theme as a function of the emergent themes.

student-centered theme as a function of statistically significant predictor variables for the 593 undergraduate students. The percentage of undergraduates who endorsed this theme was 59.9% ($n = 355$), and 40.1% ($n = 238$) did not endorse this theme. The best predictor of endorsing the student-centered theme was gender ($\chi2$ [1] = 9.304, adj. $p <= .002$), with women undergraduates (63.2%, $n = 289$) being statistically significantly more likely to endorse the student-centered theme than were the men undergraduates (48.5%, $n = 66$). The model resulted in a classification accuracy of approximately 60.5% of the sample (i.e., risk estimate = .40).

CHAID Analysis 2

The correlational element of CHAID permits the exchange of the predictor variables and the dependent variables in the analysis. In the second analysis, the four demographic variables were the dependent variables and the nine themes were the predictor variables. Figure 6.3 shows the segmentation of ethnicity as a function of the statistically significant predictor variable, specifically the enthusiasm theme for the 593 undergraduate students. The best predictor of ethnicity was the enthusiasm theme (F [1, 591] = 9.156, adj. $p = .003$). Results indicated that a higher percentage of White students (69.6%, $n = 413$) statistically significantly endorsed the enthusiasm theme when compared to non-White students (30.4%, $n = 180$). The White undergraduates (51.8%, $n = 307$) were statistically significantly more likely to endorse the ethical theme than were the non-White undergraduates (17.9%, $n = 106$; F [1, 411] = 4.681, adj. $p = .03$). The model resulted in a classification accuracy of approximately 88% of the sample (i.e., risk estimate = .12)

When interpreting the integrated results derived from the analysis, an important point to consider is that the CHAID analysis indicates a percentage of endorsement; it does not provide information about the social context surrounding the

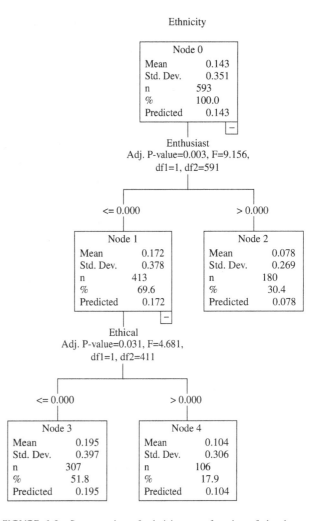

FIGURE 6.3 Segmentation of ethnicity as a function of the demographic variables.

inquiry and the varying ways that undergraduates interpret the themes of student-centered, enthusiasm, and ethical in a college classroom setting. However, the integrated analysis can be useful when triangulating results for the purpose of the development of additional research questions to be assessed in subsequent research (Bazeley & Kemp, 2012). It also can provide an advanced interpretation of the complexity characterizing the phenomenon of interest.

5 Suggested Applications of CHAID in MMR

To illustrate the application of a CHAID analysis for MMR, I have outlined a criterion sample of studies selected because qualitative data were analyzed using a CHAID analysis, thereby transforming a monomethod (e.g., qualitative) study to a MMR study through a mixed analysis. Additionally, each study addressed a different purpose, thereby illustrating the versatility of this form of analysis and suggested applications of a CHAID analysis. The individualized purposes addressed in the selected studies were aligned to topics relevant to the fields of education, sociology, sports and exercise, and business. These studies were located using the Google Scholar search engine and the quick search tool spanning multiple electronic search engines. The descriptors used to identify the studies were *CHAID* and *qualitative*.

Empirical Application 1

Education. The study designed by Shaw, Chan, and McMahon (2012) provides an illustrative example of an exhaustive CHAID analysis with a qualitative component using secondary data, a characteristic associated with data mining. Shaw et al. (2012) conducted a retrospective study analyzing secondary data. They examined the American with Disabilities Title 1 data to assess the proportion of harassment charges filed by individuals with disabilities concerning workplace harassment and the degree that a combination of personal attributes, namely gender, age, race/ethnicity, or disability, predicted the filing of the allegations. Specifically, these researchers examined how membership in more than one protected category (i.e., gender, age, race/ethnicity, or disability) interacted with the proportion of harassment charges filed in a workplace. Additionally, two workplace characteristics were assessed: type of industry and employer size. The sample comprised 25,411 individuals (11,875 men, 13,426, women, 110 other). The results of the exhaustive CHAID analysis led the researchers to conclude that the following predictors, in descending order, reflected the higher rate of harassment allegations: gender (women), type of impairment (behavioral impairments, combined sensory and neurological impairment, followed by physical impairment), and age, followed by race. Specifically, race (American Indian and Hispanic women), age (35 years or older), and impairment (behavioral impairment) yielded the higher rate of harassment allegations (Shaw et al., 2012). Manufacturing, health care, public administration, and retail work places were well represented among the top five groups filing harassment charges (Shaw et al., 2012). Shaw et al. (2012) also noted that exhaustive CHAID was the choice of analysis because it "detect[s] the strongest association between predictors and the outcome variable ... [and] show[s] the most differentiation on the outcome variable" (p. 85).

Empirical Application 2

Sociology. Balemba, Beauregard, and Mieczkowski (2012) studied the degree that specific types of victims' resistance executed during a sexual assault, such as victims' passive, verbal, or physical resistance, affected the offender's strategy to implement violence. Specifically, these researchers examined the situational variables affecting potentially the offenders' behaviors, namely, type of victim resistance, alcohol use, drug use, pornography consumption prior to the commission of the crime, offenders' premeditation, and level of offender's intimacy. They also assessed crime characteristics of which the offender had control during the crime, namely, strategies regarding violence, weapon use, nature of the sexual acts, humiliation of the victim, and time spent with the victim. Using a semi-structured questionnaire, the offenders were interviewed, and, in addition, police records, victims' statements, and institutional case files were assessed to provide information triangulation between the offenders' responses and these official sources (Balemba et al., 2012). The sample comprised 624 inmates, and data were collected during a 6-year period. The results of the exhaustive CHAID analysis led Balemba et al. (2012) to conclude that offenders' reactions to victims' resistance were strongly associated with offenders' strategic choice to implement violence, or not to implement violence, or not to have a strategy. With the choices of not having a strategy or choosing a non-violent strategy, the victim's type of resistance led to a non-violent reaction as in the cases of passive or verbal victim responses or a violent reaction in the case of victims exerting physical resistance. Additionally, the CHAID model indicated a stronger likelihood of a higher level of a violent reaction to victim resistance when the offender used humiliation or a weapon. In the case of the offender humiliating the victim, the CHAID analysis revealed that the probability of violence escalated when the victim reacted with physical resistance. Balemba et al. (2012). concluded that "the information discovered herein could have potential utility in the context of programming and policy initiatives ... [and] it could be employed to help educate potential sexual assault victims in harm reduction and situational prevention strategies" (p. 606).

Empirical Application 3

Sports and Exercise. Lavega, Alonso, Etxebeste, Lagardera, and March (2014) examined the intensity of emotions experienced by participants while engaged in traditional games with different social structures, and to assess the participants' explanations of their subjective emotions. Participants were 556 first-year undergraduate students attending Spanish universities, majoring in physical education and sports science. Quantitative data comprised students' self-reported intensity of their emotions, as measured by the Games and Emotion Scale (Lavega, Filella, Aguiló, Soldevila, & March, 2011). Qualitative data consisted of participants' explanations of their strongest emotions while engaging in play, and these data were analyzed using CHAID. Results of the quantitative analysis revealed statistically significant differences relative to type of emotion by type of results (win, lose, non-competitive), type of results by domain of motor action, and type of emotion by gender. Results of the CHAID analysis examining explanations of strongest emotions confirmed the results of the quantitative analyses. Lavega et al. (2014) concluded that "from a methodological point of view, the article illustrates the contribution that classification trees can make to the study of complex phenomena" (p. 466).

Empirical Application 4

Business. Agapito, Valle, and Mendes (2011) sought to identify attributes associated with a travel destination that contributes to tourists' inclinations to recommend a particular destination. Specifically, Agapito et al. (2011) examined the combination of the image of the tourist location, municipality of Lagos in the Alagrve region of Portugal, a location with the largest number of overnight guests, thereby elevating the likelihood that tourists would recommend it to family and friends. A cluster probabilistic scheme was implemented, resulting in the identification of a sample of 379 respondents residing in Portugal and the United Kingdom. The collected qualitative data comprised responses to open-ended items asking respondents to identity the attributes of the tourist location, municipality of Lagos. These qualitative responses were analyzed to create categorical and ordinal-scale items implemented in Phase 2, and responses were analyzed using CHAID. Results indicated that the independent variable of culture was the attribute with the strongest relationship to the dependent variable of recommendation. The results of the CHAID analysis led Agapito et al. (2011) to identify profiles of different segments revealing opposite trends in the responses. Opposing trends were based on the socio-demographics of the sample in terms of the segments of age, country of origin, and educational level. As concluded by Agapito et al. (2011), these results supported tourist destinations to diversify their tourist offers, and provided support for tourist destinations to "develop strong brands and communication strategies directed towards specific segments ... which are likely to boost tourists' desires to recommend it to their relatives and friends" (p. 40).

6 Strengths and Limitations of CHAID in MMR

CHAID, as a classification tree analysis and as a form of MMR analysis, has multiple strengths, and it offers advantages relative to more commonly used statistical analyses. CHAID allows researchers to analyze a substantial number of categorical predictor variables simultaneously, and to view the results visually in the form of classification trees. Because it applies a series of chi-square tests, it does not require a normal distribution of the predictor variables (Magidson, 1994). Subsequently, the resulting classification trees are simultaneously non-linear and non-parametric (Horner, Fireman, & Wang, 2010). A CHAID analysis allows the researcher to obtain a parsimonious representation of the statistically significant relationship between the predictor variables and the dependent variable (Magidson, 1994). As demonstrated by the illustrative example presented in this chapter, the correlational element of CHAID permits the exchange of the predictor variables and the dependent variables in the analysis. CHAID also identifies the relative predictive value of each variable in the resulting model, thereby informing decisions for future research (Song & Lu, 2015). As observed by Horner et al. (2010), CHAID is a useful analysis for conducting exploratory analysis, leading to the identification of relationships between predictor and dependent variables that might be missed using other forms of analyses. These results then can be followed by confirmatory analyses.

However, there are limitations to a CHAID analysis (Van Diepen & Franses, 2006). Specifically, the CHAID results can be unstable if a different sample is used in subsequent research using the same variable even though the characteristics of the second sample are very similar to the first sample (Van Diepen & Franses, 2006). The chi-square test assesses the degree that observed differences among groups occurred by chance. Overfitting, whereby the classification tree fits the analysis data too well, leads to a classification tree comprising random variations of the value of interest. Subsequently, the predictive accuracy is compromised when the test is conducted on a new sample (Van Diepen & Franses, 2006).

A third problem is that the categorical variables are selected strategically to differentiate among groups on the dependent variable. However, because the chi-square test takes advantage of chance in discriminating among groups, the predicted probability differences between segments are inflated and the resulting predictions can be "(severely) biased" (Van Diepen & Franses, 2006, p. 818, parentheses in the original).

7 Resources for Learning More About CHAID

The resources detailed below are recommended for learning more about CHAID.

Hand, D., Mannila, H., & Smyth, P. (2001). *Principles of data mining.* Cambridge, MA: The MIT Press.

Kass, G. (1980). An exploratory technique for investigating large quantities of categorical data. *Journal of the Royal Statistical Society. Series C (Applied Statistics) 29*(2), 119–127. doi:10.2307/2986296

Magidson, J. (1994). The CHAID approach to segmentation modeling: Chi-squared automatic interaction detection. In R. P. Bagozzi (Ed.), *Advanced methods of marketing research* (pp. 118–159). Cambridge, MA: Blackwell.

Examples of Available Software Packages and YouTube Videos

https://video.search.yahoo.com/yhs/search?fr=yhs-trp-001&hsimp=yhs-001&hspart=trp&p=chaid+youtube+videos#id=1&vid=a35db91d826f434f5f48df90fd0a6c93&actionclick
IBM SPSS Decision Trees Series: 1. Running Decision Trees
www.youtube.com/watch?v=x6i3H2CXw_Y
www.youtube.com/watch?v=0Qh8NpYhmdU
www.youtube.com/watch?v=z0WQe5_gWEc

REFERENCES

Agapito, D., Valle, P., & Mendes, J. (2011). Understanding tourist recommendation through destination image: A CHAID analysis. *Tourism & Management Studies, 7*(1), 33–42.

Balemba, S., Beauregard, E., & Mieczkowski, T. (2012) To resist or not to resist: The effect of context and crime characteristics on sex offenders' reaction to victim resistance. *Crime & Delinquency, 58,* 588–611. doi:10.1177/0011128712437914

Bazeley, P., & Kemp, L. (2012). Mosaics, triangles, and DNA: Metaphors for integrated analysis in mixed methods research. *Journal of Mixed Methods Research, 6,* 55–72. doi:10.1177/1558689811419514

Berelson, B. (1952). *Content analysis in communicative research.* New York, NY: Free Press.

Biggs, D., De Ville, B., & Suen, E. (1991). A method for choosing multiway partitions for classification and decision trees. *Journal of Applied Statistics, 18,* 49–62. doi:10.1080/02664769100000005

Collins, K. M.T. (2010). Advanced sampling designs in mixed research: Current practices and emerging trends in the social and behavioral sciences. In A. Tashakkori & C. Teddlie (Eds.), *SAGE handbook of mixed methods in social and behavioral research* (2nd ed., pp. 353–377). Thousand Oaks, CA: Sage.

Collins, K. M. T. (2015). Validity in multimethod and mixed research. In S. N. Hesse-Biber & R. B. Johnson (Eds.), *The Oxford handbook of multimethod and mixed methods research inquiry* (pp. 240–256). New York: NY. Oxford University Press.

Creswell, J. W. (2007). *Qualitative inquiry and research design: Choosing among five approaches* (2nd ed.). Thousand Oaks, CA: Sage.

Denzin, N. K., & Lincoln, Y. S. (Eds.). (2011). *Handbook of qualitative research* (2nd ed.). Thousand Oaks, CA: Sage.

Fielding, N. G., & Lee, R. M. (1998). *Computer analysis and qualitative research*. Thousand Oaks, CA: Sage.

Glaser, B. G. (1965). The constant comparative method of qualitative analysis. *Social Problems, 12*, 436–445. doi:10.1525/sp.1965.12.4.03a00070

Glaser, B. G., & Strauss, A. L. (1967). *The discovery of grounded theory: Strategies for qualitative research*. Chicago, IL: Aldine.

Guest, G., Bunce, A., & Johnson, L. (2006). How many interviews are enough?: An experiment with data saturation and variability. *Field Methods, 18*(1), 59–82. doi:10.1177/1525822X05279903

Hand, D., Mannila, H., & Smyth, P. (2001). *Principles of data mining*. Cambridge MA: The MIT Press.

Hatch, J. A. (2002). *Doing qualitative research in education settings*. Albany, NY: SUNY Press.

Hitchcock, J. H., & Onwuegbuzie, A. J. (2019). Developing mixed methods crossover analysis approaches. *Journal of Mixed Methods Research*. Advanced online publication. doi:10.1177/1558689819841782

Horner, S. B., Fireman, G. D., & Wang, E. W. (2010). The relation of student behavior, peer status, race, and gender to decisions about school discipline using CHAID decision trees and regression modeling. *Journal of School Psychology, 48*, 135–262. doi:10.1016/j.jsp.2009.12.001

Kass, G. (1980). An exploratory technique for investigating large quantities of categorical data. *Journal of the Royal Statistical Society. Series C (Applied Statistics), 29*, 119–127. doi:10.2307/2986296

Lavega, P., Alonso, J. I., Etxebeste, J., Lagardera, F., & March, J. (2014). Relationship between traditional games and the intensity of emotions experienced by participants. *Research Quarterly for Exercise and Sport, 85*, 457–467. doi:10.1080/02701367.2014.961048

Lavega, P., Filella, G., Aguiló, M. J., Soldevila, A., & March, J. (2011). Understanding emotions through games: Helping trainee teachers to make decisions. *Electronic Journal of Research in Educational Psychology, 9*, 617–640. Retrieved from http://repositorio.ual.es/bitstream/handle/10835/753/Art_24_519_eng.pdf?sequence=1

Leech, N. L., & Onwuegbuzie, A. J. (2007). An array of qualitative data analysis tools: A call for data analysis triangulation. *School Psychology Quarterly, 22*, 557–584. doi:10.1037/1045-3830.22.4.557

Magidson, J. (1994). The CHAID approach to segmentation modeling: Chi-squared automatic interaction detection. In R. P. Bagozzi (Ed.), *Advanced methods of marketing research* (pp. 118–159). Cambridge, MA: Blackwell.

Maxwell, J. A. (1992). Understanding and validity in qualitative research. *Harvard Educational Review, 62*, 279–301. doi:10.17763/haer.62.3.8323320856251826

Miles, M. B., Huberman, A. M., & Saldaña, J. (2014). *Qualitative data analysis: A methods sourcebook* (3rd ed.). Thousand Oaks, CA: Sage.

Onwuegbuzie, A. J., & Combs, J. P. (2010). Emergent data analysis techniques in mixed methods research: A synthesis. In A. Tashakkori & C. Teddlie (Eds.), *SAGE handbook of mixed methods in social and behavioral research* (2nd ed., pp. 397–430). Thousand Oaks, CA: Sage.

Onwuegbuzie, A. J., & Teddlie, C. (2003). A framework for analyzing data in mixed methods research. In A. Tashakkori & C. Teddlie (Eds.), *Handbook of mixed methods in social and behavioral research* (pp. 351–383). Thousand Oaks, CA: Sage.

Potter, W., & Levine-Donnerstein, D. (1999). Re-thinking validity and reliability in content analysis. *Journal of Applied Communication Research, 27*, 258–284. doi:10.1080/00909889909365539

Shaw, L. R., Chan, F., & McMahon, B. T. (2012). Intersectionality and disability harassment: The interactive effects of disability, race, age, and gender. *Rehabilitation Counseling Bulletin, 55*(2), 82–91. doi:10.1177/0034355211431167

Sechelski, A., & Onwuegbuzie, A. J. (2019). A call for enhancing saturation at the qualitative data analysis stage via the use of multiple qualitative data analysis approaches. *The Qualitative Report, 24*, 795–821. Retrieved from https://nsuworks.nova.edu/tqr/vol24/iss4/11

Song, Y., & Lu, Y. (2015). Decision tree methods: Applications for classification and prediction. *Shanghai Archives of Psychiatry, 27*, 130–135.

Spradley, J. P. (1979). *The ethnographic interview*. Fort Worth, TX: Holt, Rinehart & Winston.

Tashakkori, A., & Teddlie, C. (1998). *Mixed methodology: Combining qualitative and quantitative approaches* (Applied Social Research Methods Series, Vol. 46). Thousand Oaks, CA: Sage.

Teddlie, C., & Yu, F. (2007). Mixed methods sampling: A typology with examples. *Journal of Mixed Methods Research, 1*, 77–100. doi:10.1177/2345678906292430

Van Diepen, M., & Franses, P. H. (2006). Evaluating chi-squared automatic interaction detection. *Information Systems, 31*, 814–831. doi:10.1016/j.is.2005.03.002

7

Multiple Linear Regression Analysis with Qualitative Data that Have Been Quantitized

Kyle Cox, Richard Lambert, and John H. Hitchcock

This chapter introduces regression-based analytic approaches with a particular emphasis on multiple linear regression incorporating qualitative data. First, we build a conceptual definition of regression and then describe the process of quantitizing qualitative data so that it is suitable for use in regression-based analyses. The remaining sections of the chapter follow a structure similar to others in this book, starting with a technical outline that covers regression formulas, estimation, and interpretation of results. The sections after that demonstrate multiple regression with a combination of quantitative and quantitized qualitative information, suggest several applications, and summarize its strengths and limitations. Resources for further learning are listed in the conclusion of this chapter.

1 Definition of Regression and Quantitizing

Regression is a statistical technique for examining the relationship between a dependent variable (Y) and one or more independent variables (X). The purpose of regression is to statistically predict future values and/or explain variance in the dependent variable (see Field, Miles, & Field, 2012 for a more comprehensive definition). There are many types of regression, with adaptations dictated by the number and characteristics of the independent variables and dependent variable under consideration. One such extension is multiple linear regression that includes a single continuous (i.e., numeric) dependent variable and two or more (i.e., multiple) independent variables. We, the authors, believe that multiple regression is a widely used technique, in part due to its ability to accommodate many independent variables, thereby reflecting practical constraints and theoretical frameworks across many substantive fields such as education (e.g., Kelley & Bolin, 2013), the behavioral sciences (e.g., Pedhazur, 1997), organizational research (e.g., Bobko, 2001), and health and medicine (e.g., Tai & Machin, 2014). Later in this chapter, we detail bivariate regression (i.e., simple regression), multiple regression (i.e., multiple linear regression), and logistic regression; but first, we describe quantitizing. This description formalizes and justifies the process of transforming qualitative data into forms suitable for regression-based analyses.

We have referred to the variables utilized in regression as independent or dependent. This is common throughout literature but can cause confusion because the terms stem from experimental design language and regression is appropriate in a wide range of designs (e.g., experimental, quasi-experiments and observational). Other common labels for independent variables (X) include the predictor, regressor, explanatory variable, or covariate; and dependent variables (Y) may be labeled outcome, response, regressand, or criterion variable. The independent variable(s), dependent variable, terms describing capturing their relationship (i.e., coefficients), and an error term form the regression model.

Some Background on Quantitizing

There is a literature base that describes quantitizing procedures (e.g., Miles & Huberman, 1994; Newman, Onwuegbuzie, & Hitchcock, 2015; Onwuegbuzie & Combs, 2010; Onwuegbuzie & Teddlie, 2003; Sandelowski, Voils, & Knafl, 2009; Tashakkori & Teddlie, 1998); furthermore, this literature base provides broader design guidance and mixed methods frameworks that can facilitate associated analyses and integration of quantitative and qualitative methods (in addition to the previously cited sources, see for e.g., Bazeley, 2003; Hitchcock & Onwuegbuzie, 2020; Teddlie & Tashakkori, 2009). Given this literature, a basic conceptual description that justifies quantitizing is provided here for the purposes of setting the stage, not only for the remainder of this chapter, but also for the next two chapters in this book (one dealing with hierarchical linear modeling of quantitized data, and the other chapter dealing with structural equation modeling).

This conceptual description on quantitizing qualitative data is predicated on the idea that researchers routinely perform some form of quantitizing because one can rely on numerical representations of constructs to understand phenomena (cf. Berg, 2001; Onwuegbuzie & Leech, 2019). As Sandelowski et al. (2009) state:

> Quantitizing, however, refers to the process of assigning numerical (nominal or ordinal) values to data conceived as not numerical (or, following the previous discussion, to experience formed into words, visual displays, or something else conceived as qualitative). The not-numerical data typically referred to are segments of text in the form of written transcripts or field notes produced from interviews or participant observations that were themselves formed to accommodate the analyses planned. (p. 209)

That is, a number is a summary of an idea, and such ideas can only be understood by accounting for (a) context (e.g., place, time, culture), (b) the cognitive and affective meaning people attribute to a number, and (c) a number's relationship to other associated numbers, say in a scale. Moreover, there is always going to be qualitative information attached to numbers (see Onwuegbuzie & Leech [2019] for an overview of these issues in their editorial on *qualitizing*; also, see Onwuegbuzie & Leech, this volume). Therefore, we think that transforming qualitative data to some quantitative form, and vice versa, is in fact commonplace in the social sciences.

To demonstrate, if a survey includes the item: *I like donuts*, and offers the response options: Strongly Agree (4), Agree (3), Disagree (2), Strongly Disagree (1), then these options entail assigning a number to capture a person's opinion about donuts. Of course, this simple example can become quite complex when considering context, a respondent's affect, and interpretation of an item. Consider that the distance between the numerical choices in a scale might be a complex matter. In the mind of a respondent, there could be a yawning gap between the options Agree (3) and Disagree (2), but the difference between Strongly Agree (4) and Agree (3) could be seen as trivial. This is, of course, a well-known concern among researchers who attend to ordinal versus interval scales (Field, 2018). Moving past the issue of response options, qualitative researchers can use the idea of donuts potentially to engage in in-depth probing with a person about any number of topics, such as personal tastes, nutrition, dieting, sugar addiction, compulsive eating, connections between food and culture, and so on. However, such probing will typically take intensive resources. For this reason, when there is a desire to work with a large sample, researchers often rely on surveys as an alternative to interviews. When doing so, researchers are in essence practicing a trade-off between depth versus breadth. That is, researchers accept obtaining more surface-level information when conducting surveys so that they can collect data from large groups of people.

A key point to keep in mind here is that there is nothing unusual about using a number to capture some understanding of human thought and emotion. In terms of quantitizing, researchers should always remember that said understanding will be situated within a particular time, place, and culture (i.e., context). The issue at hand then is not getting caught up in quantitative versus qualitative forms of data, but instead understanding the inherent trade-offs of collecting one form of data versus another. Furthermore, from a mixed research perspective, some item writing might require researchers to work at length towards understanding constructs using qualitative methods before going through a quantification process. Hitchcock et al. (2005) present a study wherein extensive ethnographic work was conducted to generate a particular set of items and associated response options to understand self-concept among Sri Lankan youth, and each item was grounded in the qualitatively derived construct. More generally, there are longstanding survey techniques developed for distilling concepts to a numerical form while still being sensitive to context (e.g., Dillman, Smyth, & Christian, 2009), suggesting there should almost always be a strong contextual understanding of the survey effort at hand, even if qualitative methods were not formally used.

Having made the point that researchers routinely quantify ideas via survey work and other forms of social science research, now one simply needs to accept the idea that other forms of quantification can be conducted as a way to supplement or otherwise extend qualitative inquiry via concepts such as initiation, triangulation, developing, complementing, and expansion[1] (see Greene, Caracelli, & Graham, 1989). Consider that Leech and Onwuegbuzie (2008) offer a typology of four broad qualitative data sources: (a) talk, (b) observations, (c) documents, and (d) images. One can always quantify such data. For example, interview data might show clear patterns in how people respond to a series of questions, which are typically thought of as theme. Suppose one conducts interviews with students in a school and asks about the degree to which students with different sexual orientations feel safe and accepted by their peers. To begin, it is quite common practice in statistical analyses to place students in nominal categories (e.g., the letters and plus symbol in the abbreviation LGBTQ+ could itself represent up to six nominal categories, if a student identifies as being heterosexual this would be a seventh category). That is, it is typical in research to work with nominal data and, indeed, such data would form what is normally referred to in practically any introductory statistics text (e.g., Field, 2018) as a *qualitative variable* or a *categorical variable*. Taking this a little further, if one develops a safety theme, one might then rank order each interview response along a scheme such as: (1) the student always feels safe, (2) sometimes feels safe, (3) often feels unsafe, and (4) always feels unsafe. This information can then be converted into ordinal data. An even simpler scheme could be to identify whether respondents contribute to a theme; that is, researchers can assign a score of "1" for each participant who contributes to a given theme and assigning a score of "0" for those who do not, yielding binary data and a next step would be to set up a respondent by theme matrix for later analyses (see Onwuegbuzie, 2003).

On a related point, text data themselves need not be formally converted to a numerical variable because such data almost always include numerical information, such as the frequency and density of given word use. These properties can themselves be analyzed. Consider for example the idea of statistical analyses of textual data (e.g., Lacroux & Matin-Lacroux, 2019). Hence, qualitative data can be analyzed via statistical procedures without the need for quantitizing;[2] we therefore argue that there is nothing unusual about bridging qualitative data and statistical analyses. Having made this fundamental argument, we are not in any way claiming that statistical analyses of information that might have initially taken some qualitative form can or should replace qualitative inquiry. The degree to which researchers should incorporate statistical modeling is a function of one's purpose and goals. We are instead arguing that qualitative data can, at times, be subject to statistical modelling and through this chapter, we seek to establish how to deploy linear regression modeling techniques that include quantitized variables, so as to expand readers' mixed analyses repertoire. While introducing three forms of regression over the next three subsections, we primarily utilize continuous (i.e., quantitative) variables for clarity and simplicity. In subsequent sections and only after providing a basic description of regression, we integrate the complexities of working with quantitized variables.

Bivariate Linear Regression

Bivariate linear regression or simply, bivariate regression, includes a single continuous dependent variable, Y, and a single independent variable, X, that can take a continuous or binary form. This form of regression allows one to investigate the ability of a single X to predict a single Y and/or a single X to explain variance in a single Y. Consider a hypothetical university admissions example in which bivariate regression is used by university personnel to identify students ready for the rigors of a university curriculum. Admissions personnel are interested in predicting an outcome, Y, typically first-year university grade point average (GPA) with a predictor, X, a university entrance examination score. The regression analysis quantifies the degree to which an entrance examination score predicts GPA. If the exam score is a strong predictor of GPA, admissions personnel can infer students with higher examination scores will likely be more successful academically during their first year at the university. Conversely, the results might indicate that entrance examination scores do not predict GPA. In this case, the inclusion of GPA in admissions decisions is suspect because the scores do not help identify students who will be academically successful.

Regression can also be conceptualized as a technique to explain variation in a dependent variable using an independent variable. For bivariate regression, there is some variation in an outcome across cases that can be explained using another variable. University administrators might for example be interested in variation in student GPA attributable to differences in motivation. A bivariate regression would quantify the ability of student motivation to explain variation in student GPA. Explanatory investigations can provide important actionable results. If student motivation has a strong, positive relationship with student GPA, interventions, curriculum, and teaching methods that increase student motivation could be prioritized as a means to improve student academic outcomes (e.g., GPA).

Multiple Linear Regression

Multiple linear regression, or simply multiple regression, is an extension of bivariate regression that accommodates two or more independent variables but still entails explaining or predicting a single continuous dependent variable. For example, student GPA, like many outcomes of interest, has a complicated set of influences. To reflect the complexities of the real world, it is often necessary to consider multiple independent variables. Rather than relying solely on a single entrance examination score, university admissions personnel can employ multiple regression to predict first-year college GPA with an entrance examination score, high school GPA, teacher rating, and essay score as independent variables. A multiple regression analysis not only indicates the total predictive ability of all the independent variables but also their unique individual contribution to prediction while accounting for or holding constant the influence of remaining independent variables. For example, the multiple regression analysis described indicates the overall ability to predict first-year college GPA using all of the independent variables and includes the unique relationship between high school GPA and first-year GPA after accounting for college entrance examination score, teacher rating, and essay score.

Like bivariate regression, multiple regression can also serve in an explanatory capacity. In the context of the student motivation example, multiple regression allows us to consider the relationship between student GPA and different social-emotional and/or academic influences such as student motivation, student anxiety, entrance examination score, and high school GPA. Multiple regression results indicate the explanatory power of the combined independent variables on first-year GPA and include the unique explanatory ability of high school GPA on first-year GPA while accounting for student motivation, student anxiety, and entrance examination score.

Logistic Regression

The regression approaches presented so far have only included a continuous dependent variable; logistic regression can be employed when the outcome of interest is binary (extensions for ordered and unordered categorical variables are complex but also available, see Agresti, 2019). In the university admissions example, logistic regression can be employed to predict the likelihood of acceptance to the university using one or several independent variables. More generally, results from a logistic regression indicate the overall ability of independent variables to predict the dependent variable outcome and the changes in outcome likelihood (i.e., whether the outcome occurs or not) associated with each individual independent variable. The change from a continuous to categorical dependent variable and subsequent change from standard regression to logistic regression results in substantial changes to model estimation and interpretation. Although not detailed here, comprehensive descriptions of logistic regression are available in a range of resources spanning from approachable to technical (e.g., Agresti, 2019; Hosmer, Lemeshow, & Sturdivant, 2013).

2 When Multiple Linear Regression Analysis is Appropriate in Mixed Methods Research

The first and most important factor in determining the appropriateness of multiple linear regression in a mixed analysis is proper alignment between the capabilities of multiple regression and the study purpose. Any study that investigates relationships among variables is a candidate to employ regression. This, of course, includes many studies and demonstrates the wide-ranging applicability of regression approaches. Part of the alignment between study purpose and regression capabilities is matching the independent and dependent variables of interest with the regression model utilized in the analysis. For example, multiple linear regression requires a continuous dependent variable but accommodates a wide spectrum of independent variables, including those from quantitized qualitative data.

If these broad considerations indicate multiple regression as being appropriate, then it becomes necessary to check the specific assumptions and effectiveness of the multiple linear regression model. The four primary assumptions of the regression model necessary for accurate inferences are linearity, independence, homoscedasticity, and normality. Assumptions checks are typically completed after conducting the regression analysis as they require an examination of the residuals or errors produced during model estimation. The independence assumption is often an exception because assessing the independence of observations is possible in the research design phase (i.e., before data collection). These assumption checks are rarely included in published works but some mention of their consideration is warranted (see Field et al., 2012). Any regression analysis should also note the effectiveness of the regression model. A common approach is to report R^2 and/or adjusted R^2 values (i.e., coefficient of multiple determination), which indicates a regression model's ability to predict or to explain variance in the dependent variable.

Finally, multiple linear regression has sample size requirements to ensure that it consistently detects statistically significant relationships between the dependent variable and the independent variables but these requirements depend on characteristics of the regression model and studied sample (e.g., Cohen, 1988). For example, a multiple regression model including many independent variables requires a larger sample than does bivariate regression to yield adequate statistical power (i.e., 80% probability of detecting significant relationships) at a nominal level of statistical significance (e.g., Type I error or α is 0.05). When possible, an a priori statistical power analysis should be conducted to determine adequate sample size or an analogous method to investigate the sufficiency of the sample size (e.g., minimum detectable effect size). The process to determine statistical power is relatively simple with easily accessible and freely available software programs such as G*Power (Faul, Erdfelder, Buchner, & Lang, 2009).

3 Technical Outline of Multiple Linear Regression Analysis with Qualitative Data for Mixed Methods Research

The following technical outline begins with bivariate regression and then details multiple linear regression providing foundational technical knowledge for the application of regression-based approaches, including advanced approaches such as hierarchical linear modeling. This technical outline covers regression equations, interpreting results, estimating regression parameters, and assessing the regression model and its results. Examples are incorporated to improve understanding and include variables from quantitized data.

Bivariate Regression

The foundational form of regression is a line that best represents the relationship between an independent variable and a dependent variable. As such, the formula for bivariate regression is based on a linear function such that

$$Y_i = b_0 + b_1 X_i + e_i. \qquad (1)$$

A line is fit with an intercept b_0 and a slope b_1 that best captures the relationship between X, the independent variable, and Y, the dependent variable. The b_0 and b_1 terms are known as the regression coefficients (sometimes represented by B) and have a numerical subscript for identification. The outcome of each individual (Y_i) is not perfectly predicted by X_i so a residual or error term (e_i) is required to capture any deviations. The subscript i on these terms identifies specific individuals and their specific X, Y, and residual values. Assuming they meet the requirements for the regression model, Y and/or X can be a quantitized version of qualitative data.

Consider a working example from the empirical demonstration in this chapter to give these regression concepts a tangible meaning. Program implementation problems is a dichotomous independent variable coded as *1-Presence* or *0-Absence of program implementation problems* and was derived from interview data (i.e., quantitized data).[3] The dependent variable of interest is *School-level socioeconomic status* operationalized as the percentage of students in a school in the National School Lunch Program (NSLP). The coding of the implementation variable with a 1 or 0 is known as dummy coding and is necessary to conduct the regression analysis. Dummy coding involves the assignment of numerical values to categories. With a dichotomous or binary variable such as *Implementation problems*, a 0 represents absence of the trait and a 1 represents presence of the trait. The dummy coding process can be extended for categorical variables that have more than two categories. For these variables, each category is separately dummy coded as previously described, creating multiple dummy variables. One category designated as a baseline is represented by zeros in all the dummy coded variable categories (see Hardy [1993] for a detailed explanation).

Returning to the regression formula presented in Equation 1, the b_0 intercept value indicates where the regression line crosses the y-axis and indicates the value of the dependent variable when the independent variable is zero. The intercept in the working example has substantial meaning as X_i represents program implementation problems at school i coded as *absent*=0 and *present*=1. The intercept is then the average percentage of students in a school in NSLP for schools without implementation problems (i.e., Y when X is 0). If a zero value for X is nonsensical, interpretation of the intercept (b_0) is typically avoided. However, the intercept should always be included in the equation because constraining it to zero (i.e., excluding b_0 from the formula) causes inaccuracies in the other regression coefficients (Baguley, 2012, p. 182).

The regression coefficient for slope (b_1) is often of primary interest because it captures the nature of the relationship between the X and Y variables. A positive b_1 value indicates a positive relationship between X and Y (i.e., increases in X indicate increases in Y), whereas a negative b_1 indicates a negative relationship between X and Y (i.e., increases in X indicate decreases in Y). In our example, a positive b_1 value is expected because implementation problems are likely to be related to higher rates of student enrollment in the NSLP. The b_1 term can be interpreted as the amount of change expected in Y given a 1-unit increase in X. In our example with a dichotomous variable, b_1 represents the amount of expected change in the percentage of students in the NSLP given the presence of implementation problems.

Finally, the residual term e_i, captures the differences between the predicted dependent variable value and the actual value. Implementation problems might be related to the percentage of students in the NSLP, although not perfectly. Some schools will have a higher- or lower-than-expected NSLP percentage relative to their implementation levels. There are a few implications worth noting here. Every individual case will have an e_i term. A small e_i value indicates that the dependent variable was predicted precisely, whereas larger e_i values suggest less precise prediction. A broader implication is that e_i values play a crucial role in determining the quality of the regression analysis, accuracy of prediction, and even the performance of individual independent variables.

Multiple Regression

The bivariate regression formula in Equation 1 can be extended to accommodate two predictors such that

$$Y_i = b_0 + b_1 X_{1i} + b_2 X_{2i} + e_i \qquad (2)$$

or more than two predictors

$$Y_i = b_0 + b_1 X_{1i} + b_2 X_{2i} + \ldots + b_n X_{ni} + e_i. \qquad (3)$$

Equations 2 and 3 represent a specific and general formula for multiple linear regression. Every predictor (X_n) has a matching coefficient (b_n) that captures the relationship between X_n and the outcome (Y) while controlling for or holding constant the effects of other independent variables. In other words, b_n is the unique relationship between X_n and Y. Predicted dependent variable values are now a combination of all the independent variable-coefficient products and a residual term (e_i). In terms from our example, we can add the percentage students of color in a school (X_2) as a second independent variable to help explain Y, which, again, is the percentage of students in a school in the NSLP. The b_1 term represents the relationship between implementation problems (X_1) and percentage of students in the NSLP while controlling for or holding constant the effect of the percentage of students of color in a school, whereas b_2 represents the relationship between the percentage students of color in a school (X_2) and the percentage of students in the NSLP (Y) while controlling for or holding constant the effect of implementation problems. The residual, e_i, captures any deviation between the predicted percentage of students in the NSLP and actual percentage of students in the NSLP for school i. Note the additional language necessary to interpret the regression coefficients (e.g., the relationship between X and Y while controlling for or holding constant the other independent variables). In a multiple linear regression model the regression coefficients associated with the independent variables (e.g., b_1 and b_2) capture the unique relationship between X and Y. The influence of the other independent variables is accounted for when determining these coefficients—hence the additional language indicating a conditional relationship.

Multiple linear regression models can include many independent variables, requiring a process to identify the variables to include for analysis (i.e., model selection or model building). This process is both important and difficult. For example, a plethora of qualitative data may produce many quantitized variables. Which of these variables should be included in the regression model? Unfortunately, there are no universal guidelines to dictate variable selection across all possible contexts. Autonomous methods have been detailed in literature (stepwise, all-subsets, hierarchical) but also have well established issues (e.g., Hurvich & Tsai, 1989). Rather, the process requires substantive expertise while evaluating empirical, theoretical, and practical considerations. We recommend the general guidelines presented in Gelman and Hill (2007, p. 69) and the criteria for a good regression model described by Baguley (2012, p. 457). Briefly, these criteria suggest that models be fairly robust to violations of any assumption, have strong theoretical justification, and produce reasonable predictions.

Estimating Multiple Regression Equations

The process of determining the best numerical values for each parameter of interest (e.g., b_0, b_1, and b_2 in Equation 2) is referred to as estimating the regression model. So, how does one determine the best values? Where do these numbers come from? Recall, the foundational form of regression is a line that best represents the relationship between the independent variable and the dependent variable. For bivariate regression, the line should run through or near as many data points as possible. This is often referred to as fit or fitting a regression line. In more technical language, the best regression line (e.g., values for b_0, b_1, and b_2 in Equation 2) minimizes the residuals in the model (e). The most prevalent method for estimating the bivariate and multiple regression models described here is ordinary least squares (OLS). OLS minimizes the squared distance between the predicted values of the dependent variable $(\hat{Y})$ and the actual or observed values (Y). Further technical details require some algebra and calculus; therefore, they are omitted here (see Baguley, 2012).

Assessing Regression Models and Independent Variables

The regression coefficient values provided by OLS estimation are the best available for the given data but do not indicate the quality of the model or contributions from individual coefficients. In other words, OLS provides the best values for a regression model but does not indicate the predictive or explanatory ability of the model or individual independent variables. A popular measure of the degree that a model fits the data (i.e., goodness-of-fit) applicable in bivariate and multiple regression is R^2 (sometimes represented by r^2 in bivariate regression). It can vary between 0 and 1, with larger values typically indicating better regression model performance. The R^2 value indicates variation in Y that is accounted for by the regression model such that, at the extremes, a value of 1 indicates the model (i.e., the independent variables) perfectly predicts the dependent variable, whereas a value of 0 indicates the regression model is no better at predicting the dependent variable than using the dependent variable's mean. The steps to determine these R^2 values vary substantially between bivariate and multiple regression but their conceptual meanings are similar, with both indicating how well the X variables predict or explain variation in Y. In multiple linear regression R^2 may be referred to as multiple R^2 and increases as additional independent variables are included in the regression model. Adjusted R^2 avoids this arbitrary inflation by including a penalty for adding independent variables that do not fit the model (i.e., are not a significant predictor of the dependent variable) and is often utilized when considering a model with many independent variables. For a more comprehensive presentation of regression model assessment including considerations for influential cases and outliers, see Baguley (2012).

Assessing individual independent variables and their associated regression coefficients in a multiple regression model can indicate the independent variables contribution to predicting or explaining the dependent variable and its relative importance compared to other independent variables. Unfortunately, a direct comparison of regression coefficient values would not be useful because each regression coefficient (b_n) is a rate based on the accompanying X. Consider two variables measuring an individual's height with an X measured in inches (X_{inches}) and another X measured in feet (X_{feet}). These X values represent the same height but measured on different scales. In a regression equation, assuming a positive relationship between X and Y, b_{inches} would be much smaller than b_{feet} because these values capture the change in Y for every one-inch increase and one-foot increase in X, respectively. To better evaluate the relative importance of each independent variable, regression coefficients and error terms can be standardized. Standardized regression coefficients, often called beta weights (β weights), indicate the predictive or explanatory capacity of the independent variable on a comparable scale. However, when independent variables are correlated, as is the case in almost all social science research, standardized coefficients can be problematic when it comes to directly comparing their values because their values are conditional on other independent variables in the model (Courville & Thompson, 2001). Therefore, it is often beneficial to consider structure coefficients that capture the relationship between the independent variable and predicted values of the dependent variable $(\hat{Y})$, along with standardized coefficients, because this combination of results provides a more complete understanding of the importance of an independent variable to the regression model (Courville & Thompson, 2001; Onwuegbuzie & Daniel, 2003; Thompson & Borrello, 1985).

4 An Empirical Demonstration of Multiple Linear Regression Analysis with Qualitative Data for Mixed Methods Research

Assessing the Research Context

Research on implementation fidelity of educational programs has indicated several consistent themes. First, training and information dissemination alone are not considered sufficient to ensure adequate implementation of educational innovations. Teachers often need ongoing support, coaching, mentoring, and multi-tiered systems of support (Fixsen, Naoom, Blase, Friedman, & Wallace, 2005). The data for this example come from statewide implementation of a formative assessment program to support the growth and development of kindergarten children. The teachers involved in the study were provided with three levels of support after initial training. Each school was encouraged to form a School Implementation Team (SIT) to support teachers. Each school district was encouraged to form a District Implementation Team (DIT), and all districts had access to regional consultants who support multiple districts. Fidelity of implementation varied widely from teacher to teacher and from school to school, as did the effectiveness of the SITs and DITs. Some schools and districts did not even establish functioning implementation teams.

Data Sources and Design

This mixed methods research study involved the use of three sources of data to identify schools and districts that faced substantial implementation challenges. First, quantitative child assessment data were obtained for every kindergarten child in the state. Next, quantitative administrative data that include a rich variety of structural features for each elementary school were obtained from state databases and public sources. Finally, qualitative key informant interview data were captured from the regional consultants. These key informants were very experienced former teachers who work for the state education agency. They provide technical assistance to schools and districts, particularly with the implementation of new initiatives. These qualitative data were quantitized into a school-level indicator of whether or not the regional consultants identified substantial challenges with implementation at each school. For a more complete explanation of the data sources, sample, and context of this study, see the chapter in this volume on multi-level modeling.

Prior to conducting the multi-level models, researchers conducted a series of exploratory analyses to become familiar with the data sources. One of these exploratory tasks was to investigate structural differences between schools with no identified implementation issues and those with implementation challenges. Independent samples t tests were conducted using the quantitized key informant information (0=no identified implementation problems, 1=implementation challenges) as the grouping variable, and each of the quantitative school structural characteristics as dependent variables. The research question for these analyses was as follows: To what degree do schools for which the quantitized key informant data indicate substantial implementation challenges systematically different in structural characteristics from the schools not identified by key informants as struggling with implementation?

One of the results from these analyses indicated that schools in the positive implementation group had, on average, 74.9% of their students qualifying for the NSLP ($SD = 27.1$). Schools identified as having implementation challenges had, on average, 86.0% qualifying ($SD = 17.9$), and this difference of 11.1 percentage points was statistically significant ($t_{(358)} = 2.097$, $p = .037$). This difference can be expressed as a standardized mean difference effect size ($d = .41$). Next, we used multiple regression to examine whether this association would remain intact after controlling for other school structural characteristics.

Model Specification and Research Question

Multiple regression can, in general, be used in mixed methods research to examine such relationships in the context of controlling for covariates. Both quantitative variables and quantitized qualitative information can serve as covariates, explanatory variables, and dependent variables in such a model. In this example, we used quantitized key informant interview data as the explanatory variable. We used several school structural characteristics from administrative data as covariates, and the school level percentage of children enrolled in the NSLP as the dependent variable. This example examined the following research question: To what extent is school implementation level, as indicated by the quantitized key informant data, associated with the percentage of a school population that is enrolled in the NSLP, after controlling for school structural characteristics?

We identified five school structural characteristics that could be related to both school poverty and implementation fidelity: school percentage of students of color, average daily attendance, teacher turnover rate, school percentage of teachers with 0–3 years of experience, and whether or not a school had a new principal since the beginning of the study.

Multiple Regression Analyses with Quantitized Data

The results (see Table 7.1) indicate that two of the covariates, school percentage of kindergarten students who are students of color and average daily student attendance percentage, were statistically significantly associated with the school percentage of children enrolled in the NSLP. Notice that we only reported unstandardized regression coefficients, which is justified in the context of this exploratory analysis but also ensures the example remains as approachable as possible. In settings that require a more detailed understanding of independent variables and their relative and absolute performance, both standardized and structure coefficients are suitable.

The R^2 value for the first step in the sequenced, two-step process, with the covariates only in the model, was .414 (adjusted R^2 = .405). The average daily attendance was negatively associated with family poverty level. Exploration of the distribution of the reported attendance levels revealed that 86.3% of schools reported values of 94% to 96%. The bivariate scatterplot indicated that there was a subset of schools with very high poverty levels (99%–100%) that also had the lowest reported attendance levels (90%–91%), which would explain the negative association. However, 2% of schools reported average attendance values of 99% or 100%. These high values were not only uncommon, but might be implausible and might represent school-level administrative challenges with collecting valid data. Such administrative difficulties were more likely to occur in schools with high concentrations of family poverty, and in schools identified by the quantitized key informant data as having implementation challenges.

The quantitized explanatory variable (recall: high vs. low implementation as determined by consultant interviews) was entered into the model in the second step of the sequenced, two-step process. This effect showed a statistically significant positive association with family poverty levels (t = 2.274, p = .024). The coefficient was 9.391, indicating that schools identified as having implementation problems are expected to have a percentage of students enrolled in the NSLP that is approximately 9 percentage points higher than schools not identified in this category. This value was similar to, but a little smaller than the 11.1 percentage point gap identified with the independent samples t test. The R^2 value for this model was .422, indicating only a 1 percentage point increase in variance accounted for (adjusted R^2 = .412). However, this R^2 change was statistically significant.

It is always useful, when using regression as a tool for mixed methods research, to examine the diagnostic information related to assumptions and conditions for inference. In this case, there was no discernable pattern in the residual plot, indicating both the appropriateness and reasonableness of fitting a linear model to these data and the absence of any unusually influential data points. The residuals displayed a distribution that was approximately normal as indicated by both a histogram and normal probability plot. There were no outliers, as indicated by no standardized residuals greater than 3 or less than −3.

After completing the regression analysis, a very useful interpretation aid in mixed methods research can be the creation of a contingency table. This method allows the researcher to organize the model predicted values for the dependent variable so they can be examined across varying levels of the covariates and/or explanatory variables. This process can be implemented easily by entering the full regression equation into a spreadsheet cell. The equation can be set up to access values for each of the covariates and explanatory variables from specific adjacent cells in the spreadsheet. This simple strategy allows the researcher to intentionally manipulate the values of

TABLE 7.1

Association Between Family Poverty Percentages and Key Informant Ratings of Implementation Challenges

		B	se	t	p
Intercept		366.960	86.024	4.266	0.000
Covariates	School % of kindergarten students who are students of color	0.605	0.047	12.802	0.000
	Average daily student attendance percentage	−3.361	0.901	−3.730	0.000
	Teacher turnover rate, % teachers who left the previous year	−0.163	0.143	−1.140	0.255
	School % of teachers who have 0–3 years of experience	−0.130	0.104	−1.246	0.214
	New principal since start of study	1.753	2.279	0.769	0.442
Explanatory variable	Consultant indicates school has implementation problems	9.391	4.130	2.274	0.024

the covariates and explanatory variables to create the model estimates for specific combinations of conditions.

In this case, we were interested in what the regression model would yield as the expected value for schools with varying structural characteristics for the group identified by the quantitized variable as having implementation challenges, as compared to the schools that were not so identified. We chose to systematically vary the percentage of kindergarten students in the school who were children of color. The statewide average for this statistically significant covariate was 52.2% ($SD = 27.1$). We also chose to utilize fixed values of 50%, close to the state average, and values of 30% and 70% as realistic high and low values that occur in real schools within the middle two standard deviations away from the mean of schools in the state. All three school conditions are realistic, would be encountered by state regional early childhood consultants, and do not represent artificial or extreme values. For the remaining covariates, we chose to hold the values constant at the state average: attendance ($M = 94.93\%$, $SD = 1.24$), turnover ($M = 13.37\%$, $SD = 8.49$), percentage of teachers with 0–3 years of experience ($M = 22.86\%$, SD = 12.85), and new principal since the start of the study (38.0% of the schools had a new principal).

Table 7.2 shows these expected values for the percentage of students enrolled in the NSLP for the two implementation levels in combination with varying levels of the percentage of kindergarten children of color. These values answer the following question: Based on our modelling, what would we expect the percentage of children who are enrolled in the NSLP to be for schools with varying percentages of kindergarten children of color across the two levels of the quantitized variable, while controlling for the other covariates in the model?

The expectation for the highest percentage (95.16%) was for schools where 70% of the kindergarten students are children of color, and the quantitized key informant data indicate substantial implementation challenges. The expectation for the lowest value (61.57%) was for schools where 30% of the kindergarten students are children of color, and the quantitized key informant data indicate no implementation challenges.

This finding indicates a substantial difference (33.59 percentage points) in family poverty levels between two subgroups of schools. Furthermore, from a mixed methods research perspective, these subgroups of schools were identified by a combination of quantitized key informant data and school structural characteristics available from administrative data sources. Schools with high concentrations of students from economically disadvantages backgrounds often require different supports for teachers who are in the process of implementing a challenging new innovation. Furthermore, teachers might struggle with implementation due to a lack of available assessment and instructional resources that are culturally relevant to their students. This application of multiple regression illustrates how subgroups of schools needing additional supports for successful implementation were identified via a mixed methods research approach, and those subgroups could not have been recognized using quantitative administrative data alone.

5 Suggested Applications of Regression Analysis in Mixed Methods Research

We highlight several suggested applications for regression under various conceptualizations of mixed methods research. Although not comprehensive, the examples provide guidance for researchers interested in using regression with qualitative data that have been quantitized in mixed methods research. First, we noted that regression easily accommodates multiple data types, including quantitized qualitative data, which makes it well suited for investigations when the use of multiple types of data (e.g., quantitative and qualitative data) constitutes mixed methods research. Second, regression has several prevalent applications in the analysis of mixed methods studies employing both quantitative and qualitative approaches. Under this conceptualization of mixed methods research, regression is typically classified as a quantitative approach and is, therefore, applied in the quantitative phase of the broader mixed methods research study. The regression analysis may occur before, after, or during the qualitative phase.

When regression serves as the initial analysis in mixed methods research, it is followed by a qualitative phase. Here, qualitative methods can further explore the relationships identified in the regression analysis, further investigate the relationships, or provide a method to better understand the relationships. For example, randomized control trials can be analyzed using multiple regression with follow-up interviews to help elucidate the success or failure of the treatment (e.g., program, policy, or intervention). Regression applied in parallel with a qualitative approach allows a concurrent investigation of variable relationships. Here, each methodological component provides a unique perspective on the pertinent research questions and results may align or diverge. For example, results from a regression analysis based on survey data may indicate a non-significant relationship between variables while observations and interviews indicate a strong relationship when considering more personalized experiences (e.g., divergent results). Regression analysis following a qualitative research phase serves as a follow-up to investigate alternative aspects of the research questions, or the regression analysis can be formed as a direct result of qualitative findings. In the latter capacity, the regression model itself (i.e., the independent and dependent variables) might be identified in the qualitative phase with the regression analysis serving to further investigate and support the relationships identified in the qualitative phase. For example, qualitative analysis of interview data may suggest race,

TABLE 7.2

Model Estimated NSLP Percentage by Percentage of Students of Color

	% Students of Color		
	30%	50%	70%
Quantitized key informant data indicates implementation issues	70.96	83.06	95.16
Quantitized key informant does not indicate implementation issues	61.57	73.67	85.77

Note: NSLP = National School Lunch Program.

gender, and socioeconomic status are related to an outcome of interest. Based on these themes, a regression model with race, gender, and socioeconomic status as the independent variables would be analyzed.

6 Strengths and Limitations of Regression Analysis in Mixed Methods Research

In terms of mixed analyses with quantitized data, the flexibility of regression can be paired with the emergent and flexible properties of most forms of qualitative inquiry. Indeed, this can represent among the most flexible forms of analyses that we can think of, and integrating regression with qualitative inquiry can yield multiple forms of synergy. In the example we provided earlier, we simply do not know how we could have reached the type of understanding about schools in the sample that we achieved had we not used this approach.

Although flexible, using multiple linear regression with quantitized data in mixed analyses requires a high degree of knowledge and skills related to qualitative inquiry, regression, and mixed methodology. Such a combination is unlikely in one individual and even difficult to address using a team of researchers. This might limit the scope of studies that employ multiple linear regression with quantitized data in mixed analyses to larger scale studies and/or research teams with greater resources. We believe this limitation further illustrates the importance of this chapter because it directly addresses barriers to these analyses caused by limited knowledge and skills.

It is also worth noting that the quantitizing of qualitative data inherently reduces the richness or depth of information available from the data. We have stated our case that the compromise between reduction in depth and increase in breadth of information produced by regression with quantitized data is beneficial. However, this is somewhat dependent on the rigor of the qualitative analysis because the quantitized variables are a direct result of the qualitative analysis. Put differently, the value of conducting regression analysis with quantitized data in a mixed methods study is dependent on the underlying qualitative analysis and quantitizing procedure.

7 Resources for Learning More About Regression Analysis with Qualitative Data that Have Been Quantitized

In this final section, we provide a list of supplemental resources for advancing knowledge related to regression with qualitative data that have been quantitized. Resources are grouped by the concept they address.

Application and Approachable Resources

Our first collection of resources was procured for individuals still developing knowledge about regression approaches and are seeking a more thorough description of this technique. Cohen, Cohen, West, and Aiken (2003) and Miles and Shevlin (2001) provide a broad introduction to regression and related correlation analysis, whereas the resources from Field (2018) and Field et al. (2012) provide a similarly broad introduction but tailor instruction to a specified software package. All of these resources help one appropriately conduct a regression analysis. We include Hardy (1993) because the use of dummy variables or dummy coding is often necessary for categorical variables derived from quantitized data.

Technical Resources

To ensure our presentation of regression was as approachable as possible, we severely limited our discussion of technical aspects related to the regression model, analysis, interpretation, and assumptions. To supplement these discussions, we recommend three texts. First, Baguley (2012) provides a much more technical description of regression and more advanced techniques while still employing many examples and applications. Gelman and Hill (2007) represents a more technical work that also extends into considerations of multilevel and hierarchical models. Finally, we include Rencher and Christensen (2012) as a technical resource that specifically extends into multivariate regression.

Logistic Regression Resources

We noted a clear distinction between linear regression and more complex regression approaches for a categorical dependent variable (e.g., logistic regression). We suggest several resources for logistic regression and other regression approaches when the dependent variable is categorical because quantitizing qualitative data may produce categorical outcomes of interest. In these cases, it is useful to consult Agresti (2019) and Hosmer et al. (2013) regarding the application and interpretation of logistic regression.

Quantitizing, and Mixed and Qualitative Analyses Resources

The resources recommended thus far have supplemented our presentation of regression approaches, whereas this final set of resources is dedicated to quantitizing, mixed analyses, and qualitative analyses. We briefly summarized quantitizing and justified its use. However, those looking for additional information can begin with Sandelowski et al. (2009). We note resources to expand on the discussion of qualitative methods (Leech & Onwuegbuzie, 2008; Miles & Huberman; 1994) and mixed methods (Newman et al., 2015; Onwuegbuzie & Teddlie, 2003) for those looking to better understand regression in the context qualitative and mixed methods.

NOTES

1. These are formal terms from what we argue is seminal mixed methods literature. *Triangulation* refers to comparing findings from one form of analysis to other forms of analyses; *complementarity* entails seeking elaboration, illustration, and enhancement by using different forms of analyses; *development* means using findings from one type of analysis to help inform results from other types; *initiation*

deals with searching for and addressing contradictions and paradoxes across different analyses; and, finally, *expansion* involves attempting to expand the breadth of a study by using multiple forms of data analyses (Greene, Caracelli, & Graham, 1989).

2. Moving forward, the form "quantitized" is used (as in, regression or hierarchical linear modeling with quantitized data) to highlight the idea that what were once formally qualitative data were transformed to quantitative data. This is to be distinguished from data that a researcher has not considered analyzing with qualitative procedures.

3. The chapter in this text covering hierarchical linear modeling provides an example of quantitized dependent variable data.

REFERENCES

Agresti, A. (2019). *An introduction to categorical data analysis* (3rd ed.). Hoboken, NJ: Wiley-Interscience.

Baguley, T. (2012). *Serious stats: A guide to advanced statistics for the behavioral sciences*. London, England: Springer.

Bazeley, P. (2003). Computerized data analysis for mixed methods research. In A. Tashakkori & C. Teddlie (Eds.), *Handbook of mixed methods in social and behavioral research* (pp. 385–422). Thousand Oaks, CA: Sage.

Berg, B. (2001). *Qualitative research methods for the social sciences* (4th ed.). Boston, MA: Allyn & Bacon.

Bobko, P. (2001). *Correlation and regression: Applications for industrial organizational psychology and management* (2nd ed.). Thousand Oaks, CA: Sage.

Cohen, J. (1988). *Statistical power analysis for the behavioral sciences* (2nd ed.). Hillsdale, NJ: Erlbaum.

Cohen, J., Cohen, P., West, S. G., & Aiken, L. S. (2003). *Applied multiple regression/correlation analysis for the behavioral sciences* (3rd ed.). Mahwah, NJ: Erlbaum Associates.

Courville, T., & Thompson, B. (2001). Use of structure coefficients in published multiple regression articles: β is not enough. *Educational and Psychological Measurement, 61*, 229–248. doi:10.1177/0013164401612006

Dillman, D. A., Smyth, J. D., & Christian, L. M. (2009). *Internet, mail and mixed-mode surveys: The tailored design method* (3rd ed.). Hoboken, NJ: Wiley.

Faul F., Erdfelder E., Buchner A., & Lang A. G. (2009). Statistical power analyses using G*Power 3.1: Tests for correlation and regression analyses. *Behavior Research Methods. 41*, 1149–1160. doi:10.3758/BRM.41.4.1149

Field, A. (2018). *Discovering statistics using SPSS* (5th ed.). Thousand Oaks, CA: Sage.

Field, A., Miles, J., & Field, Z. (2012). *Discovering statistics using R*. London, England: Sage.

Fixsen, D., Naoom, S., Blase, K., Friedman, R., & Wallace, F. (2005). *Implementation research: A synthesis of the literature*. Tampa, FL: University of South Florida, Louis de la Parte Florida Mental Health Institute, National Implementation Research Network.

Gelman, A., & Hill, J. (2007) *Data analysis using regression and multilevel/hierarchical models*. Cambridge, England: Cambridge University Press.

Greene, J. C., Caracelli, V. J., & Graham, W. F. (1989). Toward a conceptual framework for mixed-method evaluation designs. *Educational Evaluation and Policy Analysis, 11*, 255–274. doi:10.3102/01623737011003255

Hardy, M. A. (1993). *Quantitative applications in the social sciences: Regression with dummy variables*. Newbury Park, CA: Sage.

Hitchcock, J. H., Nastasi, B. K., Dai, D., Newman, J., Jayasena, A., Bernstein-Moore, R., Sarkar, S., & Varjas, K. (2005). Illustrating a mixed-method approach for validating culturally specific constructs. *Journal of School Psychology, 43*, 259–278. doi:10.1016/j.jsp.2005.04.007

Hitchcock, J. H., & Onwuegbuzie, A. J. (2020). Developing mixed methods crossover analysis approaches. *Journal of Mixed Methods Research 14*, 63–83. doi:10.1177/1558689819841782

Hosmer, D. W., Lemeshow, S., & Sturdivant, R. X. (2013). *Applied logistic regression*. New York, NY: Wiley-Interscience.

Hurvich, C., & Tsai, C. (1989). Regression and time series model selection in small samples. *Biometrika, 76*, 297–307. doi:10.1093/biomet/76.2.297

Kelley K., & Bolin J. H. (2013) Multiple regression. In T. Teo (Ed.), *Handbook of quantitative methods for educational research* (pp. 71–102). Rotterdam, NL: SensePublishers.

Lacroux, A., & Matin-Lacroux, C. (2019). Spelling error perception during personnel selection: A mixed methods study of recruiters' judgments using lexicometric analysis. *International Journal of Multiple Research Approaches, 11*, 183–202. doi:10.29034/ijmra.v11n2a4

Leech, N. L., & Onwuegbuzie, A. J. (2008). Qualitative data analysis: A compendium of techniques and a framework for selection for school psychology research and beyond. *School Psychology Quarterly, 23*, 587–604. doi:10.1037/1045-3830.23.4.587

Miles, M., & Huberman, A. M. (1994). *Qualitative data analysis: An expanded sourcebook* (2nd ed.). Thousand Oaks, CA: Sage.

Miles, J., & Shevlin, M. (2001). *Applying regression and correlation: A guide for students and researchers*. London, England: Sage.

Newman, I., Onwuegbuzie, A. J., & Hitchcock, J. H. (2015). Using the General Linear Model to facilitate the full integration of qualitative and quantitative analysis: The potential to improve prediction and theory building and testing. *General Linear Model Journal, 41*(1), 12–28.

Onwuegbuzie, A. J. (2003). Effect sizes in qualitative research: A prolegomenon. *Quality & Quantity: International Journal of Methodology, 37*, 393–409. doi:10.1023/A:1027379223537

Onwuegbuzie, A. J., & Combs, J. P. (2010). Emergent data analysis techniques in mixed methods research: A synthesis. In A. Tashakkori & C. Teddlie (Eds.), *Handbook of mixed methods in social and behavioral research* (2nd ed., pp. 397–430). Thousand Oaks, CA: Sage.

Onwuegbuzie, A. J., & Daniel, L. G. (2003, February 12). Typology of analytical and interpretational errors in quantitative and qualitative educational research. *Current Issues in Education* [On-line], 6(2). Retrieved from https://cie.asu.edu/ojs/index.php/cieatasu/article/view/1609/651

Onwuegbuzie, A. J., & Leech, N. L. (2019). On qualitizing. *International Journal of Multiple Research Approaches, 11*, 98–131. doi:10.29034/ijmra.v11n2editorial2

Onwuegbuzie, A. J., & Teddlie, C. (2003). A framework for analyzing data in mixed methods research. In A. Tashakkori & C. Teddlie (Eds.), *Handbook of mixed methods in social and behavioral research* (pp. 351–383). Thousand Oaks, CA: Sage.

Pedhazur, E. J. (1997). *Multiple regression in behavioral research: Explanation and prediction.* Belmont, CA: Wadsworth.

Rencher, A., & Christensen, W. (2012). *Methods of multivariate analysis.* New York, NY: Wiley.

Sandelowski, M., Voils, C. I., & Knafl, G. (2009). On quantitizing. *Journal of Mixed Methods Research, 3,* 208–222. doi:10.1177/1558689809334210

Tai, B., & Machin, D. (2014). *Regression methods for medical research.* Chichester, West Sussex, England: John Wiley and Sons.

Tashakkori, A., & Teddlie, C. (1998). *Mixed methodology: Combining qualitative and quantitative approaches.* Applied Social Research Methods Series (Vol. 46). Thousand Oaks, CA: Sage.

Teddlie, C., & Tashakkori, A. (2009). *Foundations of mixed methods research: Integrating quantitative and qualitative techniques in the social and behavioral sciences.* Thousand Oaks, CA: Sage.

Thompson, B., & Borrello, G. (1985). The importance of structure coefficients in regression research. *Educational and Psychological Measurement, 45,* 203–209. doi:10.1177/001316448504500202

8

Structural Equation Modeling with Qualitative Data that Have Been Quantitized

David Newman and Shannon Constantinides

Following the structure utilized throughout this text, this chapter is organized into seven sections: (a) Defining Structural Equation Modeling (SEM), (b) When Use of Structural Equation Modeling is Appropriate in MMR, (c) Technical Outline of Structural Equation Modeling for MMR (d) Examples of SEM with Qualitative Data From the Literature, and (e) Ideas for Suggested Applications, followed by a review of the (f) Strengths and Limitations of SEM, and (g) Resources for Additional Learning of Specific SEM Techniques. It is important that the reader understands that qualitative data can include text data from interviews, themes, observational notes, or images. All of these data are *quantitized* by being assigned some numerical value.

1 Definition of Structural Equation Modeling

SEM represents a family of techniques that are frequently employed in the behavioral, health, and social sciences to explain or test theories about or including inherently unobservable (i.e., latent) or unquantifiable variables (Rahman, Shah, & Rasli, 2015). SEM is employed to test the fit of an operationalized theoretical model. Many times, these theoretical models are derived from prior qualitative research as well as from studies that utilize themes that emerge from the qualitative phase of a mixed methods research study, to create items that measure the desired latent (unobservable) construct. Tashakkori and Newman (2010), for example, stated that in exploratory sequential mixed methods research, qualitative inferences made from the first phase of a study can be used to identify quantitative indicators employed in the second phase of a study as a means of assessing the validity of a theory in terms of its overall fit. This is one demonstration of how theories that are derived from qualitative data can be assessed using SEM. This chapter, however, expands past that particular use of qualitative data to explore using *quantitized* data in various types of structural models. These types of quantitized data can potentially explain a larger proportion of the variance in both the measurement and the structural models. The quantitized qualitative data can come from texts, images, artifacts, sounds, and so forth.

One of the primary purposes of qualitative research is to develop theories. In this regard, SEM pairs well with mixed methods research because it has traditionally been considered a theory-testing methodology, wherein the researcher has been tasked with identifying the underlying congruency between the idea of a theory and the "reality the theory purports to represent" (Hogan & Schmidt, 2002, p. 620). The purpose of SEM is to test the fit of an operationalized theory and to assess whether or not it is an "accurate representation of the empirical world" (Hogan & Schmidt, 2002, p. 620).

The foundations of structural equation modeling started with Spearman's (1904) attempt to identify different dimensions of intelligence in order to generate an overall general intelligence factor. In the early 1930's, Thurstone (1934) developed multi-factor analysis and factor rotations, which became modern-day factor analysis. In 1921, after the development of Spearman's attempt to identify general intelligence and before Thurstone's development of multi-factor analysis, Wright developed a technique that represented a series of correlations among associated variables to help reflect the phenomena of interest. This technique has been termed path analysis, which consists only of manifest (i.e., observed) variables (Byrne, 2016). Despite the fact that many researchers were working on developing this technique simultaneously, Wright's research provided the groundwork for modern-day SEM. Wright's (1921) work was further developed by Jöreskog (1970), which combined path analysis and factor analysis. In 1972, Jöreskog and Van Thillo created LISREL, a well-known program that could analyze the combination of path analysis and factor analysis. Although researchers working the field of psychology were the earliest adopters of SEM, these techniques are now more widely and commonly used in educational, social science, behavioral science, healthcare and medical science, marketing, and economic research. In addition, there are now many statistical packages beyond LISREL that can run SEM procedures, including AMOS, STATA, EQS, R, M-plus, and SAS.

As mentioned earlier, SEM is a family of statistical techniques that allow researchers to assess theoretical models by testing the relationships between observed variables and unobservable latent variables (constructs) and the overall fit of the data to the theoretical model. The SEM family of techniques includes various forms of path analysis, confirmatory factor analysis, latent variable structural modeling, and latent growth modeling or latent growth curve models (Brown, 2015; Escobar, 2010). Kline (2016) simplified the categorization of SEM techniques by stating that, historically, factor analysis (in this case, confirmatory factor analysis) deals with measurement, path analysis assesses structure, and latent growth modeling deals with changes over time. Table 8.1 is a summary of the SEM categorization outlined by Brown (2015) and Escobar (2010). These SEM techniques will be discussed after a brief

TABLE 8.1

Structural Equation Modeling Techniques

Basic Types of SEM Techniques	Brief Explanation of Technique
Path Analysis (structure)	Used to describe directional dependent relationships between variables; may include a mediation model, wherein the path between a first and third variable is mediated by a second (intermediary) variable. All variables are observed.
Confirmatory Factor Analysis (measurement)	Hypothesis driven, data reduction technique used to test the directional relationships between observed variables and unobserved constructs; almost always used in psychometric evaluation of test instruments (Brown, 2015).
Latent Variable Structure Modeling (structure with latent variables)	Causal models with latent variables are a combination of path analysis and confirmatory factor analysis. It has been called a hybrid model. In essence, the measurement model is first estimated and the correlations or covariance matrix between constructs or factors then serves as input to estimate the structural coefficients between constructs or latent variables. In actuality, both models are simultaneously estimated by structural equation modeling.
Latent Growth Models (changes over time)	Also called growth curve analysis, this model of SEM allows for observation of changes in variables over time.

review of some common symbols used in SEM diagrams and a list of common terms and concepts.

Although it might be somewhat of an oversimplification, researchers can think of SEM techniques as a series of regression models used to make causal inferences or build causal models about unobservable or theoretical variables. By using SEM, researchers can test for covariance structures among observed variables and latent (unobserved) constructs being tested in the theoretical model. There are two common ways to represent structural equations models: (a) mathematically (like a series of regressions), or (b) graphically. Because this chapter is not focusing on the mathematical formulas but instead uses graphical representation of SEM to enhance understanding, a brief review of the symbols and shapes are required (see Table 8.2).

TABLE 8.2

SEM Symbols

Symbols	Represents in the SEM
○	Latent or unobserved variable (construct)
□	Measurable observed variables (predictors or covariate)
→	Direct relationships
↶	Correlated terms
X	Variables in the model
e	Error of the observed variables in relationship to the latent construct
R	Error of the one latent construct in relationship to another latent construct

TABLE 8.3

Key SEM Terms

Key SEM Terms	Definitions
Structural Coefficient	Similar to a regression coefficient, it is the amount of effect of one variable upon another.
Exogenous Variables	Similar to independent/ test/ intervention variables.
Endogenous Variables	Similar to dependent/ outcome variables.
Effect	Cause (could be indirect, direct and total).
Direct Effect	The effect of an exogenous (independent) variable on an endogenous (dependent) variable.
Indirect Effect	The effect of an exogenous (independent) variable on an endogenous (dependent) variable through a mediating variable.
Total Effect	The sum of both the indirect and direct effects.
Identified Model	Similar to goodness of fit; the model's parameters are explained by a unique solution.
Over-identified Model	A model wherein there is more than enough information in the data to estimate all unconstrained parameters.
Under-identified Model	The data are insufficient to create estimates of each of the parameters in the model, and, as such, the model cannot run.
Just-identified Model	The variance covariance's created from the manifest variables in the model are equal to the number of parameters allowing for estimation for each free parameter.
Observed/Manifest Variable	A manifest variable is a variable or factor that can be directly measured or observed.
Unobserved/Latent/ Construct	Unobserved/theoretical variables.
Path/ Structural Weights	Standardized or unstandardized estimates used, when comparing direct effects on a given endogenous variable. These are conceptually slope or partial regression coefficient.
Goodness of Fit	The degree to which the observed input matrix is predicted by the theoretical model.
Measurement Model	The measurement model represents the theory that specifies how measured variables come together to represent the theory.
Structural Model	Represents the theory that shows how constructs are related to other constructs. Structural equation modeling is also called causal modeling because it tests the proposed causal relationships.

Before the various types of structural equation models are discussed, it would be useful to review a list of common terms found in the SEM literature. As numerous authors and experts have contended in textbook chapters and other publications discussing SEM, one of the difficulties many researchers face while using SEM is the separate technical vernacular that accompanies the family of techniques. It is important to note that although the researcher may be using quantitized data, the terms are different than those used in traditional quantitative analyses. A brief summary of the terms is presented in Table 8.3.

Common SEM Techniques and Their Applications

As mentioned earlier, there are multiple techniques within the SEM family. In what follows, is a brief description of four basic SEM techniques: path analysis (PA), confirmatory factor analysis (CFA), latent (variable) structural equation models (LVSEM), and latent growth models (LGM). Each of these SEM techniques can be enhanced through the use of quantitized data.

Path Analysis

Path analysis (PA) is a special case of SEM that only contains observed variables with a more restrictive set of assumptions. The main difference between PA and LVSEM is that path analysis operates under the assumption that all variables are measured without error, whereas LVSEM involves the use of latent constructs to account for measurement error. As noted earlier, PA is the foundation of modern-day SEM. PA, like SEM, is used to test a theory when all the relationships between the independent (exogenous) variables and the dependent (endogenous) variables have been specified by a causal model. PA typically begins with the creation of a path diagram that specifies each of the relationships (Figure 8.1). In this way, direct effects, indirect effects, and the total effects of each of the variables can be calculated to assess the overall fit of the model as well as to investigate each variable's contribution to the theoretical model. Examples of direct effects depicted in Figure 8.1 are the paths between *Age* to *Health* and *Fitness* to *Health*. Examples of indirect paths in this model are from *Diet* to *Fitness* to *Health*, and from *Activity* to *Weight* to *Health*. Each of these path weights is essentially the partial regression coefficients from a regression analyses. As can be seen in the PA model, both the exogenous and endogenous variables are observed and are a direct measurement.

Confirmatory Factor Analysis

Confirmatory factor analysis (CFA) is a member of the SEM family that deals directly with and is used in the psychometric evaluation of measurement (Brown, 2015). CFA and exploratory factor analysis (EFA) are opposite sides of the same coin, wherein EFA focuses on reducing the large number of variables into a small set of the latent constructs based on the available data. CFA involves taking a theoretically derived model and assessing the overall fit of how well the theoretically assigned variables align with the data. Put more simply, CFA is a multivariate statistical technique that tests the overall fit of how well items or variables measure some underlying latent construct (e.g., depression, anxiety, knowledge). This is one of the most commonly used methods for assessing construct validity. EFA, on the other hand, is more frequently used in the earlier phases of research to examine the relationships among sets of variables without an a priori theory or hypothesis (Pallant, 2016). The exploratory nature of EFA is often helpful in the early development of the theoretical relationship when building the model, whereas CFA provides estimations confirming the fit of these theoretical relationships. It is important that researchers keep in mind that although a theoretical model might represent a good fit, a competing model might work as well as or better. The goal of the researcher is to find support for the theoretically derived/hypothetical model. Caution should be taken, however, with regard to big data. Big data have the potential—especially if streaming—to expand and multiply at a rapid and logarithmic pace. In this case, the researcher may be required to regularly build and test new models, as new insights are gained through the collection of new data. These insights and gains in data volume can then be used to design models in subsequent analyses to improve the model fit. This is the underlying premise that is found in Bayesian analytics, and one application of this will be briefly discussed in a later section.

Additionally, unstructured, qualitative data collected from open-ended questions; notes written by teachers, doctors, nurses, and technicians; industry worker interviews; historical records; images; and many more sources can be coded as binary, ordinal, or nominal categorical and can be included in CFA. Because the unit of analysis for the specific example below is person-level data, the only caveat is that each individual must have data that can be subjected to quantitization. If binary, the individual (participant/sample member) must be coded as a 0 or 1. If coded in an ordinal fashion, each individual must have an ordinal ranking, or a category in nominal categorical data. Figure 8.2 is an example of a CFA measurement model with three latent constructs of overall health and 15 indicator variables (5 per construct). As can be seen, there is a theoretical correlation among the three latent constructs of Emotional, Physical, and Mental Health.

Latent Variable Structural Equation Modeling

Structural equation models are often used to assess unobservable *latent* constructs. SEMs often involve utilization of a measurement model that defines the latent construct through two or more observed variables, and a structural model that defines the relationships among latent variables. Latent variable structural equation models (LVSEM) are causal models that include latent variables. This technique is a hybrid model that mixes path analysis (PA) and confirmatory factor analysis (CFA). Both aspects are run simultaneously; however, one can think of it as a two-step process: (a) estimating the measurement model of the CFA, and (b) then using these parameters as inputs in the structural model. In the model depicted in Figure 8.3, X1-X10 are the indicators used in the measurement component of the model, and Constructs 1–3 (plus the quantitized variables) are the aspect of the structural model with a correlation between Constructs 1 and 2. In this model, e1-e10 represents latent constructs that account for measurement error in the measurement model, wherein R1 represents the error associated with predicting the structural model.

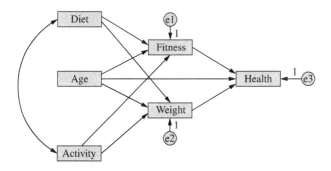

FIGURE 8.1 Path analysis.

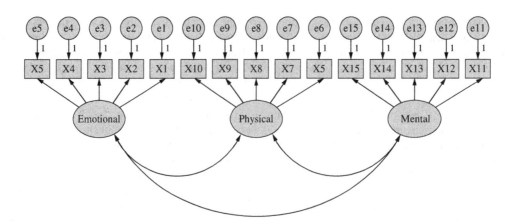

FIGURE 8.2 Graphical representation of a CFA model.

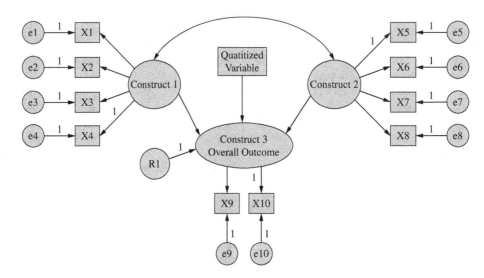

FIGURE 8.3 Latent variable structural equation model.

Latent Growth Modeling

Latent growth modeling (LGM) is the last of the SEM family of techniques to be discussed in this chapter. LGM is a longitudinal data analysis technique that produces estimated growth trajectories for a repeated measures design. These models are similar to the models presented in the following chapter on HLM. As can be seen in Figure 8.4, there are six different time points in this model, wherein there are random intercepts for each treatment group and random slopes, just as a researcher would see in Hierarchical Linear Modeling (HLM). This model also adds a quadratic time construct to assess whether the differential effect of the curvilinear growth trends differs by treatment group or if there is only a linear trend.

There are several advantages to LGM over the other repeated measures analyses. First, LGM has the capability to capture how different conditions can impact individual variability in growth as well as group variability in growth over time. Second, as with HLM, LGM can model both linear and curvilinear relationships by modeling a quadratic time parameter when there are three or more repeated measures. Third, LGM variables can simultaneously be both the independent predictors and outcomes. Both time-varying and static parameters

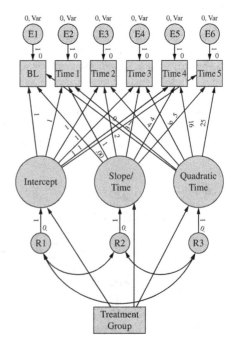

FIGURE 8.4 Latent growth model.

can be included to help address questions about the impact of development or preexisting conditions. Additionally, LGM can be used in accelerated or cohort sequential designs with multivariate outcomes, in interrupted time series models, and in hierarchically nested designs, as outlined by Duncan, Duncan, and Hops (1996), Raudenbush and Chan (1992), and Duncan and Duncan (2004). LGM is an extremely useful technique due to its flexibility in modeling growth and behavioral changes.

2 Appropriate Use of Structural Equation Modeling in MMR

In order to determine whether SEM is appropriate for use in a study, it is requisite that researchers understand both the types of SEM techniques available and also the underlying assumptions of SEM techniques. SEM has several assumptions, many of which have traditionally caused issues when using quantitized data. Thanks to advances in estimation methods and developments in computer science, some solutions to these limitations have emerged.

It is important that researchers are familiar with SEM assumptions. First, as with many other advanced techniques, a *multivariate normal distribution* is required. Typically, a maximum likelihood or restricted maximum likelihood method is used to estimate the parameters and assume a multivariate normal distribution. Small changes in multivariate normality can lead to large differences in the chi-square tests (Lei & Lomax, 2005). Second, because a linear relationship is assumed between the endogenous and exogenous variables, the data should be free of outliers. Third, there should be a *causal* relationship between the independent (exogenous) and dependent (endogenous) variables. Fourth, the *cause* has to occur prior to the effect. Fifth, all *relationships are non-spurious* and are assumed to exist in the real world. Sixth, models have to be *over identified* or *just identified* in order to estimate SEM parameters. *Under identified models* will not be calculated because there are not enough data in the observed covariance matrix to provide estimates for all the parameters. Seventh, sample size is important. Many experts suggest a sample size of 200 to 400 when there are 10 to 15 indicators (Boomsma & Hoogland, 2001; Hoogland & Boomsma, 1998; Kline, 2016, Tabachnick & Fidell, 2018). A general rule of thumb is to have 10 to 20 times as many cases as variables (Kline, 2016; Nunnally & Bernstein,1994; Tabachnick & Fidell, 2018). Lastly, error terms are assumed to be uncorrelated.

Work to enhance the flexibility of the data type in SEM models has been progressing for the past two decades. As mentioned previously, SEM has traditionally required all data be at interval level with a multivariate normal distribution and no missing values. The use of robust maximum likelihood estimates (Robust ML), developed by Satorra and Bentler (1994), was one of the earlier alternatives to using non-normally distributed data without using a non-linear transformation (e.g., log linear). Soon after, Yuan and Bentler (2000) developed the robust full information maximum likelihood (Robust FIML) method that created a possible solution for instances involving missing data, wherein data are missing at random (MAR). Robust FIML has been shown to produce unbiased parameter estimates and chi-square test statistics (Enders & Bandalos, 2001).

By the end of the 1990's and the beginning of 2000s, additional techniques like weighted least squares (Cat-WLS), diagonally weighted (Cat-DWLS), and unweighted least squares (Cat-ULS) were developed that allowed for the use of ordinal-level categorical data in the structural equation model. The drawback in using these techniques are twofold. First, when these robust techniques are used on complex models, it is difficult for the covariance matrix to converge, and so large amounts of data are required (Deng, Yang, and Marcoulides, 2018). Second, when data are categorical and missing at random, biased parameter estimates tend to be calculated (Deng et al., 2018; Tong, Zhang, & Yuan, 2014). Lee (2007) suggests that a Bayesian approach would help solve both concerns. With the development of computational algorithms like the Markov Chain Monte Carlo (MCMC) approach, many of the SEM software packages now include this Bayesian option for analyzing categorical data as well as options for imputing missing values. Bayesian estimations open the door for future research using Natural Linguistic Programming (NLP) and Deep Learning (DL) to analyze huge amounts of unstructured data and to develop coded structured themes that can be added into structural models.

3 Technical Outline of Structural Equation Modeling for MMR

Initial Structural Equation Modeling Checklist

This brings us to a general checklist of questions that need to be asked and answered when conducting or evaluating the merits of a mixed methods research study using any of the SEM family of techniques. As can be seen in Table 8.4, this checklist begins with the rationale for conducting SEM, including the specific technique being used and it progresses through the identification of the theory, models, observed variables, latent constructs, and quantized data. It also includes considerations all the way through discussing software programs and which results to display in your findings. (For a list of traditional Goodness of Fit indicators for CFA, the authors suggest referring to the work of Parry [2020] and Schreiber, Stage, King, Amaury, and Barlow [2006]; see Table 8.5.)

4 Empirical Demonstration of Structural Equation Modeling for MMR

With new technologies and the availability of big data, the use of unstructured data is emerging from previously untapped data sources. At the time that this chapter was written, there was limited research using SEM techniques with large scale quantitized text data. However, one example was the use of this type of data to improve population health outcomes with regard to rising suicide rates. In this study, researchers utilized NPL to analyze text in online social media accounts to identify

TABLE 8.4

Checklist of General Technical Points to Consider When Using SEM with Quantitized Data

Stages	Relevant Questions
1. Rationale	Did you provide a rationale and purpose for your study, including why SEM rather than another statistical analysis approach was required?
2. Describe Latent Variables	Did you describe your latent variables, thereby providing a substantive background to how they are measured?
3. Quantitized Data	Are the quantitative coded variables extracted from the qualitative data, binary, ordinal, or categorical?
4. Theory	Did you establish a sound theoretical basis for your measurement models and structural models?
5. Model	Did you indicate the type of SEM model analysis (multi-level, structured means, etc.)? Did you ensure that the appropriate estimation method is selected? In many cases, Bayesian estimates will fit the quantitized data best.
6. Alternative Models	Did you theoretically justify alternative models for comparison (e.g., nested models)?
7. Sample Size	Did you use a reasonable sample size, thereby having sufficient power in testing your hypotheses?
8. Hypotheses	Did you clearly state the hypotheses for testing the structural models?
9. Direction & Magnitude	Did you discuss the expected magnitude and direction of expected parameter estimates?
10. Diagram	Did you include a figure or diagram of your measurement and structural models?
11. Every Free Parameter	Have you described every free parameter in the models that you want to estimate? Have you considered why other parameters are not included in the models and/or why you included constraints or fixed certain parameters?
12. Software Program	Did you provide the software program used along with the version number? Keep in mind that different programs have different strengths?
13. Results	Have you included a correlation matrix, sample size, and descriptive statistics of variables? Did your interpretation of results include a description of fit indices used and why? Did you include power and sample size determination, and effect size estimates?

those with a high risk of suicide as well as to identify possible interventions (Shing et al., 2018). Some smaller studies have been published using other text analysis programs. For example, LIWC (Linguistic Inquiry and Word Count) is a program that calculates the degree to which various categories of words are used in any text document. With these types of programs already being used and with the advancements in technology making it possible to collect, store, and analyze unstructured data, it is only a matter of time before this will be common practice. Even though unstructured text data have not been analyzed using SEM, this analytical approach has been applied to diagnostic imagery data collected using functional magnetic resonance imaging to study various types of brain conductivity (i.e., working memory and movement). Schlösser, Wagner, and Sauer (2006) provided an excellent outline of the early work undertaken using SEM to analyze fMRI data. The application of SEM approaches to analyze fMRI data has increased over the past several years, and several meta-analyses have been conducted to assess the ability of SEM to model the overall effects. Guàrdia-Olmos, Peró-Cebollero, and Gudayol-Ferré (2018) conducted one of these meta-analyses by investigating 100 published fMRI works that utilized SEM and found that block design studies yielded better results in creating larger stable structural parameters with large R^2.

TABLE 8.5

CFA Goodness of Fit Indices and Suggested Criteria of Fit

Model Fit Index	Definition	Cut-off for Good Fit
X^2 Model Chi-Square	Test of global model fit/differences between expected and observed covariance matrices. X^2 values closer to zero represent a better fit, indicating less difference between the expected and observed covariance matrices.	$p > .05$
(A)GFI (Adjusted) Goodness of Fit	Similar to the R^2, the GFI represents the proportion of unique variance attributed to the estimated covariance within the sample population.	GFI > .95 (A)GFI > .9
(N)NFI/ TLI (Non)Normed-Fit Index/ Tucker Lewis Index	The NFI measures the difference between the X^2 of the hypothesized and null models. An NFI, or (N)NFI for smaller samples or to reduce negative bias, or TLI of > .95 is an indication that the fit of the model was improved by 95% when compared to the null model. Values range from 0 to 1, with ≥ .95 indicating good model fit.	NFI > .95 (N)NFI > .95 TLI > .95
CFI Comparative Fit Index	The CFI compares the fit of a target model to that of the null model, or the fit of the hypothesized model to that of the data. It is a revised form of the NFI and is considered less sensitive to sample size. Values range from 0 to 1, with ≥ .9 indicating good model fit.	CFI ≥ .9
RMSEA Root Mean Square Error of Approximation	The RMSEA uses optimally chosen parameter estimates and population covariance matrix to evaluate the differences between the null model (data) and hypothesized model. Values range from 0 to 1, with values closer to 0 indicating better fit.	RMSEA < .08
SRMR (Standardized) Root Mean Square Residual	The RMR and (S)RMR are the square root of the difference between the sample and model covariance matrices. The (S)RMR is often Preferred because it is less difficult to interpret results, especially if two varying scales are being compared (i.e., a 0-10 scale vs. a 1-5 scale). Values range from 0 to 1, with values < .08 indicating acceptable model fit.	(S)RMR < .08

Guàrdia-Olmos et al. (2018) also presented his own checklist that included specific suggestions for analyzing fMRI images that could be generalized across multiple unstructured data sources. Even though the use of quantitized data in SEM is currently minimal, it is expected that it will explode during the next several years as more and more systems are being built with NLP and DL tools already imbedded to fully utilize all aspects of the data, not just the quantitative data.

5 Suggested Applications of Structural Equation Modeling in MMR

Using Natural Linguistic Programming to Facilitate Quantitization

The ability to collect and analyze large amounts of data has continued to grow and develop. Educational systems, hospital, industry, Facebook, Twitter, Amazon, Google, and so forth, collect data continuously with approximately 80% to 90% being unstructured (Aluvalu & Jabbar, 2018). There is a tremendous amount of information that is contained in these types of data. For example, electronic health records (EHRs) can amass nearly incalculable amounts of unstructured data within just a few hours (i.e., narrative clinical notes, narrative patient histories … even imaging data). However, until recently, much of these data has been either under-utilized or not utilized at all. With the advances in augmented/artificial intelligence (AI), mixed methods researchers can go beyond simple word searches to extract contextually segmented themes and to use image recognition technology to identify commonalities imbedded within blocks of unstructured data. As Goldstein et al. (2013) stated, mixed methods researchers operating within the context of the "digital ecosystem" (p. 365) and modern online environments are able to incorporate a broad range of interactive and highly dynamic media into their works.

With the development of NLP, it is now possible to conduct data analyses on the aforementioned types of unstructured data. NLP runs on a large amount of text and extracts meaning from text to coded segments to help infer context. This can be a complex process, and if the NLP system is not trained appropriately, the process can be further complicated when attempting to obtain the correct meaning from extracted data. Additionally, NLP has a specific problem with sublanguage, which is a subset of natural language. For example, the sublanguage used in medical charting differs from that of the common language, where vocabulary and acronyms may vary by provider, location, organization, and so forth. Another example is seen in social media, wherein abbreviations and emoticons are used to express meaning instead of words. For NLP analyses to extract meaning from sublanguage, the systems must understand the rules of that language. In other words, it would not be effective to use an NLP system trained on newspapers to extract meaning from an EHR system.

The development of DL has enhanced the effectiveness of NLP for extracting meaningful contextual themes and it is now starting to be used in more meaningful ways. Deep Learning is a subset of machine learning that utilizes artificial neurological network and algorithms to learn from large amount of data. Similar to the way that the human brain processes information, DL algorithms repeat tasks with modification during each iteration to obtain better outcomes. The information that is obtained through this process is used to facilitate understanding and processing at higher, more complex layers. This process provides a more complete understanding of the information and context. Consequently, DL is self-training and the information gained is applied to overlapping constructs to improve the understanding of the content being coded. It is adaptable to fit with the overlapping nature of unstructured data, wherein aspects of the unstructured text can fall across layers and domains (Maxwell, 2017). Because of the self-learning component, deep learning can be exponentially more efficient than can nearest-neighbor-like or clustering-like models. With DL, training can be undertaken unsupervised, resulting in less time required by the computer scientist and researchers, and can greatly increase the utilization of large amounts of untapped (unstructured or streaming) data. Given the current amount of unstructured data available, there is a great need for unsupervised learning. Deep Learning is constructed through multiple levels of representation. This is one of the most important advantages of the technique, whereby the learned information is constructed level-by-level through-composition. Lower levels of extraction in this process are more general and can be shared across tasks and higher levels are more specific. This is the way that our brain processes information. Lastly, DL can be an ideal method by which researchers can manage the recursive nature of human language, which is inherently composed of words that form sentences that maintain a certain structure. Deep Learning, therefore, can capture the sequence of information, which improves the context of what is being stated and not only the exact words themselves.

6 Strengths and Limitations of Structural Equation Modeling in MMR

The primary strength of SEM is that it is a combination of techniques that allows researchers to assess causal relationships under various conditions. The flexibility of SEM to accommodate the quantitized data greatly enhances the fit of theoretical models. Additionally, SEM allows for the ability to account for measurement error when estimating parameter effects in both the measurement and structural components of the models with latent error constructs. Because of the continuous progression of data algorithms used to collect, to extract, and now to analyze data using structural equation modeling, it has become much more flexible with approaches for dealing with violations to normality, categorical level data, and missing data. These innovations have led to greater use of latent growth modeling and multilevel SEM models.

There are, however, limitations that need to be considered. First and foremost, SEM generally requires a large amount of data and/or a large sample size. The sample size required varies by the number of parameters in the model and the number of replications when using LGMs. The amount of data needed for SEM is compounded by the inclusion of quantitized data because large amounts of unstructured data are required to identify and code the themes that emerge. Even with the use of NLPs and DL, this is not an easy process. Remember that in order for any indicator to be included in the model, every case has to contain that indicator. Additionally, SEM procedures with quantitized data can be complex, and selecting the appropriated estimation method is critical to minimizing convergence issues that might occur when analyzing the model and avoiding biased parameter estimates. One needs to consider the normality of the data, level of data (categorical or interval), and proportion of and nature of missing data. Modern techniques using Bayesian estimations tend to be the most appropriate method, but it is technical and might be difficult for researchers new to SEM.

7 Resources for Learning More About Structural Equation Modeling

Due to space limitations and the general review of multiple SEM approaches and concepts already presented in this chapter, it was not possible to cover all of the nuances one needs to consider when using SEM with quantitized data. Therefore, the following resources will provide additional approach-specific guidance and additional explanations of complex topics.

Quantitizing Qualitative Data Resources

Let's begin with the quantitizing of qualitative data. For a more detailed understanding of the process as well as the strengths and weaknesses of quantitization, please refer to the foundational work conducted by Sandelowski, Voils, and Knafl (2009). Work conducted by Onwuegbuzie and Leech (2019) further develops the quantitization process using a meta-framework to answer the questions of Why, Who, What, Where, When and How. Also, Onwuegbuzie, Slate, Leech, and Collins (2007) create typologies of the quantitized data. These data can then be included in statistical modeling.

SEM Books and Online Resources

There are several good resources available to obtain more information on how to conduct specific types of SEM. To start with, there are several good books. Kline (2016) is one of the more widely used for an introduction to structural equation modeling and it is not software specific. He provides real data examples and focuses on the rationale and concepts more than the mathematical calculations. Blunch (2015) and Byrne (2016) have great books on conducting SEM using IBM's AMOS program. These books introduce complex SEM topics using real data with a step-by-step explanation of how to analyze models in AMOS. For additional guidance on the use of LGM, Duncan, Duncan, and Strycker (2013) provide an excellent introduction to growth curve models, also using real world data. Complex topics are discussed involving repeated measures designs, and the benefits of using SEM are discussed. This book builds on the reader's previous understanding of SEM to explain the complex issues involving LGM.

In addition to these books, there are several good online resources that can help, especially early in the development of your SEM knowledge. One good online resource is the David Kenny's SEM Page that can be found at http://davidakenny.net/cm/causalm.htm. This site provides a huge amount of information, from definition of terms to explanations of complex concepts. Multiple approaches to SEM are explained with links to additional resources for complex topics. In addition, many of the software programs like AMOS also have online development sites with tutorials and videos to help conduct SEM. The Amos Development Corporation website http://amosdevelopment.com/ was designed as a teaching tool that is geared to emphasizing the simplicity underlying SEM. It provides reading material and videos to help facilitate the appropriate use of SEM. Stata has a similar online resources site at www.stata.com/features/structural-equation-modeling/. Additional online help for SAS can be found at https://support.sas.com/rnd/app/stat/procedures/StructuralEquations.html and for LISREL at www.ssicentral.com/index.php/products/lisrel. These resources will help in the development of SEM knowledge and skills.

REFERENCES

Aluvalu, R., & Jabbar, M. A. (2018, April, 22–23). *Handling data analytics onunstructured data using MongoDB*. Smart Cities Symposium, Bahrain. doi:10.1049/cp.2018.1409

Blunch, N. J. (2015). *Introduction to structural equation modeling using IBM SPSS statistics and EQS*. London, England: Sage.

Boomsma, A., & Hoogland, J. J. (2001). *The robustness of LISREL modeling revisited. Structural equation models: Present and future. A Festschrift in honor of Karl Jöreskog, 2*, 139–168. Chicago, IL: Scientific Software International.

Brown, T. A. (2015). *Confirmatory factor analysis for applied research* (2nd ed.). New York, NY: The Guildford Press.

Byrne, B. M. (2016). *Structural equation modeling with Amos* (3rd ed.). New York, NY: Routledge Press.

Deng, L., Yang, M., & Marcoulides, K. M. (2018, April 25). Structural equation modeling with many variables: A systematic review of issues and developments. *Frontiers in Psychology, 9* (article 580), 1–14. Retrieved from www.frontiersin.org/articles/10.3389/fpsyg.2018.00580/full.

Duncan, S. C., Duncan, T. E., & Hops, H. (1996). Analysis of longitudinal data within accelerated longitudinal designs. *Psychological Methods, 1*, 236–248. doi:10.1037/1082–989X.1.3.236

Duncan, T. E., & Duncan, S. C. (2004). An introduction to latent growth curve modeling. *Behavior Therapy, 35*, 333–363. doi:10.1016/S0005–7894(04)80042-X.

Duncan, T. E., Duncan, S. C., & Strycker, L. A. (2013). *An introduction to latent variable growth curve modeling: Concepts, issues, and application*. New York, NY: Routledge.

Enders, C. K., & Bandalos, D. L. (2001, Nov 19). The relative performance of full information maximum likelihood estimation for missing data in structural equation models. *Structural Equation Modeling, 8*, 430–457. Retrieved from www.tandfonline.com/doi/abs/10.1207/S15328007SEM0803_5

Escobar, M. R. (2010). The four models you meet in structural equation modeling. *The Analysis Factor: Making Statistics Make Sense.* Retrieved from www.theanalysisfactor.com/four-types-sem/

Goldstein, K., Briggs, M., Oleynik, V., Cullen, M., Jones, J., Newman, E., & Narva, A. (2013). Using digital media to promote kidney disease education. *Advances in Chronic Kidney Disease, 20,* 364–369. doi:10.1053/j.ackd.2013.04.001

Guàrdia-Olmos, J., Peró-Cebollero, M., & Gudayol-Ferré, E. (2018, February 15). Meta-analysis of the structural equation models' parameters for the estimation of brain connectivity with fMRI. *Frontiers in Behavioral Neuroscience, 12*(19). doi:10.3389/fnbeh.2018.00019. Retrieved from www.frontiersin.org/articles/10.3389/fnbeh.2018.00019/full

Hogan, N. S., & Schmidt, L. A. (2002). Testing the grief to personal growth model using structural equation modeling. *Death Studies, 26,* 615–624. doi:10.1080/07481180290088338

Hoogland, J. J., & Boomsma, A. (1998). Robustness studies in covariance structure modeling: An overview and a meta-analysis. *Sociological Methods & Research, 26,* 329–367. doi:10.1177/0049124198026003003.

Jöreskog, K. G. (1970). A general method for estimating a linear structural equation system. *ETS Research Bulletin Series, 1970*(2), i-41. Retrieved from https://onlinelibrary.wiley.com/doi/pdf/10.1002/j.2333-8504.1970.tb00599.x

Jöreskog, K. G., & Van Thillo, M. (1972). LISREL: A general computer program for estimating a linear structural equation system involving multiple indicators of unmeasured variables. *Educational Testing Services, 2,* 1–71. Retrieved from https://onlinelibrary.wiley.com/doi/epdf/10.1002/j.2333-8504.1972.tb00827.x.

Kline, R. B. (2016). *Principles and practice of structural equation modeling* (4th ed.). New York, NY: The Guilford Press.

Lee, S. Y. (2007). *Structural equation modeling: A Bayesian approach.* West Sussex, England: John Wiley & Sons.

Lei, M., & Lomax R. G. (2005). The effect of varying degrees of non-normality in structural equation modeling. *Structural Equation Modeling: A Multidisciplinary Journal, 12*(1), 1–27. doi:10.1207/s15328007sem1201_1

Maxwell, A. (2017). Deep learning architectures for multi-label classification of intelligent health risk prediction. *BMC Bioinformatics, 18*(14), 523–528. doi:10.1186/s12859-017-1898-z

Nunnally, J., & Bernstein I. H. (1994). *Psychometric theory* (3rd ed.). New York, NY: McGraw-Hill Education.

Onwuegbuzie, A. J., & Leech, N. L. (2019). On qualitizing. *International Journal of Multiple Research Approaches, 11,* 98–131. doi:10.29034/ijmra.v11n2editorial2

Onwuegbuzie, A. J., Slate, J. R., Leech, N. L., & Collins, K. M. T. (2007). Conducting mixed analyses: A general typology. *International Journal of Multiple Research Approaches, 1,* 4–17. doi:10.5172/mra.455.1.1.4

Pallant, J. (2016). *SPSS survival manual: A step-by-step guide to data analysis using IBM SPSS* (6th ed.). Berkshire, England: Open University Press.

Parry, S. (2020). *Fit indices commonly reported for CFA and SEM.* Ithaca, NY: Cornell University Statistical Consulting Unit. Retrieved from www.cscu.cornell.edu/news/Handouts/SEM_fit.pdf

Rahman, W., Shah, F. A., & Rasli, A. (2015). Use of structural equation modeling in social science research. *Asian Social Science, 11,* 371–377. doi:10.5539/ass.v.11n4p371.

Raudenbush, S. W., & Chan, W. S. (1992). Growth curve analysis in accelerated longitudinal designs. *Journal of Research in Crime and Delinquency, 29,* 387–411. Retrieved from www.ncjrs.gov/App/publications/abstract.aspx?ID=141108.

Sandelowski, M., Voils, C. I., & Knafl, G. (2009). On quantitizing. *Journal of Mixed Methods Research, 3,* 208–222. doi:10.1177/1558689809334210

Satorra, A., & Bentler, P. M. (1994). Correction to test statistics and standard errors in covariance structure analysis. In A. von Eye & C. C. Clogg (Eds.), *Latent variables analysis: Applications to developmental research* (pp. 399–419). Thousand Oaks, CA: Sage.

Schlösser, R. G., Wagner, G., & Sauer, H. (2006). Assessing the working memory network: Studies with functional magnetic resonance imaging and structural equation modeling. *Neuroscience, 139*(1), 91–103. doi:10.1016/j.neuroscience.2005.06.037

Schreiber, J. B., Stage, F. K., King, J., Amaury, N., & Barlow, E. A. (2006). Reporting structural equation modeling and confirmatory factor analysis results: A review. *The Journal of Educational Research, 99,* 323–337. doi:10.3200/JOER.99.6. 323–338

Shing, H. C., Nair, S., Zirikly, A., Friedenberg, M., Daumé III, H., & Resnik, P. (2018, June). Expert, crowdsourced, and machine assessment of suicide risk via online postings. In *Proceedings of the Fifth Workshop on Computational Linguistics and Clinical Psychology: From Keyboard to Clinic* (pp. 25–36), New Orleans, LA. Retrieved from www.aclweb.org/anthology/W18-0603/.

Spearman, C. (1904). General intelligence objectively determined and measured. *The American Journal of Psychology, 15,* 201–292. doi:10.2307/1412107

Tabachnick, B. G., & Fidell, L. S. (2018). *Using multivariate statistics* (7th ed.). Boston, MA: Pearson.

Tashakkori, A., & Newman, I. (2010). Mixed methods: Integrating quantitative and qualitative approaches to research. In B. McGaw, E. Baker, & P. P. Peterson (Eds.) *International encyclopaedia of education* (3rd ed.; pp. 514–520). Oxford, England: Elsevier.

Thurstone, L. L. (1934). The vectors of mind. *Psychological review, 41*(1), 1–32. doi:10.1037/h0075959.

Tong, X., Zhang, Z., & Yuan, K. H. (2014). Evaluation of test statistics for robust structural equation modeling with non-normal missing data. *Structural Equation Modeling, 21,* 553–565. doi:10.1080/10705511.2014.919820.

Wright, S. (1921). Correlation and causation. *Journal of Agricultural Research, 20,* 557–585.

Yuan, K. H., & Bentler, P. M. (2000). Three likelihood-based methods for mean and covariance structure analysis with nonnormal missing data. *Sociological Methodology, 30,* 165–200. doi:10.1111/0081-1750.00078.

9

Hierarchical Linear Modeling with Qualitative Data that Have Been Quantitized

John H. Hitchcock, Richard Lambert, and T. Scott Holcomb

This chapter flows from the prior chapter on Ordinary Least Squares (OLS)/linear regression and follows the structure provided by the book editors. There are seven sections to this chapter, as follows: (a) Defining Hierarchical Linear Modeling (HLM) with Qualitative Data, (b) When using this Form of Analyses is Appropriate in Mixed Methods Research, (c) A Technical Outline for the Procedure, (d) An Empirical Demonstration (e) Ideas for suggested Applications, and the chapter closes with an overview of (f) Strengths and Limitations and (g) Resources for Learning More. At the outset, it is important for readers to understand that this chapter could be taken in several different directions. We, the authors, elected to focus on using HLM with data that are naturally in some qualitative form (e.g., text data from interviews, themes, observational notes) but are assigned some numerical value, meaning that they are *quantitized*. Please see the prior chapter on linear regression for a fuller overview and definition of quantitizing. Moreover, the prior chapter in this text provides a description of and literature base for understanding quantitizing.

There is prior work dealing with the concept of mixed methods HLM (e.g., Headley & Plano Clark, 2020; Onwuegbuzie & Hitchcock, 2015). There is however, to the best of our knowledge, relatively minimal guidance pertaining to the use of HLM with quantitized data. This chapter, therefore, provides guidance on how to conduct related analyses. For this chapter, readers do not necessarily need to have a command of quantitizing, but they do need to accept that prior mixed methods work has established the merits of quantitizing and even describe several worldview assumptions associated with the general practice of quantitizing.

1 Defining Hierarchical Linear Modeling (HLM) with Qualitative Data that have been Quantitized

As pointed out in the prior chapter of this book, quantitized data can be conceptualized as independent, dependent, moderating, and mediating variables, depending on the statistical modeling goal at hand. The current chapter extends upon the idea of using quantitized data as dependent variables in regression models, but now we deal with the case where data exist within a hierarchy. To explain what a hierarchy means, we ask the reader to consider that a group of people might be measured multiple times in a longitudinal study. These repeated observations of a person can be thought of as being nested by person, or put another way, there is a hierarchy of measures within a person that exist at one level, and the people within the study represent another level. Consider a study of factors that might influence blood pressure within some population of interest. If researchers measured a person's blood pressure 10 times over the course of a month, and there were 100 study participants in the sample, then there would be 1,000 observations of blood pressure. Each study participant has ten observations that, in HLM parlance, are *nested* by person. The individual blood pressure scores typically would be labeled of as *Level 1* data, and any person-level information (e.g., gender, weight, age) would be *Level 2* data. The highest level of the hierarchy here is the person, the lower level of the hierarchy are the observations within that person.

Another common form of a hierarchy (or nesting) is when people fit within some natural grouping, like a classroom, and classrooms, in turn, are organized by a larger unit such as a school. This represents a three-level hierarchy (students at Level 1, classrooms at Level 2, and schools at Level 3). Understanding hierarchies can be critically important for understanding social phenomena and this is the case for many types of designs and in many disciplines. If, for example, one wanted to study the impact of a teacher professional development approach on student learning, it is nearly impossible not to consider the hierarchy of students nested in classrooms and then schools. Moreover, it is not difficult to adopt a mixed methods way of thinking about hierarchies. In critical theory applications, hierarchies are often a basis for understanding group structures and power dynamics. One could, therefore, blend an understanding of power structures and hierarchical models. Imagine, for example, a study that entails randomly assigning schools to start to use restorative practices (see for e.g., Ashley & Burke, 2009), which, in this context, would deal with repairing relationships between students and faculty. Imagine further that there was subsequent interest in examining outcomes like the number of office discipline referrals or suspensions students receive in schools that deploy using restorative practices, versus schools that do not. In this example, there would be a clear opportunity to mix HLM because of the inherent nesting of students and schools, and ideas from critical theory given the power dynamics (and typically the need to challenge status quo dynamics) associated with restorative practices.

DOI: 10.4324/9780203729434-9

Of course, whole disciplines are practically predicated on the idea that hierarchies exist (e.g., organizational and leadership studies) and as previously demonstrated, medical researchers might be interested in hierarchies and not just observations nested by patients. Researchers might, for example, also be interested in patients nested by physicians, who are, in turn, nested within hospitals. Importantly, in standard HLM applications, the existence of these hierarchies, or levels of data, typically intertwine with research questions (Raudenbush & Bryk, 2002), and as Snijders and Bosker (1999) argue, hierarchies are often interesting concepts that can be understood via the statistical notion of *dependence*.

What does dependence mean in the context of HLM? Readers with some statistical training will remember that most statistical analyses entail making some assumptions. Furthermore, the degree to which assumptions are not met is the degree to which it becomes difficult to interpret the results of a modeling effort. Hence, when engaged in statistical analysis, it is appropriate to account for whether assumptions required of an approach are reasonable and, if not, either take on a new approach or address resulting limitations. In common parametric analyses, such as a *t* test, some of assumptions with which one deals are the degree to which data are normally distributed and the degree to which variance is similar across two groups (e.g., Field, 2018). One other assumption underlying many statistical modeling approaches is variously called the *independence assumption*, *independent observation assumption*, or *independent errors assumption*. Understanding this assumption gets to the very heart of HLM.

The issue at hand is understanding the degree to which any observation is independent of other observations in a dataset. Consider a simple randomized controlled trial (RCT) that tests the effect of some new drug on blood pressure, and there is only one measure of blood pressure per person taken at posttest. Imagine there are 100 study participants, randomly assigned to take the medication or not, and they do not know or otherwise have a connection to each other. Furthermore, study participants do not interact with each other during the course of the research. In this case, the observations (blood pressure readings) of one participant is reasonably independent of the observations of others. In this example, the independence assumption is reasonable and, assuming other assumptions were met, it would be appropriate to proceed with an independent samples *t* test. To connect back to the OLS regression chapter, readers should appreciate that an independent samples *t* test can be thought of as a special case of regression, wherein there is one independent variable and one continuous dependent variable; the dependent variable could be a quantitized variable summarizing what were originally data in a qualitative form. This chapter offers an extension to the OLS regression chapter because, in the social sciences, the independence assumption is often not tenable (Raudenbush & Bryk, 2002).

Now consider a study in education wherein elementary school teachers learn a new way to instruct mathematics. One might assign teachers to use the new approach or instead use the standard teaching methods they already know. If the outcome variable of interest is children's mathematics performance on some test (i.e., to determine whether the new teaching technique yields higher scores or not), then this study must account for the fact that the students' mathematics scores (observations) are going to be dependent, or connected, to each other within classrooms. That is, the independence assumption is not tenable. This is because we can assume that some teachers will be more effective at teaching mathematics than are others, some classrooms might have more mathematically inclined students than do others, and their behaviors might mutually pull scores in one direction or another. Indeed, different types of teachers (consider experience level, comfort with teaching mathematics) might interact differently with different classroom types. Accounting for all of this cannot be done using standard OLS analyses (incidentally, in HLM, such analyses are sometimes referred to as *single-level analyses*); one needs multi-level analyses, or HLM.

Within HLM, a key statistic for understanding dependence is the intra-class correlation (ICC). The ICC is a ratio of within group variance (a group can be a school, classroom, hospital, etc.) to the total population variance estimated from a dataset (Raudenbush & Bryk, 2002). If an ICC is equal to one, this means that all units within each group are scoring in a uniform manner (e.g., all students score exactly the same on some dependent variable test within all participating classrooms). Contrastingly, if an ICC is zero, this means there is no hierarchy at hand and scores are independent, making OLS-based analyses, such as independent samples *t* tests, appropriate. It is, however, important to keep in mind that there is generally going to be some error in ICC estimates, and so ICCs must be evaluated based on one's understanding of the research context. If, for example, a small but nonzero ICC was present in the aforementioned RCT blood pressure medication study, it would probably be reasonable to ignore it. But, then again, there could be some subtle hierarchy a researcher might not have initially considered. Suppose that a hierarchy in this example came from the fact that the 100 participants were dispersed across five hospitals (approximately 20 participants per hospital). If so, the idea that *dependence is an interesting phenomenon* missive can come in to play. One might wonder whether there is some feature about the hospital that creates a form of dependence of observations and this, in turn, can inform researchers about the nature of blood pressure scores and possibly the medication's effects. What if, for example, staff across the five hospitals varied with respect to how clear they were when it came to describing dosage procedures to patients? Consider further that following exact dosage instructions mattered greatly in terms of the medication's effectiveness. Moving past this example, some researchers can reasonably expect that the presence of hierarchies will be highly influential in the research task at hand. This is quite common in education research. If a researcher randomly assigned elementary schools to participate in a given teacher professional development program or to a comparison condition with no such program, and the dependent variable of interest is some measure of student achievement, it would be nearly impossible to conduct statistical modeling without understanding the ICC.

ICCs in Growth Modeling and Models with More than Two Levels

This notion of dependence also applies to within-participant measurements. If one longitudinally followed participants' blood pressures across repeated observations, then these participants' scores would be dependent, or nested within person. For example, a participant who started a study with high blood pressure will very likely continue to have high (or if the medication works, relatively high) blood pressure during the course of the study. Similarly, students who are strong in mathematics will probably show high scores over time. For another example, consider student sense of safety in a school. Students who express concerns in interviews during the fall term might be more prone to continue to express concern the following spring and at the end of the school year. Across these three examples (blood pressure, mathematics performance, perceptions of safety), one can conceptualize a within-person ICC, and analyzing data nested by person is typically referred to as *growth modeling*.

It is possible to mix growth modeling with HLM. For example, a design could account for repeated measures of student performance (nested or clustered by person). Call this "Level 1." The students who provide these Level 1 data can be nested by classroom. Studying growth in student performance and how this changes across classrooms would represent a three-level model. Interested in how such change occurs across schools? This would be a four-level model (i.e., scores nested within students, who are nested in classrooms, which are nested in schools). It is even possible to account for, say, communities and districts, which would entail a five-level model. For some perspective, Onwuegbuzie and Hitchcock (2015) describe how qualitative methods could be used to study larger units (e.g., schools, communities) to better understand context and interpret model findings. This chapter differs from that prior work because we focus on how to include quantitized data in a hierarchical model, yielding a different form of analysis.

2 When Using HLM with Qualitative Data that have been Quantitized is Appropriate in Mixed Methods Research

The prior section can be summarized by two key points: (a) qualitative data can be quantified and, therefore, be subject to statistical modeling and (b) it is critical to understand that hierarchies (or multiple levels/nesting) exist, especially in the social sciences. As one thinks about schools, hospitals, businesses, governments, and communities, these all represent how humans are grouped and organized, and such groupings will influence performance; hence, related data are not independent. Furthermore, when one deals with repeated observations over time within people, this also means that data are not independent; they are grouped by the person. This means that any statistical analyses of quantitized data with for example, repeated interviews, or need to attend to clustering of people within hierarchies, will likely make it necessary to consider HLM as an analytic option.

It will often be the case that quantitized data will be presented in binary, categorical, or ordinal forms. Fortunately, Raudenbush and Bryk (2002), as do other sources, offer modeling options for each of these scenarios. Although models with categorical/ordinal outcome data can be more complex, HLM can still work. Hence, most forms of quantitized data can be accommodated in models. However, a general scenario whereby HLM with quantitized data will be problematic is when dealing with small sample sizes (see the below section: "Strengths and Limitations"). For this reason, we think that HLM with quantitized data has been somewhat rare, but it seems possible that advances in microcomputing, data availability, and guidance such as what is offered in this chapter might make the procedure more common in the future. As an example, one might administer surveys to a professional group with open text-based response fields. A sample comprising verbose and opinionated respondents might yield large amounts of text data that could be emergent in nature, thereby being qualitative in nature, and such data could be analyzed using statistical procedures. Consider also a scenario wherein a researcher wishes to analyze Tweets but respondents are clustered in some fashion. If statistical treatment of such data becomes more and more feasible, then we wish to set the stage for researchers with an interest in accounting for multi-level structures and embraces the idea that dependence can be an interesting aspect to the phenomena being investigated. In that spirit, we now turn to a general technical outline.

3 A Technical Outline for HLM with Qualitative Data that have been Quantitized

Table 9.1 provides a checklist of technical points to consider when using HLM with quantitized data. Note that this table could be followed in a linear fashion (i.e., steps), but this will not always be the case because, sometimes, research is conducted on archival records and an opportunity to apply HLM with quantitized data might emerge from discussion with research stakeholders and data availability. In our experience, some technical considerations can be iterative (e.g., Do I have the sample size needed for a three-level model? If not, can we work with a two-level model?). Indeed, an emergent design approach led to the empirical demonstration presented in the next section, and so we present Table 9.1 as a checklist.

The following empirical demonstration combines some steps but, overall, addresses the checklist.

4 An Empirical Demonstration of HLM with Qualitative Data that have been Quantitized

Assessing the Research Context

In the United States, a state education agency (SEA) decided to implement an authentic, statewide formative assessment system in kindergarten classrooms. An authentic formative assessment measure does not have a standardized administration process. Rather, such measures require teachers to master a complex process of observation, collect evidence and artifacts of child growth and learning, analyze the evidence, and make placements on developmental progressions that match the current status of each child across a range of instructional objectives.

TABLE 9.1

Checklist of General Technical Points to Consider When Using HLM with Quantitized Data

Step	Elaborations
Assessing the research context	Specify whether one needs to qualitative approaches to examine some phenomena or construct because (a) there is not a ready measure or (b) because a qualiative approach emerges
Specify relevant hierarchies/clusters	Determine whether there is a hierarchical structure–Is there some rationale that a variable works differently at different levels or nested, natural/multilevel structure, measures nested by participant?
Specify your research questions/goals	Formalize your hierarchical research questions
Study Design	Identify a mixed design plan/model to guide your design thinking. Understand your variable types (e.g., are data nominal, ordinal, interval, or ratio?); Which variables are independent? Which ones are dependent? What, if any, covariates will be used? Which data are to be quantitized and why?
Data collection	Develop a data collection plan that accounts for the hierarchies of interest
Power analyses	How much data will you need for statistical modeling? See the section below, entitled, "Resources for Learning More")
Quantitizing	Specify plan for quantitizing data
Model specification	Formalize hierarchical statistical models. There are a few considerations here that are not described in this chapter.
Descriptive Analyses	After data have been collected and quantified, perform descriptive statistics, check assumptions, identify outliers and their distributional characteristics, and address any concerns with missing data. See the section "Resources for Learning More."
Model the data	Run and interpret the model
Revisit your design	Revisit your larger design plan. The analyses might be one of several steps within your study.
Assess your findings	To what degree did you answer your questions? Was the HLM procedure worth the effort?

When the formative assessment process (FAP) is working well in classrooms, it can provide teachers with rich information to understand the strengths and areas for growth that each child brings to the classroom, and can support meaningful, data-driven differentiation and individualization of instruction. Teachers who use the FAP to gather valid evidences of child status and progress can focus on what is important for the developmental progress of each child. However, making valid placements on the developmental progressions can be complex. Therefore, the SEA charged researchers with conducting a series of studies that examined implementation fidelity to better understand how to support teachers in the FAP.

As part of the statewide study of the extent to which elementary teachers were able to implement the FAP with fidelity, researchers conducted surveys of teachers, observations in classrooms, interviews with teachers, and interviews with district leaders and school administrators. At the end of the first two years of statewide implementation, the researchers decided to conduct a pilot study involving additional sources of data. These researchers sought to obtain the perspective of specific support personnel from the SEA. For some context, the state in which the study was conducted is organized into regions and the SEA employs regional consultants who are charged with providing training, technical assistance, and consultation to schools and school districts as needed. During the study period, these regional consultants focused a large amount of their time and resources on supporting district and school efforts at achieving fidelity of implementation for the authentic formative assessment initiative. These consultants were, therefore, considered key informants who had direct knowledge of requests for support from districts and schools, and they had direct interactions with teachers pertaining to implementation, across widely varying contexts within the state. With the help of these consultants, the researchers conducted a mixed methods study in an attempt to extend their understanding of the FAP implementation process.

Data Sources and Design

Three sources of data were used in this mixed methods study: (a) teacher ratings of students, (b) consultant focus groups, and (c) school-level, state administrative data. The researchers obtained ratings the teachers made about each child using the authentic formative assessment system, which included their assessment of kindergarten readiness for the children in their classrooms. Through a data-sharing agreement, de-identified data were provided to the researchers for the first two years of statewide implementation of the assessment system. The researchers also obtained data for the pilot years that preceded the two years of full state implementation. These data did not include any identifying information about students or teachers; the data did however include the placements that teachers made on all of the developmental progressions for each child in the state. Schools and school districts were identified by codes. The researchers used these data to calculate overall descriptive statistics at the state, district, and school levels. These descriptive statistics included the percentage of children assessed and the percentage of children rated as "ready" for kindergarten.

The second source of data was collected via focus groups with regional consultants. At the beginning of each focus group, the researchers presented some descriptive information about the statewide results from the early childhood assessment system. The group conversation that followed focused on the process of implementing the assessment system including the specific difficulties and challenges they observed among school districts and schools. Part of the role for the regional consultants was to support the development of District Implementation Teams (DIT) and School Implementation Teams (SIT). The conversation focused on districts and schools where teachers faced significant implementation challenges, including sites where the existing DIT or SIT functioned poorly and were unable to provide effective support to teachers. Discussions also included general comments and exchanges about districts and schools that were unable to develop a functioning DIT or SIT.

The focus group data provided rich information about the process of implementation from the perspective of the regional consultants. Consultant perspectives were critical to the study because consultants interacted with teachers and administrators from multiple schools and school districts, and they played a variety of support roles. Furthermore, consultants understood the official intentions and objectives of the SEA and their perspective was independent of the varying messaging that district and school leaders conveyed to teachers. Their comments underscored the complexity of the task given to teachers, the importance of clear messaging about the nature and purpose of the authentic formative assessment system, the value of effective teacher training, and the necessity for ongoing support to teachers.

The third source of data was administrative: the school structural characteristics obtained from state sources. The SEA offers school report cards that are publicly available resources and provide information on school, district, and state level data. The available data broadly cover student growth and proficiency in academic areas as well as other school- and student-level characteristics. Two different views of school report card information were available. For this study, we used the more detailed, analytical report cards that allowed for the selection of a single indicator for all elementary schools within a district. The analytical report cards separate indicators into five categories: (a) school profile, (b) school performance, (c) school indicators, (d) school environment, and (e) school personnel. These categories served as district- and school-level covariates of interest. For example, the covariates falling within the school personnel category were collected for an entire district and then the next district of interest was selected, and the process was repeated for all remaining covariates of interest before moving on to the next category.

The SEA follows the federal Every Student Succeeds Act (ESSA) guidelines for determining percentage of students who are economically disadvantaged at each school. Student average daily attendance is calculated based on the total number of days of attendance for all students within a school divided by the total number of school days. The teacher turnover rate provides the percentage of classroom teachers who left the school since the previous school year. It is common for schools to see a certain amount of turnover just as is experienced in other industries. The SEA also provides information on the years of teaching experience that teachers have at each school. In the school report cards, teachers are categorized based on experience as follows: 0–3 years of experience, 4–10 years of experiences, and 10+ years of experience. All of these data were used to create a rich profile of each school.

Quantitizing

At the end of each focus group, the consultants were given a homework assignment. They were asked by the researchers to identify a list of schools and districts in their regions that could be classified as "low implementers." Four of the eight consultants provided their selections with rationale in a comments field. However, the remaining four consultants reported that they did not feel comfortable making the ratings because they had only 1 year of experience providing technical assistance to the districts and schools. The four consultants who did provide ratings had each worked with their regions for at least 3 years. These four identified 32 out of 409 schools as having serious implementation problems with no functioning SIT. They also identified five out of 57 districts as also having major implementation challenges and no functioning DIT. These data were quantitized by creating 0/1 indicator variables for each school and district, whereby 1 represented implementation problems and 0 otherwise. As detailed further later, these data served as dependent variable data in our empirical demonstration.

Model Specification and the Research Question/Goal

Next, a two-level Multilevel Model was used to examine possible associations among the three sources of data. Schools represented Level-1 in the analyses and school districts were at Level-2; all schools were nested within their respective district. The model was specified to help identify structural characteristics of the schools and features of their teacher rating data that were aligned with the quantitized regional consultant ratings. In this way, the analysis could help us to address our research goal, which was to identify patterns among the low implementation schools that would extend the findings from the qualitative portion of the study to capture a more complete picture of the processes and challenges present in those schools. Although the regional consultants were important sources of school-level data, and could report from their direct subjective experiences with a range of challenges faced by the teachers, they had not analyzed either the administrative data or the teacher rating data. In addition, they rated the schools independently following the focus group. Therefore, the purpose of these analyses was to extend and amplify the qualitative data with potentially complementary patterns in the quantitative data that emerged across multiple schools and thereby could enrich understanding of the implementation challenges faced by the teachers.

Study Design: Independent and Dependent Variables and Statistical Power

The teacher rating data were used to create quantitative indicators of potential implementation problems. The administrative data were used to provide quantitative covariates for the analysis. The qualitative, binary indicator of poor school-level implementation from the regional consultants was used as the outcome measure at Level-1. Therefore, the model was a binary logistic regression model and was used to identify variables that were associated with the probability that a school was identified by a consultant as a poor implementation school. At Level-2, a district level indicator of poor implementation (from the third data source) was used as an indicator that a school was nested within a poor implementation district. This variable was also used as a predictor of the probability that a given school was identified as a poor implementation school. Of the total of 409 schools nested within 57 districts contained in the four participating regions, the sample was reduced to only those districts with at least five elementary schools. The final sample for the Multilevel Model contained 360 schools, 26 of which were identified as having poor implementation and no functioning SIT. The 360 sampled schools were nested within 33 districts, three of which were identified as having significant implementation problems and no functioning DIT.

Given the relatively modest number of level two units (33 districts), it was important to retain a minimum number of Level-1 units per Level-2 unit in order to enhance the precision of the estimates of Level-1 coefficients. Statistical power for Multilevel Models is a complex interplay between the number of Level-1 and Level-2 units, the ICC, and model specification, among other factors. For a more complete discussion of statistical power for Multilevel Models, see Maas and Hox (2005); Bell, Morgan, Schoeneberger, Kromrey, and Ferron (2014); Raudenbush, Martinez, and Spybrook (2007); and Spybrook, Raudenbush, Liu, Congdon, and Martinez (2006).

Covariates

Using the rich school profiles created from state administrative data, we decided to select covariates that could represent challenges related to the implementation fidelity of the measure. Other variables included in the analysis were selected because we wanted to rule them out as having an impact on implementation issues. Ideally, the percentage of students who were economically disadvantaged and the percentage of students of color would not relate to implementation fidelity issues. These variables were included because one is an indicator of poverty across the school population and the other represents historically marginalized groups. Average daily attendance percentage was used as a covariate because there could be instances where students were not at school sufficiently to collect valid evidence on the assessment.

The remaining covariates collected for the study dealt with personnel-related challenges. Schools with a higher turnover rate could potentially have had an issue with consistency of implementation of the assessment. The percentage of teachers who had 0–3 years of teaching experience within a school was considered because this variable could have indicated implementation challenges. New teachers typically have a more difficult time implementing authentic formative assessments, given that these assessments typically require a higher level of developmental and content expertise and experience. The final variable, whether the school had contained a new principal since the start of the study, was considered for similar reasons. New principals could be less experienced with the assessment or be focusing on other tasks that come with being a new leader of a school.

Revisiting the Design: Identifying Red Flags

The teacher rating data were used to create a series of potential implementation red flags. These Level-1 indicators were created to represent potentially implausible data patterns that might be related to teacher challenges with implementation.

The first red flag was created by identifying schools where teachers rated less than 10% of the children as being ready for kindergarten. No external objective measure of child development was included in the study, therefore, it is possible that these ratings were accurate, but it is implausible that such a small percentage of children would demonstrate the skills and abilities that qualify for the readiness designation. This indicator might, therefore, identify schools where teachers were very strict in the placements on the developmental progressions, or were incapable of collecting sufficient evidences to develop a realistic and valid sense of each child's status. The second indicator identified schools where more than 90% of the children had been rated as ready. It is plausible that a high percentage of children could be ready for kindergarten; however, these schools might also contain teachers who were very lenient in their placements on the progressions.

Schools where less than 80% of the children were assessed where also given a red flag. Naturally, if teachers are unable to complete all of the state-required assessments, implementation is not complete. Next, two indicators of potential implementation problems were created by comparing the achievement composite score from state testing to the readiness percentage. One indictor variable was assigned when the readiness percentage was 25 percentage points or more below the achievement composite, and the other represented schools where the readiness percentage was 25 percentage points higher than the achievement composite. The achievement composite score is not a perfect indicator of the general status of the children in the school. However, it uses the state standardized tests to create a schoolwide composite that is meant to represent the estimated overall school-level percentage of students performing on grade level. The rationale for these indicators is that readiness percentages below the achievement composite might indicate poor implementation due to strictness or incomplete evidence collection. Similarly, readiness percentages above the achievement composite might represent leniency in the teacher ratings. The last two indicators were formed by identifying schools with large year-to-year changes in readiness percentages. Given that schools almost always serve the same neighborhoods and families from year to year, large swings in readiness percentages seem implausible. Schools with 25 percentage point increases or decreases in readiness from Year 1 to Year 2 of implementation were given indicators.

Analyses

Due to space limitations, descriptive analyses and assumption checks are not reviewed here other than to point out that conducting a two-level model was considered by the researchers to be reasonable. The results of the Multilevel Model (see Table 9.2) indicate that only one of the covariates (see the p values) was associated with the probability that a given school was identified as having serious implementation problems. Every increase in one percentage point for the average daily attendance number was associated with a 1.566 times higher probability of having serious implementation problems.

Given the very narrow range of daily attendance figures (86.3% of schools reported 94%, 95%, or 96%), it is plausible

TABLE 9.2

Association between Quantitative Indicators of Implementation Fidelity and Key Informant Ratings of Implementation Challenges

		B	se	t	p	Exp(B)	Odds Ratio 95% LL	95% UL
Intercept		−3.696	0.224	−16.518	0.000	0.025	0.016	0.039
Level 2 predictor	District has poor implementation support	4.423	0.650	6.801	0.000	83.314	22.108	313.970
Level 1 covariates	School % of students who are economically disadvantaged	−0.001	0.014	−0.038	0.969	0.999	0.972	1.027
	School % of kindergarten students who are students of color	−0.018	0.009	−1.866	0.063	0.983	0.964	1.001
	Average daily student attendance percentage	0.448	0.163	2.743	0.006	1.566	1.135	2.160
	Teacher turnover rate, % teachers who left the previous year	0.020	0.024	0.833	0.405	1.020	0.973	1.070
	School % of teachers who have 0-3 years of experience	0.006	0.016	0.396	0.693	1.006	0.975	1.038
	New principal since start of study	0.801	0.423	1.892	0.059	2.227	0.968	5.121
Level 1 "Red Flags"	Readiness % below 10%	2.959	0.563	5.257	0.000	19.274	6.367	58.348
	Readiness % above 90%	−2.514	1.168	−2.153	0.032	0.081	0.008	0.806
	Assessed less than 80% of children	0.809	0.762	1.061	0.290	2.246	0.501	10.069
	Readiness % at least 25 percentage points above achievement composite	2.191	0.717	3.055	0.002	8.946	2.181	36.696
	Readiness % at least 25 percentage points below achievement composite	−0.181	0.648	−0.279	0.780	0.835	0.233	2.986
	Readiness % dropped by at least 25 percentage points	−0.577	0.745	−0.774	0.439	0.562	0.130	2.435
	Readiness % increased by at least 25 percentage points	1.198	0.589	2.032	0.043	3.313	1.039	10.568

that schools reporting unrealistic values such as 99% or 100% were more likely to have issues with implementation.

This finding helps rule out the possibility that the regional consultants were persuaded by any structural characteristics of the schools. Rather, it increases our confidence that their ratings were driven by their experiences with teacher implementation of the assessment system.

Four of the quantitative *Red Flags* in Table 9.2 were associated with the probability that the consultant would place a school in the poor implementation group. Schools where less than 10% of the children were identified as "ready" were over 19 times more likely to be placed in the poor implementation group. In contrast, schools where over 90% of the children were rated as "ready" were only .081 times as likely to be rated as poor implementers. Schools where teachers rated children as 25 percentage points or more below the achievement composite were almost nine times more likely to be identified as poor implementers. Finally, schools with large year-to-year increases in readiness percentages were more than three times as likely to be identified by the consultants as poor implementers.

Assessment

A key take home point for readers is that this demonstration of using HLM with quantitized focus group data, combined with the school data profiles, led to an understanding of: (a) the schools that the consultants determined were experiencing implementation problems (understood from the focus group data), (b) factors that did and did not influence these ratings, (c) the capacity to predict schools that are likely to be characterized by implementation concerns, while (d) accounting for school clustering by district in the state. Given the importance of the FAP to educating children in the state, these are valuable findings that would have been quite difficult to achieve without using HLM with quantitized focus group data. Hence, we hope that this demonstration established the potential this procedure brings to social science research.

5 Suggested Applications for HLM with Qualitative Data that have been Quantitized

Anytime one requires sensitive, emergent work that needs to be accounted for in a nested setting, this procedure might be of use. By sensitive, we mean to convey the ideas that qualitative data can, in some cases, be sensitive to measurement accuracy but also be sensitive to context and politics. Recall from our demonstration that consultants were careful to indicate when they felt comfortable with identifying schools with implementation challenges and we doubt that we would have been able to narrow down to the analytic sample without the benefit of the focus groups. We also demonstrated in the example some flexibility around identifying covariates and red flags that allowed for the development of predictive models that will inform future statewide FAP implementation efforts while working with nested analyses (i.e., schools within districts). This, in turn, shows a form of iteration between our design and emergent research questions, which, again, compelled us to present

Table 9.1 as a checklist and not as a stepwise approach to HLM analyses with quantitized data.

HLM analyses with quantitized data could, of course, be extended in a number of ways beyond the type of example presented in this chapter. For instance, this general procedure might be of use when examining Twitter data that are clustered by group. For another example, researchers might deploy surveys with open-ended response options to a large sample with different clusters (e.g., community, organizational membership). A researcher could use topic modelling to identify the topics/themes, then binarize these themes (i.e., 1 = a person contributed to the topic/theme, and 0 otherwise), and then apply HLM, whereby tweets or survey responses are nested by geographic region, or by time, or by some other backend data.

6 Strengths and Limitations of HLM with Qualitative Data that have been Quantitized

The key strength we see in this approach is that one can learn much by modeling quantized data and it is often necessary to handle clustering. To this point, we simply do not see how we could have reached the findings that were achieved in the empirical demonstration had there not been an opportunity to use HLM with quantitized data. There are, however, a few key limitations at hand. The first limitation is that this work is resource intensive. A considerable amount of data was collected and collated for the analyses presented in the empirical demonstration. HLM is, for the most part, a large sample effort; indeed, one even needs a large number of clusters. With too few clusters, it would make more sense to consider clusters as a moderating variable in an OLS model (see the related chapter on this topic in this book). Overall, HLM requires at least five Level-1 units per Level-2 cluster and, in turn, most analyses need at least 30 Level-2 clusters (cf. Raudenbush & Bryk 2002; Snijders & Bosker, 1999). This, in turn, will generally mean that a considerable amount of qualitative data will need to be collected, and/or such data will be somewhat surface in nature. In addition, the notion of quantitizing data will likely mean that some of its richness might be lost in the process. This can be overcome if one chooses to use HLM to extend but not replace qualitative analyses, but, again, this would mean using a large number of resources or some more novel approach, such as analyses using machine-learning tools.

Another limitation is that HLM procedures with quantitized data can be complex. There are multiple considerations that go into making different modeling choices such as the use of random versus fixed effects analyses (which, in essence, deals with statistical generalization from an observed sample to a population), model complexity (e.g., number of predictor variables, interaction effects, covariates), and number of levels (e.g., two-level models, three-level models). Add to this, members of a research team need to be capable of qualitative design and analyses, and it is necessary to think through how best to quantify qualitative data (unless working with datasets derived from Twitter, surveys, etc.).

7 Resources for Learning More About HLM with Qualitative Data that have been Quantitized

Due to space limitations and the fact that Sandelowski, Voils, and Knafl (2009) provide a foundational overview of quantitizing in an article that is easily accessed, we do not cover these details here. We do, however, note that Sandelowski et al. point out that most works gloss over issues of key assumptions, tradeoffs, and benefits of quantitizing. To avoid offering yet another source in the literature that skips over these important issues, the first resource we offer for learning more is to read the Sandelowski et al. article. Sandelowski et al. also point out that quantitizing data and performing subsequent analyses does not necessarily mean a study is taking a mixed methods approach. The degree to which a particular analysis is situated in a mixed methods study, or program of study, will be informed by researcher positioning. If readers wish to be highly confident that their HLM analyses with quantitized data fall within a mixed methods realm, they might review Combs and Onwuegbuzie (2010) and Onwuegbuzie and Combs (2011). These works offer what we see as four key features: (a) they are introductory in nature, (b) they provide an overview of 13 mixed analyses criteria, (c) each piece offers detailed tables and screenshots of software to offer clear guidance, and (d) both works may be accessed on-line, for free. Developing a command of these three sources will set most readers on a good path towards understanding mixed analyses.

There are numerous texts that cover HLM and qualitative analyses. In our judgement, the ones that best fit the idea of performing HLM with quantitized data would be Raudenbush and Bryk's (2002) overview of HLM. Raudenbush and Bryk's work not only covers the conceptual basis for HLM, but also it provides much needed detail around modeling decisions that an analyst will likely need to handle, such as using HLM with ordinal and dichotomous outcome variables. Fortunately, their work provides a compendium of different two-, three- and even four-level models that can be used as a starting point for hierarchical model specification in any given analytic scenario. Hox (2010) and Snijders and Bosker (1999) are additional texts that have been useful in helping us to grasp HLM procedures. Although the ideas presented in this chapter are not contingent on how one might go through the process of qualitative analyses and quantitizing qualitative data, it will still be necessary for researchers to have basic skills in these two arenas. Saldaña's (2012) work provides an accessible overview of numerous qualitative analysis approaches and, in our judgement, provides a way to quickly comprehend specific procedures in the qualitative analysis realms.

As noted earlier, statistical power is a topic that readers will need to consider in advance of conceptualizing any HLM work because this is not a small sample size arena. Two free sources that likely will be quite useful, even though they both focus on randomized controlled trial designs, are: (a) *PowerUp!* And (b) *Optimal Design. PowerUp!* Is a Microsoft Excel-based set of spreadsheets (Dong &

Maynard, 2013) and users may input various analytic expectations (e.g., variance explained by a covariate, ICC values, minimum detectable effect size) for a number of different trial designs to obtain a sense of required sample sizes. *Optimal Design* (Raudenbush et al., 2011) may be downloaded as a Zip file. It offers similar features to *PowerUp!* but, importantly, offers power analyses when dealing with dichotomous outcome variables.

The statistical software R (R Development Core Team, 2014) may be downloaded and used for free (as of this writing, see: www.r-project.org/). R also allows for graphical representation of data and this might be especially useful for HLM because one might, for example, wish to visually examine relationships within hierarchies (e.g., in the empirical example we provide, one might wish to examine the relationship between the variable "schools where less than 10% of the children were identified as ready" and the poor implementation group outcome variable within each district).

One final set of resources for learning more come in the form of specific writing about mixed methods and HLM. Onwuegbuzie and Hitchcock (2015) offers general design advice and described advantages that can be obtained from mixed methods HLM approaches. König (2019) offers an empirical example wherein he mixed qualitative data with HLM, and he demonstrates how a qualitative understanding of context can help explain data variance across different levels in a model. Finally, we would be remiss in failing to mention a recent article by Headley and Plano Clark (2020), who describe applications of multilevel mixed methods research and describe different design stages. This chapter differs from these works in that its purpose was to focus on HLM analyses of quantitized data. Therefore, whereas these resources provide details about HLM, qualitative analyses, quantitizing, and mixed method HLM design advice, the current chapter provides an example focusing on analysis. It is our hope that this combined set of resources will facilitate future mixed analyses wherein HLM is used with quantitized data.

REFERENCES

Ashley, J., & Burke, K. (2009). *Implementing restorative justice: A guide for schools*. Chicago, IL: Illinois Criminal Justice Information Authority.

Bell, B. A., Morgan, G. B., Schoeneberger, J. A., Kromrey, J. D., & Ferron, J. M. (2014). How low can you go? An investigation of the influence of sample size and model complexity on point and interval estimates in two-level linear models. *Methodology*, 10, 1–11. doi:10.1027/1614-2241/a000062

Combs, J. P., & Onwuegbuzie, A. J. (2010). Describing and illustrating data analysis in mixed research. *International Journal of Education*, 2(2), EX, 1–23. Retrieved from www.macrothink.org/journal/index.php/ije/article/viewFile/526/392

Dong, N., & Maynard, R. A. (2013). PowerUp!: A tool for calculating minimum detectable effect sizes and sample size requirements for experimental and quasi-experimental designs. *Journal of Research on Educational Effectiveness*, 6(1), 24–67. doi:10.1080/19345747.2012.673143

Field, A. (2018). *Discovering statistics using SPSS* (5th ed.). Thousand Oaks, CA: Sage.

Headley, M. G., & Plano Clark, V. L. (2020). Multilevel mixed methods research designs: Advancing a refined definition. *Journal of Mixed Methods Research*, 14, 145–163. doi:10.1177/1558689819844417

Hox, J. J. (2010). *Multilevel analysis: Techniques and applications* (2nd ed.). New York, NY: Routledge.

König, S. (2019). Fitness training in physical education: A quantitative dominated crossover mixed methods multilevel study. *International Journal of Multiple Research Approaches*, 11(1), 44–59. doi:10.29034/ijmra.v11n1a2

Maas, C. J. M., & Hox, J. J. (2005). Sufficient sample sizes for multilevel modeling. *Methodology*, 1, 86–92. doi:10.1027/1614-1881.1.3.86

Onwuegbuzie, A. J., & Combs, J. P. (2011). Data analysis in mixed research: A primer. *International Journal of Education*, 3(1): E13. Retrieved from www.macrothink.org/journal/index.php/ije/article/view/618/550

Onwuegbuzie, A. J., & Hitchcock, J. H. (2015). Advanced mixed analyses. In S. N. Hess-Biber & R. B. Johnson (Eds.), *Oxford handbook of multimethod and mixed methods research inquiry* (pp. 275–295). Oxford, England: Oxford University Press.

R Development Core Team. (2014). *R: A language and environment for statistical computing*. Vienna, Austria: R Foundation for Statistical Computing.

Raudenbush, S. W., & Bryk, A. S. (2002). *Hierarchical linear models: Applications and data analysis methods* (2nd ed.). Thousand Oaks, CA: Sage.

Raudenbush, S. W., Martinez, A., & Spybrook, J. (2007). Strategies for improving precision in group-randomized experiments. *Educational Evaluation and Policy Analysis*, 29, 5–29. doi:10.3102/0162373707299460

Raudenbush, S. W., Spybrook, J., Congdon, R., Liu, X., Martinez, A., Bloom, H., & Hill C. (2011). *Optimal design plus empirical evidence (Version 3.0)*. Retrieved from www.wtgrantfoundation.org/resources/optimal-design

Saldaña, J. (2012). *The coding manual for qualitative researchers* (2nd ed.). Thousand Oaks, CA: Sage.

Sandelowski, M., Voils, C. I., & Knafl, G. (2009). On quantitizing. *Journal of Mixed Methods Research*, 3, 208–222. doi:10.1177/1558689809334210

Snijders, T. & Bosker, R. (1999). *Multilevel analysis: An introduction to basic and advanced multilevel modeling*. Thousand Oaks, CA: Sage.

Spybrook, J., Raudenbush, S. W., Liu, X.-f., Congdon, R., Martinez, A. (2006). *Optimal design for longitudinal and multilevel research: Documentation for the "Optimal Design" software*. Ann Arbor, MI: Survey Research Center of the Institute of Social Research at University of Michigan.

10

Bayesian Analyses with Qualitative Data

Prathiba Natesan Batley

1 Definition of Bayesian

Named after the early 18th century English statistician, philosopher, and Presbyterian minister Reverend Thomas Bayes, Bayesian methodology is based on Bayes's theorem, which determines the probability of an event based on prior knowledge about information that might be related to the event. That is, Bayes' theorem states that

$$P(A|B) = \frac{P(B|A)P(A)}{P(B)} \quad (1)$$

In Formula 1, P(A|B) is the conditional probability of A given B and is the quantity in which we are interested, otherwise known as the posterior distribution. In plain language, this is the probability of obtaining the parameter estimates given the data. Thus, Bayesian methodology uses knowledge about the parameters in the form of prior information and information from the data to obtain parameter estimates. In Formula 1, prior information is given as P(A). Prior information may be obtained via previous research, researchers' educated guess about the parameter, historic data, or even an agnostic belief about the values that the parameter could possibly take (Gelman, 2002). The information obtained from the data is called likelihood and is represented using the term P(B|A) in Formula 1. In sum, the posterior is proportional to the product of the prior and the likelihood.

In the denominator is the marginal likelihood, which until 1984, rendered Bayes's theorem unsolvable (intractable) for even mildly complex models. In 1984, Geman and Geman described the algorithm devised by the physicist Josiah Willard Gibbs eight decades earlier. In the Gibbs sampler, which is a Markov chain Monte Carlo algorithm, the joint distribution of a multivariate probability distribution is approximated by sampling from the conditional distribution of each variable that forms the joint distribution. Due to this approximation, Bayesian has gained importance in recent decades in many disciplines (e.g., Ansari & Jedidi, 2000; Ansari, Jedidi, & Jagpal, 2000; Gelman, 2008; Gelman et al., 2013; Gill, 2014; Kieftenbeld & Natesan, 2012; Kruschke, 2013, 2015; Lynch, 2007; Natesan, 2015, 2019; Natesan & Hedges, 2017; Nateson Batley & Hedges, in press; Natesan, Limbers, & Varni, 2010; Natesan, Nandakumar, Minka, & Rubright, 2016; Natesan Batley, Minka, & Hedges, 2020; Natesan Batley, Shukla Mehta, & Hitchcock, 2020; Natesan Batley, Boedeker, & Onwuegbuzie, 2020; Onwuegbuzie, Hitchcock, Natesan, & Newman, 2018).

Bayesian methodology provides many advantages when compared to the more commonly used frequentist methodology (e.g., ordinary least squares, maximum likelihood). The first is the philosophical difference. We have already established that Bayesian yields the term P(A|B), which is the probability of observing the null given the data. However, in frequentist framework, we assume that the null is true in the population and compute the probability of obtaining data at least as extreme as the ones already obtained, that is P(B|A). Finally, we reject or fail to reject the null based on this probability value, concluding that this is the probability of the null being true, that is, P(A|B). Obviously, as we can see from Formula 1, P(A|B) is not the same as P(B|A). The logical equivalent of this would be to say, if the sky looks cloudy it will certainly rain is the same as if it rains the sky must be cloudy. The first statement is wrong whereas the latter is correct. Thus, this conclusion to reject or fail to reject based on equating the two conditional probabilities is a logical fallacy (Cohen, 1988).

Second, Bayesian estimation provides complete distributional information about the parameter, along with the credibility of each value the parameter can take (Kruschke, 2013). As demonstrated by Natesan Batley (in press), three distributions with the same mean and standard deviation but different shapes can yield very different information (see Figure 10.1). In the first and the third panels of Figure 10.1, we know that a mean value of 3 is not an appropriate description of the bimodal and the uniform distributions. Thus, having a distribution for the parameters allows us to determine whether the expected a posteriori (EAP) estimates that are generally reported in statistics represented an appropriate summary of the parameter of interest. Thus, posterior distributions provide us with more information than do point estimates accompanied by confidence intervals that are obtained from frequentist methodology.

Third, frequentist approaches produce point estimates that are accompanied by interval estimates called confidence intervals. A 95% confidence interval is defined as follows: When the experiment is repeated an infinite number of times and infinite such analyses are conducted for those infinite datasets, 95% of the intervals subsequently obtained will contain the true value of the parameter. However, what the 95% confidence interval at hand fails to indicate is whether this interval contains the

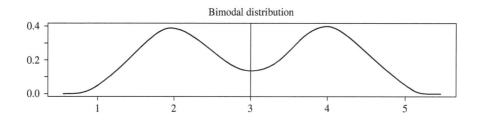
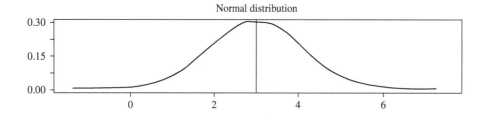

FIGURE 10.1 Three distributions with the same mean and standard deviation.

true value or not. Instead, the Bayesian credible interval is probability based (Gelman et al., 2013). A 95% credible interval indicates that the probability of finding the true value in this interval is 0.95. This is a more straightforward interpretation and is made possible because the parameter estimates are obtained in the form of posterior distributions which contain all possible values that the parameter can take (Lynch, 2007). In sum, probabilistic statements and understanding could be derived from a given credible interval that would be impossible for a given confidence interval. There are many more advantages of Bayesian methods, which will be discussed in detail in this chapter.

2 When Use of Bayesian Analysis of Qualitative Data is Appropriate in MMR

Bayesian methods have been shown to work well for small sample data because they do not depend on asymptotic or large sample theory (e.g., Ansari & Jedidi, 2000; Ansari et al., 2000; Kieftenbeld & Natesan, 2012; Natesan, 2015, 2019; Natesan & Hedges, 2017). This is particularly advantageous to the subject under discussion, which is Bayesian analysis of qualitative data. Qualitative data generally tend to have smaller sample sizes, which means that many commonly used frequentist methods might be rendered inappropriate for analysis. Bayesian methods are also free of distributional assumptions even for small data (e.g. Natesan Batley, Shukla Mehta et al., 2020). This is obviously a useful trait because qualitative data do not necessarily follow strict distributional shapes. Stevens's (1946, 1951) four scales of measurement—nominal, ordinal, interval, and ratio—are generally used in the context of quantitative data analysis. However, these categories of measurement are equally valid for qualitative observations as well (King, Keohane, & Verba, 1994, pp. 2150–2153). In fact, these scales, as commonly used, can be frequently bisected into qualitative (nominal, ordinal) and quantitative (interval, ratio) measures. Thus, data from commonly used ordinal scales, such as Likert-format scale, may be considered as qualitative data.

It is in this context of quantitising qualitative data (Sandelowski, Voils, & Knafl, 2009) that we will be using enumeration as a technique to count how often an event occurs or descriptors occur in qualitative data (Buckley, 2004). For instance, take the example of a child with autism, Sam. A behavioural researcher might be interested in designing and implementing a behavioural intervention that is targeted towards reducing these problem behaviours of Sam. The child might display one or several of these problem behaviours such as hitting, scratching, or biting others; hitting or biting self; throwing or breaking objects, eating inedible objects, running away or wandering off, tantrums, and screaming. In sum, these could manifest in the form of property destruction, physical aggression, self-injury, and/or tantrums (National Research Council, 2001).

The purpose of the research is to effectively reduce problem behaviours while also providing sufficient evidence that in this single case experimental design (SCED), it was the intervention that led to a reduction in problem behaviours. However, both in qualitative analysis and commonly used analyses such as frequentist methods (e.g., regression, *t* tests), it would be impossible to conduct any robust analysis that would show evidence to support causality. This is particularly because SCED data are typically small sample data with few participants (Gast & Ledford, 2014) and therefore, large sample quantitative methods cannot be used. Additionally, SCED data exhibit autocorrelation; that is, the observation at a particular time-point is dependent on the observation at the previous time-point (Huitema, 1985; Huitema & McKean, 1998, 2000). This is the antithesis of the independence of observations assumption that is a key assumption that commonly underlies analytical techniques such as regression, *t* test, analysis of variance (ANOVA), and so forth. In order to overcome this problem of autocorrelation, maximum likelihood estimation may be employed. However, maximum likelihood requires a large sample size and is thus rendered inappropriate for SCED data. Further exacerbating all these complications is the fact that SCED data are often count or percentage data (Natesan Batley, Shukla Mehta, et al., 2020; Rindskopf, 2014). This compounds the requirement for a technique that is robust even in the absence of asymptotic theory. Bayesian overcomes all these disadvantages. Moreover, Bayesian credible interval estimates of autocorrelation have been shown to have more accurate coverage than do ordinary least squares estimates (Shadish, Rindskopf, Hedges, & Sullivan, 2013).

This aforementioned example case of Sam is what I will expand on for the sake of demonstrating Bayesian analysis of qualitative data in this chapter. However, this is only one such scenario wherein Bayesian analysis of qualitative data is probably the only appropriate technique to use. I will not be expanding on all possible scenarios that are appropriate for Bayesian analysis of qualitative data, but I will conclude this section with the caveat that this is an area that is still in its stages of infancy and presents great possibilities for exploration for future researchers.

3 Technical Outline of Bayesian Analysis of Qualitative Data for MMR

Let us assume that the researcher is interested in showing that Sam's problem behaviours have reduced following the introduction of the intervention. For these data, we would consider an interrupted time-series model—that is a model wherein the independent variable is time and the dependent or outcome variable is the number of problem behaviours exhibited by Sam observed in a 1-hour observation period. The data are centered about a mean in the baseline phase (the first phase, also called the A phase in SCEDs) and centered about another mean value in the intervention phase (the second phase, also called the B phase in SCEDs). The interruption here is the intervention, which initiates a change in the mean in the intervention phase. As mentioned before, the data are autocorrelated. That is, the value of the outcome variable at time-point t is correlated with the value of the outcome variable at time-point (t-1). I describe this model now in statistical terms. Note that because the data are count data (i.e., number of problem behaviours), it is most appropriate to assume that they follow a Poisson distribution than a normal distribution that is more appropriate for intervally scaled data. The Poisson distribution represents a discrete probability distribution that denotes the probability of a specific number of events occurring within a fixed interval of time or space. These events have a known constant mean rate and are independent of the time since the last event (Haight, 1967). This is the equivalent of independence of observations assumption for normal data. Onwuegbuzie et al. (2018) demonstrated the Bayesian analysis of mixed data in SCEDs by using qualitative data as priors and quantitative data as likelihood. However, here, I show a Bayesian analysis of mixed data wherein the likelihood comes from qualitative data and the priors come from quantitative data.

The observed value at the first time point (y_{p1}) in Phase *p* follows a Poisson distribution with mean $\hat{y}_{p1}$, where $\hat{y}_{p1}$ is the probability of obtaining a given response on the given model. The remainder of the time series follows a Poisson procedure with 1-lag autocorrelated errors (e.g., Harrop & Velicer, 1985; Velicer & Molenaar, 2013). The predicted values in the remainder of the time series are distributed as:

$$y_{pt} \mid H_{pt-1}, \Theta \sim Po\left(\hat{y}_{pt(pt-1)}\right). \quad (2)$$

In Equation 2, H_{pt-1} is the past history, Θ is the vector of parameters, and *Po* refers to Poisson distribution. Essentially, what Equation 2 demonstrates is that the predicted value of the dependent variable at Time *t* in Phase *p* is Poisson-distributed as the probability of the predicted value of the current data point given the past history, or the value of the previous data point. The generalized linear model and the serial dependency of the residual (e_t) can be expressed as,

$$\hat{y}_{pt} = \begin{cases} \exp(\beta_{01} + e_{pt-1}), \; if \; t \leq t_b \\ \exp(\beta_{02} + e_{pt-1}), \; otherwise \end{cases} \quad (3)$$

and

$$e_{pt-1} = \rho e_{pt-2} + \varepsilon. \quad (4)$$

In Equation 3, $\hat{y}_{pt}$ is the probability of the predicted value of the dependent variable at Time *t* in phase *p*; β_{01} and β_{02} are the means or intercepts of Phase 1 and Phase 2, respectively; e_{pt} is the error at Time *t* in Phase *p*; ρ is the autocorrelation coefficient; and ε is the independently distributed error. In Equation 4, *e* is white noise created by a combination of random error (ε) and autocorrelation between adjacent time-points (ρ). Their standard deviations are derived from Equation 5.

$$\sigma_e = \frac{\sigma_\varepsilon}{\sqrt{1-\rho^2}} \quad (5)$$

Now, consider a design with only two phases: baseline and treatment. Let the time-points in the baseline phase be

1, 2,...,t_b and in the treatment phase be t_{b+1}, ..., t_n. Then, the intercept β_{0p} can be modeled as:

$$\beta_{0p} = \begin{cases} \beta_{01}, & \text{if } t \leq t_b \\ \beta_{02}, & \text{otherwise} \end{cases} \quad (6)$$

The intercepts now need to be drawn from, say normal distributions. Let us assume that the researcher considers her/his intervention to be effective only if the outcome variable is decreased to not more than 40% of the original frequency of problem behaviours. Let us also assume that, from previous research, it is known that the number of problem behaviours exhibited by someone whose symptoms closely mimic Sam's is between five and 10. This means a reduction in the number of problem behaviours to between two and four in the intervention phase would be expected. Thus, we will use this information based on previous research to specify our priors. However, we will attempt to remain a little less optimistic about the expected values. The means of these normal distributions (μ_{01} and μ_{01}) are independently drawn from normal distributions with means 7.5 and 4 (the mid-points of our ranges above), and standard deviations for each phase independently drawn from gamma distributions, which are most commonly used priors for standard deviation. The advantage of gamma distribution as a prior for standard deviation is that it contains only non-zero positive values, which is the characteristic of the standard deviation of any variable.

$$\beta_{0p} \sim norm(\mu_{0p}, \sigma_p^2); p = 1, 2 \quad (7)$$

$$\mu_{01} \sim norm(7.5, 10) \quad (8a)$$

$$\mu_{02} \sim norm(4, 10) \quad (8b)$$

$$\sigma_p \sim gamma(1, 1). \quad (9)$$

An effect-size estimate of the treatment can be obtained from the posterior distribution of the rate ratio of the mean of the distribution from which the intercepts are drawn, as given in Equation 10 (Natesan Batley, Shukla Mehta, et al., 2020).

$$\mu_{ratio} = \frac{e^{\mu_2}}{e^{\mu_1}} \quad (10)$$

This rate ratio is the ratio of the rate between the treatment and the baseline phases. Smaller rate ratio values are desirable for substantively negative outcome variables because this would indicate the effectiveness of the intervention in decreasing the occurrence of negative outcome variables in the treatment phase compared to that of the baseline phase. In our case, the outcome variable is problem behaviours, which is a substantively negative variable.

4 Empirical Demonstration of Bayesian Analysis of Qualitative Data for MMR

Figure 10.2 illustrates the data for Sam's problem behaviours. I would like to remind the reader that for a SCED to meet the optimum design requirements according to the What

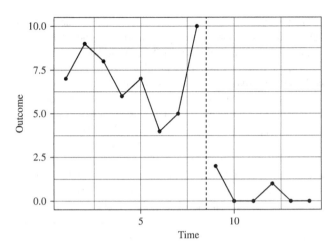

FIGURE 10.2 Plot showing the number of problem behaviours for Sam.

Works Clearinghouse standards (Kratochwill et al., 2010), there needs to be three instances of intervention effect. This can be undertaken in the form of a multi-phase design such as an ABAB or multiple baseline through staggering the intervention for three or more participants. However, the example we are considering here is only for demonstration purposes. A full ABAB design example for the same concept is given by Natesan Batley, Shukla Mehta, et al. (2020). The codes for the program for the setup discussed in this chapter are available from Github for free at https://github.com/prathiba-stat/Bayesian-qualitative. JAGS 4.0.0 (Just another Gibbs sampler; Plummer, 2003) is used by these programs to fit the data. The R package runjags (Denwood, 2016) runs parallel chains and iterates the model estimates until convergence. Runjags checks convergence using two convergence diagnostics: the multivariate potential scale reduction factor (MPSRF; Brooks & Gelman, 1998) and Heidelberger and Welch's convergence diagnostic (Heidelberger & Welch, 1983). Four chains were conducted. The corresponding JAGS code is given in Github. The estimates are shown in Table 10.1.

Level Changes

The estimated levels of the outcome variable in both baseline and intervention phases are 6.88 [i.e., exp(1.93)] and 0.5

TABLE 10.1

Descriptives of Posteriors of Parameter Estimates for Sam's Problem Behaviours

	Lower 95%	Median	Upper 95%	M	SD
rho	−0.08	0.29	0.6	0.27	0.19
mu[1]	1.61	1.93	2.24	1.93	0.16
mu[2]	−2.09	−0.66	0.49	−0.72	0.67
sigma[1]	1.43	3.72	9.61	4.55	3.25
sigma[2]	0.85	2.57	6.95	3.18	2.48
prec[1]	0	0.07	0.24	0.09	0.07
prec[2]	0	0.15	0.57	0.2	0.19
rate_ratio	0.02	0.07	0.2	0.08	0.05

[i.e., exp(-0.66)], respectively. Readers can compare the exponent of the *mu* (estimates from Table 10.1) means and quantiles with the reported means. The corresponding posterior standard deviations ranged from 0.16 to 0.67. The posterior standard deviations are rather small for all phases. The posterior mean of autocorrelations is very small for the data (−0.08).

Rate Ratio Effect Size

Posterior density plot of the rate ratio effect size is given in Figure 10.3. To recap, the rate ratio is interpreted as a reduction or increase in treatment compared to the baseline. Therefore, the decrease in the outcome variable was .07 times of what it was in baseline phase. When considering 95% of the highest density interval (HDI) of the posterior density, the outcome variable in the intervention phase is .02 to .20 times of what it was in baseline phase. This shows that problem behaviours in the first intervention phase were only 0.2% to 20% of what they were in the baseline phase. The researcher is now free to choose a region of practical equivalence (ROPE; Kruschke, 2015), wherein the null hypothesis that there was no effect can be accepted based on what values the researcher deems to be negligibly different from the null. The posterior distribution of the rate ratio in Figure 10.2 gives both the probable value of the rate ratio and its corresponding probability (i.e., probability density). For instance, the effect size between baseline phase and intervention phase is peaked at .05 (mode), with 95% of the values lying between .02 and .20. This is the 95% highest density interval.

Suppose we decide that a treatment is effective only if the outcome variable is decreased to not more than 40% of the original frequency of problem behaviours. We see that the posterior distribution for the phase change between baseline and intervention do not contain the value of 0.4 and all values are less than 0.4. This means the null can be accepted that the probabilities of the rate ratio of outcome variable being less than 4 times for phase change between baseline and intervention is 100%, as seen in Figure 10.2. The vertical line at 0.4 in the figure shows the hypothesized value chosen by the researcher and the percentage value in the figure represents the probability mass that falls on the left side of the hypothesized value for the phase changes.

5 Suggested Applications of Bayesian Analysis of Qualitative Data in MMR

I demonstrated in the previous example how Bayesian analysis of very small sample qualitative data can add to commonly used analyses such as qualitative analysis or visual analysis. The Bayesian rate ratio modelled using Poisson distribution had the following advantages: (a) it was robust to small samples; (b) it could easily incorporate non-normal distributions such as Poisson distributions, thereby giving rise to ease in modelling qualitative data; (c) it could model autocorrelations; (d) it produced an effect size that took into effect all the model complexities of SCED count data; (e) it produced posterior distributions of all the parameter estimates that gave more information about the estimates than frequentist methodologies do; (f) it provided visual representations of the distributions; (g) it produced credible intervals that are more straightforward to interpret, and (h) it allowed the researcher to reject or to accept the null or the research hypothesis instead of only being able to reject or fail to reject the null, as would be the case with frequentist approaches.

The list of advantages provided by Bayesian methodology is long and growing even further with the advent of computationally efficient technology. Qualitative data provide unique challenges to being quantitised and analysed using quantitative methodologies because they do not necessarily conform to a perfect interval scale or a distributional form. They are also generally smaller samples. Bayesian methodology overcomes all these challenges and also allows us to incorporate prior information about the parameters based on experience, previous research, data from other sources, and/or literature.

Onwuegbuzie et al. (2018) provided examples of how this quantitising of qualitative data within the Bayesian realm can lead to systematic mixed methods analysis. This is another example of Bayesian analysis of not only qualitative data, but also data collected via multiple methodologies. The realm for developing these techniques remains unexplored and offers almost infinite possibilities. The definition of data has expanded in the last few decades (e.g., to include photographs, tweets, likes, comments, views, page visits; cf. Lynch & Gerber, this volume). For instance, Leech and Onwuegbuzie (2008) offered a typology of four broad qualitative data sources: (a) talk, (b) observations, (c) documents, and (d) images. Following this, the treatment and analyses of these new types of data should also expand to meet the fast-growing expectations of how best to analyse, to interpret, and to infer from data.

6 Strengths and Limitations of Bayesian Analysis of Qualitative Data in MMR

The technical and philosophical strengths of using Bayesian methodology for qualitative data have been discussed in the previous sections. I would like to emphasize a few points

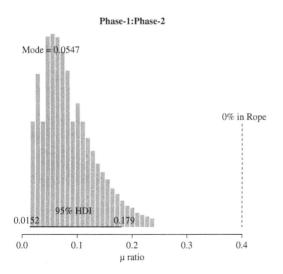

FIGURE 10.3 Posterior density plot of the rate ratio effect size for problem behaviours.

here. The use of prior supports replication research, which has become an important topic (e.g., Cook, 2014). This is because researchers should be using prior information to hypothesize (and empirically test) the size of a plausible treatment impact on some outcome measure. As more information is collected, the hypothesis can become more refined. Thus, having a Bayesian mindset entails continued thought about replication. If researchers are working with distributions of plausible treatment values, they will be in a stronger position to specify the strength of an intervention in advance of a study. The choice of priors and its study is a vast subject whose thorough discussion is beyond the scope of this study. Interested readers are referred to some seminal works on this topic (Gelman et al., 2013; Gill, 2014; Lynch, 2007). There are studies that compare the performance of various prior specifications on parameter estimates and that shed light on the importance of this area of study (de la Torre, Stark, & Chernyshenko, 2006; Kieftenbeld & Natesan, 2012). As Natesan Batley, Boedeker, and Onwuegbuzie (2020) noted, we include prior information when defining a problem, reviewing literature, drawing conclusions from our data, and comparing findings with findings from other research. However, we fail to acknowledge that the data we have are just a sample and, therefore, we should consider findings from other sources while analysing data in order to place our truth within the context of other truths. This is what Bayesian allows us to do. With more systematic inclusion of priors, we are able to push the realm of qualitative data analysis to tackle the replicability crisis that could earlier not be addressed via qualitative methods. This defiance of boundaries is the biggest advantage offered by Bayesian analysis of qualitative data.

However, Bayesian methodology is not without its limitations. It is a computationally intensive technique and until a few years ago, it could take minutes to hours to analyse reasonably complex models. However, with the advent of new technology, this limitation is being addressed rapidly. Nevertheless, there is a dearth of Bayesian representation in the curriculum (Natesan Batley, Boedeker et al., 2020). Very few academic programs train the future generations in Bayesian methodology, and the number of professional development programs in Bayesian is also few and far between. This creates a chasm between *hardcore* Bayesians who are at the helm of developing new models and algorithms, and applied researchers who desperately need such techniques to solve their data challenges in the real world. For this chasm to reduce, there needs to be a change at the educational level in curricula, and at the policy level with respect to editorial guidelines, evidence-based research guidelines, and funding guidelines. Finally, there is a learning curve associated with Bayesian. However, with the availability of Bayesian even in commonly available software programs such as SPSS and in freeware such as R, this limitation can be addressed.

7 Resources for Learning More About Bayesian Analysis of Qualitative Data

There are plenty of resources for learning Bayesian analysis (e.g., Gelman, 2008; Gelman et al., 2013; Gill, 2014; Kruschke, 2015; Lynch, 2007). The aforementioned can get an uninitiated reader started on Bayesian analysis. However, there is a need for more work on Bayesian analysis of qualitative data. This area remains widely unexplored. I found Buckley (2004) to be a nice introduction to Bayesian qualitative data analysis in the political sciences. However, this work is fairly technical. Onwuegbuzie et al. (2018) provide some good examples of quantitising qualitative data for Bayesian analysis in a mixed methods framework using general linear models and meta-analysis. Natesan Batley (2020) provided an introduction to the use of Bayesian methods in a multiple inquiry framework that also involved quantitising qualitative data for Bayesian analysis. Roberts, Dixon-Woods, Fitzpatrick, Abrams, and Jones (2002) used findings from the qualitative research studies to provide prior information to analyse their data using fully integrated Bayesian thinking (FIBT). Most of these studies involve quantitising qualitative data to be used as priors. There is a need for more studies that can explore how to use qualitative data to provide information towards likelihood and not simply for prior specification. The present chapter is one such example. In fact, it uses qualitative data as likelihood and quantitative data as prior information to analyse SCED data using the FIBT framework.

REFERENCES

Ansari, A., & Jedidi, K. (2000). Bayesian factor analysis for multilevel binary observations. *Psychometrika*, 65, 475–497. doi:10.1007/BF02296339

Ansari, A., Jedidi, K., & Jagpal, S. (2000). A hierarchical Bayesian approach for modeling heterogeneity in structural equation models. *Marketing Science*, 19, 328–347. doi10.1287/mksc.19.4.328.11789

Brooks, S., & Gelman, A. (1998). Some issues in monitoring convergence of iterative simulations. *Journal of Computational and Graphical Statistics*, 7, 434–455. doi:10.1080/10618600.1998.10474787

Buckley, J. (2004). Simple Bayesian inference for qualitative political research. *Political Analysis*, 12, 386–399. doi:10.1093/pan/mph025

Cohen, J. (1988). *Statistical power analysis for the behavioral sciences* (2nd ed.). Hillsdale, NJ: Lawrence Erlbaum.

Cook, B. G. (2014). A call for examining replication and bias in special education research. *Remedial and Special Education*, 35, 233–246. doi:10.1177/0741932514528995

de la Torre J., Stark S., & Chernyshenko O. S. (2006). Markov chain Monte Carlo estimation of item parameters for the generalized graded unfolding model. *Applied Psychological Measurement*, 30, 216–232. doi:10.1177/0146621605282772

Denwood, M. J. (2016). runjags: An R package providing interface utilities, parallel computing methods and additional distributions for MCMC models in JAGS. *Journal of Statistical Software*, 71. doi:10.18637/jss.v071.i09

Gast, D. L., & Ledford, J. R. (2014). *Single subject research methodology in behavioral sciences* (2nd ed.). New York, NY: Routledge.

Gelman, A. (2002). Prior distribution. In A. H. El-Shaarawi & W. W. Piegorsch (Eds.), *Encyclopedia of environmetrics* (Vol. 3, pp. 1634–1637). Chichester, England: John Wiley and Sons.

Gelman, A. (2008). Teaching Bayes to graduate students in political science, Sociology, Public Health, Education, Economics, ... *The American Statistician, 62*, 202–205. doi:10.1198/000313008X330829

Gelman, A., Carlin, J. B., Stern, H. S., Dunson, D. B., Vehtari, A., & Rubin, D. B. (2013). *Bayesian data analysis* (3rd ed.). Boca Raton, FL: Chapman & Hall.

Geman, S., & Geman, D. (1984). Stochastic relaxation, Gibbs distributions, and the Bayesian restoration of images. *IEEE Transactions on Pattern Analysis and Machine Intelligence, 6*, 721–741. doi:10.1109/TPAMI.1984.4767596.

Gill, J. (2014). *Bayesian methods: A social and behavioral sciences approach* (3rd ed.). Boca Raton, FL: Chapman & Hall.

Haight, F. A. (1967). *Handbook of the poisson distribution*. New York, NY: John Wiley & Sons.

Harrop, J. W., & Velicer, W. F. (1985). A comparison of alternative approaches to the analysis of interrupted time-series. *Multivariate Behavioral Research, 20*, 27–44. doi:10.1207/s15327906mbr2001_2

Heidelberger, P., & Welch, P. D. (1983). Simulation run length control in the presence of an initial transient. *Operations Research, 31*, 1109–1144. doi:10.1287/opre.31.6.1109

Huitema, B. E. (1985). Autocorrelation in applied behavior analysis: A myth. *Behavioral Assessment, 7*, 107–118.

Huitema, B. E., & McKean, J. W. (1998). Irrelevant autocorrelation in least-squares intervention models. *Psychological Methods, 3*, 104–116. doi:10.1037/1082-989X.3.1.104

Huitema, B. E., & McKean, J. W. (2000). A simple and powerful test for autocorrelated errors in OLS intervention models. *Psychological Reports, 87*, 3–20. doi:10.2466/pr0.2000.87.1.3

Kieftenbeld, V., & Natesan, P. (2012). Recovery of graded response model parameters: A comparison of marginal maximum likelihood and Markov chain Monte Carlo estimation. *Applied Psychological Measurement, 36*, 399–419. doi:10.1177/0146621612446170

King, G., Keohane, R. O., & Verba, S. (1994). *Designing social inquiry: Scientific inference in qualitative research*. Princeton, NJ: Princeton University Press.

Kratochwill, T. R., Hitchcock, J. H., Horner, R. H., Levin, J. R., Odom, S. L., Rindskopf, D. M., & Shadish, W. R. (2010). *What Works Clearinghouse: Single-case design technical documentation. Version 1.0 (Pilot)*. Retrieved from https://ies.ed.gov/ncee/wwc/Docs/ReferenceResources/wwc_scd.pdf

Kruschke, J. K. (2013). Bayesian estimation supersedes the t-test. *Journal of Experimental Psychology: General, 142*, 573–603. doi:10.1037/a0029146

Kruschke, J. K. (2015). *Doing Bayesian data analysis: A tutorial with R, JAGS, and Stan* (2nd ed.). Burlington, MA: Academic Press/Elsevier.

Leech, N. L., & Onwuegbuzie, A. J. (2008). Qualitative data analysis: A compendium of techniques and a framework for selection for school psychology research and beyond. *School Psychology Quarterly, 23*, 587–604. doi:10.1037/1045-3830.23.4.587

Lynch, S. M. (2007). *Introduction to applied Bayesian statistics and estimation for social scientists*. New York, NY: Springer.

Natesan, P. (2015). Comparing interval estimates for small sample ordinal CFA models. *Frontiers in Psychology, 6*, 1599. doi:10.3389/fpsyg.2015.01599

Natesan, P. (2019). Fitting Bayesian models for single-case experimental designs: A tutorial. *Methodology, 15*, 147–156. doi:10.1027/1614-2241/a000180

Natesan, P., & Hedges, L. V. (2017). Bayesian unknown change-point models to investigate immediacy in single case designs. *Psychological Methods, 22*, 743–759. doi:10.1037/met0000134.

Natesan Batley, P. & Hedges L.-V. (in press). Accurate model vs. accurate estimates: A study of Bayesian single-case experimental designs. *Behavior Research Methods*.

Natesan, P., Limbers, C., & Varni, J. W. (2010). Bayesian Estimation of graded response multilevel models using Gibbs sampling: Formulation and illustration, *Educational and Psychological Measurement, 70*, 420–439. doi:10.1177/0013164409355696

Natesan, P., Nandakumar, R., Minka, T., & Rubright, J. (2016). Bayesian prior choice in IRT estimation using MCMC and variational Bayes. *Frontiers in Psychology, 7*, 1422. doi:10.3389/fpsyg.2016.01422

Natesan Batley, P. (in press). Use of Bayesian estimation in the context of fully integrated mixed methods models. In J. Hitchcock & A. J. Onwuegbuzie (Eds.) *Routledge handbook for advancing integration in mixed methods research*. New York, NY: Sage.

Natesan Batley, P., Boedeker, P., & Onwuegbuzie, A. J. (2020). Adopting a meta-generative way of thinking in the field of education via the use of Bayesian methods: A multimethod approach in a post-truth and COVID-19 era. *International Journal of Multiple Research Approaches, 12*(1).

Natesan Batley, P., Minka, T., & Hedges, L. V. (2020). Investigating immediacy in multiple phase-change single case experimental designs using a Bayesian unknown change-points model. *Behavioral Research Methods*. doi:10.3758/s13428-020-01345-z.

Natesan Batley, P., Shukla Mehta, S., & Hitchcock, J. (2020). Integrating visual and statistical analyses in single case experimental research using Bayesian unknown change-point models. *Behavioral Disorders*. doi:10.1177/0198742920930704

National Research Council. (2001). *Educating children with autism*. Washington DC: The National Academies Press. doi:10.17226/10017.

Onwuegbuzie, A., Hitchcock, J., Natesan, P., & Newman, I. (2018). Using fully integrated Bayesian thinking to address the 1 + 1 = 1 integration challenge. *International Journal of Multiple Research Approaches, 10*, 666–678. doi:10.29034/ijmra.v10n1a43

Plummer, M. (2003). *JAGS: A program for analysis of Bayesian graphical models using Gibbs sampling*. In Proceedings of the 3rd international workshop on distributed statistical computing.

Rindskopf, D. (2014). Nonlinear Bayesian analysis for single case designs. *Journal of School Psychology, 52*, 179–189. doi:10.1016/j.jsp.2013.12.003

Roberts, K., Dixon-Woods, M., Fitzpatrick, R., Abrams, K., & Jones, D. R. (2002). Factors affecting uptake of childhood immunisation: An example of Bayesian synthesis of qualitative and quantitative evidence. *Lancet, 360*, 1596–1599. doi:10.1016/S0140-6736(02)11560-1

Sandelowski, M., Voils, C. I., & Knafl, G. (2009). On quantitizing. *Journal of Mixed Methods Research, 3,* 208–222. doi:10.1177/1558689809334210

Shadish, W. R., Rindskopf, D. M., Hedges, L. V., & Sullivan, K. J. (2013). Bayesian estimates of autocorrelations in single-case designs. *Behavioral Research Methods, 45,* 813–821. doi:10.3758/s13428-012-0282-1

Stevens, S. S. (1946). On the theory of scales of measurement. *Science, 103,* 677–680. doi:10.1126/science.103.2684.677

Stevens, S. S. (1951). Mathematics, measurement, and psychophysics. In S. S. Stevens (Ed.) *Handbook of experimental psychology* (pp. 1–49). New York, NY: Wiley.

Velicer, W. F., & Molenaar, P. (2013). Time series analysis: Research methods in psychology. In J. Schinka & W. F. Velicer (Eds.). *Handbook of psychology* (2nd ed., Vol. 2, pp. 628–660). New York, NY: John Wiley & Sons.

11

Item Response Theory Integrating Qualitative Data

Vanessa Scherman and Linda Liebenberg

1 Definition of Using Qualitative Data and IRT for MMR Instrument Development

Across disciplines, researchers are calling for greater inclusion of population experience and perspective in research processes, allowing for greater cultural and contextual relevance of findings (see, for e.g., American Psychological Association, Task Force on Resilience and Strength in Black Children and Adolescents, 2008; Chilisa, 2005; Robinson, 2007; Smith, 1999; Tweed & DeLongis, 2006; Walter & Anderson, 2013). Although this shift in focus has occurred predominantly in the field of qualitative research, the continuing prevalence of quantitative surveys has raised the question of how we ensure that these measures better reflect lived experience of the communities who form our research focus. Indeed, authors such as Cheung, van de Vijver, and Leong (2011) have made strong arguments for the development of psychological tools that better account for cultural and contextual relevance. As Tudge (2008) has cautioned, researchers may choose to use qualitative research approaches rather than quantitative research approaches as a means of responding to concerns of representation. In response, mixed methods researchers have advocated for the integration of qualitative and quantitative approaches in the development of scales that hold greater representational validity (Onwuegbuzie, Bustamante, & Nelson, 2010).

To strengthen validity claims, Creswell and Plano Clark (2018), for example, elaborate on exploratory mixed methods research designs that focus on instrument development. Two variations are put forward, namely, the instrument development model and the taxonomy development model (Creswell & Plano Clark, 2018). Each model typically begins with a qualitative phase, which is then followed by a quantitative phase, but the manner in which the phases are connected differs. In the instrument development model, the topic is initially explored from qualitative approaches, where qualitative findings guide the development of items for the quantitative instrument. In the second data collection phase, quantitative data are used in the validation process. Thus, instrument development connects the qualitative and quantitative phases. By contrast, in the taxonomy development model, qualitative data are normally used to identify important variables with the aim of developing a taxonomy or classification system or a theory. The qualitative phase produces specific categories that are used to direct research questions and data collection strategies for the quantitative phase. However, it should be noted that, regardless of the model selected, validity and reliability are not functions of the test but rather of the scores (cf. Onwuegbuzie & Daniel, 2002, 2004; Thompson & Vacha-Haase, 2000; Vacha-Haase, Kogan, & Thompson, 2000; Witta & Daniel, 1998).

2 When Use of Using Qualitative Data and IRT for MMR Instrument Development is Appropriate

Despite these developments, Daigneault and Jacob (2014) highlight the need for additional and continued discussion of how to use mixed methods research approaches in instrument development and validation. Although Onwuegbuzie et al. (2010) highlight the value of integrating multiple data sources in instrument development and using crossover analyses to ensure validity, as suggested earlier, a sequential (i.e. QUAL → QUAN) approach is predominantly used in ways that keep data and data analysis separate (see, for e.g., Ungar & Liebenberg, 2011). Put simply, qualitative data are analysed using qualitative approaches for item development. Once items are integrated into a scale, these are then assessed quantitatively to ensure instrument score reliability and score validity. Drawing on Onwuegbuzie and Combs's (2010) explanation of crossover analyses, we are proposing the integration of quantitative analysis at an earlier stage and an integration with qualitative data, conducting analysis of qualitative data using Item Response Theory (IRT). Specifically, in this chapter, we argue that data collected and analysed using descriptive phenomenology forms a strong foundational basis for the development of instrument items. Items then become codes to be used in a quantitative content analysis (Babbie & Mouton, 2001; Neuendorf, 2017) of the qualitative data. The resulting frequency counts linked to each item through the quantitative content analysis form the basis for an IRT analysis. It is our contention that, in this way, piloted measures are already that much stronger in terms of content validity. First, we present an argument for the use of a descriptive phenomenological approach to qualitative data collection together with a secondary analysis using quantitative content analysis. Following this, we highlight item response theory, with the focus on Rasch analysis, and the data structure required in order to undertake the analyses. We conclude with thoughts on how this type of analyses can strengthen validity claims and contribute meaningfully to the design and development of culturally and psychometrically sound instruments.

3 Technical Outline of Using Qualitative Data and IRT for MMR Instrument Development

Qualitative Data: The Basis of Instrument Content

Qualitative data allow us to integrate lived experiences into the development of scale items. Phenomenology provides a framework for the exploration of lived experiences (Eberle, 2014; Wertz, 2011), lending itself to mixed methods instrument development. As Saldaña (2015) explains, phenomenology is "the description of lived experiences" (p. 73), bringing to light what particular experiences mean to people, and of what these experiences consist.

Analysis in descriptive phenomenology involves developing a list of significant statements. Creswell and Poth (2018) explain that, although not necessary, these statements can be taken directly from the data. They also explain that each statement is treated "as having equal worth" (p. 201) in terms of establishing findings. The researcher then works with the statements to ensure that there are no repeats within the list and that the content of a statement does not overlap with the contents of other statements. This approach to analysing qualitative data aligns strongly with item development, wherein statements become the basis of items and the process of assessing for duplication and overlap supports assessment for double-barrel and redundant items. Additionally, statements developed in the course of descriptive phenomenological analysis then are brought together into larger groups, reflecting "meaning units or themes" (Creswell & Poth, 2018, p. 201). Although the intent of these groups within the process of descriptive phenomenological analysis is to establish a solid basis for interpretation, they simultaneously point to possible sub-scales of questions, reflecting theoretical constructs linked to the focus of the measure. Finally, drawing on these groups of themes, researchers then create a description of what participants' experience (i.e. a textual description) and how they experience this (i.e. structural description). Drawing on these two descriptions, researchers establish a composite description of the topic of study. This composite description would provide the theory underpinning the measure, explaining how scale items and possibly sub-scales come together to provide a complete understanding of the phenomenon under investigation.

That descriptive phenomenological analysis is a qualitative idiographic approach, means that we need to be cognizant about how we structure our sample in qualitative components of instrument development. Questions to contend with relate to the purpose of our work, as follows: What are the intentions of the scale being developed? For use with whom and in what contexts? and How representative is our qualitative sample of these populations? Whereas quantitative research approaches lend themselves to random sampling, qualitative approaches allow us to engage more effectively in purposive sampling, strengthening the representativeness of the data and resulting items developed for inclusion. Importantly, as with all qualitative research studies, the research process begins with the researcher(s) describing her/his own experiences with the focus of the study. In this way, personal perceptions and understandings can be acknowledged and set aside in the analysis of participants' experiences. This process of bracketing (Wertz, 2011) further enhances the construct validity of the items generated for the measure. Saldaña (2015) explains the process of bracketing as setting "aside your own perceptions and experiences of the phenomenon you're studying and to see it from the participants' point of view … to decentre your own values system and worldview, to listen to others carefully, and to empathize" (p. 74).

Once items have been established from the qualitative data, we are proposing that researchers establish the presence of these items in the qualitative data set and then conduct IRT analysis, with due consideration to minimum sample sizes required, on these items prior to the actual piloting of the scale. Specifically, in order to conduct an IRT analysis on the qualitative data, we are proposing the use of manifest quantitative content analysis (Kondracki & Wellman, 2002; Potter & Levine-Donnerstein, 1999) to establish the frequency of the scale items in the qualitative data. Manifest quantitative content analysis explores the tangible content of what participants have shared in their interviews (Babbie & Mouton, 2001). Although the approach to descriptive phenomenological analysis is inductively data-driven, quantitative content analysis can include deductive, theoretically driven approaches. In this way, we can assess the extent to which existing theory is represented in the qualitative data. In manifest quantitative content analysis, qualitative data are coded for the presence of each scale item, and it is coded each time the scale item appears in the qualitative data (e.g., interview, focus group). This process allows for the frequency of the code's presence to be established. The use of more than one coder and establishing inter-coder reliability is crucial in this process because researchers are not coding for the presence of exact words and phrasing, but rather for the presence of conceptual reflections of the instrument items. The resulting quantitative content analysis data then are analysed using IRT. The categories are identified by means of frequency counts for each code, by each participant, in order to identify a percentage of agreement. The percentage of agreement then can be converted into category codes from 1 to 4, depending on the data (1 = absent, 2, 3 and 4 will account for a third each). Based on the information generated from the qualitative data, simulation studies can take place that would generate the sample size required for IRT analyses. The process of simulation entails the generation of random numbers from a stochastic process that is described from by a series of distributional statements, in this case from the qualitative data (Kery & Royle, 2016). Although a simulation study of this nature is beyond the scope of this chapter, for an example of how this can be undertaken can be found in Scherman, Zimmerman, and Smit (2018).

4 Empirical Demonstration of Using Qualitative Data and IRT for MMR Instrument Development

Understanding Item Response Theory in the Instrument Development Process

In addition to the call for instruments that better reflect the diversity of lived experience across groups, the need for psychometrically sound instruments is a further theme that is repeated often in the literature and in response to the perceived weaknesses of classical test theory (Reeve & Masse, 2004). Part of the discussion and debate of instrument development centres around what Wilson (2005) calls construct modelling. Construct modelling provides a framework for instrument development, drawing our attention to the purpose of the instrument being developed and the context in which the instrument will be used. Considering the purpose and context, the theoretical construct is placed on a continuum, relevant to the purpose and context, with distinguishable qualitative levels between the extremes on the continuum. Scale items are considered to be associated with the theoretical construct and are seen as the realisation of the construct (Wilson, 2005). When thinking about validity inferences, we are essentially making deductions about the underlying structure of the scale and the possible related representativeness of scale items when considering the conceptual understanding of the scale. Thus, working within a psychometric framework, the theory behind the instrument is supported by the results obtained from the questionnaire (Scherman, 2016).

Within this process, the items associated with the construct have to be explored to ensure that they are functioning appropriately and especially in light of what would be expected in relation to the underlying theory. Item response theory allows us to do this by focussing on the item level as opposed to the test level of the scale. At the heart of IRT is the principle that there is a relationship between an individual's ability to endorse a response option and how they respond to the item (Tran, Nguyen, & Chan, 2017). As with classical test theory, IRT examines item functioning (Crocker & Algina, 1986), but uses probabilistic models to focus on the interplay between items and the respondents. In this way, IRT explores instruments on an item level, as opposed to a test level, to characterise individual respondents (termed latent traits) to identify the probability of a positive response (Hambleton, Swaminathan, & Rogers, 1991). Thus, there is an estimation of how participants of different ability levels for a specific trait should respond to an item (Crocker & Algina, 1986). Here, both the trait and the ability levels are articulated on a continuum with less or more of the trait and low to high ability, respectively. IRT is preferred by item response theorists to classical test theory (CTT) because the knowledge gained from IRT analysis can be used to compare performance on different tests and allows the analyst to apply the results of an item analysis to groups with ability levels different from those of the group used for the analysis (Crocker & Algina, 1986).

Concepts central to IRT include latent traits, item characteristics curves (ICC), the assumption of local independence, and monotonicity. A latent trait refers to the characteristics of an individual (Hambleton et al., 1991), which are unobservable and cannot be measured directly, for instance, reading ability. Latent traits are referred to as abilities or theta (θ) (Baker, 2001), and can be plotted on a continuum of ability or endorsability (Tran et al., 2017). An item characteristics curve is the visual representation of the probability of responding correctly to an item as a function of a latent trait that underlies the performance on the test (Crocker & Algina, 1986). The assumption of local independence is related to the term statistical independence, and refers to the estimation of response patterns by means of using the correct and incorrect responses (Crocker & Algina, 1986). The idea is that if items are to have statistical properties across samples, then the items must be answered independently of one another (Tran et al., 2017). In other words, items should contain no information that could be used to respond to other items. Unidimensionality, on the other hand, refers to the statistical dependence of items, which can be accounted for by a single latent trait (Crocker & Algina, 1986) or, rather, that the items represent only one latent trait or dominant factor. The final assumption is monotonicity, which, according to Tran et al. (2017, p. 102), "refers to situations in which the probability of endorsing an item continuously increases as the individual's trait increases."

Many approaches or models can be used under the umbrella term of IRT, namely, one-parameter (i.e., difficulty only), two-parameter (i.e., difficulty and discrimination), three- parameter (i.e., difficulty, discrimination, and guessing or lower asymptote), and four-parameter (i.e., difficulty, discrimination, guessing, and upper asymptote) models, each of which includes elements of difficulty, discrimination, guessing, and/or upper asymptote, depending on the model that is selected (Crocker & Algina, 1986). Although Rasch enthusiasts do not necessarily appreciate being included under the IRT umbrella, for the purposes of this illustration, Rasch modelling will be associated with the one-parameter model.

The Rasch model not only contributes to inferences made about construct validity but also indicates how well the item fits within the underlying construct (Bond & Fox, 2015). Rasch is used as interval measures and are constructed by means of a stochastic process that creates inferential stability and locates a person on the latent continuum. Thus, both person measures (i.e., abilities) and item measures (i.e., difficulties) are measured concurrently, with these measures being measured on an interval-level scale (Vaderas, Alonso, Prieto, Espallargues, & Castells, 2004). This continuum represents the hierarchical ordering of the construct, regarding the difficulty or complexity of concepts as represented by the items and the proficiency levels of the respondents. The designed rating scale used in questionnaires is essentially communication between the intentions of the developer, and the respondent attitudes, behavior, or achievement on the construct of interest (Bond & Fox, 2015) and is designed to capture degrees of one attribute (Linacre, 2004).

This analysis technique is ideal for exploratory data analysis wherein one wants to understand the structure of items or to identify those items that are functioning well. Furthermore, assessments based on Rasch analysis are item and person free in that the person's response is the dependent variable, whereas the independent variables are the person's trait score and item difficulty. In this way, Rasch enables researchers to estimate person abilities independently of the sample used and provides statistics that indicate the precision at which abilities are estimated. Accordingly, items that contribute to the sub-test are identified and poor items are eliminated (Andrich, 1988). Items that are regarded as poor are items that do not contribute to the sub-test or possibly measure another construct contrary to the construct under exploration. Rasch analysis speaks to validity claims as the items and person parameter are explored. The Rasch model also addresses several issues arising from CTT, namely, that the measurement model (Wright & Mok, 2004, p. 4):

- produces linear measures,
- overcomes the issue of missing data,
- gives estimates of precision, and
- has devices for identifying misfit.

For the purposes of this chapter, the rating scale Rasch model, originally proposed by Andrich (1978), is used. When thinking about a questionnaire, rating scales and Likert-format scales, such as strongly agree, agree, disagree and strongly disagree, are typical. For each of the categories, a number label is assigned (for e.g., 1–4). Missing data also might be an issue, as well as the issue of aligning the item difficulty to the ability level of the participants (Wright & Mok, 2004). When thinking about using qualitative data in the manner in which we have described, it is important to note that data preparation would include the calculation of point-biserial correlations, the item-category empirical measurements, and how the categories function; as well as the amount of variance explained. The point measure measure correlation (i.e., the ability of an item to discriminate between high and low performers) is interpreted in the same manner as item discrimination would in the context of CTT. This measure thus provides an indication of how well the item is discriminating among the participants included in the sample. Very often when using questionnaire data, a Likert-format scale is used to denote the categories of agreement or the item-category empirical measurements, as mentioned earlier. However, it is important to explore the category function to ascertain whether the categories as conceptualized are appropriate. For example, originally a 5-point scale may have been used but, upon inspection of the categories, it would appear as if a 4- or a 3-point scale would be more appropriate. In CTT, exploratory factor analysis typically is used to explore how well the items are fitting together or how the items cluster together. In this analysis, each of the factors (cluster of items) explains a percentage of variation. This assists in the analysis of how many of the factors makes sense to retain. In Rasch analysis, and to explore assumptions of unidimensionality, a similar analysis is undertaken to ensure that the assumptions of the Rasch analysis are appropriately met. Once this has been undertaken, the model fit is explored. Unidimensionality in this context, is understood as only one trait being measured and is considered to be a prerequisite for construct-related-validity.

Using a rating scale, data are fitted to the Rasch model to determine whether items are working as they should. Using the rating scale measurement model as described by Andrich (1978), the unidimensionality of the various scales in the questionnaire is considered because the measurement is seen as implying both order and magnitude on a dimension (Andrich, 1988). It is thus important that the data structure generated by the qualitative data analyses support the generation of the statistics required to undertake Rasch analyses. Thus, INFIT and OUTFIT statistics should be generated. The INFIT means-square (MNSQ) is associated with the response patterns, and the OUTFIT mean-square (MNSQ) is associated with response patterns that are not expected. Both INFIT and OUTFIT identify aberrant response patterns, with the former not as highly influenced by the outliers as the OUTFIT statistic. The question of fit is related to discrimination or how well the item discriminates between persons of high and low endorsability. The point-measure correlation, as explained earlier, has to be evaluated. The point-measure correlation explores whether the item aligns with the abilities of the persons. The order of the categories have to be investigated in addition to item-person maps generated. With regard to the category order, the Andrich thresholds are explored to ensure that the categories are not disordered. The item-person map, on the other hand, is a visual representation of both persons and items to be mapped together on the same graph to provide a picture of how persons correlate to respective items (Aziz et al., 2008). Ideally, items should be located at each of the scale points (Stelmack et al., 2004) and then a normal person distribution can be observed. Figure 11.1 provides an example of an item person map from a study undertaken by Stelmack et.al (2004) wherein visual impairment was explored and Rasch analysis was used as part of the validation process.

5 Suggested Applications of Using Qualitative Data and IRT for MMR Instrument Development

We propose that when considering instrument development, in order to establish psychometric and cultural value, a mixed methods research approach is followed. To date, the manner in which this can be accomplished has not be adequately interrogated in the mixed methods research literature. Although authors such as Koskey, Sondergeld, Stewart, and Pugh (2018), drawing on the work of Onwuegbuzie et al. (2010), have started to unpack what a mixed methods instrument development framework would look like, we believe that the approach put forward in this chapter adds to the discussion on instrument development principles.

Central to validity inferences is the ethical and appropriate use of instruments. This concern extends to the manner in which instruments are developed. The International Testing Commission (ITC) has put forward a number of guidelines as to how an instrument should be developed (ITC, 2020). Many of the guidelines speak to the use of qualitative and quantitative data but the data often are used in isolation each other, feeding into the development process sequentially. In this chapter, we have proposed making use of qualitative data analysis, rooted in a descriptive phenomenological approach, not only to identify items, a process that typically would have been

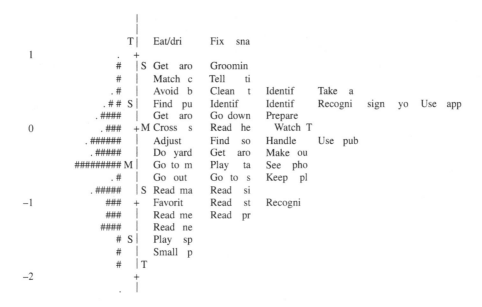

FIGURE 11.1 Item-person map.

undertaken by engaging in literature, but also to use the data to understand the appropriate category structure for the item stems. Once this has been undertaken, data can be simulated and analysed using item response theory before the questionnaire is even piloted. This approach might contribute to stronger validity claims, as well as cost-effective research wherein all data sources are optimally used and the integration of data also becomes more prominent.

6 Strengths and Limitations of Using Qualitative Data and IRT for MMR Instrument Development

Measurement essentially refers to the "assignment of numbers to categories of observations" (Wilson, 2005, p. 4). It is important to note, however, that the numbers have properties with predetermined meaning. When using mixed methods research designs, the manner in which instrument development takes place is an important consideration not only from a psychometric point of view but also from an ethical point of view. Normally, exploratory designs are used for the purpose of instrument development. The strength of these designs lies in the fact that there is a discernable two-phase structure in place, wherein one type of data is collected at a time (Creswell & Plano Clark, 2018). Challenges include deciding which data to use from the qualitative phase and how this choice impacts validity claims.

Establishing validity claims is perhaps the more important of the two challenges. Messick (1989, p. 5) stated that "to validate an interpretive inference is to ascertain the extent to which multiple lines of evidence are consonant with the inference, while establishing that alternative inferences are less well supported." Thus, the onus is on the researcher to provide the substantive evidence required to support any validity claims that are made. Further, validity claims speak to the meaningfulness as well as trustworthiness of scores derived from instruments. The scores are directly linked to the conceptualization and meaning of the construct, which, in turn, has implications for interpretation as well as for use of the instrument (Messick, 1981).

7 Resources for Learning More About Qualitative Data and IRT for MMR Instrument Development

Bond, T. G., & Fox, C. M. (2015). *Applying the Rasch model: Fundamental measurement in the human sciences* (3rd ed.). London, England: Lawrence Erlbaum Associates

Creswell, J. W., & Plano Clark, V. L. (2018). *Designing and conducting mixed methods research* (3rd ed.). Thousand Oaks, CA: Sage.

Creswell, J. W., & Poth, C. N. (2018). *Qualitative inquiry and research design* (4th ed.). Thousand Oaks, CA: Sage.

Crocker, L., & Algina, J. (1986). *Introduction to classical and modern test theory.* New York, NY: Holt, Rinehart & Winston.

Franzosi, R., Doyle, S., McClelland, L. E., Putnam Rankin, C., & Vicari, S. (2013). Quantitative narrative analysis software options compared: PC-ACE and CAQDAS (ATLAS.ti, MAXqda, and NVivo). *Quality & Quantity, 47*, 3219–3247. doi:10.1007/s11135-012-9714-3

International Testing Commission. (2020). Published guidelines. Retrieved from www.intestcom.org/page/5

Koskey, K. L. K., Sondergeld, T. A., Stewart, V. C., & Pugh, K. J. (2018). Applying the mixed methods instrument development and construct validation process: The transformative experience questionnaire. *Journal of Mixed Methods Research, 12*, 95–122. doi:10.1177/1558689816633310

Onwuegbuzie, A. J., & Daniel, L. G. (2002). A framework for reporting and interpreting internal consistency reliability estimates. *Measurement and Evaluation in Counseling and Development, 35*, 89–103.

Onwuegbuzie, A. J., & Combs, J. P. (2010). Emergent data analysis techniques in mixed methods research: A synthesis. In A. Tashakkori & C. Teddlie (Eds.), *SAGE handbook of mixed methods in social and behavioral research* (2nd ed., pp. 397–430). Thousand Oaks, CA: Sage.

Onwuegbuzie, A. J., Bustamante, R. M., & Nelson, J. A. (2010). Mixed research as a tool for developing quantitative instruments. *Journal of Mixed Methods Research, 4,* 56–78. doi:10.1177/1558689809355805

Potter, W. J., & Levine-Donnerstein, D. (1999). Rethinking validity and reliability in content analysis. *Journal of Applied Communication Research, 27,* 258–284. doi:10.1080/00909889909365539

Rasch.org. (2020). *Rasch measurement analysis software directory.* Retrieved from www.rasch.org/software.htm

Schoonenboom, J., Johnson, R. B., & Froehlich, D. E. (2018). Combining multiple purposes of mixing within a mixed methods research design. *International Journal of Multiple Research Approaches, 10,* 271–282. doi:10.29034/ijmra.v10n1a17

Thompson, B., & Vacha-Haase, T. (2000). Psychometrics is datametrics: The test is not reliable. *Educational and Psychological Measurement, 60,* 174–195. doi:10.1177/0013164400602002

Vacha-Haase, T., Kogan, L. R., & Thompson, B. (2000). Sample compositions and variabilities in published studies versus those in test manuals: Validity of score reliability inductions. *Educational and Psychological Measurement, 60,* 509–522. doi:10.1177/00131640021970682

VERBI Software. (2017). *MAXQDA 2018 [computer software].* Berlin, Germany: VERBI Software. Retrieved from www.maxqda.com

Wertz, F. J. (2011). A phenomenological psychological approach to trauma and resilience. In F. J. Wertz, K. Charmaz, L. M., McMullen, R. Josselson, R. Anderson, & E. McSpadden (Eds.), *Five ways of doing qualitative analysis: Phenomenological psychology, grounded theory, discourse analysis, narrative research, and intuitive inquiry* (pp. 124–164). New York, NY: Guilford.

REFERENCES

American Psychological Association, Task Force on Resilience and Strength in Black Children and Adolescents. (2008). *Resilience in African American children and adolescents: A vision for optimal development.* Washington, DC: Author. Retrieved from www.apa.org/pi/cyf/resilience/html

Andrich, D. (1978). Application of a psychometric rating model to ordered categories which are scored with successive integers. *Applied Psychological Measurement, 2,* 581–594. doi:10.1177/014662167800200413

Andrich, D. (1988). *Rasch models for measurement.* Thousand Oaks, CA: Sage.

Aziz, A. A., Mohamed, A., Arshad, N., Zakaria, S., Zaharim, A., Ghulman, H. A., & Masodi, M. S. (2008). Application of Rasch model in validating the construct of measurement instrument. *International Journal of Education and Information Technologies, 2,* 105–112.

Babbie, E., & Mouton, J. (2001). *The practice of social research* (South African Edition). Cape Town, South Africa: Oxford University Press.

Baker, F. B. (2001). *The basic of item response theory* (2nd ed.). Retrieved from http://ericae.net/

Bond, T. G., & Fox, C. M. (2015). *Applying the Rasch model: Fundamental measurement in the human sciences* (3rd ed.). London, England: Lawrence Erlbaum Associates.

Cheung, F. M., van de Vijver, F. J. R., & Leong, F. T.L. (2011). Toward a new approach in the study of personality in culture. *American Psychologist, 66,* 593–603. doi:10.1037/a0022389

Chilisa, B. (2005). Educational research within postcolonial Africa: A critique of HIV/AIDS research in Botswana. *International Journal of Qualitative Studies in Education, 18,* 659–684. doi:10.1080/09518390500298170

Creswell, J. W., & Plano Clark, V.L. (2018). *Designing and conducting mixed methods research.* Thousand Oaks, CA: Sage.

Creswell, J. W., & Poth, C. N. (2018). *Qualitative inquiry and research design* (4th ed.). Thousand Oaks, CA: Sage.

Crocker, L., & Algina, J. (1986). *Introduction to classical and modern test theory.* New York, NY: Holt, Rinehart & Winston.

Daigneault, P-M., & Jacob, S. (2014). Unexpected but most welcome: Mixed methods for the validation and revision of the Participatory Evaluation Measurement Instrument. *Journal of Mixed Methods Research, 8,* 6–24. doi:10.1177/1558689813486190

Eberle, T. S. (2014). Phenomenology as a research method. In U. Flick (Ed.), *The Sage handbook of qualitative data analysis* (pp. 184–202). Thousand Oaks, CA: Sage.

Hambleton, R. K., Swaminathan, H., & Rogers, H. J. (1991). *Fundamentals of item response theory.* Newbury Park, CA: Sage.

International Testing Commission. (2020). Published guidelines. Retrieved from www.intestcom.org/page/5

Kery M., & Royle, J. A. (2016). *Applied hierarchical modeling in ecology.* London, England: Academic Press.

Kondracki, N. L., & Wellman, N. S. (2002). Content analysis: Review of methods and their applications in nutrition education. *Journal of Nutrition Education and Behavior, 34,* 224–230. doi:10.1016/S1499-4046(06)60097-3

Koskey, K. L. K., Sondergeld, T. A., Stewart, V. C., & Pugh, K. J. (2018). Applying the mixed methods instrument development and construct validation process: The transformative experience questionnaire. *Journal of Mixed Methods Research, 12,* 95–122. doi:10.1177/1558689816633310

Linacre, J. M. (2004). Optimizing rating scale category effectiveness. In E. V. Smith & R. M. Smith (Eds). *Introduction to Rasch measurement.* Maple Grove, MN: JAM Press.

Messick, S. (1981). Evidence and ethics in the evaluation of tests. *Educational Researcher, 10*(9), 9–20. doi:10.3102/0013189X010009009

Messick, S. (1989). Meaning and values in test validation: The science and ethics of assessment. *Educational Researcher, 18,* 5–11. doi:10.3102/0013189X018002005

Neuendorf, K. A. (2017). *The content analysis guidebook* (2nd ed.). Thousand Oaks, CA: Sage.

Onwuegbuzie, A. J., Bustamante, R. M., & Nelson, J. A. (2010). Mixed research as a tool for developing quantitative instruments. *Journal of Mixed Methods Research, 4,* 56–78. doi:10.1177/1558689809355805

Onwuegbuzie, A. J., & Combs, J. P. (2010). Emergent data analysis techniques in mixed methods research: A synthesis. In A. Tashakkori & C. Teddlie (Eds.), *SAGE handbook of mixed methods in social and behavioral research* (2nd ed., pp. 397–430). Thousand Oaks, CA: Sage.

Onwuegbuzie, A. J., & Daniel, L. G. (2002). A framework for reporting and interpreting internal consistency reliability estimates. *Measurement and Evaluation in Counseling and Development, 35,* 89–103. doi:10.1080/07481756.2002.12069052

Onwuegbuzie, A. J., & Daniel, L. G. (2004). Reliability generalization: The importance of considering sample specificity, confidence intervals, and subgroup differences. *Research in the Schools, 11*(1), 61–72.

Potter, W. J., & Levine-Donnerstein, D. (1999). Rethinking validity and reliability in content analysis. *Journal of Applied Communication Research, 27,* 258–284. doi:10.1080/00909889909365539

Reeve, B. B., & Masse, L. C. (2004). Item response theory modeling for questionnaire evaluation. In R. M. Groves, G. Kalton, J. N. K. Rao, N. Schwarz, & C. Skinner (Eds.), *Methods for testing and evaluating survey questionnaires.* Hoboken, NJ: Wiley & Sons.

Robinson, L. (2007). *Cross-cultural child development for social workers.* London, England: Palgrave Macmillan.

Saldaña, J. (2015). *Thinking qualitatively: Methods of mind.* Thousand Oaks, CA: Sage.

Scherman, V. (2016). Methodological standards and fit for purpose: What criteria should psychologists use to evaluate of psychological assessments. In R. Ferreira (Ed.), *Psychological Assessment: Thinking innovatively in contexts of diversity* (pp. 72–85). Cape Town, South Africa: Juta.

Scherman, V, Zimmerman, L., & Smit, B. (2018). Mixed method data analysis: An exploratory approach to strengthening inferences about relationships and affinities. *International Journal of Multiple Research Approaches, 10,* 57–76. doi:10.29034/ijmra.v10n1a4

Stelmack, J., Szlyk, J. P., Stelmack, T., Babcock-Parziale, J., Demers-Turco, P., Williams, R. T., & Massof, R. W. (2004). Use of Rasch person-item map in exploratory data analysis: A clinical perspective. *Journal of Rehabilitation Research & Development, 41,* 233–242. doi:10.1682/JRRD.2004.02.0233

Smith, L. T. (1999). *Decolonising methodologies: Research and Indigenous peoples.* London, England: Zed Books.

Thompson, B., & Vacha-Haase, T. (2000). Psychometrics is datametrics: The test is not reliable. *Educational and Psychological Measurement, 60,* 174–195. doi:10.1177/0013164400602002

Tran, V. T., Nguyen, T. H., & Chan, K. T. (2017). *Developing cross-cultural measurement in social work research and evaluation* (2nd ed.). New York, NY: Oxford University Press.

Tudge, J. (2008). *The everyday lives of young children: Culture, class, and child rearing in diverse societies.* Cambridge, MA: Cambridge University Press.

Tweed, R. G., & DeLongis, A. (2006). Problems and strategies when using rating scales in cross-cultural coping research. In P. T. P. Wong & L. C. J. Wong (Eds.), *Handbook of multicultural perspectives on stress and coping* (pp. 203–221). New York, NY: Springer.

Ungar, M., & Liebenberg, L. (2011). Assessing resilience across cultures using mixed-methods: Construction of the Child and Youth Resilience Measure-28. *Journal of Mixed-Methods Research, 5,* 126–149. doi:10.1177/1558689811400607

Vacha-Haase, T., Kogan, L. R., & Thompson, B. (2000). Sample compositions and variabilities in published studies versus those in test manuals: Validity of score reliability inductions. *Educational and Psychological Measurement, 60,* 509–522. doi:10.1177/00131640021970682

Vaderas, J. M., Alonso, J., Prieto, L., Espallargues, M., & Castells, X. (2004). Content-based interpretation aids for health-related quality of life measures in clinical practice. An example for the visual function index (VF-14). *Quality Life Research, 13,* 35–44. doi:10.1023/B:QURE.0000015298.09085.b0

Walter, M., & Anderson, C. (2013). *Indigenous statistics: A quantitative research methodology.* Walnut Creek, CA: Left Coast Press.

Wertz, F. J. (2011). A phenomenological psychological approach to trauma and resilience. In F. J. Wertz, K. Charmaz, L. M., McMullen, R. Josselson, R. Anderson, & E. McSpadden (Eds.), *Five ways of doing qualitative analysis: Phenomenological psychology, grounded theory, discourse analysis, narrative research, and intuitive inquiry* (pp. 124–164). New York, NY: Guilford.

Wilson, M. (2005). *Constructing measures using an item modeling approach.* New York, NY: Taylor and Francis.

Witta, E. L., & Daniel, L. G. (1998, April). *The reliability and validity of test scores: Are editorial policy changes reflected in journal articles?* Paper presented at the annual meeting of the American Educational Research Association, San Diego, CA.

Wright, B. D., & Mok, M. M. C. (2004). An overview of the family of Rasch measurement models. In E. V. Smith & R. M. Smith (Eds.), *Introduction to Rasch measurement* (pp. 1–24). Maple Grove, MN: JAM Press.

12
Diachronic Analysis of Qualitative Data

M. Teresa Anguera, Mariona Portell, Antonio Hernández-Mendo,
Pedro Sánchez-Algarra, and Gudberg K. Jonsson

Acknowledgements

The authors gratefully acknowledge the support of the Spanish government subprojects *Integration ways between qualitative and quantitative data, multiple case development, and synthesis review as main axis for an innovative future in physical activity and sports research* [PGC2018-098742-B-C31] (2019–2021) and *Mixed methods research approach on performance analysis (in training and competition) in elite and academy sport* [PGC2018–098742-B-C33] (2019–2021) (Ministerio de Ciencia, Innovación y Universidades/Agencia Estatal de Investigación/Fondo Europeo de Desarrollo Regional), that are part of the coordinated project *New approach of research in physical activity and sport from mixed methods perspective* (NARPAS_MM) [SPGC201800X098742CV0].

1 Definition of Diachronic Analysis of Qualitative Data

Qualitative Data and the Integration with Quantitative Elements

In recent scientific literature, different proposals have been published regarding the quantitative analysis of qualitative data and, in this sense, we highlight the extensive and rigorous compilation work carried out by Onwuegbuzie (2016), which shows the amplitude of possibilities, depending on the specific characteristics of each study. Mixed methods research (MMR) offers different possibilities in studies carried out on spontaneous or habitual behavior in natural contexts (Portell, Anguera, Hernández-Mendo, & Jonsson, 2015), or in intervention programs with low interventive intensity (Chacón-Moscoso, Sanduvete-Chaves, Portell, & Anguera, 2013). The option we propose is systematic observation, both direct (Anguera, 2003; Portell, Anguera, Chacón-Moscoso, & Sanduvete-Chaves, 2015; Sánchez-Algarra & Anguera, 2013) and indirect (Anguera, Portell, Chacón-Moscoso, & Sanduvete-Chaves, 2018), grounded in observational methodology (Anguera, 2003). Direct observation focuses on obtaining records of behavior in natural situations wherein behaviors occur spontaneously, when the perceptivity of the coded behavior is guaranteed. And indirect observation, of more recent structuring, focuses on diverse material of verbal, vocal, graphic, or objectual nature: in-depth interviews, focal groups, information that was originally in text format (e.g., newspapers, handwritten notes, reports), graphics, photographs, texts from digital magnetic recording of formal and informal conversations, group discussions, sounds that accompany speech, handled objects, and so forth.

There are many situations wherein the information provided by the systematic observation is irreplaceable. Examples include the study of various communicative flows (Anguera, Jonsson, & Sánchez-Algarra, 2017), such as between therapist and patient (Del Giacco, Anguera, & Salcuni, 2020; Del Giacco, Salcuni, & Anguera, 2019), between teacher and student (García-Fariña, Jiménez Jiménez, & Anguera, 2018), social competence among adolescents of the autistic spectrum (Alcover et al., 2019), intra-family interaction (Gimeno, Anguera, Berzosa, & Ramírez, 2006), interpersonal relationships among autistic children (Rodríguez-Medina, Rodríguez-Navarro, Arias, Arias, & Anguera, 2018), physical activities (Camerino, Castañer, & Anguera, 2012), individual sports (Menescardi et al., 2019), collective sports (Vázquez-Diz, Morillo-Baro, Reigal, Morales-Sánchez, & Hernández-Mendo, 2019), and prevention programs in the workplace (Portell, Sene-Mir, Anguera, Jonsson, & Losada, 2019).

This broad empirical coverage, and the heterogeneity that it entails, requires clear and flexible methodological guidelines, which make it possible to follow the process that goes from qualitative data to diachronic analysis. Diachronic study implies making a successive collection of (qualitative) data from the same participants along several sessions in a period of time (hours, days, weeks, months, years), with the objective of managing and, in the context of our chapter, analyzing data using quantitative techniques for categorical data (Bakeman & Quera, 2011; Magnusson, 2020; Sackett, 1980). To apply diachronic analysis, we should distinguish between intersessional following (Escolano-Pérez & Blanco-Villaseñor, 2015; Portell, Anguera, Chacón-Moscoso, et al., 2015), when two or more sessions are studied during a period of time, and intrasessional following (Portell, Anguera, Chacón-Moscoso, et al., 2015), which allows to collect the data from the beginning to the end of each session. Intrasessional following is of relative importance, because it can measure order and sequence, a differential trait in relation to other studies during a period of time that only measure frequency (number of occurrences). Concerning this intrasessional following, Sackett (1978) referred to a continuous real-time measurement, affirming that the "recording device preserves the order of codes" (p. 26), and Bakeman (1978) used the expression "describe changes from moment to moment" (p. 64). In a parallel sense, Magnuson (2005) stated that "All this is occurring at the same time as numerous events of various types occur concurrently and sequentially within and across individuals in countless ways" (p. 4). The diachronic analysis is very useful in several fields, such as program intervention (Anguera, 1992), sport (Ardá & Anguera, 2000; Ardá, Casal, & Anguera, 2002), clinical psychology (Arias & Anguera, 2005), and so on. The requirement that must be met to perform each of the diachronic analysis that are described in this chapter is that we have an intrasessional following record, which implies the continuous record of each observational session.

As we have argued in previous works (Anguera, Blanco-Villaseñor, Losada, Sánchez-Algarra, & Onwuegbuzie, 2019; Anguera, Camerino, Castañer, Sánchez-Algarra, & Onwuegbuzie, 2017; Anguera & Hernández-Mendo, 2016), observational methodology could be considered as *mixed methods* itself. We take as a starting point the notion established by Creswell and Plano Clark (2007) regarding the *connecting* option, that is "connecting two datasets by having one build on the other" (p. 7). Taken both literally and from a broader perspective, it constitutes an essential foothold for a rethinking of *quantitizing*, which involves the systematization of initial descriptive records—first dataset—through an observation instrument (mainly a field format combined with category systems) in order to obtain an equivalent code matrix—second dataset—that is built on the first (still qualitative data, where columns are dimensions/subdimensions, and rows are the successive units), which will be analyzed through specific quantitative techniques for categorical data. Moreover, we take into account that Onwuegbuzie and Teddlie (2003) discussed a model for mixed methods data analysis, where one step is data transformation, although it is not the same as the data analysis conducted by ourselves, which implies transforming qualitative data into quantitative data or vice versa. And our proposal consists of organizing qualitative data in a systematized structure (matrix of codes), that is qualitative, but that is possible to analyze quantitatively considering their temporal organization. This is the innovative potential of our proposal in this chapter. Such transformation must guarantee the maintenance of the informational quality of the data, even if its appearance varies. In addition, from a more molar perspective, the connecting allows the alternation of QUAL-QUAN-QUAL stages, which is consistent with the generic approach of MMR, while achieving a total integration between qualitative and quantitative elements.

Connections between Qualitative Data and Bayesian Analysis

Integration plays a crucial role in the diachronic analysis of qualitative data within the framework of mixed methods. According to O'Cathain, Murphy, and Nicholl (2010, p. 341): "Integration—the interaction or conversation between the qualitative and quantitative components of a study—is an important aspect of mixed methods research, and, indeed, is essential to some definitions." One of the integration frameworks with the greatest potential and future perspective that we want to mention is the one developed by Onwuegbuzie, Hitchcock, Natesan, and Newman (2018), which is located in the "radical middle" (Onwuegbuzie, 2012, p. 192), and which is situated within the wide space existing between what we conventionally call *qualitative* and *quantitative*, without considering the borders mentioned by Fetters and Freshwater (2015) in their 1 + 1 = 3 as an integration formula, but surpassing them from a continuous integration perspective, until reaching *full integration* (Creamer, 2018).

Onwuegbuzie et al. (2018) further developed the initial conceptualization of Onwuegbuzie (2017) regarding the full integration of qualitative and quantitative elements in the stages of data collection and analysis, as well as in the interpretation of the results, based on their 1 + 1 = 1 integration formula. This formula built on Newman, Onwuegbuzie, and Hitchcock's (2015) conceptualization of full integration via the general linear model. Recently, Onwuegbuzie et al. (2018) have demonstrated the usefulness of Bayesian analysis as a mixed analysis, on which other authors have discussed (Crandell, Voils, & Sandelowski, 2012; Creamer, 2018), considering it an extension to classical (i.e., frequentist) statistics for the solution of typical statistical problems, such as estimation, hypothesis contrast, and prediction.

In Bayesian estimation, unlike frequentist statistics, each value of a distribution is associated with the probability that the parameter adopted that value—this is called the *posterior distribution*. This posterior distribution allows for the inclusion of very diverse contextual information, which can involve qualitative data, and makes possible its subsequent quantitative analysis, as the researchers can make a justification about *prior information* (Onwuegbuzie et al., 2018), given that they know the route -basic in diachronic analysis- over time, as well as the various elements that qualify the information obtained through qualitative data. Some researchers reject the claim that *prior information* should be included in a process of scientific inference (Hernández Solano, 2008), but this circumstance can be avoided by establishing a prior non-informative or reference distribution, especially when there is not much prior information about the problem, or at least, from a diachronic perspective.

The basic equation of Bayes theorem, and following the notation used by Onwuegbuzie et al. (2018), is as follows:

$$p(\theta|Data) = \frac{p(Data|\theta)\, p(\theta)}{p(Data)},$$

where p is the probability, θ is the parameter(s) of interest, $p(\theta|Data)$ is the posterior distribution of the parameters, $p(Data|\theta)$ is the plausibility of the data, or, in other words, the information contained in the data, $p(\theta)$ is the prior information, that is, the researcher's belief about the parameters, and $p(Data)$ is the marginal probability of the data. When a researcher has prior knowledge of an aspect to be studied—in the form of qualitative data, this prior knowledge can be quantified in a probability model, and it would not be helpful to disqualify it. If we apply it, for example, to the therapist-patient interaction, coach-athlete interaction, teacher-student interaction, peer interaction, or the like, it might seem difficult to capture this prior knowledge through a distribution a priori, but it is a practical difficulty, and the researcher must be aware of the relevance of this information, and should be conscious of the rich qualities that qualitative data provide in a diachronic process.

The conceptual advantage is that these probabilities *a posteriori* are the true (subjective) probabilities of the hypotheses that reflect the observed data and the distribution a priori, which allows us to reach a conclusion that is more intuitive and close to common sense than the one that involves the use of frequentist statistics. For the moment, and while waiting to apply the Bayesian approach in the near future, we propose an integration that has already been repeatedly tested and used that allows us to perform quantitative analysis (i.e., lag sequential analysis, polar coordinate analysis, and T-pattern analysis) from qualitative data, and which, in our opinion, also allows us to position ourselves towards a *middle* that contemplates a symmetry between qualitative and quantitative approaches.

Transformation to Code Matrix (Using Several Software as Prototypes)

In MMR, various proposals have been made to integrate qualitative and quantitative elements, but not without controversy (Anguera, Blanco-Villaseñor, Losada, & Sánchez-Algarra, 2019). The proposals involve different types of data, which include the transformation of quantitative data into qualitative data (Onwuegbuzie & Teddlie, 2003; Sandelowski, Voils, & Knafl, 2009), of qualitative data into quantitative data (Anguera, Camerino, et al., 2017; Sandelowski et al., 2009), or any other type of information. We are committed to the transformation of qualitative data so that it can be quantitatively analyzed (Anguera & Hernández-Mendo, 2016; Anguera, Camerino, et al., 2017).

Our proposal, adaptable to all situations that allow the use of observational methodology as a scientific method, will be based on a clear delimitation of the behaviour(s) and observation situation, observational design, context-adapted instrument construction, recording and coding, data quality control, and data analysis. This methodological approach prioritizes the use of observation instruments that are fully adapted to the context of interest, and this generally requires the design of *ad hoc* (i.e., custom made) tools (Anguera, Magnusson, & Jonsson, 2007).

Two key decisions will have to be taken and an observation instrument will have to be built (Anguera, Blanco-Villaseñor, Losada, et al., 2019; Anguera, Portell, et al., 2018), as follows:

- *First decision*: Establish the dimensions of the study (also referred to as response levels or criteria). This concept, relative to the different facets or aspects that are to be taken into account, was initially proposed by Weick (1968), and is considered as a "categorical variable" (Bakeman, Adamson, & Strisik, 1995, p. 281). We include an example in Table 12.1. Each dimension can be hierarchized establishing, for example, macrodimension, dimension, and subdimension.

- *Second decision*: Propose the segmentation criteria of the continuum of the interactive sequence in successive observation units (Anguera, 2020), in order to facilitate the structuration of the qualitative initial information. Because behavioral events necessarily take place in time "a relationship between the analysis of their temporal and qualitative aspects

TABLE 12.1

Example of Dimensions (Fragment) in a Patient-Therapist Relationship in a Psychotherapy Process[a]

Verbal Mode-Structural Form (VeM-SF) dimension
Courtesies
Assertion
Question
Agreement
Denial
Direction
Verbal Mode-Communicative Intent (VeM-CI) dimension
Acknowledging
Informing
Exploring
Deepening
Focusing
Temporizing
Attuning
Resignifying
Extracted from Del Giacco, Salcuni and Anguera (2019, Supplementary Material, p. 1-3). It does not include the definition of the categories or the corresponding examples that illustrate each one.

Note: [a] For each of the dimensions, the codes that make up the observation instrument have been developed.

TABLE 12.2

Tabular Structure Prepared to Obtain the Code Matrix Corresponding to the Systematized Record, with Various Dimensions (Breaking Down into Subdimensions) and Units Resulting from Applying the Segmentation Criteria—Both Direct and Indirect Observation[a]

		Dimensions (also called **Criteria** and **Response levels**)					
		Dimension 1		Dimension 2	Dimension 3		
		Subdimension 11	Subdimension 12		Subdimension 31	Subdimension 32	Subdimension 33
Units	Unit 1	Code	Code	Code	Code	Code	Code
	Unit 2	Code	Code	Code	Code	Code	Code
	Unit 3	Code	Code	Code	Code	Code	Code
	Unit 4	Code	Code	Code	Code	Code	Code
	...	...	...	...	...	...	...
	Unit n	...	...	...	...	...	...

Note: [a] There is an example where there are three Dimensions: First is unfolded in two Subdimensions, second is not unfolded, and third is unfolded in three Subdimensions. The rows referred to units. The cells should contain the codes corresponding to a hypothetical record.

sometimes results from the choice of unit" (Fassnacht, 1982, p. 59). It is a very relevant decision, and some years ago, Dickman (1963) and Birdwhistell (1970) proposed that the behavioral flow should be segmented into units. Schegloff (2000) considers that it is possible to establish a gradation of *granularization*, and more recently, Anguera and Izquierdo (2006) proposed the so-called "rule of the three Ds" (<u>D</u>elimitation, <u>D</u>enomination, and <u>D</u>efinition).

Both concepts (dimension and observation unit) have subsequently been developed, both for direct (Anguera & Izquierdo, 2006) and indirect (Anguera, 2020; Casarrubea el al., 2018) observation, and integrated as basic pieces for the preparation of the observational instrument. Once this instrument has been constructed, it is possible to carry out the recording, which comprises qualitative data, and which will preferably be structured as a code matrix that contains qualitative data but that allows for its subsequent quantitative treatment. Table 12.2 shows the format of a code matrix that will be obtained from the established dimensions (Table 12.1) and the segmentation into observation units.

The code matrix is essential for the process of *quantitizing* the qualitative data (Anguera, 2020; Anguera, Jonsson, et al., 2017). This matrix will have, by rows, the successive units in which the behavior episode is fragmented, and the corresponding dimensions by columns. Consequently, the resulting code matrix is formed from the assignment of each of the observation units to the respective code. Therefore, each row of the table contains the code chain corresponding to the co-occurrences of each of the units of the studied behavior (see example in Table 12.3). This code matrix constitutes the blueprint of how the data record will be characterized, although still qualitative (QUAL phase). Figuratively speaking, it is necessary to have, from the beginning, the architectural pillars and the framework of this *building*. From this code matrix, we can also incorporate various data modalities such as drawings, sounds, and photographs, a still incipient issue, but which fits into the most advanced codifying proposals, and for which computer software programs have been developed to facilitate their analyses.

The following free computer programs are highly helpful to facilitate the formal structure of the record in the form of a code matrix:

- *HOISAN*. The HOISAN program was designed to code and to transcribe in observational methodology (Hernández-Mendo, López-López, Castellano, Morales-Sánchez, & Pastrana, 2012; Hernández-Mendo et al., 2014). This program allows users to export data to other statistical programs (e.g., EduG, TG, SAGT, SAS, SPSS, THEME) to perform a corresponding analysis. Among the export possibilities, those related to the Atlas.ti program (www.youtube.com/channel/UCYR-VG5Ar7-Idr0W1WWy6Yw) are highlighted. The possibilities of Atlas.ti for the qualitative analysis of large unstructured bodies of textual, graphic, audio and video data are well known. Version 8 of this program offers the option of exporting data through the "Statistical Data" option that generates an Excel file. In this sense, the HOISAN program exports in Excel format the verbal production collected that can be imported by Atlas-ti through the "Survey" option. HOISAN can be downloaded from www.menpas.com

- *LINCE*. The free LINCE program (Gabin, Camerino, Anguera, & Castañer, 2012; Soto, Camerino, Iglesias, Anguera, & Castañer, 2019) allows users to make a Microsoft Excel record in the form of a code matrix, admitting observation instruments with one or several dimensions/subdimensions, and recording the duration of each behavior (if there is one dimension) or each co-occurrence of behaviors (if there are several dimensions/subdimensions) in seconds or in frames. It allows for the import of records to HOISAN, and the export of them to GSEQ5 and to THEME Edu. LINCE can be downloaded from http://lom.observesport.com/ and can be found on YouTube www.youtube.com/watch?v=gVF5GuXW-ow.

TABLE 12.3

Simulated Example of a Record Obtained from the Dimensions/Subdimensions and Units of Table 12.2 in Matrix Code Format

```
114 123 21 311 326 334
112 122 22 312 324 332
114 124 22 314     334
111     25 311 321
```

- *GSEQ5.* This free program (Bakeman & Quera, 2011) supports five types of data, which are configured as a code matrix: *sequential event data* (one dimension and order parameter in the record), *sequential state data* (various dimensions/subdimensions and order parameter in the record), *sequential event data with time* (various dimensions/subdimensions and order and duration parameters in the record), *sequential interval data* (various dimensions/subdimensions and order parameter in the record; in addition, the session is segmented in intervals), and *sequential multievent data* (various dimensions/subdimensions and order parameter in the record). GSEQ5 can be downloaded from http://bakeman.gsucreate.org/
- *THEME Edu.* The Theme/ThemeEdu (Magnusson, 1996, 2000, 2016, 2020) data format is simple, using only two columns, for time and event, and can import data from, for example, Lince, Elan, and Microsoft Excel. ThemeEdu is available free and can be downloaded from http://patternvision.com/products/theme/

Diversification of Quantitative Analysis

Once the systematized record in the form of a code matrix is available, we have qualitative data whose structure has been modified since its collection by means of *connecting* (Creswell & Plano Clark, 2007), as we have indicated previously.

In previous works (Anguera, Portell, et al., 2018; Blanco-Villaseñor, Losada, & Anguera, 2003), we have referred to the diachronic approach in research as a broad perspective that refers to studies that are focused in a period of time and using intrasessional following. The interest in diachronic studies has been evidenced in various ways and, here, we are particularly interested in highlighting the quantitative analysis of qualitative data from direct and indirect systematic observation. We propose to showcase it via three diachronic analytical techniques of demonstrated efficacy: lag sequential analysis, polar coordinate analysis, and T-pattern detection and analysis. All of them, heterogeneous with each other, have a common background and share two essential premises: On the one hand, a diachronic analysis is intended, and, therefore, we will search the underlying structure from the dataset collected during time and using intrasessional following; and, on the other hand, the data must be of a qualitative nature. (It can come, for example, from open interviews, discussion groups, behavioral observation, transcription of conversations, and so forth.)

2 When the Use of Lag Sequential Analysis, Polar Coordinate Analysis, and T-Pattern Analysis is Appropriate in MMR

Lag Sequential Analysis

Lag sequential analysis (Bakeman, 1978) is used when the researcher needs to know how a behavior works at a first level of abstraction. The succession of sessions over time drives researchers to delve into the search for common elements that present with a greater or lesser degree of presence and consolidation, and that connect sequentially with each other. This analysis allows us to study processes over time, yielding a dynamic vision about how the behavior patterns obtained allow researchers to know the evolution produced, with elements of these patterns that could be modified, and with connections among them that can remain stable or evolve.

An interesting aspect of the lag sequential analysis is that the study can be conducted prospectively (i.e., forward) or retrospectively (i.e., backward). They are two perspectives of diachronic analysis that can give answers to very different approaches, starting always from qualitative data.

Polar Coordinate Analysis

Polar coordinate analysis (Sackett, 1980) is used when it is required to obtain a map that shows the relationships among all the codes of conduct that we consider relevant, specifying in each case, one of them as *focal behavior*, and the others as *conditioned behaviors*. Such a map allows researchers *to take the pulse*, over the course of time, of a training process, a type of relationship, a context, and so forth, because we can know diachronically (i.e., during a period of time and using intrasessional following) how these relationships are modified.

At a conceptual level, the concepts of prospectivity and retrospectivity are handled in a complementary manner. Concerning retrospectivity, as per Sackett's (1980) work, we proposed (Anguera, 1997) an optimization, differentiating his approach (which we call *classical retrospectivity*) from another new (*genuine retrospectivity*) that authentically performs the calculation backwards. The in-depth knowledge of a process can materialize not only from the beginning to the end, or from the end to the beginning, but it is possible to focus on a specific moment of the process, and to analyze it prospectively from this point forward and retrospectively backward.

T-pattern Analysis

T-pattern analysis (TPA) is a multivariate approach for the detection and description of recurring sequences of behavioral events. Researchers use T-pattern analysis to search for hidden repeated patterns in behavior and interactions, based on a model of the temporal organization of behavior. This unique algorithm which was developed by Magnusson in 1978 (Magnusson, 1978), who first presented the T-pattern concept during an AI workshop at the University of Uppsala, Sweden (1981), and which has been embedded into the THEME™ software (1981, 1996, 2000, 2016, 2020) (Patternvision Ltd., Iceland). It considers both the order and the time distances between behavioral event types as well as hierarchical organization.

THEME™ can detect complex repeated patterns that are hidden to observers and very difficult or impossible to detect using other available methods. The software program includes various tools for the filtering and analysis of detected patterns on the basis of their frequency, complexity, structure, actor identity, and behavioral content. THEME™ has been used extensively in studies of human communication, spoken dialogue, gestures, protocol analysis, and so forth.

3 Technical Outline of Lag Sequential Analysis, Polar Coordinate Analysis, and T-pattern Analysis for MMR

Lag Sequential Analysis

Lag sequential analysis was initially proposed by Bakeman (1978), and has been progressively developed (Bakeman & Gottman, 1986; Bakeman & Quera, 2011). Its essence lies in knowing to what extent a sequence of behaviors occurs more frequently than expected, if everything is left to chance. If so, the resulting behavior patterns will show the connection among them. The main elements of lag sequential analysis are focal behavior, conditioned behavior, and lag. The *focal behavior* can be established from a specific research problem, as a behavior that can initiate and promote some regularity along time, and the researchers want to examine the consistency of these regularities; the *conditioned behaviors* are those that can be statistically significantly associated with the focal behavior, forming part of the resulting behavior pattern; and lag is the place of order that occupies a certain conditioned behavior compared to the focal behavior. In each study that we discuss, we will propose as premises what the focal behaviors, the conditioned behaviors, and the lags will be.

Based on the focal behavior, the matched frequencies are calculated, taking into account the conditioned behaviors and the lag, whether positive or negative (see Section 4). The matching frequency is a parameter consisting of the number of times that a certain behavior (conditioned behavior) appears after (if the lag is positive) or before (if the lag is negative) the focal behavior. We can work with all the focal and conditioned behaviors that we deem necessary.

By initially proposing an example corresponding to the vocal emotional responses of a patient in a psychotherapy session, we start from the following category system:

Vocal behavior = {Speech Laugh Yell Sigh Weep}

Let us assume that the record of vocal behavior in a session is: Speech, Yell, Sigh, Weep, Speech, Yell, Weep, Speech, Laugh, Sigh. Now, if we consider *Yell* as the focal behavior, and all other categories as conditioned behaviors, we would have that the matching frequency of *Yell* with *Weep* in lag 1 is 1, because *Weep* only once occupies the lag +1 regarding *Yell*. We have the simple frequencies of each behavior, and all the matching behaviors corresponding to each focal behavior with respect to the conditioned behaviors, and for each lag (in the next section, we present an empirical demonstration).

From the simple and matched frequencies, and their totals, we found, respectively, the expected probabilities (which only refer to the effect of chance) and the conditional probabilities (which refer to the probability of occurrence of each conditioned behavior, in a certain lag, from a certain focal behavior). From here, the conditional probability values that are higher than the expected probability, in the respective lags, are statistically significant, and show us the behaviors that will be part of the behavior pattern because their probability of occurrence does not depend on chance, but on a demonstrated sequential association regarding the focal behavior.

Polar Coordinate Analysis

Polar coordinate analysis constitutes a second stage of the lag sequential analysis because the adjusted residues obtained in the lag sequential analysis are the starting data of this analysis. Polar coordinate analysis was proposed by Sackett (1980) as a data-reduction system. The main objective is to obtain a complete map of interrelationships among behaviors (direct observation) or among textual units (indirect observation), and to represent it graphically through vectors. Based on the adjusted residue values obtained in the lag sequential analysis, the corresponding z scores are found, as relative indices of sequential dependence, both when the focal behavior acts as a criterion as when it acts as conditioned, and both prospectively (lags +1, +2, …) and retrospectively (lags −1, −2, …), and that it must be undertaken with at least 5 lags (from −5 to −1 and from +1 to +5), according to Sackett (1980). The z scores that connect the focal behavior with each conditioned behavior are independent values for each of the lags because they start from different matching frequencies.

However, a greater reduction of data is still possible, by representing these values in vectors, knowing that each of them has a length and an angle. Indeed, by distributing the codes in the different quadrants according to the type of relationship established in each case between the focal and conditioned behaviors, it is possible to find the distance between the origin (0,0) of coordinates Z_{sum} and the intersection point (or length of the vector), which corresponds to $\sqrt{X^2 + Y^2}$, where X is the Z_{sum} corresponding to the prospective values and Y corresponding to the retrospective values, as well as the angle, whose trigonometric function of the sine arc is Arc sin $= \frac{Y}{length}$, after taking into account the number of degrees to be added or subtracted in the different quadrants (Table 12.4), while indicating

TABLE 12.4

Profile of the Vectors of Each Quadrant

Quadrant	Relations between focal behavior and conditioned behavior	Angle
Quadrant I	Prospective and retrospective activation	$(0 < \varphi < 90) = \varphi$
Quadrant II	Prospective inhibition and retrospective activation	$(90 < \varphi < 180) = 180 - \varphi$
Quadrant III	Prospective and retrospective inhibition	$(180 < \varphi < 270) = 180 + \varphi$
Quadrant IV	Prospective activation and retrospective inhibition	$(270 < \varphi < 360) = 360 - \varphi$

Diachronic Analysis of Qualitative Data

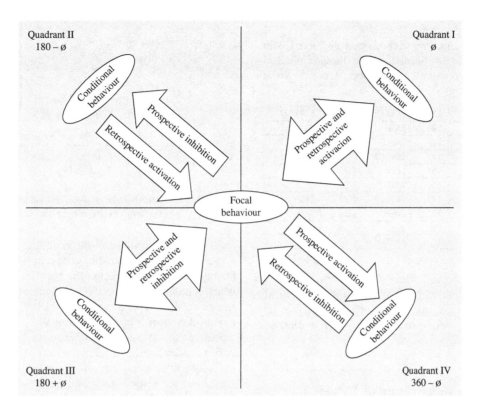

FIGURE 12.1 Relationships between focal behavior and conditioned behaviors in each quadrant. [Extracted from Aragón, Lapresa, Arana, Anguera, & Garzón, 2017, p. 30]

the type of relationships established. Figure 12.1 shows graphically the relationships between focal behavior and the conditioned behaviors in each quadrant.

T-pattern Analysis

The theoretical and methodological background of a T-pattern analysis (TPA) is mostly based on research in ethology, psychology, and linguistics, but also has roots in multivariate statistics and artificial intelligence (Casarrubea et al., 2015). After exploring existing methods and software programs and identifying their limitations concerning the analysis of behavior as complex real-time processes, Magnusson (the creator of Theme/TPA) set out to develop new structural concepts and tools and, in particular, for the discovery of its hidden patterns (Magnusson, 1978).

A T-pattern (see Figure 12.2) is defined as a self-similar tree-like structure repeated with statistically significant translation symmetry. Originally proposed as a model for temporal structure in behavior, the T-pattern, together with a number of other structural aspects and terms, is called the T-system (Magnusson 1996, 2000, 2006, 2016, 2017). In terms of ranges (intervals) of variation of distances between consecutive terms, a T-pattern can be characterized as follows:

$$Q = X_1[d_1,d_2]_1 X_2[d_1,d_2]_2 .. X_i[d_1,d_2]_i X_{i+1}..X_{m-1}[d_1,d_2]_{(m-1)} X_m,$$

with X as an event-type or a T-pattern, the general term $X_i[d_1,d_2]_i X_{i+1}$ means that within occurrences of the pattern, after X_i occurring at t, statistically significantly more often than expected by chance, X_{i+1} occurs within interval $[t + d_1, t + d_2]$, or short $[d_1, d_2]$, called a critical interval (CI).

Because Q can be recursively split into a statistical binary tree of critical intervals, as follows:

$$Q = Q_{Left}[d_1,d_2]Q_{Right}; \text{ with } X_1X_2.X_m \text{ as its terminals,}$$

detection goes in the opposite direction, starting with the series of (1D) locations of a number of potential terminals and connecting those with critical interval relations to form ever more complex T-patterns. To avoid combinatorial explosions during

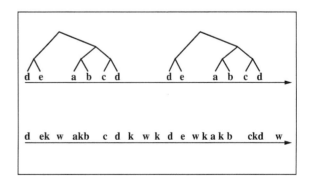

FIGURE 12.2 The lower part of this figure shows a simple real-time behavior record containing a few occurrences of several event types, a, b, c, d, e, k and w indicating their respective instances within the observation period. The upper line is identical to the lower one, except that occurrences of k and w have been removed. A simple t-pattern (abcd) then appears, that was difficult to see when the other events were present.

TABLE 12.5

Code Matrix Corresponding to the Systematic Record, with One Column (Vocal Emotional Response Dimension) and 30 Rows (Each Corresponds to an Occurrence of Vocal Emotional Response)

1	SPEECH	11	SPEECH	21	SPEECH
2	SIGH	12	SIGH	22	SIGH
3	YELL	13	WEEP	23	YELL
4	SPEECH	14	SPEECH	24	SPEECH
5	WEEP	15	SIGH	25	WEEP
6	SPEECH	16	YELL	26	SPEECH
7	SIGH	17	SPEECH	27	SIGH
8	YELL	18	SIGH	28	YELL
9	SPEECH	19	YELL	29	SIGH
10	YELL	20	LAUGH	30	YELL

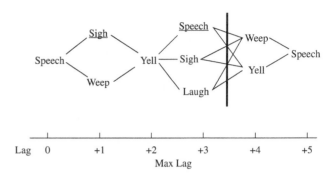

FIGURE 12.3 Structure extracted from the lag sequential analysis realized in its basic form by manual calculation.

the search and construction of complex T-patterns, all are compared, deleting redundant or partial ones. Although cyclicality of occurrence is not a defining aspect of T-patterns, they often occur cyclically and even when none of their components does.

4 Empirical Demonstration of Detection of Lag Sequential Analysis, Polar Coordinate Analysis, and T-Pattern Analysis for MMR

Lag Sequential Analysis

To facilitate understanding, an empirical demonstration carried out manually from the data in Table 12.5 is included, corresponding to the succession of emotional responses given by a patient in a psychotherapy session. From this code matrix, the simple frequencies and the matching frequencies have been manually found (Table 12.6, left side), considering the lags +1 to +5. Also, because the totals are available, on the right side of Table 12.6, the expected probabilities (i.e., quotient between each simple and total frequency) and the conditioned probabilities (i.e., quotient between each matching frequency and the total) have been obtained. The expected probabilities indicate only the effect of chance, whereas the conditional probabilities correspond to the situation studied.

This illustration corresponds to the basic diagram of lag sequential analysis, in which no optimization of the procedure is performed. In accordance with this warning, Table 12.6 highlights the conditional probabilities whose values are higher than the corresponding expected probability, and will be the codes that form part of the behavior patterns obtained, when considered statistically significant. Interpretive guidelines should be applied to said structure to allow researchers to consider where it ends conventionally. These interpretative guidelines are as follows: (a) When there are no more lags with statistically significant behaviors; (b) when you have two consecutive empty lags; and (c) when in two consecutive lags, there are several statistically significant behaviors, and in this case, the first of these two lags is considered the MAX LAG, and with this ends the interpretive purposes of the structure obtained. Figure 12.3 shows the structure that has been extracted through this basic manual calculation, along the five lags considered, and SPEECH being the focal behavior. The MAX LAG is in the +3 lag because in the +3 and +4 consecutive lags, there are several statistically significant behaviors. This analysis could be undertaken through the free program GSEQ5 (Bakeman & Quera, 2011) or HOISAN (Hernández-Mendo et al., 2012).

Polar Coordinate Analysis

Polar coordinate analysis is extremely labor-intensive when carried out manually, and, until recently, there was no free computer program with the ability to facilitate this analysis. HOISAN (Hernández-Mendo et al., 2012) is the first and the only one available to the scientific community. We present an example that corresponds to a study on autistic children, and which is partially published by Alcover et al. (2019), with HOISAN being used for the calculation of the adjusted

TABLE 12.6

Simple and Matching Frequencies (on the Left Side) and the Expected and Conditioned Probabilities (on the Right Side)

	Simple and matching frequencies table						Expected and conditional probabilities table					
Lag	Speech	Sigh	Weep	Yell	Laugh	TOTAL		Speech	Sigh	Weep	Yell	Laugh
	10	8	3	8	1	30	Expected probabilites	0.33	0.26	0.1	0.26	0.03
+1	0	7	2	1	0	10		0	**0.7**	**0.2**	0.1	0
+2	3	0	1	6	0	10	Conditional probabilites	0.3	0	**0.1**	**0.6**	0
+3	5	4	0	0	1	10		**0.5**	**0.4**	0	0	**0.1**
+4	1	2	3	4	0	10		0.1	0.2	**0.3**	**0.4**	0
+5	5	2	0	2	0	9		**0.55**	0.22	0	0.22	0

Diachronic Analysis of Qualitative Data

TABLE 12.7

Z Values Obtained Through the HOISAN Program (Hernández-Mendo, López-López, Castellano, Morales-Sánchez, & Pastrana, 2012), Corresponding to the Gest_GEDES Focal Behavior and the Conditioned Behaviors (the Remaining Codes of the First Column) in the Lags −1 to −5 and +1 to +5

Code	Lag-5	Lag-4	Lag-3	Lag-2	Lag-1	Lag+1	Lag+2	Lag+3	Lag+4	Lag+5
Near_PX	0	0	0	0	0	0	0	0	0	0
Gest_affirm_neg_YES_NOT	0	0	0	0	0	0	0	0	0	0
Play_JF	-0,725	-0,722	-0,718	-0,715	-0,712	-0,712	-0,693	-0,674	-0,654	-0,657
Gest_GEMO	-0,154	-0,154	-0,153	-0,152	-0,216	-0,216	-0,216	-0,217	4,545	-0,219
Func_COMFU	-0,292	-1,491	0,859	-0,311	0,884	-0,3	2,054	-1,504	-0,333	0,835
Gest_GESEN	0,355	0,329	0,337	-1,027	0,32	-1,021	-1,027	1,639	0,295	0,286
Gest_GESEÑ	2,68	0,997	-0,718	0,954	-0,712	0,962	-0,715	-0,718	0,937	-0,725
Gest_GECONV	-0,791	0,775	-0,784	0,792	0,8	0,8	-0,78	-0,784	-0,787	-0,769
Gest_GEDES										

TABLE 12.8

Length and Angle Parameters Corresponding to the Focal Behavior Gest_GEDES and the Conditioned Behaviors (the Remaining Codes in the First Column)[a]

Code	Quadrant	Prospective Zsum	Retrospective Zsum	Lengh	Angle
Play_JF	III	-1,52	-1,61	2,21 (*)	226,66
Gest_GEMO	IV	1,64	-0,37	1,69	347,29
Func_COMFU	IV	0,34	-0,16	0,37	334,98
Gest_GESEN	I	0,08	0,14	0,16	61,29
Gest_GESEÑ	II	-0,12	1,43	1,44	94,63
Gest_GECONV	II	-1,04	0,35	1,1	161,15

Note: [a]The statistically significant vector is indicated by (*), the length being >1.96 (for p<.05). The length and angle are calculated from the prospective and retrospective Z_{sum} values.

residues (results of the lag sequential analysis previously carried out, which, at the same time, are data of the polar coordinate analysis). From the adjusted residues obtained in a previous lag sequential analysis, wherein Gest_GEDES (last code of the first column of Table 12.7) is the focal behavior, and the conditioned behaviors correspond to the other codes of said first column, the HOISAN program has obtained the Z_{sum} values for each conditioned behavior, differentiated by prospective and retrospective approaches, as well as the parameters of length and angle of the vectors (Table 12.8). Figure 12.4 includes the graphic representation, which is obtained with the R program (Rodríguez-Medina, Arias, Arias, Hernández-Mendo, & Anguera, 2019).

T-pattern Analysis

To give an example on how the Theme/ThemeEdu works, we provide an example from a Doctor-Suicidal Patient Interview study (Haynal-Reymond, Jonsson, & Magnusson, 2005). According to authors, current techniques of repeated suicide risk assessment are not reliably predictive, and research into new methods were needed. The judgment of clinicians has relied partly on nonverbal signs such as facial expressions. If differences in patients and/or interviewer's facial expressions appeared between subjects who were to make subsequent attempts (Repeaters) and those who were not (Non-Repeaters), this could lay the foundations for new ways of prediction.

In this study, 59 patients admitted to the Geneva University Hospitals after a suicide attempt were video-recorded during an interview with a psychiatrist. After the interview, the therapist was asked to assess the suicide risk on a 4-point scale. At a 24-month follow-up, the authors identified ten Repeaters, who were matched with 11 of the 48

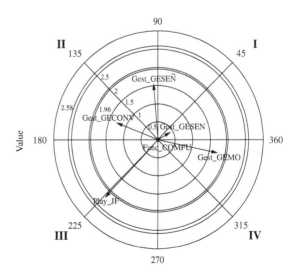

FIGURE 12.4 Graphical representation of the vectors corresponding to the focal behavior Gest_GEDES and the conditioned behaviors of the first column of Table 12.7.

Non-Repeaters, with respect to gender, age, and number of previous suicide attempts. To code the doctor's and patient's facial behavior, the authors used Ekman and Friesen's *Facial Action Coding System* (FACS; Ekman & Friesen, 1978; Friesen & Ekman, 1984) and analyzed the behavioral differences in both groups. To analyze the structure of the interactive behavior, they used THEME.

Results indicated an average activation of all coded units, peri-ocular activation, and duration of the doctor's gaze straight at the patient, which were all statistically significantly higher, distinguishing correctly 81.8% to 90.9% of the patients. In contrast, the doctor's written predictions were erroneous: only 22.7% of the patients were correctly classified. This fact reflects the doctor's perception of risk, without awareness. Different types of behavioral patterns were found to occur exclusively by either repeaters or non-repeaters and statistically significant differences were found in the complexity of patterns between groups (see Figures 12.5 and 12.6). These provide a sense of the nonverbal communication quality.

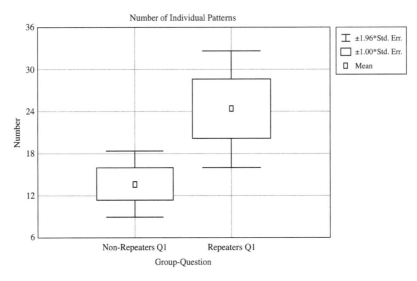

FIGURE 12.5 Number of individual patterns detected in Question 1 for groups Non-Repeaters and Repeaters (t = −2,23; df = 19; p < .03).

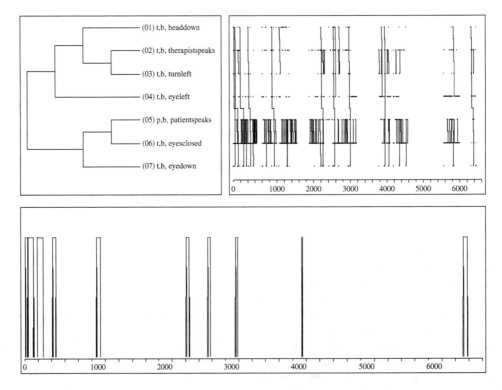

FIGURE 12.6 Pattern found in the Repeaters group concerning Questions 1 and 2. Events (a) Therapist, begin, headdown; (b) Therapist, begin, therapistspeaks; (c) Therapist, begin, turnleft; (d) Therapist, begin, eyeleft; (e) Patient, begin, patientspeaks; (f) Therapist, begin, eyesclosed; and (g) Therapist, begin, eyedown.

5 Suggested Applications of Detection of Lag Sequential Analysis, Polar Coordinate Analysis, and T-Pattern Analysis in MMR

The lag sequential analysis can be used with five types of data proposed by Bakeman (1978) and Bakeman and Quera (2011), and polar coordinate analysis can now be used with *multievent data* (but in the near future we expect to use it with other types of data). The behavior of all living beings consists of patterns in time; consequently, its nature and its underlying dynamics are difficult to be perceived and detected by the unaided observer. This calls for means of detection, data handling, and analysis. By using T-pattern detection, it is possible to reveal hidden relationships among the behavioral events in time. Casarrubea et al. (2015) review the use of TPA in different fields. In particular, Table 12.1 presents a summary of the applications of T-pattern analysis, with their respective references, in animal and human behavior.

6 Strengths and Limitations of Detection of Lag Sequential Analysis, Polar Coordinate Analysis, and T-pattern analysis in MMR

In the framework of MMR, the strength of lag sequential analysis is that it can be used to obtain behavior patterns with both direct and indirect observation. Therefore, not only when we record visually perceptible behaviors, but also when we start from life stories, repeated conversations, successive episodes in a person, in a dyad, in a small group, and so forth, it is possible to look for the structure through lag sequential analysis. In a similar vein, the strength of polar coordinate analysis is that it allows behavior to be vectorized. A requirement for the applicability of the lag sequential analysis and polar coordinate analysis is related to the sample size of recorded data. As a minimum, there should be at least 30 data points (Bakeman & Gottman, 1986), but in a diachronic study, it is foreseeable that a much larger number will be available.

TPA has all the strengths of lag sequential analysis, but involves less assumptions. TPA is hierarchical and multiordinal and can deal with parallel data streams because the mutual exclusion of events in time is not required because it is based on real-time temporal locations of events rather than sequential/serial positions. Just two occurrences even of the same behavior might allow detection of a statistically significant T-pattern because real-time plays a major role. TPA was developed to deal effectively with even the smallest data and possibly occurring within very short observation intervals, again, thanks to the implication of real-time. TPA does not deal directly with behavioral alternatives or substitutes; for example, if A is followed statistically significantly by B or C or D within some window but not by any single one of them, then no relation is detected. This weakness is now being worked on to eliminate it from TPA.

We want to highlight the complementarity among lag sequential analysis, polar coordinate, and TPA as a strength of these approaches. The range of possibilities is very wide, and the only limits would be found in those cases where it was not possible to obtain an orderly systematic record, regardless of whether it is direct or indirect observation.

7 Resources for Learning more about Lag Sequential Analysis, Polar Coordinate Analysis and T-Pattern Analysis

In addition to the works that have been cited when presenting each technique, the reader can delve into the lag sequential analysis in greater depth through the publications associated with the GSEQ5 (e.g., Bakeman & Quera, 2011). The publications associated with HOISAN (Hernández-Mendo et al., 2012) are also a resource that helps to get started in the application of polar coordinate analysis. On the other hand, multiple studies that combine these two techniques can be found in Anguera, Blanco-Villlaseñor, Jonsson, Losada, and Portell (2019).

The website http://lom.observesport.com/ has a repository (*Publicaciones*), where it is possible to download articles that have used lag sequential analysis, polar coordinate analysis, and T-pattern analysis in the sports field.

Moreover, in Table 12.9, we add more resources in order to be able to learn HOISAN software, lag sequential analysis, polar coordinate analysis, and generalizability analysis. Generalizability analysis, although not directly discussed in this chapter, is used in observational studies at a stage prior to diachronic analysis, while we manage data quality control.

A comprehensive review of TPA already has been published, demonstrating its usefulness in the study of various aspects of human or animal behavior, such as behavioral modifications in neuro-psychiatric diseases, route-tracing stereotypy in mice, sport and movement science, interaction between human subjects and animal or artificial agents, hormonal-behavioral interactions, patterns of behavior associated with emesis and, in laboratories, exploration and anxiety-related behaviors in rodents (Casarrubea et al., 2015). Further information on

TABLE 12.9

Resources to Learn HOISAN Software, Lag Sequential Analysis, Polar Coordinate Analysis, and Generalizability Analysis

Title of YouTube resource and link	Language
HOISAN software www.youtube.com/watch?v=QtmHgU_Bud0	Spanish
cLag sequential analysis (HOISAN software) www.youtube.com/watch?v=ZuNh3GzUlZQ	Spanish
Polar coordinate analysis (HOISAN software) www.youtube.com/watch?v=zarMVSDyWKY	Spanish
Generalizability analysis (SAGT software) www.youtube.com/watch?v=1_GFnEMaY28&t=7s	Spanish
Generalizability analysis: Optimization of measure design (SAGT software) www.youtube.com/watch?v=P6r_5D3_KTg	Spanish
Generalizability analysis through square sums (SAGT software) www.youtube.com/watch?v=a_RhY-ubYCc	Spanish

Theme/ThemeEdu, TPA, and publications can be found on www.patternvision.com and http://hbl.hi.is/.

Conclusions

In this chapter, we have presented three techniques of diachronic quantitative analysis that apply to qualitative data, showing how they represent a mixed methods research approach via the *connecting* technique, by transforming qualitative data from direct and/or indirect observation into matrices of codes, having previously built an *ad hoc* observation instrument.

The lag sequential analysis, the analysis of polar coordinates, and the TPA offer three different ways for a diachronic analysis, always involving scrutinizing the structure of behavior, and from rigorous quantitative analyses that are very suitable for qualitative data. The suggested analysis can help mixed method researchers both design their mixed analysis as well as analyze their data coherently. We hope that this chapter represents an important step started by Onwuegbuzie, Slate, Leech, and Collins (2009) on the way to "the quest to demystify the mixed analysis process" (p. 31).

REFERENCES

Alcover, C., Mairena, M. A., Mezzatesta, M., Elías, N., Díez, M., Balañá, G., González, M., Rodríguez-Medina, J., Anguera, M. T., & Arias-Pujol, E. (2019). Mixed methods approach to describe social interaction during a group intervention for adolescents with autism spectrum disorders. *Frontiers in Psychology, 10*, 1158. doi:10.3389/fpsyg.2019.01158

Anguera, M. T. (1992). Diseños diacrónicos en programas de intervención [Diachronic designs in intervention programs]. *Bordón (Madrid), 43* (4), 421–429.

Anguera, M. T. (1997). From prospective patterns in behavior to joint analysis with a retrospective perspective. In *Colloque sur Invitation Méthodologie d'Analyse des Interactions Sociales*. Paris, France: University of Paris V, Sorbonne.

Anguera, M. T. (2003). Observational methods (general). In R. Fernández-Ballesteros (Ed.), *Encyclopedia of psychological assessment* (Vol. 2, pp. 632–637). London, England: Sage.

Anguera, M. T. (2020). Is it possible to perform "liquefying" actions in conversational analysis? The detection of structures in indirect observation. In L. Hunyadi and I. Szekrényes (Eds.), *The temporal structure of multimodal communication* (pp. 45–67). Intelligent Systems Reference Library book series, Vol. 164. Cham, Switzerland: Springer.

Anguera, M. T., Blanco-Villaseñor, A., Jonsson, G. K., Losada, J. L., & Portell, M. (Eds.) (2019). *Systematic observation: Engaging researchers in the study of daily life as it is lived*. Lausanne, Switzerland: Frontiers Media.

Anguera, M. T., Blanco-Villaseñor, A., Losada, J. L., & Sánchez-Algarra, P. (2019, Julio). Análisis del intercambio comunicativo: Planteamiento innovador del *quantitizing*. *Congresso Ibero-Americano em Investigação Qualitativa (CIAIQ2019)*. Lisboa, Portugal: CIAIQ.

Anguera, M. T., Blanco-Villaseñor, A., Losada, J. L., Sánchez-Algarra, P., & Onwuegbuzie, A. J. (2018). Revisiting the difference between mixed methods and multimethods: Is it all in the name? *Quality & Quantity, 52*, 2757–2770. doi:10.1007/s11135–018–0700–2

Anguera, M. T., Camerino, O., Castañer, M., Sánchez-Algarra, P., & Onwuegbuzie, A. J. (2017). The specificity of observational studies in physical activity and sports sciences: Moving forward in mixed methods research and proposals for achieving quantitative and qualitative symmetry. *Frontiers in Psychology, 8*, 2196. doi:10.3389/fpsyg.2017.02196.

Anguera, M. T., & Hernández-Mendo, A. (2016). Avances en estudios observacionales en Ciencias del Deporte desde los *mixed methods*. *Cuadernos de Psicología del Deporte, 16*(1), 17–30. doi:10.4321/S1578-84232015000100002

Anguera, M. T., & Izquierdo, C. (2006). Methodological approaches in human communication: From complexity of perceived situation to data analysis. In G. Riva, M. T. Anguera, B. K. Wiederhold, and F. Mantovani (Coord.), *From communication to presence. Cognition, emotions and culture towards the Ultimate Communicative Experience* (pp. 203–222). Amsterdam, Netherlands: IOS Press.

Anguera, M. T., Jonsson, G. K., & Sánchez-Algarra, P. (2017). Liquefying text from human communication processes: A methodological proposal based on t-pattern detection. *Journal of Multimodal Communication Studies, 4*(1–2), 10–15.

Anguera, M. T., Magnusson, M. S., & Jonsson, G.K. (2007). Instrumentos no estándar [Non-standard instruments]. *Avances en Medición, 5*, 63–82.

Anguera, M. T., Portell, M., Chacón-Moscoso, S., & Sanduvete-Chaves, S. (2018). Indirect observation in everyday contexts: Concepts and methodological guidelines within a mixed methods framework. *Frontiers in Psychology, 9*, 13. doi:10.3389/fpsyg.2018.00013

Aragón, S., Lapresa, D., Arana, J., Anguera, M. T., & Garzón, B. (2017). An example of the informative potential of polar coordinate analysis: Sprint tactics in elite 1500 m track events. *Measurement in Physical Education and Exercise Science, 16*, 279–286. doi:10.1080/1091367X.2016.1245192

Ardá, T., & Anguera, M. T. (2000). Evaluación prospectiva en programas de entrenamiento de fútbol a 7 mediante indicadores de éxito en diseños diacrónicos intensivos retrospectivos [Prospective evaluation in soccer 7 training programs using indicators of success in intensive retrospective diachronic designs]. *Psicothema, 12* (Supl. N° 2), 52–55.

Ardá, T., Casal, C. A., & Anguera, M. T. (2002). Evaluación de las acciones ofensivas de éxito en fútbol 11 mediante diseños diacrónicos intensivos retrospectivos [Evaluation of successful offensive actions in soccer 11 using intensive retrospective diachronic designs]. *Metodología de las Ciencias del Comportamiento*, vol. especial, 48–51.

Arias-Pujol, E., & Anguera, M. T. (2005). Análisis de la comunicación en un grupo terapéutico de adolescentes: estudio diacrónico [Communication analysis in a therapeutic group of adolescents: diachronic study]. *Revista de Psicopatología y Salud Mental del Niño y del Adolescente, M1*, 25–36.

Bakeman, R. (1978). Untangling streams of behavior: Sequential analysis of observation data. In G. P. Sackett (Ed.), *Observing behavior* (Vol. 2, pp. 63–78). Baltimore, MD: University of Park Press.

Bakeman, R., Adamson, L. B., & Strisik, P. (1995). Lags and Logs: Statistical Approaches to Interaction (SPSS version). In J. M. Morgan (Ed.), *The analysis of change* (pp. 279–308). Mahwah, N. J.: Lawrence Erlbaum Associates.

Bakeman, R., & Gottman, J. M. (1986). *Observing interaction: An introduction to sequential analysis.* Cambridge, England: Cambridge University Press.

Bakeman, R., & Quera, V. (2011). *Sequential analysis and observational methods for the behavioral sciences.* Cambridge, England: Cambridge University Press.

Birdwhistell, R. L. (1970). *Kinesics and context: Essays and body motion communication.* Philadelphia, PA: University of Pennsylvania Press.

Blanco-Villaseñor, A., Losada, J. L., & Anguera, M. T. (2003). Analytic techniques in observational designs in environment-behavior relation. *Medio Ambiente y Comportamiento Humano, 4*, 111–126.

Camerino, O., Castañer, M., & Anguera, M. T. (Coords.). (2012). *Mixed methods research in the movement sciences: Case studies in sport, physical education and dance.* Abingdon, England: Routledge.

Casarrubea, M., Jonsson, G. K., Faulisi, F., Sorbera, F., Di Giovanni, G., Benigno, A., Crescimanno, G., & Magnusson, M. S. (2015). T-pattern analysis for the study of temporal structure of animal and human behavior: A comprehensive review. *Journal of Neurosciences Methods, 239*, 34–46. doi:10.1016/j.jneumeth.2014.09.024

Casarrubea, M., Magnusson, M. S., Anguera, M. T., Jonsson, G. K., Castañer, M., Santangelo, A., Palacino, M.,.... Crescimanno, G. (2018). T-pattern detection and analysis for the discovery of hidden features of behaviour. *Journal of Neurosciences Methods, 310*, 24–32. doi:10.1016/j.jneumeth.2018.06.013

Chacón-Moscoso, S., Sanduvete-Chaves, S., Portell, M., & Anguera, M. T. (2013). Reporting a program evaluation: Needs, program plan, intervention, and decisions. *International Journal of Clinical and Health Psychology, 13*(1), 58–60. doi:10.1016/S1697-2600(13)70008-5

Crandell, J. L., Voils, C. I., & Sandelowski, M. (2012). Bayesian approaches to the synthesis of qualitative and quantitative research findings. In K. Hannes and C. Lockwood (Eds.), *Synthesizing qualitative research* (pp. 137–159). Oxford, England: Wiley & Sons.

Creamer, E. G. (2018). *An introduction to fully integrated mixed methods research.* Thousand Oaks, CA: Sage.

Creswell, J. W., & Plano Clark, V. L. (2007). *Designing and conducting mixed methods research* (2nd ed.). Thousand Oaks, CA: Sage.

Del Giacco, L, Anguera, M. T., & Salcuni, S. (2020). The action of verbal and non-verbal communication in the therapeutic alliance construction: A mixed methods approach to assess the initial interactions with depressed patients. *Frontiers in Psychology, 11*, 234. doi:10.3389/fpsyg.2020.00234

Del Giacco, L., Salcuni, S., & Anguera, M. T. (2019). The communicative modes analysis system in psychotherapy from mixed methods framework: Introducing a new observation system for classifying verbal and nonverbal communication. *Frontiers in Psychology, 10*, 782. doi:10.3389/fpsyg.2019.00782

Dickman, H. R. (1963). The perception of behavioral units. In R. Barker (Ed.), *The stream of behavior* (pp. 23–41). New York, NY: Appleton-Century-Crofts.

Ekman, P., & Friesen, W. V. (1978). *Facial action coding system: A technique for the measurement of facial movement.* Palo Alto, CA: Consulting Psychologists Press, Inc.

Escolano-Pérez, E., & Blanco-Villaseñor, A. (2015). The longitudinal measurement of change: Intraindividual variability in behavior and interindividual differences observed in childhood. *Anales de Psicología, 31*, 545–551. doi:10.6018/analesps.31.2.166361

Fassnacht, G. (1982). *Theory and practice of observing behaviour.* London, England: Academic Press.

Fetters M. D., & Freshwater, D. (2015). The 1 + 1 = 3 integration challenge. *Journal of Mixed Methods Research, 9*, 115–117. doi:10.1177/1558689815581222

Friesen, W. V., & Ekman, P. (1984). *EMFACS-7.* Unpublished manual.

Gabin, B., Camerino, O., Anguera, M. T., & Castañer, M. (2012). Lince: Multiplatform sport analysis software. *Procedia - Social and Behavioral Sciences, 46*, 4692–4694. doi:10.1016/j.sbspro.2012.06.320

García-Fariña, A., Jiménez Jiménez, F., & Anguera, M. T. (2018). Observation of physical education teachers' communication: Detecting patterns in verbal behavior. *Frontiers in Psychology, 9*, 334. doi:10.3389/fpsyg.2018.00334

Gimeno, A., Anguera, M. T., Berzosa, A., & Ramírez, L. (2006). Detección de patrones interactivos en la comunicación de familias con hijos adolescentes. *Psicothema, 18*, 785–790.

Haynal-Reymond, V., Jonsson, G. K., & Magnusson, M. S. (2005). Nonverbal communication in doctor-suicidal patient interview. In L. Anolli, S. Duncan, M. Magnusson, and G. Riva (Eds.), *The hidden structure of social interaction. From genomics to culture patterns* (pp. 142–149). Amsterdam, Netherlands: IOS Press.

Hernández-Mendo, A., Castellano, J., Camerino, O., Jonsson, G., Blanco-Villaseñor, A., Lopes, A., & Anguera, M. T. (2014). Programas informáticos de registro, control de calidad del dato, y análisis de datos [Observational software, data quality control and data analysis]. *Revista de Psicología del Deporte, 23*(1), 111–121.

Hernández-Mendo, A., López-López, J. A., Castellano, J., Morales-Sánchez, V., & Pastrana, J. L. (2012). Hoisan 1.2: programa informático para uso en metodología observacional [Hoisan 1.2: software for observational methodology]. *Cuadernos de Psicología del Deporte, 12*, 55–78. doi: 10.4321/S1578-84232012000100006

Hernández Solano, A. M. (2008). *Desarrollo de un software para el análisis estadístico bayesiano* [TRADUCIR]. Master Thesis. Oaxaca, México.

Magnusson, M. S. (1978). *The human ethological probabilistic structural multivariate approach to the study of children's nonverbal communication* (Unpublished doctoral dissertation). University of Copenhagen's Silver Medal.

Magnusson, M. S. (1996). Hidden real-time patterns in intra- and inter-individual behavior: Description and detection. *European Journal of Psychological Assessment, 12*, 112–123. doi:10.1027/1015-5759.12.2.112

Magnusson, M. S. (2000). Discovering hidden time patterns in behavior: T-patterns and their detection. *Behavior Research Methods, Instruments, & Computers, 32*, 93–110. doi:10.3758/BF03200792

Magnusson, M. S. (2005). Understanding social interaction: Discovering hidden structure with model and algorithms. In L. Anolli, S. Duncan, M. S. Magnusson, and G. Riva (Eds.), *The hidden structure of interaction. From neurons to culture patterns* (pp. 3–22). Amsterdam, The Netherlands: IOS Press.

Magnusson, M. S. (2006). Structure and communication in interaction. In G. Riva, M. T. Anguera, B. K. Wiederhold, and F. Mantovani (Eds.), *From communication to presence: Cognition, emotions and culture towards the ultimate communication experience* (pp. 127–146). Amsterdam, The Netherlands: IOS Press.

Magnusson, M. S. (2016) Time and self-similar structure in behavior and interactions: From sequences to symmetry and fractals. In M. S., Magnusson, J. K. Burgoon, and M. Casarrubea (Eds.), *Discovering hidden temporal patterns in behavior and interaction, Neuromethods* (Vol. 111, pp. 3–35). New York, NY: Springer.

Magnusson, M. S. (2017). Why search for hidden repeated temporal behavior patterns: T-pattern analysis with theme. *International Journal of Clinical Pharmacology & Pharmacotherapy*, 2, 128. doi:10.15344/2017/2456–3501/128.

Magnusson, M. S. (2020). T-Pattern Detection and Analysis (TPA) with THEME™: A mixed methods approach. *Frontiers in Psychology*, 10, 2663. doi:10.3389/fpsyg.2019.02663

Menescardi, C., Falco, C., Estevan, I., Ros, C., Morales-Sánchez, V., & Hernández-Mendo, A. (2019). Is it possible to predict an athlete's behavior? The use of polar coordinates to identify key patterns in taekwondo. *Frontiers in Psychology*, 10, 1232. doi:10.3389/fpsyg.2019.01232

Newman, I., Onwuegbuzie, A. J., & Hitchcock, J. H. (2015). Using the general linear model to facilitate the full integration of qualitative and quantitative analysis: The potential to improve prediction and theory building and testing. *General Linear Model Journal*, 41(1), 12–28. Retrieved from www.glmj.org/archives/articles/Newman_v41n1.pdf

O'Cathain, A., Murphy, E., & Nicholl, J. (2010). Three techniques for integrating data in mixed methods studies. *British Medical Journal*, 341, c4587. doi:10.1136/bmj.c4587

Onwuegbuzie, A. J. (2012). Putting the MIXED back into quantitative and qualitative research in educational research and beyond: Moving towards the 'radical middle'. *International Journal of Multiple Research Approaches*, 6, 192–219. doi:10.5172/mra.2012.6.3.192

Onwuegbuzie, A. J. (2016). A call for conducting multivariate mixed analyses. *Journal of Educational Issues*, 2(2), 1–30. doi:10.5296/jei.v2i2.9316

Onwuegbuzie, A. J. (2017, March). *Mixed methods is dead! Long live mixed methods!* Invited keynote address presented at the Mixed Methods International Research Association Caribbean Conference, Montego Bay, Jamaica.

Onwuegbuzie, A. J., Hitchcock, J., Natesan, P., & Newman, I. (2018). Using fully integrated thinking to address the 1+1=1 integration challenge. *International Journal of Multiple Research Approaches*, 10(1), 666–678. doi:10.29034/ijmra.v10n1a43

Onwuegbuzie, A. J., Slate, J. R., Leech, N. L., & Collins, K. M. T. (2009). Mixed data analysis: Advanced integration techniques. *International Journal of Multiple Research Approaches*, 3, 13–33. doi:10.5172/mra.455.3.1.13

Onwuegbuzie, A. J., & Teddlie, C. (2003). A framework for analyzing data in mixed methods research. In A. Tashakkori and C. Teddlie (Eds.), *Handbook of mixed methods in social and behavioral research* (pp. 351–383). Thousand Oaks, CA: Sage.

Portell, M., Anguera, M. T., Chacón-Moscoso, S., & Sanduvete-Chaves, S. (2015). Guidelines for reporting evaluations based on observational methodology (GREOM). *Psicothema*, 27, 283–289.

Portell, M., Anguera, M. T., Hernández-Mendo, A., & Jonsson, G. K. (2015). Quantifying biopsychosocial aspects in everyday contexts: An integrative methodological approach from the behavioral sciences. *Psychology Research and Behavior Management*, 8, 153–160. doi:10.2147/PRBM.S82417

Portell, M., Sene-Mir, A. M., Anguera, M. T., Jonsson, G. K., & Losada, J. L. (2019). Support system for the assessment and intervention during the manual material handling training at the workplace: Contributions from the systematic observation. *Frontiers in Psychology 10*, 1247. doi:10.3389/fpsyg.2019.01247

Rodríguez-Medina, J., Arias, V., Arias, B., Hernández-Mendo, A., & Anguera, M. T. (2019). *Polar Coordinate Analysis, from HOISAN to R: A Tutorial Paper*. Unpublished manuscript. Retrieved from: https://jairodmed.shinyapps.io/HOISAN_to_R/

Rodríguez-Medina, J., Rodríguez-Navarro, H., Arias, V., Arias, B., & Anguera, M. T. (2018). Non-reciprocal friendships in a school-age boy with autism: The ties that build? *Journal of Autism and Developmental Disorders*, 48, 2980–2994. doi:10.1007/s10803-018-3575-0

Sackett, G. P. (1978). Measurement in observational research. In G. P. Sackett (Ed.), *Observing behavior* (Vol. 2, pp. 25–43). Baltimore, MD: University of Park Press.

Sackett, G. P. (1980). Lag sequential analysis as a data reduction technique in social interaction research. In D. B. Sawin, R. C. Hawkins, L. O. Walker, and J. H. Penticuff (Eds.), *Exceptional infant. Psychosocial risks in infant-environment transactions* (pp. 300–340). New York, NY: Brunner/Mazel.

Sánchez-Algarra, P., & Anguera, M. T. (2013). Qualitative/quantitative integration in the inductive observational study of interactive behaviour: Impact of recording and coding predominating perspectives. *Quality & Quantity. International Journal of Methodology*, 47, 1237–1257. doi:10.1007/s11135-012-9764-6

Sandelowski, M., Voils, C. I., & Knafl, G. (2009). On quantitizing. *Journal of Mixed Methods Research*, 3, 208–222. doi:10.1177/1558689809334210

Schegloff, E. A. (2000). On granularity. *Annual Review of Sociology*, 26, 715–720. doi:10.1146/annurev.soc.26.1.715

Soto, A., Camerino, O., Iglesias, X., Anguera, M. T., & Castañer, M. (2019). LINCE PLUS: Research software for behavior video analysis. *Apunts. Educación Física y Deportes*, 137, 149–153. doi:10.5672/apunts.2014–0983.es.(2019/3).137.11

Vázquez-Diz, J. A., Morillo-Baro, J. P., Reigal, R. E., Morales-Sánchez, V., & Hernández-Mendo, A. (2019). Mixed methods in decision-making through polar coordinate technique: Differences by gender on beach handball specialist. *Frontiers in Psychology*, 10, 1627. doi:10.3389/fpsyg.2019.01627

Weick, K. E. (1968). Systematic observational methods. In G. Lindzey and E. Aronson (Eds.), *Handbook of social psychology* (Vol. II, pp. 357–451), Reading, MA: Addison-Wesley.

Part II

Qualitative Approaches to Quantitative Data

13

Qualitizing Data

Anthony J. Onwuegbuzie and Nancy L. Leech

The evolution of mixed methods research has been characterized by the emergence of several integration equations. The original equation, which can be traced back to at least the early 20th century, "before QUAN [quantitative research] became the dominant paradigm in social science" (Johnson & Gray, 2010, p. 86), could be expressed as follows:

$$1+1=2 \qquad (1)$$

In such mixed methods research studies, one or more qualitative research components/phases and one or more quantitative research components/phases are conceptualized, planned, and implemented to address related aspects (i.e., sub-research questions) of research questions that underlie the same phenomenon. Therefore, this 1 + 1 = 2 integration formula implies that both qualitative data and quantitative data are collected, analyzed, and interpreted. However, the qualitative and quantitative components occur in a parallel and separate manner. That is, the qualitative data are qualitatively analyzed and interpreted separately, whereas the quantitative data are quantitatively analyzed and interpreted separately. As such, these mixed methods research approaches (i.e., representing whole systems of a research study) have been known as *parallel mixed methods research approaches* (cf. Onwuegbuzie & Johnson, 2006)[1]. At the conclusion of these parallel mixed methods research studies, it is not unusual for the researchers to publish the qualitative and quantitative results separately (i.e., via different outlets)—which represents the lowest level of integration (e.g., the latter published work citing the former published work), if integration occurs at all. In contrast, a slightly higher level of integration would involve both the qualitative and quantitative findings being presented within the single report but in different sections with minimal integration. At the level of analysis, the 1 + 1 = 2 integration formula leads to the qualitative analysis and quantitative analysis not interacting with each other—coined as "non-cross-over mixed analyses" by Onwuegbuzie and Combs (2010, p. 423) and a "within-tradition analysis" by Onwuegbuzie, Slate, Leech, and Collins (2007, p. 12). Moreover, this integration maintains a demarcation between qualitative and quantitative research approaches—yielding what we refer to as *low integration*.

At the turn of the 21st century, the period of institutionalization of mixed methods research as a distinct methodological approach (Teddlie & Johnson, 2009) saw the development of a more integrated model that involved use of the following integration formula:

$$1+1=3 \qquad (2)$$

Fetters and Freshwater (2015) describe this formula as "qualitative + quantitative = more than the individual components" (p. 115). A major characteristic of this integration equation is the notion of meta-inferences, which represent inferences stemming from both the qualitative and quantitative findings being combined into a coherent whole (Tashakkori & Teddlie, 1998). It is these meta-inferences that change the mathematical expression from a "2" on the right-hand side of Equation 1 to a "3" on the right-hand side of Equation 2. However, like the 1 + 1 = 2 integration formula, the 1 + 1 = 3 formula "reifies a quantitative–qualitative dichotomy" (Onwuegbuzie, Hitchcock, Natesan, & Newman, 2018, p. 666). As such, they represent a *partial integrated mixed methods research approach—yielding what we refer to as medium integration*.

In 2017, Onwuegbuzie introduced an integration formula that represented a synechist (i.e., antidualistic) stance (cf. Johnson & Gray, 2010), wherein the quantitative–qualitative analysis dichotomy is replaced by continua that facilitate the full integration of qualitative and quantitative elements at the data collection, data analysis, and data interpretation phases. This formula is encapsulated by the following formula:

$$1+1=1 \qquad (3)$$

Accordingly, we refer to this form of integration as representing a *fully integrated mixed methods research approach*—yielding what we refer to as *high integration*. Broadly speaking a fully integrated mixed methods research approach represents an approach wherein the qualitative and quantitative elements (e.g., methods, methodologies, ontologies, epistemologies, axiologies, analyses, positionalities, quality criteria) are maximally interactive, often from the onset of the research process (see, for e.g., Onwuegbuzie et al., 2018). Figure 13.1 shows a visual representation comparing 1 + 1 = 3 partial integration (i.e., medium integration) and the alternative 1 + 1 = 1 full integration (i.e., high integration) as a function of degree of integration.

It should be noted that this integration formula advances the use of what Onwuegbuzie and Combs (2010) referred to as *crossover mixed analyses*—wherein one or more analysis types associated with one tradition (e.g., quantitative analysis) are used to analyze data associated with a different tradition (e.g., qualitative data).

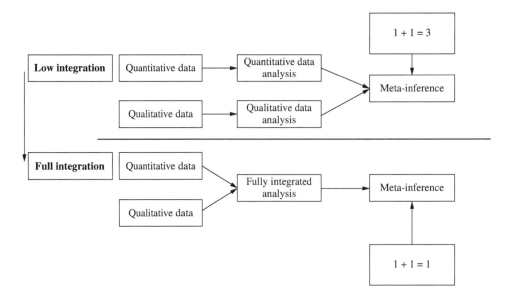

FIGURE 13.1 Contrasting 1 + 1 = 3 partial integration and 1 + 1 = 1 full integration in mixed methods research.
Adapted from Onwuegbuzie, Hitchcock, Natesan, and Newman, 2018.

Onwuegbuzie and Combs (2010, p. 422) coined this *crossing* of traditions as representing *crossover mixed (methods) analyses*. Importantly, crossover mixed analyses can be used to reduce, to display, to transform, to correlate, to consolidate, to compare, to integrate, to assert, and/or to import data (Hitchcock & Onwuegbuzie, 2020; Onwuegbuzie & Combs, 2010; Onwuegbuzie & Hitchcock, 2019a). As noted by Tashakkori, Johnson, and Teddlie (2021), crossover mixed analyses represent "one of the more fruitful areas for the further development of MM [mixed methods] analytical techniques" (p. 285).

Even more recently, two additional formulae have come to the fore. These formulae involve the integration of mixed methods research approaches and multiple methods (i.e., multimethod) research approaches within the same study. As defined by the editors of the *International Journal of Multiple Research Approaches* (*IJMRA*), whereas mixed methods research involves between-tradition mixing (i.e., one or more qualitative research elements integrated with one or more quantitative research elements), multiple methods research involves within-tradition mixing (i.e., two or more qualitative research elements only OR two or more quantitative research elements) (IJMRA, 2020, ¶ 1–3). Here, *elements* refer to methods, methodologies, paradigms, analyses, and the like.

Onwuegbuzie and Hitchcock (2019b) introduced the concept of *multi-mixed methods research* (i.e., partial or medium integration). In a nutshell, we define multi-mixed methods research as an approach that comprises *both* a multiple methods research component(s) (i.e., multiple quantitative elements and/or multiple qualitative elements) *and* a mixed methods research component(s) (i.e., qualitative *and* quantitative research elements), wherein the qualitative and quantitative components represent a true dichotomy. We characterize multi-mixed methods research by the following formula:

$$\sum_{i=2}^{L} L^i + \sum_{j=2}^{N} N^j = 3 \qquad (4)$$

where L is the number of qualitative data sources from which to choose (e.g., interview data, focus group discussion data, observations, blogs, documents, still images, moving images, poems, sound, smell, taste), and the researcher(s) chooses all L of them; and N is the number of quantitative data sources (e.g., standardized test data, rating scale responses, Likert-format scale responses, questionnaire responses, symptom checklist data, personality inventory data) from which to choose, and the researcher chooses all N of them. For both the qualitative data sources and quantitative data sources, repetition of data sources can occur and the order of analyzing the broad data sources matters (Onwuegbuzie & Hitchcock, 2019b). Therefore, for example, with four qualitative data sources (or quantitative data sources), there are a total of 336 (i.e., $4^2 + 4^3 + 4^4 = 16 + 64 + 256$) ways (i.e., permutations) to analyze the qualitative data (or quantitative data) sequentially for multi-mixed methods research designs wherein repetition is allowed. Indeed, as determined by Onwuegbuzie and Hitchcock (2019b), for multi-mixed methods research that involve sequential analyses, it only takes a combined total of eight sources of qualitative and/or quantitative data (e.g., 5 qualitative data sources and 3 quantitative data sources) to exceed 1 million permutations of multiple data sources, 10 data sources to exceed the U.S. definition of 1 billion permutations, and 12 data sources to exceed the U.K. definition of 1 billion permutations. The "3" on the right-hand side of Equation 4 indicates a concretizing of the quantitative–qualitative dichotomy. Therefore, whereas the right-hand side of this equation represents a real mathematical formula, the left-hand side of the equation represents a metaphor. As a whole, Equation 4 implies that the L qualitative data sources contribute to the qualitative component set and the N quantitative data sources contribute to the quantitative component set, and the interaction (i.e., integration) between the qualitative component set and the quantitative component set, which can occur during the data analysis phase and/or the data interpretation phase, contributes to the ensuing meta-inferences.

In contrast, the second formula that involves the integration of mixed methods research approaches and multiple methods research approaches, represent a synechist (anti-dualistic) stance. We present this formula as follows:

$$\sum_{i=2}^{L} L^i + \sum_{j=2}^{N} N^j = 1 \qquad (5)$$

where, again, L and N are the number of qualitative data sources and quantitative data sources, respectively, from which to choose and the researcher(s) chooses all L and N of them, repetition of data sources can occur, and the order of analyzing the data sources matters (Onwuegbuzie & Hitchcock, 2019b). As is the case for Equation 4, in Equation 5, whereas the right-hand side of this equation represents a real mathematical formula, the left-hand side of the equation represents a metaphor. Further, as is the case for multi-mixed methods research approaches, it only takes a combined total of eight sources of qualitative and/or quantitative data sources to exceed 1 million combinations of multiple data sources. This Equation 5 formula implies that the integration of data can begin from the onset—namely, at the data conceptualization stage. An example of this is using Bayesian methodology simultaneously to collect and to analyze one or more qualitative data sources *and* one or more quantitative data sources—using what Johnson (2017) refers to as *both/and* logic—such as might be used to conduct a Bayesian meta-analysis that involves the collection, analysis, and interpretation of both quantitative and qualitative works from the extant literature in an integrated manner (cf. Natesan Batley, Boedeker, & Onwuegbuzie, 2020; Onwuegbuzie et al., 2018). Because this integration formula represents the fullest integration among all such formulae to date, the approach that it characterizes has been coined by Onwuegbuzie and Hitchcock (2019b) as representing a *meta-methods research approach*. Broadly speaking, a meta-methods research as an approach that comprises both a multiple methods research component(s) (i.e., multiple quantitative elements and/or multiple qualitative elements) and a mixed methods research component(s) (i.e., qualitative and quantitative research elements), wherein the qualitative and quantitative components are maximally interactive, typically from the onset of the research process.

1 Definition of Qualitizing

With the exception of parallel mixed methods research approaches (Equation 1), what all of these formulae have in common is that they can involve crossover mixed analyses, albeit to varying degrees. Now, of the arsenal of crossover mixed analyses available (cf. Hitchcock & Onwuegbuzie, 2020), the two most common analytic methods available are *quantitizing* and *qualitizing*. Broadly speaking, quantitizing entails transforming qualitative data into numerical codes that can, in turn, be subjected to statistical analyses (Miles & Huberman, 1994; Sandelowski, Voils, & Knafl, 2009; Tashakkori & Teddlie, 1998). Various ways of quantitizing data have been discussed in the chapters in Section 1 of this volume.

In contrast, traditionally, qualitizing has been defined as converting quantitative data into data that can be analyzed qualitatively (Tashakkori & Teddlie, 1998). Although this definition has served mixed methods researchers well for more than two decades now, it is in need of expansion. To this end, Onwuegbuzie and Leech (2019) expanded its definition in the following way:

> The technique of qualitizing involves transforming data into qualitative form. The data that are qualitized can either stem directly from quantitative data, or from qualitative data that are converted to numeric form (i.e., quantitized), or both. The qualitizing process can involve one or more qualitative analysis and/or one or more quantitative analysis (e.g., descriptive analyses, exploratory analyses, inferential analyses) that represent either a single analysis (i.e., single qualitizing) or multiple analyses (i.e., multi-qualitizing), which, optimally, involves the full integration of qualitative and quantitative research approaches (i.e., 1 + 1 = 1 integration formula) that yield fully integrated analysis. Some form of qualitizing can be undertaken by quantitative researchers, qualitative researchers, and mixed researchers that represent a variety of ontological, epistemological, and methodological assumptions and stances. The qualitizing process can yield numerous representations that include codes, categories, sub-themes, themes, figures of speech, meta-themes, and narratives (i.e., prose or poetry). (p. 122)

This definition will be deconstructed in the section entitled "Technical Outline of Qualitizing for Mixed Methods Research."

2 When Use of Qualitizing is Appropriate in Mixed Methods Research

Researchers should use qualitizing approaches when it has the potential to help address one or more of the research questions. Moreover, the type of research questions plays an important role in determining the appropriateness of qualitizing (Onwuegbuzie & Leech, 2019). For instance, using the typology of Plano Clark and Badiee (2010), because qualitizing occurs either on quantitative data or qualitative data that have been quantitized, qualitizing is much more relevant for *dependent research questions*—which represent questions that depend on the results stemming from addressing another question—than for *independent research questions*, which are two or more research questions that are connected around the same phenomenon, but with each question not depending on the results of the other question[s]). Additionally, the use of qualitizing is relevant for both *predetermined research questions* (i.e., questions based on literature, personal tendencies, practice, and/or disciplinary considerations that are posed at the beginning of the study) and *emergent research questions* (i.e., new or modified research questions that arise during the design, data collection, data analysis, or interpretation phase). Further, qualitized techniques are more pertinent for *general overarching mixed methods research questions* (i.e., broad questions that are addressed using both qualitative and quantitative research approaches), *hybrid mixed methods issue research questions* (i.e., one question that has two or more distinct parts such that a qualitative research approach is used to address one part and a quantitative research approach is used to address the other part), *mixed methods procedural/mixing research questions* (i.e., narrow research questions that direct the integration of the qualitative and quantitative components of the study), and *combination research questions* (i.e., at least one mixed methods research question combined with separate qualitative and quantitative research questions), than they are for *separate research questions* (i.e., involving one or more qualitative research questions and one or more qualitative research questions).

3 Technical Outline of Qualitizing for Mixed Methods Research

Let us now unpack Onwuegbuzie and Hitchcock's (2019b) expanded definition of qualitizing. The first sentence (i.e., "The technique of qualitizing involves transforming data into qualitative form") is the same as the traditional definition. But this is where the similarity ends. Unlike the traditional definition wherein qualitizing only occurs on data that were originally quantitative, Onwuegbuzie and Leech's (2019) expanded definition implies that qualitizing also can occur on data that were originally qualitative but then were subsequently quantitized. For instance, themes extracted from an open-ended survey item (i.e., qualitative data) via a qualitative analysis (e.g., constant comparison analysis; Glaser, 1965) could be quantitized by determining the percentage of participants who fall under each theme—which yields quantitative data. Then, some form of narrative profile can be developed from these percentages—representing the qualitizing of quantitative data. As described by Onwuegbuzie and Leech (2019),

> Narrative profile formation includes modal profiles, average profiles, holistic profiles, comparative profiles, and normative profiles. Broadly speaking, modal profiles are detailed narrative descriptions of a group of individuals that are based on the most frequently occurring attributes in the group that they represent. Average profiles are profiles that are based on the average of a number of attributes of the individuals or situations. Holistic profiles represent the overall impressions of the researcher pertaining to the unit of investigation. Comparative profiles are obtained by comparing one unit of analysis to one or more other units, and includes possible similarities/differences between/among them. Finally, normative profiles are similar to narrative profiles but are based on the comparison of an individual or group with a standard, such as a normative group (cf. Onwuegbuzie & Teddlie, 2003; Tashakkori & Teddlie, 1998). (p. 103)

The first part of the third sentence (i.e., "The qualitizing process can involve one or more qualitative analysis and/or one or more quantitative analysis") indicates that qualitizing can involve qualitative analyses and/or quantitative analyses. Although the word *qualitizing* might imply the exclusive use of *qualitative* analyses, in much the same way that the word *quantitizing* implies and is actualized as the exclusive use of quantitative analyses, the expanded definition is much more flexible. Now, virtually any of the 34 qualitative analysis approaches identified by Onwuegbuzie and Denham (2014) (e.g., constant comparison analysis, classical content analysis, domain analysis, qualitative comparative analysis), many of Miles and Huberman's (1994) 37 qualitative analysis methods (i.e., 19 within-case analyses and 18 cross-case analyses) (see also Miles, Huberman, & Saldaña, 2014), and many of Saldaña's (2016) 33 qualitative data analysis techniques (i.e., coding techniques; see also Saldaña's excellent chapter in this volume) can be utilized to qualitize data that were either originally collected in quantitative form or that were quantitized after being originally collected in qualitative form. However, as will be illustrated in the heuristic example, *quantitative* analysis also can be used to qualitize data that were either originally collected in quantitative form or that were quantitized after being originally collected in qualitative form. In particular, clustering techniques, such as cluster analysis, (ipsative) factor analysis, multidimensional scaling, correspondence analysis, latent class analysis, and Q methodology, can play an important role in the qualitizing process.

The second part of the third sentence (i.e., "that represent either a single analysis (i.e., single qualitizing) or multiple analyses [i.e., multi-qualitizing]") indicates that qualitizing can represent either a single analysis (i.e., *single qualitizing*; Onwuegbuzie & Leech, 2019, p. 115) or multiple analyses (i.e., *multi-qualitizing*; Onwuegbuzie & Leech, 2019, p. 115). Single qualitizing represents the most basic form of qualitizing, involving one analytic operation (i.e., qualitative analysis or quantitative analysis) on one set of data (i.e., data that were originally collected in quantitative form or data that were quantitized after being originally collected in qualitative form). Contrastingly, multi-qualitizing represents a more complex form of qualitizing, which involve two or more iterations of qualitizing on one or more sets of data. For example, in the heuristic example, the qualitizing process involved both a twostep cluster analysis (i.e., exploratory analysis) and a series of inferential analyses (i.e., chi-square analyses).

The third part of the third sentence (i.e., "which, optimally, involves the full integration of qualitative and quantitative research approaches [i.e., 1 + 1 = 1 integration formula] that yield fully integrated analysis") indicates that at its most integrated form, the qualitizing process involves adoption of full(er) integration of qualitative and quantitative approaches, using either a fully integrated mixed methods research approach or a meta-methods research approach. As explained by Onwuegbuzie and Leech (2019),

> Although the standard single qualitizing yields some degree of integration because it represents a form of crossover mixed analysis, the qualitizing process

can be made to move toward even fuller integration by multi-qualitizing ... [which is] what we refer to as *fully integrated qualitizing* (*FIQ*) because both quantitative data and qualitative data as well as qualitive analysis and quantitative analysis were used to inform the qualitizing process. (p. 115)

The fourth sentence of the expanded definition of qualitizing (i.e., "Some form of qualitizing can be undertaken by quantitative researchers, qualitative researchers, and mixed researchers that represent a variety of ontological, epistemological, and methodological assumptions and stances") makes it clear that some form of qualitizing can be undertaken by qualitative researchers, quantitative researchers, and mixed methods researchers. That is, qualitizing also can occur in qualitative research and quantitative research without having to frame the study as a mixed methods research study. Further, qualitizing is compatible with various research philosophies that represent all three traditions of research. For example, as demonstrated by Onwuegbuzie, Johnson, and Collins (2009), because the ontological, epistemological, and axiological stances underlying many, if not most, conducting a qualitative research study does not prevent qualitative researchers from using, as appropriate, any form(s) of qualitative analysis techniques and quantitative analysis techniques that include both descriptive statistics and inferential statistics. Therefore, their philosophical stance does not prevent researchers from using qualitizing, at least in theory. In particular, qualitative analysis approaches that generate some form of numbers, such as classical content analysis (Berelson, 1952) and qualitative comparative analysis (Ragin, 1987, 1989, 1994, 2008), could be qualitized, for example, by forming narrative profiles, especially comparative profiles and holistic profiles. Similarly, quantitative researchers identifying themselves as belonging to a postpositivist-based philosophical tradition, by using clustering techniques, should consider qualitizing their data, Indeed, qualitizing outcomes, such as modal profiles, average profiles, and normative profiles, should have intuitive appeal for quantitative researchers. For examples of narrative profiles, see Onwuegbuzie and Teddlie (2003).

The final sentence of the expanded definition of qualitizing (i.e., "The qualitizing process can yield numerous representations that include codes, categories, sub-themes, themes, figures of speech, meta-themes, and narratives [i.e., prose or poetry]") makes it clear that the qualitizing process can yield numerous representations. These representations include codes, categories, sub-themes, themes, figures of speech, meta-themes, and narratives. As outlined by Onwuegbuzie and Leech (2019), the appropriate representation to use depends on several factors, such as the following:

- research question(s) (e.g., general overarching mixed methods research questions likely would necessitate richer qualitizing representations [e.g., prose or poetry] than would mixed methods procedural/mixing research questions because the latter type of questions are narrower in nature for the purpose of integrating the qualitative and quantitative strands of the study)
- research design (e.g., qualitative-dominant mixed research studies likely would necessitate richer qualitizing representations than would quantitative-dominant mixed research studies because the former is more likely to privilege case-oriented interpretation, whereas the latter tends to involve a focus on variable-oriented interpretations)
- sample size (e.g., smaller sample sizes are more likely to involve a focus on case-oriented interpretations—thereby motivating richer qualitizing representations [e.g., prose or poetry] per participant/group—than would larger sample sizes)
- space restrictions for the report (e.g., less space limitations would afford more space to produce richer qualitizing representations than would more space limitations)
- intended outlet for the report (e.g., an outlet that routinely publishes mixed methods research studies likely would allow richer qualitizing representations than would an outlet that publishes monomethod research studies)
- audience (e.g., consumers familiar with the concept of qualitizing likely would be more welcoming of richer qualitizing representations than would consumers who are unfamiliar with the notion of qualitizing). (p. 113)

Regardless, we recommend that, whenever possible, mixed methods researchers who are involved in the qualitizing process should consider providing qualitizing representations that are as rich as possible because such richness allows researchers to contextualize their findings to a greater extent. Narratives stemming from the qualitizing process provide (substantially) more richness than do representations such as codes, categories, sub-themes, themes, figures of speech, meta-themes, and the like.

As a summary, the expanded definition of qualitizing involves the following five major elements:

- Element 1. Qualitizing can stem not only from quantitative data but also from qualitative data.
- Element 2. Qualitizing can involve qualitative analyses and/or quantitative analyses.
- Element 3. Qualitizing can involve a single analysis or multiple analyses.
- Element 4. Qualitizing can yield a fully integrated analysis.
- Element 5. Qualitizing can yield numerous representations.

4 Empirical Demonstration of Qualitizing for Mixed Methods Research

In this section, we provide a heuristic example from the extant literature that exemplifies both a multi-mixed methods research approach and a meta-methods research approach in which qualitizing was an important phase of the analysis and meaning-making process. This example represents a study conducted by Ojo and Onwuegbuzie (2020) to examine the perceptions and attitudes of students regarding online learning in an era of disruption of the COVID-19 pandemic, uniquely using both multi-mixed methods research approaches and meta-methods study approaches. This study involved students enrolled at the University of the Witwatersrand (i.e., Wits University)—a South African university that was the joint highest ranked university in Africa. At the time of the study, Wits University was closed due to the COVID-19 virus—as was the case for all South African universities and colleges; however, teaching and learning took place online.

A total of 4,419 Wits University students completed an online survey. The survey instrument, which was developed specifically for this study, contained four parts: (a) Section I: demographic information; (b) Section II: a 5-point, Likert-format scale (1 = Strongly Disagree, 2 = Disagree, 3 = Neutral, 4 = Agree, and 5 = Strongly Agree) measuring university students' perceptions of readiness and motivation for online teaching, learning, and assessment (i.e., Scale 1); (c) Section IIII: a 5-point Likert-format scale (1 = Strongly Disagree, 2 = Disagree, 3 = Neutral, 4 = Agree, and 5 = Strongly Agree) measuring students' attitudes towards COVID-19 and its impact on higher education (i.e., Scale 2); and (d) Section IV: containing the following three open-ended items: "To what extent do you consider your current home situation suitable for online learning?" (i.e., Item 1); "What personal challenges do you have that could hinder your ability to successfully learn online?" (i.e., Item 2); and "Please provide any general comment that you think might be useful to share" (i.e., Item 3). For the purpose of their article, and keeping in mind the amount of data generated by this survey instrument, the authors analyzed only responses to Scale 2 and the open-ended Item 1.

A principal components analysis and score reliability analysis (i.e., *quantitative analyses of quantitative data*) of Scale 2, namely, the Attitude of Students Towards COVID-19 and its Impact on Higher Education scale, revealed the following two subscales: Students' Self-regulation Towards COVID-19-Based Higher Education and Attitudes Toward Teaching, Learning, and Assessment in COVID-19-Based Higher Education. A series of nonparametric analyses (i.e., *quantitative analyses of quantitative data*) revealed that scores on these measures discriminated gender, age group, level of student (i.e., undergraduate vs. postgraduate), locality status (i.e., local vs. international student), and registration status (i.e., full-time vs. part-time). An analysis of the open-ended responses (i.e., *quantitative analysis of qualitative data*) by the VOSviewer 1.6.14 text mining software program—which was used to construct and to display co-occurrence networks (i.e., network maps) of important words extracted from the 4,419 sets of responses (Van Eck & Waltman, 2014, 2017)—led to the identification of six co-word clusters (see Figure 13.2), which, in turn, led to the identification of six metathemes (i.e., *qualitative data*). A sentiment analysis of these six metathemes (i.e., *quantitative analysis of qualitative data*) distinguished the positive sentiments and negative sentiments

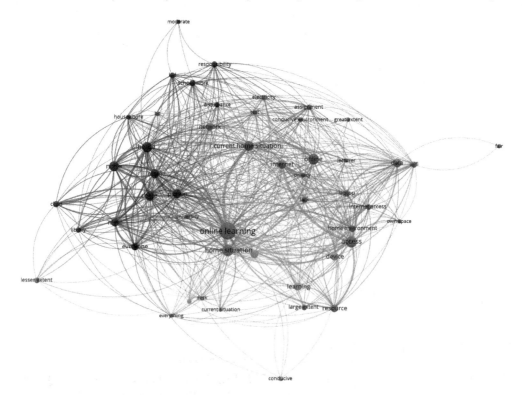

FIGURE 13.2 Keyword co-occurrence map of responses to the following question.

Adapted from Ojo and Onwuegbuzie, 2020, p. 35.

Note: Keyword threshold was set at a minimum of 20 with 50 keywords selected for display.

(i.e., *quantitative data*). For the purpose of quantitizing, the positive sentiments were coded as "1," whereas the negative sentiments were codes as "0." In particular, the negative sentiments identified not only the biggest challenges for students but also the characteristics of students who experience these challenges. The text mining analysis (i.e., *quantitative analysis*) of the 4,419 sets of open-ended responses (i.e., *qualitative data*), followed by the sentiment analysis (i.e., *qualitative analysis*) and chi-square analyses (i.e., *quantitative analysis*), led the authors to create what Onwuegbuzie and Dickinson (2008) referred to as a *crossover display* (see Table 13.1), which we define later. Ojo and Onwuegbuzie (2020) referred to it as a crossover display because not only did this display contain quantitative findings and qualitative findings but also it represented findings that emerged from quantitative analyses (text mining) of qualitative data (open-ended responses) (see left column of Table 13.1) and qualitative analysis of quantitized data (see right column of Table 13.1). That is, the crossover display contained findings from a series of crossover mixed analyses.

Next, a twostep cluster analysis (i.e., *quantitative analysis of quantitative data*) led to the identification of four attitudinal clusters of students with respect to their self-regulation towards COVID-19-based higher education and their attitudes toward teaching, learning, and assessment in COVID-19-based higher education. Finally, a series of chi-square analyses (i.e., *quantitative analyses*) of these four clusters (i.e., nominal variable with 4 levels) with respect to their attitudes (i.e., *quantitative data*) and experiences with online learning in their homes (i.e., *qualitative data*) revealed how these four clusters differed. As a result, the authors developed comparative narrative profiles (i.e., *qualitizing* based on both *quantitative data* and *qualitative data*). In building these profiles (i.e., *qualitative data*), the authors determined (i.e., via *quantitative analyses*) that the students' online experiences (i.e., *qualitative data*) were much more important than were the demographic variables (i.e., *quantitative data*) in discriminating the four attitudinal clusters of students. The authors concluded that these clusters provided important information about which negative experiences are most likely to co-exist, thereby informing the development of interventions.

In summary, with respect to Onwuegbuzie and Leech's (2019) five-component typology of qualitizing, Ojo and Onwuegbuzie's (2020) qualitizing process involved the following elements:

- Element 1. The qualitizing process involved both *quantitative data* (i.e., students' self-regulation towards COVID-19-based higher education; students' their attitudes toward teaching, learning, and assessment in COVID-19-based higher education; students' demographic information) and *qualitative data* (i.e., students' experiences with online learning in their homes).
- Element 2. The qualitizing process involved both quantitative analyses (e.g., principal components analysis, text mining, twostep cluster analysis, chi-square analysis) and qualitative analyses (i.e., sentiment analysis, narrative profile analysis).
- Element 3. The qualitizing process involved multiple analyses (see Element 2).
- Element 4. The qualitizing process yielded a fully integrated analysis that included a series of crossover analyses.
- Element 5. The qualitizing process yielded comparative narrative profiles.

TABLE 13.1

Crossover Display of the Sentiment Analysis Findings Pertaining to the Metathemes and Select Themes Extracted from the VOSviewer 1.6.14 Text Mining.

Metatheme/Theme	Groups that were statistically significantly more likely to provide negative statements
Metatheme 1: *Non-Academic Home Characteristics*	No statistically significant findings
Metatheme 2: *Current Home Situation*	Undergraduate students (60.0%) were 1.23 times more likely than were the postgraduate students (33.3%)
Metatheme 3: *Technology*	men students (37.1%) were 1.50 times more likely than were women (24.4%)
	the postgraduate students (40.0%) were 1.69 times more likely than were the undergraduate students (23.1%)
	students in the 25-35 age group (38.9%) were 1.80 times more likely than were the students in the 18–24 age group (23.4%)
Metatheme 4: *Online Learning*	students in the 18-24 age group (55.7%) were 1.08 times more likely than were the students in the 25–35 age group (39.3%)
	the undergraduate students (56.3%) were 1.17 times more likely than were the postgraduate students
	full-time students (54.7%) were 3.75 times more likely than were the part-time students (24.4%)
Metatheme 5: *Device*	No statistically significant findings
Internet connection Theme of the Device Metatheme	No statistically significant findings
Metatheme 6: *Network*	No statistically significant findings
Electricity Theme of the Network Metatheme	No statistically significant findings

Adapted from "University Life in an Era of Disruption of COVID-19: A Meta-Methods and Multi-Mixed Methods Research Study of Perceptions and Attitudes of South African Students," by E. O. Ojo and A. J. Onwuegbuzie, 2020, *International Journal of Multiple Research Approaches, 12*(3), p. 49. Copyright 2020 by Dialectical Publishing PLC.

5 Suggested Applications of Qualitizing in Mixed Methods Research

As recognized by Onwuegbuzie and Leech (2019), the framework of Greene, Caracelli, and Graham (1989) can be used by researchers to get more out of their data. In particular, qualitizing can be used to address each of Greene et al.'s five goals, as follows:

- *complementarity* (i.e., seek elaboration, illustration, enhancement, and clarification of the findings from the quantitative data or qualitative data that are subsequently quantitized with results from the qualitizing process or vice versa)
- *triangulation* (i.e., compare findings from the qualitized data with results of qualitative data extracted from one or more other data sets)
- *initiation* (i.e., discover paradoxes and contradictions that emerge when findings from the qualitized data and the results of qualitative data are compared that might lead to a re-framing of the research question[s])
- *development* (i.e., use the finding from the qualitizing process to help inform findings from the quantitative data or qualitative data that are subsequently quantitized)
- *expansion* (i.e., expand the breadth and range of a study by using multiple analytical strands [i.e., findings from quantitative data or qualitative data that are subsequently quantitized representing one strand and results from the qualitizing for different study phases representing another strand]).

In terms of applications, we encourage mixed methods researchers to be as creative as possible in their qualitizing representations. One way of being creative is via the use of poetry. Poems that lend themselves to narrative representations, in alphabetical order, include the following: ABC Poem, Acrostic, Bio Poem, Cinquain, Concrete, Diamante, Emotion Poem, Epic, Free Verse, Haiku, I-Poem, Limerick, Narrative, Pantoum. Sonnet, Tanka, and Villanelle (cf. Archibald & Onwuegbuzie, 2020). Crossover displays and joint displays provide another way to provide rich representations from the qualitative process. As coined by Onwuegbuzie and Dickinson (2008), crossover displays are "visual extensions to summarize and integrate both qualitative and quantitative results within the same framework" in order to "enhance[e] researchers' understanding (i.e., increased Verstehen) of social and behavioral phenomena in general and the meaning that underli[e] these phenomena in particular" (p. 204). Indeed, crossover displays are compatible with fully integrated mixed methods research approaches and meta-methods research approaches. In contrast, joint displays (Fetters, Curry, & Creswell, 2013; Guetterman, Fetters, & Creswell, 2015; Johnson, Grove, & Clarke, 2017) provide ways to "integrate the data by bringing the data together through a visual means to draw out new insights beyond the information gained from the separate quantitative and qualitative results" (Fetters et al., 2013, p. 10).

Because joint displays maintain the quantitative–qualitative analysis dichotomy, they are compatible with partial integrated mixed methods research approaches and multi-mixed methods research approaches.

6 Strengths and Limitations of Qualitizing in Mixed Methods Research

A limitation of qualitizing is that there is scant methodological guidance in the extant literature on this topic (Nzabonimpa, 2018). Indeed, Onwuegbuzie and Leech (2019), who conducted an extensive review of the literature, did not find a single work devoted exclusively, or even partially, to the technique of qualitizing. And in the more than 60 books devoted, at least in part, to mixed methods research (Onwuegbuzie, 2020), at best, the topic of qualitizing is given a cursory mention. Perhaps, then, it should not surprising that there are relatively few examples of the traditional view of qualitizing in the empirical mixed methods research literature, and virtually no examples of the expanded notion of qualitizing. Consistent with this assertion, Onwuegbuzie and Leech (2019) reported that of the 145 empirical research articles published in the *Journal of Mixed Methods Research* (*JMMR*) during a 12-year time period (i.e., its onset in 2007 to 2019), only 10 articles (i.e., 6.9%) included the word qualitize and/or qualitizing. Further, of the 95 methodological/conceptual/theoretical research articles published in *JMMR* in this timeframe, only 10 articles (i.e., 10.5%) included the word qualitize and/or qualitizing. Therefore, we encourage authors of mixed methods research books to provide a richer discussion of the topic of qualitizing in their books.

With respect to the conduct of qualitizing, a limitation stems from the fact that the vast majority of mixed methods research studies involve lower level quantitative analysis approaches that comprise either descriptive analyses (i.e., measures of central tendency [e.g., mean, median, mode]; measures of variability [e.g., standard deviation, variance]; measures of position [e.g., percentile ranks, z scores, t scores]) or univariate analyses (e.g., correlations, independent samples t tests, one-way analysis of variance, analysis of covariance) (Ross & Onwuegbuzie, 2014). Yet, knowledge of clustering techniques is needed in order to conduct some of the more in-depth qualitizing techniques, especially those involving multi-qualitizing techniques. Therefore, it is clear that courses and other forms of training in qualitizing techniques are needed.

Nevertheless, as noted by Onwuegbuzie and Leech (2019), when researchers use qualitizing techniques, they have the potential to add descriptive precision (e.g., via rich narrative profiles) to the empirical precision yielded by a quantitative measure(s), to add interpretive richness to the quantitative phase/component of a mixed methods research study, to translate quantitative data into a more reader-friendly form(s), to facilitate pattern matching across data sets via the creation of narrative categories, to serve as a form of reliability or trustworthiness check (e.g., by comparing the qualitized data with other qualitative data), to assist in making quantitative data be more transparent, and to increase the mixed methods researcher's level of creativity (e.g., via the creation of poems and visual displays). Moreover, via the conduct of crossover mixed analyses that are consistent with fully integrated mixed methods research approaches and meta-methods research approaches, qualitizing has the potential "to answer questions in a more in-depth manner, as well as to answer more complex and complicated questions" (Onwuegbuzie & Leech, 2019, p. 127).

7 Resources for Learning More About Qualitizing

Qualitizing techniques are discussed extensively in Onwuegbuzie and Leech's (2019) editorial. Also, an excellent discussion of qualitizing, alongside quantitizing, can be accessed from Nzabonimpa's (2018) work.

Here is a link to a YouTube video that provides a short explanation of meta-inferences:
www.youtube.com/watch?v=QByPTUjWd9c
Here are links to two useful YouTube videos on joint displays:
www.youtube.com/watch?v=U6KvCN-7ZKM&t=134s
www.youtube.com/watch?v=jnJe0Vo2vVM

NOTE

1. Whereas some authors do not consider these designs as representing mixed methods research (e.g., Yin, 2006) but rather quasi-mixed designs (e.g., Teddlie & Tashakkori, 2006), other authors do (e.g., Onwuegbuzie & Leech, 2004). Also, some other researchers (e.g., Tashakkori, Johnson, & Teddlie, 2021) define parallel mixed methods research designs somewhat differently.

REFERENCES

Archibald, M., & Onwuegbuzie, A. J. (2020). Poetry and mixed methods research. *International Journal of Multiple Research Approaches*, *12*(2), 153–165. doi:10.29034/ijmra.v12n2editorial3

Berelson, B. (1952). *Content analysis in communicative research*. New York, NY: Free Press.

Fetters, M. D., Curry, L. A., & Creswell, J. W. (2013). Achieving integration in mixed methods designs: Principles and practices. *Health Services Research*, *48*, 2134–2156. doi:10.1111/1475-6773.12117

Fetters M. D., & Freshwater, D. (2015). The 1 + 1 = 3 integration challenge. *Journal of Mixed Methods Research*, *9*, 115–117. doi:10.1177/1558689815581222

Glaser, B. G. (1965). The constant comparative method of qualitative analysis. *Social Problems*, *12*, 436–445. doi:10.1525/sp.1965.12.4.03a00070

Greene, J. C., Caracelli, V. J., & Graham, W. F. (1989). Toward a conceptual framework for mixed-method evaluation designs. *Educational Evaluation and Policy Analysis*, *11*, 255–274. doi:10.3102/01623737011003255

Guetterman, T. C., Fetters, M. D., & Creswell, J. W. (2015). Integrating quantitative and qualitative results in health science mixed methods research through joint displays. *Annals of Family Medicine*, *13*, 554–561. doi:10.1370/afm.1865

Hitchcock, J. H., & Onwuegbuzie, A. J. (2020). Developing mixed methods crossover analysis approaches. *Journal of Mixed Methods Research*, *14*, 63–83. doi:10.1177/1558689819841782

Johnson, R. B. (2017). Dialectical pluralism: A meta-paradigm whose time has come. *Journal of Mixed Methods Research*, *11*, 156–173. doi:10.1177/1558689815607692

Johnson, R. B., & Gray, R. (2010). A history of philosophical and theoretical issues for mixed methods research. In A. Tashakkori & C. Teddlie (Eds.), *Sage handbook of mixed methods in social and behavioral research* (2nd ed., pp. 69–94). Thousand Oaks, CA: Sage.

Johnson, R. E., Grove, A. L., & Clarke, A. (2017). Pillar Integration Process: A joint display technique to integrate data in mixed methods research. *Journal of Mixed Methods Research*, doi:10.1177/1558689817743108

Miles, M., & Huberman, A. M. (1994). *Qualitative data analysis: An expanded sourcebook* (2nd ed.). Thousand Oaks, CA: Sage.

Miles, M., Huberman, A. M., & Saldaña, J. (2014). *Qualitative data analysis: A methods sourcebook* (3rd ed.). Thousand Oaks, CA: Sage.

Natesan Batley, P. Boedeker, P., & Onwuegbuzie, A. J. (2020). Adopting a meta-generative way of thinking in the field of education via the use of Bayesian methods: A multimethod approach in a post-truth and COVID-19 era. *International Journal of Multiple Research Approaches*, *12*(1).

Nzabonimpa, J. P. (2018). Quantitizing and qualitizing (im-)possibilities in mixed methods research. *Methodological Innovations*, *11*(2), 1–16. doi:10.1177/2059799118789021

Ojo, E. O., & Onwuegbuzie, A. J. (2020). University life in an era of disruption of COVID-19: A meta-methods and multi-mixed methods research study of perceptions and attitudes of South African students. *International Journal of Multiple Research Approaches*, *12*(3), 4–19. doi:10.29034/ijmra.v12n1editorial2.

Onwuegbuzie, A. J. (2017, March). *Mixed methods is dead! Long live mixed methods!* Invited keynote address presented at the Mixed Methods International Research Association Caribbean Conference at Montego Bay, Jamaica.

Onwuegbuzie, A. J. (2020). *The landscape of mixed methods research books*. Unpublished manuscript.

Onwuegbuzie, A. J., & Combs, J. P. (2010). Emergent data analysis techniques in mixed methods research: A synthesis. In A. Tashakkori & C. Teddlie (Eds.), *Handbook of mixed methods in social and behavioral research* (2nd ed., pp. 397–430). Thousand Oaks, CA: Sage.

Onwuegbuzie, A. J., & Denham, M. A. (2014). Qualitative data analysis techniques. In L. Meyer (Ed.), *Oxford Bibliographies in education*. Oxford, England: Oxford University Press. Retrieved from www.oxfordbibliographies.com/view/document/obo-9780199756810/obo-9780199756810-0078.xml

Onwuegbuzie, A. J., & Dickinson, W. B. (2008). Mixed methods analysis and information visualization: Graphical display for effective communication of research results. *The Qualitative Report*, *13*, 204–225. Retrieved from www.nova.edu/ssss/QR/QR13-2/onwuegbuzie.pdf

Onwuegbuzie, A. J., & Hitchcock, J. H. (2019a). Toward a fully integrated approach to mixed methods research via the 1 + 1 = 1 integration approach: Mixed Research 2.0. *International Journal of Multiple Research Approaches*, *11*, 7–28. doi:10.29034/ijmra.v11n1editorial1

Onwuegbuzie, A. J., & Hitchcock, J. H. (2019b). Using mathematical formulae as proof for integrating mixed methods research and multiple methods research approaches: A call for multi-mixed methods and meta-methods in a mixed research 2.0 era. *International Journal of Multiple Research Approaches, 11*, 213-234. doi:10.29034/ijmra.v11n3editorial2

Onwuegbuzie, A. J., Hitchcock, J. H., Natesan, P., & Newman, I. (2018). Using fully integrated Bayesian thinking to address the 1 + 1 = 1 integration challenge. *International Journal of Multiple Research Approaches, 10*, 666–678. doi:10.29034/ijmra.v10n1a43

Onwuegbuzie, A. J., & Johnson, R. B. (2006). The validity issue in mixed research. *Research in the Schools, 13*(1), 48–63.

Onwuegbuzie, A. J., Johnson, R. B., & Collins, K. M. T. (2009). A call for mixed analysis: A philosophical framework for combining qualitative and quantitative. *International Journal of Multiple Research Methods, 3*, 114–139. doi:10.5172/mra.3.2.114

Onwuegbuzie, A. J., & Leech, N. L. (2004). Enhancing the interpretation of "significant" findings: The role of mixed methods research. *The Qualitative Report, 9*, 770–792. Retrieved from https://nsuworks.nova.edu/tqr/vol9/iss4/10/Onwuegbuzie.pdf

Onwuegbuzie, A. J., & Leech, N. L. (2019). On qualitizing. *International Journal of Multiple Research Approaches, 11*, 98–131. doi:10.29034/ijmra.v11n2editorial2

Onwuegbuzie, A. J., Slate, J. R., Leech, N. L., & Collins, K. M. T. (2007). Conducting mixed analyses: A general typology. *International Journal of Multiple Research Approaches, 1*, 4–17. doi:10.5172/mra.455.1.1.4

Onwuegbuzie, A. J., & Teddlie, C. (2003). A framework for analyzing data in mixed methods research. In A. Tashakkori & C. Teddlie (Eds.), *Handbook of mixed methods in social and behavioral research* (pp. 351–383). Thousand Oaks, CA: Sage.

Plano Clark, V. L., & Badiee, M. (2010). Research questions in mixed methods research. In A. Tashakkori & C. Teddlie (Eds.), *Handbook of mixed methods in social and behavioral research*(2nd ed., pp. 275–304). Thousand Oaks, CA: Sage.

Ragin, C. C. (1987). *The comparative method: Moving beyond qualitative and quantitative strategies*. Berkeley, CA: University of California Press.

Ragin, C. C. (1989). The logic of the comparative method and the algebra of logic. *Journal of Quantitative Anthropology, 1*, 373–398.

Ragin, C. C. (1994). Introduction to qualitative comparative analysis. In T. Janoski & A. M. Hicks (Eds.), *The comparative political economy of the Welfare State: New methodologies and approaches* (pp. 299–319). New York, NY: Cambridge University Press.

Ragin, C. C. (2008). *Redesigning social inquiry: Fuzzy sets and beyond*. Chicago, IL: The University of Chicago Press.

Ross, A., & Onwuegbuzie, A. J. (2014). Complexity of quantitative analyses used in mixed research articles published in a flagship mathematics education journal. *International Journal of Multiple Research Approaches, 8*, 63–73. doi:10.5172/mra.2014.8.1.63

Saldaña, J. (2016). *The coding manual for qualitative researchers* (3rd ed.). London, England: Sage.

Sandelowski, M., Voils, C. I., & Knafl, G. (2009). On quantitizing. *Journal of Mixed Methods Research, 3*, 208–222. doi:10.1177/1558689809334210

Tashakkori, A., Johnson, R. B., & Teddlie, C. (2021). *Foundations of mixed methods research: Integrating quantitative and qualitative approaches in the social and behavioral sciences*(2nd ed.). Thousand Oaks, CA: Sage.

Tashakkori, A., & Teddlie, C. (1998). *Mixed methodology: Combining qualitative and quantitative approaches*. Applied Social Research Methods Series (Vol. 46). Thousand Oaks, CA: Sage.

Teddlie, C., & Johnson, R. B. (2009). Methodological thought since the 20th century. In C. Teddlie & A. Tashakkori (Eds.), *Foundations of mixed methods research: Integrating quantitative and qualitative techniques in the social and behavioral sciences* (pp. 62–82). Thousand Oaks, CA: Sage.

Teddlie, C., & Tashakkori, A. (2006). A general typology of research designs featuring mixed methods. *Research in the Schools, 13*(1), 12–28.

Van Eck, N. J., & Waltman. L. (2014). Visualizing bibliometric networks. In Y. Ding, R. Rousseau, & D. Wolfram (Eds.), *Measuring scholarly impact: Methods and practice* (pp. 285–320). Dordrecht, Netherlands: Springer.

Van Eck, N. J., & Waltman, L. (2017). Citation-based clustering of publications using CitNetExplorer and VOSviewer. *Scientometrics, 111*, 1053–1070. doi:10.1007/s11192-017-2300-7

Yin, R. K. (2006). Mixed methods research: Are the methods genuinely integrated or merely parallel? *Research in the Schools, 13*(1), 41–47.

14

Coding Techniques for Quantitative and Mixed Data

Johnny Saldaña

The purpose of this chapter is to review and display selected applications of qualitative coding methods onto quantitative and mixed data generated from mixed methods research studies.

1 Definition of Qualitative Coding

A code in qualitative analysis is most often a word or short phrase that symbolically assigns a summative, salient, essence-capturing, and/or evocative attribute for a portion of narrative or visual data. The data can consist of qualitative empirical materials such as interview transcripts, participant observation field notes, photographs, and so on, but this chapter focuses on the qualitative coding of quantitative data in their various forms (e.g., descriptive statistics, test scores, quantitative survey results). Just as a title represents and captures a book, film, or poem's primary content and essence, so does a code represent and capture a datum's primary content and essence. The initial purpose of qualitative coding is data *condensation* (not "reduction") for later purposes of pattern detection, categorization, assertion or proposition development, theory building, and other analytic processes (Miles, Huberman, & Saldaña, 2020; Saldaña, 2016).

In qualitative data analysis, a code is a researcher-generated interpretation that both symbolizes and "translates" data (Vogt, Vogt, Gardner, & Haeffeke, 2014, p. 13), and thus attributes new meaning to each individual datum. Mixed methods researchers use comparable *translation* terms in the literature when data are paradigmatically altered: conversion, transformation, quantitizing, qualitizing, and so on. In this chapter, the qualitative coding of quantitative data representations will be termed *qualitizing*. Seen graphically, the process of quantitative data *translated* into qualitative codes is fundamentally:

How Much / Many → What Kind / Quality

2 When Use of Qualitative Coding is Appropriate in MMR

There is perhaps more methods guidance available on quantitizing qualitative data than there is on qualitizing the quantitative. Traditional content analysis studies typically rely on a qualitative review of empirical materials followed by an appropriate quantitative analytic approach (Neuendorf, 2017). A methodological strategy such as this colloquially *counts what counts*. But there are also qualitative or thematic approaches to content-analytic studies (Schreier, 2012), and qualitative cousins of statistical meta-analysis termed *meta-ethnography*, *meta-summary*, and *meta-synthesis* (Major & Savin-Baden, 2010; Sandelowski & Barroso, 2007).

Some qualitative researchers not involved with content-analytic studies might nevertheless feel the need to quantitize—to convert qualitative data into quantitative representations such as percentages to better ensure a sense of validity to their analyses, although that argument might be methodologically flawed because numbers do not always suggest rigor (Sandelowski, Voils, & Knafl, 2009). Thus, qualitative researchers are encouraged to ask themselves *why* they are changing words into numbers in the first place. A parallel question can be posed to quantitative and mixed methods researchers: Why should you qualitize quantitative data?

First, "Qualitizing is a mixed methods analytical strategy where measures on quantitative instruments are summarized in narrative form for the purposes of further analysis and cross-case comparison" (Creamer, 2018, p. 107). Thus, coding or qualitizing enables data from both paradigms to *talk to one another* in a compatible, mediated language, better insuring not just a mixing but a fusion or *integration* of both qualitative and quantitative strands of the study during the data analytic merger.

Second, "qualitizing quantitative numeric data by creating narrative categories based on the distribution of scores" provides indexing and classification functions across data sets (Plano Clark & Ivankova, 2016, p. 120). Qualitative coding serves to construct patterns into such groupings as categories, themes, or theoretical constructs. When quantitative data are qualitatively coded and examined, patterns may arise as well—not from statistical techniques such as scatterplots, but from a particular combination of qualitized codes that "look alike" and "feel alike" when combined together (Lincoln & Guba, 1985, p. 347).

Third, qualitizing articulates in meta-inferential language not just the statistical properties but the qualitative nuances interpreted from a quantitative data set. The symbols used for quantitative reasoning and display (e.g., N, $\pm$, %) can be decoded easily when read silently to oneself. But in oral presentations or an author's written commentary, numbers sometime lose their supposed objectivity when a statistical result is voiced with proud emphasis to an audience, or phrased as "surprisingly little" or "significantly high" in a journal article. Qualitizing provides interpretive texture to quantitative data.

Fourth, qualitizing can provide what is termed *concordance* or *paradigmatic corroboration*—a "reality check" of sorts between results from separate quantitative and qualitative data analyses. Some mixed methods studies may involve examination of the same phenomenon in different ways and achieve results in both numeric and narrative forms. Paradigmatic corroboration assesses whether there is congruency, discrepancy, or contradiction between the two data sets (Leal et al., 2018). The goal is not necessarily to correlate findings but to *triangulate* them—that is, to generate results: (a) quantitatively, (b) qualitatively, and then, (c) in comparison and ideally in combination with each other. When quantitative data are qualitized, integration becomes much easier with their qualitative cousins.

3 Technical Outline of Qualitative Coding for MMR

First, I provide a simple illustration of coding qualitative data, followed by examples of qualitizing the quantitative.

Qualitative Process Coding

Below is an interview excerpt with its researcher-assigned qualitative code (using uppercase letters) for the data unit. The superscript numbers connect the beginning of the data unit with its corresponding code. Saldaña (2016) profiles more than 30 different qualitative coding methods with each one serving a different analytic purpose, depending on the research questions of interest and the adopted research methodology (e.g., grounded theory, phenomenology, case study). The particular coding method chosen for this datum is *Process Coding*, which utilizes a gerund-based ("ing"-word) phrase that connotes observable or conceptual action for studies in which phases, stages, and cycles of social process are examined. The research study explores the daily experiences of people living with COPD (Chronic Obstructive Pulmonary Disease) at various stages of progression.

In this example, qualitative coding was applied to qualitative data. Now, imagine that 50 participants living with COPD had been interviewed, and a collection of codes is assembled that summarizes their responses to the open-ended prompt, "What concerns, if any, do you have about your COPD?" The collection may include such varied codes as LIVING WITH WORRY, REGRETTING EARLY CHOICES, PAYING FOR PRESCRIPTIONS, BECOMING HOSPITALIZED, RESIGNING TO END-STAGE, and so on. Comparable codes would be grouped into appropriate categories and thematically analyzed. They may even be quantitized or transformed into numeric representations such as category percentages (e.g., 48% of respondents indicated daily "worries" of some kind).

Now, examine a series of facts and descriptive statistics about COPD from a U.S. Centers for Disease Control and Prevention (CDC) webpage (CDC, 2019):

- In the United States, tobacco smoke is a key factor in the development and progression of COPD.
- Chronic lower respiratory disease, primarily COPD, was the third leading cause of death in the United States in 2014.
- Almost 15.7 million Americans (6.4%) reported that they have been diagnosed with COPD.
- More than 50% of adults with low pulmonary function were not aware that they had COPD, so the actual number may be higher.

A greater amass of facts such as these is available from additional sources such as the American Lung Association, *The Journal of the American Medical Association*, and the World Health Organization. With a barrage of information from so many sources, a way of not just organizing or indexing but *consolidating* the facts might be useful for literature reviews or summary reports. Qualitizing the data in various ways is one way to make consolidation happen for mixed methods work.

Descriptive Coding

For example, *Descriptive Coding* summarizes in a word or short phrase—most often a noun—the basic topic of a passage of qualitative data. Thus, this coding method serves an *indexing* function by qualitizing:

INTERVIEWER: What concerns, if any, do you have about your COPD?
WILLIAM: [1]Is it going to get worse, which from what I understand, it will. So far so good. It's not excellent but it's good. I worry if I'm ever going to have a really bad attack where I can't breathe at all. I worry about whether I'll ever need an oxygen tank. I just take it easy now, don't strain myself, but I can't control what happens inside my lungs. So, I've just gotta live with that.

[1] LIVING WITH WORRY

---

[1]In the United States, tobacco smoke is a key factor in the development and progression of COPD.

[1] SMOKING OUTCOME

Structural Coding

Structural Coding applies a content-based or conceptual phrase representing a topic of inquiry to a segment of data that relates to a specific research question used to frame the study. Structural Coding categorizes units of data into comparable segments to examine the corpus's commonalities, differences, and interrelationships:

> *Research Question: What are the current major health issues in the United States?*
> *Structural Code:* [1] CAUSES OF DEATH
>
> ---
> [1] Chronic lower respiratory disease, primarily COPD, was the third leading cause of death in the United States in 2014.

Magnitude Coding

Another example (and the one used most frequently in mixed methods research studies) is *Magnitude Coding*, which adds a supplemental alphanumeric or symbolic code or subcode (sometimes called a "tag") to an existing coded datum or category to indicate its intensity, frequency, direction, presence, or evaluative content. Magnitude Codes can be qualitative, quantitative, and/or nominal or ordinal indicators to enhance description. It is a method that strategically *qualitizes and quantitizes* within the same code:

> [1]Almost 15.7 million Americans (6.4%) reported that they have been diagnosed with COPD. More than 50% of adults with low pulmonary function were not aware that they had COPD, so the actual number may be higher.
>
> ---
> [1] RELATIVE PREVALENCE: MODERATE

Evaluation Coding

Yet another method possible with these descriptive data is *Evaluation Coding*, which applies (primarily) non-quantitative codes to qualitative data that assign *judgments* about the merit, worth, or significance of programs or policy (Rallis & Rossman, 2003, p. 492). Imagine that the four bullet points of information are being used to assess the current success of and future plans for a smoking cessation campaign. The Evaluation Code below consists of several components. First, there is a symbolic Magnitude Code (±) that the analyst applies to suggest current program efficacy as low (−), moderate (±), or high (+). Following the Magnitude Code is a Descriptive Code, referring to a specific subprogram of the smoking cessation project: television public service announcements (TV-PSA CAMPAIGN). Following the Descriptive Code is a recommendation (REC) code for project follow-up or action by the research team's clients.

Miles et al. (2020) illustrate various ways of quantitizing qualitative evaluation through rubric-based codes that can be compatibly transferred and applied to quantitative data and statistical results. A qualitizing rating/ranking/positioning system like the examples below can be applied to both QUAL and QUAN data to assess their comparability. The method is an adaptation of Magnitude Coding and assigns to a range of data a continuum of researcher observations and judgments such as:

> - [1]In the United States, tobacco smoke is a key factor in the development and progression of COPD.
> - Chronic lower respiratory disease, primarily COPD, was the third leading cause of death in the United States in 2014.
> - Almost 15.7 million Americans (6.4%) reported that they have been diagnosed with COPD.
> - More than 50% of adults with low pulmonary function were not aware that they had COPD, so the actual number may be higher.
>
> ---
> [1] ±TV-PSA CAMPAIGN; REC: ENCOURAGE SMOKERS TO GET TESTED FOR COPD

> Quantities
>
> - MINOR, MODERATE, MAJOR
> - A LITTLE, IT DEPENDS, A LOT
> - NIL, UNCERTAIN, LOW, HIGH
> - NOT APPLICABLE, MISSING DATA, INCOMPLETE DATA, DATA COMPLETE
>
> Qualities
>
> - POOR, MODERATE, GOOD
> - UNFAVORABLE, NEUTRAL, FAVORABLE
> - MISSING, WEAK, ADEQUATE, STRONG
> - INEFFECTIVE (−), MIXED EFFECTIVE (±), EFFECTIVE (+), VERY EFFECTIVE (++)
>
> Change
>
> - DROPPED, REVISED, ADDED/CREATED
> - NOT PERTINENT (1), PERTINENT, BUT NOT IMPORTANT IN CAUSING CURRENT SITUATION (2), IMPORTANT FACTOR IN CAUSING CURRENT SITUATION (3)
> - ANTECEDENT CONDITION(S), MEDIATING VARIABLE(S), OUTCOME(S)
>
> Effects
>
> - NEGATIVE EFFECTS, POSITIVE EFFECTS
> - WEAK INFLUENCE, STRONG INFLUENCE, RECIPROCAL INFLUENCE
> - NOT IMPORTANT, SOMEWHAT IMPORTANT, QUITE IMPORTANT, VERY IMPORTANT
> - NO IMPACT, LITTLE TO NO IMPACT, SOME IMPACT/IMPACTS IN COMBINATION, HIGH IMPACT, VERY HIGH IMPACT

Affective Coding Methods

Descriptive and Structural Coding methods aim for the basic organization of data, whereas Magnitude and Evaluation Coding rely on the data analyst's inferential interpretation of data. In other words, assessing whether given statistical information suggests "moderate" concern is a matter of professional judgment. The supposed objectivity of a number should not imply that qualitizing the quantitative must always have some sense of neutrality. On the contrary, other available coding methods venture into affective domains of analysis such as emotions, metaphors, values, attitudes, and beliefs—benchmark goals for algorithmically driven text mining and sentiment analysis software (Ignatow & Mihalcea, 2017; Liu, 2015).

The not-for-profit Gun Violence Archive website (gunviolencearchive.org) documents the number of mass shooting incidents (4+ victims, not including the shooter) in the United States for the past five years:

- 2014: 268
- 2015: 335
- 2016: 382
- 2017: 346
- 2018: 340

A Magnitude Code applied to these data might be RISING VIOLENCE. Yet, descriptive statistics such as these generate a variety of reader reactions depending on his or her sociopolitical ideologies, previous history (if any) with gun violence, and other affective factors such as one's personal values system. Selected coding methods are available that do not shy away from but overtly label the subjective domains of interpretation.

Emotion Coding

Emotion Coding labels the emotions recalled and/or experienced by the participant or researcher, or inferred by the researcher about the participant. An investigator with a socially conscious perspective might code the aforementioned gun death data array as DISTRESSING, whereas an official from the National Rifle Association might assign the code DECREASING CURVE to the statistics. Two different observers with different sets of sensibilities will each react to (and thus code) the data in two completely different ways. This variance is not a liability but a *given* of the conditions of Emotion Coding. Subjective experiences and interpretations generate subjective codes.

Metaphor Coding

Metaphor Coding identifies the participants' use of metaphors or vivid comparisons to related ideas and imagery in narrative, visual, and even quantitative data. Similes and other literary devices that compare or represent one thing to another (e.g., analogy, allusion, synecdoche, metonymy, symbol) are also considered part of Metaphor Coding. Metaphors are conceptual and thus hold transferable properties. When we qualitize through metaphor, we create a code that can be compared with other codes at an evocative level.

As with Emotion Coding, Metaphor Coding is a personal interpretation by the analyst. A few that might be applied to the gun death statistics presented earlier are DEADLY VIRUS or A HOUSE ON FIRE. When compared to qualitative codes, perhaps there is some congruence with related imagery. Qualitative interview data can be rife with metaphors, and they deserve particular notice in our general analyses. And don't forget that statistics themselves are symbols of mathematical meaning and metaphors for analytic insight.

Values Coding

Values Coding is the application of codes to qualitative data that reflect a participant's or researcher's values, attitudes, and beliefs, representing his or her perspectives or worldview. Briefly,

> a value [V:] is the importance people attribute to themselves, other people, things, or ideas, and the principles, moral codes, and situational norms people live by. An attitude [A:] is the way people think and feel about themselves, other people, things, or ideas—evaluative perceptions and sets of cumulative reactions, reflecting the beliefs they've learned through time. A belief [B:] includes interrelated values and attitudes, plus personal knowledge, experiences, opinions, prejudices, morals, and other interpretive perceptions of the social world. (Saldaña & Omasta, 2018, p. 128)

As an affective coding method, Values Coding depends on whose values system is being represented. Also, values, attitudes, and beliefs are part of an intricately interconnected system; so, it is sometimes difficult to distinguish among the three constructs. Just a few of the possible qualitized codes that might be applied to the gun death data are:

V: TRAGIC LOSS
A: DISTURBING TREND
B: NOT SURPRISING

In Vivo Coding

The earlier examples are the researchers' values, not those of the participant. An interesting, yet too little, employed method is to share simple descriptive statistics to participants to collect *their* responses to data. Participant reactions to relevant quantitative data can generate some interesting interpretations and perspectives as part of the mixed methods data base.

Saldaña and colleagues conducted an online mixed methods survey (discussed later in this chapter) and presented core statistical results and a brief report of the qualitative findings to participants as a member check and for additional response. Their written responses to the research team provided us with *In Vivo Codes*—codes derived from the language used by the participants themselves. The survey respondents offered comments about the results in progress such as "ON-TARGET," "I AGREE," and "THIS VALIDATES." These codes supported the analyst's interpretations of the mean survey ratings and a few statistical tests undertaken. In Vivo Codes remain grounded in the participants' point of view and are placed in quotation marks to remind the researcher of their origin.

The Difference Between Codes and Themes

There are no standardized definitions of the terms *code* and *theme*, and some researchers use the terms interchangeably in reports. I, however, make the distinction that a code is a word or short phrase; a theme is an extended phrase or sentence. Aside from length, a theme identifies what a unit of data is *about* and/or what it *means*. To Rubin and Rubin (2012), themes are statements qua (in the role of) ideas that summarize what is going on, explain what is happening, or suggest why something is done the way it is (p. 118).

One example of how qualitized data were transformed into themes can be seen in a mixed methods school improvement study by Jang, McDougall, Pollon, Herbert, and Russell (2008), who initiated a factor analysis of quantitative survey data administered to teachers and principals of 20 schools that resulted in nine factors qua codes (e.g., SCHOOL GOALS, SHARED DECISION MAKING, COLLECTIVE TEACHER EFFICACY). These nine factors were then compared with the 11 themes constructed from qualitative interview and focus group data (e.g., in categories such as Distributed Leadership, Communication, Parental Involvement). Five of the factors and themes overlapped, so to "make data comparison more transparent, we transformed the results from the quantitative data by creating narrative descriptions of the nine factors" (p. 233). Thus, a factor such as SCHOOL CULTURE, which appeared in both the quantitative and qualitative data analyses, was compared and hence integrated with their respective thematic narratives:

> **SCHOOL CULTURE**
>
> *Quantitative theme (derived from a survey):* Teachers support collaborative inquiry and are dedicated to constant improvement.
> *Qualitative theme (derived from interviews and focus groups):* A positive school culture has a sense of welcoming and an attitude that learning is a goal. (p. 234)

Another example of a paradigmatically corroborated theme was DISTRIBUTED LEADERSHIP:

> **DISTRIBUTED LEADERSHIP**
>
> *Quantitative theme (derived from a survey):* School leaders provide a supportive climate for the development of teacher capacity.
> *Qualitative theme (derived from interviews and focus groups):* Many school participants, rather than just the principal, are involved in leadership activities (p. 234).

Data were further consolidated in the analysis to reveal the varying levels of school improvement practices among the 20 school sites. Methodologically, the research team observed that data analysis through comparison of common and dissimilar quantitatively and qualitatively derived themes was not only helpful but also necessary because

> The survey data alone would not have been sufficient to effectively capture the interplay of the unique sociodemographic circumstances of the schools with various factors associated with school success. The qualitative data would not have been sufficient to systematically examine such dynamics based on the data from a large sample. (p. 238)

If you have difficulty condensing or qualitizing quantitative data into a word or short phrase, consider how an extended thematic statement is also an option for translating statistical data from numeric representations into narrative form.

Profiled earlier were just a few qualitizing approaches to quantitative data. One qualitative coding method not yet applied to mixed methods studies is Causation Coding (Saldaña, 2016), which identifies the antecedent condition(s), mediating variable(s), and outcome(s) of a social process(es) as a "triplet" code—for example, COMPETITION → WINNING → SELF-ESTEEM; or, "FEAR OF SPEAKING" → SPEAKING EVENTS + SPEECH CLASS → JOURNALISM CAREER + SUCCESS. Johnson, Russo, and Schoonenboom's (2017) theoretical discussion of causation in mixed methods research sets forth selected principles awaiting testing through Causation Coding.

In sum, the particular coding method(s) chosen for a mixed methods research study should harmonize with the project's overall research design. But most important is to strategically select a qualitizing method(s) that enables cross-paradigmatic comparison and integration for mixed methods data analysis. This principle is illustrated next.

4 Empirical Demonstrations of Qualitative Coding for MMR

In this section, I provide two empirical demonstrations of qualitizing the quantitative to illustrate the diverse approaches available for mixed methods researchers. The first example employed Magnitude Codes for a medical study. The second employed qualitized codes with accompanying analytic memos for an educational study.

MMR with Qualitized Magnitude Codes

Leal et al. (2018) conducted "An Exploration of the Effects of Tibetan Yoga on Patients' Psychological Well-Being and Experience of Lymphoma: An Experimental Embedded Mixed Methods Study." For quantitative measures, each cancer patient/participant in the experiment (both treatment and control groups) took a varied selection of psychological tests at a baseline and various post-intervention points in time to measure their anxiety, depression, sleep quality, spirituality, and self-reported personal well-being (i.e., finding meaning from cancer experiences). For qualitative data, each participant provided written reflections prompted by three open-ended questions at two post-intervention points in time. The analyses of the quantitative and qualitative data explored how their integration could "generate a synergistic approach providing a more comprehensive and insightful analysis of complex interventions not available through either method alone" (p. 2).

The researchers examined each participant's quantitative scores on the psychological tests taken across four points in time and *qualitized their variation patterns*. They then compared these patterns with respective qualitative data codes from each patient that were congruent, divergent, or contradictory with the quantitative profile. This enabled an integrated analysis of the patients' psychological trends through time, and reinforced the overarching theme of cancer experience—*living with paradox*, described as

> a contradictory experience of positive and negative emotional states occurring concurrently. Respondents expressed fear of death, loss, and being out of control, while simultaneously expressing spirituality and acceptance of death. The experience of contradiction participants report has been characterized as inherent to the cancer journey as a traumatic and life-threatening event consistent with posttraumatic growth, the seeming contradiction of growth through suffering. (p. 18)

The research team examined each participant's psychological test scores across time and noted the variation patterns in order to construct qualitized "themes" (i.e., codes). As described by the researchers, "Codifying quantitative scores transformed numerical data into observable patterns, facilitating comparison and integration of the distinct data sets" (p. 10). These themes were then examined with the corresponding qualitative data codes generated from the participants' written reflections. Four examples of the words and phrases used to code/theme the quantitative data, followed by the series of qualitative codes applied to participants' open-ended responses, were:

Patient #102
Pattern: Minimum variation
Qualitized Theme: CONSISTENCY (Extremely stable scores)
Qualitative Data Codes: EQUILIBRIUM, DOUBT, INCONGRUOUS—FEELING HEALTHY/BEING ILL

Patient #38
Pattern: Maximum variation
Qualitized Theme: TRANSFORMATION (Marked positive changes)
Qualitative Data Codes: GROWING, TAINTED, LOSS/OUT OF CONTROL

Patient #63
Pattern: Congruent—Little variation
Qualitized Theme: MODERATE (Slight positive change)
Qualitative Data Codes: ACCEPTANCE, FUNDAMENTALLY TRANSFORMATIVE, MIXED EMOTIONS

Patient #19
Pattern: Incongruent—Internal contradiction between measures
Qualitized Theme: CONFLICT (Both positive and negative changes)
Qualitative Data Codes: POSITIVE, SHIFTING PRIORITIES, INCONGRUOUS (pp. 15–16; adapted)

The full report details the logistics and nuances of the researchers' analyses, but the discussion here focuses on the qualitizing of psychological test score variations across time.

Leal et al. smartly derived their qualitative themes/codes from statistical and holistic interpretation of observed patterns. Themes such as CONSISTENCY, TRANSFORMATION, MODERATE, and CONFLICT honed in on changes (if any) in quantitative scores, which could then be compared with qualitative codes suggesting change (if any) or paradox—e.g., EQUILIBRIUM, GROWING, FUNDAMENTALLY TRANSFORMATIVE, SHIFTING PRIORITIES. Sleep quality was the variable that quantitative measures revealed was the most significantly different between treatment and control groups. Qualitatively, the yoga treatment participants documented more acceptance of self, others, and life in the open-ended survey responses.

The take-away from this profile is to consider how qualitative Magnitude Codes can be applied to statistical data for comparison with codes derived from qualitative empirical materials and data analysis. This strategy was employed in the next study profiled in the next section, but with additional coding methods used as springboards for analytic memo writing.

MMR with Qualitized Affective Codes and Analytic Memos

In the "Lifelong Impact: Adult Perceptions of Their High School Speech and/or Theatre Participation" study, McCammon, Saldaña, Hines, and Omasta (2012) conducted a mixed methods online survey with 234 adult respondents:

> The primary purpose of the "Lifelong Impact" study was to determine in what ways participation in high school theatre/speech classes and/or related extracurricular activities (e.g., play productions, speech tournaments) may have positively influenced and affected adults after graduation. The second purpose was to identify, describe, and advocate the potentially beneficial and "lifelong" impacts speech/theatre participation during adolescence can contribute to adulthood. (pp. 2–3)

Respondents ranged in age from 18 to 70+ and lived in North America. The e-mailed survey contained 14 items in total, five of which solicited numeric ratings and open-ended responses to a series of prompts such as the following:

> *Quantitative*
> My participation in high school speech and/or theatre has affected the adult I am now:
> 4 = Strongly Agree, 3 = Agree, 2 = Disagree, 1 = Strongly Disagree: _____
>
> *Qualitative*
> In what ways do you think your participation in speech and/or theatre as a high school student has affected the adult you have become? _____

The mean rating from all 234 survey respondents to the quantitative prompt above was 3.82 out of 4.00. Four qualitative categories were constructed from their open-ended responses: Lifelong Self-Confidence, Lifelong Thinking and Working, Lifelong Living and Loving, and Lifelong Legacy.

All survey responses, both quantitative and qualitative, were entered into an Excel data base in individual cells (see Figure 14.1). Means of quantitative ratings were calculated by the software in various sample configurations for comparison (e.g., by total data base of respondents, by gender, by graduation cohort [2000s, 1990s, 1980s, etc.], by types of high school experiences [theatre only, speech only, or both], and by current adult occupation [theatrical or non-theatrical]). Quantitizing by calculating the percentages of qualitative categories was also conducted—for example,

> Thirty-six percent of respondents [to this item] testified a sense of *self-confidence* was a significant outcome of their participation in high school theatre and/or speech programming. (The percentage is much higher if comparable *confidence* comments from other survey questions were pooled here.) (McCammon & Saldaña, 2011, pp. 53–54).

Not featured in the final published report due to space limitations but described in the unpublished technical report was Saldaña's backstage analytic work with the data. The Excel spread sheet was a *playground* for inductive queries because the software quickly enabled various configurations of data arrays. Numbers and narratives were always kept close together. Quantitative and qualitative survey responses plus their codes in adjacent cells created a true sense of data integration. Qualitative coding of the open-ended responses took more time, of course, whereas various mean ratings and *p* values were calculated quickly. This discussion will focus on the qualitizing components of the analysis.

In survey research such as this, Vogt et al. (2014) recommend that analysts "link the numerically coded to the categorically coded answers" (p. 34). Five survey items with their quantitative and qualitative data arrayed by gender, current occupation, and so on, enabled a

> mixed-methods analysis to the reconfigured data—comparing means between two groups and applying a two-tailed *t*-test to discern any significant statistical differences ($p < .05$), followed by a qualitative comparison of codes. After a few initial queries, we

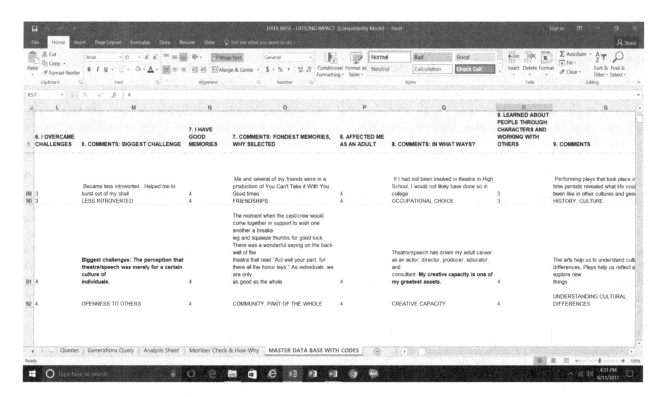

FIGURE 14.1 An Excel spreadsheet of quantitative and qualitative data for the "Lifelong Impact" study.

observed *paradigmatic corroboration*—in other words, the lower … the *p* level, the more qualitative differences seemed to appear between groups; conversely, when the *p* level was moderate or high, the less qualitative differences we could detect between groups. (McCammon & Saldaña, 2011, p. 77)

After each mean was calculated and each *t* test *p* value was ascertained, a "so what?" qualitative code was added to the statistical result. The "so what?" code was a first impression jotting with an accompanying analytic memo (explained below) that would be used as a comparison against the qualitative analysis of the narrative data. A 3.82 out of a possible 4.00 mean rating from 234 respondents to the prompt, "My participation in high school speech and/or theatre has affected the adult I am now," generated the qualitized Magnitude Code: HIGH!-LIFELONG AFFECTS. This code was an *interpretation*, based on the analyst's knowledge of means calculated thus far and initial coding of the qualitative data.

Saldaña (2016) notes that codes are nothing more than a list of labels until they are analyzed in some way, and *analytic memos* are methods for getting the researcher's thoughts and ideas about the codes documented in print. Codes serve as prompts or triggers for the deeper meanings they evoke, and analytic memos about them are "roughly equivalent to a lab notebook in experimental research" (Vogt et al., 2014, p. 394). The goal is not just to summarize the data but to reflect and expound on them, as suggested by the coding choices.

HIGH!-LIFELONG AFFECTS generated the following brief memo from the data analyst. Note that it is dated with a memo category as its heading. The memo is intended as a for-the-researcher's-eyes-only jotting and is permissibly *messy* in its composition. Also notice how the memo places the self-standing statistic in context—this is, in comparison to other statistics generated thus far.

> November 15, 2010
> PATTERN: HIGH!-LIFELONG AFFECTS
> A 3.82 out of 4.00 mean is pretty high, especially when compared to the other means. This sort of clinches what we suspected all along. What'll be interesting is to see why those who felt they had a bad teacher in high school from question #3 still rated this question so high.

Qualitized codes and brief analytic memos were composed after each statistical test had been conducted. For example, the research team hypothesized that there would be statistically significant differences—both quantitative and qualitative—between men and women respondents, based on previous audience reception research with live theatre experiences. However, the mean ratings of each group to the survey prompt, "My participation in high school speech and/or theatre has affected the adult I am now," showed no statistically significant difference. The analyst's qualitative code for the *p* < .64 result generated the (unabashedly subjective) qualitized code: THIS CAN'T BE RIGHT. An analytic memo reflected on this unexpected finding, as follows:

> December 3, 2010
> PROBLEM: THIS CAN'T BE RIGHT
> Hmmmm. Didn't turn out the way we thought it was going to. Gender differences in theatre response research are all over the place, so why didn't we get the same result? Something's going on, so check out what happens with the qual analysis—I bet there'll be differences there. *p* < .64?!

Surprisingly, the qualitative data analysis comparing men's and women's responses to the open-ended prompt, "In what ways do you think your participation in speech and/or theatre as a high school student has affected the adult you have become?" also revealed no discernable differences between genders. Major Descriptive Codes constructed for the qualitative responses and analysis included (SELF-)CONFIDENCE, PUBLIC SPEAKING, FRIENDSHIPS, OCCUPATIONAL CHOICE, and LEGACY. Yet, none of them appeared with more noticeable frequency in one group over another, and neither group had a set of subcodes unique to them. This observation prompted another analytic memo:

> January 16, 2011
> PATTERN: NO GENDER DIFFERENCES
> Both the quant and qual results showed that there was no significant difference between men and women in the study. This wasn't what we expected, but it's good to know that both the quant test and qual results corroborate. Maybe theatre and speech are "equalizers" of some kind. We say it's an inclusive space, so maybe aside from race and sexual orientation, gender is embraced and brings the same outcomes regardless of whether you're male or female.

Research methodologist Robert Stake (1995) wisely observes, "Good research is not about good methods as much as it is about good thinking" (p. 19). Some mixed methods researchers might feel the need to devise qualitized codes that possess quantitative properties—that is, Magnitude Codes exclusively. But a THIS CAN'T BE RIGHT code is just as legitimate, for it stimulates "good thinking" via reflection and reflexivity on the data's possible meanings as they are separately analyzed then later integrated.

A few qualitative research methodologists advocate that analytic memos should be truly open-ended, and they offer no prescriptive guidelines for their contents. Saldaña and Omasta (2018), however, recommend a series of specific prompts for analytic memos as guidelines for novices to the field. Although originally designed for qualitative inquiry, the prompts can also serve the quantitative and mixed methods researcher when reflecting on statistical and mixed data. Analytic memos are opportunities for investigators from all paradigms and research approaches to reflect on and write about:

1. a descriptive summary of the data
2. how the researcher personally relates to the participants and/or the phenomenon

3. the participants' actions, reactions, and interactions
4. the participants' routines, rituals, rules, roles, and relationships
5. what is surprising, intriguing, or disturbing (Sunstein & Chiseri-Strater, 2012, p. 115)
6. code choices and their operational definitions
7. emergent patterns, categories, themes, concepts, and assertions
8. the possible networks and processes (links, connections, overlaps, flows) among the codes, patterns, categories, themes, concepts, and assertions
9. an emergent or related existent theory
10. any problems with the study
11. any personal or ethical dilemmas with the study
12. future directions for the study
13. the analytic memos generated thus far (i.e., meta-memos)
14. tentative answers to the study's research questions
15. the final report for the study

For mixed methods researchers in particular, when comparing and integrating quantitative with qualitative data, I add the following prompt for analytic memo writing:

16. how qualitized codes/themes interrelate (i.e., congruency, divergence, contradiction, explanation) with qualitative codes/themes

5 Suggested Applications of Qualitative Coding in MMR

According to Creamer (2018), "Converting is a strategy for data consolidation where qualitative data are converted to quantitative data or quantitative data are converted to qualitative data so they can be analyzed together" (p. 104). One of the most common critiques of selected mixed methods research studies is that the quantitative and qualitative data sets are analyzed separately, albeit well, but without a true mixing for rich meta-inferencing. Conversion of statistical results into qualitative forms for comparison and integration with qualitative analyses in progress better guarantees true consolidation of the empirical materials and findings.

The coding method(s) chosen for a particular qualitative research study is based on several factors, such as the nature of the research question, the methodology adopted (grounded theory, phenomenology, case study, etc.), a priori goals, and other considerations. The specific coding method(s) selected for qualitizing the quantitative should also serve a purpose—preferably, aligned with or related to in some way with the mixed methods research design and analyses. For example, the Leal et al. (2018) research team knew that "paradox" was inherent in cancer patient experiences, and the quantitative and qualitative data collected from them would also reflect that paradox—sometimes consistent, sometimes inconsistent, and sometimes contradictory. Qualitizing the idiosyncratic *variation* in participants' test scores and written responses harmonized with one of the research team's frameworks for studying people whose lives are in constant flux.

When a consequential statistic of some kind (a score, mean, Pearson's r, $p <$ value, etc.) has been generated, qualitatively code its meaning or significance followed by an analytic memo. Magnitude Codes such as HIGH, LOWER THAN HYPOTHESIZED, WIDELY VARIED RESPONSES, and so on (a method I facetiously call "quantitizing the quantitative—again") are perhaps the statistician's initial go-to researcher responses. But these, too, are quantitatively driven; think outside the paradigmatic box. "So what?" codes are honest analyst impressions of quantitative results. Analytic memos—a private experience—elaborate on those labels for good thinking at the moment and during later integration.

Finally, qualitizing might also assist researchers conducting meta-analyses of quantitative studies, particularly if the pool includes related qualitative studies. Meta-analysis, meta-ethnography, meta-summary, and meta-synthesis each have their own methods for consolidating results from a combination of studies. But if boundaries are blurred and borders redrawn, richer and more comprehensive compendia of previous research from a variety of paradigms can be developed. See Sandelowski, Trimble, Woodard, and Barroso (2006) for an exemplar of qualitative meta-synthesis and data transformation.

6 Strengths and Limitations of Qualitative Coding in MMR

Creamer (2018) posits that in "the highest-caliber mixed methods studies, the qualitative and quantitative strands are often so cleverly and iteratively interwoven that it becomes an exercise in semantics to disentangle the two" (p. 100). Qualitizing is one analytic strategy to better ensure that the quantitative strand of a mixed methods study does not remain an isolated component. The method better ensures compatibility and blended interchange between both data sets—an ideal goal of a truly *mixed* methods study.

A second strength of qualitizing is seeing a quantitative data set in a fresh way. The transformation of numbers into words may provide a different interpretive dimension to the study. A new researcher lens, filter, and angle on the findings can bring to light a unique perspective not possible from statistical analysis alone.

In some studies, quantitizing the qualitative for an additional statistical analysis opportunity may value-add to the findings. But a potential drawback to qualitizing the quantitative is forcing numeric representations into condensed narrative forms *when unnecessary*. Certainly, statistics do not speak for themselves, and narrative explanations are always needed to emphasize their meaning and significance for an audience. But it should be acknowledged that sometimes numbers *are* the best answer to a particular research question. Qualitizing can serve as a worthwhile for-the-researcher's-eyes-only exploration in the privacy of one's office. But if nothing new is discovered or if no compatibility can be logically constructed, then leave the experiment out of the report. As the contemporary folk saying goes, "If it ain't broke, don't fix it."

One principle that is both a strength and limitation of qualitizing is its dependence on the analyst's creativity. The precision of quantitative research rests with numeric accuracy. In qualitative research, precision rests with word choices. When words are selected for codes or themes, the vocabulary must consist of the best choices the researcher can make that interpretively symbolize and capture the essence of a datum's meaning. Whether the qualitized choice is straightforwardly descriptive, evocatively metaphoric, or unabashedly values-laden is the analyst's judgment call. Interrater reliability notwithstanding, there is no one *right* way to code data, and mixed methods researchers must accept that as a given when qualitizing the quantitative. Each paradigm has its own representational traditions and methodological canons, and the qualitative generally emphasizes heuristic meaning making more than algorithmic deduction. To me, the absence of methods standardization in qualitative inquiry is not a limitation but its strength. To adapt an insightful research principle by Patton (2015), "Because each [mixed methods] study is unique, the analytical approach used will be unique" (p. 522).

7 Resources for Learning More About Qualitative Coding

Coding and analytic memos are discussed extensively in Saldaña's (2016) *The Coding Manual for Qualitative Researchers*, with applications illustrated through matrices, diagrams, and graphics in Miles et al. (2020) *Qualitative Data Analysis: A Methods Sourcebook*. One of the best discussions of mixed methods research principles can be accessed from Creamer's (2018) *An Introduction to Fully Integrated Mixed Methods Research*. Access Vogt et al.'s (2014) *Selecting the Right Analyses for Your Data: Quantitative, Qualitative, and Mixed Methods* for extensive discussions on coding across the paradigms and expert analytic guidance. Finally, for an exemplar journal article whose mixed methods study utilizes qualitizing, see Leal et al.'s (2018) "An Exploration of the Effects of Tibetan Yoga on Patients' Psychological Well-Being and Experience of Lymphoma: An Experimental Embedded Mixed Methods Study."

REFERENCES

Centers for Disease Control and Prevention. (2019). Chronic Obstructive Pulmonary Disease (COPD). Retrieved March 10, 2019 from www.cdc.gov/copd/index.html

Creamer, E. G. (2018). *An introduction to fully integrated mixed methods research*. Thousand Oaks, CA: Sage.

Ignatow, G., & Mihalcea, R. (2017). *Text mining: A guidebook for the social sciences*. Thousand Oaks, CA: Sage.

Jang, E. E., McDougall, D. E., Pollon, D., Herbert, M., & Russell, P. (2008). Integrative mixed methods data analytic strategies in research on school success in challenging circumstances. *Journal of Mixed Methods Research 2*, 221–247. doi:10.1177/1558689808315323

Johnson, R. B., Russo, F., & Schoonenboom. J. (2017). Causation in mixed methods research: The meeting of philosophy, science, and practice. *Journal of Mixed Methods Research*. Advance online publication. doi:10.1177/1558689817719610

Leal, I., Engebretson, J., Cohen, L., Fernandez-Esquer, M. E., Lopez, G., Wangyal, T., & Chaoul, A. (2018). An exploration of the effects of Tibetan yoga on patients' psychological well-being and experience of lymphoma: An experimental embedded mixed methods study. *Journal of Mixed Methods Research 12*, 31–54. doi:10.1177/1558689816645005

Lincoln, Y. S., & Guba, E. G. (1985). *Naturalistic inquiry*. Newbury Park, CA: Sage.

Liu, B. (2015). *Sentiment analysis: Mining opinions, sentiments, and emotions*. New York, NY: Cambridge University Press.

Major, C. H., & Savin-Baden, M. (2010). *An introduction to qualitative research synthesis: Managing the information explosion in social science research*. London, England: Routledge.

McCammon, L. A., & Saldaña, J. (2011). *Lifelong impact: Adult perceptions of their high school speech and/or theatre participation*. Unpublished manuscript.

McCammon, L., Saldaña, J., Hines, A., & Omasta, M. (2012). Lifelong impact: Adult perceptions of their high school speech and/or theatre participation. *Youth Theatre Journal 26*(1), 2–25. doi:10.1080/08929092.2012.678223

Miles, M. B., Huberman, A. M., & Saldaña, J. (2020). *Qualitative data analysis: A methods sourcebook* (4th ed.). Thousand Oaks, CA: Sage.

Neuendorf, K. A. (2017). *The content analysis guidebook* (2nd ed.). Thousand Oaks, CA: Sage.

Patton, M. Q. (2015). *Qualitative research and evaluation methods* (4th ed.). Thousand Oaks, CA: Sage.

Plano Clark, V. L., & Ivankova, N. V. (2016). *Mixed methods research: A guide to the field*. Thousand Oaks, CA: Sage.

Rallis, S. F., & Rossman, G. B. (2003). Mixed methods in evaluation contexts: A pragmatic framework. In A. Tashakkori & C. Teddlie (Eds.), *Handbook of mixed methods in social & behavioral research* (pp. 491–512). Thousand Oaks, CA: Sage.

Rubin, H. J., & Rubin, I. S. (2012). *Qualitative interviewing: The art of hearing data* (3rd ed.). Thousand Oaks, CA: Sage.

Saldaña, J. (2016). *The coding manual for qualitative researchers* (3rd ed.). London, England: Sage.

Saldaña, J., & Omasta, M. (2018). *Qualitative research: Analyzing life*. Thousand Oaks, CA: Sage.

Sandelowski, M., & Barroso, J. (2007). *Handbook for synthesizing qualitative research*. New York, NY: Springer.

Sandelowski, M., Trimble, F., Woodard, E. K., & Barroso, J. (2006). From synthesis to script: Transforming qualitative research findings for use in practice. *Qualitative Health Research 16*, 1350–1370. doi:10.1177/1049732306294274

Sandelowski, M., Voils, C. I., & Knafl, G. (2009). On quantitizing. *Journal of Mixed Methods Research 3*, 208–222. doi:10.1177/1558689809334210

Schreier, M. (2012). *Qualitative content analysis in practice*. London, England: Sage.

Stake, R. E. (1995). *The art of case study research*. Thousand Oaks, CA: Sage.

Sunstein, B. S., & Chiseri-Strater, E. (2012). *Fieldworking: Reading and writing research* (4th ed.). Boston, MA: Bedford/St. Martin's.

Vogt, W. P., Vogt, E. R., Gardner, D. C., & Haeffeke, L. M. (2014). *Selecting the right analyses for your data: Quantitative, qualitative, and mixed methods*. New York, NY: Guilford.

15

Mixed Methodological Discourse Analysis[1]

Zsuzsanna Géring

Discourse is one of the most heavily used concepts in contemporary social science. Sometimes it refers to the distinction between talk and text, sometimes it is treated as a complex system of text and sometimes it designates a cluster of relevant texts, events and social relations. Consequently, its meaning is manifold and its definitions are numerous. Accordingly, its analysis, that is, discourse analysis (DA), too covers a broad range of methodological and analytical procedures from the examination of speech patterns in individual sentences to the examination of social power and suppression in clusters of news. This means that discourse analysis is not a methodological process with highly elaborated technical details, but rather a collection of approaches and methodological tools with shared theoretical background.

In the literature, discourse analysis is often treated as an inherently qualitative method, although there can be found some scattered references in a few DA books about a slight possibility of quantitative approaches mentioned in relation to discourse (Fairclough, 2003; Tonkiss, 2012). However, they do not elaborate how quantitative methods could enhance DA. In this chapter, I try to take this additional step and apply the pragmatic approach of mixed methodology to the field of DA. I emphasize that we should shift from the standpoint that places DA solely in the frame of the qualitative paradigm; instead, we might also incorporate considerations from the quantitative realm. This is in line with the pragmatist position of mixed methods, which argues that while analysts aim to understand social phenomena, the emphasis should not just be on methodology and research procedure but, more importantly, on the very problem examined (more about pragmatism in Johnson, de Waal, Stefurak, & Hildebrand, 2017; Johnson, Onwuegbuzie, de Waal, Stefurak, & Hildebrand, 2017). In order to do so, researchers might utilise all available theoretical (e.g., postpositivist, constructivist, participatory) and methodological (both qualitative and quantitative) frameworks (for mixed methods research see among others Creswell, 2009; Creswell & Plano-Clark, 2011; Frels & Onwuegbuzie, 2013; Hesse-Biber, 2010; Onwuegbuzie & Leech, 2005a; Tashakkori & Teddlie, 2010; Teddlie & Tashakkori, 2009).

The focus of this chapter is to demonstrate through some interesting examples, how the mixed methodological approach can enrich the field of DA, offset its weaknesses, and strengthen its applicability in order to reach better understanding of our world. It is not as if the DA landscape is not complex enough, as the following short introduction of the different DA approaches and schools will show.[2]

1 Definition of Discourse Analysis and Mixed Methodological Discourse Analysis

When we are looking for a DA-definition, we should widen our scope and take into consideration some important aspects of the theoretical field in which DA is embedded.

The first among these is the *linguistic turn* of social sciences (for a short summary see Jorgensen & Phillips, 2002). The linguistic turn questioned the viewpoint of a language as a neutral and transparent transmitter medium with which reality can be described objectively and completely (see for example Austin, 1975; Carver, 2004). In contrast, the discourse or discursive approach emphasises the meaning-making function of the language, and states that reality is constructed through the communication itself, due to the communicating actors' social relations and interaction (Kress, 2001). Therefore, language is not treated as a neutral medium, because we define and understand our world and society through and with it. That is, the *language is* not a static transmitter system but a dynamic and *active field* of social meaning-making (Hall, 2001). In this aspect, discourse analysis can be defined as the analysis of *language in its use* (Taylor, 2001).

This also means that the analysed *discourse is always situated*, that is, embedded in a social context (Fairclough, 2003, Potter, 2004) as well as in an intertextual context, which refers to the numerous other texts and discourses connected with the analysed one (Titscher, Meyer, Wodak, & Vetter, 2003). For example, in case of news-analysis we should take into consideration the characteristics of the given newspapers, the social background of the analysed phenomena, and other texts, such as, policy documents, political speeches etc. that are connected to the examined news.

These two characteristics point out that discourse is always *constructive* through the meaning-making processes of language use *and at the same time it is constructed* because it is embedded in a social and textual context and framed by linguistic and social rules and routines.

Discourse analysts (like Gill, 2000) emphasize that language use, both in its spoken and written form, is social action in the sense that it exerts a social influence even if it is also constrained by society having codified and non-codified rules that can be linked to the social contexts and characteristics of the speakers/writers. Theorists also point to the roles and functions discourses play in processes of social construction and to how they might serve as tools (both in negative and positive sense) to define societal processes and institutions (Bryman, 2012).

TABLE 15.1

Summary of the Three DA-Approaches.

Attributes	Linguistics Approach	Discursive Psychology	Critical Discourse Analysis
Focus of research	language use	identity	social patterns, ideology, power
Analysed level of construction	social interaction	social actor	social system
Connected disciplines	sociolinguistics, ethnography, ethnomethodology	psychology, social psychology, linguistics	sociology, cultural studies, political sciences
Some of the main founders	Sapir, Whorf, Hymes, Gumperz, Labov, Halliday	Gergen, Harré, Davis, Henriques, Hollway, Sarbin, Josselson, Leiblich, Wetherell, Potter	Kress, Fowler, Hodge, Fairclough, van Dijk, Wodak

The different schools and approaches (see below) highlight how analysing discourses can contribute to the understanding of social phenomena, actions, actors, processes, or even the operation of organisations. Regardless of the analysed phenomena, one of the basic common features of DA is that the analysis focuses on the discourse itself (Potter & Wetherell, 1987), on the role and function it is playing in its social context, on the way it is constructed, and on the layers with which it is linked to its intertextual and social context.

Despite a shared theoretical and methodological background across traditions and approaches, there are some distinguishable DA approaches and schools of thought based on the different levels of construction and the examined function of discourses. Their number varies from author to author in the literature; Potter (2004) mentioned three main approaches like Gill (2000), while Leech and Onwuegbuzie (2008) distinguished five major traditions. I will differentiate three main DA approaches based on their topic, main method, and related theoretical considerations (Table 15.1):[3]

1. The first is the *linguistic approach* concentrates on the examination of talk and interaction as social actions. It is rooted mainly in sociolinguistics, ethnography, and ethnomethodology. Discourse analysis here means the exploration of language use in social interactions, with special focus on the relation between the language use and its context (e.g., Brown & Yule, 2003; Schriffin, 2002; Tannen, Hamiliton, & Schriffin, 2015)

2. The second main school is *discursive psychology*. Its main question addresses how social actors construct their own identities in and through a social interaction. This approach emerged from the interlocking of psychology, social psychology, and linguistics. Its focus is how people talk about themselves, how they present themselves and others in interactions, and how they construct their identities in these processes (e.g., Edwards & Potter, 1992; Parker, 2002; Potter & Wetherell, 1987).

3. The third approach is *critical linguistics or critical discourse analysis* (CDA). This approach is committed to the analysis of the discursive features of social institutions. Discourse analysts in this field shift the focus from social actors or from social interaction in its strict sense to the level of social patterns, ideology and social institutions mobilised in and constructed through discourses. It is connected especially to sociology, cultural studies, and political science. One of the distinctive features of this school is its strong critical viewpoint, which often takes shape in ideology critics and examination of power relations in social interaction (for CDA see Fairclough, 1998, 2003, 2013; Wodak, 2015; Wodak & Chilton, 2005; Wodak & Meyer, 2002). CDA criticizes inequality in nearly all of its forms.

In sum, discourse analysis can be treated as a theoretical and methodological approach that concentrates on language in use, and it focuses on the functions that discourse plays in our social world at different (individual, interactive, and social) levels. At the same time, it is a collection of methodological tools and procedures—stemming from these considerations—used to analyse the formation and production of meaning-making processes, and individual and collective representations in and through communication that is crystallized in discursive and social structures.

Based on these considerations my definition of mixed methodological discourse analysis is as follows:

> Mixed methodological discourse analysis (MMDA) is a methodological standpoint in the field of discourse analysis. Its main feature is the incorporation of quantitative and qualitative processes into the analysis of discourses. Therefore, it is not a new school or new theoretical approach in discourse analysis, rather the expansion of the methodological toolbox of DA with the consideration of mixed methods research. It is applicable to all of the mentioned discursive fields and could be combined with other textual or non-textual methods.

The field of DA is complex and diverse, but none of these attributes indicates that it should be rendered solely to the qualitative paradigm. Therefore, in the following sections, we show when and how the mixed methodological DA approach can help enrich traditional discourse analytical thinking and methodology.

2 When Use of Discourse Analysis is Appropriate in MMR

Applying discourse analyses in a mixed methods research study is appropriate when discourse in itself is the topic of the examination. That is, we could use DA when the analysis of textual data is not a phase of the research with which we would like to gain information about something else, but when we would like to analyse the textual data exactly to understand how the actors produce meaning, identity, opposition, power relations, and so forth, or how a given phenomenon is constructed in the given texts (e.g., in an interview, in news, in everyday talk). In the case of discourse analysis through the examination of the textual data, we would like to gain information about the rhetorical tools applied, the relation of text and its context, the function of the discourse, its effect, and so on.

In the following section, we demonstrate the possibility and advantage of mixed methodological DA at different phases of research. The list is not exhaustive, but it focuses on those points of the research, where the incorporation of typically quantitative considerations and the applying of quantitative methods can best enhance the traditional qualitative DA.

Some possible mixing points in DA include the following:

- *Sampling.* In a typical DA, sampling is based on the so-called qualitative sampling-principles, mainly on purposive sampling, with a relatively small sample of texts. Nonetheless, with MMDA we can manage bigger samples, which improves the possibility of generalisability. Therefore, even at the phase of sampling, we should also consider quantitative sampling methods that is, representativeness and/or randomisation.[4]
- *Refine the research question.* In the case of DA, even a small sample can lead to an enormous amount of data and interesting features. At this point, applying quantitative methods, that is, the measurement of characteristics can help. For example, one might attempt to find the most frequent topics or meaning-making patterns, find *outliers* among the different characteristics, and so on.
- *Turning textual DA data into numeric data.* The translation of texts into quantitative data is the special characteristic of some textual methods, such as for example, quantitative content analysis. Mixed methodological discourse analysis can also be useful in that.
- *Connecting DA results with non-textual data.* In case of discourse analysis, especially in its critical and social-level-oriented form, the involvement of context is extremely important in the interpretation of the results. The researcher should analyse the social, historical, legal, and political background of the analysed discourse. However, a lot of information may be in quantitative form. In order to connect the textual data with the contextual data, a lot of times we need quantitative discursive data (see prior point) or we need to transform the qualitative data into quantitative ones.
- *Verification.* In traditional discourse analysis, researchers work with smaller samples in order to be able to analyse them thoroughly. Even in that case, it is important to verify the results in a large and independent sample to filter out *researcher bias*. With

this goal in mind, the quantification of DA results may be a necessary step, to verify the data on a large independent sample (see earlier points).

The advantages of MMDA are similar to the advantages of mixed methods research in general. Here it can be mentioned the importance of mixing the different approaches, because typically qualitative methods help avoid oversimplification, and quantitative methods play important role in verification and generalisation. With a mixed methods research design, the movement between texts and quantitative data could be easier, because the applied quantitative methods could render textual data into quantitative form or could offer quantitative outputs about texts. Another important aspect of MMDA is that it leads to a deeper understanding without sacrificing validity, since it can provide a more comprehensive picture of the analysed phenomena by covering (or comparing) large corpus of texts.[5]

MMDA offers a change of approach inside the textual analytical realm because DA is traditionally treated as a small-scale deep and inherently qualitative analysis. With the incorporation of quantitative DA and the mixed methodological DA approach, we can break away from the norm, and, as in the pragmatic approach, should place the research question into the focus of the analysis and apply the available methodological tools, that are the best to answer it, may it be quantitative or qualitative DA or both.

3 Technical Outline of Discourse Analysis for MMR

There are several different outlines of the discourse analysis process in different books and chapters on DA (e.g. Gee, 2011a; Gill, 2000; Potter, 2004; Potter & Wetherell, 1987; Schneider, 2015; Tonkiss, 2012). But these descriptions do not deal with mixed methodological DA, even if they mention the possibility of combining quantitative and qualitative methods (e.g. Fairclough, 2003; Tonkiss, 2012). In the following, I provide a short technical description of a typical DA research process based mainly on Tonkiss (2012) referring at each phase to the possibilities and processes of mixed methodological DA designs.

Tonkiss (2012) identified four phases of the discourse analytical process, which she treated as a qualitative textual analysis approach: defining the research problem, collecting data, coding and analysing data, presenting the analysis. At each of these phases, I introduce the main concerns and a possible mixing point. However, it is important to highlight that in many cases these phases are not separated so easily, because discourse analysis is always an iterative process based on the reading and multiple rereading of the analysed texts.

1 Defining the Research Problem

In the case of DA the discourse itself is the topic of the research; that is, the research question should focus on the construction and function of the discourse (Potter &

Wetherell, 1987). In most cases this indicates a rather broad research problem, which can be narrowed to specific questions, or in the case of MMDA sometimes to hypotheses. Sometimes the exact research questions or hypotheses might be articulated only during the text-analysing process because the important features and interesting characteristics (like outliers) emerge only by reading and analysing the relevant materials.

2 Collecting Data

Data-collection is determined by the research question. There are endless sources of texts (e.g., books, newspapers, transcription of political speeches or everyday conversations, tweets, blogs etc.) and other discourse elements (e.g., visual element, photos, videos), and the choice depends on the relevance of the different text types, the available data collection methods, and the researcher's personal interest (for example it is aimed at offline or online sources).

In MMDA the data gathering processes and a general data analysis can be arranged by quantitative methodological considerations and automated software programs. These computer-assisted procedures contribute to the collecting and/or to the analysis of large amounts of texts within a short time.

3 Coding and Analysing Data

Tonkiss (2002) considers coding and data-analysis as one phase of DA. However, other scholars strictly separate them, even emphasising that in the case of coding "the goal is not to find results but to squeeze an unwieldy body of discourse into manageable chinks" (Potter & Wetherell, 1987). Although coding and analysis are not the same, sometimes at the end of a coding process the identified code list (like a theme list or a map of topics) can be viewed as a result in and of itself. This is even more true for MMDA designs where the coding process could be—at least partly—automated.

During data analysis, researchers can choose different approaches, like identifying main topics, looking for similarities and differences, searching for patterns, studying the actors and their special discursive features, and connecting textual data to contextual data. All of these examinations can include quantitative assessments (like frequencies, significance, correlations etc.) as well as qualitative assessments (like different legitimation strategies, language use patterns etc.), or both (for examples see the next section). The analysis of discourses should focus on the function of discourse. That is, the researcher should take into account the roles that different discursive features play in the given context and search for evidence in the data.

4 Presenting the Analysis

During interpretation of results and presentation of findings, the researcher has to pay close attention to validity, reliability, and coherence. MMDA can be extremely useful at this phase, whether the results of a small sample qualitative analysis are validated on a large corpus quantitatively, or the data gathering process includes validating statistical measurement regarding significance. Naturally, there are other ways of validation, which do not necessarily require quantitative measurement, such as deviant case analysis, comparing participants' understanding, and coherence or readers' evaluations (for detailed discussion see Potter, 2004 or Gill, 2000).

4 Empirical Demonstration of Discourse Analysis for MMR

Discourse analysis provides a methodological toolbox with different procedures and levels of analysis. To demonstrate some of its complexity, I will introduce four different illustrations of possible fields for mixed methodological DA next. It is important to mention that none of the following researchers used the concept or definition of MMDA. It is a new concept defined in this chapter. Nonetheless, they applied and combined DA methods and procedures that way, which can indicate when, how and why MMDA can be applied.

Example 1: Sampling, Generalising and Focusing of Research-Scope Issues—Analysing Corporate Website Texts

The purpose of research carried out by me (see Géring 2015a, 2015b) was to answer the question of "What and how do Hungarian middle-sized and large companies communicate on their websites in terms of their role and responsibility in society?". In order to answer this research question on the social level—as opposed to an individual level analysis of certain companies' discourses, or the investigation of the language use of particular corporate actors—a wider discursive frame was necessary. These considerations, combined with concerns for accessibility led to the investigation of corporate homepages. I built a representative stratified random sample of the population of Hungarian medium-sized and large companies and analysed their homepages. The final sample consisted of 146 homepages.

In order to understand how the concept and content of the social role of companies are presented in corporate discourse, I analysed the introductory web-texts of companies. The steps of the research design were as follows:

1. In step one; with the help of iterative coding, I examined how the social roles of companies are defined through actors' language use, in this case, the homepage introductory texts of companies. There was no pre-fixed coding scheme prior to text analysis, but it developed throughout the analysis. In this process, the codes do not refer to specific words but instead to higher-level units (such as sentences or paragraphs). The result was a thematic map of 48 articulated corporate goals (e.g., sustainability, competitiveness, knowledge sharing, importance of tradition) that emerged from the introductory texts. This provided not only a list of topics, but also the frequencies

(e.g., the percentage of companies that mentioned the goal or social role in their introductory text). This helped me to gain a richer account about the rate of their diffusion and enabled me to separate the generally used topics from those that were rarely voiced.

2. The next step was the development of a thematization typology from the varieties of roles found in website texts. Subsequently, using the cluster-forming procedure of the NVivo software, the social roles thus identified were integrated into 11 clusters. These clusters of identified and coded social roles led to 11 sub-discourses, namely the collection of those textual segments (typically sentences or short paragraphs) where the given roles appeared. The frequencies of the clusters provided important information about the generality or particularity of a given sub-discourse. This information was easily translated into quantitative data,[6] and was added to the SPSS database of quantitative data for the companies in the sample. This way, I was able to analyse with standard statistical methods whether different features of the analysed companies (e.g., revenue, number of employees, foreign or domestic owner) had significant relationship with the communicated goals.

3. Among the defined clusters, one contained those identified roles which were in correspondence with the main theoretical concepts of corporate social responsibility (e.g., sustainability, responsibility, environment protection). Therefore, at the last phase, I focused on what types of discursive methods and legitimation strategies the companies used in this sub-discourse (i.e., in those parts of the texts where these conceptions were used). For example, it was shown how the companies could reach very different meaning applying the same word, like sustainability, using it for environmental sustainability but also in connection with competitiveness and "financial sustainability," which covers wholly different meanings and areas while mobilising the power of legitimation associated with the environmental-friendly concept.

In this research, the mixed DA approach helped to gain not only a comprehensive picture about the conceptualisation of companies' social role and goals on a representative sample of the Hungarian medium- and large sized enterprises, but also lead to a sub-discourse containing the most relevant texts related to the research question, what I was able to analyse qualitatively to get deeper understanding of the applied discursive strategies and meaning-making processes in connection with corporate social responsibility.

Example 2: Connecting Contextual and Textual Data—Arab Women in News Headlines and in Students' Perceptions

Context plays an extremely important role in discourse analysis. The knowledge about the wider social, political, legal, and economic context of the given discourse is crucial during the coding and categorising process and at the interpretative phase of the analysis. Sometimes, these are in textual forms (like legal documents, news, political speeches etc.), but sometimes these data are quantitative. Therefore, mixed discursive data can be easier connected to quantitative contextual data.

An interesting example can be found in Mustafa-Awad and Kirner-Ludwig's (2017) research. They examined how Arab women are perceived in German news headlines and connected these results with students' perceptions about the same topic. Their research purpose was to investigate the conceptualisation of Arab women among German university students and to study whether it is affected by news discourse. The researchers based the time period on social context, that is, the so-called Arab Spring. They analysed the news between October 2010 and December 2014. However, before the newspaper selection they asked the university students which news media they read. This way the connection revealed (or the lack of it) between images of press and the students' perception was relevant and reliable. Their methodological design contained three major phases:

1. The student questionnaire was circulated, and data were collected about the students' backgrounds, the news media they read, their perception of Arab women, and their standpoint regarding critical reading and the role of media. The answers were measured on a 5-point scale when appropriate. The results served as input to the newspaper selection and as a contextual factor for comparison with the textual results from phase 3.

2. The second phase was text-corpus building. Based on the results of the questionnaire, Mustafa-Awad and Kirner-Ludwig (2017) were able to choose the relevant newspapers, and collect the appropriate news reports with Arab women being mentioned. They limited their research to the news headlines as important indicators of the mobilised conceptions. They found 836 relevant headlines between October 2010 and December 2014.

3. Data analysis and comparison were the focus in the third phase. They identified eight main topical frames: activism, violence, oppression, rights, empowerment, marriage, dress regulation and restriction, and religion. These frames (each of them containing 8–10 keywords) indicated the most common topics and themes appearing in the corpus in connection with Arab women. Furthermore, they calculated the frequencies of the given topics and keywords.

The results of the three phases were interesting in themselves. Moreover, they provided data for the comparison of news headlines with the readers' perceptions. With this mixed DA approach the researchers were able to connect the analysis of the texts with the analysis of the audience—which is a very important aspect of discourse analysis.

Example 3: Chilean Press Analyses with Qualitative and with Quantitative Ways of DA

Sayago (2015) provided an excellent case study comparing the differences between qualitative and quantitative DA. He conducted both DA research processes addressing the same research question: 'How does the Chilean written press represent the actions of resistance of a specific community before a mega-mining business that threatens their way of life?'.

Sayago (2015) at first described the customary qualitative way of discourse analysis in relation to these actions and its surrounding news. That meant of course the data-gathering, then the coding process where the researcher tags the relevant parts of the texts with the connected codes. He focused his attention to three aspects, namely, justification of the conflict, description of the actions, and characterisation of the actors, and used them as categories. After sorting the relevant textual parts into these categories, he moved into deeper analysis of the collected texts. This way he was able to identify the different justification strategies, differentiate between actors and mediums.

Next, Sayago (2015) demonstrated how to analyse the same texts with quantitative DA. Applying the same three categories, we can treat them as variables. In this case, we should provide indicators with which we can measure the behaviour of each variable. For this, Sayago (2015) suggested a rating (an ordinal scale) for each of the three variables. For example, in the case of justification, the text can be measured as superficial, medium or in-depth, based on the rigorousness of the applied arguments. Or in the case of the characterisation of the actors, the text could be negative, neutral, or positive. These are ordinal scales, where the levels can be signalled with numbers.[7] This way, the texts can be measured at different levels, from arguments (applying the ordinal scale) to whole texts of a given medium (e.g. analysing the proportion of superficial, medium or in-depth justifications). At the end of this kind of coding, the results will be data matrices (for example three variables at every news report) analysable with standard statistical processes and software.

Example 4: Validity Issues and Dealing with a Large Set of Data—Analysis of the Level of Civility and Argumentation in Online Political Comments

Jimarkon and Todd (2011, 2013) analysed online forum texts in order to reveal agonism and antagonism in online discussions connected to political unrest in Thailand in 2010. They applied DA "to explore the constructs of civility and argumentation in the population of online postings" (Jimarkon & Todd, 2011, p. 47). Almost 400 messages comprised the data set, which included more than 24,000 words. They drew attention to two possible problems during discourse-analysis.

The first problem is about capturing the change of civility level over time when there is a huge amount of texts, therefore the qualitative analysis is too time-consuming. To solve this, at first Jimarkon and Todd (2013) gave a civility and an argumentation measurement to every message, which required thorough read and a clearly defined 4-point scale for both aspects (for details see Jimarkon and Todd, 2013). After that, they divided the corpus into two halves in time and compared the average level of civility and the average level of argumentation of the first half of the forum to the second half of the forum. On both dimensions, the average level increased over time; that is, communication moved toward more civil form of dialogue and was based more and more on clear and two-sided arguments rather than feelings and one-sided claims.[8]

This type of quantitative measurement can also help to eliminate the so-called researcher-bias, when the researcher involuntarily selects those textual units that are richer and more interesting from her or his point of view. For example, in this research, the qualitative analysis of a small sample of threads showed that there was a (politically defined) group which posted more civil messages than others. However, Jimarkon and Todd (2011) coded all of the messages with their quantitative scale of civility in the whole sample, therefore they were able to analyse the differences between groups, and this way verify the findings of the small-scale qualitative analysis phase of their research.

5 Suggested Applications of Discourse Analysis in MMR

DA in general is the appropriate method when the discourse is to be analysed, that is, when we would want to gain information about the function and working of a given discourse. Furthermore, there are cases when the research question, special research requirements and/or the researcher's own attitude make mixed methodological discourse analysis a suitable research design.

MMDA refers to the combination of quantitative and qualitative data gathering and data-analysis processes in a discourse analytical study. Nonetheless, in discourse analysis, the quantification processes require constant hermeneutic and interpretative work from the researcher, that is, they could not be as easily automated as non-textual quantitative methods (see Box 15.1 about this topic).

Additionally, in the application of MMDA there is the possibility of *analysing large set of texts*. A lot of cases the researcher has to deal with huge amount of texts. With the help of MMDA, this becomes manageable and can lead to much more complex results then a general quantitative description of textual features (like in quantitative content analysis).

Also, *enhanced reliability and validity* is a further feature of MMDA. MMDA can be used to validate results of small-sample qualitative analysis on a large corpus of texts with quantitative procedures. Alternatively, it can also explain the most interesting and/or outlier data based on general quantitative analysis, which could be examined deeper with qualitative discourse analysis in order to understand its specialty.

Lastly, *statistical analysis of discursive characteristics* can help to compare and/or link contextual and textual data, which plays crucial role in discourse analysis especially in critical discourse analysis.

> **BOX 15.1**
>
> **THE QUESTION OF COMPUTER-ASSISTED ANALYTICAL PROCEDURES IN MMDA**
>
> Numerous software and programmes are available used to carry out MMDA processes.[9] There are three main parts of the research where computer-assisted procedures can support the researcher: data gathering, data analysis and management, and statistical analysis of textual data.
>
> In the case of data gathering, text-mining and text-selection programmes (e.g., LexisNexis or Aika) are helpful. There are automated built-in processes for searching and listing relevant texts based on the given searching terms. Unfortunately, most of these programmes or software are optimized to the English language. Furthermore, the researcher has to be very careful with the searching terms and making interpretations because these are automated processes without reflection on the meaning of words and their connotations.
>
> At the data-analysis phase, programmes like NVivo, Atlas.ti, MAXQDA, QDA Miner, WordStat and other qualitative data analysis software can be used for coding, thematising, and segmenting the texts. These programmes can also provide quantitative data or information easily converted into quantitative data. (For list, see for example Wikipedia: https://en.wikipedia.org/wiki/Computer-assisted_qualitative_data_analysis_software).
>
> Finally, WordStat, SPSS, R and similar programmes can be used for statistical analysis of the quantitative data as well as to convert textual data to quantitative forms (like nominal or categorical variables) and provide quantitative features of the analysed texts. (More information: https://en.wikipedia.org/wiki/List_of_statistical_software).
>
> However, these computer-assisted procedures can only supplement the researcher's own efforts during the text analysis. The researcher has to read and reread the analysed texts, and continually interpret and reinterpret their features and connection to the context both in qualitative and quantitative DA procedures.

6 Strengths and Limitations of Discourse Analysis in MMR

Many strengths of discourse analysis stem from its theoretical background and its complex methodological approach. That is, due to the special focus on the discourse itself, DA can reveal discursive features that often remain hidden without detailed analysis and refined methodological tools. With discourse analysis, the researcher acquires a *more complex comprehension of the function of discourse* and the discursive strategies that contribute to meaning making, identity development, and construction of social institutions. This leads to a *deeper understanding* of the analysed phenomena.

Another strength of discourse analysis is its *special focus on the context* of the analysed material. This methodology emphasises the role of context in the analysis and during the interpretation of the results.

These advantages could be further strengthened by MMDA. As demonstrated before, the applied methods in MMDA can complement each other providing both a general picture and deeper details and understanding, and both quantitative and qualitative descriptions about the subject of the research.

Complexity constitutes the major impediment to the DA methodology, namely, its *time-consuming* nature, whether it is qualitative or mixed methodological DA. Even with a small sample of texts, the emerging discursive features can be numerous and diverse. This fact requires great discipline from the researcher if she or he does not want to be lost among them. The support of textual and statistical software programs helps to systematize the data but cannot substitute the long time and enormous energy needed to configure coding, measuring, and data-interpretation.

As mentioned before, the diversity of methods and tools provides an excellent opportunity to articulate the relevant research design to our research problem, especially in case of MMDA, when numerous combinations of quantitative and qualitative methods are available. However, at the same time, it can *overburden the researcher with possibilities* and require many decision points.

Last, due to this complexity both in the theoretical and in the methodological arenas, discourse analysis is a so-called *craft-skill*. Namely, with the lack of an exclusive outline of the methodological procedure, discourse analysis in general refers to a skill which can be learned and mastered only by doing—like riding a bicycle (Potter & Wetherell, 1987) or journalism Gee (2011a). In the case of MMDA some of the applied procedures can be more easily learned or copied from other research or from textbooks (especially the quantitative procedures), but the skill of noticing interesting discursive features or identifying discursive strategies cannot be easily translated into rules or processes.

7 Resources for Learning More about Discourse Analysis

There are numerous resources for gathering information about DA. In the following, I introduce a few from the different types and formats. Among the usual reading materials are the extensive books about the field like James Paul Gee's books (2011a, 2011b) 'An introduction of discourse analysis' and 'How to do discourse analysis. A toolkit' with tools and samples. Jorgensen and Phillips's book (2002) 'Discourse analysis as theory and method' is based on Laclau and Mouffe's approach, focusing on critical DA and discursive psychology. Norman Fairclough's book (2003) *Analysing discourse. Textual analysis for social research* provides a comprehensive overview of the main concepts of the field. In their book *Methods of text and discourse analysis* Stefan Titscher and his colleagues (2003) provide an overview of 12 text- and discourse analysis methods. Other widespread outline of the field can be found in the *Handbook of Discourse Analysis* book edited by Deborah Tannen and her colleagues (2015), in Margaret Wetherell and her colleagues' (2001) edited two volumes (*Discourse theory and practice* and *Discourse as Data*), as well as in Teun A. van Dijk's edited book (1997) *Discourse studies. A multidisciplinary introduction.*

Shorter versions of general introductions can be found in book-chapters, as in the case at Potter (2004), Tonkiss (2012), or Gill (2000).

Further important resources are the main journals of the field, namely *Discourse and Society, Discourse and Communication, Discourse Studies, Discourse Processes, Critical Discourse Studies* and *Discourse, Context & Media*.

There are a lot of online resources as well in different formats. Like a short summary about the linguistic approach from Richard Nordquist (www.thoughtco.com/discourse-analysis-or-da-1690462), or a definition of DA from Linguistic Society of Amerika (www.linguisticsociety.org/resource/discourse-analysis-what-speakers-do-conversation). Among the numerous videos a good example is a short video introduction about critical DA from Florian Schneider at www.politicseastasia.com/research/video-introduction-to-discourse-analysis/. Furthermore, online courses are available in the field of textual and discourse analysis, for example a corpus linguistics course with an outlook to corpus-based DA, at Futurelearn by Lancaster University (www.futurelearn.com/courses/corpus-linguistics).

Although mixed methodological discourse analysis (MMDA) is a new concept defined in this chapter, there are examples of mixed methodology in the field besides the ones introduced above. Among others, Allyson Holbrook and Sid Bourke (2004) applied mixed methods in analysing PhD processes in Australia, or Florian Schneider (2015) combined DA with social network analysis. Also, there is a methodological textbook about mixed methods in Applied Linguistics by Zoltán Dörnyei (2007).

NOTES

1. This chapter was prepared as part of the project 'The future of business education' funded by National Research, Development and Innovation Office, Hungary (FK127972).
2. It should be mentioned, that despite the intention of neutrality, the details and examples might mirror my own approach, who is primarily a sociologist with a social constructionist point of view.
3. Naturally, these three disciplines refer to a broader research area than could be introduced here, and their boundaries are not so clear and precise. I use this trio, despite its oversimplification, to picture the broad range of DA approaches with their main characteristics and simultaneously the variance of the field. It is based mainly on the approach in Wetherell, Taylor, & Yates (2001), but it corresponds with the three levels of DA in Grant, Harvey, Oswick & Putnam (2004).
4. We should mention that the best way of mixed research is what Onwuegbuzie and Leech (2005b) wrote as 'taking the Q out of Research'. In case of sampling, this means that we should put an end to the distinction of qualitative and quantitative sampling and we should treat sampling, as a phase of research with the necessary restrictions and possibilities derived from the research questions not as a choice based on a methodological paradigm.
5. One of the DA methods which is trying to address the problem of analyzing huge amount of texts with DA approach is corpus-based discourse analysis. The main advantage of corpus-based DA is its capability of examining a large amount of text (even millions of words) and identifying some of their basic discursive characteristics numerically. These kinds of results provide the bases of deeper (in a lot of cases even critical) discourse analysis by connecting contextual and textual data and enabling the researcher to also scrutinize smaller samples with qualitative DA. For examples see Biber et al., 2007; Upton & Cohen, 2009; Baker et al., 2008; Mulderrig, 2011.
6. To turning my textual information related to the 11 sub-discourses into quantitative data the applied software (in this case NVivo) was quite helpful. After I finalized the 11 clusters of the identified and coded social roles, I gathered and coded those textual parts which they contained. This way, with the help of the software, which contained the source of every text (here, the name of the company), I was able to collect the names of the companies, whose texts appeared in a given cluster. These company-lists provided the base for a dummy-code in SPSS, where '0' meant, that a given company does not mentioned any of the given cluster's social roles, and '1' meant that at least one social role of the given cluster appeared in the company introductory text. Accordingly, I had 11 variables (the 11 cluster), with these 0 and 1 codes at every company.
7. Sayago (2015) even moved forward, and operationalized the measurement of these levels, with further quantitative weights.
8. The researchers analyzed numerous other aspects of the discourse, with both quantitative and qualitative procedures (see Jimarkon and Todd 2013).
9. For a comparison of the 63 text-analysis, text-mining software see: www.predictiveanalyticstoday.com/top-software-for-text-analysis-text-mining-text-analytics/. For a technical description of MAXQDA in relation with mixed methods approaches see Kuckartz (2010).

REFERENCES

Austin, J. L. (1975). *How to do things with words*. Oxford, England: Oxford University Press.

Baker, P., Gabrielatos, C., Khosravinik, M., Krzyzanowski, M., Mcenery T., & Wodak, R. (2008). A useful methodological synergy? Combining critical discourse analysis and corpus linguistics to examine discourses of refugees and asylum seekers in the England press. *Discourse & Society, 19,* 273–306. doi:10.1177/0957926508088962

Biber, D., Connor, U., & Upton, T. (Eds.) (2007). *Discourse on the move: Using corpus analysis to describe discourse structure*. Amsterdam/Philadelphia: John Benjamins.

Bryman, A. (2012). *Social research methods* (4th ed.). Oxford, England: Oxford University Press.

Carver, T. (2004). Discourse analysis and the linguistic turn. *European Political Science, 2,* 50–53. doi:10.1057/eps.2002.46

Creswell, J. W. (2009). *Research design. Qualitative, quantitative, and mixed methods approaches.* London, England: Sage.

Creswell, J. W., & Plano-Clark, V. L. (2011). *Designing and conducting mixed methods research.* London, England: Sage.

Brown, G., & Yule, G. (2003). *Discourse analysis.* Cambridge, England: Cambridge University Press.

Dörnyei, Z. (2007). *Research methods in applied linguistics. Quantitative, qualitative, and mixed methodologies.* Oxford, England: Oxford University Press.

Edwards, D., & Potter, J. (1992). *Discursive psychology.* London, England: Sage.

Fairclough, N. (1998). *Language and power.* London, England: Longman.

Fairclough, N. (2003). *Analysing discourse. Textual analysis for social research.* London, England: Routledge.

Fairclough, N. (2013). *Critical discourse analysis: The critical study of language.* New York, NY: Routledge.

Frels, R. K., & Onwuegbuzie, A. J. (2013). Administering quantitative instruments with qualitative Interviews: A mixed research approach. *Journal of Counseling & Development 91*, 184–194. doi:10.1002/j.1556-6676.2013.00085.x

Gee, J. P. (2011a). *An introduction to discourse analysis. Theory and method*(3rd ed.). New York, NY: Routledge.

Gee, J. P. (2011b). *How to do discourse analysis. A toolkit.* New York, NY: Routledge.

Géring, Z. (2015a). Content versus discourse analysis. Examination of corporate social responsibility in companies' homepagetexts. In *Sage Research Methods Cases.* London, England: Sage Publications. Online ISBN: 9781446273050 doi:10.4135/9781446273050014556732

Géring, Z. (2015b). The online discourse of corporate social responsibility. What and how Hungarian medium-sized and large companies communicate about their corporate social role and responsibility. PhD thesis. Available at http://phd.lib.uni-corvinus.hu/883/3/Zsuzsanna_Gering_ten.pdf

Gill, R. (2000). Discourse analysis. In M. W. Bauer & G. Gaskell (Eds.), *Qualitative researching with text image and sound: A practical handbook* (pp. 172–190). London, England: Sage.

Grant, D., Hardy, C., Oswick, C., & Putnam, L. L. (2004). Introduction: Organizational Discourse: Exploring the Field. In D. Grant, C. Hardy, C. Oswick, & L. Putnam (Eds.), *The Sage handbook of organizational discourse* (pp. 1–36) London, England: Sage.

Hall, S. (2001). Foucault: Power, knowledge, and discourse. In Wetherell, M., Taylor, S., & Yates, S. J. (Eds.) *Discourse theory and practice* (pp. 72–80). London, England: Sage.

Hesse-Biber, S. N. (2010). *Mixed methods research: Merging theory with practice* New York, NY: The Guilford Press.

Holbrook, A., & Bourke, S. (2004). An investigation of PhD examination outcome in Australia using a mixed method approach. *Australian Journal of Educational & Developmental Psychology, 4*, 153–169. Available at https://files.eric.ed.gov/fulltext/EJ815560.pdf

Jimarkon, P., & Todd, R. W. (2011). *Using quantitative methods as a framework for qualitative analysis. Proceedings of the International Conference on Doing Research in Applied Linguistics* (pp. 45–51). April 21–22, 2011. Bangkok, Thailand: King Mongkut's University of Technology Thonburi.

Jimarkon, P., & Todd, R. W. (2013). Red or yellow, peace or war. Agonism and antagonism in online discussion during the 2010 political unrest in Thailand. In A. De Rycker & Z. Mohd Don (Eds.), *Discourse and crisis: Critical perspectives* (pp. 301–322). Amsterdam, Netherlands: John Benjamins Publishing Company.

Johnson, R. B., Onwuegbuzie, A. J., de Waal, C., Stefurak, T., & Hildebrand, D. (2017). Unpacking pragmatism for mixed methods research: The philosophies of Peirce, James, Dewey, and Rorty. In D. Wyse, N. Selwyn, E. Smith, & L. Suter (Eds.), *The BERA/Sage handbook of educational research* (pp. 259–279). London, England: Sage.

Johnson, R. B., de Waal, C., Stefurak, T., & Hildebrand, D. (2017). Understanding the philosophical positions of classical and neopragmatists for mixed methods research. *Kölner Zeitschrift für Soziologie und Sozialpsychologie, 69*, 63–86. doi:10.1007/s11577-017-0452-3

Jorgensen, M. W., & Phillips, L. J. (2002). *Discourse analysis as theory and method.* London, England: Sage.

Kress, G. (2001). From Saussure to critical socio-linguistics: The turn towards a social view of language. In M. Wetherell, S. Taylor, & S. J. Yates (Eds.), *Discourse theory and practice* (pp. 29–38) London, England: Sage.

Kuckartz, U. (2010). Realizing mixed-methods approaches with MAXQDA. Philipps-Universität, Marburg. Available at www.maxqda.de/download/MixMethMAXQDA-Nov01-2010.pdf

Leech, N., & Onwuegbuzie, A. J. (2008). Qualitative data analysis: A compendium of techniques and a framework for selection for school psychology research and beyond. *School Psychology Quarterly, 23*, 587–624. doi:10.1037/1045-3830.23.4.587

Mulderrig, J. (2011) Manufacturing consent: A corpus-based critical discourse analysis of New Labour's educational governance. *Educational Philosophy and Theory, 43*, 562–578. doi:10.1111/j.1469-5812.2010.00723.x

Mustafa-Awad, Z., & Kirner-Ludwig, M. (2017). Arab women in news headlines during the Arab Spring: Image and perception in Germany. *Discourse & Communication 11*, 515–538. doi:10.1177/1750481317714114

Onwuegbuzie, A. J., & Leech, N. L. (2005a). On becoming a pragmatic researcher: The importance of combining quantitative and qualitative research methodologies. *International Journal of Social Research Methodology, 8*, 375–387. doi:10.1080/13645570500402447

Onwuegbuzie, A. J., & Leech, N. L. (2005b). Taking the "Q" out of research: Teaching research methodology courses without the divide between quantitative and qualitative paradigms. *Quality & Quantity 39*, 267–296. doi:10.1007/s11135-004-1670-0

Parker, I. (Ed.) (2002). *Critical discursive psychology.* London, England: Palgrave McMillan.

Potter, J. (2004). Discourse analysis. In M. Hardy & A. Bryman (Eds.), *Handbook of data analysis* (pp. 607–624). London, England: Sage.

Potter, J., & Wetherell, M. (1987). *Discourse and social psychology. Beyond attitudes and behaviour.* London, England: Sage.

Sayago, S. (2015). The construction of qualitative and quantitative data using discourse analysis as a research technique. *Quality & Quantity, 49*, 727–737. doi:10.1007/s11135-014-0020-0

Schneider, F. (2015). China's info-web: How Beijing governs online political communication about Japan. *New Media and Society*, *18*, 2664–2684. doi:10.1177/1461444815600379

Schriffin, D. (2002). *Approaches to discourse*. Oxford, England: Blackwell.

Tannen, D., Hamilton, H. E., & Schiffrin, D. (2015). *The handbook of discourse analysis*. Oxford: John Wiley & Sons.

Tashakkori, A., & Teddlie, C. (Eds.) (2010). *Handbook of mixed methods in social & behavioral research* (2nd ed.). London, England: Sage.

Taylor, S. (2001). Locating and conducting discourse analytic research. In M. Wetherell, S. Taylor & S. J. Yates (Eds.), *Discourse as a data: A guide for analysis* (pp. 5–48). London, England: Sage.

Teddlie, C., & Tashakkori, A. (Eds.) (2009). *Foundations of mixed methods research: Integrating quantitative and qualitative approaches in the social and behavioral sciences*. London, England: Sage.

Titscher, S., Meyer, M., Wodak, R., & Vetter, E (2003). *Methods of text and discourse analysis*. London, England: Sage.

Tonkiss, F. (2012). Discourse analysis. In C. Seale (Ed.), *Researching society and culture* (3rd ed., pp. 405–419). London, England: Sage.

Upton, T. A., & Cohen, M. A. (2009) An approach to corpus-based discourse analysis: The move analysis as example. *Discourse Studies*, *11*, 585–625. doi:10.1177/1461445609341006

Van Dijk, T. A. (Ed.) (1997). *Discourse studies. A multidisciplinary introduction*. London, England: Sage.

Wetherell, M., Taylor, S., & Yates, S. J. (Eds.) (2001). *Discourse theory and practice*. London, England: Sage.

Wodak, R. (2015). *The politics of fear—what right-wing populist discourses mean*. London, England: Sage.

Wodak, R., & Chilton, P. (Eds.) (2005). *A new agenda in (critical) discourse analysis: Theory, methodology and interdisciplinarity* (Vol. 13). Amsterdam, Netherlands: John Benjamins Publishing.

Wodak, R., & Meyer, M. (Eds.) (2002). *Methods of critical discourse analysis*. London, England: Sage.

Part III

"Inherently" Mixed Analysis Approaches

16

Ethnographic Decision Models with Qualitative Data: A Thoroughly Mixed Method[1]

Gery W. Ryan and H. Russell Bernard

1 Introduction: Definition

Ethnographic decision models (EDMs) are a multimethod approach that predicts episodic behaviors, like choosing among alternative treatments during illness (Ryan and Martinez 1996) or deciding whether to evacuate during a hurricane (Gladwin et al. 2001). EDMs are based on a deep understanding of the cultural rules and nuances that people use to make decisions. As an approach, EDM consists of an ordered, rigorous set of data collection and analysis techniques. To start, researchers use semi-structured interviews to collect qualitative data on people's decision-making process and then use qualitative methods to identify decision criteria. Next, researchers develop and administer a survey instrument to collect more structured—i.e., quantitative—data on people's actual choices and the circumstances under which they made those choices. These survey data are used to build an ethnographically grounded decision model that anticipates or accounts for the decision outcomes. Constructing the initial model can be done by building from one case to another—a thoroughly qualitative approach—or it can be done using machine learning—a quantitatively intensive approach (Murthy 1998; Zhang 2016). Finally, researchers test the accuracy of the model quantitatively, with a new sample, by estimating the degree to which it predicts the reported actual outcomes at or better than chance and qualitatively by testing its content validity (e.g., to what degree does the model conform to how participants describe their own decision processes). Because EDM inherently relies on both qualitative and quantitative approaches, it is classified in this book as an inherently mixed analysis approach.

2 When Use of EDMs Is Appropriate in Mixed Methods Research (MMR)

EDMs are used when a researcher wants to understand individual decision-making processes leading to outcomes of interest. Any recurring decision—to buy or not buy a computer; to use (or demand the use of) a condom during sex; to stay home sick from work or not—can be modeled with the EDM method. As with any binary outcome, yes–no decisions can be modeled and tested with logistic regression and there are computer programs for modeling decisions, but crucially, ethnographic decision models illuminate *how choices are made from the perspective of those making those choices*. To generate and test EDMs, researchers use a multi-staged approach to combine many of the exploratory data collection and preliminary model building techniques used in grounded theory (Corbin and Strauss 2015; Glaser and Strauss 1967) with the confirmatory and validating techniques used in classic content analysis (Krippendorf 2013). Typically, EDMs are built and tested on small, ethnographic samples of interviews with 20–60 people with one sample being used to build the model and another independent sample used to test the model. Even with such small samples, EDMs typically predict 80%–90% of all outcomes and do better than what would be predicted by chance.

Overall, EDMs predict aggregate, group decision making, but with the appropriate ethnographic data, EDMs can also tell us about the rationales behind the 10%–20% of errors in a model. (More on this later.)

Ethnographic decision trees have a long history in the social sciences. Early EDMs were used to examine how farmers decided what to plant (Barlett 1980; Gladwin 1976, 1983, 1989b); how fish sellers set prices (Quinn 1978), how fisherman decided where to fish (Gatewood 1983); and how laypeople decided what to do when they or their children get sick (Mathews and Hill 1990; Young 1980). For more early examples, see Gladwin (1989a), Hill (1998), and Bernard et al. (2017).

The method of ethnographic decision tree modeling was made accessible in a landmark book by Christina Gladwin (1989a). Since then, the method has been applied to many kinds of choices. In addition to studies of illness decisions (Montbriand 1995; Ryan and Martínez 1996; Weller et al. 1997), researchers have used EDMs to explain: whether Navajo mothers breast-feed or use formula (Bauer and Wright 1996); when farmers in New Zealand use organic or conventional agricultural methods (Fairweather 1999); under what circumstances Houston's intravenous drug users decide to share needles or not (Johnson and Williams 1993); the decision to evacuate or not in the face of hurricanes (Gladwin et al. 2001); and how clinicians make outpatient referrals for patients with substance abuse (Breslin et al. 2000).

More recently, EDMs have been used to describe whether or not to use a telecenter for entrepreneurial endeavors in Jamaica (Bailey and Ngwenyama 2013); how injured farmworkers make treatment timing choices (Thierry et al. 2015); whether women in rural Bangladesh give birth at a medical facility or at home (Edmonds 2010); and farmers' decisions in Uzbekistan to adopt agroforestry (Djalilov et al. 2016).

3 Technical Outline of EDMs for MMR: How to Build EDMs

Christina Gladwin (1989a) laid out five steps for building and testing EDMs: (1) select a specific behavioral choice to model; (2) elicit decision criteria from a purposive or convenience sample of respondents; (3) elaborate and verify the decision criteria on a purposive, heterogeneous sample of informants; (4) use the ethnographic data from Step 1 and the survey data from Step 2 to build a hierarchical decision model; and finally, (5) test the model on an independent and, if possible, representative sample from the same population. We (Ryan and Bernard 2006) added a sixth step in our study of people's decisions to recycle (or not) the last aluminum beverage can they had in their hand: (6) validate the model with responses from people about why they acted as they did. (For other clear descriptions of the steps, see Ryan and Martínez [1996], Hill [1998], and Beck [2005].)

Step 1 Selecting a Behavioral Choice to Investigate

The first step to building EMDs is for the researcher to identify the key decision to be explored and what alternatives are available. Fort (2011), for example, modeled whether people living in a protected forest reserve in southern Malawi decided to produce charcoal, an illegal livelihood activity; and Mwangi and Brown (2015) used the EDM approach to understand whether or not small and medium enterprises in Kenya decided to register for mobile banking services.

EDMs are not limited, however, to binary decisions. EDMs can also be used to predict choices among different alternatives. Oh and Park (2004) built models to predict whether cancer patients used hospital-only treatments or hospital-plus-alternative therapies. In a classic study, Young and Garro (1994) modeled how laypeople in a small rural town in Mexico decided among four treatment modalities: home treatments, treatment by folk curers (i.e., *curanderas*), treatment by local, unlicensed biomedical practitioners (i.e., *practicantes*), and treatment by a certified doctor.

Nor are EDMs limited to static descriptions. Following the lead of Young and Garro (1994), Ryan and Martínez (1996) modeled which of seven treatment alternatives (teas, carbonated beverages, rice water, sugar–salt solutions [SSS], pills, physical manipulations, and Western medical personnel) people living in San José, Mexico, used when their children had diarrhea. In addition to predicting whether a mother would use or not use each of treatment modalities, the Ryan–Martínez model also predicted which treatments mothers would use first, second, third, and fourth. In another example, Keshavarz and Karami (2014) built and tested three separate models to predict which of multiple coping mechanisms farmers in India would use when responding to initial, middle, and end stages of a prolonged drought.

Step 2 Eliciting the Decision Criteria

The second step is to identify the decision criteria that might influence individual choices. The objective is to elicit as many reasons as possible for why people make the choices that they do and to begin to understand *how* the criteria interact with each other to influence choices. Success in this step is determined by both the data elicitation techniques used as well as by who is selected to be interviewed.

There is no correct way to elicit decision criteria. Instead, researchers have used a variety of techniques, including informal interviews (Young and Garro 1994), in-depth ethnographic interviews (Shuk et al. 2012), more formal semi-structured interviews (Beck 2000), free listing tasks (Weller et al. 2016), paired comparisons (Keshavarz and Karami 2014 Young and Garro 1994), hypothetical scenarios (Roberts 2000), and participant observation (Bailey and Ngwenyama 2013; Beck 2000). Some elicitation protocols emphasize asking informants hypothetical questions such as "Why do people do or not do X?" while others ask about real past events, such as "The last time you had to choose between X and Y, what did you do and why?"

Most researchers use combinations of techniques to complement the strengths and offset the weaknesses of each particular method. For example, in Young and Garro's (1994) study in Mexico, they began with ethnographic fieldwork and had opportunities to observe how illness episodes unfolded. Then, in addition to informal talks and interviews, they used structured interview protocols including frame substitution, where they asked about the relationships between a set of propositions (Can you use X to cure A? Can you use X to cure B?) and a set of illnesses. They also used paired comparisons where they asked informants to compare pairs of treatment alternatives to each other (Is A better than B for curing X? For curing Y?).

From this combination of elicitation techniques, Young and Garro identified four criteria that consistently arose as important considerations in the choice of treatment: (1) illness gravity; (2) whether an appropriate home remedy was known; (3) faith in the effectiveness of the treatment for a given illness; and (4) expense of treatment and the availability of resources. For more on frame substitution and paired comparison techniques, see Weller and Romney (1988) and Borgatti (1994, 1999). For essential interviewing tips, see Spradley (1979), Becker (2008), and Bernard (2017).

To understand how Indian farmers coped with drought, Keshavarz and Karami (2014) conducted in-depth ethnographic interviews. They asked farmers to tell them how they had responded to the recent drought and recorded what the farmers did and the order in which they did it during the initial, middle, and end stages of the drought. To ensure that they didn't miss anything, they used a checklist of the drought management strategies they had compiled earlier to identify behaviors the farmers might have forgotten to mention. After collecting all the behaviors, they asked the farmers to explain why they decided to use particular strategies. They also used the paired comparison technique and asked under what circumstances the farmers would prefer one drought management strategy over another.

To elicit decision criteria from clinicians about whether to refer a patient to a substance abuse program, Breslin et al. (2000) conducted semi-structured interviews, but used a combination of hypothetical and real scenarios. They began by asking participants to explain in general the guidelines they use to make these choices. Next, they asked participants to think about a patient that they had recently referred to Program A and to describe (without identifying the patient) why they decided this particular program was appropriate. Then they asked participants to think about a patient that they had recently referred to Program B and to describe the factors that lead to that referral decision.

To identify how first-degree relatives of melanoma survivors made decisions about sun-protection behaviors, Shuk et al. (2012) conducted in-home, ethnographic interviews with 25 participants. In addition to observing the setting in which participants were making decisions, interviewers also asked participants to recall two separate recent sun-exposure periods when they were outdoors for an hour or more. For each sun-exposure event, they asked participants to report on whether they (1) used sunscreen; (2) sought shade; (3) put on a hat; and (4) used sun-protective clothing. They also asked participants to describe the event, including the outdoor activity and setting, who else was present, weather conditions, time of day, and the length of time they spent outdoors. Next, they asked informants for the reasons they used sun protection and reasons they did not use sun protection. Finally, they asked each person to answer a set of demographic questions. They used the information from the interviews to construct four meta decision-tree models (one for each sun-protection behavior).

Data collection at this point can also be broken into stages. Roberts (2000), for example, used a two-stage approach to elicit the factors that elder Jewish women in North Carolina who lived independently considered most significant when considering end-of-life decisions. Roberts first conducted unstructured and semi-structured qualitative interviews with a convenience sample of adults in their 50s. From these interviews, she identified six key conditions associated with end-of-life choices: (1) differing degrees of pain; (2) whether there was a cure for the disease; (3) reliance on others; (4) mental abilities; (5) financial burden worries; and (6) alternative living situations. She then used combinations of conditions to develop seven hypothetical scenarios that would be presented to older women. For instance, one scenario described a person living "in a nursing home with severe loss of intellectual functions and memory (i.e., Alzheimer's Disease) thus were totally reliant on others with no known cure with fairly-well controlled pain and no worry about being a financial burden" (Roberts 2000: 130).

In the second stage, Roberts conducted semi-structured interviews with a new sample of 13 Jewish women—nine women in their 50s, four women in their 70s, and one woman in her 90s. For each of the seven scenarios she had identified in the first stage, Roberts asked these 13 women whether they would (1) use aggressive treatment and life support measures; (2) not use aggressive treatment and life support measures (passive euthanasia); or (3) terminate one's life (active euthanasia). Roberts recorded each nominal response. Each scenario generated a lot of discussion (two–four hours), which Roberts audio-taped and transcribed verbatim. From these interviews, Roberts used the quantitative data from the responses to the scenarios, as well as the qualitative data from the discussions to identify pain and financial worries as being the most important conditions affecting whether women would choose euthanasia.

4 Empirical Demonstration of EDMs for MMR

For our study of whether to recycle cans, we asked 21 informants in North Dakota and Florida the following: (1) Think about the last time you had a can of something to drink in your hand-soda, juice, water, beer, whatever. When was that? (2) What did you do with the can when you were done? And (3) Why did you [didn't you] recycle? The first question generated a qualitative answer that we could dichotomize into "Recycled" or "Didn't Recycle." The second question generated a response that we could quantify into "Number of Days Ago." And the last question usually generated a short qualitative justification for their behavior. Recent literature on non-probability sampling shows that 20–60 knowledgeable people are enough to uncover and understand core themes for a topic (Francis et al. 2010; Fugard and Potts 2015; Guest et al. 2006, 2017; Hagaman and Wutich 2017; Mason 2010; Morgan et al. 2002; Morse 1989; Sandelowski 1995; Weller et al. 2018).

We reached saturation (few new rationales mentioned for recycling or not). Table 16.1 shows the list of 27 reasons we retrieved for recycling and the 13 we retrieved for not cycling. Some people surely reported having recycled when they hadn't, but this doesn't affect the building of a preliminary model since good ethnographic informants know about the target behavior and can knowledgeably respond to questions about their own behavior (in this case, getting rid of an empty beverage can) and about their reasons for their behavior. The bottom line on sampling, then, is to maximize diversity (age, sex, ethnicity, education, area of the country, occupation) to elicit as wide a range of decision criteria as possible.

While convenience and purposive samples are common in the making of EDMs, Weller et al. (2016) were able to use the equivalent of a case-control comparison design to understand why some residents of Galveston, Texas, evacuated while others stayed behind during Hurricane Ike in 2008. Weller et al. began by identifying a sample of people from across the city who had evacuated. For each person interviewed, they matched them with a neighbor who did not evacuate. They chose the match-design so that "socioeconomic status and property damage would be distributed similarly in the two groups to allow a clearer focus on the rationale for evacuation." The researchers then conducted in-depth qualitative interviews, with open-ended questions, to elicit reasons, motives, and beliefs about evacuation, including why someone did or did not comply with evacuation orders, what they might do next time and why, and what they would like others to know who might be given an evacuation order in the future. They were careful to ask everyone the same questions. This allowed them to quantitatively compare the relative importance of all reasons in the decision-making process.

Step 3 Collecting Data for a Preliminary Model

The next step is to use the data from Step 2 to develop a structured elicitation instrument—one that asks everyone the same set of questions—and use these data to build a preliminary model of the behavior. Here again, yes/no questions produce data that make building a model easier. Ordering is also important. Ask about the behavior first—the thing you are trying to predict—then ask people to explain why they did what they did, and finally, ask about the conditions you wish to consider. In our (2006) study of recycling, we asked a purposive sample of 70 people 31 questions derived from Table 16.1. The 31 questions are shown in Table 16.2. Note that some of the questions generate dichotomous answers (e.g., yes, no); others generate nominal or qualitative response (e.g., at home, at work, etc.); and others generate quantitative responses (e.g., not at all, a little, some, a lot).

Why a sample of 70 at this stage? From our experience, we anticipated that our final decision model—pictured as a branching, bifurcating tree diagrams below, in Figure 16.1—would be at least three levels deep. To ensure that each of the decision's endpoints would contain at least five people, the minimum sample size would be $5*2^{(\text{\# of Levels})}$, or $5*2^3 = 40$. Perfect bifurcation at each decision rarely happens, so we try to more-or-less double the minimum sample size to ensure that we wind up some cases at each endpoint, and hence, our 70 survey cases for building the model.

Some researchers use vignettes at this stage. Roberts (2000) wanted to model what an older Jewish woman would want to happen if she had an incurable illness and couldn't communicate. She recruited 91 women who identified as Reform Jews and 102 who identified as Conservative Jews, two of the main sects of American Judaism. Based on her initial elicitation interviews, Roberts developed ten hypothetical scenarios. For example, in the first scenario, Roberts asked, consider a situation where:

> You are in a coma and the doctors have said you are brain dead.
> You have no money left, all your financial resources have been exhausted and your only way to pay is through public benefits (Medicaid) and/or charity.
> Which choice would you make?
>
> 1. Use aggressive treatments and life supports to stay alive;
> 2. Not use aggressive treatments and no life supports to stay alive; or
> 3. Choose to terminate your life. (Roberts 2000: 41)

In the second scenario, Roberts asked: Consider a slightly different scenario where:

> You are in a coma and the doctors have said you are brain dead.
> There are enough funds to cover any of your needs, either through your own funds and/or your families' funds.
> Which choice would you make?
>
> 1. Use aggressive treatments and life supports to stay alive;

TABLE 16.1

Reasons for Recycling or not Recycling from 21 Informants

1. It's wasteful to just throw it away.	1. I was traveling and I had no place to recycle it.
2. The city has a recycling program. The garbage man picks it up.	2. Bins aren't around. I didn't have a recycling bin. There aren't enough recycling bins available.
3. To help save the environment.	3. There's no recycling program where I live. No city recycling program
4. Recycling bins are conveniently located.	4. Because I don't have big blue.
5. That's what big blue is for.	5. I didn't think about it.
6. My kid made a pact with a TV club so she now recycles.	6. I gave it to kids who turn it in for money.
7. I'm concerned about the environment.	7. Forgot.
8. It's environmentally sound.	8. Recycling is not available to me.
9. Land is not a renewable resource.	9. Laziness.
10. I save cans to get money for them.	10. The recycling bin was not conveniently located.
11. The people I'm staying with recycle, so I do, too.	11. Because I have to separate out cans from my garbage and that's a problem.
12. The bins were around.	12. Lack of education.
13. It's useful and can be used again.	13. I don't have enough time.
14. To keep the environment clean.	
15. Because of habit; we usually put it in big blue.	
16. Because I'm environmentally conscious.	
17. To preserve the environment for my kids.	
18. It's not biodegradable.	
19. It's no good in the landfill.	
20. Because it's just good to recycle.	
21. It's easy to do.	
22. Because it's the right thing to do.	
23. Because it's the big thing to do these days.	
24. Because someone told me to.	
25. We shouldn't cover the land up with garbage.	
26. To buy more beer.	
27. Because if you don't you have to pay a fee.	

Ethnographic Decision Models

2. Not use aggressive treatments and no life supports to stay alive; or
3. Choose to terminate your life. (Roberts 2000: 41)

By examining how women's choices varied across the ten scenarios, Roberts concluded that in situations where a woman could no longer speak for herself and had little medical hope for recovery, pain was a greater influence than finances in end-of-life decisions.

Step 4 Building the Model

Figure 16.1 shows our preliminary model for recycling when people decide to recycle or throw away the last aluminum can they had in their hand. This step, described by Gladwin (1989a), takes a lot of trial and error. It involves taking each question from the survey in Step 3 and asking the following, for each one: If we could ask only this question, how many errors (that is, outcomes that are not predicted by the model) would result. For our study of whether people recycled the last aluminum beverage can they had in their hands, it turned out that question 7a in Table 16.2 (Were you at home at the time?) produced the fewest errors. That question became the first branch of our proposed model.

As you can see in Figure 16.1, guessing that everyone at home recycled and that everyone not at home did not recycle produces six errors (the four errors the model correctly predicts that people don't recycle and the two errors the model erroneously predicts that people will recycle) on the left-hand branch. On the right-hand branch, the model produces 11 errors (the 7 + 2 = 9 errors where the model correctly predicts people will recycle and the 1 + 1 = 2 errors where the model erroneously predicts that people don't recycle). Combined, this is a total of 17 errors (6 + 11) and an accuracy rate of 53 out of 70 cases, or 76%. As you can also see, building models involves selecting different combinations of decision criteria (a qualitative process) and checking these combinations for accuracy (a quantitative process).

What this means is that by asking just one question (Were you home when you had that last can in your hand?) we can predict (for this sample) correctly 76% of the time. We try to improve on this by repeating the process and asking: What's the best predictor of recycling for each of the two branches of the model?

Of the 27 informants who were at home, the best predictor of who did or who did not recycle was to ask question 26 in Table 16.2: Do you recycle any materials besides cans? As you can see in Figure 16.1, of the 23 people who said they recycled other products, the model correctly predicts that 21 people (91.3%) recycled the last can they had in their hand and erroneously predicts that two people recycled when they didn't. And conversely, of the four people who said they didn't recycle other products, the model correctly predicts that all four (100%) didn't recycle. So, the rule here is this: For those at home who recycle other products, guess "recycled the can"; otherwise guess "didn't recycle the can." This results in just two errors out of 27 cases, or 92.6% correct.

On the right-hand branch of the model, just guessing that nobody recycled produced 32 out of 43 correct answers, or 74.4% correct. (Note, to calculate the total correct answers, we counted all the cases where the model correctly predicted that people didn't recycle (11 + 18 = 29), plus all the cases that the model erroneously predicted that people would recycle (1 + 2 = 3).) This improves to 88.4% correct by distinguishing whether those not at home were at work or elsewhere, and then asking: "Was a recycling bin conveniently located nearby?"

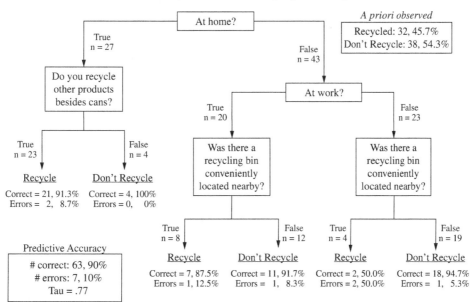

FIGURE 16.1 Decision to recycle cans (ethnographic sample, N=70).

TABLE 16.2

Questions Asked in the Recycling Study

After asking about the last can and the reasons for recycling, ask each of the following:
1. Does your city have a recycling program?
2. Can you return aluminum cans for redemption in your town or city?
3. Did you live in a house or apartment?
4. If you live in a house, is there a special pickup for recycled materials (e.g., big blue)?
5. Are there special bins for recycled materials in your apartment building etc.?
6. Are there recycling bins for cans where you work?
7. The last time you drank from an aluminum can were you:
   7a. at home?
   7b. at work?
   7c. driving in your car?
   7d. inside or outside?
   7e. at someone else's house?
8. The last time you drank from an aluminum can did you get the can from a vending machine?
9. The last time you drank from an aluminum can was there a recycling bin conveniently located nearby?
10. The last time you drank from an aluminum can were you busy?
11. The last time you drank from an aluminum can were there other people around when you finished your drink?
12. If so, do these people usually recycle cans?
13. If so, did anyone suggest that you recycle the can?
14. Do you have children?
15. Do you habitually recycle material such as cans, newspapers, and plastics at home?
16. Do you habitually recycle material such as cans, newspapers, and plastics at work?
17. Do you consider yourself environmentally conscious (not at all, a little, some, a lot)?
18. How much do you think that recycling helps to save the environment (not at all, a little, some, a lot)?
19. How much are you concerned about the environment (not at all, a little, some, a lot)?
20. How much do you think recycling helps to keep the environment clean (not at all, a little, some, a lot)?
21. How important is it for you to preserve the environment for children (not at all, a little, some, a lot)?
22. Do you think it's wasteful to throw away an aluminum can?
23. Do you think that there is a lot of social pressure nowadays to recycle?
24. Do you think that cans are bad for landfills?
25. Do you think that recycling aluminum cans is useful?
26. Do you recycle any materials besides cans?
27. If so, what other materials do you recycle?

Note: Questions 1–16 and questions 22–26 were answered Yes or No. Questions 7–11 are expansions of the question "Where were you when you had that used beverage can in your hand?" into five binary questions. This ensures that all informants are given the same set of cues as the data are collected to build the preliminary model. Questions 17–21 produced ordinal data (not at all, a little, some, a lot). Question 27 produced text.

First, as shown in Figure 16.1, when people were at work and bins were nearby, seven of the eight respondents who were at work recycled (the eight includes the seven people who the model correctly predicted would recycle and the one person the model erroneously predicted didn't recycle). When people were at work and bins were unavailable, 11 of the 12 respondents said that they didn't recycle (the 12 includes the 11 people who the model correctly predicted didn't recycle and the one person the model erroneously predicted didn't recycle). This branch of the model gets 18 out of 20, or 90% correct. Second, among the 23 respondents who were neither at home nor at work, asking if a recycling bin was nearby produces a model with just three errors, or 87% correct. Overall, on the right-hand branch, the model produces five errors (88.4% correct), and the accuracy of the complete model (both left- and right-hand branches) is 63 right out of 70, or 90%.

So overall, how did we do? In Figure 16.1, the box labeled "a priori observed," refers to the how many people reported recycling (32 out of 70 or 45.7%) and how many people reported not recycling (38 out of 70 or 54.3%). If this was all we knew and we had to guess whether a can gets recycled or not, then, without any information about the circumstances (being at home, having a recycling bin nearby, etc.), our best guess on any individual case would have been that people didn't recycle and we would have been correct 54.3% of the time and wrong 45.7% of the time. We refer to this as "a priori" because this tells us how accurate we would be before we built our model. But if we use the model described here, then we do much better. In fact, the model predicts 77% better than expected by chance (and is indicated by Klecka's tau = .77 in Figure 16.1. (See Klecka 1980: 50–51 for details on how to calculate this statistic.)

As it happens, if the only criterion for success is reducing the number of errors to a minimum, the model in Figure 16.1 is actually more complicated than it needs to be. As Figure 16.2 shows, we can collapse the two paths "At Work?" and "Not at Work?" without any loss of predictive power—it's the same 90% for the models in both Figure 16.1 and Figure 16.2. The reason is this: Most of the predictive power on the right side of the model is based on a bin being nearby. The extra criterion in the model, however (at work–not at work in Figure 16.1), with its two extra paths, shows that people at work recycle more than do those who are neither at home nor at work—40% (7 + 1 = 8 of 20), compared to 13% (2 + 1 = 3 of 23). The extra criterion thus provides information on the size and location of the problem—information that suggests where to put recycling bins if we don't have an unlimited supply of them.

Step 5 Testing the Model on an Independent Sample

An accuracy rate of 90% may seem high, but it's hardly a surprise when a model accounts for the data on which it is built. All we are in doing in Figure 16.1 is representing graphically what people told us they did. Models, however, are tentative theories, or hypotheses. Their validity doesn't depend on how they are derived but on how well they stand up to tests on an independent sample of people who were not involved in building the model in the first place. Model confirmation on independent samples is typically done in EDM studies to increase their internal and external validity.

Strong agreement between two or more, independently derived EDMs is similar to repeating a laboratory experiment in terms of reliability and internal validity. For example, assume another group of independent researchers followed the process describe above but collected data from different people at each step. If after all the steps and decisions the

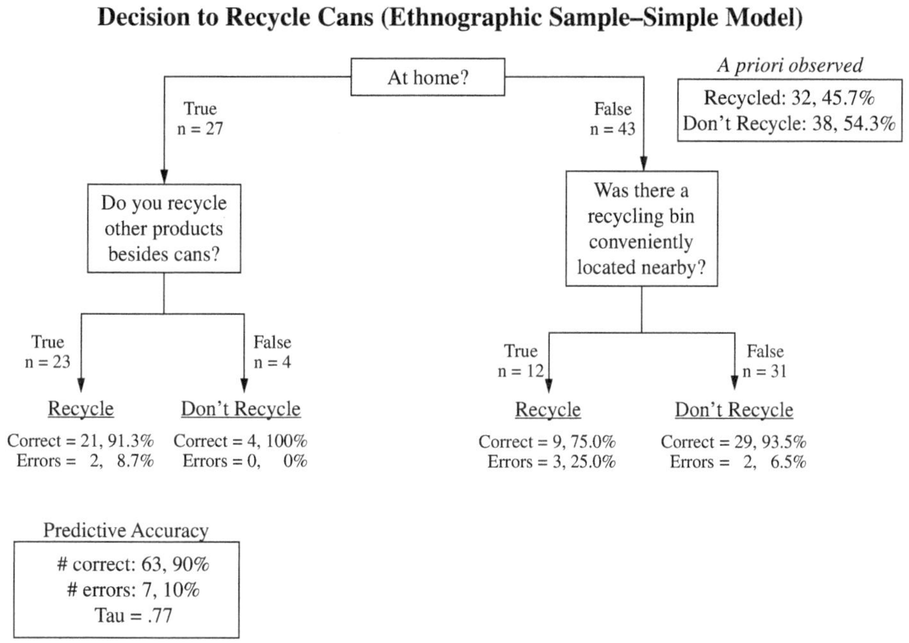

Decision to Recycle Cans (Ethnographic Sample–Simple Model)

```
                              At home?
                    True                  False
                    n = 27                n = 43
                      |                     |
         Do you recycle              Was there a
         other products              recycling bin
         besides cans?               conveniently
                                     located nearby?
      True        False           True         False
      n = 23      n = 4           n = 12       n = 31
        |          |                |            |
     Recycle  Don't Recycle      Recycle    Don't Recycle
  Correct = 21, 91.3%  Correct = 4, 100%   Correct = 9, 75.0%   Correct = 29, 93.5%
  Errors  =  2,  8.7%  Errors  = 0,   0%   Errors  = 3, 25.0%   Errors  =  2,  6.5%
```

A priori observed
Recycled: 32, 45.7%
Don't Recycle: 38, 54.3%

Predictive Accuracy
# correct: 63, 90%
# errors: 7, 10%
Tau = .77

FIGURE 16.2 Decision to recycle cans—simplified model (ethnographic sample, N=70).

other research team made, the prediction based on their data resulted in a model that resembled ours, we would have a lot of confidence that the results were relatively robust and unlikely to be spurious. Still, as with all ethnographically derived findings, there is doubt about external validity—whether the results can be generalized to a larger population (Weller et al. 1997). This is just another reason why it is so important to collect detailed information about the characteristics of your participants.

To see how our model EDM did on a larger population, we tested it on a representative, national phone survey of 386 respondents in the United States. The results are in Figure 16.3.

Comparing Figures 16.1 and 16.3, there are many differences in the distribution of answers. For the ethnographic model, we interviewed people wherever we could find them, while for the national survey, we called people at home. Sure enough, 58% of the national respondents said they were at home when they had that last beverage can in their hand, compared to only 39% of our ethnographic informants.

And still, the ethnographic model held up well in a national test. Of the 173 people who were at home and who also said they recycled other products besides cans, 160 (93%) recalled recycling the can, compared to 91% in the ethnographic sample. Of the 55 people at home who reported not recycling other products besides cans, 45 (82%) recalled not recycling the can, compared to 100% for the ethnographic sample. And the overall accuracy of the national model is 85%, compared to 90% for the ethnographic model.

What this means is that there is likely to be a strong consensus, across the United States, about the decision to recycle aluminum beverage cans. We had a glimpse of this when we got the same model in North Dakota and Florida, but of course, it didn't have to turn out that way. Multiple ethnographically derived models on small samples could easily turn up cultural or regional differences for any given decision—like when to take a sick child to the doctor or when to report child abuse.

Just as with the ethnographic model, adding the question in the national model about where the behavior took place (at work vs. at home) had no effect on prediction power. It did, however, corroborate the policy-relevant information produced in the ethnographic model regarding where to put scarce resources if we want to increase recycling behavior. Of the 158 people in the national sample who said they were not at home when they had that last beverage can in their hands, 20% (20 + 1 = 21 out of 104 in Figure 16.3) said they didn't recycle if they also said they were at work.

By contrast, 50% (25 + 2 = 27 out of 54 in Figure 16.3) of the not-home people said they didn't recycle if they also said they were not at work. It may be tempting to try to reduce the 50% error rate by further modifying the model, but the not-home/not-at-work condition covers people at who are football games, or driving on the freeway, or visiting other people's houses, or window shopping. With so many conditions, and limited resources with which to put out recycling bins, it is going to be tough to have an impact on that 50% error rate. In the short term, it's easier to imagine incentives for getting employers to put out those bins.

Step 6 Assessing the Validity of Ethnographic Decision Models

Thus far, we have focused on the quantitative measure of model error rate. We can take the process one step further and bring qualitative information into assessing the model's validity.

We asked 33 of our ethnographic informants to tell us, in their own words, why they recycled, before we asked systematically about the decision-criteria. For these informants, we examined the fit between their justifications of their choice to recycle or not and the model's predictions. We did this by

Decision to Recycle Cans (National Sample)

A priori observed
Recycled: 277, 71.8%
Don't Recycle: 109, 28.2%

```
                              At home?
              True                          False
              n = 228                       n = 158

       Do you recycle                            At work?
       other products                  True                False
       besides cans?                   n = 104             n = 54

    True         False            Was there a          Was there a
    n = 173      n = 55            recycling bin       recycling bin
                                   conveniently        conveniently
   Recycle     Don't Recycle       located nearby?     located nearby?
Correct = 160, 92.5%  Correct = 45, 81.8%
Errors =  13,  7.5%   Errors = 10, 18.2%
                              True      False      True      False
                              n = 61    n = 43     n = 15    n = 39

  Predictive Accuracy        Recycle  Don't Recycle  Recycle  Don't Recycle
   # correct: 326, 84.5%   Correct = 60, 98.4%  Correct = 23, 53.5%  Correct = 13, 86.7%  Correct = 25, 64.1%
   # errors:   60, 15.5%   Errors =  1,  1.6%   Errors = 20, 46.5%   Errors =  2, 13.3%   Errors = 14, 35.9%
   Tau = .59
```

FIGURE 16.3 Decision to recycle cans (national sample, N=386).

following individual recycling cases down the decision tree and examining the degree to which each end point in the tree (each final decision) corresponded to our informants' own accounts. The results are shown in Table 16.3.

The top right-most cell of Table 16.3 contains the rationales from people who reported that they were at home and recycled other things besides cans. At home, only one person said it was easy to do. Three people, however, said it was a good thing to do or that it was mandatory. Nowhere else in the rationales do these latter two themes arise.

The next cell down shows the rationales from people who reported that they were at home but did not recycle other things. The model correctly predicted that the first three of the respondents would not recycle. Unlike those who had recycled, none of the three mentioned that it was important or good to recycle-nor that it was mandatory. The three cases that were misclassified more closely resemble the rationales in the cell above.

The rationales for those at work are clearly divided between those respondents who reported having a recycling bin conveniently located nearby and those who did not. Those who had a bin nearby reported its availability and the ease with which one could recycle. Those who didn't have a bin spontaneously mentioned not being able to keep cans on the job or not having a recycling center.

The last cell shows the rationales for those who were not at home or at work and who did not have a recycling bin nearby. Of the eight cases that the model predicted correctly, half spontaneously mentioned either the lack of convenience or the lack of a recycling bin. The other half mentioned explicitly where they were and clearly implied that place had something to do with their behavior. The two people who said that they threw the can out of the car identified a factor we hadn't thought of before—that laws against drinking and driving might have an impact on environmentally friendly behaviors.

Resolving Errors with Ethnography

Why do some people recycle when the model predicts that they shouldn't and other people don't recycle when the model predicts that they should? We turn to the verbatim comments of our informants. Those who recalled recycling a can despite not being at home or at work and not having a bin conveniently located were likely to justify their behavior by citing their beliefs in environmentalism or citing financial benefits for doing it. This may be the result of positive attitudes about recycling—attitudes that give people the extra impetus they need for recycling when bins aren't handy.

This is worth testing, but note that attitudes (or whatever else is at work) can account for no more than 10% of responses in the local sample (since the model predicts 90% of responses there) and no more than 15% of responses in the national sample (since the model predicts 85% of responses there).

We don't have ethnographic data to account for those not at home who reported not recycling a can despite having a recycling bin handy because none of our 33 informants were in that category. In fact, only three out of 76 people in our national sample reported not recycling despite having a bin handy. Just putting a lot of recycling bins around will likely increase recycling behavior. This has been known for some time, of course, but the fact that we can validate a well-understood piece of information like this gives us confidence in the EDM method for answering questions that are not this obvious.

5 Suggested Applications of EDMs in MMR

In principle, ethnographic models can be used to study complex choices, but in practice they are most commonly used for binary (yes/no) or categorical (A, B, or C) decisions. Binary decisions can, of course, be modeled statistically,

TABLE 16.3

Verbatim Justifications for 33 Recycling Choices from Ethnographic Sample

Decision Rules	Choice	Verbatim Justification
At home? Yes Recycle other things? Yes	Yes	I know you can recycle it and the bin was easy to get to. I believe in it, and it's good for the environment. I feel that it's some form of token effort in trying to protect the environment and keep stuff out of landfills. I recycle as much as I can. For recycling—because garbage just doesn't disappear—if you recycle there is less garbage then. They pick it up on Wednesday—because it's a good thing to do. It is required to recycle cans. It is mandatory, and I believe in recycling. It is mandatory.
At home? Yes Recycle other things? No	No	*Correct* I don't recycle. I didn't think about it and I don't like storing it around home because it brings pests. I was too lazy. Sometimes I keep em' for my brother but ... I give them to him.... I just didn't this time. *Incorrect* I take them to a place where they take aluminum cans and gets money for em'. I did it to recycle ... no reason just to recycle. It's easy to do and they pick em' up.
At work? Yes Bin nearby? Yes	Yes	I always recycle aluminum cans. ... I don't know ... because I can, because it's available. It's an automatic thing at work; we all recycle there. I wasn't gonna mess with it—it was easy. One of the operator collects them at work, and she takes the bag weekly to put it ... to take in for recycling.
At work? Yes Bin nearby? No	No	We're not allowed to keep cans on the job. There was no recycling center nearby. A lady at work collects them—so I put them in the bag to give to this one lady.
At work? Yes Bin nearby? Yes	No	*Correct* It wasn't convenient I guess. There was no obvious place to put it for recycling. I don't know—I didn't have a container to put it in. I was not home—I was someplace in town. I was at someone's house. I was driving—I threw it out the window—it was a beer can—the environment—I'm down with it but there are too many rules—I threw it out so I wouldn't get caught with it in my car. I wasn't at home—at home I would've put it in the recycling bucket — If it weren't illegal to put it in my car.... I'd've taken it home with me—more people would recycle if it weren't for those open container laws. *Incorrect* Well I didn't know what to do with it. That's better on the environment. I take em' in and turns em' in for money. I think it's a good thing—why use new things when you can reuse old things.

with logistic regression and categorical decisions can be modeled statistically with multinomial logit models or conditional logit models, but *ethnographic* decision models (as contrasted with purely statistical ones) are particularly good for understanding real-life, discrete choices and the rationales behind those choices. Unlike most purely probabilistic models, EDMs depend on a series of related if-then choices—things that we think make a lot of sense in real-world settings.

6 Strengths and Limitations of EDMs in MMR

EDMs are based on mixed methods during the full inquiry process—from exploratory data collection and analysis, to initial model building and hypothesis generation, to confirmatory analysis for model accuracy and validation. EDMs involve fully inductive work—inducing rules from a set of real-life events—and fully deductive work—generating and confirming hypotheses. On the other hand, while EDMs are typically generated on small samples and have high internal validity, they require testing on large samples in order to check external validity. Without this second step, EDMs are not likely to be convincing in applications research, where the goal is to get people to change their behavior—to recycle beverage cans, for example, as in the case reported in this chapter.

7 Resources for Learning More about EDMs

Gladwin (1989a) remains the key source for anyone who want to learn more about EDMs. Other overviews include Beck 2005, Bernard et al. (2017), and Hill (1998). See Ryan and Martínez (1996) and Weller et al. (1997) for more nuances in regard to accuracy and predictability.

NOTE

1. Parts of this chapter are adapted from Ryan and Bernard (2006). Used by permission, Society for Applied Anthropology.

REFERENCES

Bailey, A., and O. Ngwenyama. 2013. Toward entrepreneurial behavior in underserved communities: An ethnographic decision tree model of telecenter usage. *Information Technology for Development* 19: 230–248. doi:10.1080/02681102.2012.751571

Barlett, P. F. 1980. Cost-benefit analysis: A test of alternative methodologies. In *Agricultural decision making*, edited by P. Barlett, 137–160. New York: Academic Press.

Bauer, M., and A. Wright. 1996. Integrating qualitative and quantitative methods to model infant feeding behavior among Navajo mothers. *Human Organization* 55: 183–192. doi:10.17730/humo.55.2.p55g316v70572732

Beck, K. A. 2000. A decision making model of child abuse reporting. Doctoral dissertation, Vancouver, University of British Columbia. Retrieved from https://open.library.ubc.ca/cIRcle/collections/ubctheses/831/items/1.0089769

Beck, K. A. 2005. Ethnographic decision tree modeling: A research method for counseling psychology. *Journal of Counseling Psychology* 52: 243. doi:10.1037/0022-0167.52.2.243

Becker, H. S. 2008. *Tricks of the trade: How to think about your research while you're doing it*. Chicago: University of Chicago Press.

Bernard, H. R. 2017. *Research methods in anthropology* (6th ed.). Lanham, MD: Rowman & Littlefield.

Bernard, H. R., A. Wutich, and G. W. Ryan. 2017. *Analyzing qualitative data: Systematic approaches* (2nd ed.). Thousand Oaks, CA: Sage.

Borgatti, S. P. 1994. Cultural domain analysis. *Journal of Quantitative Anthropology* 4: 261–278. Retrieved from http://works.bepress.com/steveborgatti/44/

Borgatti, S. P. 1999. Elicitation techniques for cultural domain analysis. *Enhanced Ethnographic Methods* 3: 115–151.

Breslin, F. C., C. H. Gladwin, D. Borsoi, and J. A. Cunningham. 2000. Defacto client-treatment matching: How clinicians make referrals to outpatient treatments for substance use. *Evaluation and Program Planning* 23: 281–291. doi:10.1016/S0149-7189(00)00014-8

Corbin, J., and Strauss, A. L. 2015. *Basics of qualitative research. Techniques and procedures for developing grounded theory* (4th ed.). Thousand Oaks, CA: Sage.

Djalilov, B. M., A. Khamzina, A. K. Hornidge, and J. P. Lamers. 2016. Exploring constraints and incentives for the adoption of agroforestry practices on degraded cropland in Uzbekistan. *Journal of Environmental Planning and Management* 59: 142–162. doi:10.1080/09640568.2014.996283

Edmonds, J. K. 2010. Social networks, decision making and use of skilled birth attendants to prevent maternal mortality in Matlab, Bangladesh. Doctoral dissertation, Atlanta, Emory University. Retrieved from https://etd.library.emory.edu/

Fairweather, J. R. 1999. Understanding how farmers choose between organic and conventional production: Results from New Zealand and policy implications. *Agriculture and Human Values* 16: 51–63. Retrieved from https://link.springer.com/journal/10460

Fort, J. D. 2011. The role of factors involving the environment in a forest livelihood decision of Malawian villagers. Master's thesis, Gainesville, University of Florida. Retrieved from http://ufdc.ufl.edu/UFE0043443/00001

Francis, J. J., M. Johnston, C. Robertson, L. Glidewell, V. Entwistle, M. P. Eccles, and J. M. Grimshaw. 2010. What is an adequate sample size? Operationalising data saturation for theory-based interview studies. *Psychology and Health* 25: 1229–1245. doi:10.1080/08870440903194015

Fugard, A. J., and H. W. Potts. 2015. Supporting thinking on sample sizes for thematic analyses: A quantitative tool. *International Journal of Social Research Methodology* 18: 669–684. doi:10.1080/13645579.2015.1005453

Gatewood, J. B. 1983. Deciding where to fish: The skipper's dilemma in southeast Alaskan salmon seining. *Coastal Management* 10: 347–67. doi:10.1080/08920758309361928

Gladwin, C. H. 1976. A view of the Plan Puebla: An application of hierarchical decision models. *American Journal of Agricultural Economics* 58: 881–887. Retrieved from https://academic.oup.com/ajae

Gladwin, C. H. 1983. Contributions of decision-tree methodology to a farming systems program. *Human Organization* 42: 146–57. Retrieved from www.sfaa.net/publications/human-organization/

Gladwin, C. H. 1989a. *Ethnographic decision tree modeling*. Newbury Park, CA: Sage.

Gladwin, C. H. 1989b. Modeling farmers' decisions to change: Using cognitive science in the design of agricultural technology. In *Social science perspectives on managing agricultural technology*, edited by D. Groenfeldt and J. W. Mook, 127–141. IWMI Books, International Water Management Institute, number 113863.

Gladwin, C. H., H. Gladwin, and W. G. Peacock. 2001. Modeling hurricane evacuation decisions with ethnographic methods. *International Journal of Mass Emergencies and Disasters* 19: 117–143. Retrieved from http://ijmed.org/

Glaser, B., and A. Strauss. 1967. *The discovery of grounded theory. Strategies for qualitative research*. Chicago: Aldine.

Guest, G., A. Bunce, and L. Johnson. 2006. How many interviews are enough? An experiment with data saturation and variability. *Field Methods* 18: 59–82. doi:10.1177/1525822X05279903

Guest, G., E. Namey, and K. McKenna. 2017. How many focus groups are enough? Building an evidence base for nonprobability sample sizes. *Field Methods* 29: 3–22. doi:10.1177/1525822X16639015

Hagaman, A., and A. Wutich. 2017. How many interviews are enough to identify metathemes in multi-sited and cross-cultural research? Another perspective on Guest, Bunce, and Johnson's (2006) landmark study. *Field Methods* 29: 23–41. doi:10.1177/1525822X16640447

Hill, C. E. 1998. Decision modeling: Its use in medical anthropology. In *Using methods in the field*, edited by V. C. de Munck and E. J. Sobo, 139–64. Walnut Creek, CA: AltaMira Press.

Johnson, J., and M. L. Williams. 1993. A preliminary ethnographic decision tree model of injection drug users' (IDUs) needle sharing. *International Journal of the Addictions* 28: 997–1014. Retrieved from www.tandfonline.com/toc/isum19/25/sup1?nav=tocList

Keshavarz, M., and E. Karami. 2014. Farmers' decision-making process under drought. *Journal of Arid Environments* 108: 43–56. doi:10.1016/j.jaridenv.2014.03.006

Klecka, W. R. 1980. *Discriminant analysis*. Beverly Hills, CA: Sage

Krippendorf, K. 2013. *Content analysis* (3rd ed.). London: Sage.

Mason M. 2010. Sample size and saturation in PhD studies using qualitative interviews. *Forum: Qualitative Social Research*, 2010; 11. doi:10.17169/fqs-11.3.1428

Mathews, H. F., and C. Hill. 1990. Applying cognitive decision theory to the study of regional patterns of illness treatment choice. *American Anthropologist* 91: 155–170. doi:10.1525/aa.1990.92.1.02a00110

Montbriand, M. J. 1995. Decision tree model describing alternate health care choices made by oncology patients. *Cancer Nursing* 18: 117. Retrieved from https://journals.lww.com/cancernursingonline/pages/default.aspx

Morgan, M. G., B. Fischoff, A. Bostrom, and C. J. Atman. 2002. *Risk communication: A mental models approach*. New York: Cambridge University Press.

Morse, J. M. 1989. Strategies for sampling. In *Qualitative nursing research: A contemporary dialogue*, edited by J. M. Morse, 117–31. Rockville, MD: Aspen Press.

Murthy, S. K. 1998. Automatic construction of decision trees from data: A multi-disciplinary survey. *Data Mining and Knowledge Discovery* 2: 345–389. Retrieved from https://link.springer.com/journal/10618

Mwangi, B. J., and I. Brown. 2015. A decision model of Kenyan SMEs' consumer choice behavior in relation to registration for a mobile banking service: A contextual perspective. *Information Technology for Development* 21: 229–252. doi:10.1080/02681102.2013.874320

Oh, H. S., and H. A. Park. 2004. Decision tree model of the treatment-seeking behaviors among Korean cancer patients. *Cancer Nursing* 27: 259–266. Retrieved from https://journals.lww.com/cancernursingonline/pages/default.aspx

Quinn, N. 1978. Do Mfantse fish sellers estimate probabilities in their heads? *American Ethnologist* 5: 206–226. doi:10.1525/ae.1978.5.2.02a00020

Roberts, E. 2000. Women's choices for end of life care: How older Jewish women make clinical decisions. Doctoral dissertation, Columbia, University of South Carolina. Retrieved from https://search.proquest.com/pqdtglobal/index?accountid=10920

Ryan, G. W., and H. R. Bernard. 2006. Testing an ethnographic decision tree model on a national sample: Recycling beverage cans. *Human Organization* 65: 103–114. doi:10.17730/humo.65.1.884p8d1a2hxxnk79

Ryan, G. W., and H. Martinez. 1996. Can we predict what mothers do? Modeling childhood diarrhea in rural Mexico. *Human Organization* 55: 47–57. doi:10.17730/humo.55.1.p0n23832j8q34743

Sandelowski, M. 1995. Sample size in qualitative research. *Research in Nursing and Health* 18: 179–183. doi/pdf/10.1002/nur.4770180211

Shuk, E., J. E. Burkhalter, C. F. Baguer, S. M. Holland, A. Pinkhasik, M. S. Brady, and J. L. Hay. 2012. Factors associated with inconsistent sun protection in first-degree relatives of melanoma survivors. *Qualitative Health Research* 22: 934–945. doi:10.1177/1049732312443426

Spradley, J. 1979. *The ethnographic interview*. New York: Holt, Rinehart and Winston.

Thierry, A. D., and S. A. Snipes. 2015. Why do farmworkers delay treatment after debilitating injuries? Thematic analysis explains if, when, and why farmworkers were treated for injuries. *American Journal of Industrial Medicine* 58: 178–192. doi:10.1002/ajim.22380

Weller, S. C., R. Baer, and J. Prochaska. 2016. Should I stay or should I go? Response to the Hurricane Ike Evacuation order on the Texas Gulf Coast. *Natural Hazards Review* 17: 04016003. doi:10.1061/(ASCE)NH.1527-6996.0000217

Weller, S. C., and A. K. Romney. 1988. *Systematic data collection*. Newbury Park: Sage.

Weller, S. C., T. R. Ruebush, and R. E. Klein. 1997. Predicting treatment-seeking behavior in Guatemala: A comparison of the health services research and decision–theoretic approaches. *Medical Anthropology Quarterly* 11: 224–45. doi:10.1525/maq.1997.11.2.224

Weller, S. C., B. Vickers, H. R. Bernard, A. M. Blackburn, S. Borgatti, C. C. Gravlee, and J. C. Johnson. 2018. Open-ended interview questions and saturation. *PLoS ONE* 13(6): e0198606. doi:10.1371/journal.pone.0198606

Young, J. C. 1980. A model of illness treatment decisions in a Tarascan town. *American Ethnologist* 7: 106–131. doi:10.1525/ae.1980.7.1.02a00070

Young, J. C., and L. C. Garro. 1994. *Medical choice in a Mexican village*. New Brunswick, NJ: Rutgers University Press.

Zhang, Z. 2016. Decision tree modeling using R. *Annals of Translational Medicine* 4: 275. doi.org/10.21037/atm.2016.05.14

17

Qualitative Comparative Analysis (QCA)

An Integrative Approach Suited for Diverse Mixed Methods and Multimethod Research Strategies

Benoît Rihoux, Priscilla Álamos-Concha, and Bojana Lobe

1 Defining QCA[1]: An Integrative Approach

QCA was launched by Charles Ragin, a sociologist and political scientist, through an agenda-setting book (Ragin, 1987). He first presented it as a research *approach* ambitioning to reconcile the qualitative and quantitative approaches, which he preferred to label *case-oriented* and *variable-oriented* (Ragin, 1997). Indeed, from the outset, he questioned the qualitative and quantitative labels. He also questioned mainstream quantitative approaches for their emphasis on given populations and standard sampling procedures, instead advocating more qualitative case selection strategies (*versus* random sampling) and more careful definitions of 'what is a case?' (Ragin & Becker, 1992).

QCA was then also gradually developed in a series of techniques, with attached protocols and software programs, now brought under the label of *configurational comparative methods* (CCMs) (Rihoux & Ragin, 2009) or *set-theoretic methods* (STMs) (Schneider & Wagemann, 2012).

The main drive for Ragin to initiate QCA was the emphasis that the bulk of quantitative (read: statistical) research laid on the identification of the net effect of each independent variable on the dependent variable. This did not enable one to tap the richness of historical cases in terms of causal mechanisms, and statistically framed interaction effects did not enable more complex forms of causality to be modelled (Marx, Rihoux, & Ragin, 2013). The search for alternatives to net effects thinking has remained a core preoccupation of Ragin and other QCA developers (Ragin, 2006).

As spelled out by Ragin in his 1987 volume, and still largely standing today with some refinements and nuances (Rihoux, 2013, 2017; Rihoux & Marx, 2013), QCA is an approach and set of techniques that: (1) is case-oriented, with each case being considered as a whole (holistic approach); (2) represents cases as configurations of *conditions* and *outcome* variables,[2] with combinations of conditions being causally linked to the outcome; (3) systematically identifies similarities and differences across comparable cases via *truth tables* (tables of configurations[3]); (4) promotes frequent iterations to theoretical and case-based knowledge, so as to enhance the dialogue between ideas and evidence; (5) identifies, through minimization algorithms, the key combinations of conditions leading to the presence or absence of the outcome, framing complex causation in terms of *multiple conjunctural causation*;[4] (6) systematizes the analysis in terms of (combinations of) necessary and/or sufficient conditions; (7) seeks to achieve some parsimony while also maintaining the complexity of each individual case; and (8) enables one to process more than a few cases, via intermediate n designs enabling multiple cross-case comparisons, to move beyond the idiosyncrasies of single case studies and to conduct forms of modest generalization.

In Ragin's quest for tools enabling one to model and process cases as complex combinations of traits, the decisive impulse leading to the development of QCA as a set of techniques was his intuition that non-statistical mathematical tools could suit that purpose: Boolean algebra and set theory. Together with criminologist and programmer Kriss Drass who also co-authored some of the very first empirical applications (e.g. Drass & Spencer, 1987), Ragin developed the first software program (QCA). It was based on Boolean logic and therefore required one to code each variable in a binary way (0 or 1), placing one clear dichotomization threshold for each variable and each case. The user thus had to establish fundamental distinctions—differences in kind, not in degree—in each variable (for example, revolutionary situation yes/no, low/high welfare state development, etc.). This corresponded to what is now labeled as the csQCA (*crisp-set QCA*) technique.

In the wake of vivid debates around QCA (De Meur, Rihoux, & Yamasaki, 2009), and also following the increasing use of QCA in larger n settings (Fiss, Sharapov, & Cronqvist, 2013), Ragin turned to another framing of QCA: as a set-theoretic approach, fundamentally distinct from the correlational (read: mainstream statistical) approach (Ragin, 2008). Indeed, set-theoretic methods focus on membership scores of elements in sets (versus linear measurement), with causal relations being modelled as subset or superset relations (versus correlations), etc. (Schneider & Wagemann, 2012: 3–12). Some critiques of the limitations of csQCA as a dichotomous technique also pushed for further innovation, through the development of finer-grained *multivalue QCA* (mvQCA) (Cronqvist & Berg-Schlosser, 2009) and especially of the more technically elaborate *fuzzy-set QCA* (fsQCA) that has become the main technique besides csQCA.

The last decade has witnessed a multitude of QCA developments and innovations, both conceptual and technical, including: (a) more elaborate models such as two-step QCA distinguishing remote from proximate conditions (Schneider, 2019; Schneider & Wagemann, 2006); (b) technical ways to include the time dimension in QCA (Caren & Panofsky, 2005; Hino, 2009; Pagliarin & Gerrits, 2020); (c) software programs among which TOSMANA, fs/QCA as well as some increasingly powerful R modules; (d) more sophisticated model-building strategies through the formulation of configurational hypotheses (that is, hypotheses combining different conditions); (e) more refined strategies for threshold-setting in crisp sets and calibration of fuzzy sets; (f) robustness analyses of QCA results; (g) the development of coefficients in the QCA procedure, among which a relevance coefficient (enabling one to separate genuine from trivial necessary conditions) and a coverage coefficient (evaluating the empirical coverage of the QCA solution); (h) benchmarks regarding the number of conditions/number of cases ratio (Marx, Cambré, & Rihoux, 2013; Marx & Dusa, 2011); (i) more diverse modes of data visualization, through Venn diagrams, scatterplots, decision trees and other visual forms (Rubinson, 2019); (j) more varied strategies to obtain different types of complex, intermediate, or parsimonious QCA solutions; etc. Another important trend is the recent development of other neighboring techniques such as Coincidence Analysis (CNA), a close neighbor (Baumgartner & Epple, 2014), or Necessary Condition Analysis (NCA), a more distant relative (Dul, 2016).

QCA itself constitutes an integrative research approach, as it rests among other things on the integration of case-based and other forms of substantive knowledge (Ragin, 2014). Indeed, while being *sui generis* in a way, it is also fed by several methods and traditions, both on the qualitative (case-oriented) and on the quantitative (mathematical, albeit non-statistical) sides (Blanchard, Rihoux, & Álamos-Concha, 2017). More specifically, QCA is about case-based evidence, which is compatible with multiple data collection techniques (see Section 3.1), but also about mathematical formalization in the research process.

2 When Use of QCA is Appropriate in Mixed Methods or Multimethod Research: Five Main Strategies

Because of its integrative nature, QCA can be quite smoothly inserted in a mixed methods research (MMR) or in a multimethod research; this is in fact often recommended as a good practice (Rihoux, Ragin, Yamasaki, & Bol, 2009: 170–172; Schneider & Wagemann, 2012). We define here *mixed methods research* as research that integrates at least one qualitative and at least one quantitative data collection and/or data analysis method (Johnson, Onwuegbuzie, & Turner, 2007), and *multimethod research* as a broader term that includes any use of more than one type of method, including, for example, two qualitative methods or two quantitative methods.

QCA is itself a data analysis—not a data collection—method. Considering this fundamental distinction, and building upon previous, more focused attempts (Blatter & Haverland, 2012: 231–235; Meuer & Rupietta, 2017; Rihoux & Lobe, 2009), we may distinguish five main strategies for inserting QCA in mixed methods and multimethod research (see Table 17.1).

The first two strategies include QCA as the only *data analysis* method—that is: no other data analysis method is exploited. Strategy 1 consists in exploiting different types of *data collection* methods, qualitative and/or quantitative, upstream of the QCA, whereas strategy 2 consists in ensuring that the whole QCA procedure (pre-QCA, QCA proper, and post-QCA) is informed by case-based knowledge. Both strategies can be implemented following a mixed methods or a multimethod logic. Indeed, when QCA is combined with *qualitative* data collection (strategy 1) and/or with *qualitative* case-based knowledge throughout the procedure (strategy 2), given the epistemological proximity between case-based research and QCA as a research approach (the latter also being 'qualitative' in that sense), this corresponds to a multimethod strategy. By contrast, when one also resorts to quantitative data and/or to numerical case-based knowledge in these two strategies, one then follows a MMR approach.

The further three strategies involve at least one other *data analysis* method besides QCA: conducting more thorough case studies before the QCA phase (strategy 3—again: mixed methods or multimethod); conducting in-depth case studies of targeted cases, in particular via causal process tracing (CPT),

TABLE 17.1

Five Main Strategies for Inserting QCA in Mixed Methods and Multimethod Research

Strategy	Mixed Methods	Multi-method	Description
1. Mixed data-informed QCA	X	X	QCA preceded by qualitative and/or quantitative rounds of data collection methods
2. Case-informed QCA	X	X	QCA informed by case-based knowledge throughout the procedure: pre-QCA steps, QCA analytical steps, and post-QCA steps
3. In-depth case-informed QCA	X	X	QCA preceded by at least one in-depth case study
4. QCA-CPT		X	QCA followed by at least one in-depth case study, in particular via CPT
5. QCA-statistical	X		QCA preceded or followed by at least one statistical data analysis

after the QCA phase (strategy 4—multimethod); and sequencing a QCA analysis with at least one statistical data analysis method (strategy 5—mixed methods). In the next two sections, we unpack these respective five strategies in terms of concrete protocols.

Short Introduction to QCA Steps—and Mixed Methods or Multimethod Strategies with QCA as Data Analysis Method

It goes beyond the scope of this chapter to examine in detail the QCA technical steps (see Section 8 for textbooks and other resources). The generic sequence of main steps is however discussed further below (Section 3.2; strategy 2). In a nutshell, the implementation of QCA consists in three main phases: (1) a pre-QCA phase that includes case selection, model building, data collection and data preparation; (2) the QCA phase proper, including software treatment and logical minimization procedures to produce QCA solutions; and (3) a post-QCA phase that includes interpretation of the QCA solutions as well as some forms of modest generalization.

Strategy 1: Mixed Data-informed QCA

As a *data analysis* method, QCA is compatible with virtually all types of *data collection* methods, which should logically precede it. Whatever the n of cases, that is, relatively small n, intermediate n or larger n, QCA typically requires quite a diverse set of data for the respective cases. This also enables the user to gain at least some level of case-based knowledge before engaging in QCA proper (see also strategies 2 and 3 below).

In concrete terms, this translates into a mixed database or dataset, based on some rounds of qualitative and/or quantitative data collection or compilation. At least three variants are available at this mixed data collection stage: (1) exploiting mixed data sources, that is, both qualitative and quantitative; (2) exploiting multiple qualitative data sources; (3) exploiting multiple quantitative data sources (see Figure 17.1). These three variants are naturally not mutually exclusive and may be combined via several data collection loops.

This mixed data then feeds into the QCA via the successive data transformation steps (see strategy 2, steps 3 to 6). It is thus integrated in the core of the QCA procedure, as it eventually feeds into the QCA *truth table* (see strategy 2, step 7) that can be processed via software in order to obtain the QCA solutions.

Strategy 2: Case-informed QCA

Case-based knowledge is supposed to be a crucial companion to QCA, especially in smaller n and intermediate n situations in which each case matters. At the very least, it is necessary to gain some level of familiarity with relevant cases before engaging in QCA (Berg-Schlosser, 2012: 55–84; Ragin, 1987: 121). Beyond this, it is even better if case-based knowledge informs the whole sequence of pre-QCA, QCA and post-QCA concrete steps (see Figure 17.2). In the next subsections, we briefly discuss each one of these steps (for a more detailed discussion, see Rihoux & Lobe, 2009, 2015).

Pre-QCA steps

1. The first step of *comparative research design and case selection* involves purposeful selection of each case (Berg-Schlosser & De Meur, 2009). This requires at least some level of case-based knowledge, as the delineation of the population of comparable cases is often not so straightforward, especially as one encounters borderline cases and has to choose whether to include them or not.

2. The next step, *gaining further within-case knowledge*, is a challenging one in a multiple-case setting, as there is always a trade-off between the number of cases considered (breadth) and the degree of intimacy gained with regard to each individual case (depth). This is even more challenging when one engages in cross-national comparisons, across different cultural contexts, with sources in different languages and of different quality. One should anyhow strive to become well-acquainted with each individual case.

3. The third is *defining the outcome of interest*. This does not only stem from theory and the research question, as case-based knowledge can feed into this definition process. For example, Scouvart et.al. (2007) exploit field observation of the cases (specific sub-regions with settlers in the Amazon basin) to refine both the definition and the operationalization of the speed of deforestation (the outcome of interest for the QCA), complementing the quantitative measurement of this outcome.

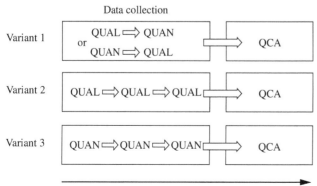

Source: own elaboration

FIGURE 17.1 Mixed data-informed QCA strategy

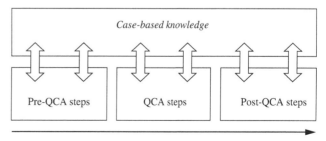

Source: own elaboration

FIGURE 17.2 Case-informed QCA strategy

This step also goes along with operationalization and data collection for the outcome.

4. *Model specification and selection of conditions* is the next key step. In principle, this depends more on theory if one uses QCA mostly for theory testing. However, in order to decide whether the theory to be tested is applicable to the cases under scrutiny, one must also rely on case-based knowledge. If QCA is mostly used for exploratory purposes and/or for theory- or conjecture-building, knowledge about individual cases plays a central role. This step also comprises the operationalization and data collection for each condition.

5. The fifth pre-QCA step, *visualizing/synthetizing cases and the model*, requires one to get a better, global view of each of the cases, which requires case-based knowledge, as each case constitutes in effect a sort of complex system (Gerrits & Verweij, 2018). One way to do this is to construct graph-like synthetic case descriptions, with a time line and the key changes on the outcome and on the conditions for the whole period considered (e.g. Rihoux, 2001: 135–174; Thomann, 2019: 60–69). By producing and observing such descriptions, one can already intuitively grasp some cross-case commonalities, some core differences, as well as some puzzling case profiles.

QCA analytical Steps

6. The next, challenging step is *calibration*, which consists in different operations depending on the QCA variant used: csQCA, mvQCA or fsQCA. It often requires informed judgment, and therefore case-based knowledge plays a crucial role here, especially because purely theory-derived cut-off points are seldom undisputed.

7. The seventh step is the exploration of the *truth table*— that is, the table of configurations. A configuration is simply a combination of conditions leading to a certain outcome value (see Section 1). One frequently meets *contradictory configurations*, that is, empirical cases which, although they share the same condition values, display different outcome values (see Section 1). A qualitative re-examination of the cases involved often constitutes a very efficient strategy to solve such contradictions (Rihoux & De Meur, 2009: 48–49).

8. The eighth, core step is the key QCA operation of *logical minimization* via an analysis of sufficiency, preceded by an analysis of necessity (Schneider & Wagemann, 2012), and the treatment of *logical remainders* (non-empirically observed configurations), using the QCA software. Here the choice of the adequate strategy also requires case-based knowledge, especially if one opts for the *intermediate solution*, that is, considering only those logical remainders that are consistent with one's theoretical and/or substantive knowledge.

9. Similarly, during the ninth step of solving *contradictory simplifying assumptions*, one may exploit case knowledge to orientate the problematic logical remainders' outcome value (for an empirical demonstration, see Vanderborght & Yamasaki, 2004).

10. The tenth step is *arbitrating between different (terms of) QCA solutions*. Here one must again intervene and select the *solution terms* (parts of the QCA solutions) that make the most sense. Although this can be a theory-driven process, it is also advisable to rely on case-based knowledge in certain clusters of cases.

Post-QCA steps

11. The first post-QCA step in terms of interpretation consists in *factoring out conditions* from the QCA solutions, that is, manually singling out some conditions in those solutions. This often relies on case-based criteria.

12. The next, crucial step of *case-by-case interpretation* is by definition case-oriented, because QCA is conceived as a lever to better understand purposefully selected cases (Curchod, Dumez, & Jeunemaître, 2004; see also step 1 above). This consists in re-examining more in-depth some individual case narratives, using the core conditions comprised in the QCA solutions. One often discovers that the same combination of conditions should be translated into different narratives for different cases. This step can be formalized further with causal process tracing (see strategy 4).

13. During the step of *cross-case patterns interpretation*, one identifies similarities or differences across the case narratives, building upon the terms of the QCA solutions. This enables one to make sense out of multiple-case narratives— i.e. to identify common (bits of) causal narratives across several cases. Via these focused, case-based comparative interpretations, one also frequently discovers other unsuspected elements that were not comprised as conditions in the QCA model, which could lead one to revise the model (back to step 4).

14. Beyond the empirical cases comprised in the QCA, one may perform *limited historical generalizations* (also labelled as *modest* or *contingent* generalizations), that is, formulating propositions that can be applied, with appropriate caution, to other cases that are sufficiently close to the initially selected cases. This requires some substantive knowledge about these other, neighboring cases.

15. Finally, one engages in *robustness tests* and *theory evaluation*. Robustness tests enable one to evaluate how robust the QCA findings are when modifying previous choices (case selection, condition selection, calibration strategy, consistency thresholds, etc.). This frequently requires some case-based judgment—for instance: to what extent is it meaningful, considering specific cases, to modify this or that calibration threshold? As for theory evaluation, it consists in analyzing the intersections between prior theoretical hunches and the QCA empirical findings, which may lead one to either corroborate a theory or to reformulate it by either increasing or reducing its parsimony (Schneider & Wagemann, 2012: 297–304). Again, this requires some re-examination of the empirical cases comprised in the QCA.

Summing up: this case-informed strategy entails rich dialogue with the cases at literally every research step. It enables one to consolidate the whole QCA protocol so that it is both theory- and case-informed, and to ensure that the QCA solutions are useful for both within-case and cross-case interpretations. Yet, this MMR strategy does not entail the sequencing or articulation of QCA with another *data analysis* method—contrary to the next three MMR or multimethod research strategies.

3 Technical Outline: QCA in Mixed Methods or Multimethod Research with Another Data Analysis Method

Strategy 3: In-depth Case-informed QCA

This strategy consists in first conducting an in-depth study of one specific case—or of a few handpicked cases, if feasible and felt useful—before engaging in QCA. The starting point is a crucial case, because it stands out as a typical case with regard to the theory. It could however also be selected because it is a particularly puzzling one, for instance a case that would have been expected to display a negative outcome according to the theory and that displays the positive outcome instead (Rohlfing, 2012) (see Figure 17.3).

The advantages of conducting such a pre-QCA in-depth case study are manifold, as this helps one to (1) fine-tune the delineation of the population, starting from that crucial case as a point of reference and looking for comparable cases; (2) consolidate the casing (what is a case?); (3) gain a deeper understanding of the empirical phenomenon under study before turning to systematic, cross-case comparison via the QCA; (4) consolidate the core concepts; (5) clearly delineate the outcome variable, conceptually and empirically; (6) confirm the fit between the envisaged theory and the case at hand, to potentially also look for other (segments of) theories to feed the model that will then be evaluated with QCA, thereby making a more case-informed and context-informed selection of conditions); and (7) get a first grip on some potential causal mechanisms—for the latter purpose, one could conduct a *theory-building causal process tracing* analysis on this particular case (that is, a "PT first" design; see Beach & Rohlfing, 2018: 13–14)—to be distinguished from a post-QCA *theory-testing causal process tracing* analysis as discussed in strategy 4.

There is not one standard way to conduct such a pre-QCA in-depth case study. One may refer to established case study methods (see e.g. Gerring, 2007; Rohlfing, 2012; Yin, 2017)—and obviously one needs good access to both secondary and primary data. One should use a case study method that is in some way compatible with analytic thinking, i.e., with reflecting in terms of (condition and outcome) variables and causal mechanisms. If so, normally one must choose a typical case in order to find evidence of a causal relationship that can pave the way for the cross-case analysis via QCA. If no such evidence is found, one must turn to another typical case for further exploration (Beach & Rohlfing, 2018: 13–14).

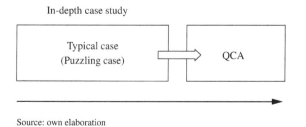

FIGURE 17.3 In-depth case-informed QCA strategy.

Note that this third MMR strategy is distinct from, but very compatible with, mixed- or multimethod strategies 1 and 2 discussed above: the in-depth case study may constitute a useful preparatory step before engaging in systematic qualitative and/or quantitative data collection across all cases selected for the QCA (strategy 1), and it may also help consolidating the whole sequence of pre-QCA steps (strategy 2).

Strategy 4: QCA-causal Process Tracing

This strategy consists in first conducting a QCA, and then handpicking specific cases that are examined in-depth through causal process tracing (CPT), more precisely the *theory-testing process tracing* variant, that is, 'a theory-first research method, testing whether a hypothesized causal mechanism exists in a positive case or set of positive cases by exploring whether the predicted evidence of a hypothesized causal mechanism exists in reality' (Beach, 2017: 18). This is one of the three core variants of CPT as defined and further refined by Beach and Pedersen, besides *theory-building process tracing*, an inductive variant, and *explaining outcome process tracing*, an iterative, abductive variant (Beach, 2017; Beach & Pedersen, 2019). We are recommending Beach's approach to CPT because it unpacks causal mechanisms more precisely than other approaches, both conceptually and in terms of operationalization (for a less demanding approach, see in particular Bennett & Checkel, 2014).

The main purpose of this QCA-CPT strategy is to unpack causal mechanisms at play within selected positive cases. One is then able to address both why-questions with QCA (core combinations of conditions leading to the outcome) and how-questions with CPT (causal mechanisms at play between some core conditions). The sequencing of CPT after a QCA is currently being refined as a powerful research strategy and is subject of much elaboration and debate (Beach, 2018; Beach & Pedersen, 2016, 2018, 2019; Beach & Rohlfing, 2018; Beach & Siewert, 2020; Goertz, 2017; Williams & Gemperle, 2017).

The logic of the sequence is quite straightforward: QCA is first used to identify the core combinations of conditions that lead to the outcome of interest in a given set of selected cases, thereby identifying cross-case patterns; then CPT is conducted on specific cases that share the same combination of conditions, the presence of the outcome and also similar features (contextual conditions), so as to (a) provide evidence of a *causal* relationship between a given combination of conditions and the outcome, and to (b) *understand* how a that combination of conditions produces the outcome by tracing the causal mechanisms linking them together under certain contextual (*scope*) conditions.

One may handpick two main types of cases for post-QCA CPT (see Figure 17.4), depending on one's main goal (Beach & Pedersen, 2019; Beach & Rohlfing, 2018; Rohlfing & Schneider, 2018; Rohlfing & Schneider, 2013; Schneider & Rohlfing, 2013, 2016). The first option is *typical cases*, that is, cases that display membership in the same condition(s), the outcome of interest and also the possible contextual condition(s) (Beach & Pedersen, 2018, 2019). The unpacking of causal mechanisms within these cases with CPT either leads to discovering that a particular case is idiosyncratic (another typical case must then be selected), or to confirm that the theorized mechanism is indeed at play between the combination of condition(s) (the theory can then be confirmed, and the analysis can be terminated), or to disconfirm that these theorized mechanisms are at play—that is, at least a part of the chain of mechanisms is broken—(the theory must then be modified by searching for other causal conditions and contexts).

Following the second option, one handpicks three potential types of *deviant cases*: (1) a *deviant case consistency in kind* that displays some of the theory-congruent core combinations of conditions in the QCA solution, but yet does not display the outcome; (2) a *deviant case consistency in degree* that displays both a theory-congruent combination of conditions and the outcome, but however violates the subset relation, as it displays a higher membership in the conjunction (Beach & Pedersen, 2019: 111); or (3) a *deviant case coverage*, where the outcome is present in spite of the absence of some theory-congruent core combinations of conditions. One then discovers that this deviant case is idiosyncratic (another deviant case must then be selected), that the theory cannot be improved (the analysis can then be terminated), or that the theory can in fact be improved, typically by re-framing some conditions or by adding some other conditions and contexts that had been overlooked and that are revealed by the CPT analysis.

In complement to these two main types of cases, one could also focus on two further specific types (these are not displayed in Figure 17.4, as their use is more limited): (1) some *individually irrelevant cases* that display neither the outcome nor the expected core combinations of conditions; such cases are not really useful for single-case analyses but could be useful for some comparative within-case analyses, especially contrasting them with *typical cases* or with *deviant cases coverage* (Rohlfing & Schneider, 2018; Schneider & Rohlfing, 2016); and (2) *counterfactual cases* where the hypothesized cause is present but the outcome is different (Emmenegger, 2011); one could then look for other conditions and contexts potentially enabling the occurrence of a certain outcome of interest (Rihoux & De Meur, 2009: 48–56) and reformulate or complement the QCA model.

It has to be stressed that in order to perform a CPT type of analysis, one may select those cases that are relevant for building and testing theories, i.e. the *typical cases*. Similarly, *deviant cases consistency* are also relevant for CPT because they can help us to identify omitted contexts or causal conditions that can explain why a process did not work as theorized (Beach & Pedersen, 2019: 90). By contrast, *deviant cases coverage* and *irrelevant cases* are not adequate cases for CPT, because they tell us nothing about the mechanisms linking causes and outcomes (Ibid.).

It goes beyond the reach of this chapter to present in detail the concrete steps of a CPT analysis (Beach & Pedersen, 2016, 2019). In a nutshell, when focusing on typical cases in a post-QCA phase: one needs to (1) select a typical case that is particularly relevant for the purpose of generalization, (2) conceptualize the hypothesized causal mechanism between the configuration of conditions and the outcome, (3) implement the empirical tests for each part of a causal mechanism, that is, the operationalization of the conceptualized causal mechanism (fingerprints, priors, theoretical uncertainty and uniqueness), (4) collect empirical data based on the empirical predictions (fingerprints) for each part of the mechanism, as observations, and (5) assess whether these observations may be considered as evidence of the presence of each part of the causal mechanism and of the causal mechanism as a whole (empirical certainty and uniqueness).

This fourth strategy is a very promising and potentially very powerful one. It is however particularly challenging in terms of concept formation and operationalization: in order to avoid the risk of generating mechanistic heterogeneity, one must construct the concepts used for the QCA in alignment with the CPT approach. This places quite a constraint on the use of QCA, because the CPT approach to concepts is more stringent (Pattyn, Álamos-Concha, Cambré, Rihoux, & Schalembier, 2020).

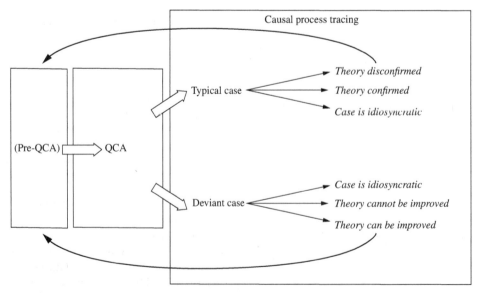

Source: own eleboration, based on Schneider & Rohlfing (2013:561)

FIGURE 17.4 QCA-causal process tracing strategy

Strategy 5: QCA-statistical

This fifth strategy is quite different from the previous ones, as it also comprises quantitative (read: statistical) data *analyses* alongside QCA. As has been amply discussed (Fiss et al., 2013; Meuer & Rupietta, 2017), statistical analyses and QCA differ deeply in terms of epistemological and methodological assumptions and in terms of concrete goals. In terms of foundational assumptions, the bulk of statistical methods take on board assumptions of linearity, additivity, causal symmetry, permanent causality, etc., whereas QCA is in essence non-linear, non-additive, causally asymmetric and causally non-permanent, assumes equifinality, etc.

In terms of concrete goals, even though it is possible, with statistical techniques, to tap interactions effects between the independent variables, to engage in more complex forms of modeling (e.g. structural equation modeling) and to test other types of linear models (e.g. curvilinear), one core goal pursued is still to identify the net effect of each independent variable on the dependent variable; in many statistical analyses, the goal is also to perform statistical inference from a sample to the full population. By contrast, QCA is geared towards the identification of complex causal patterns (combinations of conditions, within configurations) that produce a given phenomenon, via the identification of set relations (not correlations) framed in terms of necessity and sufficiency. It therefore does not aim at identifying the net effect of single conditions on the outcome. Neither does it aim at producing statistical inference—it rather focuses on making *modest historical* generalizations.

However, in the process of diversification of QCA applications (see Section 1), there have been an increasing number of empirical applications in larger n settings, and also an increasing proportion of fsQCA applications, some of which are exploiting more fine-grained, interval- or ratio-level data. This has opened up further QCA-statistical MMR possibilities (see Meuer & Rupietta, 2017 for a review).

There are two main variants: either first run some statistical analyses and then a QCA, or start with a QCA and pursue with some statistical analyses (see Figure 17.5). Both variants typically allow one to exploit a given dataset both from a correlational and a set-theoretic perspective—but, as discussed below (see Sections 5 and 6), it is also possible to cross-feed both analyses in more refined ways.

The first type of MMR sequence is to first conduct a standard statistical analysis—for instance, a multiple regression analysis—that provides results in terms of net effects of respective independent variables on the dependent variable. This is then followed by a QCA framing the research question in terms of combinations of conditions and providing a different and complementary view (equifinal paths leading the outcome) through the QCA solutions. Another way to exploit such a sequence is, for instance, to exploit the statistical analyses in order to measure the outcome variable that will be used in the QCA (see also Section 5).

The second type of MMR sequence is to first conduct a QCA, and then some statistical analyses. Such post-QCA statistical analyses can be exploited in a least five ways: (1) controlling for alternative explanations, in particular by considering a larger number of independent variables, that is, beyond the limited number of conditions that can be comprised in the QCA; (2) quantifying the QCA solutions, for instance by determining the relative importance of the respective solution terms; (3) quantifying the representativeness of the QCA solution; (4) conducting focused analyses, especially descriptive ones, on sub-populations identified via the QCA; and (5) extending configurational theories tested via the QCA by also considering linear hypotheses via complementary statistical analyses (Meuer & Rupietta, 2017).

4 Empirical Demonstrations of QCA in Mixed Methods or Multimethod Research

Given the multiple ways in which QCA can be inserted in a mixed methods or multimethod design, we have chosen to handpick a number of published empirical illustrations corresponding to the five main strategies discussed above—and to highlight some core good practices.

Our informed guess is that roughly one third of all published QCA empirical applications meet the criteria, at least to some extent, of strategies 1, 2 and 3—that is: they involve diverse data sources (strategy 1) and/or seriously engage with some level of case-based knowledge throughout the research process or at least in the pre-QCA phase (strategies 2 and 3). We may mention, by means of illustration, two empirical applications that tick both boxes:

- Bauwens, Lobe, Segers and Tsaliki (2009) investigate the core combinations of factors contributing towards a high degree of online risk by children using the Internet in 20 European countries. This

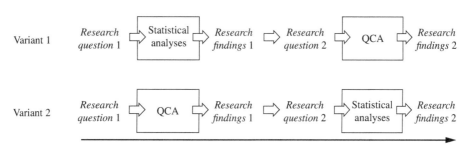

Source: own elaboration

FIGURE 17.5 QCA-statistical strategy

QCA application builds on a wealth of diverse qualitative and quantitative data systematically collected in each country, including surveys, expert and user interviews, official statistics, policy documents, focus groups etc. In addition, as this is embedded in a larger collaborative EU-funded project (EUKidsOnline), the QCA can also rely on extensive country monographs compiled by the respective country experts.

- Pagliarin, Hersperger and Rihoux (2020) examine the combinations of conditions that lead to a form of concordance between strategic urban projects and spatial plans in 38 diverse large-scale urban development projects in 9 Western European urban regions. The data gathered are very diverse: archival material, official reports, in-depth interviews with experts and practitioners (analyzed via the MAXQDA software), an online expert survey, grey literature and site visit notes—which enabled the lead author to gain some quite in-depth knowledge about the respective cases, also feeding this into the interpretation of the QCA solutions.

Regarding strategy 4, to the best of our knowledge, there are still very few publications comprising a QCA followed by a full-fledged CPT analysis—indeed this strategy is just beginning to be developed. One rare example is Álamos-Concha's (2018) research on the factors that have led to the success of 'large-scale contentious politics' in some Middle East and North Africa (MENA) countries in the 2010–2012 period. She first covers 14 MENA countries via a QCA, which enables her to identify four core conditions operating in conjunction, within a specific context, and then performs a CPT on the typical case of Tunisia, unpacking three specific and integrated causal mechanisms at play—exploiting a wealth of primary data, including interviews and ethnographic fieldwork in different Tunisian locations.

Beyond this, some published applications feature in-depth case analyses in a post-QCA phase, mostly in order to consolidate the interpretation of the QCA solutions, that is, a multimethod strategy that is quite proximate to strategy 4—though not engaging in a full-fledged CPT analysis. Here are two illustrations:

- Cooper and Glaesser (2012) first perform a QCA in a large n design (a subgroup of 790 respondent from the German Socio-Economic Panel), where the outcome is the type of school young people attended at the age of 17. They then focus on two types of 'deviant' cases, respectively regarding the necessity of a core expected condition and the sufficiency of a core combination of conditions, and exploit four in-depth interviews with young people. This enables them to identify some particular mechanisms at play for these specific 'deviant' individuals.
- Aversa, Furnari and Haefliger (2015) perform a csQCA of 28 firms competing in Formula One racing, which enables them to identify business model configurations associated with high and with low performance respectively. They then focus on two specific cases—with particularly high and particularly low performances—on which they conduct in-depth case studies via *case histories*, that is, a less formalized form of causal process tracing. To this end, they exploit diverse sources, including extensive interviews with expert informants.

Finally, among the growing number of research pieces corresponding to strategy 5, we have handpicked three publications to illustrate different types of articulation between QCA and statistical analyses:

- In their analysis of the determinants of social inequality and poverty in the US, Ragin and Fiss (2016) first perform a re-analysis of existing data via a refined logistic regression model, using a moderate number of independent variables, then use the latter as conditions for several rounds of fsQCA analyses. This enables them identify set-theoretic connections between some core conditions (e.g. family background and test scores), which reveals a distinct pattern of racial confounding that was not identified via the statistical analyses.
- Schneider and Makszin (2014) also first exploit statistical analyses before a QCA. In a comparative analysis across 37 capitalist democracies, they examine whether the degree of political inequality between social groups (the outcome for the QCA) is shaped by features of the welfare capitalist system. Using individual-level data, they first run regressions for each one of the country cases in order to obtain a beta coefficient of a specific independent variable, which is then used as the outcome of the fsQCA.
- Ali, Seny Kan and Sarstedt (2016) analyze how firms can achieve high levels of organizational performance under different configurations of absorptive capacity and organizational innovation. To this end, exploiting the same dataset, they use partial least squares structural equation modeling (PLS-SEM) to test five directional hypotheses, and fsQCA to test a more encompassing, sixth hypothesis phrased in terms of expected combinations of absorptive capacity (with four sub-dimensions) and organizational innovation (with three sub-dimensions), that is, via a seven-condition fsQCA model.

5 Suggested Applications of QCA in MMR

The five main strategies that have been outlined and illustrated here above are by no means limitative. They can be exploited in a complementary manner, as building blocks of richer and more multi-stage mixed methods designs—also resorting to some other methods not discussed above:

- One particularly rich illustration is the MMR implemented by Berg-Schlosser (2012), building upon a research project on the survival or collapse of democracies (the outcome of interest) in Europe between the two World Wars. This multi-step MMR includes in-depth case studies, csQCA and fsQCA analyses,

an MSDO/MDSO analysis (a specific technique that establishes distance matrixes across multiple cases and a large number of conditions (Berg-Schlosser & De Meur, 1997)) as well as several rounds of statistical analyses.
- Such multi-step MMR that sequences in-depth case studies, QCA and statistical analyses can also be found in other book-length publications, such as Mc Bride and Mazur (2010) on state feminism in Western democracies or Glaesser (2015) on young people's educational careers in England and Germany.
- Another type of rich combination is exemplified by Woodside, Schpektor and Xia's (2013) elaborate work on management models. They combine three distinct methods in order to process marketing field experiments data: statistical (multiple regression analyses), fsQCA and isomorphic modeling, and demonstrate that each method brings some complementary information in the analysis of marketing performance.
- Beyond this, it is also possible to combine or sequence QCA with various other analytical methods, for instance Social Network Analysis (Fischer, 2011; Stevenson & Greenberg, 2000; Yamasaki & Spreitzer, 2006) and Game Theory (Brown & Boswell, 1995).

The bottom line is that it is possible to fruitfully sequence and cross-fertilize QCA with diverse methods, in multiple ways, depending on one's research goals. One may also include close neighbors of QCA such as set-theoretic counterfactual analysis (Mahoney & Barrenechea, 2019) or analyses of necessity (Goertz, 2017).

6 Strengths and Limitations of QCA in Mixed Methods or Multimethod Research

The core strength of including QCA in mixed methods or multimethod research is that it enables one to gain more leverage, in a specific way, in one's research project. That specific leverage is all about tapping conjunctural causes—causal complexity—in multiple-case settings, from relatively small n to larger n research situations. When combined with statistical analyses, QCA enables one to move beyond net effects thinking and to get more out of the data. When combined with case studies and in particular with CPT, QCA enables one to both address a why-question, uncovering cross-case patterns of core conditions leading to some outcome of interest, and a how-question, opening the black box of mechanisms linking (or not) these core conditions to the outcome in single cases.

QCA can therefore potentially bring a lot of added value, as it can complement correlational thinking and single case thinking. For these reasons, we recommend that researchers try and move beyond the single-method use of QCA, and especially to combine it with some form of case studies focusing on causal mechanisms. Indeed QCA by itself does not really establish strong causal links (Blatter & Haverland, 2012). Some deeper, case-based evidence is needed to do so, and CPT is a particularly powerful—albeit demanding—method to that end.

This said, the endeavor of inserting QCA in mixed methods or multimethod research can bump into at least three types of limitations. The first two are generic to any mixed methods or multimethod research. On the one hand, such a design is bound to be more time-consuming, more demanding in terms of methods skills, less easy to manage and therefore also potentially more high-risk than a single-method research (Lobe, 2008). On the other hand, for MMR specifically, it often proves challenging to bridge (or at least to sequence) methods that are built on different epistemological assumptions—the contrast between conventional statistical techniques and QCA is a case in point. Gladly, the epistemological jump is less difficult when combining QCA with case studies, because QCA already includes quite a number of case-oriented features (see above), and also because, in essence, both QCA and case studies are grounded in set-theoretical thinking (Rohlfing & Schneider, 2018).

The third type of limitation is not specific to QCA proper. It has more to do with the challenge of conducting systematic cross-case research, that is, conducting empirical research across multiple and diverse cases (breadth, that can be achieved with QCA as an analytic and complexity reduction tool) while also gaining sufficient intimacy with each and every case considered (depth) (Berg-Schlosser & De Meur, 2009; Peters, 2013). This entails at least five concrete challenges:

- Gathering rich information on each case—which means gathering at least *some* form of primary data on each case, beyond the already available secondary data, existing case monographs etc. This is particularly difficult in cross-country and cross-cultural research projects;
- Avoiding bias in the data. This difficulty is of course obvious when having to rely on secondary data, as pre-existing databases may be biased in many ways. It is also obvious when collecting primary data, for instance through interviews or ethnographic work, when the researcher often injects some of his or her own cultural or normative biases in the data;
- Balancing in-depth knowledge of each case with the number of cases considered. The more the researcher invests time and resources into gathering information on each single case, the more he or she knows about each case's specificity, context, historicity, and what makes it special—and the less time he or she can devote to covering a diversity of cases. Our recommendation is that one should, *ex ante*, decide on the minimal threshold of within-case 'intimacy' one wants to reach across all cases considered for the QCA;
- Balancing one's knowledge of the respective cases. In most research situations, within a given population, sub-population, or sample/selection of cases, the researcher has more privileged access to some cases, with more diverse and more solid data, and/or more skills to better grasp some cases. This challenge has

to be addressed because knowledge gaps on some cases are likely to make the QCA more fragile at different steps of the procedure, in particular threshold-setting/calibration, solving contradictions and arbitrating between terms in QCA solutions;

- Gathering data at the micro-level (agents) in all cases, especially if the cases are located at macro- or meso-levels (for instance: political systems, urban areas, policy processes, firms, etc.). In principle, such data are needed if one ambitions to unpack mechanisms with CPT in the post-QCA phase, but it is often very difficult to obtain, at least in terms of direct, first-hand data.

In spite of these challenges and caveats, inserting QCA in mixed methods or multimethod research has already proven very powerful as a research strategy. The various innovations currently under way in the field of QCA, both at the conceptual and technical levels, will undoubtedly provide multiple opportunities for further refinements, both for fundamental and applied research.

7 Resources for Learning More About QCA in Mixed Methods and Multimethod Research

There are still very few specific sources unpacking QCA in mixed methods and multimethod research, let alone providing practical guidance. Diverse chapters in the *The Sage Handbook of Case-Based Research* (Byrne & Ragin, 2009) provide useful reflections on the epistemological foundations of research involving QCA and case studies, and a piece in this same handbook approaches this from a more hands-on perspective (Rihoux & Lobe, 2009).

There are also rather short sections devoted to this in the main QCA textbooks (Oana, Schneider, & Thomann, 2021: 166–173; Rihoux et al., 2009: 170–172; Schneider & Wagemann, 2012: 305–312); the latter also provide precise guidance for QCA proper (see also other textbooks: Dusa, 2018; Mello, 2021). Meuer and Rupietta (2017) provide a quite extensive review of QCA-statistical MMR applications, and numerous pieces discussing research combining QCA with case studies—in particular via CPT—are cited here above (see strategies 2, 3 and 4).

Regarding published empirical applications: a dozen examples, showcasing diverse QCA uses in mixed methods or multimethod research, are discussed in short in Sections 5 and 6 above. Depending on one's discipline, substantive topics and methodological interests besides QCA, many more published pieces may be found via the COMPASSS international resource website (https://compasss.org/), in particular via its searchable bibliographical database.

NOTES

1. The authors express their thanks to the following colleagues who have offered very useful feedback on a previous draft of this chapter: (A–Z) Derek Beach, Dirk Berg-Schlosser, Burke Johnson, Tony Onwuegbuzie, Ingo Rohlfing and Carsten Schneider. The usual disclaimer applies.

2. In QCA terminology, the *outcome* corresponds to the dependent variable in statistical analysis. A *condition* is an explanatory variable (or factor, determinant, stimulus, ingredient) that is expected to affect the outcome, in combination with other conditions (see *multiple conjunctural causation*, below)—therefore it is not the equivalent of a dependent variable in statistical analysis.

3. A *configuration* is a combination of conditions relevant to a given outcome. It may correspond to one, more than one, or no empirical case(s), and it constitutes one row of the *truth table*. It typically displays an outcome value of 0 or 1, or it is a *contradictory* configuration if some cases display a 0 outcome while some others display a 1 outcome in spite of sharing the same combination of condition values.

4. A conception of causality according to which (1) most often, it is a combination of conditions that generates the outcome, (2) different combinations of conditions may produce the same outcome, (3) a given outcome may result from a condition when it is present and also when it is absent, depending on how this condition is combined with other conditions (no permanent causality), and (4) the presence and the absence of the outcome may require different explanations (no causal symmetry) (Berg-Schlosser, De Meur, Rihoux, & Ragin, 2009: 8–9).

REFERENCES

Álamos-Concha, P. (2018). *Conditions and causal mechanisms of large-scale contentious politics in authoritarian regimes. A multimethod analysis of Middle East and North Africa Countries, 2010–2012.* Louvain-la-Neuve, Belgium: Presses Universitaires de Louvain.

Ali, M., Seny Kan, K. A., & Sarstedt, M. (2016). Direct and configurational paths of absorptive capacity and organizational innovation to successful organizational performance. *Journal of Business Research*, 69(11), 5317–5323. doi:10.1016/j.jbusres.2016.04.131

Aversa, P., Furnari, S., & Haefliger, S. (2015). Business model configurations and performance: A qualitative comparative analysis in Formula One racing, 2005–2013. *Industrial and Corporate Change*, 24(3), 655–676. doi:10.1093/icc/dtv012

Baumgartner, M., & Epple, R. (2014). A coincidence analysis of a causal chain: The Swiss minaret vote. *Sociological Methods & Research*, 43(2), 280–312. doi:10.1177/0049124113502948

Bauwens, J., Lobe, B., Segers, K., & Tsaliki, L. (2009). A shared responsibility. *Journal of Children and Media*, 3(4), 316–330. doi:10.1080/17482790903233325

Beach, D. (2017). Process-tracing methods in social science. In W. R. Thompson (Ed.), *Oxford Research Encyclopedia of politics* (pp. 1–29). Oxford, UK: Oxford University Press.

Beach, D. (2018). Achieving methodological alignment when combining QCA and process tracing in practice. *Sociological Methods & Research*, 47(1), 64–99. doi:10.1177/0049124117701475

Beach, D., & Pedersen, R. B. (2016). *Causal case study methods. Foundations and guidelines for comparing, matching, and tracing.* Ann Harbour, MI: University of Michigan Press.

Beach, D., & Pedersen, R. B. (2018). Selecting appropriate cases when tracing causal mechanisms. *Sociological Methods & Research*, 47(4), 837–871. doi:10.1177/0049124115622510

Beach, D., & Pedersen, R. B. (2019). *Process tracing methods. Foundations and guidelines* (2nd ed.). Ann Arbor, MI: University of Michigan Press.

Beach, D., & Rohlfing, I. (2018). Integrating cross-case analyses and process tracing in set-theoretic research: Strategies and parameters of debate. *Sociological Methods & Research, 47*(1), 3–36. doi:10.1177/0049124115613780

Beach, D., & Siewert, M. (2020). 'Hic sunt dracones': The consequences of overlooked causal heterogeneity in Set-Theoretic Multimethod Research and what to do about it. (under review).

Bennett, A., & Checkel, J. (2014). *Process tracing: From metaphor to analytic tool.* Cambridge, UK: Cambridge.

Berg-Schlosser, D. (2012). *Mixed methods in comparative politics: Principles and applications* London, UK: Palgrave Macmillan.

Berg-Schlosser, D., & De Meur, G. (1997). Reduction of complexity for a small-n analysis: A stepwise multi-methodological approach. *Comparative Social Research, 16*, 133–162.

Berg-Schlosser, D., & De Meur, G. (2009). Comparative research design: case and variable selection. In B. Rihoux & C. C. Ragin (Eds.), *Configurational comparative methods. Qualitative Comparative Analysis (QCA) and related techniques* (pp. 19–32). Thousand Oaks, CA: Sage.

Berg-Schlosser, D., De Meur, G., Rihoux, B., & Ragin, C. C. (2009). Qualitative Comparative Analysis (QCA) as an approach. In B. Rihoux & C. C. Ragin (Eds.), *Configurational comparative methods. Qualitative Comparative Analysis (QCA) and related techniques* (pp. 1–18). Thousand Oaks, CA: Sage.

Blanchard, P., Rihoux, B., & Álamos-Concha, P. (2017). Comprehensively mapping political science methods: An instructors' survey. *International Journal of Social Research Methodology, 20*(2), 209–224. doi:10.1080/13645579.2015.1129128

Blatter, J., & Haverland, M. (2012). *Designing case studies: Explanatory approaches in small-n research.* Basingstoke, UK: Palgrave Macmillan

Brown, C., & Boswell, T. (1995). Strikebreaking or solidarity in the Great Steel Strike of 1919: A split labor market, game-theoretic, and QCA analysis. *American Journal of Sociology, 100*(6), 1479–1519. doi:10.1086/230669

Byrne, D., & Ragin, C. C. (Eds.). (2009). *The Sage handbook of case-based methods.* London, UK: Sage.

Caren, N., & Panofsky, A. (2005). TQCA: A technique for adding temporality to Qualitative Comparative Analysis. *Sociological Methods & Research, 34*(2), 147–172. doi:10.1177/0049124105277197

Cooper, B., & Glaesser, J. (2012). Qualitative work and the testing and development of theory: Lessons from a study combining cross-case and within-case analysis via Ragin's QCA. *Forum Qualitative Sozialforschung/Forum: Qualitative Social Research, 13*(2), 1–24 (article 24). doi:10.17169/fqs-13.2.1776

Cronqvist, L., & Berg-Schlosser, D. (2009). Multi-value QCA (MVQCA). In B. Rihoux & C. C. Ragin (Eds.), *Configurational comparative methods. Qualitative Comparative Analysis (QCA) and related techniques* (pp. 69–86). Thousand Oaks, CA: Sage.

Curchod, C., Dumez, H., & Jeunemaître, A. (2004). Une étude de l'organisation du transport aérien en Europe: les vertus de l'AQQC pour l'exploration de la complexité. *Revue Internationale de Politique Comparée, 11*(1), 85–100. doi:10.3917/ripc.111.0085

De Meur, G., Rihoux, B., & Yamasaki, S. (2009). Addressing the critiques of QCA. In B. Rihoux & C. C. Ragin (Eds.), *Configurational comparative methods. Qualitative Comparative Analysis (QCA) and related techniques* (pp. 147–166). Thousand Oaks, CA: Sage.

Drass, K. A., & Spencer, J. W. (1987). Accounting for presentencing recommendations: Typologies and Probation Officers' Theory of Office. *Social Problems, 34*(3), 277–293. doi:10.2307/800767

Dul, J. (2016). Necessary Condition Analysis (NCA): Logic and methodology of "Necessary but Not Sufficient" causality. *Organizational Research Methods, 19*(1), 10–52. doi:10.1177/1094428115584005

Dusa, A. (2018). *QCA with R. A comprehensive resource.* Cham, Switzerland: Springer.

Emmenegger, P. (2011). How good are your counterfactuals? Assessing quantitative macro-comparative welfare state research with qualitative criteria. *Journal of European Social Policy, 21*(4), 365–380. doi:10.1177/0958928711412222

Fischer, M. (2011). Social network analysis and Qualitative Comparative Analysis: Their mutual benefit for the explanation of policy network structures. *Methodological Innovations Online, 6*(2), 27–51. doi:10.4256/mio.2010.0034

Fiss, P. C., Sharapov, D., & Cronqvist, L. (2013). Opposites attract? Opportunities and challenges for integrating large-n QCA and econometric analysis. *Political Research Quarterly, 66*(1), 191–198. doi:10.1177/1065912912468269e

Gerring, J. (2007). *Case study research: Principles and practices.* Cambridge, UK: Cambridge University Press.

Gerrits, L., & Verweij, S. (2018). *The evaluation of complex infrastructure projects: A guide to Qualitative Comparative Analysis.* Cheltenham, UK: Edward Elgar.

Glaesser, J. (2015). *Young people's educational careers in England and Germany. Integrating survey and interview analysis via Qualitative Comparative Analysis.* Basingstoke, UK: Palgrave Macmillan.

Goertz, G. (2017). *Multimethod research, causal mechanisms, and case studies: An integrated approach.* Princeton, NJ: Princeton University Press.

Hino, A. (2009). Time-Series QCA: Studying temporal change through Boolean analysis. *Sociological Theory and Methods, 24*(2), 219–246.

Johnson, R. B., Onwuegbuzie, A. J., & Turner, L. A. (2007). Toward a definition of mixed methods research. *Journal of Mixed Methods Research, 1*(2), 112–133. doi:10.1177/1558689806298224

Lobe, B. (2008). *Integration of online research methods.* Ljubljana, Slovenia: Faculty of social sciences, University of Ljubljana.

Mahoney, J., & Barrenechea, R. (2019). The logic of counterfactual analysis in case-study explanation. *British Journal of Sociology, 70*(1), 306–338. doi:10.1111/1468-4446.12340

Marx, A., Cambré, B., & Rihoux, B. (2013). Crisp-set Qualitative Comparative Analysis in organizational studies. *Research in the Sociology of Organizations, 38 [Configurational Theory and Methods in Organizational Research]*, 23–47. doi:10.1108/S0733-558X(2013)0000038006

Marx, A., & Dusa, A. (2011). Crisp-set Qualitative Comparative Analysis (csQCA), contradictions and consistency benchmarks for model specification. *Methodological Innovations Online, 6*(2), 103–148. doi:10.4256/mio.2010.0037

Marx, A., Rihoux, B., & Ragin, C. C. (2013). The origins, development and applications of Qualitative Comparative Analysis (QCA): The First 25 Years. *European Political Science Review*, *6*(1), 115–142. doi:10.1017/S1755773912000318

McBride, D. E., & Mazur, A. G. (Eds.). (2010). *The politics of state feminism. Innovation in comparative research*. Philadelphia, PA: Temple University Press.

Mello, P. (2021). *Qualitative Comparative Analysis: Research design and application*. Washington, DC: Georgetown University Press.

Meuer, J., & Rupietta, C. (2017). A review of integrated QCA and statistical analyses. *Quality & Quantity: International Journal of Methodology*, *51*(5), 2063–2083. doi:10.1007/s11135-016-0397-z

Oana, I.-E., Schneider, C. Q., & Thomann, E. (2021). *Qualitative Comparative Analysis (QCA) using R: A beginner's guide*. Cambridge, UK: Cambridge University Press.

Pagliarin, S., & Gerrits, L. (2020). Trajectory-based Qualitative Comparative Analysis: Accounting for case-based time dynamics. *Methodological Innovations* (Online first). doi:10.1177/2059799120959170

Pagliarin, S., Hersperger, A. M., & Rihoux, B. (2020). Implementation pathways of large-scale urban development projects (lsUDPs) in Western Europe: A qualitative comparative analysis (QCA). *European Planning Studies*. doi:10.1080/09654313.2019.1681942

Pattyn, V., Álamos-Concha, P., Cambré, B., Rihoux, B., & Schalembier, B. (2020)). Policy effectiveness through configurational and mechanistic lenses: Lessons for concept development. *Journal of Comparative Policy Analysis: Research and Practice* (Online first). doi:10.1080/13876988.2020.1773263

Peters, B. G. (2013). *Strategies for comparative research in political science: Theory and methods*. Basingstoke, UK: Palgrave Macmillan.

Ragin, C. C. (1987). *The comparative method: Moving beyond qualitative and quantitative strategies*. Berkeley, CA: University of California Press.

Ragin, C. C. (1997). Turning the tables: How case-oriented methods challenge variable-oriented methods. *Comparative Social Research*, *16*, 27–42.

Ragin, C. C. (2006). The limitations of net-effects thinking. In B. Rihoux & H. Grimm (Eds.), *Innovative comparative methods for policy analysis* (pp. 13–41). New York, NY: Springer.

Ragin, C. C. (2008). *Redesigning social inquiry: Fuzzy sets and beyond*. Chicago, IL: Chicago University Press.

Ragin, C. C. (2014). Comment: Lucas and Szatrowski in critical perspective. *Sociological methodology*, *44*(1), 80–94. doi:10.1177/0081175014542081

Ragin, C. C., & Becker, H. S. (Eds.). (1992). *What is a case? Exploring the foundations of social inquiry*. New York, NY: Cambridge University Press.

Ragin, C. C., & Fiss, P. C. (2016). *Intersectional inequality. Race, class, test scores, and poverty*. Chicago, IL: University of Chicago Press.

Rihoux, B. (2001). *Les partis politiques: Organisations en changement. Le test des écologistes*. Paris, France: L'Harmattan.

Rihoux, B. (2013). Qualitative Comparative Analysis (QCA), Anno 2013: Reframing *The Comparative Method*'s seminal statements. *Swiss Political Science Review*, *19*(2), 233–245. doi:doi.org/10.1111/spsr.12031

Rihoux, B. (2017). Configurational Comparative Methods (QCA and Fuzzy Sets): Complex causation in cross-case analysis. In J. Woldendorp & H. Keman (Eds.), *Handbook of Research Methods and Applications in Political Science* (pp. 383–399). Cheltenham, UK: Edward Elgar.

Rihoux, B., & De Meur, G. (2009). Crisp-set Qualitative Comparative Analysis (csQCA). In B. Rihoux & C. C. Ragin (Eds.), *Configurational comparative methods. Qualitative Comparative Analysis (QCA) and related techniques* (pp. 33–68). Thousand Oaks, CA: Sage.

Rihoux, B., & Lobe, B. (2009). The case for qualitative comparative analysis (QCA): Adding leverage for thick cross-case comparison. In D. Byrne & C. Ragin (Eds.), *The Sage handbook of case-based methods* (pp. 222–243). London, UK: Sage.

Rihoux, B., & Lobe, B. (2015). The case-orientedness of Qualitative Comparative Analysis (QCA): Glass half-empty or half-full. *Teorija i praksa*, *52*(6), 1039–1055. doi:10.13140/RG.2.1.1919.1529

Rihoux, B., & Marx, A. (2013). Qualitative Comparative Analysis at 25: State of play and agenda. *Political Research Quarterly*, *66*(1), 167–171. doi:10.1177/1065912912468269a

Rihoux, B., & Ragin, C. C. (Eds.). (2009). *Configurational comparative methods. Qualitative Comparative Analysis (QCA) and related techniques*. Thousand Oaks, CA: Sage.

Rihoux, B., Ragin, C. C., Yamasaki, S., & Bol, D. (2009). Conclusions: The ways ahead. In B. Rihoux & C. C. Ragin (Eds.), *Configurational comparative methods. Qualitative Comparative Analysis (QCA) and related techniques* (pp. 167–178). Thousand Oaks, CA: Sage.

Rohlfing, I. (2012). *Case studies and causal inference: An integrative framework*. Basingstoke, UK: Palgrave Macmillan.

Rohlfing, I., & Schneider, C. (2018). A unifying framework for causal analysis in set-theoretic multimethod research. *Sociological Methods & Research*, *47*(1), 37–63. doi:10.1177/0049124115626170

Rohlfing, I., & Schneider, C. Q. (2013). Improving research on necessary conditions: Formalized case selection for process tracing after QCA. *Political Research Quarterly*, *66*(1), 220–230. doi:10.1177/1065912912468269i

Rubinson, C. (2019). Presenting qualitative comparative analysis: Notation, tabular layout, and visualization. *Methodological Innovations*, *12*(2), online first. doi:10.1177/2059799119862110

Schneider, C. Q. (2019). Two-step QCA revisited: The necessity of context conditions. *Quality & Quantity*, *53*(3), 1109–1126. doi:10.1007/s11135-018-0805-7

Schneider, C. Q., & Makszin, K. (2014). Forms of welfare capitalism and education-based participatory inequality. *Socio-Economic Review*, *12*(2), 437–462. doi:10.1093/ser/mwu010

Schneider, C. Q., & Rohlfing, I. (2013). Combining QCA and process-tracing in set-theoretic multimethod research. *Sociological Methods & Research*, *42*(4), 559–597. doi:10.1177/0049124113481341

Schneider, C. Q., & Rohlfing, I. (2016). Case studies nested in fuzzy-set QCA on sufficiency: Formalizing case selection and causal inference. *Sociological Methods & Research*, *45*(3), 526–568. doi:10.1177/0049124114532446

Schneider, C. Q., & Wagemann, C. (2006). Reducing complexity in Qualitative Comparative Analysis (QCA): Remote and proximate factors and the consolidation of democracy. *European Journal of Political Research*, *45*(5), 751–786. doi:10.1111/j.1475-6765.2006.00635.x

Schneider, C. Q., & Wagemann, C. (2012). *Set-theoretic methods for the social sciences: A guide to Qualitative Comparative Analysis*. Cambridge, UK: Cambridge University Press.

Scouvart, M., Adams, R. T., Caldas, M., Dale, V., Mertens, B., Nédélec, V., ... Lambin, E. F. (2007). Causes of deforestation in the Brazilian Amazon: A Qualitative Comparative Analysis. *Journal of Land Use Science*, 2(4), 257–282. doi:10.1080/17474230701785929

Stevenson, W. B., & Greenberg, D. (2000). Agency and social networks: strategies of action in a social structure of position, opposition, and opportunity. *Administrative Science Quarterly*, 45(4), 651–678. doi:10.2307/2667015

Thomann, E. (2019). *Customized implementation of European Union food safety policy: United in diversity?* Cham, Switzerland: Palgrave Macmillan.

Vanderborght, Y., & Yamasaki, S. (2004). Des cas logiques... contradictoires? Un piège de l'aqqc déjoué à travers l'étude de la faisabilité politique de l'allocation universelle. *Revue Internationale de Politique Comparée*, 11(1), 51–66. doi:10.3917/ripc.111.0051

Williams, T., & Gemperle, S. M. (2017). Sequence will tell! Integrating temporality into set-theoretic multi-method research combining comparative process tracing and qualitative comparative analysis. *International Journal of Social Research Methodology*, 20(2), 121–135. doi:10.1080/13645579.2016.1149316

Woodside, A. G., Schpektor, A., & Xia, X. (2013). Triple sensemaking of findings from marketing experiments using the dominant variable based-logic, case-based logic, and isomorphic modeling. *International Journal of Business and Economics*, 12(2), 131–153.

Yamasaki, S., & Spreitzer, A. (2006). Beyond methodological tenets. The worlds of QCA and SNA and their benefits to policy analysis. In B. Rihoux & H. Grimm (Eds.), *Innovative comparative methods for policy analysis* (pp. 95–120). New York, NY: Springer.

Yin, R. K. (Ed.) (2017). *Case study research and applications. Design and methods* (6th ed.). Thousand Oaks, CA: Sage.

18

Q Methodology as Mixed Analysis

Susan Ramlo

1 Definition of Q Methodology

More than 80 years ago, William Stephenson created Q methodology [Q] as a scientific way to measure subjectivity (Brown, 1980; McKeown & Thomas, 2013; Ramlo, 2016a; Stephenson, 1935, 1953a). Essentially, the stages within any Q study are as follows: create a concourse of items that represent the broad communications of the topic, select a subset of the concourse called the Q-sample, collect Q-sorts wherein participants sort the Q-sample items into a grid based upon their viewpoint of the topic, analyze the sorts via factor analysis and correlation, and interpret the multiple divergent perspectives and consensus that emerge (Brown, 1980; McKeown & Thomas, 2013; Newman & Ramlo, 2010; Ramlo, 2015a, 2016a, 2016b). Oftentimes, researchers are familiar with only Q's technique (the Q-sort) or its method (factor analyzing to group people instead of items like R factor analysis). But it is important to note that Q is a complete methodology comprising a set of procedures, theory, and philosophy that focuses on the study of subjectivity (Brown, 1980, 2008). Further detail about Q's procedures, theory, and philosophy are provided within the Technical Outline section of this chapter. But for now, suffice to say, the processes of Q include investigating subjectivity, collecting conversations and/or dialogue, factor analysis, correlation, and interpretation. Certainly, these processes constitute an interactive continuum of qualitative and quantitative research (Newman & Ramlo, 2010).

Although some researchers (e.g., Block, 2008; Nunnally, 1978) have used Q's use of factor analysis to frame it as a quantitative research methodology, others (e.g., Brown, 1996, 2008; Watts & Stenner, 2005) have used Q's focus on measuring and describing subjective viewpoints to identify it as a qualitative research methodology. Yet, other researchers have focused on Q's mixture of qualitative and quantitative research, declaring it as mixed (e.g., Ramlo, 2016a, 2016b; Ramlo & Newman, 2011), inherently mixed (e.g., Newman & Ramlo, 2010; Ramlo, 2015a), and even a qualiquantology (Stenner & Stainton-Rogers, 2004), with the explanation that mixed methods is insufficient a term to describe the mixture of qualitative and quantitative in Q. Here, I accept Q as inherently mixed methods across the multiple stages within the larger methodology, including mixed analysis within the factor-analytic stage.

2 When Use of Q Methodology is Appropriate

Because Q involves the use of factor analysis to reveal the multiple, divergent viewpoints within a group of people or an individual sorting under multiple conditions of instruction with rich descriptions that enable the researcher both to describe and to differentiate those viewpoints (Brown, 1980; McKeown & Thomas, 2013; Stephenson, 1953a), Q is an appropriate choice whenever the research question involves investigating the multiple perspectives, as well as consensus, regarding any topic (Brown, 1980). Without a doubt, the broader research community more typically uses Likert-format scales (Flake, Pek, & Hehman, 2017) to determine viewpoints but there are numerous disadvantages to the Likert-format scale approach compared to Q. The Q-sort, unlike a Likert-format scale, empowers participants to provide their own views based upon their own interpretations of the statements. In other words, each Q-sort represents an internal snapshot of each person's viewpoint based on their preferences, experiences, and interpretations (Brown, 1980; Ramlo & Newman, 2011; Stephenson, 1953a). As such, there is no need for researcher-provided operational definitions to consider during the sorting process because it is the sorter's responsibility to interpret the meanings contained in the statements/items of the Q-sample (Brown, 1980; Stephenson, 1953a).

Therefore, Q does not require establishing validity and reliability of the statements used in the Q-sample. Instead, post-sort interviews often are used to clarify the thinking of participants and their placements of items, especially at the extreme ends of the sorting grid (Brown, 1980; Newman & Ramlo, 2010; Stephenson, 1953a). These post-sort interviews and other information often are used by the Q researcher to use factor analysis to find the best theoretical significance for the study (Brown & Robyn, 2004; Kramer & Gravina, 2004; McKeown & Thomas, 2013; Ramlo, 2015a, 2016b). In other words, in Q, the goal is to find an operant solution (Brown, 1980; Ramlo, 2015a).

Another substantial difference is how participants interact with the items of a Q-sort opposed to responding to a Likert-format scale. In Q-sorting, each item is compared to all other items as they are placed along the grid continuum. Each participant interacts with these items as they decide where to place each item relative to the others based upon her/his viewpoint. Those items placed at either end of that continuum represent those items with the most salience for the sorter. Alternatively, in a Likert-format scale, participant responses to each item is independent of their responses to the other items (Baas, Rhoads, & Thomas, 2016).

Surveys often require a large sample of participants and researchers typically seek to generalize survey responses to a larger population (Baas et al., 2016; Brown, 1980), wherein all participants are exposed to standard stimuli. Within Q, the focus is on determining the "similarity or dissimilarity of *operations* under controlled *conditions* [emphasis in original] of instruction" (Brown, 1980, p. 150), whereby the term "operations" speaks to the process of manipulating the Q-sample. The number of statements in the Q-sample is the sample size and a Q researcher must have sufficient items within this sample to represent all the communications on the topic (Brown, 1980; McKeown & Thomas, 2013; Newman & Ramlo, 2010). The set of participants, P-set, is often small and theoretically relevant to the problem under investigation (Brown, 1980). In fact, a single person may represent the P-set with multiple sorts under different conditions of instruction, which could include how they perceive other people in their lives view them (Brown, 1980; McKeown & Thomas, 2013). Thus, not surprisingly, Q has been used in psychoanalysis (Brown, 1980).

Finally, Likert-type scales result in a loss of meaning compared to the results from Q (McKeown, 2001). Whereas such scales provide aggregate values for statements across all participants, Q offers descriptive results that offer differentiation of the diverse viewpoints that exist (Brown, 1980; McKeown, 2001). Thus, when a researcher is interested in the multiple perspectives within a group of people and desires to describe those viewpoints as well as the consensus among those viewpoints, Q methodology is the most appropriate choice.

3 Technical Outline of Q Methodology for MMR

Q methodology is a set of procedures, theory, and philosophy that focuses on the study of subjectivity (Brown, 1980, 2008). The stages of Q exist within a broad philosophical, ontological, and epistemological framework. Brown (1980) describes Q as "the body of theory and principles that guides the application of technique, method, and explanation" (p. 6). Here, within this section, I will describe each stage of any Q methodology study in the form of a technical outline that focuses on Q as an inherently mixed method.

Concourse

Every Q study commences with the collection of communications on the topic. The sources for these communications often include focus groups, interviews, or printed materials such as newspaper articles (McKeown & Thomas, 2013). This collection is called the concourse. Although most often a collection of statements, the concourse also can consist of other means of communications, including pictures and scents. The concourse should represent a universe of communications on the topic (Brown, 1980; Newman & Ramlo, 2010; Ramlo & Newman, 2011; Stephenson, 1953a).

Q-sample

The Q-sample is a subset of the larger concourse. When the participants sort items, they sort all the items from the Q-sample. The goal for selecting the Q-sample is to preserve the range of communications represented in the larger concourse. To accomplish this, Fisher's Design of Experiments (i.e., theoretical modeling using an analysis of variance design) is frequently used to select the Q-sample from the concourse (Brown, 1980). The Q-sample typically consists of 30 to 60 items (Brown, 2008).

Q-sort

The Q-sort provides Q researchers the ability to collect subjective, self-referential measurements of subjectivity. This process often is called Q technique and should not be confused with the larger methodology that is Q. Participants place the individual items of the Q-sample into a grid provided by the researcher. This grid represents a continuum that often has a range such as +5 (i.e., Most Like My View) to −5 (i.e., Most Unlike My View) (Brown, 1980; McKeown & Thomas, 2013). The participants are asked to sort based upon a condition of instruction such as "sort the 46 statements in the envelope based upon your views of this course." Specifically, each Q-sort represents a participant's interaction with the Q-sample based upon their understanding of the topic being studied and, therefore, allows each participant to provide their views (Brown, 1980; Ramlo & Newman, 2011; Stephenson, 1953b). Each Q-sample item is contained on a separate slip of paper with a numerical identifier that is used for recording the final sort in the grid. These numerical identifiers are entered for each sort within a specialized software program such as PQMethod (Schmolck, 2002) for analysis.

Q Analysis

PQMethod is a freeware program specifically designed for Q studies (Brown, 2008; Newman & Ramlo, 2010; Schmolck, 2002). Although factor analysis can be performed within other statistical software, such as SPSS, such software provides the quantitative rather than the additional qualitative aspects of the factor-analytic stage in Q (Newman & Ramlo, 2010). Thus, specialized software is necessary to address the mixed analysis within Q.

After the sorts have been entered into the specialized software, they are factor analyzed to group people with similar views, each type of view represented by a factor (Brown, 1980; Ramlo & Newman, 2010; Stephenson, 1953a). Like R factor analysis, that groups items rather than people, the factor analysis in Q consists of factor extraction and factor rotation. In Q, the preferred factor extraction and rotation choices might seem out of step for those researchers familiar with R factor analysis (Ramlo, 2016b). However, in Q, the factor-analytic goal is to find theoretical significance rather than statistical significance, like in R (Brown, 1980; McKeown & Thomas, 2013; Ramlo, 2016b).

Centroid is the preferred factor extraction choice in Q methodology. It is preferred over the more common choice in R of principle components analysis (PCA). PCA offers a best mathematical solution whereas centroid is indeterminate, meaning that there is not a single best mathematical solution (Brown, 1980; McKeown & Thomas, 2013; Ramlo, 2015a, 2016b). In Q methodology, indeterminate solutions within the factor-analytic stage align with how Q reveals states of mind, which are indeterminate and probabilistic functions. Subjective communications are inherently indeterminate (McKeown & Thomas, 2013). Stephenson (1988) believed that psychology needed to move from a Newtonian framework to one that is quantum mechanical (Ramlo, 2015a; Stephenson, 1988). Thus, Q's probabilistic functions and indeterminate solutions exist within a quantum mechanical framework and combine Stephenson's two disciplines of psychology and physics. Brown (1980) and Ramlo (2015a, 2016b) contain more information about how the centroid is calculated.

Although varimax is commonly used for factor rotation in R factor analysis, hand rotation is the preferred method in Q (Brown, 1980; McKeown & Thomas, 2013; Ramlo, 2015a, 2016b). Theoretical and judgmental rotation are alternative names for hand rotation in Q. However, the term graphical rotation used by Tucker and MacCallum (1997) might provide the best physical description. In hand rotation, each sort is plotted within a two-dimensional axis, wherein each axis represents one of the factors. The locations are based upon the factor loadings on each factor. It is important to note that the interrelationships among the sorts are preserved during factor rotation because the rotation only serves to change the axes and does not rotate the sorts (Brown, 1980; Stephenson, 1953a).

Within the software, the researcher can select pairs of factors for rotation. The axes are rotated within the software, often guided by the researcher's insight about those who sorted the items (Brown, 1980; Ramlo, 2015a, 2016b). Sometimes this insight is provided through post-sort interviews or comments (Ramlo, 2016c, 2019). Other times, the rotations may be guided by a unique quality or position of one of the participants such as a leadership role. In other words, in Q, researchers often use abductory principles to follow hunches and to explore solutions. Stephenson (1953a) stressed that the combination of centroid extraction, hand rotation, and abduction offers researchers the ability to perform scientific explorations. By seeking operant solutions, new understandings can be discovered (Stephenson, 1961).

Interpretation

Once the best theoretical factor solution has been found, the factors are interpreted based on the tables produced as part of the analyses. Most specialized Q software programs provide an extensive report with a variety of tables including factor arrays, distinguishing statements, and consensus statements (Newman & Ramlo, 2010; Ramlo, 2016b). The factor arrays provide a representative sort for each viewpoint that emerged during the analyses. Additionally, the tables of distinguishing statements provide those statements that distinguish each viewpoint from the others that emerged. The factor arrays and tables of distinguishing statements in conjunction with the post-sort questionnaires or interviews facilitate creating a detailed description of each viewpoint. Finally, a table of consensus, which contains the statements with similar grid positions between pairs of factors, enables the researcher, and even the stakeholders, to see what the divergent viewpoints have in common (Brown, 1980; McKeown & Thomas, 2013; Newman & Ramlo, 2010; Ramlo, 2016b). Within the interpretation stage of Q, a researcher does something unique when compared to those who use scaled tests wherein interpretation is not necessary—within the use of scaled tests the meanings have been previously specified. Instead, the researcher creates a "new gestalt" (p. 52) based on the meanings presented within the Q sorts and represented by the factors that emerged from her/his analysis (Brown, 1980).

More on Mixed Analysis in Q

Within this technical outline of the procedures of Q, it is worthwhile to discuss more the inherently mixed analysis stage. It might be obvious at this point that, within Q, the complex mixture of qualitative and quantitative approaches does not represent the simplistic claim that qualitative research has its foundation in words and quantitative research has its foundation in numbers (Newman & Ramlo, 2010). Instead, qualitative research's foundation is based on rich description and the seeking of meaning of phenomena based on perspectives of whoever is under examination (Ridenour & Newman, 2008). However, compared to typical qualitative research, Q uses complex statistical analysis, including correlation and factor analysis (Brown, 1980; Stephenson, 1953a) while also minimizing the impact of the researcher's frame of reference—yet maintaining the relationship among themes within the data (Stainton-Rogers, 1995).

Some quantitative-focused researchers have criticized Q based on statistical considerations (Kampen & Tamás, 2014; Wittenborn, 1961). In particular, some statisticians suggest that Stephenson was simply naïve about factor analysis (Kampen & Tamás, 2014). Yet, these same critics seem to miss the fact that Stephenson was a student of the creator of factor analysis, Charles Spearman (Brown, Danielson, & van Exel, 2015; Good, 2010). Additionally, Kampen and Tamás (2014) criticize Stephenson for not understanding science; yet, he possessed PhDs in both physics and psychology (Brown, 1980; Brown et al., 2015; Good, 2010; Newman & Ramlo, 2010). Thus, Stephenson possessed scientific, mathematical, and statistical expertise with a deep interest in using these skills to create a scientific means of measuring subjectivity (Brown et al., 2015). Additionally, Kampen and Tamás (2014) seem to misunderstand that there is a difference between seeking statistical significance, within R factor analysis, and seeking theoretical significance, within Q's factor-analytic stage (Brown, 1980; Kramer & Gravina, 2004; Ramlo, 2015a, 2016b; Stephenson, 1961). In other words, there seems to be a misunderstanding of inherently mixed analysis within Q primarily by those who are focused on objectivity.

Stephenson was aware of the involvement of subjectivity in the physical sciences and rejected the claim that scientific inquiry was purely objective (Ramlo, 2015a; Stephenson, 1986a). Stephenson (1986b) understood that Q's mixing of laws, theory, instrumentation, and application was both complex and contrary to popular and sometimes dogmatic objective positions. Many Q researchers seem to accept Q as being mixed (Ramlo, 2017a). However, some of those Q methodologists who accept Q as being mixed do so within a structure that represents a kind of quantitative and qualitative dichotomy within the methodology. Specifically, these Q researchers see the qualitative aspects of Q separate from the quantitative stage of factor analysis. In other words, these researchers classify each distinct stage in Q as either qualitative or quantitative. Thus, these researchers see the factor-analytic stage as one that fits into a postpositivistic framework. Other Q researchers, especially those more accepting of the complexity of Q's philosophical, epistemological, and ontological framework, see a more inherent mixture of qualitative and quantitative within Q (Ramlo, 2017a). I agree with this later type of classification. I consider Q as existing within an interactive continuum of qualitative and quantitative research (Newman & Ramlo, 2010; Ramlo & Newman, 2010) like that described by Ridenour and Newman (2008) and representing an inherently mixed method, including the analysis stage of Q (Newman & Ramlo, 2010; Ramlo, 2016b). Understanding this, a reader of this chapter might want to reread this technical outline section with the idea of Q representing inherently mixed research.

4 Empirical Demonstration of Q Methodology for MMR

As might be obvious at this point, there are some differing opinions about the factor-analytic stage of Q methodology. Perhaps surprisingly, divergent viewpoints and practices about this stage even exist within the Q community and have appeared in various media, including the Q METHOD email listserv as well as discussions at the annual conferences of the International Society for the Scientific Study of Subjectivity (ISSSS). The purpose of the study presented here was to investigate and to describe the multiple viewpoints about the factor-analytic stage of Q that exist within the Q community. This demonstration lacks the detail of the full study (Ramlo, 2017a) but is presented in sufficient detail to provide an empirical demonstration of Q.

Concourse, Q-sample, and Q-sort

In this study, the concourse was developed by offering an online survey with various prompts about the factor-analytic stage of Q. The open-ended responses resulted in a concourse of 123 items. These items were distributed across the following eight themes: Comparisons; Dependent on specifics; Easy/Difficult; External authority; Not understood; Objectivity/R factor analysis; Other options (at the factor-analytic stage); and Personal conviction. Fisher's design of experiments was used to select the 51 items for the Q-sample (Ramlo, 2017a, 2019).

The following example is an adaptation from Ramlo (2019). These were the items sorted by the participants using the grid provided in Figure 18.1. Participants provided some information about their Q experience prior to sorting and then responded to open-ended questions about their sorting choices post-sort.

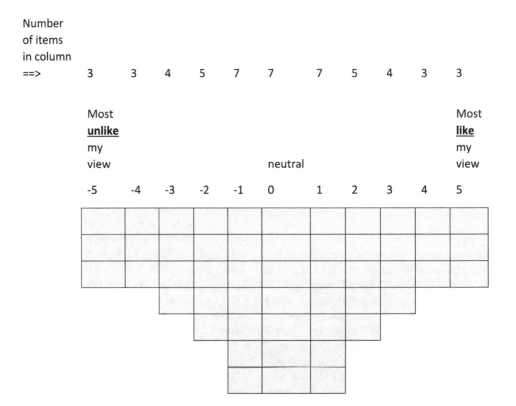

FIGURE 18.1 Sorting grid used in the views of factor analysis in Q study

Source: **Based on the grid in Ramlo (2019)**

P-set

In Q, the sample size is the number of statements sorted, the Q-sample. The sorters make up the P-set. In this study, the researcher sought Q methodologists with a range of experience and practice at the factor-analytic stage of Q. The P-set was recruited during the 2016 ISSSS conference, emails to specific methodologists, and the Q METHOD listserv. A diverse set of 29 Q methodologists provided sorts for the study.

Q Analysis

The Q-sample and Q-sorts were entered into PQMethod (Schmolck, 2002) for analysis. Although objective rotation procedures have their place, for statistical reasons (Brown, 1980), the researcher used the preferred option of hand rotation for this Q study. Because only centroid extraction does not violate the statistical assumptions of a singular best solution (Brown, 1980; McKeown & Thomas, 2013; Ramlo, 2015a, 2016b), the factors were first extracted using centroid then rotated using hand rotation while seeking an operant (i.e., genuinely functional) factor solution.

Abductory principles were used during the hand rotation based upon information gleaned from reading the post-sort comments. Specifically, one of the participants, #9, seemed very knowledgeable about Stephenson's writings and Q's philosophical, ontological, and epistemological aspects. Alternatively, Participant #8 provided a very naïve understanding of Q and seemed frustrated about the software and those who share their expertise on the Q METHOD listserv, among other aspects. Thus, Participants #8 and #9 seemed to be in great contrast to each other and represented the two extreme ends of the Q expertise of the P-set. Therefore, hand rotation focused on ensuring that each of these participants was strongly associated with a unique factor.

How strongly a sort/participant is associated with a factor is given within the factor matrix where +1.00 would be a perfect positive correlation, −1.00 would be a perfect negative correlation, and 0.00 would indicate no association with a factor/perspective (Brown, 1980, 2008). When a sort has sufficient correlation with a factor/viewpoint with minimal correlation with the other factors/viewpoints, it is identified with that factor using *flagging* within the Q software. The necessary correlations can be calculated as shown in Brown (1980). Only those sorts that are flagged on a factor are used for the remaining analyses that produce the various tables in Q. Table 18.1 includes the flagging on factors, indicated by an X, as well as the preferences for factor extraction and rotation provided by the participants.

TABLE 18.1

Factor Array with Xs Indicating Association with a Single Factor

Q sort	Preferred Extraction	Preferred Rotation	Year started using Q	Factor 1	Factor 2	Factor 3
1	Centroid	Hand	2004	X		
2	No response	No response			X	
3	Centroid	Hand	2010	X		
4	PCA	Hand or Varimax	1968		X	
5	Centroid, PCA	Varimax	1975		X	
6	PCA	Varimax	2008		X	
7	Centroid, PCA	Hand	2007	X		
8	PCA	Varimax	2015			X
9	Centroid	Hand	1963	X		
10	Centroid, PCA	Hand or Varimax	1987	X		
11	PCA	unsure	2012		X	
12	PCA	Varimax	2003		X	
13	PCA	Hand or Varimax	1975		X	
14	Centroid	Hand	2014	X		
15	Centroid, PCA	Hand or Varimax	1972			
16	Centroid, PCA	Hand or Varimax	No response	X		
17	Centroid (1), PCA (2)	Hand or Varimax	1996	X		
18	PCA	Hand	2013	X		
19	Centroid	Hand	2011	X		
20	Centroid, PCA	Varimax	2014			
21	Centroid	Hand	2010	X		
22	Centroid	Hand	2012	X		
23	Both (dependent on study)	Varimax or Quartimax	2004			
24	PCA	Varimax	1997		X	
25	Centroid	Hand	2011	X		
26	PCA	Varimax	1992		X	
27	Both	Hand	1990	X		
28	PCA	Varimax	2000		X	
29	Centroid	Hand	2013	X		

Note: Preferred factor extraction and rotation was self-reported by the sorter. Based on table in Ramlo (2019).

Certainly, dealing with these correlation coefficients within the factor matrix is a mathematical one, as is the creation of the tables. However, as part of this inherently mixed analysis stage, the process of factor rotation and interpretation is one of exploration of descriptive results presented in these tables and participant dialogue provided post-sorting (Ramlo, 2015a, 2016b). These descriptions and explanations offer the ability to seek operant solutions with theoretical significance (Brown, 1980; Ramlo, 2015b, 2016a) while using abductory principles within scientific explorations (Brown, 1980, 2008; Stephenson, 1961). Undoubtedly, such a complex interaction between qualitative and quantitative within this analysis stage indicates that not only is Q inherently mixed but also it uses inherently mixed analysis.

Interpretation

In this study, three divergent viewpoints, each represented by a factor, emerged. All but three of the 29 sorts were associated with a single factor/viewpoint. Factor interpretation was based upon the factor arrays, distinguishing statements, participants' written comments, and the factor extraction and rotation preferences that the participants provided.

Inherently Mixed Viewpoint

Factor 1 represents 15 participants including Sorter #9. These Q methodologists all prefer hand rotation, although some stated that they use varimax for initial explorations of factor structure. All but #18 use centroid factor extraction. Although the factor array for this viewpoint was used for interpretation in conjunction with the distinguishing statements, and participants' post-sort comments, Table 18.2 focuses solely on those statements that distinguish this viewpoint from the other two.

For instance, unlike the other two viewpoints, Statement #29 is salient (grid positions 4, −2, −1 for Factors 1, 2, & 3, respectively). Therefore, those on Factor 1 see the embrace of automatic solutions such as using PCA extraction, scree tests, and varimax rotation as a "default position that is taken as a way to avoid taking responsibility." Factor 1 sorters also agree that hand rotation allows for more detailed inspection of data (Statement 33; at 5, 1, 1) and reject those statements that castoff the use of hand rotation (Statements 28 and 9; at −5, 2, 4 and −5,−2, 3, respectively). Instead this view involves the belief that the factor-analytic stage is about the search "for an operant solution, which is best found using theory and judgment" (Statement 42; at 5, 0, 1). Regarding factor extraction, this view involves the acceptance of the centroid as the "only method that is compatible with the principles of Q methodology. Stephenson explicitly recommended against principal components" (Statement 6; at 3, −5, −5). Thus, this viewpoint appears to accept the inherently mixed analysis of Q methodology as well as Stephenson's recommendation to use centroid extraction, hand rotation, and abduction within a Q factor-analytic stage while following scientific principles.

Utilitarian Postpositivist Viewpoint

This viewpoint represents ten of the participants. These Q methodologists expressed confidence in their knowledge and use of factor

TABLE 18.2

Statements that Distinguish Factor 1 from the Other Factors

No.	Statement	Grid Position	Grid Position	Grid Position
33	Hand rotation allows more detailed inspection of data.	5	1	1
42	The search is for an operant solution, which is best found using theory and judgment. Simple structure is sometimes acceptable.	5	0	1
29	The embrace of automatic solutions--PCA, scree test, varimax, etc.--is too often the default position that is taken as a way to avoid taking responsibility.	4	−2	−1
6	Centroid is the only method that is compatible with the principles of Q methodology. Stephenson explicitly recommended against principal components.	3	−5	−5
38	I prefer centroid because it is the method used by Stephenson and Brown.	2	−5	−5
19	My interest is conceptual not statistical. The differences between the two, although statistically important, invalidates neither in my opinion. Sometimes one is better, sometimes the other.	2	−1	−2
14	I love the philosophy that underpins Q methodology but since I'm not a 'natural' statistician I never feel confident about factor analysis.	0	−3	5
3	I usually rely on PCA because it typically serves my purposes.	−1	4	−4
46	In the studies I have done, my goal in rotation is to find "simple structure," rather than to test hypotheses about the relationships between specific study participants. Varimax accomplishes that goal in a quicker and simpler fashion.	−2	5	2
1	Hand-rotation doesn't seem to deliver much more than the varimax solution.	−3	0	0
26	In P-samples, I don't have specific participants whom I consider singular. And I don't know what factors will emerge, or how many, so I don't want to guess which interesting or powerful person I might rotate through. So I prefer PCA and Varimax.	−4	2	4
28	Usually I have no grounds for doing hand rotation.	−5	2	4
9	I choose to avoid hand-rotation on the grounds that it involves a virtual molding of the data/outcome driven by the researcher, whereas my preference is to have minimal investigator interference, again in the interests of greater objectivity.	−5	−2	3

TABLE 18.3

Statements that Distinguish Factor 2 from the Other Factors

No.	Statement	Grid Position	Grid Position	Grid Position
16	PCA provides acceptable factor extraction solutions.	1	5	0
3	I usually rely on PCA because it typically serves my purposes.	−1	4	−4
37	I think PCA is suitable for someone with limited knowledge with Q methodology.	1	4	−1
15	I think it makes more sense to conceptualize the results as components (summarizations of trends in the data) than factors in the strict sense (latent variables).	−1	2	−2
17	My factor analytic choices are easier to defend to non-Q journals.	0	2	−1
43	Usually I settle on using PCA because the results are usually more highly expressed.	−3	1	−3
50	There's really no need for much of the complications and arcane methods; judgmental rotation might have its place, maybe even flagging – but these come later. The "factor analytic" (sic) stage of Q, to me, should really be considered as a data reduction step. Nothing else.	−4	1	−2
2	PCA is more straightforward and descriptive than centroid extraction.	−1	1	−3
34	The difference between PCA and centroid is not well-understood by me and many other Q-researchers.	0	−1	2
9	I choose to avoid hand-rotation on the grounds that it involves a virtual molding of the data/outcome driven by the researcher, whereas my preference is to have minimal investigator interference, again in the interests of greater objectivity.	−5	−2	3
14	I love the philosophy that underpins Q methodology but since I'm not a 'natural' statistician I never feel confident about factor analysis.	0	−3	5
35	I still feel most comfortable when working in tandem with someone to analyze the factors.	0	−4	0
10	I use centroid just because I think/thought that it was common for Q methodology to use centroid.	1	−4	−1

analysis. Based on the factor-analytic preferences of those on this factor, this viewpoint rejects the use of centroid and hand rotation while accepting PCA and varimax. The acceptance of using PCA factor extraction is clear in the distinguishing Statements 16, 3, and 37 (1, 5, 0; −1, 4, −4; 1, 4, −1). Those with this view reject the use of centroid in Q (Statement #10; at 1, −4, −1). The distinguishing statements for Factor 2 are provided in Table 18.3.

Those on Factor 2 want to be able to defend their statistical choices and thus feel the need to avoid what they perceive as mathematical impropriety. Although this view seeks useful results, their focus on statistical correctness has led them to use PCA extraction with varimax rotation. Factor 2 participant comments reinforce the Q results. In their post-sort comments, Sorter #26 makes it clear why they reject the idea of theoretical significance but accepts the use of statistical significance in Q. Participant #12 explains that their experimentation with centroid with hand rotation versus PCA with varimax produces similar mathematical results. This participant sees the factor-analytic debate as "a lot of smoke with very little fire." Participant #20 agrees that they see little mathematical difference between centroid with hand rotation solutions and PCA with varimax solutions. They deem the PCA with varimax combination much easier to defend to non-Q journals. Thus, this viewpoint is focused on the mathematical aspects of the factor-analytic stage of Q but these sorters also want utilitarian solutions. However, they seem to see proper use of statistics connected to the most useful solutions.

Skeptical Novice Viewpoint

Although this factor represents only one participant, it resonates with many of the statements made during the survey-stage of this study (Ramlo, 2017a). Therefore, the researcher decided that ascribing to this viewpoint was still warranted. The participant is #8, mentioned earlier within the Q analysis section. They had used Q for approximately one year at the time of the study. This view accepts PCA with varimax presumably because it is perceived as being easier to use. This participant complains about the archaic software and the lack of short, accessible explanations about the factor-analytic stage of Q. Only this view did not completely involve rejection of the idea that "Q methodology's statistical process is just 'smoke and mirrors.'" (Statement #21 at −5, −5, −1). They are also "skeptical about the cult of personality around the Q celebrities." Finally, this view includes rejection of the idea that the creator of a method should "dictate how it should be implemented." This viewpoint does not seem to be concerned with aspects such as the philosophical framework of Q. Instead, this view is more concerned with the procedural performance of a Q study.

Consensus

There were 12 consensus statements and these also provided insight. In Q, consensus is determined between pairs of factors. In other words, a consensus statement may have the same or similar grid placement for Factors 2 and 3 but not for Factor 1. Yet, similar placement does not mean that both factors involve interpretations of the statement in the same way. For instance, Statement #5, "I prefer PCA because it offers more factors than centroid," is at −3 for each of the three factors. However, Factor 1 participants reject the use of PCA and Factor 2 participants accept PCA as being more statistically correct than centroid. Factor 3 participants seem unsure about statistical differences among the various factor-analytic options. Still, participants representing all three viewpoints appear to see the Statement 36, "I prefer other options than PCA/centroid and varimax/hand-rotation that three factors placed," as most unlike their view symbolized by its placement at −4.

Conclusions

Of the three viewpoints discovered, only one, Factor 1, is accepting of the inherently mixed statistical, philosophy-of-science, and psychological principles of Q. The inherently mixed viewpoint involves Q being seen as a complete methodology that offers a scientific approach to studying subjectivity. Alternatively, the Factor 2 viewpoint seems to support Stenner and Stainton-Rogers's (2004) contention that some researchers might feel uncomfortable with Q's qualitative-quantitative hybridity and that familiarity with quantitative research and statistics might accentuate this discomfort. The Factor 2 viewpoint is obviously more focused on the quantitative aspects of the factor-analytic stage of Q and seemingly involves rejection of the more qualitative characteristics of this stage. Additionally, this study demonstrates how perspectives about the factor-analytic stage of Q are directly connected to factor-analytic behavior in Q. However, this study also raises the question about what needs to be undertaken within the Q community to help Q methodologists and new Q researchers understand and accept the inherent qualitative-quantitative hybridity of Q, especially within Q's factor-analytic stage.

5 Suggested Applications of Q Methodology in MMR

Q has been applied to a broad range of fields related to the social and behavioral sciences. Stephenson used Q to study within the fields of psychology, journalism, advertising, philosophy, education, and marketing (Good, 2010). Today, the annual conference of the ISSSS, which represents the international Q methodology community, often features papers from fields that include education, environmental science, urban planning, counseling, sports science, political science, popular culture, and more. In each case, Q was used to determine the divergent opinions about a topic. Thus, the applications of Q are boundless whenever investigating subjectivity is the purpose. The strengths of using Q is discussed next and provides additional examples of Q applications.

6 Strengths and Limitations of Q Methodology in MMR

Strengths

The strengths of using Q have been presented throughout this chapter but it is good to summarize them here. Stephenson (1953a) explained that one of the differences between other data collection methods and Q technique is that the participant provides their internal viewpoint with their sort without need of a priori assumptions, whereas other methods provide only the external observations of the researcher. This allows behavior to be dealt with on its own terms (Brown, 1980).

Q also allows researchers to use a relatively small number of participants without the additional need for determining instrument score validity and score reliability (Brown, 1980; McKeown & Thomas, 2013; Newman & Ramlo, 2010; Stephenson, 1953a). Within Q studies, consensus is determined as well as the divergent viewpoints. Oftentimes, there is more consensus among a group than is realized and this can facilitate dialogue about a topic such as organizational change (Ramlo, 2005), including curriculum changes (Ramlo, 2011).

Q's ability to provide descriptions of the divergent viewpoints and consensus can provide important information for program evaluation (Cerrone, Nicholas, & Ramlo, 2013; Ramlo, 2012, 2015c; Ramlo & McConnell, 2008; Ramlo, McConnell, Duan, & Moore, 2008; Ramlo & Newman, 2010; Ramlo & Nicholas, 2010) and assessment (Naspetti, Mandolesi, & Zanoli, 2016; Pike, Wright, Wink, & Fletcher, 2015; Richardson, Fister, & Ramlo, 2015; Ramlo, 2015b, 2017b). Q research also can demonstrate that divergent viewpoints can affect other types of assessments, including those of medical practitioner clinical performance (Gingerich, Ramlo, van der Vleuten, Eva, & Regehr, 2016) and student evaluation of teaching (Ramlo, 2017b).

Limitations

Although Q methodology offers a way to circumvent the limitations of other studies that investigate subjectivity, there are some limitations. Q methodology is not generalizable in the typical sense of that term. The issue of generalizability as well as replicability in Q methodology has been addressed by Thomas and Baas (1993). Thomas and Baas differentiate between *statistical inference*, where the purpose is generalizing to a larger audience from a large, random sample of participants, and *substantive inference*, where the focus is a more qualitative one *about* phenomena. The latter inference, about phenomena, applies to Q methodology. Q factors represent generalizations such that they describe how persons of a certain perspective think about the topic under investigation (Brown, 1980; Thomas & Baas, 1993). In fact, the Q factors that emerge are generalizations based on the responses of several people. In this way, generalizations in Q relate to general principles such as the relations of and between factors (Brown, 1980). Certainly, the results of Q studies have been found to be replicable (Brown, 1980; Thomas & Baas, 1993). The test-retest reliability of the Q sorts has been shown to be 0.80 or higher (Brown, 1980).

Yet, reviewers and researchers often are unfamiliar with Q methodology. With some exceptions, Q methodology is not a typical research methodology introduced in social or behavioral science graduate programs. Qualitative-focused researchers might not explicitly understand the mathematical details of factor analysis. Alternatively, quantitative-focused researchers might misinterpret the qualitative aspects of Q. Thus, familiarity with both qualitative and quantitative approaches is beneficial to anyone undertaking a Q study. Additionally, Q methodologists must be prepared to defend against reviewer and dissertation-member misconceptions.

Frequently, Q listserv participants ask for help with various aspects of their Q studies as well as help with disparaging comments from journal reviewers and dissertation committee members (Ramlo, 2017a).

7 Resources for Learning More About Q Methodology

The ISSSS is the international Q methodology society. ISSSS was created in 1985 to promote the scientific study of subjectivity based on the ideas and concepts of Q methodology as enunciated by William Stephenson. The society's website (i.e., www.qmethod.org) contains numerous resources, including videos, unpublished articles, information about the annual conference, and access to their journal, *Operant Subjectivity: The International Journal of Q Methodology* (*OS*). A free-access listserv, Q-Method, also is available and is a moderated forum for the exchange of information related to Q Methodology (Ramlo, 2016a). The listserv membership has continuously grown and currently contains approximately 900 individuals. Several YouTube channels feature Q instruction, including Sue-Z Q [1] by Ramlo.

Four instructional texts on Q methodology currently exist. The first text on Q was written by Stephenson (1953a), *A Study of Behaviour: Q-Technique and Its Methodology*. Stephenson lays out his methodology within this text with a focus on the statistical, philosophy-of-science, and psychological principles that make up Q's methodology. This text is currently out of print.

Political Subjectivity: Applications of Q Methodology in Political Science by Brown (1980) contains a great deal of information about Q. Although this text uses applications of concern to political scientists, it is a superior resource for any social or behavioral scientist interested in Q. Although this text is also out of print, it is freely available as a PDF on the ISSSS website.

There are also two more current texts on Q: "The little green book on Q" by Bruce McKeown and Dan Thomas (1988, 2013), *Q Methodology*, is one in a series from the Sage Series on Quantitative Applications in the Social Sciences. This text is written as an introduction to Q's procedural, technical, and statistical aspects. The second edition has an entire chapter dedicated to the complexities of Q's factor-analytic stage. The fourth Q text is *Doing Q Methodological Research: Theory, Method & Interpretation* (Watts & Stenner, 2012). Designed as an introduction to Q and written as a narrative, this text focuses more on the procedures of Q rather than on the deeper methodological aspects. In other words, this text resembles a Q cookbook.

NOTE

1. Available at www.youtube.com/channel/UCeGHkvwvjCwV2FKtxEZ6OqA

REFERENCES

Baas, L., Rhoads, J., & Thomas, D. (2016). Are quests for a "culture of assessment" mired in a "culture war" over assessment? A Q-methodological inquiry. *SAGE Open*, 6(1), 1–17. doi:10.1177/2158244015623591

Block, J. (2008). *The Q-sort in character appraisal: Encoding subjective impressions of persons quantitatively*. Washington, DC: American Psychological Association.

Brown, S. R. (1980). *Political subjectivity: Applications of Q methodology in political science*. New Haven, CT: Yale University Press.

Brown, S. R. (1996). Q methodology and qualitative research. *Qualitative Health Research*, 6, 561–567. doi:10.1177/104973239600600408

Brown, S. R. (2008). Q methodology. In L. M. Given (Ed.), *The SAGE encyclopedia of qualitative research methods* (pp. 700–704). Thousand Oaks, CA: Sage.

Brown, S. R., Danielson, S., & van Exel, J. (2015). Overly ambitious critics and the Medici Effect: A reply to Kampen and Tamás. *Quality & Quantity*, 49, 523–537, doi:10.1007/s11135–014–0007-x

Brown, S. R., & Robyn, R. (2004). Reserving a key place for reality: Philosophical foundations of theoretical rotation. *Operant Subjectivity*, 27, 104–124.

Cerrone, K., Nicholas, J., & Ramlo, S. (2013). Perspectives contributing to early college high school student persistence. *Operant Subjectivity: The International Journal for Q Methodology*, 36, 342–352. doi:10.15133/j.os.2012.019

Flake, J. K., Pek, J., & Hehman, E. (2017). Construct validation in social and personality research: Current practice and recommendations. *Social Psychological and Personality Science*, 8, 370–378. doi:10.1177/1948550617693063

Gingerich, A., Ramlo, S., van der Vleuten, C. P. M., Eva, K. W., & Regehr, G. (2016). Inter-rater variability as mutual disagreement: Identifying raters' divergent points of view. *Advances in Health Sciences Education*, 22, 819–838. doi:10.1007/s10459-016-9711-8

Good, J. M. M. (2010). Introduction to William Stephenson's quest for a science of subjectivity. *Psychoanalysis & History*, 12, 211–243. doi:10.3366/pah.2010.0006

Kampen, J. K., & Tamás, P. (2014). Overly ambitious: Contributions and current status of Q methodology. *Quality & Quantity*, 48, 3109–3126. doi:10.1007/s11135-013-9944-z

Kramer, B., & Gravina, V. (2004). Theoretical rotation as a tool for identifying points of leverage in people's perspectives for program improvement. *Operant Subjectivity: The International Journal for Q Methodology*, 27, 125–144.

McKeown, B. (2001). Loss of meaning in Likert scaling: A note on the Q methodological alternative. *Operant Subjectivity*, 24, 201–206.

McKeown, B., & Thomas, D. (1988). *Q methodology*. Newbury Park, CA: Sage.

McKeown, B., & Thomas, D. (2013). *Q methodology* (2nd ed.). Newbury Park, CA: Sage.

Naspetti, S., Mandolesi, S., & Zanoli, R. (2016). Using visual Q sorting to determine the impact of photovoltaic applications on the landscape. *Land Use Policy*, 57, 564–573. doi:10.1016/j.landusepol.2016.06.021

Newman, I., & Ramlo, S. (2010). Using Q methodology and Q factor analysis to facilitate mixed methods research. In A. Tashakkori & C. Teddlie (Eds.), *Handbook of mixed methods in social & behavioral research* (2nd ed., pp. 505–530). Thousand Oaks, CA: Sage.

Nunnally, J. C. (1978). *Psychometric theory* (2nd ed.). New York, NY: McGraw-Hill.

Pike, K., Wright, P., Wink, B., & Fletcher, S. (2015). The assessment of cultural ecosystem services in the marine environment using Q methodology. *Journal of Coastal Conservation: Planning and Management, 19*, 667–675. doi:10.1007/s11852–014–0350-z)

Ramlo, S. (2005). An application of Q methodology: Determining college faculty perspectives and consensus regarding the creation of a school of technology. *Journal of Research in Education, 15*(1), 52–69.

Ramlo, S. (2011). Facilitating a faculty learning community: Determining consensus using Q methodology. *Mid-Western Educational Researcher24*(1), 30–38.

Ramlo, S. (2012). Inservice science teachers' views of a professional development workshop and their learning of force and motion concepts. *Teaching and Teacher Education, 28*, 928–935. doi:10.1016/j.tate.2012.04.002.

Ramlo, S. (2015a). Theoretical significance in Q Methodology: A qualitative approach to a mixed method. *Research in the Schools, 22*(1), 68–81.

Ramlo, S. (2015b). Q methodology as a tool for program assessment. *Mid-Western Educational Researcher, 27*, 207–223. Retrieved from www.mwera.org/MWER/volumes/v27/issue3/v27n3-Ramlo-FEATURE-ARTICLE.pdf

Ramlo, S. (2015c). Student views about a flipped physics course: A tool for program evaluation and improvement. *Research in the Schools, 22*(1), 44–59.

Ramlo, S. (2016a). Mixed method lessons learned from 80 years of Q methodology. *Journal of Mixed Methods Research, 10*, 28–45. doi:10.1177/1558689815610998

Ramlo, S. (2016b). Centroid and theoretical rotation: Justification for their use in Q methodology research. *Midwestern Researcher, 28*(1), 73–92. Retrieved from www.mwera.org/MWER/volumes/v28/issue1/v28n1-Ramlo-SPECIALIZED-RESEARCH-STATISTICAL-METHODS.pdf

Ramlo, S. (2016c). Students' views about potentially offering physics courses online. *Journal of Science Education and Technology, 25*, 489–496. doi:10.1007/s10956-016-9608-6.

Ramlo, S. (2017a). The preferences of Q methodologists at the factor-analytic stage: An examination of practice. *Research in the Schools, 24*(2), 40–55.

Ramlo, S. (2017b). Improving student evaluation of teaching: Determining multiple perspectives within a course for future math educators. *Journal of Research in Education, 27*, 49–78. Retrieved from https://docs.wixstatic.com/ugd/baaa29_d1bed31fc9434fb6b3f701e986f0c8b6.pdf

Ramlo, S. (2019). *Divergent viewpoints about the statistical stage of a mixed method: Qualitative versus quantitative orientations*. Manuscript submitted for publication.

Ramlo, S., & McConnell, D. (2008). Perspectives of university faculty regarding faculty reading circles: A study using Q methodology. *The Journal of Faculty Development, 22*(1), 25–32.

Ramlo, S., McConnell, D., Duan, Z., & Moore, F. (2008). Evaluating an inquiry-based bioinformatics course using Q methodology. *Journal of Science Education and Technology, 17*, 219–225. doi:10.1007/s10956–008–9090-x

Ramlo, S., & Newman, I. (2010). Classifying individuals using Q Methodology and Q Factor Analysis: Applications of two mixed methodologies for program evaluation. *Journal of Research in Education, 21*(2), 20–31. Retrieved from www.eeraonline.org/journal/files/v20/JRE_v20n2_Article_3_Ramlo_and_Newman.pdf

Ramlo, S., & Newman, I. (2011). Q methodology and its position in the mixed methods continuum. *Operant Subjectivity: The International Journal for Q Methodology, 34*, 173–192. doi:10.15133/j.os.2010.009

Ramlo, S., & Nicholas, J. (2010). In-service science teachers' views about learning physics after a one week workshop. *Human Subjectivity, 1*, 109–120.

Richardson, L., Fister, C., & Ramlo, S. (2015). Effect of an exercise and weight control curriculum: Views of obesity among exercise science students. *Advances in Physiology Education, 39*(2), 43–48. doi:10.1152/advan.00154.2014

Ridenour, C. S., & Newman, I. (2008). *Mixed methods research: Exploring the interactive continuum*. Carbondale, IL: Southern Illinois University Press.

Schmolck, P. (2002). *PQMethod manual mirror*. Unpublished manuscript. Retrieved from www.rz.unibw-muenchen.de/~p41bsmk/qmethod/

Stainton-Rogers, R. (1995). Q methodology. In J. A. Smith, R. Harré, & L. van Langenhove (Eds.), *Rethinking methods in psychology* (pp. 178–192). London, England: Sage.

Stenner, P., & Stainton-Rogers, R. (2004). Q methodology and qualiquantology: The example of discriminating between emotions. In Z. Todd, B. Nerlich, S. McKeown, & D. D. Clarke (Eds.), *Mixing methods in psychology* (pp. 103–117). New York, NY: Psychology Press.

Stephenson, W. (1935). Technique of factor analysis. *Nature, 136*, 297. doi:10.1038/136297b0

Stephenson, W. (1953a). *The study of behavior: Q-technique and its methodology*. Chicago, IL: University of Chicago Press.

Stephenson, W. (1953b). Postulates of behaviorism. *Philosophy of Science, 20*, 110–120. doi:10.1086/287250

Stephenson, W. (1961). Scientific creed, 1961: Philosophical credo. Abductory principles. The centrality of self. *The Psychological Record, 11*, 1–26. doi:10.1007/BF03393380

Stephenson, W. (1986a) William James, Niels Bohr, and complementarity: I – Concepts. *Psychological Record, 36*, 519–527. doi:10.1007/BF03394970

Stephenson, W. (1986b) William James, Niels Bohr, and complementarity: II – Pragmatics of a thought. *Psychological Record, 36*, 529–543. doi:10.1007/BF03394971

Stephenson, W. (1988). Quantum theory of subjectivity. *Integrative Psychiatry, 6*(3), 180–187.

Thomas, D. B., & Baas, L. R. (1993). The issue of generalization in Q methodology: "Reliable schematics" revisited. *Operant Subjectivity, 16*, 18–36. doi:10.15133/j.os.1992.014

Tucker, L., & MacCallum, R. C. (1997). *Exploratory factor analysis*. Unpublished manuscript. Retrieved from www.unc.edu/~rcm/book/factor.pdf

Watts, S., & Stenner, P. (2005). Doing Q methodology: Theory, method and interpretation. *Qualitative Research in Psychology, 2*(1), 67–91. doi:10.1191/1478088705qp022oa

Watts, S., & Stenner, P. (2012). *Doing Q methodological research: Theory, method and interpretation*. London, England: Sage.

Wittenborn, J. R. (1961). Contributions and current status of Q methodology. *Psychological Bulletin, 58*, 132–142. doi:10.1037/h0045018

19

Social Network Analysis as Mixed Analysis

Dominik E. Froehlich and Jasperina Brouwer

Social network analysis (SNA) has become an important theoretical and methodological framework to investigate research questions in both the social and natural sciences. This is illustrated by the surge in SNA-related publications, for example in the domain of learning and instruction research: from 37 publications in 2003 to more than 400 a decade later in the Education Resources Information Center database (Froehlich, Rehm, & Rienties, 2020a; Froehlich, Van Waes, & Schäfer, 2020). In this chapter, we will discuss the foundations of social network analysis as mixed analysis.

1 Definition of Social Network Analysis

In order to review an SNA manuscript, there are three important points we need to understand about the nature of the analysis to be reviewed: the perspective SNA has on social phenomena, the different types of networks one may investigate, and the "mixed nature" of SNA as a method.

Social Network Analysis as a Lens to See the World

Researchers use SNA if they are interested in the relationships and structural features of networks (Wellman, 1983). A *network* is defined as a set of *nodes* (or vertices, or actors)—for example, pupils in a classroom—and *edges* (or ties, or relationships)—for instance, conversations or friendship relationships between pupils. Nodes may contain *attributes* (e.g., gender, age, motivation). Edges may be weighted (e.g., weighted by the frequency of interaction) or directed (i.e., having a specified direction). In social networks the nodes are active agents, such as individuals or teams (Borgatti, Everett, & Johnson, 2013).

The term SNA itself is somewhat misleading because SNA is not only about analytical procedures but also describes an integrated set of theories ("network theory," e.g., Borgatti & Halgin, 2011) and research methods. The SNA perspective differs from other approaches in several ways (Wasserman & Faust, 1994). First, the focus is on relational theories and concepts (Monge & Contractor, 2003). The unit of analysis is not simply the characteristic or attribute of an individual (although SNA can produce input for such analyses), but rather dyads (two nodes), triads (three nodes), or groups (Froehlich, Galey, Mejeh, & Schoonenboom, 2020; Froehlich, Rehm, & Cornelissen, Forthcoming). Actors and their behavior are seen as interdependent. The actors' relationships and behaviors, or personal characteristics—attributes—can influence each other. Relationships with others make certain behaviors more likely and limit others. For example, it is more likely that adolescents who smoke are likely to be friends to other smokers (Mercken, Snijders, Steglich, Vartiainen, & de Vries, 2010).

Types of Networks

There are two distinct types of networks that can be analyzed, each with their own set of methods and theories: namely, sociocentric and egocentric networks. In a *sociocentric network*, the relationships among all the actors within previously defined boundaries are measured and analyzed. For instance, all the pupils within a specified class may be surveyed about their friendship relationships in the class. However, in an *egocentric network* (Crossley et al., 2015), the emphasis is on one individual—the ego—and his or her relationship to others—the *alters* (and potentially about the relationship between alters). For instance, one pupil is asked about their contacts with other class members (an *ego-alter question*) and whether he or she thinks relationships exist between the other class members (an *alter-alter question*). The main difference with egocentric measures is that in the ego network the information about the relationships comes from one individual rather than from all of the class members who can nominate each other (Prell, 2012). The difference between the types of networks is represented in Figure 19.1.

So far, we have only discussed relationships among actors of one kind; for instance, interactions among pupils (another example would be e-mails sent between managers). This is called a *one-mode network* with similar types of nodes. Another variant of social network analysis called *two-mode networks* or bipartite graphs allows researchers to study ties between dissimilar types of nodes (Agneessens & Everett, 2013). A two-mode network features two sets of nodes; for example, adding teachers to a network of pupils. A special type of a two-mode network is an *affiliation network*, in which the nodes/sets are actors and events (Wasserman & Faust, 1994). An example is the study of Davis, Gardner, and Gardner (1941), who investigated a group of 18 women (first node set) who joined a series of 14 society events (second node set). Other examples are members joining different clubs in a city (Wasserman & Faust, 1994).

The Nature of Social Network Analysis

SNA is often considered to be a quantitative technique (Hollstein, 2014). However, this does not appropriately capture the highly qualitative origins of the method (Freeman, 2000, 2004) or the

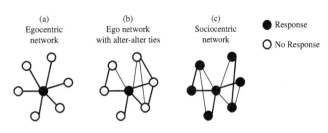

FIGURE 19.1 Egocentric and sociocentric networks.

current breadth of methods that go under the banner of SNA. Onwuegbuzie and Hitchcock (2015) highlighted the potential to integrate qualitative and quantitative strands of network research, and described the method as quantitative-dominant crossover mixed analysis. Other researchers agree with this requirement to include more qualitative information to produce more meaningful research (Bolíbar, 2015; Domínguez & Hollstein, 2014; Franke & Wald, 2006; Rienties, Johan, & Jindal-Snape, 2015). As noted by Hollstein (2011), qualitative data collection and analysis can facilitate social network analysis because qualitative data can "explicate the problem of agency, linkages between network structure and network actors, as well as questions relating to the constitution and dynamics of social networks" (p. 404). More specifically, Hollstein identified six areas in which qualitative research can enhance SNA: the exploration of networks, network practices, network orientation and assessments, how and why networks matter, understanding network dynamics, and the validation of network data and field access.

Carrington (2014) describes SNA as neither qualitative or quantitative but mathematical and structural. This is echoed in the SNA community, where quantitative approaches are commonly referred to as *formal network analysis*. This term is more focused on the perspective taken than the underlying type of data.

2 When the Use of Social Network Analysis is Appropriate in MMR

Social network analysis has his roots in several disciplines, including mathematics, psychology, and sociology. From there, the method has been adapted and applied in virtually all academic domains: for instance, history (Elo, 2015), politics (Ansell, Bichir, & Zhou, 2016; Apkarian, Bowler, Hanneman, & Martin, 2015), economics (Harris, Louis, & Baker, 2014), music (Vlegels & Lievens, 2015), health (Yang, Latkin, Muth, & Rudolph, 2013), and education (Rienties, Héliot, & Jindal-Snape, 2013). More information about the historical development of social network analysis can be found in Freeman (2004).

It is appropriate to use SNA whenever the research question addresses (perceived) structures or (perceived) connections or relationships between any entities, that is, social or non-social entities. For instance, friendships between students, trust between managers and employees, or the spread of a virus via personal contacts. Social network theory has led to a few frequently researched concepts and theories in the past, including social capital, homophily/similarity attraction, and contagion. These three theories will be discussed in more detail in this section to provide a brief overview of some of the most important network theories and concepts.

Social Capital

The concept of social capital became popular in the late 20th century and is frequently used by researchers. Social capital is the advantage one obtains from a certain position in a network (Burt, 2005). For instance, social networks permit access to variable resources, such as information, trust, practical or emotional support, community values and norms (Kadushin, 2012). Through the use of these resources an individual can reach personal goals that could not be reached without these resources (Coleman, 1988). Coleman (1988) has suggested that people also build networks of trust, reputation, obligation, norms, and values through social exchanges. For example, as a form of students' social capital, students create informal support networks (Hommes et al., 2012). In these informal peer networks, students inform each other, help one another, collaborate, and share trustworthy information when they become friends. These peer relationships among first-year university students might facilitate both their adjustment to university life and their academic performance (Brouwer, Jansen, Flache, & Hofman, 2016; Brouwer, 2017).

Social capital and social networks share similar dimensions of social structures and content. The position in the networks and the type of ties determines the amount of social capital. Granovetter (1973) emphasized that to create new ideas, or to get a job, an individual needs connections he or she does not know very well (weak ties). These weaker ties are a bridge to other, different information. In this respect, Putnam (2001) has distinguished between bridging social capital and bonding social capital, which is linked to the social network structure. Bridging social capital refers to weak ties and less dense networks, whereas bonding social capital refers to strong ties and dense, knitted networks.

Homophily and Propinquity

Lazarsfeld and Merton (1954) introduced the principle of *homophily*, which means that it is more likely that a close relationship will develop between people who are similar than between people who are dissimilar. Or, to put it colloquially, "birds of a feather flock together" (McPherson, Smith-Lovin, & Cook, 2001). To define homophily in a more formal way, when two people are randomly drawn from a population or from a network they belong to, there is a larger chance that they will have similar characteristics (Verbrugge, 1977). This means that people within networks are likely to be more homogeneous in their backgrounds, attitudes, and opinions. Homophily exists in all types of close relationships, such as within student groups (Brouwer, Flache, Jansen, Hofman, & Steglich, 2018; Lomi, Snijders, Steglich, & Torló, 2011) or between colleagues in a small organization (Froehlich & Messmann, 2017).

Proximity (or propinquity) makes it more likely that there will be a relationship between spatially close actors (Monge & Contractor, 2003), for instance, when the actors are sharing the same office or sitting next to each other in the same classroom. The effects of proximity and distance were also discussed by Festinger, Schacter, and Back (1950; cited by Kadushin, 2012), who gave the example of a housing project for World War II military veterans. Festinger, Schacter, and Back found that the veterans became friends more often when they lived near each other, whereas the veterans in the corner houses frequently became isolated.

Regarding the attraction between two individuals, Lazarsfeld and Merton (1954) distinguished between status homophily and value homophily (Frieling & Froehlich, 2017). Status homophily can be ascribed to a person based on their background characteristics, such as gender or age; or status homophily can be acquired, based on, for example, the person's education or occupation. Value homophily, on the other hand, refers to similarity in attitudes, beliefs, or stereotypes. Two of the main characteristics of homophily are that people are similar when they meet (the selection effect), or they become similar when they interact (the influence effect) (McPherson et al., 2001). This can be addressed with stochastic actor-based models to investigate longitudinally collected social network data (Snijders, Van de Bunt, & Steglich, 2010).

Contagion or Diffusion in Networks

Diffusion means that certain aspects or components are transmitted through a social system, such as ideas, opinions, and diseases (Valente, 1996). When graphically depicted, the diffusion usually follows an S-curve, which means that in the beginning only a few people adopt, for example, an idea. Then, people share this idea with others, who also adopt the idea. The proportion of people who adopt the idea increases when more people transmit the idea (diffusion), but the increase slows down when there are fewer people to adopt the idea (Kadushin, 2012).

Epidemiology diffusions should be distinguished from social diffusions. Social influence and social diffusion exist in different forms, and the term means that at the social level something has been transmitted through social contacts, for example through influence, or persuasion to buy something, or to influence opinions in a certain way. Epidemiology or biology diffusions refer to the spread of diseases or health risks. Social network analysis also appears a useful method to investigate the contagion among people (see Kadushin, 2012).

3 Technical Outline of Social Network Analysis for MMR

Defining Research Questions at Different Levels of Analysis

Social network research questions differ from commonly used research questions in that we are not interested in only personal perceptions or characteristics but in the actual social relationships. Social networks can be either the independent variable or the dependent variable. When social networks are investigated as an independent variable, social network theory can be used to explain or predict certain outcomes, such as individual performance or organizational benefits. When social networks are investigated as a dependent variable, individual or group characteristics, behaviors, or attitudes can be used to explain social structures (Borgatti et al., 2013). Here are examples of research questions at different levels: (1) Do students who have higher grades have more friends? (actor level, social network as a dependent variable); (2) Are students who sit next to each other more likely to become friends? (dyad level, social network as a dependent variable); (3) Do well-connected networks tend to spread information faster? (network level, social network as an independent variable).

Defining the Network

Before we can measure and analyze a network, we need to define what the network actually is—the so-called *boundary-decision* (Laumann, Marsden, & Prensky, 1983; S. S. Smith, 2013). Based on the definition of networks given above, this means that we need to define who the actors are (e.g., pupils within a classroom, any people in a region) and what the focal type of the relationship is (e.g., trade between countries, intimate relationships among teenagers, seeking feedback among employees). In other words, we need to define the boundary of the set of actors (nodes), which allows researchers to investigate a specific population. The boundary of members in a network is commonly contrasted with non-members and defined based on the frequency of interactions (e.g., pupils in a class) or the strength of the relationships (e.g., family or friendship; Wasserman & Faust, 1994). There are two approaches to this question (Smith, 2013): the nominalist and the realist way. The *nominalist approach* is theory-driven: Based on theoretical considerations, the researcher defines who or what is to be considered in the network. For example, when researching the development of occupational expertise we might want to focus on an employee's relationship with colleagues and not with friends and other emotional contacts outside the company or field of occupation (Froehlich, 2015; Froehlich, Beausaert, Segers, & Gerken, 2014). Conversely, the *realist approach* considers the network and its boundaries as perceived by the actors themselves. This openness on the side of the researcher may lead to unexpected findings, such as Granovetter's (1973) discovery that often the "weak ties" (in terms of emotional intensity, time spent with each other, reciprocal service, and intimacy) are more important than "strong ties," for instance, when getting a job via one's network.

Many network studies include social entities or communities of a manageable size, for example neighborhoods, clubs, or classrooms. Most often, these networks have a plain boundary of actor sets. When the network can be clearly defined, sociometric (full network) and egocentric measures are appropriate for making inferences about the population of networks. Sometimes the boundaries of the network are not as clearly defined or it is not possible to include all actors. In this case, a sample can be taken from the larger population. This can be done by snowball or chain sampling, which is a non-probabilistic sampling technique. It starts with the report of a key actor about the actors with whom they have a certain connection. This will be continued by approaching the actor's connections, and so on, up to several waves; for example, there have been studies of the connections of gang members (Borgatti et al., 2013; Wasserman & Faust, 1994).

Collecting Data

A large number of social network studies use different methods for data collection, either quantitative or qualitative or both (cf. Froehlich, 2020a). The diversity of data collection methods applied in social network research varies from text analysis to contact diaries for collecting data about ego networks. Researchers can investigate the type of ties, the strength of the ties, the frequency of interactions, and also information about the actors' personal attributes (Wasserman & Faust, 1994).

When it comes to drawing samples, and collecting data, another difference from traditional approaches exists. For sociocentric network analysis to work as intended, a census of the defined network is desirable. This emphasizes a high response-rate of ideally above 80%, or even 90% (Wasserman & Faust, 1994). It is also important to highlight the ethical considerations concerning SNA data collection. Since we are mostly interested in some feature of a relationship between people, asking respondents for evaluations of that other person's or their joint relationship is often required (even if the other party does not take part in the research!). These "third parties" may be affected by the conclusions. Therefore, a thorough ethical review of the data collection procedures and the potential implications for participants and third parties is a must.

For data collection, SNA is open to both qualitative and quantitative methods. For quantitative data collection, sociometric questionnaires are the method used most often. These questionnaires differ from psychometric questionnaires in so far as they contain two separate parts. First, the researcher needs to identify relevant alters that the ego has relationships with. Second, more detailed information about these relationships must be acquired. There are two prominent methods for finding out about relevant alters. One can provide a list of all potentially relevant persons; for example, all the pupils in a class. This approach is usually referred to as the "roster method," as a full roster of relevant alters is provided to the respondent. An alternative, and more open-ended, approach is the "free recall" method, in which the respondents are asked for names via a name-generator (Burt et al., 2012) or, more abstractly, for relevant other positions the respondent has been in contact with (position generator; see Van Der Gaag, Snijders, & Flap, 2008). After providing or collecting relevant other names or positions, the relationship to each alter is specified through a so-called name interpreter question. For instance, this could mean indicating the frequency of contact for each alter. The number of alters to be enlisted may or may not be limited by the researchers (Wasserman & Faust, 1994).

Data mining approaches (especially from online networks such as Twitter) are gaining momentum (Barbier & Liu, 2011; Srivastava, 2008). Also, other technologies may be used to track relationships, such as electronic badges (Pentland & Heibeck, 2010) or contact logs.

On the qualitative side, the method of concentric circles is a popular approach to collecting data (Kahn & Antonucci, 1980). Here, an interviewee (as the ego) is asked to place alters on a map of concentric circles that represent closeness (or some other defined feature) of the relationship. Information from the interview can then be used to corroborate or aid the interpretation of the different positions. This process can be augmented with software (Hollstein & Pfeffer, 2010).

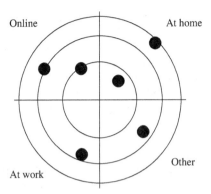

FIGURE 19.2 Example of using the concentric circles method for qualitative data collection.

As a qualitative approach to data collection, face-to-face interviews are commonly used. This is a popular way to collect ego network data (Froehlich, 2020b). The procedure is similar to the sociometric questionnaire, in that name generating questions (e.g., "Who do you ask for advice when you do not understand the study material?") are followed by name interpreting questions (e.g., "Is this person older than you?").

Another qualitative data-collection approach is observation, which can be used to study small groups (Wasserman & Faust, 1994). The advantage of the observation approach is that it is not necessary to rely on the memory of the interviewee or the respondent. The researcher can simply observe who is interacting with whom. However, the type of interaction should be defined and coded as such. Another issue is that several interactions can take place at the same time. Finally, diary data or archiving data (e.g., newspapers, minutes of gatherings) can also be used for collecting network data. An example is the use of citations of scientific articles.

Analyzing the Data

Visual analysis plays an important role in SNA (Brandes, Indlekofer, & Mader, 2012; Freeman, 2000). Indeed, an image of a network often shows its distinct features very well and offers a great basis for discussions with stakeholders. The depicted positions and networks can also be expressed in more quantitative terms—for example (Carrington, 2014; Schoch & Brandes, 2016; Wasserman & Faust, 1994) density (the proportion of actual connections to potential connections), geodesics (the shortest path between two actors), node centrality (a measure of how well connected an actor is to the rest of the network), or centralization (the overall consolidation of the network).

Traditional inferential statistics are often not applicable in SNA, since the data usually violates the assumption of independent cases. Alternative descriptive statistics that can be used are correlations and regressions using quadratic assignment procedures (QAP; Dekker, Krackhardt, & Snijders, 2003; Krackhardt, 1992). Also, for data synthesis across studies, specialized procedures exist (e.g., Krackhardt & Kilduff, 1999). Exponential random graph modeling (ERGM; Robins, Pattison, Kalish, & Lusher, 2007) is another approach that compares the features of an observed network (e.g., reciprocity) with other potential instances of the same network. For dynamic longitudinal networks, stochastic actor-based models are most frequently used (Snijders et al., 2010).

The qualitative methods applied for data analysis are less proprietary to SNA; "standard" qualitative methods are often applicable. An example for an adapted qualitative method is qualitative structural analysis (QSA; Herz, Peters, & Truschkat, 2015), a "combination of the analytical perspective of structural analysis and analytical standards taken from qualitative social research" (p. 1).

4 Empirical Demonstration of Social Network Analysis for MMR

As an empirical demonstration, research performed using first-year students at a university in the Netherlands is described below (see Brouwer, Jansen, Flache, & Hofman, 2018). A mixed methods SNA approach was used to combine the collection and analysis of complete social networks with open-ended questions.

Interactive small group learning approaches, such as learning communities, have been increasingly implemented at universities worldwide. A learning community is a group of about twelve students who take the same courses. The rationale behind learning communities is that students can collaborate with each other, get to know each other easily, and learn from each other through shared knowledge construction (Brouwer, 2017). In fact, the learning communities facilitate building a new social peer network after the transition from high school to university. There were two major research questions:

1. How do learning communities contribute to academic help-relationships and friendship relationships?
2. How do students appreciate the learning communities in term of peer network formation?

Previous research investigated the benefits of learning communities for individual outcomes, such as academic performance (Hotchkiss, Moore, & Pitts, 2006) and student satisfaction (Zhao & Kuh, 2004), but learning communities were rarely investigated from a social network perspective.

The sample included 95 first-year social sciences students who were part of learning communities. The network boundary was defined as the complete degree program, because Brouwer et al. (2018) were interested in the students' contacts with their fellow students in their learning community compared to their contacts outside their learning community. Complete social network data were collected online at the end of the first and at the end of the second semester (longitudinal measurements). This means that students could nominate fellow students from the complete degree program. The names of their learning community members were shown on a roster, and students could add additional names from other learning communities of the degree program.

Each student was asked two social network questions that were adapted from Van de Bunt (1999). The first item was, "I ask this fellow student (name) for help when I do not understand the study material?" The second question was, "What kind of relationship do you have with (name)?" The questions could indicate whether the students are best friends, friends, possible friends, have a neutral relationship, or an unknown relationship (you know only the other person's name or face), or even indicate not knowing the person at all. For the given analysis, it was a technical requirement to dichotomize the answer categories and indicate best friend, friend, and possible friend as one category (friends) and the other answer categories as zero (not friends). An open question was asked about the students' opinion of learning communities and suggestions for improvement at the end of the year and coded these as a positive or negative evaluation. The other question concerned the students' perceived contribution of learning communities on relationship formation and the learning process.

The social network data were analyzed descriptively for the first research question regarding how learning communities contribute to network formation. The statistical network statistics showed that the students had more relationships with fellow students in their learning community compared to students outside the learning community. The density of seeking help in friendship networks, which is the ratio of the actual relationships divided by the possible relationships, was ten times higher in the learning communities than outside the learning communities. The degree centrality (the number of an actor's ties) indicated that students asked on average two to three students for help from their learning community in the first semester, which decreased in the second semester. In the second semester, students asked relatively more students outside their learning community for help. The same held true for friendship, but the decrease in the number of friendships in the learning communities was less strong than in the help-seeking network. The graphs of the results showed that learning communities formed dense subgroups in the degree program, particularly in the first semester. Evidence for this came from the qualitative analysis (the second research question): Students indicated that they found learning communities helpful for building relationships with their peers, mentioning that they get to know each other easily in this safe environment.

This example shows the contribution of an analysis of complete social networks using a mixed methods design. Social networks were analyzed descriptively and based on graphical presentations. The open-ended question was added to investigate the students' opinions in addition to what we learned about in the social network structure.

5 Suggested Applications of Social Network Analysis in MMR

SNA and its focus on relationships and structures has helped advance science in many fields. It also lends itself very well to more applied research projects to drive change on a local level. This is especially true for SNA's capability to produce network charts that can mostly be understood intuitively by the participants (see Technical Outline in this chapter).

6 Strengths and Limitations of Social Network Analysis in MMR

Despite the strength of social network data and analysis, we need to also consider some limitations of the resulting data. First of all, let us consider the reliability of the data. Social network data can change rapidly, because social relationships are often volatile. However, some social network questions lead to more reliable results than others. In SNA, the mutual or reciprocal ties are more reliable when the two actors of this specific relationship perceive the relationship similarly. Reciprocated ties occur more often in close relationships, such as friendships. This means that social network measures tend to be more reliable in close networks with reciprocated ties (Marsden & Campbell, 1984). The same holds true for the questions about close ties, because in close connections reciprocated ties exist more often (Wasserman & Faust, 1994).

Another limitation of social networks is missing data. The most common problem is that a possible respondent does not participate in the study even though he or she belongs to the target population. Such missing values can make the network seems less connected and dense than it actually is. When central persons in the network are missing, it is even more problematic (Smith & Moody, 2013; Smith, Moody, & Morgan, 2017). In sum, the data collected for sociometric network analysis must be very inclusive regarding achieving large samples and high response rates. For certain populations, this may not be feasible.

The theoretical definition of a network—a set of nodes and edges—is straightforward. However, applying this thought to (research) practice triggers a host of open questions, and most prominently the boundary specification problem (Laumann et al., 1983). Basically, the boundary question is what is in the network and what is not (which is discussed in the technical outline of SNA in this chapter).

A problem commonly identified in MMR is the (mixed) competencies required by the researchers (cf. Onwuegbuzie & Hitchcock, 2015; Froehlich, Mamas, & Schneider, 2020). This problem can be aggravated when applying mixed approaches to SNA, as the quantitative methods are—compared to "standard" statistics—even more sophisticated. This, and the fact that few researchers get formal training in the field of SNA early in their career, results in a steep learning curve that may be difficult to master along with a diffuse set of interests and learning goals. Being acquainted with the quantitative side of SNA, however, can be very important, at least for academics, as the field is very much driven by quantitative analyses (Hollstein, 2014). Qualitative approaches have existed from the beginning of SNA, and—also thanks to the massive amount of data available online (e.g., Twitter networks)—there has been an emphasis on quantitative methods to conduct SNA research.

Anonymity is important in social science research, but in full network designs it is hard to guarantee anonymity. Although cover names can be used, in full network designs it is necessary that the actors be identified. In this case, the researcher needs to promise and maintain confidentiality.

Another problem occurs when a person who should be part of the sample is not willing to participate. Even if this actor does not participate, he or she may still be nominated by other actors. Deleting this specific actor leads also to ethical concerns, because the data are not representative of the population under study anymore and, therefore, the study becomes biased and of lower quality.

Data visualization is often applied and informative. However, a researcher needs to take care that the actors in the graphs cannot be traced to the specific individuals, for example by limiting the background information in the graph and by making node labels invisible (Borgatti et al., 2013). Merely deleting the names is not enough, as the social structures often make it easy for "insiders" to reveal identities (Palonen & Froehlich, 2020).

7 Resources for Learning More About Social Network Analysis

Associations, Conferences, Journals

The International Network for Social Network Analysis (INSNA, 2017) is the largest association for social network analysts. It organizes annual, method-focused conferences around the globe—including the international Sunbelt conference and also more local conferences, such as the European Conference on Social Networks (EUSN)—and promotes dedicated journals such as *Connections and Social Networks*. For the purpose of learning more about SNA, the SOCNET listserv hosted by INSNA is an excellent resource.

Important Texts

Borgatti et al. (2009) have written an important introductory article about SNA in the social sciences. The book by Wasserman and Faust (1994) is a very complete classic on SNA. Borgatti, Everett, and Johnson (2013), Crossley et al. (2015), and Scott (2000) are important textbooks for (application oriented) social network analysis. Freeman (2004) sketches the development of SNA from a historical perspective. The books by Domínguez and Hollstein (2014) and Froehlich, Rehm and Rienties (2020b) zero in on mixed methods approaches to SNA. As previously mentioned, SNA comes not only with tools for analysis, but also has a strong theoretical foundation of its own. To learn more about theories of networks, the texts of Monge and Contractor (2003) are important starting points.

Software

A host of different software packages exist to aid in the conduct of social network analysis. One of the most popular stand-alone applications is probably UCINet and its integrated visualization software Netdraw (Borgatti, Everett, & Freeman, 2002). Also, R packages and Python libraries exist for analyses and visualization work—statnet (Karlsson, 2006) and igraph (Csardi & Nepusz, 2006) are often used. In addition to these rather general applications, specialized software, for example for longitudinal analysis, exist (e.g., SIENA by Ripley, Boitmanis, & Snijders, 2015). Mixed approaches to SNA may not require the emphasis on analysis that all of the mentioned programs have; more visualization oriented software packages like Gephi (Bastian, Heymann, & Jacomy, 2009) or visone (Brandes & Wagner, 2004) are easy to learn alternatives.

A more complete and in-depth overview of software packages in the field of SNA is provided by (Huisman & Van Duijn, 2005).

REFERENCES

Agneessens, F., & Everett, M. G. (2013). Introduction to the special issue on advances in two-mode social networks. *Social Networks*, 35(2), 145–147. https://doi.org/10.1016/j.socnet.2013.03.002

Ansell, C., Bichir, R., & Zhou, S. (2016). Who says networks, says oligarchy? Oligarchies as "rich club" networks. *Connections*, 35(2), 20–32. https://doi.org/10.17266/35.2.2

Apkarian, J., Bowler, S., Hanneman, R., & Martin, B. (2015). Donor motivations in the California State Legislature: A social network analysis of campaign contributions. *Connections*, 35(1). https://doi.org/http://dx.doi.org/10.17266/35.1.3

Barbier, G., & Liu, H. (2011). Data mining in social media. In Charu C. Aggarwal (Ed.), *Social Network Data Analytics* (pp. 327–352). Boston, MA: Springer. https://doi.org/10.1007/978-1-4419-8462-3_12

Bastian, M., Heymann, S., & Jacomy, M. (2009). Gephi: An open source software for exploring and manipulating networks. *International AAAI Conference on Weblogs and Social Media*.

Bolíbar, M. (2015). Macro, meso, micro: Broadening the "social" of social network analysis with a mixed methods approach. *Quality & Quantity*, 3, 2217–2236. https://doi.org/10.1007/s11135-015-0259-0

Borgatti, S. P., Everett, M. G., & Freeman, L. C. (2002). *UCINet for Windows: Software for social network analysis*. Harvard, MA: Analytic Technologies.

Borgatti, S. P., Everett, M. G., & Johnson, J. C. (2013). *Analyzing social networks*. London, England: Sage.

Borgatti, S. P., & Halgin, D. S. (2011). On network theory. *Organization Science*, 22, 1168–1181. https://doi.org/10.1287/orsc.1110.0641

Borgatti, S. P., Mehra, A., Brass, D. J., & Labianca, G. (2009). Network analysis in the social sciences. *Science*, 323(5916), 892–895. https://doi.org/10.1126/science.1165821

Brandes, U., Indlekofer, N., & Mader, M. (2012). Visualization methods for longitudinal social networks and stochastic actor-oriented modeling. *Social Networks*, 34(3), 291–308. https://doi.org/10.1016/j.socnet.2011.06.002

Brandes, U., & Wagner, D. (2004). visone—Analysis and visualization of social networks. In M. Jünger & P. Mutzel (Eds.), *Graph drawing software* (pp. 321–340). Heidelberg, Germany: Springer.

Brouwer, J. (2017). *Connecting, interacting and supporting. Social capital, peer network and cognitive perspectives on small group teaching*. (Doctoral thesis). University of Groningen, Groningen.

Brouwer, J., Flache, A., Jansen, E., Hofman, A., & Steglich, C. (2018). Emergent achievement segregation in freshmen learning community networks. *Higher Education*, 76(3), 483–500. doi: 10.1007/s10734-017-0221-2

Brouwer, J., Jansen, E., Flache, A., & Hofman, A. (2016). The impact of social capital on study success among first-year university students. *Learning and Individual Differences*, 52, 109–118. doi: 10.1016/j.lindif.2016.09.016

Brouwer, J., Jansen, E., Flache, A., & Hofman, A. (2018). Leergemeenschappen en de vorming van hulp- en vriendschapsrelaties van eerstejaarsstudenten in het hoger onderwijs [Learning Communities and the formation of help relationships and friendships of first-year students in higher education]. *Tijdschrift voor Hoger Onderwijs*, 35(4), 52–66.

Bunt, G. G. V. D., Duijn, M. A. J. V., & Snijders, T. A. B. (1999). Friendship networks through time: An actor-oriented dynamic statistical network model. *Computational & Mathematical Organization Theory*, 5(2), 167–192. https://doi.org/10.1023/A:1009683123448

Burt, R. S. (2005). *Brokerage and Closure: An Introduction to Social Capital*. Oxford, England: Oxford University Press.

Burt, R. S., Meltzer, D. O., Seid, M., Borgert, A., Chung, J. W., Colletti, R. B., … Margolis, P. (2012). What's in a name generator? Choosing the right name generators for social network surveys in healthcare quality and safety research. *BMJ Quality & Safety*, 21(12), 992–1000. https://doi.org/10.1136/bmjqs-2011-000521

Carrington, P. J. (2014). Social network research. In S. Domínguez & B. Hollstein (Eds.), *Mixed methods social networks research: Design and applications* (pp. 35–64). New York, NY: Cambridge University Press.

Coleman, J. S. (1988). Social capital in the creation of human capital. *American Journal of Sociology*, 94, S95-S120. https://doi.org/10.1086/228943

Crossley, N., Bellotti, E., Edwards, G., Everett, M. G., Koskinen, J., & Tranmer, M. (2015). *Social network analysis for egonets: Social network analysis for actor-centred networks*. Thousand Oaks, CA: Sage.

Csardi, G., & Nepusz, T. (2006). The igraph software package for complex network research. *InterJournal Complex Systems*, 1695.

Davis, A., Gardner, B. B., & Gardner, M. R. (1941). *Deep South: A social anthropological study of caste and class*. Chicago, IL: University of Chicago Press.

Dekker, D., Krackhardt, D., & Snijders, T. A. B. (2003). *Multicollinearity robust QAP for multiple-regression*. Nijmegen, The Netherlands.

Domínguez, S., & Hollstein, B. (2014). *Mixed methods social networks research: Design and applications*. (S. Domínguez & B. Hollstein, Eds.). New York, NY: Cambridge University Press.

Elo, K. (2015). The content structure of intelligence reports. *Connections*, 35(1). https://doi.org/10.17266/35.1.2

Franke, K., & Wald, A. (2006). Möglichkeiten der Triangulation quantitativer und qualitativer Methoden in der Netzwerkanalyse [Opportunities for triangulating quantitative and qualitative methods in social network analysis]. In B. Hollstein & F. Straus (Eds.), *Qualitative Netzwerkanalyse: Konzepte, methoden, anwendungen [Qualitative network analysis: Concepts, methods, applications]* (pp. 153–175). Wiesbaden, Germany: VS Verlag für Sozialwissenschaften.

Freeman, L. C. (2000). Visualizing social networks. *Journal of Social Structure*, 1.

Freeman, L. C. (2004). *The development of social network analysis*. Vancouver, Canada: Empirical Press. Retrieved from http://aris.ss.uci.edu/ lin/book.pdf

Frieling, M., & Froehlich, D. E. (2017). Homophilie, diversity und feedback: Eine soziale netzwerkanalyse [Homophily, diversity, and feedback: A social network analysis]. In *Internationales Personalmanagement: Rollen—Kompetenzen—Perspektiven. Implikationen für die Praxis [International human resource management: Roles—competencies—perspectives]*. Wiesbaden, Germany: SpringerGabler.

Froehlich, D. E. (2015). *Old and Out? Age, employability, and the role of learning* (Doctoral thesis). Maastricht, Netherlands: Maastricht University.

Froehlich, D. E. (2020a). Mapping Mixed Methods Approaches to Social Network Analysis in Learning and Education. In D. E. Froehlich, M. Rehm, & B. C. Rienties (Eds.), *Mixed methods social network analysis: Theories and methodologies in learning and education*. London: Routledge.

Froehlich, D. E. (2020b). Exploring social relationships in "a mixed way": Mixed Structural Analysis. In D. E. Froehlich, M. Rehm, & B. C. Rienties (Eds.), *Mixed methods social network analysis: Theories and methodologies in learning and education*. London: Routledge.

Froehlich, D. E., Beausaert, S. A. J., Segers, M. S. R., & Gerken, M. (2014). Learning to stay employable. *Career Development International*, 19(5), 508–525. https://doi.org/10.1108/CDI-11-2013-0139

Froehlich, D. E., Galey, S., Mejeh, M., & Schoonenboom, J. (2020). Integrating units of analysis: Applying mixed methods social network analysis. In D. E. Froehlich, M. Rehm, & B. C. Rienties (Eds.), *Mixed methods social network analysis: Theories and methodologies in learning and education*. London: Routledge.

Froehlich, D. E., Mamas, C., & Schneider, H. W. (2020). Automation and the journey to mixed methods social network analysis. In D. E. Froehlich, M. Rehm, & B. C. Rienties (Eds.), *Mixed methods social network analysis: Theories and methodologies in learning and education*. London: Routledge.

Froehlich, D. E., & Messmann, G. (2017). The social side of innovative work behavior: Determinants of social interaction during organizational innovation processes. *Business Creativity and the Creative Economy*, 3(1). https://doi.org/10.18536/bcce.2017.10.3.1.03

Froehlich, D. E., Rehm, M., & Cornelissen, F. (Forthcoming). *Investigating Informal Learning via Social Media using Mixed Methods Social Network Analysis: A Case Study. MedienPädagogik: Zeitschrift Für Theorie Und Praxis Der Medienbildung*.

Froehlich, D. E., Rehm, M., & Rienties, B. C. (2020a). Mixed Methods Social Network Analysis. In D. E. Fröhlich, M. Rehm, & B. C. Rienties (Eds.), *Mixed methods social network analysis: Theories and methodologies in learning and education*. London: Routledge.

Froehlich, D. E., Rehm, M., & Rienties, B. C. (2020b). *Mixed methods social network analysis: Theories and methodologies in learning and education*. London: Routledge.

Froehlich, D. E., Van Waes, S., & Schäfer, H. (2020). Linking Quantitative and Qualitative Network Approaches: A Review of Mixed Methods Social Network Analysis in Education Research. Review of Research in Education, 44(1), 244–268. https://doi.org/10.3102/0091732X20903311

Granovetter, M. S. (1973). The strength of weak ties. *American Journal of Sociology*, 78(6), 1360–1380. https://doi.org/10.1086/225469

Harris, J. K., Louis, S., & Baker, E. A. (2014). Employment networks in a high-unemployment rural area. *Connections*, 34(1&2). https://doi.org/10.17266/34.1.1

Herz, A., Peters, L., & Truschkat, I. (2014). How to do qualitative structural analysis: The qualitative interpretation of network maps and narrative interviews. *Forum Qualitative Sozialforschung/Forum: Qualitative Social Research*, 16(1). https://doi.org/10.17169/fqs-16.1.2092

Hollstein, B. (2011). Qualitative approaches to social reality: The search for meaning. In J. Scott & P. J. Carrington (Eds.), *The Sage handbook of social network analysis* (pp. 404–416). London: Sage Publications.

Hollstein, B. (2014). Mixed methods social networks research: An introduction. In S. Domínguez & B. Hollstein (Eds.), *Mixed methods social networks research: Design and applications* (pp. 3–34). New York, NY: Cambridge University Press.

Hollstein, B., & Pfeffer, J. (2010). Netzwerkkarten als Instrument zur Erhebung egozentrierter Netzwerke [Network maps as instrument to collect data of egocentric networks]. In *Unsichere Zeiten* (pp. 1–13). Wiesbaden, Germany: VS Verlag für Sozialwissenschaften.

Hommes, J., Rienties, B. C., Grave, W. de, Bos, G., Schuwirth, L., & Scherpbier, A. (2012). Visualising the invisible: A network approach to reveal the informal social side of student learning. *Advances in Health Sciences Education*, 17(5), 743–757. https://doi.org/10.1007/s10459-012-9349-0

Hotchkiss, J. L., Moore, R. E., & Pitts, M. M. (2006). Freshman learning communities, college performance, and retention. *Education Economics*, 14(2), 197–210. https://doi.org/10.1080/09645290600622947

Huisman, M., & Van Duijn, M. A. J. (2005). Software for social network analysis. *Models and Methods in Social Network Analysis*, 270, e316.

INSNA. (2017). International network for social network analysis. Retrieved October 24, 2017, from www.insna.org/

Kadushin, C. (2012). *Understanding social networks: Theories, concepts, and findings*. Oxford, England: Oxford University Press.

Kahn, R. L., & Antonucci, T. C. (1980). Convoys over the life course: attachment, roles, and social support. In P. B. Baltes & O. Brim (Eds.), *Life span development and behavior* (Vol. 3) (pp. 253–286). New York, NY: Academic Press.

Karlsson, A. (2006). statnet: Software tools for the representation, visualization, analysis and simulation of network data. *Journal of Statistical Software*, 17, 1–11. https://doi.org/10.18637/jss.v069.i12

Krackhardt, D. (1992). A caveat on the use of the quadratic assignment procedure. *Journal of Quantitative Anthropology*, 3(4), 279–296.

Krackhardt, D., & Kilduff, M. (1999). Whether close or far: Social distance effects on perceived balance in friendship networks. *Journal of Personality and Social Psychology*, 76(5), 770–782. https://doi.org/10.1037/0022-3514.76.5.770

Laumann, E. O., Marsden, P. V., & Prensky, D. (1983). The boundary specification problem in network analysis. In R. S. Burt & E. Minor (Eds.), *Applied network analysis: A methodological introduction* (pp. 18–87). Beverly Hills, CA: Sage.

Lazarsfeld, P. F., & Merton, R. K. (1954). Friendship as a social process: A substantive and methodological analysis. In M. Berger (Ed.), *Freedom and control in modern society* (pp. 18–66). New York, NY: Van Nostrand.

Lomi, A., Snijders, T. A. B., Steglich, C. E. G., & Torló, V. J. (2011). Why are some more peer than others? Evidence from a longitudinal study of social networks and individual academic performance. *Social Science Research*, 40(6), 1506–1520. https://doi.org/10.1016/j.ssresearch.2011.06.010

Marsden, P. V., & Campbell, K. E. (1984). Measuring tie strength. *Social Forces*, 63(2), 482–501. https://doi.org/10.2307/2579058

McPherson, M., Smith-Lovin, L., & Cook, J. M. (2001). Birds of a feather: Homophily in social networks. *Annual Review of Sociology*, 27, 415–444. https://doi.org/10.1146/annurev.soc.27.1.415

Mercken, L., Snijders, T., Steglich, C., Vartiainen, E., & de Vries, H. (2010). Dynamics of adolescent friendship networks and smoking behavior. *Social Networks*, 32(1), 72–81. https://doi.org/10.1016/j.socnet.2009.02.005

Monge, P. R., & Contractor, N. S. (2003). *Theories of communication networks*. New York, NY: Oxford University Press.

Onwuegbuzie, A. J., & Hitchcock, J. H. (2015). Advanced mixed analysis approaches. In S. Hesse-Biber & R. B. Johnson (Eds.), *The Oxford handbook of multimethod and mixed methods research inquiry* (pp. 275–295). New York, NY: Oxford University Press.

Palonen, T., & Froehlich, D. E., Van Waes, S., & Schäfer, H. (2020). Linking Quantitative and Qualitative Network Approaches: A Review of Mixed Methods Social Network Analysis in Education Research. *Review of Research in Education*, 44(1), 244–268. https://doi.org/10.3102/0091732X20903311, D. E. (2020). Mixed-Methods Social Network Analysis to Assist HR Practices and Consultancy. In D. E. Froehlich, D. E., Van Waes, S., & Schäfer, H. (2020). Linking Quantitative and Qualitative Network Approaches: A Review of Mixed Methods Social Network Analysis in Education Research. Review of Research in Education, 44(1), 244–268. https://doi.org/10.3102/0091732X20903311, M. Rehm, & B. C. Rienties (Eds.), *Mixed methods social network analysis: Theories and methodologies in learning and education*. London: Routledge.

Pentland, A., & Heibeck, T. (2010). *Honest signals: How they shape our world*. Boston, MA: MIT Press.

Prell, C. (2012). *Social network analysis: History, theory and methodology*. SAGE.

Putnam, R. D. (2001). *Bowling alone: The collapse and revival of American community*. New York, NY: Simon and Schuster.

Rienties, B. C., Héliot, Y., & Jindal-Snape, D. (2013). Understanding social learning relations of international students in a large classroom using social network analysis. *Higher Education*, 66(4), 489–504. https://doi.org/10.1007/s10734-013-9617-9

Rienties, B. C., Johan, N., & Jindal-Snape, D. (2015). Bridge building potential in cross-cultural learning: A mixed method study. *Asia Pacific Education Review*, 16(1), 37–48. https://doi.org/10.1007/s12564-014-9352-7

Ripley, R., Boitmanis, K., & Snijders, T. A. B. (2015). *Siena— Simulation investigation for empirical network analysis*. Oxford: University of Oxford.

Robins, G., Pattison, P., Kalish, Y., & Lusher, D. (2007). An introduction to exponential random graph (p*) models for social networks. *Social Networks*, 29(2), 173–191. https://doi.org/10.1016/j.socnet.2006.08.002

Schoch, D., & Brandes, U. (2016). Re-conceptualizing centrality in social networks. *European Journal of Applied Mathematics*, 27(06), 971–985. https://doi.org/10.1017/S0956792516000401

Scott, J. (2000). *Social network analysis: A handbook*. Thousand Oaks, CA: Sage Publications.

Smith, J. A., & Moody, J. (2013). Structural effects of network sampling coverage I: Nodes missing at random. *Social Networks*, 35(4), 652–668. https://doi.org/10.1016/j.socnet.2013.09.003

Smith, J. A., Moody, J., & Morgan, J. H. (2017). Network sampling coverage II: The effect of non-random missing data on network measurement. *Social Networks*, 48, 78–99. https://doi.org/10.1016/j.socnet.2016.04.005

Smith, S. S. (2013). Social network boundaries and tricky to access populations: A qualitative approach. *International Journal of Social Research Methodology*, 17(6), 613–623. https://doi.org/10.1080/13645579.2013.820076

Snijders, T. A. B., van de Bunt, G. G., & Steglich, C. E. G. (2010). Introduction to stochastic actor-based models for network dynamics. *Social Networks*, 32(1), 44–60. https://doi.org/10.1016/j.socnet.2009.02.004

Srivastava, J. (2008). Data mining for social network analysis. In *2008 IEEE International Conference on Intelligence and Security Informatics* (pp. xxxiii–xxxiv). https://doi.org/10.1109/ISI.2008.4565015

Valente, T. W. (1996). Social network tresholds in the diffusion of innovations. *Social Network*, 18(95), 69–89. https://doi.org/10.1016/0378-8733(95)00256-1

Van Der Gaag, M., Snijders, T. A. B., & Flap, H. D. (2008). Position generator measures and their relationship to other social capital measures. In N. Lin & B. Erickson (Eds.), *Social capital: An international research program* (pp. 27–48). Oxford, England: Oxford University Press. https://doi.org/10.1093/acprof:oso/9780199234387.001.0001

Verbrugge, L. M. (1977). The structure of adult friendship choices. *Social Forces*, 56(2), 576–597. https://doi.org/10.1093/sf/56.2.576

Vlegels, J., & Lievens, J. (2015). Music genres as historical artifacts: The case of classical music. *Connections*, 35(1). https://doi.org/10.17266/35.1.4

Wasserman, S., & Faust, K. (1994). *Social network analysis: Methods and applications*. New York, NY: Cambridge University Press.

Wellman, B. (1983). Network analysis: Some basic principles. *Sociological Theory*, 1(1), 155–200.

Yang, C., Latkin, C., Muth, S. Q., & Rudolph, A. (2013). Injection drug users' involvement in drug economy: Dynamics of sociometric and egocentric social networks. *Connections*, 33(1), 24–34. https://doi.org/10.1097/MPG.0b013e3181a15ae8.Screening

Zhao, C.-M., & Kuh, G. D. (2004). Adding value: Learning communities and student engagement. *Research in Higher Education*, 45(2), 115–138. https://doi.org/10.1023/B:RIHE.0000015692.88534.de

20

Social Media Analytics as Mixed Analysis

Tom Liam Lynch and Hannah R. Gerber

1 Definition of the Ontological Imperative with Social Media Data

A word as frequently and easily used as *digital* hardly appears to need definition. However, before we proceed, it is necessary to be clear about we mean by *digital*. In order to accurately and critically frame what is possible in digital methods and analysis, it is important to dispel common misconception. One popular misconception is that the digital lacks physicality. In fact, although the digital does refer to the electrical and radio transmission of information, such transmission requires very real devices, wires, servers, and so on, as well as, at least to-date, humans to mine the materials needed for conduction and to build and to install the devices, wires, and servers. Another popular misconception is that the digital refers to *smart* devices and magical algorithms. In fact, devices are better described as dumb insofar as they can only do precisely what human beings have programmed them to do. Similarly, algorithms might appear magical but are also just the products of what human beings have instructed computer processors to do based on a variety of variables that humans deem important. What one might describe as *smart* automation is actually the result of computational and human languages that comprise software systems. Finally, the digital is often regarded as a mysterious black box, something that simply exists and behaves the way it does because of what it is. In fact, digital devices, applications, and systems are intentionally designed by human beings; the languages, logics, and assumptions of those who create such devices, applications, and systems can be explicated. The world of computers is not antonymous to the world of human beings. To be digital is itself a social, linguistic, and creative human undertaking. As the etymology of *digital* reminds us, the digital originally referred to the fleshy fingers one used to count or to play the keys of musical instruments (Digital, 2016).

When it comes to digital methods of research and analysis, there exists what we termed an *ontological imperative* (Lynch & Gerber, 2018) to consider. The ontological imperative refers to the necessity of researchers who are invested in understanding digital spaces and communications to take into account the nature of the digital itself when collecting, analyzing, and reporting data. To be clear, most data used in research today are either themselves digitally collected or are mediated digitally when analyzed or reported. What we argue is that researchers must exercise greater explicit reflexivity when conducting and presenting research in order to identify precisely how the digital data and tools used in their work impacts their epistemological claims. In this chapter, we are particularly interested in the implications of the ontological imperative as it relates to the way researchers collect and analyze data. Of particular interest in this chapter is what it means to conduct a *mixed analysis* of social media data. In fact, we would argue all research that works with social media data is inherently mixed because such data always include both quantitative data (i.e., time stamps) and qualitative data (i.e., text or media). When it comes to social media data, quantitative and qualitative data are inextricably tied together.

2 When Use of the Ontological Imperative with Social Media Data is Appropriate in MMR

The question of when to employ digital methods within multiple approaches—qualitative, quantitative, and mixed (see Leech, Collins, & Onwuegbuzie, 2017; Onwuegbuzie, Gerber, & Abrams, 2017; Rogers, 2013)—is rapidly becoming an unnecessary question to ask. As digital technologies increasingly mediate the way people and institutions communicate formally and informally, the availability of digital data is great. Further, even data that are gathered via analogue methods often eventually are analyzed and reported via digital applications like qualitative, quantitative, and mixed methods analytical software and even word processors. In terms of mixed methods research, as briefly suggested earlier, it is reasonable to suggest that any research involving digital data and analysis is inherently mixed. The digital is necessarily both human and computational, qualitative and quantitative. For example, social media data might appear to be purely digital, but researchers would be remiss not to make explicit the fact that such data come from very human users via software applications and devices that are designed by other human beings using both computational and human languages. Again, when it comes to social media data, the qualitative and the quantitative are inseparable. If it seems otherwise, it is only because one does not account sufficiently for the ontology of the digital itself.

Digital methods of analysis always transduce what Lynch (2015) called *software space*. Software space consists of social, political, and economic contexts in which software is positioned as a necessary component of one's life or work. There are five layers to software space that are helpful to consider:

devices, networking infrastructure, user interfaces, code, and information systems (Lynch, 2015). An illustration will make the heuristic clearer. Imagine a user of Twitter who participates in an ongoing conversation online about her favorite soccer (i.e., football) team using a designated hashtag #NYCFC. She wishes to connect with other users who share her interest. When tweeting, she uses her mobile phone (the device), which connects to a wireless signal (the networking infrastructure) and on which she taps different buttons and types (the user interface) in order to send a tweet. When the phone is on and as she uses it, myriad applications are enacted based on programming languages (the code) that include sending and receiving packets of data to and from many servers (the information systems). To refer to such an activity simply as "digital" would be to oversimplify the phenomenon and betray one's misunderstanding of digitality. The design of the device, the technical specifications of the network, the ease of the user interface, the elegance and efficiency of the code, and the kinds of data sent and received are all human decisions and have a direct impact on the kinds of things our user can (and cannot) do—what she experiences and what researchers observe.

When collecting and analyzing digital data, researchers can gather many different types of information. For example, were we to collect data from our soccer fan, the kinds of data we could gather would be determined in part by whether we used a third-party tool (an application designed by someone else) or if we collected data ourselves directly from Twitter (using an Application Programming Interface or API). As discussed elsewhere (Gerber & Lynch, 2017), one available third-party tool used by researchers makes 33 fields of data about users available, whereas Twitter itself allows users of its API to collect well over 100 fields. (To be clear, the data that Twitter makes available through their API is likely a very small portion of all the data the company actually collects on users.) Once collected, such data must be cleaned, organized, and analyzed, which is possible via a wide array of methods. Mixed methods researchers are likely comfortable with such work because it resembles traditional methods. Filtering data and running various kinds of analyses are often par for the course. However, it is also necessary to note methodologically the analytical implications of the ontological imperative. For instance, a researcher would want to disclaim how the data available for analysis are limited based on the method of collection. What data were made available to the researcher? Did the tool used limit such available data? Would such data likely be available to another researcher attempting to replicate the study or might things like Twitter's Terms of Service and the tool's availability change over time?

Once data have been collected, many forms of analysis exist that, again, demonstrate the inherently mixed nature of working with social media. For instance, tweets can be collected and analyzed for sentiment scores. Referred to as *sentiment analysis*, researchers can employ a number of formulas to computationally calculate the positivity or negativity of any text. The result might be a simple positive or negative designation, or it might be a numerical score. Sentiment analysis is a popular method in fields like marketing, for example, where agencies use it to give companies a sense of their brand's status with customers.

It is not uncommon for researchers to visualize their data (Evergreen, 2017; Tufte, 2001), particularly because new tools have made data visualization more accessible. However, visualizing data is not quite as innocuous as it sometimes seems. For instance, it has been argued that researchers must take caution when using visualization techniques as part of the analysis process rather than simply reporting one's findings (Rieder & Rohle, 2012). Whereas visualizations used to be part of how one reported one's findings—that is, an epistemological technique—today, the prevalence of products often make visualization part of one's analysis—that is, a methodological and analytical tool. In addition, researchers have found that the lack of use of visual displays can be a predictor of a publication's rejection (Onwuegbuzie & Hwang, 2019a) and the overall vagueness and readability of a manuscript (Onwuegbuzie & Hwang, 2019b).

To underscore, we argue that the question of when to use of the ontological imperative is appropriate with social media data for mixed methods research only has one acceptable answer: always. Social media data are always mixed, always the result of both human and computational influence at a particular moment in time.

3 Technical Outline of Ontological Imperative with Social Media Data for MMR

The ontological imperative consists of posing five essential questions of one's research methodology that, when done well, offer a context for one's epistemological findings that take into account a critical understanding of the nature of the digital. The five questions are as follows:

1. What digital tools, systems, and services are at play in my study? Who created them and why?
2. What data do these digital tools, systems, and services render?
3. What hidden limitations might there be to the data rendered via these digital tools, systems, and services?
4. What are the epistemological implications of this ontological analysis?
5. What are the axiological implications of this ontological analysis?

Allow us to explain further what these questions attempt to address.

Question 1: All digital technologies are created by human beings whose motivations, assumptions, and biases must be accounted for. The purpose of this question is to provide researchers an opportunity to scrutinize how the human beings behind the technology might have allowed their own personal motivations and paradigms to influence their digital product. Such influence can extend from the design of the digital product to the computational logic of computer code to the decisions in composing an algorithm. The purpose of this question is not to criticize, but rather to critique.

Question 2: Digital data are generated in both seen and hidden ways. Right now, if you have one nearby (as you likely do), your smartphone is sending and receiving packets of data at a rapid pace. Some of those data are encrypted; some are not. When you move locations, your phone likely updates several service providers of your movement. When you post a photo to social media, many dozen data points about that single photo are also shared with the social media company and any partners (like advertisers) with which they might work. Data are being rendered constantly.

Question 3: Data rendered by different digital services and products are always partial. The amount of data that could be generated, stored, and manipulated by companies and service providers is infinite. As a result, whatever data are generated or made available to researchers for use are always only a small portion of what could be accessed. As a result, researchers must view the data offered to them skeptically: Why these data and not other data? Companies make decisions about what data to collect, use, and make available publicly. Scrutinizing why some data are available—and why others are not—is a crucial consideration in understanding the limitations and affordances of one's methodology and findings.

Question 4: Accounting for the nature of digital data, products, and services deepens the validity of one's epistemological findings. When researchers have accounted for the nature of the digital, one is able to spot weaknesses and strengths in what they can claim to know. Unlike collecting and analyzing data in non-digital settings, where one individual can observe and gather data and analyze oneself, to engage with digital data and tools necessarily involves other faceless human beings whose decisions can influence one's methods, analyses, and findings.

Question 5: The way digital data and products operate raise myriad ethical concerns that researchers must consider. Again, when imagining an individual researcher collecting data, say, in a classroom without the aid of any digital tools, we can see clearly what ethical responsibilities she has. A researcher might complete an Institutional Review Board (IRB) application, prepare permission documentation for parents and students, and de-identify and take confidentiality steps in any work she/he collects. However, when data are collected and analyzed digitally, the ethical lines are not so clear. For instance, do social media data require IRB approval to use in research? Must usernames be de-identified? Those questions and many more emerge when engaging in research in the digital space.

4 Empirical Demonstration of Ontological Imperative with Social Media Data for MMR

Allow us now to apply the ontological imperative to a sample data set. Let's build on the aforementioned example in which we imagine a social media user engaging with her favorite sports team: the New York City Football Club (NYCFC). As researchers, we might have a range of inquiries involving such data: how networks of users engage with each other, how positively or negatively different players are discussed, or how users subvert formal power structures associated with professional soccer. The range is extensive. We might then pull a dataset of tweets from Twitter during a specific, bounded period of time related to our topic of inquiry. On September 7, 2019, NYCFC had a particularly interesting game where they conceded a goal in the first two minutes, equalized well over one hour later, and then won on a penalty kick in the final minute of overtime. Surely, a dataset of tweets would provide some rich fodder for study?

In order to pull the data, we used the R programming language to write a simple script that imported tweets containing #NYCFC between September 3 and September 11—four days leading up to the game, the game, and four days afterwards. The result were 8,879 tweets, each containing a possible 88 categories of data with a potential of 781,352 data points. As suggested earlier, there are many ways one might explore such data. For present purposes, however, let us focus on applying the ontological imperative to these data themselves.

1. **What digital tools, systems, and services are at play in my study? Who created them and why?** There are four main tools, systems, and services at play in the collection of #NYCFC Twitter data. First, we used the R programming language. R is created and maintained by a community of volunteers all over the world. Like all popular computer languages, R is a human-readable language meant to allow people to communicate directly with computers. The motivation behind the creation of R appears to have been greatly academic, rather than commercial, its origins rooted in the desire of a small group of professors to create a specific language for statistics. Second, in order to efficiently access Twitter's data archives, we used a package in R called "rtweet." A package is like a prewritten block of code that someone else wrote in order to make a complicated task a bit easier. The motivation behind the creation of packages range from hobbyists looking for a side project to community members earnestly committed to creating efficient code to others who wish to monetize their packages or services in some direct or indirect way. Third, Twitter makes some of their data available for mass extraction. They do so via a protocol called an API (meaning *application programming interface*) that regulates communications and requests between the outside world and Twitter's servers and databases. A key motivation for Twitter is, of course, to be profitable. The kinds of data collected, stored, and made available to others reflects its business bottom line. They have a range of *premium* services for individuals or institutions looking to have advanced access to their data. Fourth, we downloaded the data from R into Excel so that we could more manageably engage with them. A motivation for Microsoft, creators of Excel, is profit as well as attempting to keep users in the Microsoft ecosystem of products.

2. **What data do these digital tools, systems, and services render?** By using the R programming language and rtweet package to collect Twitter data, we

were able to gather nearly 8,000 tweets in approximately 10 seconds. The data include 88 categories of data, not all of which is necessarily collected for every tweet. The reason for incomplete data for some Tweets could simply be because that user did not generate that data due to their privacy settings or other factors. Categories of data include the following: screen name of user; date and time of creation, text in the tweet, number of characters, hashtags used, links included, whether or not the tweet is a reply to another user, and much more. Importantly, some of the data required cleaning upon import. The use of special characters or emojis in tweets do not always appear correctly in a standard spreadsheet.

3. **What hidden limitations might there be to the data rendered via these digital tools, systems, and services?** The hidden limitations that one might consider relate to the digital products and tools one uses to access, collect, and analyze data, including the motivations, assumptions, and biases that the products' and tools' creators might have literally encoded into them. First, as a programming language, R is in a constant state of revision. That is, all programming languages have to be updated regularly to address changes to industry standards. In addition, programming languages are updated to include new features. In both cases, the version of R used to conduct our data pull will certainly be out-of-date for many readers of this chapter. Second, the package rtweet also comprises programming languages and it too undergoes revisions. The latest version, for example, is offering a premium function that makes it easier for users to search within more refined windows of dates and times. It is possible that such features could make a considerable difference to the kinds of data one can retrieve from social media platforms like Twitter. Third, Twitter itself uses protocols for requesting and receiving data from their databases. Those wishing to collect Twitter data must agree to their Terms of Service (ToS), the details of which many users will skim or skip but which contain important ethical and legal information. Further, Twitter chooses to make some—not all—of their data available for free retrieval. We observed 88 types of data. Twitter very likely has access to many times more categories of data that they do not share with the public via their API. For example, Twitter will share a link to pictures that users uploaded. They do not, however, provide access to any of the metadata associated with an individual photo, like the phone used to take it, longitude and latitude, shutter speed, and direction facing when taken, although these types of data are most certainly available to the company. As this example illustrates, the choice of which data to share, with whom, how, and why are all part of Twitter's business-driven motivation. Fourth, when we imported data from R into Excel, we observed instances of gibberish in the text data, which, upon further inspection, seemed to relate to users' use of special characters. Technically speaking, it seems possible to avoid such errors in importing. Nevertheless, observing its occurrence required that we take time to attempt cleaning the data before any further work.

4. **What are the epistemological implications of this ontological analysis?** One of the most important epistemological implications of the aforementioned analysis is this: other researchers looking to replicate our data collection might never be able to do so. Replicability, a hallmark of epistemological confidence and academic rigor, is very challenging. Why? The reason has everything to do with the nature of the digital. All four digital components used in our collection and cleaning of data are in flux. One might not understand them to be so, but they are. The R programming language gets updated every few months. It is possible that they will develop new functions, for example, to enable users to more easily engage with social media platforms. Similarly, at the time of writing, the rtweet package had received upgrades to its functionality that suggested more sophisticated kinds of searches of Twitter data were not so far away. As such upgrades take shape, the methods we used to collect our data might be depreciated. Not only might the methods and tools used to collect data change, but the kinds of data that are available might also shift. There is nothing preventing Twitter from expanding or restricting the kinds of data they make available to users in the future. What data one can access, how, and with what ethical or legal implications are all malleable. And finally, Excel updates multiple times a year. In the future, it will likely be able to read data imported from R with fewer errors, which will directly affect the integrity of the data researchers can work with—hopefully for the better. In sum, researchers' fundamental assumption that methodological replicability yields epistemological integrity is fading in the Digital Age.

5. **What are the axiological implications of this ontological analysis?** Although axiology refers broadly to issues of value, we focus here more narrowly on issues of ethics that arise when working with social media data. One of the key questions researchers must ask when working with digital data like the aforementioned tweets shared is this: To what extent is the collection and analysis of such data ethical? Those social media users whose data were collected earlier did not sign any specific permission-granting document to us. They checked a box agreeing to the Terms of Service (ToS) for Twitter, and those terms, at the time of this writing, gave Twitter all the legal leeway they needed to collect, share, and make available users' tweets to others. However, there is complexity at play that should be noted. First, the ToS for any technology company change over time. It is possible that the terms laid out when one signs up

for an account with a company change drastically in successive years as the company attempts to identify new ways to raise revenue. This can happen when least expected. Gerber, Abrams, Curwood, and Magnifico (2017) highlighted one such instance wherein the publisher Random House acquired Figment.com, a fanfiction writing site, and made all privately searchable posts publicly searchable. Although users might be informed of such changes, it is unlikely that users are actively required to grant new permission and generally speaking, users cannot opt out of new changes. Whereas initial enrollment requires an active opting in to the terms, remaining enrollment requires actively opting out, if opting out is even an option. Second, the kinds of data that are collected include sensitive information that merits consideration. Should researchers preserve usernames or do they have an ethical obligation to create fictitious names and practice modes of concealment (Bruckman, 2002)? Or, because the data that are collected include the information about other users as well—like which users might have quoted and retweeted a tweet—one might expand one's ethical questions not only to the primary users but also to secondary users.

5 Suggested Applications of Ontological Imperative with Social Media Data in MMR

Applying the ontological imperative to one's research might most fruitfully be undertaken by creating a subsection for the ontological imperative in one's methodology section, providing a subheading for each of the five questions. Then, one might synthesize one's insights by adding a subsection called "Implications of the Ontological Imperative." Using the data from the aforementioned #NYCFC Twitter collection, one might identify several important statements that one should make in one's methodology section. First, researchers might note that the data themselves both represent a specific time and cultural phenomenon, but for many reasons, might not be able to be collected in precisely the same way in the future. Twitter, for instance, might change the parameters of the way data are accessed, limiting collection to only recent data, say, within the last 7 days. Second, the data that are collected might vary from those collected in our example, either because Twitter adjusts its parameters or because the tools that are used to collect the data are updated and functionality is lost. This phenomenon adds additional shape to what Onwuegbuzie (2012) calls *the radical middle* in conducting research,

> which should not be a passive and comfortable middle space wherein the status quo among quantitative and qualitative epistemologies is maintained, but rather a new theoretical and methodological space in which a socially just and productive coexistence among all research traditions is actively promoted, and in which mixed research is consciously local,

dynamic, interactive, situated, contingent, fluid, strategic, and generative. (p. 192)

Digital data, as discussed earlier, is both humanly and computationally constructed, humanly and computationally distributed, and human and computationally adjusted in perpetuity. But what is important to note is that digital data are always both "consciously local" and subliminally global. That is, although digital data are generated intentionally in local contexts (a fan watching a live soccer game in The Bronx), those data are sent electronically all over the world to networks of servers, acted upon by algorithms and scripts written by international teams of programmers, and then physically distributed on servers across the planet wherein hardware can be subject to the unique laws of the host country (see also World Intellectual Property Copyright Treaty [1996]). One could argue that the historical meaning of *local* no longer exists in the Digital Age, certainly not as it pertains to digital data. There is no local. There is only global distribution that can be initiated and received locally and temporarily.

6 Strengths and Limitations of Ontological Imperative with Social Media Data in MMR

There are strengths and limitations to all analytical methods. The ontological imperative is no different. In the following sections, we identify some of the main strengths and limitations of the ontological imperative, ultimately arguing that its strengths far outweigh its limitations.

Strengths

1. The ontological imperative explicitly accounts for a greatly underappreciated aspect of conducting research in the Digital Age: that all digital data and tools are *mixed* so to speak and all are unstable. As we argued prior, far too many researchers—and people generally—appear to lack a critical understanding of the nature of digital phenomena. They believe that the digital is ethereal when it is quite concrete, mechanical when it is human, and objective when it is the product of myriad postlapsarian human beings' efforts. By accounting for the ontology of the digital, researchers will find that they can more confidently conduct research and assert what they do and do not know.

2. The ontological imperative offers a clear series of steps to systematically identify and account for the mixed and unstable nature of digital data and tools. It would be one thing to conceptually point out that the nature of the digital is problematically misunderstood. But what we propose goes further. We provide a series of discrete steps that are specific enough to help researchers outline the contours of how digitality impacts their research, while remaining sufficiently nimble to be applied to a wide range of research topics and methodological paradigms.

3. The goal of the ontological imperative is realistically focused on qualifying one's research methods and epistemology, not overthrowing the possibility of knowing at all. That is, we attempt to walk a fine line between rupturing one's fundamental assumptions about digital phenomena while simultaneously arguing that ontological instability does not necessitate epistemological ennui. We anticipate that some who read this work will argue that the ontological imperative is a case for the impossibility of knowing in the Digital Age. That would be a mistake. Rather, by explicitly accounting for the nature of the digital, we argue that researchers strengthen the quality of newly created knowledge when they undergo the steps outlined earlier.

4. The ontological imperative is framed in a way that will make it applicable despite changes in the digital landscape because the fundamental nature of what constitutes digitality does not change radically over time. We expect that some researchers might be quick to suggest that because digital phenomena appear to change so frequently, the applicability of ontological imperative will necessarily expire quickly as well. But to suggest so is incorrect and betrays one's limited understanding of the nature of the digital. Picture the way trees sway in the breeze. Yes, what one sees toward the tops move with some frequency, like leaves and branches. But as one observes the lower parts of the tree and its systems of roots, one sees far less movement. This stability metaphor is furthered when one considers that a tree's roots extend up to three times the height and breadth of the tree itself! It is an apt metaphor for the nature of digital phenomena. Yes, software constantly updates and new apps appear to launch and close with daily frequency. New features come out regularly. So too do new devices. But the actual nature of what it means to be digital—the interplay between software and hardware—really does not change radically, very greatly, nor very often.

5. The ontological imperative can be applied across fields and methodological leanings. As suggested earlier, because the nature of the digital itself applies nimbly across fields and methodologies, the same is true of the ontological imperative. However, we believe that, over time, it is possible that some researchers will begin to surface patterns in the ways the ontological imperative applies to specific fields. For example, health researchers who study social media data for indications of how diseases spread nationally and internationally might find themselves more concerned with the way geographical metadata are captured and shared by social media companies as well as advances in tools and packages that allow one to analyze such data. The ontological imperative sections of their research works might well reflect such disciplinary leaning, which we would view as an appropriate and exciting refinement.

Limitations

1. The ontological imperative requires becoming familiar with (and to be unintimidated by) the complexity of digital spaces. We acknowledge that some researchers might find the complexity of the digital surprising and indeed overwhelming. Some might reach a kind of digital saturation point, choosing to leave unaddressed the ontological issues described earlier in favor of a more ignorance-is-bliss attitude. Doing so is understandable, but ultimately weakens the quality of research as a whole. We would argue that editors of journals and books could assist in the field in strengthening digitally conscious research by adding clauses to their manuscript review processes that require the ontological imperative to be addressed when dealing with social media data. Furthermore, future style guides like APA Publication Manuals could require, or at least encourage, researchers to account for the ontological imperative as well.

2. The ontological imperative requires examining documents and language that researchers often take for granted, like developer documentation. In fact, we understand that some researchers might find developer documentation intimidating or beyond their comprehension. However, we would also argue that such documentation is written by human beings in order to communicate with other human beings about the nature of digital products and phenomena. Developer documents might be an unfamiliar genre, but they are not wholly uninterpretable. The more one reads and reflects and writes about such documentation, the clearer it becomes both how to access developers' insights and why doing so is invaluable.

3. The ontological imperative might feel to some like it is too great a departure from the research itself. As one colleague remarked, "this is way beyond me and out of my field of expertise." With all due respect to our peer, digital phenomena and tools increasingly mediate all of our lives and fields. To suggest that focusing explicitly on the ontological imperative would distract from one's research is to suggest that the nature of the digital is unimportant. As we have argued earlier, that is untrue. Including focused reflection on the nature of the digital by using the steps outlined earlier is no more *beyond* researchers than composing thorough and thoughtful methodology sections.

4. In journal articles especially, concision is so important that accounting for the ontological imperative might seem like an indulgence. We acknowledge that there is a linguistic economics to writing up one's research. However, the ever-present challenge for all researchers is to ensure that their methodology builds readers' confidence in the epistemological implications of their work. As the research community builds their collective understanding of the complexity of the digital world, one should expect that editors and readers will come to expect a level of conceptual and methodological sophistication

commensurate with the sophistication of digital phenomena themselves. In short, addressing the ontological imperative will be necessary.

Moving Forward

In the coming years, we anticipate that the research community will become more collectively informed about the complexity of digital phenomena. The more headlines describe attempts to *hack* public agencies and elections or breaches in data security at well-known private companies, the more collective consciousness will rise. Eventually, researchers will be expected to account for digital phenomena and tools in ways they have heretofore avoided. The ontological imperative provides ready at hand a methodological tool that can demonstrate to the field how to account for what is known and unknown about digital phenomena.

7 Resources for Learning More About Ontological Imperative with Social Media Data

In this chapter, we have made the case that the ontological imperative is an invaluable—and increasingly necessary—instrument for any researcher who examines digital phenomena or uses digital tools. At the heart of our argument is the fact that the very nature of the digital is sufficiently complex that it merits scrutiny in one's methodology section. One might wonder, however, where to begin exploring the ontological imperative further. Fortunately, we have penned an essay (Lynch & Gerber, 2018) that explores more thoroughly the nature of the digital and how to begin implementing the ontological imperative in one's research. That essay is a sound resource to explore next. (We are including at this chapter's end a list of additional resources created with the book's editors.)

In addition, we might encourage you to try this exercise. After reviewing the five steps of the ontological imperative once more, choose a research work that focuses on digital phenomena. Reread it. Then, try posing each of the aforementioned five questions, perhaps even imagining you were writing a section for the author's methodology section on the ontological imperative. Ask yourself: How did addressing the ontological imperative affect the quality of the author's findings? We have done this in workshops and classes, where attendees and students are often surprised by the weakness of the epistemological claims and the validity threats that could, in fact, shape alternate explanations to the phenomena at hand. We suspect that your own review of methodology sections will reveal previously unacknowledged epistemological gaps, and in so doing, demonstrate the worthwhileness of the ontological imperative in your own research.

Additional Resources
Tools for Data Analysis

- Lumify is a big data fusion, analysis, and visualization platform that helps users to discover connections and to explore relationships in their data via a host of analytic options.
- Plotly is an analytics tool that allows users to create charts and dashboards to share online.
- Python is a language used widely for different forms of social media and text analysis, including natural language processing.
- R is a language for statistical computing and graphics that is used for big data analysis and that provides a wide variety of statistical tests.

Tutorials

- "Text Analytics with R | Sentiment Analysis with R" is an excellent introductory video: www.youtube.com/watch?v=y21yWgMWMc8
- "Topic modeling with R and tidy data principles" by Julia Silge, walks users through an accessible and smart introduction: www.youtube.com/watch?v=evTuL-RcRpc
- "Introduction to Exploring Social Network Structure with Visualization in R" provides exactly what it says, accessibly and smartly: www.youtube.com/watch?v=N_mMXvNPE8Y

REFERENCES

Bruckman, A. (2002). Studying the amateur artist: A perspective on disguising data collected in human subjects research on the Internet. *Ethics and Information Technology, 4*, 217–231. doi:10.1023/A:1021316409277

Digital. (2016). In *OED Online*. Retrieved from www.oed.com.rlib.pace.edu/view/Entry/52611?redirectedFrom=digital

Evergreen, S. D. H. (2017). *Presenting data effectively: Communicating your findings for maximum impact* (2nd ed.). Thousand Oaks, CA: Sage.

Gerber, H. R., Abrams, S. S., Curwood, J. C., & Magnifico, A. M. (2017). *Conducting qualitative research of learning in online spaces*. Thousand Oaks, CA: Sage.

Gerber, H. R., & Lynch T. L. (2017). Into the meta: Research methods for moving beyond social media surfacing techniques. *Tech Trends, 61*, 263–272. doi:10.1007/s11528-016-0140-6

Leech N. L., Collins K. M. T., & Onwuegbuzie A. J. (2017) Collecting qualitative data to enhance social network analysis and data mining. In R. Alhajj & J. Rokne (Eds.), *Encyclopedia of social network analysis and mining* (pp. 1–11). New York, NY: Springer.

Lynch, T. L. (2015). *The hidden role of software in educational research: Policy to practice*. New York, NY: Routledge.

Lynch, T. L., & Gerber, H. R. (2018). The ontological imperative when researching in the digital age. *International Journal of Multiple Research Approaches, 10*, 112–123. doi:10.29034/ijmra.v10n1a7

Onwuegbuzie, A. J. (2012). Introduction: Putting the mixed back into quantitative and qualitative research in educational research and beyond: Moving toward the radical middle. *International Journal of Multiple Research Approaches, 6*, 192–219. doi:10.5172/mra.2012.6.3.192

Onwuegbuzie, A. J., Gerber, H. R., & Abrams, S. S. (2017). Mixed methods research. In J. Mathes (Ed.), *International encyclopedia of communication research methods* (pp. 1–33). doi:10.1002/9781118901731.iecrm0156

Onwuegbuzie, A. J., & Hwang, E. (2019a). Editorial: Frequency in the use of visual displays and its predictability of the editor's decision of manuscripts submitted to *Research in the Schools*. *Research in the Schools, 26*(1), i–x.

Onwuegbuzie, A. J., & Hwang, E. (2019b). Writing style, readability, and communication vagueness as a predictor of the use of visual displays among manuscripts submitted to *Research in the Schools*. *Research in the Schools, 26*(2), i–x.

Rieder, B., & Rohle, T. (2012). Digital methods: Five challenges. In D. M. Berry (Ed.), *Understanding digital humanities* (pp. 67–84). New York, NY: Palgrave Macmillan.

Rogers, R. (2013). *Digital methods*. Cambridge, MA: MIT Press.

Tufte, E. R. (2001). *The visual display of quantitative information* (2nd ed.). Cheshire, CT: Graphics Press.

World Intellectual Property Copyright Treaty. (1996). *Understanding copyright and related rights.* WIPO Publication No. 909(E). Retrieved from www.wipo.int/edocs/pubdocs/en/wipo_pub_909_2016.pdf

21

Geographic Information Systems as Mixed Analysis

Nigel G. Fielding and Joan M. Verd

1 Definition of GIS as Mixed Analysis

A distinctive trait of researchers drawn to mixed methods is their respect for context (Holdenab, Eriksson, Andreasson, Williamsson, & Dellvecd, 2015). This respect has motivated analytically fruitful combinations of quantitative data and qualitative data, and has had a substantial impact on how Mixed Methods have developed, bearing in mind the dominance of quantitative methods and postpositivist assumptions in social science at the time that contemporary forms of multimethod designs first emerged (between approximately 1945 and 1970). Bringing context back in has been a major contribution of the mixed methods movement, but methodological developments do not proceed in isolation from analytical developments. The latter saw in the 1990s the *re-discovery* of time as a neglected feature of social analysis (Adam, 1994), facilitated both by new applications of long-established methodologies (e.g., diary methods) and by new methods enabled by the Internet. So it is with another inescapable feature of the social world, that of space. Our social world is dominated by the relentless flow across our news feeds of issues relating to space in one way or another, from the mass migrations occasioned by war, drought, and poverty to the criminogenic effect of our attempts to confine offenders to the space of the prison cell, and the *postcode lottery* of healthcare under policies of austerity and neoliberalism. Space, it seems, is the essential context for many of our contemporary social woes. Perhaps furthest advanced in application to emergent forms of sociality associated with the urban, the spatial dimension is one of the most fruitful contemporary sites of methodological, conceptual, and empirical development. For example, in police research, there is a substantial literature on change in officer attitudes over time, from training to late career, but there are few comparative studies of variations in attitudes at different career stages across different countries. Those few studies suggest that what have been taken as universal characteristics of officer attitudes are not universal at all. Taking the spatial into account provides new tests of our assumptions and accepted wisdom.

When we engage intellectually with context, it is implicit that we seek to draw on more than one factor and more than one kind of evidence to address the issue at hand. Few social problems reduce to a single factor. Usually, the *essential* evidence has more than one dimension and its empirical manifestations take more than one form. Accordingly, when contemporary researchers explore and visualize in geographic space, they use not only statistical data (such as that derived from Census returns or the incidence of crime events) but also qualitative data derived from and about the people who live in or move through such geographic space. A principal means to perform such work is to employ a Geographic Information System (GIS). A GIS is a sophisticated database of layers of spatially related data, which may be manipulated, either statistically or qualitatively, to reveal patterns or display relationships using the cartographic aesthetic of the map. The transparent overlays that helped 1960s schoolchildren build up a multi-layered understanding of an issue from the textbooks used in history and civics lessons (such as the incidence of slavery across the pre-Civil War states and its relationship to the region's principal staple crops) can be seen as a homely precursor of the GIS. The affordances of contemporary software, in tandem with those of the continuous online environment of the Internet, provide powerful ways to build profoundly *mixed* analyses of social problems drawing on an array of information sources that no textbook could support.

GIS databases help us to think and reflect spatially in ways that extend the depth and scope of our understanding of context. GIS provides context for at least three different elements in research projects: (a) for the places/locations mentioned by people observed, interviewed, or surveyed; (b) for the places from which informants originate or perform the activities that are of interest to the researcher(s) (in the long run, providing some biographical-spatial context, and in the short run, identifying how the place where they live/work/study influences their responses); and (c) for the places where data were produced (so we can better understand the effects of location on the responses obtained). Thus, we can see how space shapes data and we can connect what people do or say with where they do or say it, along with where they are from. These uses are captured by the terms *geo-referencing* or *geo-tagging*. Geo-referenced or geo-tagged information helps to enhance interpretation or understanding because GIS data bring in more meaning. Researchers become more aware and sensitive to the *places where things happen* (S. J. Steinberg & S. L. Steinberg, 2006).

However, as the textbook example suggests, to render a GIS purely as a form of software is too narrow. The history or civics lesson required knowledge from the teacher and textbook as well as the overlays. A GIS is likewise multifaceted, comprising not only the software and technologies but methods.

Quantitative methods long predominated in the integration of social and spatial information but, latterly, qualitative methods have joined the picture, and their impact has been substantial. Technology has helped here, in the form of software to facilitate qualitative analysis (i.e., Computer-Assisted Qualitative Data Analysis Software [CAQDAS]), with modern qualitative software being *geo-referenced* and *geo-coded*. MAXQDA provides an external link to Google Earth, so users can geolocate any entity in the program by means of a hyperlink. The 'Links' function in NVivo is similar but cannot distinguish links to GIS software and is restricted to geo-locating social media content produced, for example, from Facebook or Twitter. ATLAS.ti offers particularly full support for qualitative work involving geo-data because it integrates geo-coding as a function of the program. QDA Miner also offers powerful support for work with geo-data. A valuable feature is its Integrated Geocoding, which assigns geographical coordinates to geographical entities such as cities, counties, and states/provinces, and to postal codes and IP addresses. QDA Miner also supports geo-data representation with tools in its 'GISViewer' module that enable users to create heat maps (shading matrices), data point maps, and distribution maps. The program also supports the space/time heuristic with geo-tagging and time-tagging tools. These associate geographical and time coordinates to text segments or graphical areas, and allow users to retrieve coded data based on time or location. Events can also be plotted in space and time (e.g., the dates when, and the places where, the 'Unabomber'—Theodore Kaczynski—committed terrorist acts across the United States between 1978 and 1995). Moreover, QDA Miner provides tools with which to create dynamic maps and interactive timelines (so putative copycat attacks similar to those committed by the 'Unabomber' could be successively placed at different points on the timeline to test potential patterns). A step beyond what is offered in standalone CAQDAS involves qualitative programs that are directly integrated into a GIS package (discussed further later).

Although software has had a considerable impact on work with a geo-spatial dimension, arguably the greatest impact has been from the emergence of *Qualitative Geography* (or *Critical GIS*), which has brought new methods and new perspectives to work with GIS. Qualitative Geography incorporates spatially relevant information sources beyond GIS per se; these include the mapping of individuals' use of GPS, mobile devices, wireless infrastructures, and the Internet. Such traces can comprise a quantitized map of social activities (Girardin, 2009). Mixing quantitative and qualitative geospatial information can reveal new dimensions of a research topic. In this sense, it can be considered as a kind of observational data (Onwuegbuzie, Leech, & Collins 2010). For instance, the shape of a rural landscape, the way streets are designed, or the kind of shops in a quarter can be treated as variables/factors that can be part of the data set—not just context. They may be seen as *traces* of past activity, in the ethnographic sense. Of course, this kind of information can be collected and registered by means of field notes or photographs, in the case of qualitative information, or using geographic databases in the case of quantitative information, but GIS can provide both quantitative and qualitative information *all-in-one*, organized as different layers of the same database. Rather than being used to provide context to other kinds of data or to see how space shapes other kinds of data, geospatial information is treated as data in its own right; for example, a cartographic representation of a particular distribution of retail shops (indicating how densely concentrated they are, and their distance from adjacent residential areas) can be treated as the unit of analysis, with each instance of that distribution assigned the same geo-code, enabling searches across a geographical database to locate instances of that distribution of shops. Such searches could, for instance, be useful in analyzing what kinds of shop distribution are associated with survival on Main Street in an age of Internet retail.

A pioneering example of full integration of software tools and mixed methods was a study of the lives of Muslim women in Columbus, Ohio after 11 September, 2001 (*9/11*, the attack on the Twin Towers in New York City). This study involved the adoption of narrative analysis as the qualitative element, a 3D GIS-based time-geographic approach as the representational framework, and direct incorporation into the GIS (in this case ArcGIS ©) of a qualitative analysis tool based on the principles of CAQDAS to facilitate the geo-visualization of the narrative data (Kwan & Ding, 2008). Geographers continue to innovate in convergence between CAQDAS and GIS, against evidence that social scientists who adopt CAQDAS largely use it in pedestrian ways, as a data management tool (White, Judd, & Poliandri, 2012). Thus, Jung (2014) demonstrates the use of *code clouds* to spatially visualize analytic codes generated using CAQDAS and derived from geographically referenced tweets. Rather than transforming the qualitative data into categories or numbers, code clouds preserve the context of data as a locational visual image.

2 Appropriate use of GIS in Mixed Methods Research

Thus, both intellectual currents and technological developments have played a part in the new analytical reach of geography. But the new potential they have created is not confined to cartography and territorial analysis *per se*. Being able to represent geographic information through interactive maps is not only transformative for geography. Digital simplification of the fundamentals of collecting, handling, and analyzing spatial information means that what was the province of the geography discipline is now available to the mixed method social researcher (Longley, Goodchild, Maguire, & Rhind, 2005). Given the pervasiveness of the spatial dimension across a range of social questions, the appropriate uses of GIS in mixed methods research are extensive. We want to address this not only in terms of substantive matters (e.g., health, crime, education) but also of the purposes and pursuits of social research.

To start with substantive matters, GIS is a highly appropriate approach to understanding patterns in the distribution of social resources. We can see this from the earliest days of social research onwards. Charles Booth mapped where rich and poor people lived in London, and by also mapping morbidity and mortality by area of residence and mapping places associated with particular commercial and industrial activities, he could examine the varying health effects of the occupations pursued by different social classes (see https://booth.lse.ac.uk/ for a digitized collection of Booth's maps). As this suggests, the resources of interest may be physical (e.g., the availability of uranium in land around the Grand Canyon owned by the federal government and land owned by Native Americans, and the differing drilling rights associated with such ownership), economic (e.g., regional variation in employment between Eire and Northern Ireland under post-Brexit border arrangements), or about fundamental social divisions (e.g., health inequalities between the prosperous Nordic fringe of the European Union and the deprived post-Soviet east of Europe). The point of these examples is, of course, that each of them involves patterns that are spatially manifest but behind which stand a constellation of causes with social, economic, and political dimensions. Mapping resources is also a way to identify and assess the constraints provoked by territory, such as neighborhoods. Mapping life events or residential mobility can also show the biographical constraints faced by different social groups. Where interest lies in understanding causality, GIS stands alongside mixed methods as a way to make complex interactions more visible and explicable.

We mentioned that we construe *appropriate use* not only as a matter concerning the disciplinary agenda of the social sciences but also as a matter of its purposes and pursuits. GIS can be a significant resource in the decision process relating to social change. We might take the instance of a Rust Belt town whose community is seeking ways to improve its socioeconomic fortunes. A host of information must be organized in order to examine and weigh the various consequences of different forms of redevelopment initiative. What, for instance, might be the health and wellbeing consequences of re-developing the former town center as a night-time economy locale featuring a gambling casino? What planning law and zoning restrictions would need to be considered? What demands on medical services do such locales make and what collateral effects are there from, for instance, increased late night traffic and vehicle movements? How far should primary schools be located from the locale to avoid risk and other negative effects impacting schoolchildren? Multiple information sources are available to inform the response to each question, each with a geographical dimension. Historical health data and vehicle particulate pollution data are available from other jurisdictions where casinos have been introduced as an engine of economic recovery. Zoning is explicitly geographical (but implicitly political). Crime statistics tied to police precincts are available such that risks can be estimated from precincts similar to those of the town in question.

If this approach sounds familiar to mixed methods readers, it is because, aided by GIS, geographers have latterly become closet mixed methodologists. Things get really interesting, though, where we recognize that the fully worked GIS project can be used as a means of decision support for the citizens of our Rust Belt town. By *fully worked*, we mean that the necessary information to support an understanding of the several dimensions of a decision (social, economic, political) has been used to populate the GIS. This helps us to make a further point, which is that GIS projects can be *iterative*. Like the distinction between a cross-sectional and a longitudinal research design, rather than a one-shot time slice, the decision process can indeed be supported as a *process*, something where we form different, evolving, better informed views as our knowledge grows and we become alert to how one dimension interacts with another. Where urban planning departments have often operated in a way that seems to be hermetically sealed from the community they serve, offering a plan for consultation when many of the important decisions have already been made behind closed doors, the GIS model offers an approach wherein citizens can discuss and debate the different consequences of different approaches to redevelopment. A GIS can serve as an accessible, real-time decision model without the complexities of traditional social science models.

This is, perhaps, to emphasize the instrumental, applied returns from work with GIS. But the further value of adopting GIS techniques is the contribution they can make in terms of extending the generalizability of social science analysis. Incorporating the spatial dimension can help us build *contextualized generalizations* (J. Fielding & N. Fielding, 2015). We do this by identifying the features of social phenomena that exercise persistent influence, which we recognize by their occurring in every setting where the phenomenon manifests, and by identifying features around which variation occurs in the particular form of the phenomenon present in a specific local setting. Ultimately, the appropriate uses of GIS include helping social science be cumulative while sensitively attuned to context.

3 Techniques and Skills in Using GIS in Mixed Methods Research

Maps and other spatial representations are best regarded as both qualitative and quantitative, the former because often the only numbers on a map are the scale to which they have been drawn, the latter because images such as contours or streets are based on measurements and projections. Thus, the researcher seeking to use GIS will benefit from having both qualitative and quantitative skills. Contemporary researchers want to explore in geographic space using both statistical data such as crime and detection rates and qualitative data about the people who reside in or move through geographic space such as a police precinct. The qualitative data might be text from an interview transcript or an observational fieldnote or an official document, but may also be a photograph, a video, or a flow chart summarizing a timeline.

Both statistical data and textual data are non-spatial and must be linked to spatial coordinates. Such data may be *point* data linking one position in space, or lines, such as roads, or may be defined by areas, such as high crime rate *hotspots*. A map with two layers of information might have one based on area classifications derived from a census and a second layer of points, for instance, exact locations where crime incidents have occurred. The former often takes the form of a *choropleth* map, which uses graduated symbols and colors to indicate the magnitude or presence of a characteristic of the phenomenon in question. For instance, the color green applied to part of a town map may indicate a middle-income area and a triangle symbol on a street may indicate a specific income quartile. To hold different layers, each containing particular information, GIS software such as ESRI ArcMap© is used. The software can be manipulated both statistically or qualitatively to seek patterns or express relationships, in this case, between income and crime rates in a residential area.

Researchers using GIS draw on a vocabulary that includes *geo-referencing*, *geo-linking*, and *geo-coding*, as discussed earlier. In the terms of the geography discipline, geo-referencing and geo-linking mean aligning geographic data to a coordinate system (e.g., longitude and latitude), that is, a paper map. This allows different geographic datasets to be matched within a common geographical framework. Geo-referencing or geo-linking is a process that links data, such as an extract from an interview transcript, to locations in Cartesian space, perhaps the location where the interview took place or which the interview discusses. Geo-coding is a term used to indicate the process that assigns coordinates to postal addresses, which enables point locations to be added to maps.

Having compiled a GIS with layers containing relevant information, the researcher is in a position to exploit *geo-visualization*. Geo-visualization has four principal purposes. Visualization may be used to explore unknown data. For instance, a paradox in the fear of crime is that those with the lowest statistical risk—older persons—often have the greatest fear of crime. We might want to explore cartographic data to determine whether this relationship varies according to the kind of housing in which older persons live—it might be lower in a retirement community that is gated and has a full-time caretaker than it is in single tenure households. A second use of visualization is analytical. We might, for example, wish to test the accepted relationship among crime fear, crime risk, and age in a new location. In that sense, visualization can be a form of theory testing. A third application of visualization involves synthesis of the results of the analysis. Superimposing layers from several different cities, each with choropleth maps showing the relationship among age, crime fear, and crime risk, can help us tease out hypotheses about variations or similarities. Or we may draw on several different kinds of data held in the GIS, such as a map of income distribution, an interview about the cost of commuting to work, and a set of photographs of traffic congestion, to pursue an interpretation of physical barriers to gaining employment in a low-income area. The fourth purpose of visualization is the obvious one, which is to present and communicate spatial information.

Despite the considerable affordances of GIS and other forms of information with a spatial dimension, our use of such resources and methods should be discriminating. The seductive appeal of maps and other visualizations can obscure the importance of avoiding the reification of GIS information. The ease with which these kinds of data are obtained and used could lead us to neglect the fact that maps are sometimes based on data that are old, partial or unreliable. One blatant and widespread example is the (in)accuracy of maps that include the locations and type of military installations. Even advanced countries with highly educated populations and highly developed research communities indulge in false information when it is considered that it may be useful to an enemy. It is a good discipline to remember that maps "are as good as the data on which they are based" (Ball & Petsimeris, 2010, p. 40). This is why authors such as S. J. Steinberg and S. L. Steinberg (2006) or Matthews, Detwiler, and Burton (2005) recommend that researchers pursue some means of *ground truthing* to double check the quality of information provided by GIS, which suggests a further benefit of mixing methods.

4 Empirical Demonstration of GIS in MMR

Case Study: GIS in the Analysis of Urban Transformation in Barcelona

Urban planning in Barcelona since the end of the Francoist dictatorship has been internationally recognized for its capacity to reshape the landscape of a city that was, at the end of the 1970s, a mishmash of grey quarters, with a lack of green areas and cut off from the seaside. However, the presumed success of the *Barcelona model* of planning has been criticized for the dominance of private agents over the political agenda and for the use of international macro-events to promote large urban transformations (Charnock, Purcell, & Ribera-Fumaz, 2014), which, in fact, had been a characteristic of the evolution of urban planning in Barcelona since the Universal Exhibition of 1888 (Delgado, 2005, 2007). Other authors highlight the flexible and pragmatist approach of urban planning in the city, being the result of an interaction "between the institutional wills, the political or economic opportunities that appear, the legal and financial constraints, and the demands or reactions of different social actors" (translated from Borja, 2010, p. 175). This style of governance seems to be the badge of urban planning in Barcelona, flexibility first and foremost, for good or for bad.

The following sections will explain the role played by GIS in a mixed methods research project (Porcel, 2010; Verd & Porcel, 2012) conducted by researchers interested in the process of agreeing and re-setting the urban planning of the Parc dels Tres Turons—literally, in the Catalan language, Three Hills Park—in Barcelona. The history of the urban planning of the Parc dels Tres Turons area since its re-launch in 2000 is an example of the aforementioned pragmatism and flexibility of urban regeneration in Barcelona. However, unlike other large urban transformation operations that took place during the 1980s and 1990s, the planning of the Parc dels Tres Turons project entirely followed a public management model. Therefore, the actors who participated in the process of urban reorganization in this area were, on the one hand, the different instances of the City Council of Barcelona competent in the matter and, on the other hand, the list of many neighborhood entities that had different views on how the park should be redesigned. The focus of the study was the construction and transformation of urban space, understood as a dialectical and conflictual process resulting from the struggle among designers, planners, traders, policymakers, and users (Lefebvre, 1991). This implied, at a methodological level, collecting information on the opinions, proposals, and counter-proposals of the different actors involved and, at the same time, considering the spatial and geographical characteristics of the area. These latter characteristics are important not only in terms of its centrality (or not) in the city of Barcelona, which would have its effects not only on the interest of private capital for investing in the area, but also in terms of the features of the terrain and buildings in the area, which determine their market value and the potential loss for owners in the event of expropriation.

Context

The Tres Turons area in Barcelona has been subject to controversy for years. In the planning approved in 1907, it was considered a rural area. Notwithstanding, until 1953, constructions were allowed in the area provided that they met the criteria established by the Barcelona Urbanization Plan of 1917 (Bou & Gimeno, 2007). In 1953, the area was first zoned as an urban park, considering its hilly characteristics, thereby placing many privately owned houses and plots under the threat of expropriation. From then on, the area required a specific project for its transformation into a park. In 1967, a partial development plan, the "Plan Parcial de Ordenación de los Cerros de la Montaña del Carmelo, Turó de Rubira y Montaña Pelada y sus zonas adyacentes," was approved, but it was never implemented, mainly because of the large number of properties that would be expropriated. In the 1960s, a period of explosive growth and housing deficit in Barcelona, thousands of immigrants from other parts of Spain started to build huts in Tres Turons (Bou & Gimeno, 2007). Over the years, self-built houses came to share the space with the earlier summer residences of bourgeois origin, and some parts of the area were rezoned to allow the construction of apartment blocks (Fabre & Huertas Clavería, 1976). This mixture of urban processes resulted in a highly heterogeneous urban setting and made intervention in the area increasingly complex.

In 1976, at the end of the dictatorship, a general metropolitan plan that is still in force today, confirmed the classification of Tres Turons as a green area but left it once more pending a plan for conversion into a park. All dwellings that had been built up to that time were threatened with expropriation. This situation lasted for decades, until in 2000, the City Council launched the definitive plan to convert Tres Turons into a green lung for the city. However, the Pla del Parc dels Tres Turons was opposed right from the start by a large proportion of the affected residents. Initially, this plan involved the expropriation and demolition of more than 800 houses that had been inhabited for decades. The neighborhood organizations rejected this proposal and called for a mixed park that conserved the existing homes. After nearly 10 years of unsuccessful negotiations, in 2009, the Council achieved the initial approval of an amendment to the 1976 General Development Plan for Tres Turons. The new development proposal introduced a dual zoning, with a core of green park and a perimeter defined as a transition zone where homes were authorized. This significant change to the existing development plan was aimed at removing the obstacles that had long hindered the project. The new proposal reduced the number of homes expropriated to less than one half of the existing number and satisfied many of the organizations of residents affected by the plan. This final period of discussions and proposals that led to the ultimate reconfiguration of the urban development of Tres Turons was the one considered in the research. The steps followed in the research are described next.

Step 1 Collecting and Preparing the Appropriate Data

In this research, no initial hypotheses to be tested were developed. Rather, it was decided to adopt an open approach to data collection in order to obtain a broader view of the process leading to the planning outcome that was finally agreed. Nevertheless, because the focus of the research question was on the conflictual construction of urban space, it was clear that three kinds of information had to be obtained: (a) data on the spatial characteristics of the area, including the different kinds of buildings distributed within the theoretical boundaries of the projected park; (b) data on the views and strategies of the actors involved in the process of negotiation; and (c) data on the evolution of conflict, the subjects at stake, and the successive proposals up to the final one approved in 2009.

To obtain all the aforementioned data, a combination of ethnographic and documentary research was carried out. Many visits to the area were made, in which photographs and field notes were obtained, including informal conversations with neighbors. In addition, both official documents and press releases were searched as a strategy to identify the evolution of conflict and negotiations. Finally, representatives of all the neighborhood entities and relevant Barcelona City Council decision-making areas were interviewed. As a result of this combination of research strategies, the analytical corpus of the study was made up of the following data types:

- Field notes from observation
- Photographs
- In-depth interviews with key actors
- Press releases
- Urban documents and plans
- Documents of formal communications among the actors

Regarding the preparation and handling of the data, ArcGIS 9 was initially used to map the location and boundaries of the Parc dels Tres Turons in the city of Barcelona (see Figure 21.1). GIS software proved to be a valuable tool because of the predominantly geographical nature of much of the information analyzed and the fact that the object of study was urban space. However, the main program used was not ArcGIS, but Google Earth as a plug-in of ATLAS.ti version 6. In version 6, Google Earth was embedded as an external application and remained operative throughout the analysis. Because most of the data considered relevant for the research was qualitative, as a qualitative software program, ATLAS.ti version 6 had the advantage of allowing users to store all the data in a single file while also letting users directly access Google Earth.[1]

Step 2 Data Handling and Analysis

The type of analysis conducted in any study must be a direct consequence not only of the research question, but also of the type of data that have been collected. It has already been mentioned that in this study, ATLAS.ti was the software around

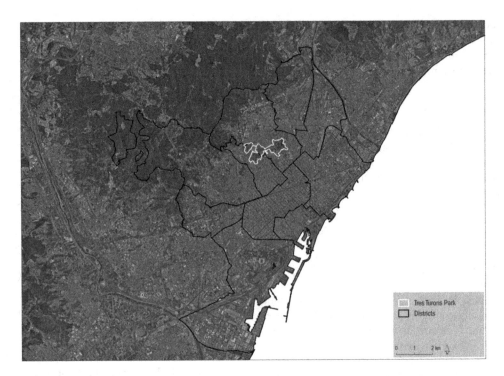

FIGURE 21.1 Location and boundaries of the Parc dels Tres Turons in relation to the city districts of Barcelona.

Source: Verd and Porcel (2012): Figure 1. Map elaborated using ArcGIS 9 on the basis of the ortophoto image of Catalonia 1:5.000 from the Cartographic Institute of Catalonia.

which the data were brought together, but, in other circumstances, using several different programs might be preferable—GIS software for socio-spatial data, statistical software for the analysis of numerical data, and CAQDAS software for qualitative data.

In this case, the data to be handled were related primarily to two types of information: urban planning documents and photographs taken in the locale. Because of the highly technical tone of urban planning documents, textual analysis was not very productive. Therefore, only the information most relevant to the research objectives was selected and Google Earth was used from within ATLAS.ti to anchor it to the part of the territory to which it applied. This way, the spatial information related to urban planning was connected to the morphology of the urban space. This procedure can be described as geo-referencing in the terms mentioned in Sections I and III. A similar process was used for the photographs, although their function was analytically different. Google Earth was used to embed them directly in the territory in the places where they were taken. This procedure enriched the analysis by relating the information contained in photographs with information from their geographical context. The use of ATLAS.ti also allowed the researchers to enter comments on the photographs, which was very useful for adding ethnographic memos. Once the information had been geo-referenced, it was integrated into Google Earth in layers that could be enabled or disabled by the researcher.

In later stages of the analysis, the press releases and the transcriptions of the interviews were integrated as primary documents in ATLAS.ti. The contents of these documents referring to specific locations were also geo-referenced. The integration of Google Earth within ATLAS.ti also enabled the codes generated with ATLAS.ti to be associated to specific points of the territory defined as *territorial quotations*. Technically, this was achieved by considering the aerial maps offered by Google Earth—actually, the screenshots of the maps—as documents to be analyzed and coded. As discussed in Sections I and III, this procedure is referred to as geo-coding. Indeed, the coding function in ATLAS.ti was used to mutually connect all types of data.

Finally, when it was considered necessary to further develop the analytical and explanatory power of the graphic presentations of the area, the KMZ file generated by Google Earth with all the elements worked on in ATLAS.ti was exported to ArcGIS. This possibility was used to make maps such as the one presented in Figure 21.2, where the changes in the boundaries of the park and the residents' demands for exemption from expropriation that were met in the final planning are represented.

Step 3 Obtaining and Interpreting Results

The combination of GIS and CAQDAS software made it possible to manage all the different types of data within a single file and to apply the same code or notation to various types of information. This served also to strengthen the analytical process and the integration of the different elements of the corpus analyzed. At a methodological level, this facilitation of integration resulted in a perfect blend of the ethnographic work—whose most palpable results were the field notes and photographs—with the work based on the collection and

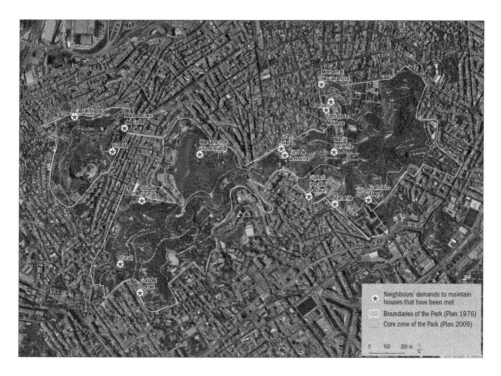

FIGURE 21.2 Amendments to the boundaries of the park and the expropriation of houses met in 2009 with regard to the General Metropolitan Plan of 1976.

Source: Verd and Porcel, 2012: Figure 9. Map elaborated using ATLAS.ti 6.0 and ArcGIS 9 on the basis of the ortophoto image of Catalonia 1:5.000 from the Cartographic Institute of Catalonia.

analysis of the planning documents and the textual analysis of interviews and media news.

This mixed approach to the data analysis also allowed a contextualized and multidimensional reading of the results, providing analytical density (Fielding, 2008) to the categories that were appearing through the interpretation process. As can be seen from the following list, most of the categories that emerged had a multifaceted nature (linking actors, space, and time):

negotiating history, park model, park's core, transition zone, urban consolidation, expropriation management, legality of houses ...

The final picture of the process of negotiation and construction of urban space obtained in the study reflects the dialectical and conflictual nature of the urban planning. In Figure 21.3, dotted lines indicate the compromise finally achieved among actors

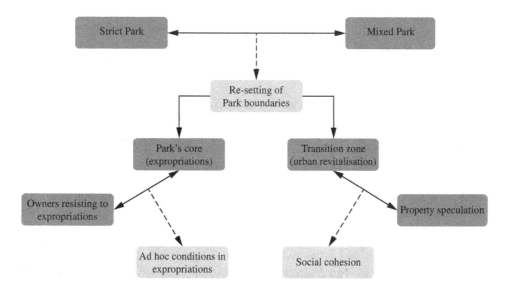

FIGURE 21.3 Adjustment sequence between different options in the urban reordering of the Parc dels Tres Turons.

Source: Own elaboration, adapted from Porcel 2010: Figure 5.1.

regarding conflictual issues. The compromise between the aim of the City Council of demolishing all the houses within the limits of the park and the neighbours' proposal that they be allowed to stay in their houses (therefore re-setting a mixed park) was to modify the boundaries of the park, thereby saving many houses in the new transition zone from expropriation. The way to overcome the resistance shown by the vast majority of residents in the new *core zone* of the park to being expropriated and rehoused was by proposing three different types of procedures to manage the expropriations of the houses, and even leaving some houses inside the park's core. The way to address the new status of the houses in the transition zone, and especially the expectations of monetary gains among the owners of the houses no longer subject to the risk of expropriation, was by ensuring that the disaffection did not result in the regularization of substandard or low-quality housing and the owners could not speculate with their newly unaffected properties. All these outcomes allow us to see that the production of urban space involves a complex social process, where the structural elements, as well as the interactions among the actors involved in the process, are decisive.

5 Some Suggested Applications of GIS in MMR

The use of GIS in MMR is not without context. Mainstream GIS is a multi-billion-dollar-a-year industry important to for-profit corporate interests and for-control State interests. Critical GIS scholars seek to widen the interests served, and their agenda has included a methodological eclecticism that they see as a counter to the domination of GIS by quantitative methods and a means of modernizing the pragmatist paradigm that accompanied early mixed methods. *Public Participation GIS* seeks to support grassroots movements and neighborhood struggles, *counter mapping* has become a strategy of resistance, and post-structuralist research has highlighted how mainstream GIS discourse shapes our worlds by selective representation (Pavlovskaya, 2006). These themes are illustrated in the following brief exemplars.

Citizen Research in Urban Community-Building: Community Gardens

Much GIS work, and social geography more generally, is orientated to urban planning and struggles over contested space. An example of such work involving GIS is Knigge and Cope's (2006) work on community gardens in Buffalo, New York. These researchers created a web-based multimedia environment with a map of community resources at its center, surrounded by boxes showing relevant quantitative, qualitative, and spatial data, such as neighborhood ethnic composition, attributes of land parcels, photographs of neighborhoods, field-note descriptions of local features, and audio files of interviews with residents. This resource proved important when planners held community meetings about redeveloping the area of Buffalo where Knigge and Cope's study was based. Residents who identified with the area but whose properties were not on the planners' maps used the resource to get the planners' maps re-drawn. By bicycling around the area, the researchers built up a sense of how the built environment related to the associations that local people felt with the locale. Knigge's ride took her past spaces that clearly featured productive vegetable and fruit cultivation but were shown on the planning maps as wasteland. Far from derelict, these areas had communal BBQ pits, resident-built benches, and other features indicating their use as an informal social space. The discovery led the researchers to pursue questions about the area's informal economy using quantified information like labor market statistics. This was added to the multimedia map resource. GIS was used to visualize land use, count vacant land parcels, and relate this information to house values. Here, mixing methods including GIS added analytical power. Without the bicycle ride fieldwork, the researchers would have been reliant on the published statistical data about land use, whereas the impact of the community gardens on house values would not have been discoverable purely by fieldwork. Alerting planners to the community gardens gave residents more sway over redevelopment decisions.

Town Planning and Public Health: Sexual Health in Latin America

The value of GIS for discovery in a mixed methods project is also illustrated by work on sexual health in Latin America (Fielding & Cisneros-Puebla, 2009). Like planning, the field of health has long made use of spatial techniques. Nongovernmental organizations (NGOs) with an interest in preventing unplanned pregnancies and sexually transmitted infections in Paraguay needed to answer questions like "Why aren't adolescents seeking clinical services?" and "How do we reach out to them?" More formally, they wanted to (a) build an understanding of factors influencing use or non-use of condoms, contraceptives, and clinical services; (b) identify places in the community where youths spend time and understand how those places were associated with high-risk behaviors and/or protective activities; and (c) develop an understanding of adolescent relationships and how they relate to sexual activity/abstinence. HIV/Aids researchers use a rapid assessment technique to identify high-risk venues for HIV transmission so as to target interventions. It involves asking informants to name places where people go to meet new sexual partners, and locations where condoms are available. These are then visited and characterized, and individuals frequenting the sites are interviewed about their sexual risk behaviors. Here, a preliminary mapping was prepared before contacting informants and mapping sites mentioned by them. The preliminary mapping included GPS points for churches, schools, neighborhood associations, social service organizations, cooperatives, sports clubs, restaurants, malls, bars, discos, plazas, clinics, general practitioner surgeries, pharmacies, and shops where contraceptives/condoms could be purchased. Some 500 non-residential sites were identified and mapped using ArcView software. The resulting digital maps of each neighborhood were used as visual aids in small group discussions. Group discussion participants were asked about places that youths frequented or avoided, who they typically saw in various locations, and the activities conducted when they were there. Directing participants' attention to the maps elicited explanations of why some (indeed, most) sources of contraceptives/condoms were avoided.

6 Strengths and Limitations of GIS in Mixed Methods Research

Where the issue of concern to the researcher has a geo-spatial dimension, then GIS is squarely in frame. This does not mean that every geo-spatial question that researchers might want to answer can be answered via GIS. For example, the online world has opened up a wide range of new topics for investigation, with social media, in particular, offering new resources for researchers who want to understand communication flows, social influence, the functioning of social networks, the effects of expressed opinion on the attitudes of others, the patterns of behavior and mood as they vary through the 24-hour cycle, and so on. Yet, we recognize some fundamental limits that represent the flip side of the affordances of online artefacts, such as the fact that unless we are co-present (either literally or via a surveillance technology) we can never be certain of the identity of the sender or other participant in an online interaction. Similarly, many of the things we most want to know are partially present but remain tantalizingly hidden in the online world. For instance, the DOLLY archive of geo-located tweets is a considerable resource (see Resources section below), but it comprises only those tweets from devices whose owners have enabled geo-tagging. It is known that there are substantial demographic differences between those who opt in to geo-services and who geo-tag their tweets and those who do not (Sloan & Morgan, 2015).

The issues posed by commensurability of research design, method, and approach to data analysis that continue to make mixed methods a controversial practice for some (Fielding, 2009) remain present when incorporating GIS in a mixed method research design. The *pedigree* of the GIS is very much one that originated with a strong affinity for quantitative information. It took a number of years, and the emergence of a Qualitative Geography *movement*, to see GIS researchers begin to orientate to the inclusion of qualitative information alongside quantitative information and geo-spatial information. It is interesting that, despite the mainstream emphasis on quantification, most GIS software has only basic quantitative tools and the statistical techniques do not involve advanced mathematics (Pavlovskaya, 2006), but the GIS community is still dominated by quantitative work and poses questions and research agendas that are best prosecuted using quantitative techniques. However, the projects mentioned in Sections IV and V give some idea of what has been achieved by those who have adopted a fully mixed methods approach, wherein the techniques used are driven by the multiple dimensions of the research question rather than those that are most readily supported technically or for which social geographers are most often trained. Like any other methodological combination, it is critical that we mix methods because it increases their explanatory power rather than simply because there is a vogue for mixing or the researcher has such skills.

Those who do include geo-referenced techniques within a mixed methods research design find that the key issue is one of data integration (Bazeley, 2017). To date, this issue has been most hotly debated in respect of the conversion of qualitative data into quantitative data—a technique referred to as *quantitizing* (Tashakkori & Teddlie, 1998)—in order to enable a synthesizing analysis employing statistical techniques. Many are uncomfortable with the conversion of data from one form to another in such a fundamental way. The care and wide range of considerations that Bazeley (2017) explains as being necessary to safely perform the fullest forms of data integration demonstrate the numerous dimensions the researcher must consider in assessing the exact alignment of data whose elicitation involves substantially dissimilar processes. However, bringing geo-data into encounter with, for example, extracts from a non-standardized interview, does not generally pose that degree of challenge, assuming the geo-spatial location information is clear and can be assigned with reasonable precision to a map, and there is some indication in the interview data that the participant is talking about that location or that kind of location. Moreover, a measure of verification or validity checking is often enabled by such mixing. A participant's claim to have been able to see a particular locational feature can be assessed by inspecting the map. Indeed, there are cases where analytical puzzles have been solved by such procedures, as where a doubtful classification of the socio-economic status of residents of a particular neighborhood was found to be the result of the fieldworker having taken an incorrect turn and strayed out of the study area. Information in the fieldnotes was compared to physical features apparent on the map of the study area and the troublesome classification was identified as a sampling error.

Such cases reinforce the message that robust mixed methods work requires measurement precision, an understanding of the weaknesses as well as the strengths of the methods being combined, and an appreciation of how a facile multiple methods analysis can multiply error. Although these are classic considerations in the delivery of good research whatever the method, it is the case that GIS brings to the party an openness to scrutiny that is often lacking in social research. That is, the physical features represented by mapped space—the built environment as well as land contours—are more readily inspected for validity than are, say, an individual's inner beliefs. No human representation is unimpeachable—even the *picture* that says more than a thousand words might have been photo-shopped—but some representations are more susceptible to evaluation than are others.

7 Resources to Learn More about GIS

Online Resources

1. ArcGIS (www.arcgis.com): An industry standard Geographic Information System that supports creating maps and analyzing mapped information.
2. QGIS (www.qgis.org): A free, Open Source cross-platform desktop GIS application supporting viewing, editing, and analysis of geospatial data.
3. Mapshaper (www.mapshaper.org): Application that supports map-making tasks like simplifying shapes, editing attribute data, clipping, erasing, and more.
4. ColorBrewer (colorbrewer2.org/): Application supporting choosing effective color schemes for thematic maps (choropleths).

5. American Factfinder (https://data.census.gov/cedsci/): A data retrieval product by the U.S. Census Bureau; in addition to the U.S. Census, it draws information from several recurrent surveys focused on the USA.
6. Carto (formerly CartoDB; https://data.census.gov/cedsci/ Provides GIS and web mapping tools for display in a web browser, enabling data analysis and visualization by those without previous GIS experience.
7. Mapbox (www.mapbox.com): An Open Source mapping platform for custom designed maps.
8. DOLLY (Digital Online Life and You; www.floatingsheep.org): An archive at the University of Kentucky providing a repository of billions of geolocated tweets (updated daily), enabling real-time analysis, indexing, and coding.
9. OpenStreetMap (www.openstreetmap.org): A free wiki map of the world.

Reading Resources

1. Zook, Poorthuis, and Donohue (2017) provides an overview of the principles of cartographic design for social research and outlines stages and techniques for mapping online data that contains geographic coordinates.
2. Abernathy (2016) has a strong focus on 'Big Geodata' and quantitative approaches to work with geographical data but also covers CLAVIN, a 'geoparser' program that extracts geographical information from qualitative data.
3. S. J. Steinberg and S. L. Steinberg (2006) explains in a clear way the steps to be followed when using quantitative and qualitative GIS in social research. Although the authors do not specify the research process to be followed in a mixed methods GIS project, they provide strong arguments for mixing quantitative and qualitative data.
4. Cope and Elwood (2009) is an edited volume with chapters featuring Critical Geography projects. Some are purely qualitative, but most combine quantitative and qualitative GIS data. It provides a good idea of the many different applications of GIS to social science research.

NOTE

1. In ATLAS.ti 9, the present version of the program, geospatial information is handled by opening the maps produced by OpenStreetMap (OSM), a collaborative project to create a free editable map of the world. Among other possibilities, this map allows selecting a region as a quotation which can be opened with the Google Maps browser outside of ATLAS.ti.

REFERENCES

Abernathy, D. (2016). *Using geodata and geolocation in the social sciences*. Thousand Oaks, CA: Sage.

Adam, B. (1994). *Time and social theory*. Cambridge, England: Polity.

Ball, S., & Petsimeris, P. (2010). Mapping urban social divisions. *Forum Qualitative Sozialforschung/Forum: Qualitative Social Research*, *11*(2), Art. 37. Retrieved from www.qualitative-research.net/index.php/fqs/article/view/1480/2991

Bazeley, P. (2017). *Integrating analyses in mixed methods research*. London, England: Sage.

Borja, J. (2010). *Llums i ombres de l'urbanisme de Barcelona*. Barcelona, Spain: Editorial Empuries.

Bou, L., & Gimeno, E. (2007). *El Carmel ignorat: Historia d'un barri impossible*. Barcelona, Spain: Ajuntament de Barcelona and Agencia de Promocio del Carmel i Entorns

Charnock, G., Purcell, T. F., & Ribera-Fumaz, R. (2014). City of rents: The limits to the Barcelona model of urban competitiveness. *International Journal of Urban and Regional Research*, *38*, 198–217. doi:10.1111/1468-2427.12103

Cope, N., & Elwood, S. (Eds.). (2009). *Qualitative GIS: A mixed methods approach*. London, England: Sage.

Delgado, M. (2005). *Elogi del vianant: Del "model Barcelona" a la Barcelona real*, Barcelona, Spain: Edicions de 1984

Delgado, M. (2007). *La ciudad mentirosa: Fraude y miseria del "modelo Barcelona"*, Barcelona, Spain: Catarata.

Fabre, J., & Claveria, J. H. (1976). *Tots els barris de Barcelona Vol. IV: Els Tres Turons i els barris de Montjuic*. Barcelona, Spain: Edicions 62.

Fielding, J., & Fielding, N. (2015). Emergent technologies in mixed and multimethod research. In S. Hesse-Biber & B. Johnson (Eds.), *Oxford handbook of multimethod and mixed methods research inquiry* (pp. 561–584). Oxford, England: Oxford University Press.

Fielding, N. (2008). Analytic density, postmodernism, and applied multiple method research. In M. Bergman (Ed.), *Advances in mixed method research: Theories and applications* (pp. 37–52). London, England: Sage.

Fielding, N. (2009). Going out on a limb: Postmodernism and multiple method research. *Current Sociology*, *57*, 427–447. doi:10.1177/0011392108101591

Fielding, N., & Cisneros-Puebla, C. (2009). CAQDAS-GIS convergence: Towards a new integrated mixed method research practice? *Journal of Mixed Methods Research*, *3*, 349–370. doi:10.1177/1558689809344973

Girardin, F. (2009). *Aspects of implicit and explicit human interactions with ubiquitous geographic information*. Unpublished doctoral Thesis. Department of Technology. Barcelona, Spain: Universitat Pompeu Fabra.

Holdenab, R. J., Eriksson, A., Andreasson, J., Williamsson, A., & Dellvecd, L. (2015). Healthcare workers' perceptions of lean: A context-sensitive, mixed methods study in three Swedish hospitals. *Applied Ergonomics*, *47*, 181–192. doi:10.1016/j.apergo.2014.09.008

Jung, J-K. (2014). Code clouds: Qualitative geovisualization of geotweets. *The Canadian Geographer*, *20*, 1–17. doi:10.1111/cag.12133

Knigge, L., & Cope, M. (2006). Grounded visualization: Integrating the analysis of qualitative and quantitative data through grounded theory and visualization. *Environment and Planning A*, *38*, 2021–2037. doi:10.1068/a37327

Kwan, M.-P., & Ding, G. (2008). Geo-narrative: Extending geographic information systems for narrative analysis in qualitative and mixed method research. *The Professional Geographer*, *60*, 443–465. doi:10.1080/00330120802211752

Lefebvre, H. (1991). *The production of space*, Oxford, England: Blackwell Publishers.

Longley, P., Goodchild, M., Maguire, D., & Rhind, D. (2005). *Geographic information systems and science*, Chichester, England: Wiley.

Matthews, S., Detwiler, J., & Burton, L. (2005). Geo-ethnography: Coupling geographic information analysis techniques with ethnographic methods in urban research. *Cartographica, 40*(4), 75–90. doi:10.3138/2288-1450-W061-R664

Onwuegbuzie, A. J., Leech, N. L., & Collins, K. M. T. (2010). Innovative data collection strategies in qualitative research. *The Qualitative Report, 15*, 696–672. Retrieved from https://nsuworks.nova.edu/cgi/viewcontent.cgi?article=1171&context=tqr

Pavlovskaya, M. (2006). Theorizing with GIS: A tool for critical geographies? *Environment and Planning A, 38*, 2003–2020. doi:10.1068/a37326

Porcel, S. (2010). *La producción social del espacio urbano. Tensiones y ajustes en la (re)ordenación urbana de los Tres Turons de Barcelona*. Research Dissertation for the Diploma of Advanced Studies (Doctoral Studies). Department of Sociology. Barcelona, Spain: Universitat Autònoma of Barcelona.

Sloan, L., & Morgan, J. (2015). Who tweets with their location? Understanding the relationship between demographic characteristics and the use of geoservices and geotagging on twitter. *PLOS One, 10*(11). e0142209. doi:10.1371/journal.pone.0142209. Retrieved from https://journals.plos.org/plosone/article?id=10.1371/journal.pone.0142209

Steinberg, S. J., & Steinberg, S. L. (2006) *Geographic information systems for the social sciences*. London, England: Sage.

Tashakkori, A., & Teddlie, C. (1998). *Mixed methodology: Combining qualitative and quantitative approaches*. Applied Social Research Methods Series (Vol. 46). Thousand Oaks, CA: Sage.

Verd, J.-M., & Porcel, S. (2012). An application of qualitative geographic information systems (GIS) in the field of urban sociology using ATLAS.ti: Uses and reflections. *Forum Qualitative Sozialforschung/Forum: Qualitative Social Research, 13* (2), Art. 14. doi:10.17169/fqs-13.2.1847. Retrieved from http://nbn-resolving.de/urn:nbn:de:0114-fqs1202144

White, M., Judd, M., & Poliandri, S. (2012). Illumination with a dim bulb? What do social scientists learn by employing qualitative data analysis software in the service of multi-method designs. *Sociological Methodology, 42*, 43–76. doi:10.1177/0081175012461233

Zook, M., Poorthuis, A., & Donohue, R. (2017). Mapping spaces: Cartographic representations of online data. In N. Fielding, G. Blank, & R. M. Lee (Eds.), *The Sage handbook of online research methods* (2nd ed.) (pp. 542–560). London, England: Sage.

22

Nonverbal Communication Analysis as Mixed Analysis

Anthony J. Onwuegbuzie and Sandra Schamroth Abrams

Despite its utility, the analysis of nonverbal communication (NVC)—in both offline and online spaces—is underutilized by many, if not most, researchers representing the social, behavioral, and health science fields. As evidence for this claim, with respect to qualitative research articles, Denham and Onwuegbuzie (2013), who examined the use of NVC data in *The Qualitative Report* journal over a 22-year period, documented that only 24% of articles mentioned NVC and, in most cases, this mention took place in only one or two sentences. Moreover, some of these authors merely discussed the collection of NVC in general terms, such as stating that "The researcher did make notes of nonverbal communication where necessary during the interviews" (Denham & Onwuegbuzie, 2013, p. 12), but did not provide or specify: (a) the *type(s)* of NVC data that were collected or how or when they were collected; (b) any *evidence* that NVC analysis took place; or (c) any *findings* related to NVC. With regard to quantitative research, as an example, an examination of the *Journal of Educational and Psychological Measurement*—an exclusively quantitative-based journal with a focus on the study of measurement theory, problems, and issues—reveals that, in among the more than 1,000 articles published over its 79-year history, only 117 articles (less than 10%) include any discussion of NVC. In terms of the mixed methods research field, of the 273 articles (excluding editorial and media review) articles published in the *Journal of Mixed Methods Research*, from its inception through the third issue of 2020—the latest issue at the time of writing—only 21 works (7.69%) discuss NVC to any degree.

Perhaps this lack of NVC analysis should not be surprising, bearing in mind that there is limited or no discussion on NVC in research methodology textbooks. Therefore, with a few exceptions (e.g., Onwuegbuzie & Byers, 2014), there is scant methodological guidance in the extant literature on this topic. To this end, in this chapter, we begin formally the conversation on NVC analysis by providing a methodological discussion of this concept.

1 Definition of Nonverbal Communication Analysis

According to Merriam-Webster (2020) dictionary, "verbal" means "of, or relating to, or consisting of words; consisting of or using words only and not involving action" (¶1, 3). It stands to reason, therefore, that *nonverbal* would signify anything that involves action, including, but not limited to, gesture, gaze, facial expressions, movement, stance, and body position. Only the spoken word is included as verbal communication because there is an ongoing stream-of-consciousness that accompanies informal (i.e., non-rehearsed) speech; spoken language that, once voiced, cannot be unvoiced (Cope & Kalantzis, 2020). However, when written words are read aloud, that communication would be classified as nonverbal because these written words, which are the basis of the speech, stem from an active process of constructing and reconstructing communication. Writing—be it alphanumeric text or images—can be erased, edited, clarified, and, thus, filtered. *It is the action of such filtering that makes written communication nonverbal.*

The concept of multimodalities—or making and conveying meaning through more than one mode (e.g., image, sound, gesture)—also helps to clarify forms of nonverbal entities, especially because the literacies field has recognized and honored the presence and importance of linguistic, visual, aural, gestural, textural, and spatial modes (Jewitt, 2013; Kress, 2010, Rowsell, 2013). Multimodal meaning making—the act of making sense of the world—involves communication through multiple modes, as well as sensory-based experiences of the sender and receiver or communication target: (a) tones and vibrations; (b) lighting, color, and shading (this also extends to line curvature, thickness, and font selection); (c) temperature or weather and bodily and perceptive responses (e.g., sluggish movements and oppressive heat); (d) scents and odors; (e) flavors and textures; (f) material textures; and (g) one's physical position in an environment. Multimodal meaning making for the sender and receiver is complicated and it is layered (Abrams, 2015); it involves various perspectives (e.g., objective, subjective, intersubjective) and digital and nondigital tools and technologies (e.g., pen, paper, computer, phone). Embracing an expansive definition of texts to include any mode—a definition we adopt in this chapter—Kress (2010) contended that "texts are always multimodal" (p. 157), thereby suggesting that the tangible—writing or image—and the intangible—sensory-based experiences—are interconnected and meaning making cannot be divorced from nonverbal elements.

Kress's understanding also builds on an expansive definition of *text* initially set forth by qualitative researchers in the late 20th century (cf. Heath, 1983; New London Group, 1996; Street, 1984, 1995). Literacy was no longer understood as a siloed event—a child reading a book, for instance—but, instead, became envisioned as *literacies*, a concept that accounted for experiences, values, and contexts that shape meaning making. It stands to reason, then, that the theoretical underpinnings of multimodal data analysis—the examination of all modes, in addition to speech—underscore the inherent marriage of perception and embodiment (Norris, 2019). Norris (2019) explained that there is a responsibility to account for communication that occurs in the mind, through the body, and within a particular context:

> it is impossible to investigate people as they act or interact through language and/or non-verbal modes alone. The reason for this is that people do not communicate with each other by acting and interacting only verbally, but act and interact with each other with and through their entire bodies *and* the environment they inhabit. (p. 31)

To illustrate her point, Norris used the example of someone sitting in a cafe, drinking coffee, and texting a friend, folding in assumptions others might have: the person is part of a larger socially accepted practice; the person is waiting for someone to join; the half-finished cup of coffee can signify the passage of time, and so on. What is clear is that communication that is nonverbal cannot be severed from environmental and contextual factors—half empty cups of coffee, noisy cafes, embodied and perceived meaning.

As much as multimodality (i.e., multiple modes) helps to support expansive understandings of text and meaning making, it also complicates analyses of communication. If the premise is that *everything*—verbal and nonverbal—is a part of a whole, then how and why should parsing them and studying them individually be of merit? Such parsing does not undermine the value of the whole or privilege one form of communication over another. Rather, parsing verbal and nonverbal, and, respectively, texts (i.e., what is written vs. what is not) supports nuanced discussions and analyses of NVC. In what follows is an expansive definition of NVC and a conceptual framework to support analyses.

Nonverbal Communication

In the context of offline spaces, Onwuegbuzie and Abrams (in press) define NVC as the nonvocal and multimodal expression of information that emanates cognitively, affectively, physically, metaphysically, and/or spiritually, which is internal or external to the sender; NVC can be observed by the sender and receiver objectively, subjectively, and/or intersubjectively by oneself or one or more persons and/or animals, via messages, gestures, and/or signals that occur through environmental, dispositional, and/or situational cues, such as the following:

- distance (i.e., proxemics),
- use of time (i.e., chronemics),
- body language/movements (i.e., kinesics),
- touch (i.e., haptics),
- appearance of voice (i.e., paralanguage),
- eye contact (i.e., oculesics),
- smell (i.e., olfaction),
- taste (i.e., gustation),
- literary communication (i.e., linguistics), and/or
- appearance (i.e., phenotypic traits).

These cues serve as points for NVC analysis. NVC yields qualitative data, quantitative data, and multidata (e.g., data that are neither exclusively qualitative nor quantitative; Onwuegbuzie, Gerber, & Abrams, 2017) that are generated consciously, subconsciously, or unconsciously; deliberately or accidentally; once or multiple times, representing some level of continuity or discontinuity; representing some level of learned or innate behavior; that lies somewhere on the structured-unstructured continuum; that are audible or inaudible, visual or non-visual. Built on Greene, Caracelli, and Graham's (1989) five purposes for combining qualitative and quantitative data, the final communicative product either can stand alone or can be combined or integrated with verbal information/data to (a) *repeat* the message (i.e., repetition), (b) *corroborate* speech narrative (i.e., "triangulation"; Greene et al., 1989, p. 258); (c) *capture* underlying messages (i.e., "complementarity"; Greene et al., 1989, p. 258); (d) *accentuate* the underlying message (i.e., accentuation); (e) *substitute* the underlying message (i.e., substitution); (f) *expose* nonverbal behaviors that contradict the verbal communication (i.e., "initiation"; Greene et al., 1989, p. 260); (g) *broaden* the scope of the understanding (i.e., "expansion"; Greene et al., 1989, p. 260); (h) *moderate* the underlying message (i.e., *moderation;* e.g., regulation); (i) *mediate* the underlying message (i.e., mediation; e.g., filter); and/or (j) *create new directions* based on additional insights (i.e., "development"; Greene et al., 1989, p. 260). NVC can yield numerous representations that include, but are not limited to, numbers, symbols, codes, categories, sub-themes, themes, figures of speech, meta-themes, and narratives (i.e., prose or poetry).

In online spaces (e.g., any space that is digital and virtual and exists via a wired or wireless connection), NVC operates in a similar fashion, but multimodal interaction (e.g., gesture, performance, embodied movement) is heightened and privileged because the primary method of communication is not verbal. Technological advancements that have improved graphics and supported the layering of alphanumeric text with moving text (e.g., GIFs or movies) and sound, which complicates the meaning-making landscape and, thus, NVC analysis.

Although the concept of "online spaces" can be problematic in light of the blurred boundaries between offline and online meaning making (Burnett & Merchant, 2014), as well as the range of resources that go "online"—from smartphones to global positioning systems (GPS) to videogame consoles to computers—the vastness of what is online warrants a definition that acknowledges the evolving and often nebulous nature of meaning making. Burnett and Merchant (2020), in their discussion of "the ongoing reassembling of the human and more than human" (p. 46), explained how bounding meaning making to a particular time and place (e.g., a literacy event) runs contrary to the fluid nature of emergent meaning: "The act of writing then involves the ongoing realisation of potentialities, many of which may never have been consciously apparent beforehand. And as certain meanings and manifestations are realised, others disperse or are left behind" (p. 51). This concept challenges traditional heuristics and acknowledges the complexity of meaning making that is not tied to a specific context and time. Such expansive thinking supports and complicates the analysis of NVC because it suggests that we might not be able fully to document and to evaluate data that *might* represent "multiple potentialities, including multiple possibilities for what might materialise as well as what does not" (Burnett & Merchant, 2020, p. 49).

In an effort to avoid artificial bifurcations and to address the complex and evolving components of communication, we turn to the image of a three-dimensional cube and embrace the interconnected nature of three continua: (a) context and culture, (b) meaning, and (c) modalities (see Figure 22.1; Onwuegbuzie & Abrams, 2020). Similar to Burnett and Merchant (2020), we recognize that the collective use of images and alphanumeric text can exemplify how the analysis of communication exists within, across, and in between offline and online spaces, and how cultural norms and contextualized practices mediate and situate the meaning making of the sender and receiver and/or the researcher.

Inspired by Onwuegbuzie and Combs's (2010) three-dimensional model for categorizing and organizing orientations for mixed analysis, the nonverbal communication analysis model calls attention to the complexity of meaning making. The first dimension accounts for the nuances of context and culture, which can stimulate harmony or discord, understanding or confusion, and inclusion or exclusion. The emic-etic continuum accounts for gradations of intimate knowledge of context(s) and culture(s). In the middle of this continuum is an emtic (Onwuegbuzie, 2012), or a maximally interactive, perspective. This second dimension addresses intentional and unintentional meaning that is created, perceived, and communicated in accordance with one's degree of knowledge of the context and culture. The third dimension attends to the modalities of communication that exist on a verbal-nonverbal continuum. Although one might communicate solely verbally or nonverbally, in general, communication involves a combination of words and action, and an emic or etic understanding of culture and context can impact the conveyance and perception of intended or unintended meaning.

For example, one with an emic perspective of a specific religious sect might be able to place from where someone lives or originates, what the person's practices entail, and even what the person's level of observance might be; alternatively, one with an etic perspective might be able to recognize that individual as being "religious" but might not be able to discern the nuances of practice and religiosity. Even within cultures, there are nuances of normative practices. For instance, within the Igbo tribe in Nigeria, one is not allowed to pass anything to an elder using one's left hand; anyone without a semblance of this knowledge could risk disrespecting an elder. Likewise, proficiency in one videogame space is not universal, and knowledge of specialist language and practices related to a particular videogame situates a player's degree of participation and belongingness (Abrams & Lammers, 2017).

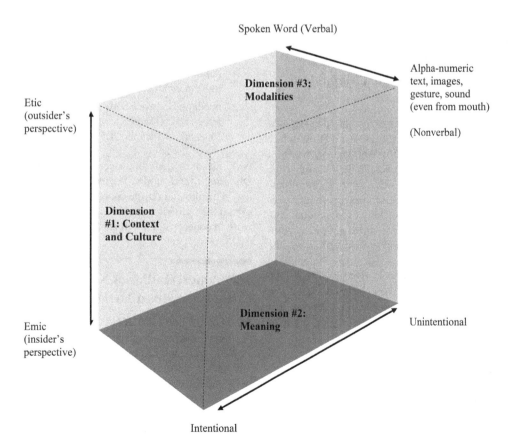

FIGURE 22.1 Dimensions of the Nonverbal Communication Analysis Model.

Adapted from Onwuegbuzie and Abrams, 2020, unpublished manuscript.

Similarly, nonverbal gestures represented by emojis, bitmojis, or any image or symbol, are not universal, suggesting that emojis are not a "global lingua franca" (Rawlings, 2018, ¶3). Emojis have profound variations in meanings across cultures: "the applause emojis are used in the West to show praise or offer congratulations. In China, however, this is a symbol for making love, perhaps due to its resemblance to the sounds 'pah pah pah'" (Rawlings, 2018, ¶11). It is common, however, for disconnects to occur due to the multiplicity of intentional or unintentional meanings that stem from cultural nuances in verbal and nonverbal communication. Even in business, "a relatively harmless Western business practice can become undesirable when implemented in the complex cultural milieu of the Eastern markets" (Kim & Aggarwal, 2016, p. 198). One's emic or etic perspective of contextually and culturally specific meaning—and their (un) intentional actions and speech—can impact the quality and effectiveness in communication. Thus, the emphasis is not on the particular dimension, but on the fact that there are multiple dimensions and subsumed into each dimension is a continuum. Although there are times when communication is primarily verbal or nonverbal, often, facets of both work in concert, and sometimes, there are contradictions between what is expressed verbally and nonverbally. An example of this would be an individual stating everything is "fine" while maintaining a grimace. Such a disconnect, especially when not contextualized, can lead to confusion and miscommunication.

2 When Use of Nonverbal Communication Analysis is Appropriate in Mixed Methods Research

The value of NVC analysis had been a topic of research well before the digital world, as we know it, existed (Bonoma & Felder, 1977; Reusch & Kees, 1956; Watzlawick, Bavelas, & Jackson, 1967), with marketing researchers citing three "value added" components of NVC: (a) the "'amplifier' phenomenon," or the ways NVC reinforces or underscores verbal messaging and meaning; (b) the "'unintentional display' effect," or the nature of NVC that reveals more truthful instantiations of preferences and emotions; and (c) the "'consistency' phenomenon," or the (dis)connection between verbal and nonverbal discourse (Bonoma & Felder, 1977, p. 170). At its core, researchers of NVC have acknowledged the complexity of NVC, and its analysis opens up meaning that otherwise might have been obfuscated by attention solely to verbal means.

In light of the three dimensions of NVC (e.g., context and culture, meaning, and modalities), NVC extends beyond discourse (with a lowercase "d")—which specifically addresses language—to include Gee's concept of Discourses "with a capital 'D'" (Gee, 1989, 1996, 2001), which acknowledges socially situated ways of being-doing-valuing that are enacted through more than language; Discourses include "integrate[d] ways of talking, listening, writing, reading, acting, interacting, believing, valuing, and feeling (and using various objects, symbols, images, tools, and technologies) in the service of enacting meaningful socially situated identities and activities" (Gee, 2001, p. 719). Thus, the concept of Discourses underscores the complexity and multidimensionality of NVC and its analysis.

NVC analysis—which focuses primarily on NVC—is appropriate in both offline and online spaces because NVC is pervasive. In the simple movement of the lips and tongue to speak, the direction of gaze—even possibly averting one's eyes, the raising and lowering of eyebrows, the vocal inflection (or lack thereof), to name a few indicators—NVC is present. In online spaces, NVC appears to be the primary driver of meaning making because *to be* online includes, but is not limited to:

- digital inscription—the combination of alphanumeric and image representations;
- digital recordings—videos of speech and/or movements, environments, contexts;
- digital embodiment—avatars and "skins" become representations of self via online and/or projective identities, wherein the player senses an emotional connection to the avatar (Gee, 2003/2007), as well as nuances of player purpose and avatar connection (McCreery, Krach, Schrader & Boone, 2012);
- digital residues—traces of one's participation online and connection to others (Grimes & Fields, 2012);
- digital, linguistic fingerprints—the use of specific alphanumeric combinations and rhythmic patterns that distinguish particular users (Turner, Abrams, Katic, & Donavan, 2014);
- haptics—nondigital articulation connected to digital movement and touch; and
- nondigital associations—connections between on-screen and off-screen ways of being vis-à-vis associative, I/identities (Abrams, 2011).

NVC analysis, therefore, needs to account for the methods, Discourses, and modalities used in being and communicating in offline and online spaces, with the understanding that, even if the individual practices and modalities are parsed, they work in concert and not in isolation.

3 Technical Outline of Nonverbal Communication Analysis for Mixed Methods Research

Based on the definition of NVC previously noted in this chapter, everything *except* for spoken language could be categorized as NVC and analyzed better to understand meaning making. Although a more comprehensive discussion of how to conduct NVC analysis is developed in other work (Onwuegbuzie & Abrams, in press; Onwuegbuzie & Byers, 2014), as a starting point for discussing NVC analysis, six important questions for information collection and problem solving should be answered—known as the Six Ws or 5W1H—namely, Why?, Who?, Where?, When?, What?, and How? Each of these questions will be answered in the following subsections.

Why Should Researchers Conduct NVC Analysis?

Verbal and nonverbal data contextualize each other and can be analyzed concurrently or sequentially. However, for the purpose of this chapter, the focus on NVC enables us to concentrate on the features of mixed methods analysis, also known as mixed analysis. At its optimum level, NVC analysis entails the analysis of multiple forms of nonverbal behavior data that represent both qualitative data and quantitative data, thereby yielding full[er] methodological integration (for more information, see Onwuegbuzie & Leech, this volume). As asserted by Creamer (2018), in "the highest-caliber mixed methods studies, the qualitative and quantitative strands are often so cleverly and iteratively interwoven that it becomes an exercise in semantics to disentangle the two" (p. 100). Under conditions of full(er) integration, NVC analysis can accomplish the following:

- enrich analysis with descriptive precision (i.e., via qualitative analyses) and numeric precision (i.e., via quantitative analyses);
- add interpretive richness to the verbal data (i.e., thick description; Ryle, 1949), thereby allowing researchers better to understand and to describe the context of the underlying behavior(s), experience(s), or phenomenon (Geertz, 1973; Ryle, 1971);
- facilitate the translation of verbal data into comprehensive form(s);
- enable a trustworthiness check, for example, by comparing the NVC data with verbal data;
- increase the transparency of verbal data; and
- increase the researcher's level of creativity (e.g., via integrating verbal and NVC analyses).

Who Should Conduct NVC Analysis?

At its most flexible level, NVC analysis can be conducted by qualitative researchers, quantitative researchers, and mixed methods researchers. In other words, NVC analysis is compatible with various research philosophies that represent all three traditions of research. Indeed, as demonstrated by Onwuegbuzie, Johnson, and Collins (2009), the ontological, epistemological, and axiological stances underlying many, if not most, researchers' qualitative or quantitative studies do not prevent researchers from using, as appropriate, all forms of analysis approaches. Therefore, importantly, both qualitative researchers and quantitative researchers can conduct NVC analysis without having to reframe their studies as mixed methods research studies (cf. Onwuegbuzie et al., 2009). In particular, qualitative researchers also can use quantitative analysis approaches to analyze NVC, especially those quantitative analysis approaches that involve descriptive analyses (e.g., descriptive statistics that include frequency counts, proportions, means). Conversely, quantitative researchers can use qualitative analysis approaches to analyze NVC, especially those qualitative analysis approaches that generate some form of numbers, including classical content analysis (Berelson, 1952) and qualitative comparative analysis (Ragin, 1987, 1989, 1994, 2008).

Where Should Researchers Conduct NVC Analysis?

NVC analysis can take place on NVC data generated in both offline (e.g., any space inhabited or traversed outside or beyond the screen) and online (e.g., any space inhabited or traversed on the screen via digital methods). Online spaces include situated communication that arise via microblogging or video social networking platforms, such as Twitter, TikTok, or Facebook, and can extend to other collaborative, socially populated spaces, such as wikis and forums (cf. Gerber, Abrams, Curwood, & Magnifico, 2016). And in the age when big data abound (cf. Gerber, Lynch, & Onwuegbuzie, in press), the scope for analyzing NVC is increasing exponentially.

When Should Researchers Conduct NVC Analysis?

Simply put, researchers should collect, analyze, and interpret NVC data whenever possible. In fact, as stated by Onwuegbuzie and Abrams (in press), NVC data lurk in almost every form of data. Consequently, researchers should collect and analyze NVC data whenever possible. For instance, with respect to quantitative research, even a purely quantitative survey can yield NVC data, such as chronemics (e.g., noncompletion of survey items that yields a form of silence) and paralinguistics (e.g., a pattern of responses on a Likert-format scale or rating scale that suggests socially desirable responses). With regard to qualitative research, for example, sometimes more meaning can be extracted from silence than from what a person utters. Interestingly, when Mazzei (2008) examined the nature and intent of, what she labelled as, "racially inhabited silences" (p. 1125) in two teacher education courses that predominantly contained White preservice teachers, she concluded that "In the course of the research these silences were shown to be both purposeful and meaningful in reaffirming the espoused perspective of the participants" (p. 1126). More specifically, as outlined earlier, NVC analysis should be conducted alongside verbal data analysis when the goal of the former is repetition, triangulation, complementarity, accentuation, substitution, initiation, expansion, moderation, mediation, and/or development.

What NVC Data Should Researchers Analyze?

Using the typology of Onwuegbuzie and Abrams (in press), NVC data can be identified using the following nine components:

1. Appearance Cues
2. Contact Cues
3. Movement Cues
4. Chemosensory Cues
5. Psychosomatic Cues
6. Language Cues
7. Temporal-Spatial Cues
8. Positionality Cues
9. Artifact Cues

Appearance cues represent cues that depict an individual's appearance, such as facial features, physique, attire, adornments, and make-up. In online spaces, appearance cues include an image (e.g., avatar, picture, icon) that the user portrays, which can be similar to or different from an offline representation of self. Appearance cues in offline and online space have a sociocultural context (Onwuegbuzie & Abrams, in press).

Contact cues include proxemics (i.e., physical distance between researcher [e.g., interviewer, observer] and participants [e.g., interviewee]) and haptics (i.e., use of touch). Fontana and Frey (2005) address proxemics alongside other nonverbal cues.

Movement cues include kinesics (i.e., body movements or postures) and optics (i.e., also known as oculesics; use of eyes by the participant). A useful framework that characterizes movement cues is McNeill's (1992) Classification Scheme of Gestures. McNeill (1992) conceptualized the following five gesture types:

1. Iconics (i.e., gestures that simulate movements, or depict objects or movements of the whole or large parts of the body);
2. Metaphorics (i.e., visual cues that portray abstract ideas or thoughts but that do not involve use of the whole or large parts of the body);
3. Beats (i.e., visual cues that exhibit abstract ideas which distinguish word[s] or phrases from other words/phrases with regard to both semantic content and discourse-pragmatic content; e.g., repetitive up-and-down movements of a finger, hand, and/or head);
4. Deictics (i.e., an abstract level of pointing to ideas portrayed in a metaphorical space); and
5. Emblems (i.e., the traditional notion of gestures that have specific linguistic labels; e.g., shaking the head left to right to indicate disagreement with a response).

Another useful framework is that of Krauss, Chen, and Chawla's (1996) typology of lexical movements that vary in lexicalization, namely: adapters (i.e., representing the low lexicalization end of the continuum: non-meaningful meaningful gestures that involve manipulations either of the person or of some object such as clothing, spectacles, or jewelry); symbolic gestures (i.e., representing the high lexicalization end of the continuum: nonverbal communication data, such as hand configurations [e.g., thumbs up] and facial expressions, which represent specific, conventional, and popularized meanings that are recognized by cultural groups); and conversational gestures (i.e., lying between these two extremes of the lexicalization continuum: nonverbal behaviors that accompany speech, that appear to be connected to the speech that they accompany, and that manifest themselves by not taking place in the absence of speech, by being temporally coordinated with speech, and by being related, to some degree, to the semantic content of the speech that they accompany).

Chemosensory cues include olfaction (i.e., smell) and gustation (i.e., taste). Relatedly, psychosomatic cues (e.g., sweating due to stress; flushed cheeks in response to embarrassment) include stimulus-induced bodily changes. Contrastingly, language cues include paralinguistics (i.e., all variations in volume, pitch, and quality of voice) and linguistics (i.e., include language form [e.g. morphology, syntax, phonology, phonetics], language meaning [i.e., semantics, pragmatics], and/or language in context [e.g., evolutionary linguistics, historical linguistics, sociolinguistics, psycholinguistics, neurolinguistics, language acquisition, discourse analysis]).

Temporal-spatial cues include chronemics (i.e., involves the use of pacing of speech and length of silence in conversation, pacing of game play in nondigital and digital games). The speed with which one speaks or moves in offline or online spaces can suggest ways of being that can be interpreted to be, but not be limited to, frenetic, calculated, phlegmatic, stoic, sanguine, or despondent. Temporal-spatial cues also account for environmental and cultural contexts, and Bronfenbrenner's (1979) theory of human development—which addresses the ecological environment and ways that "the person's development is profoundly affected by events occurring in settings in which the person is not even present" (p. 3)—suggests that temporal-spatial cues are embedded in actions, milestones, and arrested development. Finally, temporal-spatial cues provide insight into positionality at (and in) a particular time and place (i.e., a player's or a researcher's positioning and co-presence with others in a digital space). Merchant (2010) co-inhabited an immersive world with students and studied their movement, interactions, hyperlinked text, and chat logs. In online spaces, temporal-spatial cues address how and where an individual—via one's avatar or print text (or both)—is situated in practice and functions in the space. In the videogame, *Call of Duty*, players use in-game maps to visualize where they are in relation to other players (e.g., teammates or opponents) and goals (Abrams & Gerber, in press).

Finally, artifact cues can be exhibited via tools that include objects and images. In offline spaces, people use items to represent themselves in some way. For instance, many, if not most, homes worldwide are decorated with objects and images that communicate the value system of the members of the household. In online contexts, for example, people often select avatars to represent or to extend their (offline and/or online) identities and memes to express their feelings.

Although addressing these cues individually helps to identify NVC, when it comes to analyzing NVC, these cues work in concert. For instance, computer use might include the pace and movement of finger, hand, and eye; a rounded-shoulder posture due to the positioning of the body and hands; and the presence of stress-induced sweat. Thus, movement, temporal-spatial, and psychosomatic cues would help the researcher identify and analyze these features. Add to this scenario one's inherent simultaneous inhabitation of an offline and online space, and appearance cues can converge or diverge (e.g., one might identify as female in offline spaces and as male in online spaces).

How Should Researchers Conduct NVC Analysis?

NVC analysis can involve quantitative analysis, qualitative analysis, and mixed analysis. Firstly, with respect to quantitative analyses, descriptive analyses, exploratory analyses, and inferential analyses can be used. Descriptive analyses include measures of central tendency (e.g., mean, median, mode), measures of variability (e.g., range, standard deviation, variance), and measures of position (e.g., percentile, quartile, decile, z score, T score). As presented by Hitchcock and Onwuegbuzie (2020), examples of using descriptive analyses for analyzing NVC, include the following:

- Proxemics (e.g., measuring the physical distance between one or more participants, or between a participant and some object)
- Chronemics (e.g., measuring the number of words spoken per minute, the length of silence in conversation, the time that elapses between the utterances of a participant, the time that elapses between the researcher's question and the participant's response)
- Kinesics (e.g., measuring the angle of the participant's torso when talking)
- Haptics (e.g., counting the number of times the participant touches herself or himself or another person)
- Paralinguistics (e.g., measuring the noise level of a location in decibels)
- Oculesics (e.g., measuring the number of times the participant blinks per minute as an indicator of levels of stress during an interview)
- Olfaction involves the kind and degree of smell detected (e.g., determining the number or proportion of participants who appear to be affected by a certain smell)
- Gustation involves taste (e.g., determining the number or proportion of participants who appear to like the taste of a certain food or drink)

Secondly, with respect to qualitative analyses, many of the 34 qualitative analysis approaches identified by Onwuegbuzie and Denham (2014) (e.g., constant comparison analysis, classical content analysis, domain analysis, qualitative comparative analysis), many of Miles and Huberman's (1994) 37 qualitative analysis methods (i.e., 19 within-case analyses and 18 cross-case analyses; Miles & Huberman, 1994), and many of Saldaña's (2016) 33 qualitative data analysis techniques (e.g., coding techniques) can be employed to analyze NVC. A qualitative data analysis approach that lends itself particularly to NVC analysis is conversation analysis because it facilitates the analysis of turns rather than utterances (Sacks, Schegloff, & Jefferson, 1974). As presented by Hitchcock and Onwuegbuzie (2020), examples of using qualitative analyses for analyzing NVC include the following:

- Proxemics (e.g., identifying the antecedents to any changes in proxemics or examining the reaction to changes in proxemics)
- Chronemics (e.g., examining the role of the speaker's rate of speech on the listener's ability to understand what is being stated)
- Kinesics (e.g., documenting the types of body movements displayed by the participant)
- Haptics (e.g., assessing the reaction of a participant to touching or being touched by someone else)
- Paralinguistics (e.g., evaluating the tone of a participant's voice)
- Oculesics (e.g., observing the tendency for gaze aversion of a participant as an indicator of shyness)
- Olfaction involves the kind and degree of smell detected (e.g., observing the smell of location being observed; observing the reaction of participants to a certain smell)
- Gustation involves taste (e.g., observing the taste a certain stable food product of a culture being studied in an ethnographic study; observing the reaction of participants after tasting a certain food or drink)

Conversation analysis is especially useful for analyzing NVC data stemming from focus groups because it allows researchers to examine the how and the what of members' interactions, the interactions among the members themselves, and the interactions between the moderator and the focus group members. As noted by Onwuegbuzie, Dickinson, Leech, and Zoran (2010),

> Within each focus group, conversation analysis allows researchers to analyze an array of emotions and actions such as joking, frowning, agreeing, debating, using sarcasms, and the like. In addition, researchers are able to examine how participants attempt to portray themselves in the focus group setting in order to impress, flirt, complain, or criticize—to name but a few actions. (p. 265)

Therefore, conversation analysis enables researchers to analyze—either simultaneously or sequentially—both verbal and nonverbal data.

Thirdly, the fact that NVC data can be analyzed both quantitatively and qualitatively implies that mixed analysis approaches can be used for NVC analysis. For instance, in terms of proxemics, mixed analysis may include both measuring distance and examining reactions to that distance. And, consistent with mixed analysis theory (Onwuegbuzie & Combs, 2010; Onwuegbuzie & Teddlie, 2003), nonverbal communication data can be:

- reduced (i.e., condensing the dimensionality of qualitative NVC data using quantitative analysis [e.g., exploratory factor analysis of qualitative data] and/or quantitative NVC data using qualitative techniques [e.g., thematic analysis of quantitative data; Onwuegbuzie, 2003a; Onwuegbuzie & Teddlie, 2003]);
- displayed (i.e., presenting visually qualitative and quantitative NVC data within the same display; Onwuegbuzie & Dickinson, 2008);
- transformed (i.e., involving converting quantitative NVC data that can be analyzed qualitatively [e.g., qualitizing data; Onwuegbuzie & Leech, 2019; Onwuegbuzie & Leech, this volume], and/or qualitative NVC data into numerical codes that can be analyzed statistically [e.g., quantitizing data; Sandelowski, Voils, & Knafl, 2009; Tashakkori & Teddlie, 1998]);

- correlated (i.e., linking qualitative NVC data with quantitized NVC data or verbal communication data and/or quantitative NVC data with qualitized NVC data or verbal communication data [Onwuegbuzie & Teddlie, 2003; see also Onwuegbuzie & Leech, this volume]);
- consolidated (i.e., merging NVC data and/or verbal communication data to create new or consolidated codes, variables, or data sets; Onwuegbuzie & Teddlie, 2003);
- compared (i.e., examining side by side qualitative and quantitative NVC data and verbal communication data; Onwuegbuzie & Teddlie, 2003);
- integrated (i.e., incorporating qualitative and quantitative NVC data and verbal communication data either into a coherent whole or two separate sets [i.e., qualitative and quantitative] of coherent wholes; Onwuegbuzie & Teddlie, 2003);
- asserted (i.e., reviewing all qualitative and quantitative NVC and verbal data to yield meta-inferences; Smith, 1997); and/or
- imported (i.e., utilizing follow-up findings from qualitative analysis of NVC data and/or verbal data to inform the quantitative analysis [e.g., qualitative contrasting case analysis, qualitative residual analysis, qualitative follow-up interaction analysis, and qualitative internal replication analysis; Onwuegbuzie & Teddlie, 2003] or follow-up findings from quantitative analysis of NVC data and/or verbal communication data to inform the qualitative analysis [e.g., quantitative extreme case analysis, quantitative negative case analysis; Onwuegbuzie & Teddlie, 2003]).

Integrated Data Displays

Of all the available mixed analysis techniques, integrated data displays appear to have the most potential for incorporating NVC analysis. In particular, the combining of findings stemming from verbal communication and NVC data can be used to generate integrated data displays one participant (e.g., interviewee, focus group member) at a time via within-case displays or two or more participants (e.g., interviewees, focus group members) at a time via cross-case displays. In their classic data analysis textbook, Miles and Huberman (1994) categorized the following four broad types of within-case displays: partially ordered displays (i.e., visual representations that uncover and portray what is occurring in a local setting or context by imposing minimal conceptual structure on the data; e.g., context charts, checklist matrices), time-ordered displays (i.e., visual representations that order data by time and sequence, maintaining the historical chronological order of events and facilitating an analysis of when the events occurred and their antecedents; e.g., event listing, critical incident chart, event-state network, activity record, decision modeling flowchart, growth gradient, time-ordered matrix), role-ordered displays (i.e., order information according to the participant's roles in a formal or informal setting; e.g., role-ordered matrix, role-by-time matrix), and conceptually ordered displays (i.e., order the display by concepts or variables; e.g., conceptually clustered matrix, thematic conceptual matrix, folk taxonomy, cognitive maps, effects matrix, case dynamics matrix, causal network). With regard to cross-case displays, Miles and Huberman (1994) categorized the following four broad types: partially ordered displays (e.g., partially ordered meta-matrices), case-ordered displays (e.g., case-ordered descriptive meta-matrix, two-variable case-ordered matrix, contrast table, scatterplot, case-ordered effects matrix, case-ordered predictor-outcome matrix, predictor-outcome consequences matrix), time-ordered displays (e.g., time-ordered meta-matrix, time-ordered scatterplots, composite sequence analysis), and conceptually ordered displays (e.g., content-analytic summary table, substructing, decision tree modeling, variable-by-variable matrix, causal models, causal networks, antecedents matrix) (Miles & Huberman, 1994). An illustration of an integrated display will be shown later in the heuristic example.

Another useful technique for generating integrated displays is correspondence analysis. Generally speaking, correspondence analysis is an exploratory multivariate technique of factoring nominal (i.e., categorical) variables and displaying them in a property space that maps their associations in multiple dimensions (Michailidis, 2007). A correspondence analysis can be used to map codes or themes extracted from NVC behaviors as a function of the participants or a subset of participants. This mapping can be displayed as a two-dimensional representation. For instance, Ekman (1999) identified 15 fundamental and distinct emotions that are associated with innate facial expressions—amusement, anger, contentment, contempt, embarrassment, excitement, disgust, fear, guilt, pride in achievement, relief, sadness/distress, satisfaction, sensory pleasure, and shame—and the frequency of expressions could be mapped as a function of the participants.

4 Empirical Demonstration of Nonverbal Communication Analysis for Mixed Methods Research

Empirical Demonstration 1

For her doctoral dissertation, Byers (2019) conducted a phenomenological research study to understand better (a) adjunct faculty instructors' self-perceived roles within their positions within a select community college system and (b) the emphasis that these adjunct faculty members placed on different aspects of these roles in terms of their levels of performance and effectiveness. A third purpose was to build on the qualitative body of research for understanding the roles and experiences of adjunct faculty members in community college systems. Using Harré and van Langenhove's (1999) positioning theory, Holmes's (2013) claim-affirmation model of modalities of emergent identity, and Leech and Onwuegbuzie's (2010) 13-step process for qualitative data analysis, Byers conducted semi-structured interviews of 12 adjunct faculty members at the select community college system. As part of her analysis of the interview data, she collected, analyzed, and interpreted NVC data. In particular, she documented NVC following each interview by completing matrices of Ekman's (1999) expanded list of basic emotions and McNeill's (1992) classification of gestures, as developed by Onwuegbuzie et al. (2010).

TABLE 22.1

Nonverbal Communication Data: Emotions x Participants

Emotion	Angela	Anne	Irene	Karl	Laura	Matthew	Nathaniel	Neil	Noah	Sandra	Total
Amusement	28	14	28	28	32	37	24	36	27	37	291
Anger	18	61	43	4	1	0	0	0	0	0	127
Contempt	72	128	75	17	7	23	6	2	4	3	337
Contentment	29	4	24	17	40	22	41	24	23	29	253
Disgust	0	28	17	0	0	0	10	2	0	0	57
Embarrassment	1	2	0	8	0	1	1	4	0	1	18
Excitement	16	5	18	3	8	11	20	4	26	17	128
Fear	0	11	0	1	7	0	0	0	0	0	19
Guilt	0	1	0	2	1	1	0	2	2	9	18
Pride in achievement	46	16	92	36	49	32	34	44	42	48	439
Relief	6	2	0	7	34	1	3	0	2	7	62
Sadness/distress	49	132	3	34	28	26	15	8	31	12	338
Satisfaction	30	10	38	18	39	32	39	26	29	31	292
Sensory Pleasure	0	1	4	0	0	0	0	8	3	3	19
Shame	0	1	0	0	0	0	0	0	0	0	1
Total	295	416	342	175	246	186	193	160	189	197	2399
Prevalence Rate of Participant	12.30	17.34	14.26	7.29	10.25	7.75	8.05	6.67	7.88	8.21	

Adapted from "Self-Perceptions of Adjunct Faculty About Their Roles at a Select Community College System," by V. T. Byers, Unpublished doctoral dissertation, Sam Houston State University, Huntsville, TX, pp. 169-170. Copyright 2019 by V. T. Byers.

Table 22.1 presents the matrix that Byers (2019) developed that documents the emotions exhibited by her participants using Ekman's (1999) framework. Even though her study was qualitative in nature, this did not prevent her from using descriptive analyses (i.e., frequency counts) to document the NVC that she had observed.

Based on Table 22.1 and other nonverbal observations, Byers (2019) concluded the following:

> Of Ekman's (1999) 15 fundamental emotions, the participants exhibited between 10 (Angela, Irene, Matthew, Nathaniel, and Noah) and all 15 (Anne) of these emotions throughout their interviews. The three most dominant emotions displayed were that of pride in achievement, with a 18.30% prevalence rate; sadness/distress, with a 14.30% prevalence rate; and contempt, with a 14.05% prevalence rate. There were seven emotions displayed by all participants; these were amusement, contempt, contentment, excitement, pride in achievement, sadness/distress, and satisfaction. Only one participant, Anne, displayed shame. Each of the adjunct professors interviewed expressed enjoyment in the work that they do with their students, and their nonverbal language confirmed their satisfaction. (p. 168)
>
> Of my participants, Anne, Irene, Angela, and Matthew were the four most expressive. They were also the participants most likely to show dissatisfaction with their position in terms of how they were treated and compensated. They spoke the most passionately about the work that they do and its importance, but were also adamant that the institution only recognized their importance in name, but not in any meaningful way. Each of these participants started off their interviews more reserved, but built up into a fervor once we had established a rapport....
>
> Overall, each adjunct vocalized a pride in their achievement and felt their work was worthwhile, which was supported by their eyes lighting up, enthusiastic gesturing, and smiling. Of all my participants, Anne had the most distinct turnaround in her nonverbal demeanor. Although smiling and happy when talking about her subject matter and commitment to students, she immediately turned dour when asked about her satisfaction level. She would look away, look down, sigh, and several times approached tears as she exhibited nonverbal communicators of disgust, contempt, anger, sadness/distress, guilt, and shame. There was a great deal of regret and defeat in her posturing. (p. 171)

Byers (2019) developed several other tables that illustrated the NVC data that she had collected. For example, she created what mixed methods researchers refer to as a joint display table. Joint displays provide ways for researchers to "integrate the [qualitative and quantitative] data by bringing the data together through a visual means to draw out new insights beyond the information gained from the separate quantitative and qualitative results" (Fetters, Curry, & Creswell, 2013, p. 10; see also Guetterman, Fetters, Creswell, 2015; Johnson, Grove, & Clarke, 2019). Table 22.2 depicts her joint display. It can be seen from this table that the first column represents each participant's pseudonym; the second column provides a brief description of the NVC data exhibited by each participant (i.e., qualitative data); the third column presents the most prevalent emotion(s), using Ekman's (1999) framework (i.e., qualitative data); and the final column provides the frequency of the most prevalent emotion(s) (i.e., quantitative data).

TABLE 22.2

Participant Observations

Participant	Brief Description of Nonverbal Communication	Most Prevalent Emotion	Prevalence Rate (%)
Angela	She appeared very nervous at first and kept her hands folded on the table in front of her, occasionally taking a drink of water when feeling especially nervous or unsure how to answer. Once she had felt comfortable, the conversation flowed more freely. An increase in vocal volume and pace occurred when speaking about what she enjoyed about her work and when speaking about what distressed or angered her about her position. She banged down her cup at one point in emphasis of area of contention. She also demonstrated excitement about being able to talk about her concerns by leaning in and smiling.	Contempt	24.41%
Anne	She had downcast eyes most of the time and her vocal expressions were continually tinged with distress, contempt, and anger. She drank from her cup or used her lip balm when feeling nervous or overwhelmed. She only smiled or showed enjoyment when discussing interacting with her students, but also demonstrated fear and embarrassment when discussing difficult students. She seemed wistful and full of regret.	Sadness/distress	31.73%
Irene	She began with her hand on her knee, but eventually began using gestures as the interview progressed. She sat back in her chair, but leaned forward when giving more detail in her answers. Speech was emphatic and quick when delivering her viewpoints, although pauses also were used to denote importance. She demonstrated confidence in her abilities and much contempt for how the institution treated adjunct faculty.	Pride in Achievement	26.90%
Karl	He held his hands clasped in front of him on his lap throughout the interview, but occasionally made gestures. His voice and rocking motion in his chair conveyed some nervousness. Overall, he was very hopeful.	Pride in Achievement	20.57%
Laura	She had very animated features and her voice was strong and positive when discussing her position, only wavering when she discussed the insecurity she still felt with regard to her employment. She used frequent hand gestures to emphasis her responses.	Pride in Achievement	19.92%
Matthew	He was very reserved at first, but opened up as interview continued. He kept his hands in his lap or nearly the entire interview, but communicated nonverbally with head movement, facial expression, and paralinguistic changes. He showed a significant amount of care and concern for his students and joy in their accomplishments.	Amusements	19.17%
Nathaniel	He sat with his hands in his lap and was more reserved, but lit up when talking about working with his students. His speech pace, which began slow and measured, would increase with excitement and pride when talking about the students, along with an increase in smiling and laughing.	Contentment	21.24%
Neil	He kept his left hand on the back of the chair next to him for the majority of the interview. He made good eye contact, smiled, and nodded his head frequently and was overall very pleasant and agreeable.	Pride in Achievement	27.50%
Noah	He began the interview with hands down to his side. He utilized head nodding as his main nonverbal communication at the start of the interview but progressed to more gestures with his hands as the interview progressed. He shifted in his seat throughout the interview, but remained very matter of fact in his responses. His words were slow and deliberate to show the deep thought he put into answering the interview questions. He felt very satisfied in being called to teach as a public service but showed distress when talking about students "giving up" and his desire to reach them.	Pride in Achievement	22.22%
Sandra	She had a cough from a dry throat from teaching, but still managed to convey her satisfaction and enjoyment with her position through laughter, smiles, and gestures. She had a great appreciation for her position.	Pride in Achievement	24.37%

Adapted from "Self-Perceptions of Adjunct Faculty About Their Roles at a Select Community College System," by V. T. Byers, Unpublished doctoral dissertation, Sam Houston State University, Huntsville, TX, pp. 173-176. Copyright 2019 by V. T. Byers.

Empirical Demonstration 2

This second example illustrates how NVC data can be extracted from the words spoken by participants. Byers, Smith, Angrove, McAlister-Shields, and Onwuegbuzie (2015) conducted a mixed methods research study that was guided by feminist standpoint theory to understand the experiences of eight women doctoral students. Two men doctoral students also were included in the study for comparison purposes. Interestingly, some of the participants served as participant-researchers in the study, thereby yielding *emtic* viewpoints that allow for maximum interaction between *emic* (i.e., insider; participant-researchers) and *etic* (i.e., outsider; researchers who were not participants) viewpoints (Onwuegbuzie, 2012). These participants were interviewed individually, and their responses were analyzed using a sequential mixed analysis that comprised both qualitative analyses (e.g., constant comparison analysis, classical content analysis) and quantitative analyses (e.g., descriptive analyses, correspondence analysis). The qualitative analyses led to the identification of four themes, which indicated that although the women doctoral students received support and encouragement to tackle the multitude of challenges with which they were confronted—particularly with respect to balancing one's academic identity with other identities—they still felt a strong sense of remorse and guilt towards the sacrifices that they had to make in order to succeed within their doctoral programs. This finding was in contrast to the men doctoral students who, although they felt some guilt, faced their challenges more by focusing on achieving their goals and the implied results (i.e., career success) of that achievement.

Interestingly, these authors also used the verbal responses of these 10 doctoral students to identify latent (i.e., hidden, unobservable) NVC data via the literary communication (i.e., linguistics) used. To accomplish this, these researchers examined the vagueness of words spoken by each participant during the interviews—specifically, what Hiller, Fisher, and Kaess (1969) referred to as *communication vagueness*, which they defined as a "psychological construct, which refers to the state of mind of a performer who does not sufficiently command the facts or the understanding required for maximally effective communication" (p. 670). Hiller et al. (1969) identified the following 10 categories of communication vagueness:

1. Ambiguous Designation (i.e., something potentially specifiable is stated but not definitely identified; e.g., stuff, and so on);
2. Negated Intensifiers (i.e., negations can represent evasions; e.g., not necessarily; not quite);
3. Approximation (i.e., use reflects real or referential vagueness or imprecise knowledge; e.g., sort of, pretty much);
4. Bluffing and Recovery (i.e., when a speaker/writer is not communicating effectively and attempts to shift responsibility for making sense of content to the listener/reader; e.g., actually, anyway);
5. Admission of Error (i.e., repeated admissions of error that indicate a lack of confidence or competence; e.g., I made a mistake, I don't know);
6. Indefinite Amount (i.e., an amount that is potentially knowable but is not specified; e.g., a little, a lot, some, a couple);
7. Multiplicity (i.e., pseudospecification or glossing over of complexity; e.g., types, kinds);
8. Probability and Possibility (i.e., suggests lack of clarity or lack of definite knowledge; e.g., generally, at times);
9. Reservations (i.e., expressions of doubt reticence, or reluctance to commit to a specific point of view; i.e., appears, seems); and
10. Anaphora (i.e., excessive and repetitious use of pronouns instead of direct references, which makes the narrative more difficult to follow; e.g., she, he, it, them, latter, former).

WordStat 6.0 (Provalis, 2011) was used to assess the vagueness of each participant's story with respect to the aforementioned ten categories of communication vagueness. Specifically, frequency of the vague phrases made by each participant was computed across all 10 categories. The authors described the resultant frequencies as follows:

> Thaddeus, Delores, and Beatrice provided relatively high frequencies of vague phrases, whereas Calvin and Constance provided relatively low frequencies of vague phrases. Interestingly, although no pattern was apparent between the level of communication vagueness and the demographic variables of gender, number of children, and occupation, there appeared to be somewhat of a link between the level of communication vagueness and age, wherein, with one exception (i.e., Beatrice, who had the third highest level of communication vagueness), the participants in their 30s had the lowest levels of communication vagueness, those in their 40s had the highest levels, whereas those in their 50s had moderate levels of communication vagueness. Also, there appeared to be somewhat of a link between the level of communication vagueness and ethnicity, with three minority participants having moderate levels of communication vagueness and the non-minority students—with one exception (i.e., Agnes)—having either low or high levels of communication vagueness. Thus, our analysis of communication vagueness allowed us to differentiate participants who were most clear about their experiences and perceptions regarding being a doctoral student from those who were less clear about these experiences and perceptions, which further facilitated our within-case analyses by providing additional nonverbal cues (cf. Denham & Onwuegbuzie, 2013). (p. 280)

Byers et al. (2015) went further with their NVC analysis. Specifically, as described in a previous section, they used correspondence analysis to map the 10 participants onto the space that displays the 10 categories of communication vagueness. Figure 22.2 presents this correspondence plot.

The authors described Figure 22.2 as follows:

> This figure shows how the participants related to each other with respect to these 10 categories. In the top left quadrant, it can be seen that Sophia, Beatrice, Delores, and Thaddeus clustered together nearest to the categories of indefinite amount, anaphora, and ambiguous designation, with Delores also clustering close to probability and possibility. In the bottom left quadrant, Hazel clustered nearest to the categories of probability and possibility, multiplicity, negated identifiers, and approximation. In the top right quadrant, it can be seen that Calvin clustered together with Matilda, with Calvin being near to the categories of ambiguous designation and reservations and Matilda being near to the category of reservations. Finally, in the bottom fight quadrant, Constance, Agnes, and Dixie clustered together, with Constance occupying a position close to the origin and near to approximation, multiplicity, probability and possibility, anaphora, and ambiguous designation; Agnes being near approximation and bluff and recovery; and Dixie being near bluff and recovery. (pp. 280–281)

What was most interesting about these NVC findings was that Calvin, who presented the lowest number of vague phrases during his interview—that is, who exhibited the least communication vagueness—was the first participant in the cohort to complete

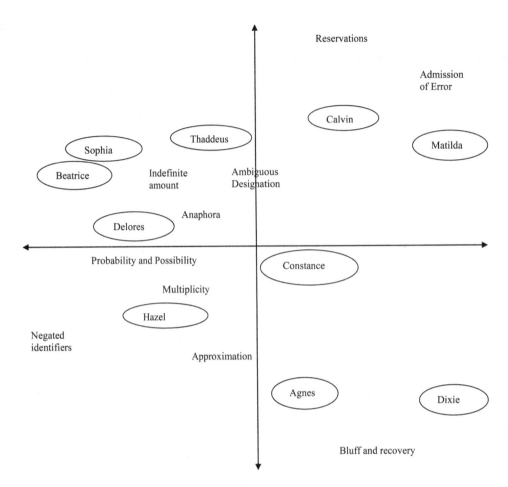

FIGURE 22.2 Correspondence analysis of the ten categories of communication vagueness.
Adapted from Byers, Smith, Angrove, McAlister-Shields, and Onwuegbuzie, 2015.

the program and to graduate, thereby providing incremental validity to the NVC analysis of communication vagueness.

Empirical Demonstration 3

Studies of NVC in online spaces involve analyses of multimodal meaning making, and examinations of NVC related to or informed by digital technologies also can include the exploration of human behavior in the offline space. For instance, in their study of adolescents coding and creating electronic textiles (a.k.a. e-textiles), Lui, Kafai, Litts, Walker, and Widman (2020) video recorded and photographed students' interactions, diagrams, and digital and nondigital tool use. They then coupled these data with interviews and field observations to address the interactive nature of crafting e-textiles, albeit primarily through offscreen behavior.

The use of digital and nondigital tools to collect NVC data has been demonstrated as being a common approach for researchers of online or digital meaning making. When examining power structures in online spaces, Abrams (2013) used interview and email-based data, as well as screenshots to document and to discuss the affordances and constraints of a particular online tool. This approach—combining in-person qualitative interviews with screenshots of asynchronous work and participant-generated email feedback—offered a methodological mix that captured the in-person learning space (i.e., the classroom) and transcended it as well; screenshots of students' asynchronous work on a collaborative digital platform not only shed light on a space that students accessed in and beyond the school building, but also helped to identify features of the space that afforded peer-mediated feedback and learning.

Likewise, Walsh and Simpson (2013) used video and still images to explore elementary school children's use of gesture to design, to read, and to interact with digital texts. More specifically, these researchers focused on the youths' use of touch pads, and they complemented their digital recordings with field notes and the teacher's reflective journal. Rooting their investigation in case study methodology, Walsh and Simpson followed the sequencing of students' gestures. In one case, the authors juxtaposed the photographs of a student's use of an iPad—sliding a finger along the screen, gesturing to an image—with the student's spoken (verbal) explanation of the on-screen information. In so doing, the authors exemplified the role of NVC in the student's "explanation text that demonstrates his learning with written language, images and graphics, which are organised in a non-linear way" (p. 152).

Empirical Demonstration 4

Research of learning in online spaces, however, can hinge on data collected solely in an online space. Abrams (2012) explored the meaning making of university students who were present in a face-to-face class while simultaneously and synchronously inhabiting an online discussion forum with their classmates. In this study, Abrams looked to several features to capture NVC vis-à-vis the rapidity of writing, the agency in modified turn-taking (e.g., communicating without interruption), the vocabulary and tone of the digital posts (e.g., colloquialisms ["math sucks"] and abbreviated language ["lol"]), and the use of images (e.g., a smiley face emoticon; emojis were not available on the forum) and colored font in represented interaction to explain how an online forum's "narrative third space represents a combination of students' personal/social and academic realms" (p. 119). For instance, Abrams noted that six students posted 33 times within 27 minutes. Although this time cannot be evenly distributed to suggest a post every 49 seconds—and Abrams did not examine the timestamps of each post to determine the length of time between them—the data, nonetheless, provide a chronemic understanding of an ongoing pace of interaction.

Additionally, Abrams (2012) distinguished the examination of online discussion forum posts from traditional interview data, suggesting that the NVC of the former can reveal a degree of agency in meaning making that might appear in a student-driven third space (i.e., an alternate, shared, and evolving environment; cf. Soja, 1996) that otherwise is absent from a traditional teacher-driven classroom:

> online text is viewed by the author before submission, and, as opposed to interview data that are spoken and not seen by the participant, there is a metalevel of review and perhaps analysis before the student presses the Submit button. Further, the action of making a response "public" suggests that there is agency in the act of posting, in that the student determines when to submit the information and then is physically responsible for clicking the virtual button. In so doing, knowledge landscapes include an understanding of virtual worlds and Discourses, and there is a sense of ownership and control that may not exist within academic or professional landscapes. (p. 115)

The nature of the discussion forum—the ability to embed responses and to follow the thread related to the original post—builds on features of digital messaging and social networking, wherein users can "like," share, and/or respond to the initial post. In this online third space, the students were afforded the opportunity to:

- engage in "shared tellership" (Ware, 2006, p. 46)
- use emoticons and symbols to express emotion
- discover commonalities among their posts
- wrestle with pedagogy and practice

The examination of NVC in the online discussion space contributed to a greater understanding of how the teacher candidates co-constructed narratives of teaching.

Other research of online spaces has generated important theories of learning in and across digital education landscapes. Cope and Kalantzis's (2013) examination of the online *Scholar* platform brought to light how an online space supported the integration of alphanumeric text, image, sound, and video; *Scholar* accommodated shifts in communicational practices and offered a new context in which to examine NVC vis-à-vis the lens of students as creators and producers.

Cope and Kalantzis (2013) addressed technology-induced changes to education practices through seven principles— "seven openings, seven affordances" (p. 333):

- *Ubiquitous Learning* that can take "any time, any place" (Cope & Kalantzis, 2013, p. 334; see also Cope & Kalantzis, 2009);
- *Active Knowledge Production* generated by participatory and collaborative creation and sharing of knowledge;
- *Multimodal Knowledge Representations* that draw on the synesthetic nature of drawing on and moving across various modes to make meaning;
- *Recursive Feedback* that is social, interactive, and constructive and supports the development of a knowledge economy "where teamwork and networked collaborations are more valuable than ever" (Cope & Kalantzis, 2013, p. 348);
- *Collaborative Intelligence* that stems from peer interaction and scaffolded discourse wherein learners help one another;
- *Metacognitive Reflection* via self- and peer-assessment of knowledge representations; and
- *Differentiated Learning* that is interest- and needs-driven.

This conceptual frame helps to situate NVC analyses in that it underscores that NVC not only is a primary entity of expression in online spaces, but also, inherently, is nuanced, complex, and multimodal.

5 Suggested Applications of Nonverbal Communication Analysis in Mixed Methods Research

The study of NVC has occurred routinely outside the world of academe for a long time. For example, although not framed as a detector of NVC, one of the most famous tools for NVC analysis is the polygraph, which is more commonly known as a lie detector test. This device was invented in 1921—almost exactly 100 years ago at the time of writing—by John Augustus Larson, a medical student at the University of California, Berkeley and a police officer of the Berkeley Police Department in Berkeley, California (International League of Polygraph Examiners, 2020). He was the first person simultaneously to record multiple physiological parameters in order to detect deception. Dr. Larson developed and utilized the continuous method of concurrently registering changes in pulse rate, blood pressure, and respiration—which represent aspects of NVC. Although considered to be (somewhat) controversial in some countries (e.g., Australia; New South Wales Government, 2009), the polygraph is considered officially as being "one of the greatest inventions of all time" (International League of Polygraph Examiners, 2020, ¶3). Being used while a person is asked and answers a series of questions, the assumption underlying the use of the polygraph is that deceptive answers will yield physiological (i.e., NVC via movement cues) responses that can be distinguished from those responses associated with nondeceptive answers. With polygraphs being used as a psychophysiological detection tool in some countries, not only with criminal suspects, but also with candidates for sensitive public or private sector employment, it is likely that development of this tool will continue, opening up further avenues for NVC research in general and NVC mixed analysis in particular.

However, the area that appears to have the most potential for the study of NVC analysis pertains to what was coined in 1956 by John McCarthy, an American computer scientist and cognitive scientist, as Artificial Intelligence (AI). In short, AI is intelligence demonstrated by machines. There are almost a countless number of AI applications. For instance, automatic number-plate recognition (i.e., ANPR; also known as [vehicle] license-plate recognition) is a technology that involves the use of optical character recognition on images to read vehicle registration plates in order to create vehicle location data. ANPR is used by law enforcement agencies worldwide for a variety of purposes that facilitate the analysis of nonverbal behaviors of drivers, including whether drivers register/license their vehicles and whether drivers are driving within the official speed limit—yielding both qualitative data (e.g., location data) and quantitative data (e.g., speed data). AI cameras also have been used to monitor the nonverbal behavior of texting while driving.

One application that is gaining widespread attention is the use of facial recognition, which was invented in the 1960s. Facial recognition technology is capable of identifying or verifying a person via a still (i.e., digital image) or moving (i.e., a video) source. Most commonly, facial recognition technology involves comparing selected facial features from a given image with faces stored in a database. However, recent years has seen a rapid increase in Biometric AI-based applications that uniquely can identify a person by analyzing patterns on individuals' faces via their facial textures and shape. As an example, schools in China are now using facial recognition technology to monitor how attentive students are in class, whereby every movement of students is watched by cameras positioned at strategic places in a classroom, such as above the blackboard (e.g., Connor, 2018)—yielding what is called a smart classroom behavior management system or smart eye. This system has led to some students positively changing their classroom behaviors. However, as a cautionary tale, we hope that data collected from such systems are used for constructive outcomes (e.g., helping teachers improve student engagement in their classrooms) and not for punitive purposes (e.g., punishing teachers for whom smart eye evidence suggests that students in their classrooms are not "adequately" engaged). Notwithstanding, as long as participants' rights are not being violated (e.g., privacy rights), this system has a lot of potential for enhancing NVC research, in general, and NVC analysis, in particular, in both offline and online spaces.

Another area that has much potential for NVC analysis is that pertaining to eye-tracking. Broadly speaking, eye-tracking is the process of measuring either the point of gaze (i.e., where an individual is looking) or the motion of an eye relative to the head. Eye-tracking occurs via an eye-tracker, which is a device for measuring eye positions and eye movement. Therefore, eye-tracking research has much potential for studying nonverbal behaviors, such as attention, reading patterns, engagement with learning material, decision-making processes, sense-making strategies, and behaviors. For example, Beach and McConnel (2019), who conducted a review of the literature on eye-tracking methodology in the context of learning, concluded that that "eye-tracking technology has the potential to provide important information about teachers' behavioural patterns and cognitive processes that may or may not be occurring during learning experiences" (p. 485).

As an example of recent research conducted in the area of eye-tracking, Sharma, Giannakos, and Dillenbourg (2020) combined eye-tracking and AI to examine 40 students who watched a Massive Open Online Course (MOOC) lecture while recording their eye movements. These researchers "identified a significant mediation effect of the content coverage, reading patterns and the two levels of with-me-ness on the relation between students' motivation and their learning performance" (p. 1).

Nevertheless, eye-tracking is still in its infancy, with the current uses of eye-tracking often being limited to laboratory environments. However, the fact that eye-trackers are becoming less invasive, eye-tracking software is improving, and eye-tracking technology is becoming miniaturized and costing less, has made eye-tracking research more accessible—thereby providing another rich avenue for NVC research and NVC analysis in both offline and online spaces.

As illustrated in our second offline example, words uttered by humans can be subjected to an NVC analysis. With the development of natural language processing (NLP), it is now possible to conduct NVC analyses on large amounts of unstructured data. NLP, which is a component of linguistics, information engineering, computer science, and AI, pertains to the interactions between computers and human (natural) languages. Moreover, NLP focuses on how to program computers to read, to process, to analyze, and to understand a large corpus of natural language data. Sentiment analysis is an analysis that involves the use of NLP, alongside text analysis, text mining, statistics (e.g., multidimensional scaling, cluster analysis, factor analysis, topic modeling techniques), machine learning, computational linguistics, and biometrics, systematically to identify, to extract, to examine, and to quantify affective states and subjective information. An important goal of sentiment analysts is to classify the polarity of a corpus of text at various levels (e.g., document level, paragraph level, sentence level)—determining, for example, whether the analyzed text reveals emotional states (e.g., angry, sad, and happy) or whether it is positive, negative, or neutral.

There are many other suggested applications for NVC analysis that we could provide. However, because we are writing this chapter at a time of the COVID-19 pandemic worldwide, we will end this section on suggested applications with a discussion of the COVID-19 tools released by Apple Inc. and Google to public health organizations. These tools use Bluetooth technology to learn to whom persons who have tested positive for the COVID-19 virus have come into contact, and then notify those people of a possible exposure. These tools facilitate NVC analysis because they allow the tracking of the previous movements of infected individuals, which include data on all the locations visited by the infected person during a specified period, with whom they contacted, the duration of each contact, and so forth. That is, these tools yield backend data that include both qualitative and quantitative data, thereby allowing for NVC mixed analyses.

6 Strengths and Limitations of Nonverbal Communication Analysis in Mixed Methods Research

NVC analysis bears its strengths in its specificity and its humanistic approach. Throughout this chapter, examples of NVC call attention to linguistic and behavioral nuances that can strengthen triangulation and the credibility of the data analysis. NVC analysis also acknowledges that communication, itself, is multimodal and multidimensional, thereby opening possibilities for research to extend beyond the confines of verbal communication. Because the majority of this chapter showcases the affordances of capturing various forms of NVC, this section primarily will address its limitations. In what follows are methodological and technological constraints.

Methodological Constraints

In quantitative research, there are several limitations that pose a threat to both *internal validity* (i.e., "approximate validity with which we infer that a relationship between two variables is causal"; Cook & Campbell, 1979, p. 37) and *external validity* (i.e., the extent to which the results of a study "can be generalized to and across populations of persons, settings, times, outcomes, and treatment variations"; Johnson & Christensen, 2020, p. 278). In qualitative research, threats can exist to both *internal credibility* (i.e., "the truth value, applicability, consistency, neutrality, dependability, and/or credibility of interpretations and conclusions within the underlying setting or group"; Onwuegbuzie & Leech, 2007, p. 234) and *external credibility* (i.e., "pertain[ing] to the confirmability and transferability of findings and conclusions"; Onwuegbuzie & Leech, 2007, p. 235). In the discourse of mixed methods researchers, reactive arrangements pose a threat to *multiple validities legitimation*, which is "the extent to which addressing legitimation of the quantitative and qualitative components of the study result from the use of [the relevant/pertinent] quantitative, qualitative, and mixed validity types, yielding high quality meta-inferences" (Onwuegbuzie & Johnson, 2006, p. 57). In the context of NVC, internal and external threats to validity/credibility include the following: reactive arrangements, observation bias, researcher bias, and cultural myopia. The latter is defined as being unwilling and/or unable to embrace progressive Discourses (Gee, 1989), or being-doing-valuing combinations.

With respect to NVC analysis, internal validity/credibility and external validity/credibility can be impacted by *reactive arrangements* (Cook & Campbell, 1979). In the parlance of quantitative researchers, reactive arrangements refer to the (potential) reactions of the participants whose NVC is being analyzed. More specifically, reactive arrangements pertain to changes in individuals' behaviors that can come to the fore as a direct result of being aware that one might be or is being observed. For example, the mere presence of observers during a study might alter participants' typical nonverbal behaviors such that rival explanations for the behaviors prevail, which, in turn, threaten multiple validities, in general, and internal validity, internal credibility, external validity, and external credibility, in particular. More specifically, reactive arrangements include, but are not limited to, the following five major components: (a) the Hawthorne effect, (b) resentful demoralization, (c) the novelty effect, (d) identity performance (Goffman, 1959), and (e) what we call, *cultural myopia*. The Hawthorne effect represents the situation when individuals interpret being observed as receiving special attention. As a result, the participants' reactions to their perceived special treatment are confounded with the effects of the NVC observation. In the context of NVC, resentful demoralization (Cook & Campbell, 1979) is similar to the Hawthorne effect inasmuch as it involves the feeling of being singled out. However, instead of welcoming knowledge of being observed, participants become resentful about being observed and become demoralized, thereby changing their nonverbal behaviors. In reference to NVC, the novelty effect refers to a change in NVC behaviors merely because participants are being observed while undertaking a different or novel activity. Identity performance involves the purposeful enactment of Discourses to present a specific identity to a particular audience or audiences. Finally, cultural myopia is a shortsighted, nonprogressive disposition (e.g., NVC) that can affect the trustworthiness of data collection, analysis, and interpretation.

One kind of observational bias occurs when the observer has not obtained a sufficient sampling of the nonverbal behavior(s) of interest. Such inadequate sampling of behaviors might happen if either persistent observation or prolonged engagement does not occur (Lincoln & Guba, 1985). Additionally, researcher bias can occur when the observer has a personal bias in favor of or against one or more nonverbal behaviors. Unfortunately, this bias might be transferred subconsciously to the participants in such a way that their nonverbal behaviors are unduly affected.

Researcher bias can be either active or passive. Active sources include mannerisms and statements made by the observer that provide an indication of the observer's behavior preferences, whereas passive sources include attributes or personality traits of the observer (e.g., gender, ethnicity, age, type of clothing worn) (Onwuegbuzie, 2003b). Another form of researcher bias is when the observer's prior knowledge of the participants (i.e., emic perspective) differentially affects the participants' nonverbal behaviors. Threats to validity/legitimation—such as observational bias or researcher bias—can be mitigated via the use of member checking approaches wherein the researcher purposefully attempts to confirm, to challenge, to clarify, and/or to expand researcher interpretations of the data.

Finally, a culturally progressive NVC observer does not refer to an observer who has a mastery of a particular culture being studied, but, instead, one who focuses on a stance taken toward respecting diversity of cultures. Moreover, a culturally progressive NVC observer who avoids making deficit nonverbal behavior observations and maintains a high degree of self-awareness for understanding how her/his/their own background and other experiences might serve as assets or limitations when observing participants. Conversely, cultural myopia refers to the lack of awareness of the observer's own biases and personal values and how these elements might influence observations. As such, cultural myopia can pose as a threat to internal validity/credibility and external validity/credibility.

Technological Constraints

A researcher is unlikely to capture NVC cues (e.g., appearance, contact, movement, chemosensory, language, temporal-spatial, positionality, and artifact) comprehensively without various technologies. At the very least, the researcher will need a computer to jot down noticings of nonverbal cues, and it is more than likely the inclusion of one or more video recording devices (such as camera) will be required to capture NVC cues. This can be a costly pursuit and is but one limitation associated with NVC analysis. Other limitations specific to the use of video recording equipment and related data include, but are not limited to, the following:

1 Resource Limitations

A camera's speed, aperture, positioning, focal distance, and lens type can impact the clarity and breadth of what is recorded. The inclusion of multiple cameras might capture additional angles, but the equipment can be costly and can alter the physical environment.

2 Behavioral Limitations

Although the dramaturgical perspective of identity performance and related "frontstage" (i.e., formal, in front of an audience) and "backstage" (i.e., informal, in private) language and conduct permeate social settings (Goffman, 1959, p. 128), cameras add another dimension that indirectly or directly can impact human behavior. Research (Jansen, Giebels, van Rompay, & Junger, 2018; van Rompay, Vonk, & Fransen, 2009) suggests that human behavior becomes normalized with the presence of camera surveillance. This understanding also can be informed by Foucault's (1977) examination of Bentham's Panopticon prison, which was designed "to induce in the inmate a state of conscious and permanent visibility that assures the automatic functioning of power" (Foucault, 1977, p. 201). Foucault concluded that the mere intimation of hierarchical surveillance regulates human behavior through an internal turn; self-regulation occurs via "an inspecting gaze, a gaze which each individual under its weight will end by interiorising to the point that he is his own overseer, each individual thus exercising this surveillance over, and against himself" (Foucault, 1980, p. 155). Therefore, it is possible that NVC can become contrived through self-regulation based on imposed environmental factors.

3 Sustainability Limitations

As with any research, triangulation (e.g., of procedures, of data collection, of data analysis) is essential to supporting the credibility of the data. Beyond the use of cameras, researcher observation notes, participant interviews, and participant self-selected artifacts can shed light on NVC and the dimensions of it. However, the data corpus can become unwieldy. Multimodal discourse analysis techniques (Norris, 2019) support the sectioning of data in frame-by-frame-style, enabling the researcher to code moments and movements. Although this is a useful approach, it might not be sustainable for larger projects completed by a small research team. Likewise, researchers will need to be trained accordingly to identify, to code, and to analyze NVC. (For more details about identifying, coding, and analyzing NVC, see Onwuegbuzie & Abrams, in press.)

7 Resources for Learning More About Nonverbal Communication Analysis

There are several resources for learning about NVC analysis. One such resource is the *Journal of Nonverbal Behavior*. Published by SpringLink, as of the time of writing, this open-access journal was launched (i.e., Volume 1 Issue 1) in September 1976—yielding a 44-year history. It has a high impact factor, with a 2019 impact factor of 1.767 and a 5-year impact factor (2019) of 2.233. According to its website,

> The Journal of Nonverbal Behavior publishes peer-reviewed original theoretical and empirical research papers on all major areas of nonverbal behavior. The coverage extends to paralanguage, proxemics, facial expressions, eye contact, face-to-face interaction, and nonverbal emotional expression, as well as other relevant topics which contribute to the scientific understanding of nonverbal processes and behavior.
>
> - Original research on all areas of nonverbal behavior
> - Covers paralanguage, proxemics, facial expressions, eye contact, face-to-face interaction and nonverbal emotional expression
> - Includes other relevant topics contributing to scientific understanding (Journal of Nonverbal Behavior, 2020, ¶1)

Examination of this journal reveals that it contains articles addressing both offline and online spaces. For example, the most current issue at the time of writing (i.e., Volume 44, Issue 2, June 2020) includes an article representing online spaces by Franco and Fugate (2020) entitled, "Emoji face renderings: Exploring the role emoji platform differences have on emotional interpretation." These authors conclude that there is a "need for future emoji perception research to examine how different platform renderings of the same emoji might lead to miscommunication and interpretation discrepancies" (p. 301). In this same issue, and representing one of the offline spaces articles, is the article by Picó et al. (2020), entitled, "How visible tears affect observers' judgements and behavioral intentions: Sincerity, remorse, and punishment." In this study, participants were exposed to photographs of tearful people and the same pictures with the tears digitally removed, alongside brief descriptions of everyday transgressions for Study 1 (n = 71) and crimes for Study 2 (n = 359). The dependent variables were the judgment of the model's emotionality (Study 1 only); sincerity (situational in Study 1 and trait in Study 2); and kindness, remorse, and proposed punishment (Study 2 only). Based on their findings, the authors concluded that although tears make transgressors appear to be more sincere, kind, reliable, and remorseful, with the exception of the drunk driving transgression, these tears do not necessarily affect the proposed punishments for the transgression. As are some of the other articles in this issue, both these articles are extremely relevant for the topic of this chapter because they involve analysis and interpretation of emoji face renderings (first article) and tears (second article). Therefore, readers should be able to increase their knowledge and understanding of NVC analysis by reading at least some of the articles published in this journal. Indeed, we encourage readers, at the very least to peruse the table of contents of as many issues as possible so that they will be in a position to select the most appropriate articles for them to read.

Another set of resources can be obtained via YouTube, which has more than 2 billion users or "almost one-third of the internet" logging in to the site each month ("YouTube for Press," n.d.) and hosts amateur through professional videos and slide shows. YouTube boasts that people watch more than 1,000,000,000 hours of videos daily ("YouTube for Press," n.d.). Thus, we turn to this media outlet to share two possible TEDx talks that can be a resource for readers.

Technology, Entertainment, Design (TED) talks, and TEDx talks—those that are independently organized—feature a host of topics directly and peripherally relevant to NVC analysis. For instance, the TEDxManchester video, *The Power of Nonverbal Communication*, spotlights former FBI agent Joe Navarro's (2020) discussion of NVC and the transmission of self, beliefs, and values. The examples and activities (e.g., shaking a stranger's hand, reviewing images—focusing on the furrowed glabella, or movement of lips) can be of service to researchers interested in developing initial techniques for NVC analysis techniques. Navarro also underscored that, based on his experience conducting approximately 13,000 interviews during his time with the FBI, there is no "Pinocchio effect…not one single behavior indicative of deception." Although Navarro did not specifically address emic or etic perspectives—rather he geared his talk to discussing NVC and empathy—what could be understood is that interpreting meaning requires more than a first glance; it requires situated understandings.

Similarly, Janine Driver's (2019) TEDxDeerPark video, *Reading Body Language*, draws on her experiences as a federal law enforcement agent and trainer to the FBI and CIA to discuss the power of body language. However, unlike Navarro, Driver contended that body language is "everyone's second language" and that people communicate intentionally and unintentionally with eye blocking, shoulder shrugging, and lip locking—or what Driver called, "ESL":

- Eye blocking, or when one's eyes are hidden (e.g., by a hat) or when one speaks with his/her/their eyes closed for an extended period (e.g., 9 seconds), suggests a purposeful removal of stimuli.
- Shoulder shrugging, even if slight, suggests uncertainty.
- Lip locking, or when lips disappear, often suggests that one does not like what one sees or hears.

Drawing on research by university professor Spencer Kelly, Driver addressed "N400," or, what Driver called, a "brain hiccup," wherein the brain realizes that one's body language does not align with the spoken language and, thus, materializes via ESL. Driver contended that ESL helps others to perceive potentially hidden messages, and she urged her audience to "see and code" body language as a way to communicate better with and to understand others.

Resources, such as Navarro's and Driver's TEDx talks, can inspire further exploration and development of methods to (de)code NVC. However, the ideas should be taken up with caution; NVC involves culturally and contextually situated nonvocal behavior that can be intentional or unintentional and draw on a variety of modalities. NVC analysis can and should be methodical and attend to multiple meanings, including those that challenge, clarify, and/or contradict verbal communication.

REFERENCES

Abrams, S. S. (2011). Association through action: Identity development in real and virtual video game environments. *Teachers College Record Yearbook, 110*, 220–243.

Abrams, S. S. (2012). Digital narratives by digital natives: Online inquiry and reflective practices in a third space. In R. W. Blake & B. E. Blake (Eds.), *Becoming a teacher: Using narrative as reflective practice. A cross-disciplinary approach* (pp. 112–133). New York, NY: Peter Lang.

Abrams, S. S. (2013). Peer review and nuanced power structures: Writing and learning within the age of connectivism. *E-Learning and Digital Media, 10*, 395–406. doi:10.2304/elea.2013.10.4.395

Abrams, S. S. (2015). *Integrating virtual and traditional learning in 6–12 classrooms: A layered literacies approach to multimodal meaning making*. New York, NY: Routledge.

Abrams, S. S., & Gerber, H. R. (in press). *Videogames, libraries, and the feedback loop: Learning beyond the stacks*. Bingley, England: Emerald Publishing.

Abrams, S. S., & Lammers, J. C. (2017). Belonging in a videogame space: Bridging affinity spaces and communities of practice. *Teachers College Record, 119*(2), 1–34.

Beach, P., & McConnel, J. (2019). Eye tracking methodology for studying teacher learning: A review of the research. *International Journal of Research & Method in Education, 42*, 485–501. doi:10.1080/1743727X.2018.1496415

Berelson, B. (1952). *Content analysis in communicative research.* New York, NY: Free Press.

Bonoma, T. V., & Felder, L.C. (1977). Nonverbal communication in marketing: Toward a communicational analysis. *Journal of Marketing Research, 14,* 169–180. doi:10.1177/002224377701400204

Bronfenbrenner, U. (1979). *The ecology of human development: Experiments by nature and design.* Cambridge, MA: Harvard University Press.

Burnett, C., & Merchant, G. (2014). Points of view: Reconceptualising literacies through an exploration of adult and child interactions in a virtual world. *Journal of Research in Reading, 37*(1), 36–50. doi:10.1111/jrir.12006

Burnett, C., & Merchant, G. (2020). Literacy-as-event: Accounting for relationality in literacy research. *Discourse: Studies in the Cultural Politics of Education, 41*(1), 45–56. doi:10.1080/01596306.2018.1460318

Byers, V. T. (2019). *Self-perceptions of adjunct faculty about their roles at a select community college system.* Unpublished doctoral dissertation, Sam Houston State University, Huntsville, TX.

Byers, V. T., Smith, R. N., Angrove, K. E., McAlister-Shields, L., & Onwuegbuzie, A. J. (2015). Experiences of select women doctoral students: A feminist standpoint theory perspective. *International Journal of Education, 7*(1), 266–304. Retrieved from www.macrothink.org/journal/index.php/ije/article/view/6982/6070

Connor, N. (2018, May 17). Chinese school uses facial recognition to monitor student attention in class. *The Telegraph.* Retrieved from www.telegraph.co.uk/news/2018/05/17/chinese-school-uses-facial-recognition-monitor-student-attention/

Cook, T. D., & Campbell, D. T. (1979). *Quasi-experimentation. Design and analysis issues for field settings.* Chicago, IL: Rand McNally.

Cope, B., & Kalantzis, M. (2009). Ubiquitous learning: An agenda for educational Transformation. In B. Cope & M. Kalantzis (Eds.), *Ubiquitous learning* (pp. 3–14). Champaign, IL: University of Illinois Press.

Cope, B., & Kalantzis, M. (2013). Towards a new learning: The scholar social knowledge workspace, in theory and practice. *e-Learning and Digital Media, 10,* 332–356. doi:10.2304/elea.2013.10.4.332

Cope, B., & Kalantzis, M. (2020). Meaning without borders: From translanguaging to transposition in the era of digitally-mediated, multimodal meeting. In K. K. Grohmann (Ed.), *Multifaceted multilingualism.* Amsterdam, NL: John Benjamins.

Creamer, E. G. (2018). *An introduction to fully integrated mixed methods research.* Thousand Oaks, CA: Sage.

Denham, M. A., & Onwuegbuzie, A. J. (2013). Beyond words: Using nonverbal communication data in research to enhance thick description and interpretation. *International Journal of Qualitative Methods, 12,* 670–696. doi:10.1177/160940691301200137

Driver, J. (2019, Sept. 13). Reading body language. *TEDxDeerPark.* Retrieved from www.youtube.com/watch?v=lvxJoUuG018

Ekman P. (1999). Basic emotions. In T. Dalgleish & M. Power (Eds.), *Handbook of cognition and emotion* (pp. 45–60). Sussex, England: John Wiley & Sons, Ltd.

Fetters, M. D., Curry, L. A., & Creswell, J. W. (2013). Achieving integration in mixed methods designs: Principles and practices. *Health Services Research, 48*(6 Pt 2), 2134–2156. doi:10.1111/1475-6773.12117

Foucault, M. (1977). *Discipline and punish: The birth of the prison.* (A. Sheridan, Trans.). New York, NY: Pantheon.

Foucault, M. (1980). *Power/knowledge: Selected interview and other writings 1972–1977.* (C. Gordon, Ed., C. Gordon, L. Marshall, J. Mepham, & K. Soper, Trans.). New York, NY: Pantheon Books.

Fontana, A., & Frey, J. H. (2005). The interview: From neutral stance to political involvement. In N. K. Denzin & Y. S. Lincoln (Eds.), *The Sage handbook of qualitative research* (2nd ed., pp. 695–727). Thousand Oaks, CA: Sage.

Franco, C. L., & Fugate, J. M. B. (2020). Emoji face renderings: Exploring the role emoji platform differences have on emotional interpretation. *Journal of Nonverbal Behavior, 44,* 301–328. doi:10.1007/s10919-019-00330-1

Gee, J. P. (1989). Literacy, discourse, and linguistics: Introduction. *Journal of Education, 171*(1), 5–17. doi:10.1177/002205748917100101

Gee, J. P. (1996). *Social linguistics and literacies: Ideology in discourses* (2nd ed.). London, England: Taylor & Francis.

Gee, J. P. (2001). Reading as situated language: A sociocognitive perspective. *Journal of Adolescent & Adult Literacy, 44,* 714–725. doi:10.1598/JAAL.44.8.3

Gee, J. P. (2003/2007). *What video games have to teach us about learning and literacy.* New York, NY: Palgrave McMillan.

Geertz, C. (1973). Thick description toward an interpretive theory of culture. In C. Geertz (Ed.), *The interpretation of cultures* (pp. 3–30). New York, NY: Basic Books.

Gerber, H. R., Abrams, S. S., Curwood, J. S., & Magnifico, A. (2016). *Conducting qualitative research of learning in online spaces.* Thousand Oaks, CA: Sage.

Gerber, H. G., Lynch, T. L., & Onwuegbuzie, A. J. (in press). *Making big data small: Designing integrated digital approaches for social science research.* Thousand Oaks, CA: Sage.

Goffman, E. (1959). *The presentation of self in everyday life.* Garden City, NY: Doubleday.

Greene, J. C., Caracelli, V. J., & Graham, W. F. (1989). Toward a conceptual framework for mixed-method evaluation designs. *Educational Evaluation and Policy Analysis, 11,* 255–274. doi:10.3102/01623737011003255

Grimes, S. M., & Fields, D. A. (2012). *Kids online: A new research agenda for understanding social networking forums.* New York, NY: The Joan Ganz Cooney Center. Retrieved from https://joanganzcooneycenter.org/publication/kids-online-a-new-research-agenda-for-understanding-social-networking-forums/

Guetterman, T. C., Fetters, M. D., & Creswell, J. W. (2015). Integrating quantitative and qualitative results in health science mixed methods research through joint displays. *Annals of Family Medicine, 13,* 554–561. doi:10.1370/afm.1865

Harré, R., & van Langenhove, L. (1999). *Positioning theory.* Oxford, England: Blackwell.

Heath, S. B. (1983). *Ways with words: Language, life and work in communities and schools.* New York, NY: Cambridge.

Hiller, J. H., Fisher, G. A., & Kaess, W. A. (1969). A computer investigation of verbal characteristics of effective classroom lecturing. *American Educational Research Journal, 6,* 661–675. doi:10.3102/00028312006004661

Hitchcock, J. H., & Onwuegbuzie, A. J. (2020). Developing mixed methods crossover analysis approaches. *Journal of Mixed Methods Research, 14*, 63–83. doi:10.1177/1558689819841782

Holmes, L. (2013). Competing perspectives on graduate employability: Possession, position or process? *Studies in Higher Education, 38*, 538–554. doi:10.1080/03075079.2011.587140

International League of Polygraph Examiners. (2020). Polygraph/lie detector FAQs. Retrieved from www.theilpe.com/faq_eng.html

Jansen, M. Giebels, E., van Rompay, T. J. L., & Junger, M. (2018). The influence of the presentation of camera surveillance on cheating and pro-social behavior. *Frontiers in Psychology, 9*, 1937. doi:10.3389/fpsyg.2018.01937

Jewitt, C. (2013). *The Routledge handbook of multimodal analysis* (2nd ed.). Abingdon, England: Routledge.

Johnson, R. B., & Christensen, L. (2020). *Educational research: Quantitative, qualitative, and mixed approaches* (7th ed.). Thousand Oaks, CA: Sage.

Johnson, R. E., Grove, A. L., & Clarke, A. (2019). Pillar Integration Process: A joint display technique to integrate data in mixed methods research. *Journal of Mixed Methods Research, 13*, 301–320. doi:10.1177/1558689817743108

Journal of Nonverbal Behavior. (2020). Home page. Retrieved from www.springer.com/journal/10919

Kim, C. S., & Aggarwal, P. (2016). The customer is king: Culture-based unintended consequences of modern marketing. *Journal of Consumer Marketing, 33*, 193–201. doi:10.1108/JCM-01-2015-1273

Krauss, R. M., Chen, Y., & Chawla, P. (1996). Nonverbal behavior and nonverbal communication: What do conversational hand gestures tell us? In M. Zanna (Ed.), *Advances in experimental and social psychology* (pp. 389–450). San Diego, CA: Academic Press.

Kress, G. (2010). *Multimodality: A social semiotic approach to contemporary communication.* New York, NY: Routledge.

Leech, N. L., & Onwuegbuzie, A. J. (2010). *Qualitative data analysis: A step-by-step approach.* Unpublished book, Sam Houston State University, Huntsville, TX.

Lincoln, Y. S., & Guba, E. G. (1985). *Naturalistic inquiry.* Beverly Hills, CA: Sage.

Lui, D., Kafai, Y., Litts, B., Walker, J., & Widman, S. (2020). Pair physical computing: High school students' practices and perceptions of collaborative coding and crafting with electronic textiles. *Computer Science Education, 30*(1), 72–101. doi:jerome.stjohns.edu/10.1080/08993408.2019.1682378

Mazzei, L. A. (2008). Silence speaks: Whiteness revealed in the absence of voice. *Teaching and Teacher Education: An International Journal of Research and Studies, 24*, 1125–1136. doi:10.1016/j.tate.2007.02.009

McCreery, M., Krach, S. K., Schrader, P. G., & Boone, R. (2012). Defining the virtual self: Personality, behavior, and the psychology of embodiment. *Computers in Human Behavior, 28*, 976–983. doi:10.1016/j.chb.2011.12.019

McNeill, D. (1992). *Hand and mind.* Chicago, IL: Chicago University Press.

Merchant, G. (2010). 3D virtual worlds as environments for literacy learning. *Educational Research, 52*, 135–150. doi:10.1080/00131881.2010.482739

Merriam-Webster. (2020). *Verbal.* Retrieved from www.merriam-webster.com/dictionary/verbal

Michailidis, G. (2007). Correspondence analysis. In N. J. Salkind (Ed.), *Encyclopedia of measurement and statistics* (pp. 191–194). Thousand Oaks, Sage.

Miles, M., & Huberman, A. M. (1994). *Qualitative data analysis: An expanded sourcebook* (2nd ed.). Thousand Oaks, CA: Sage.

Navarro, J. (2020, March 31). The power of nonverbal communication. *TEDxManchester.* Retrieved from www.youtube.com/watch?v=fLaslONQAKM

New London Group. (1996). A pedagogy of multiliteracies: Designing social futures. *Harvard Educational Review, 66*(1), 60–92. doi:10.17763/haer.66.1.17370n67v22j160u

New South Wales Government. (2009). Lie Detectors Act 1983 No 62. Retrieved from www.legislation.nsw.gov.au/#/view/act/1983/62

Norris, S. (2019). *Systematically working with multimodal data: Research methods in multimodal discourse analysis.* Hoboken, NJ: John Wiley & Sons, Inc.

Onwuegbuzie, A. J. (2003a). Effect sizes in qualitative research: A prolegomenon. *Quality & Quantity: International Journal of Methodology, 37*, 393–409. doi:10.1023/A:1027379223537

Onwuegbuzie, A. J. (2003b). Expanding the framework of internal and external validity in quantitative research. *Research in the Schools, 10*(1), 71–90.

Onwuegbuzie, A. J. (2012). Introduction: Putting the mixed back into quantitative and qualitative research in educational research and beyond: Moving towards the radical middle. *International Journal of Multiple Research Approaches, 6*, 192–219. doi:10.5172/mra.2012.6.3.192

Onwuegbuzie, A. J., & Abrams, S. S. (in press). *An integrated mixed methods approach to nonverbal communication data: A practical guide to collection and analysis in online and offline spaces.* New York, NY: Routledge.

Onwuegbuzie, A. J., & Abrams, S. S. (2020). *Dimensions of the nonverbal communication analysis.* Unpublished manuscript. Plano, TX: Dialogic R & D.

Onwuegbuzie, A. J., & Byers, V. T. (2014). An exemplar for combining the collection, analysis, and interpretations of verbal and nonverbal data in qualitative research. *International Journal of Education, 4*(1), 183–246. doi:10.5296/ije.v6i1.4399

Onwuegbuzie, A. J., & Combs, J. P. (2010). Emergent data analysis techniques in mixed methods research: A synthesis. In A. Tashakkori & C. Teddlie (Eds.), *Handbook of mixed methods in social and behavioral research* (2nd ed., pp. 397–430). Thousand Oaks, CA: Sage.

Onwuegbuzie, A. J., & Denham, M. A. (2014). Qualitative data analysis techniques. In L. Meyer (Ed.), *Oxford Bibliographies in education.* Oxford, England: Oxford University Press. Retrieved from www.oxfordbibliographies.com/view/document/obo-9780199756810/obo-9780199756810-0078.xml

Onwuegbuzie, A. J., & Dickinson, W. B. (2008). Mixed methods analysis and information visualization: Graphical display for effective communication of research results. *The Qualitative Report, 13*, 204–225. Retrieved from www.nova.edu/ssss/QR/QR13–2/onwuegbuzie.pdf

Onwuegbuzie, A. J., Dickinson, W. B., Leech, N. L., & Zoran, A. G. (2010). Toward more rigor in focus group research in stress and coping and beyond: A new mixed research framework for collecting and analyzing focus group data. In G. S. Gates, W. H. Gmelch, & M. Wolverton (Series Eds.) & K.M.T. Collins, A. J. Onwuegbuzie, & Q. G. Jiao (Vol. Eds.), *Toward a broader understanding of stress and coping:*

Mixed methods approaches (pp. 243–285). The Research on Stress and Coping in Education Series (Vol. 5). Charlotte, NC: Information Age Publishing.

Onwuegbuzie, A. J., Gerber, H. R., & Abrams, S. S. (2017). Mixed methods research. *The International Encyclopedia of Communication Research Methods*, 1–33. doi:10.1002/9781118901731.iecrm0156

Onwuegbuzie, A. J., & Johnson, R. B. (2006). The validity issue in mixed research. *Research in the Schools*, *13*(1), 48–63.

Onwuegbuzie, A. J., Johnson, R. B., & Collins, K. M. T. (2009). A call for mixed analysis: A philosophical framework for combining qualitative and quantitative. *International Journal of Multiple Research Methods*, *3*, 114–139. doi:10.5172/mra.3.2.114

Onwuegbuzie, A. J., & Leech, N. L. (2007). Validity and qualitative research: An oxymoron? *Quality & Quantity: International Journal of Methodology*, *41*, 233–249. doi:10.1007/s11135–006–9000–3

Onwuegbuzie, A. J., & Leech, N. L. (2019). On qualitizing. *International Journal of Multiple Research Approaches*, *11*, 98–131. doi:10.29034/ijmra.v11n2editorial2

Onwuegbuzie, A. J., & Teddlie, C. (2003). A framework for analyzing data in mixed methods research. In A. Tashakkori & C. Teddlie (Eds.), *Handbook of mixed methods in social and behavioral research* (pp. 351–383). Thousand Oaks, CA: Sage.

Picó, A., Gračanin, A., Gadea, M., Boeren, A., Aliño, & Vingerhoets, A. (2020). How visible tears affect observers' judgements and behavioral intentions: Sincerity, remorse, and punishment. *Journal of Nonverbal Behavior*, *44*, 215–232. doi:10.1007/s10919–019–00328–9

Provalis Research. (2011). *WordStat 6.0. User's guide*. Montreal, QC, Canada: Author.

Ragin, C. C. (1987). *The comparative method: Moving beyond qualitative and quantitative strategies*. Berkeley, CA: University of California Press.

Ragin, C. C. (1989). The logic of the comparative method and the algebra of logic. *Journal of Quantitative Anthropology*, *1*, 373–398.

Ragin, C. C. (1994). Introduction to qualitative comparative analysis. In T. Janoski & A. M. Hicks (Eds.), *The comparative political economy of the Welfare State: New methodologies and approaches* (pp. 299–319). New York, NY: Cambridge University Press.

Ragin, C. C. (2008). *Redesigning social inquiry: Fuzzy sets and beyond*. Chicago, IL: The University of Chicago Press.

Rawlings, A. (2018, December). Why emoji mean different things in different cultures. *BBC*. Retrieved from www.bbc.com/future/article/20181211-why-emoji-mean-different-things-in-different-cultures

Reusch, J., & Kees, W. (1956). *Nonverbal communication: Notes on the visual perception of human relations*. Berkeley, CA: University of California Press.

Rowsell, J. (2013). *Working with multimodality: Rethinking literacy in a digital age*. Oxon, England: Routledge.

Ryle, G. (1949). *Concept of the mind*. London, England: Hutchinson and Company.

Ryle, G. (1971). *Collected papers. Volume II collected essays, 1929–1968*. London, England: Hutchinson.

Sacks, H., Schegloff, E. A., & Jefferson, G. (1974). A simple systematics for the organization of turn-taking for conversation. *Language*, *50*, 696–735. doi:10.1353/lan.1974.0010

Saldaña, J. (2016). *The coding manual for qualitative researchers* (3rd ed.). London, England: Sage.

Sandelowski, M., Voils, C. I., & Knafl, G. (2009). On quantitizing. *Journal of Mixed Methods Research*, *3*, 208–222. doi:10.1177/1558689809334210

Sharma, K., Giannakos, M., & Dillenbourg, P. (2020). Eye-tracking and artificial intelligence to enhance motivation and learning. *Smart Learning Environments*, *7*(13). doi:10.1186/s40561-020-00122-x

Smith, M. L. (1997). Mixing and matching: Methods and models. In J. C. Greene & V. J. Caracelli (Eds.), *Advances in mixed-method evaluation: The challenges and benefits of integrating diverse paradigms* (New Directions for Evaluation No. 74, pp. 73–85). San Francisco, CA: Jossey-Bass.

Soja, E. W. (1996). *Thirdspace: Journeys to Los Angeles and other real-and-imagined places*. Malden, MA: Blackwell.

Street, B. V. (1984). *Literacy in theory and practice*. Cambridge, England: Cambridge University Press.

Street, B. V. (1995). *Social literacies: Critical approaches to literacy in development, ethnography, and education*. New York, NY: Longman.

Tashakkori, A., & Teddlie, C. (1998). *Mixed methodology: Combining qualitative and quantitative approaches*. Applied Social Research Methods Series (Vol. 46). Thousand Oaks, CA: Sage.

Turner, K. H., Abrams, S. S., Katic, E., & Donavan, M. J. (2014). Demystifying digitalk: The what and why of the language teens use in digital writing. *Journal of Literacy Research*, *46*, 157–193. doi:10.1177/1086296X14534061

Van Rompay T. J., Vonk D. J., Fransen M. L. (2009). The eye of the camera: Effects of security cameras on pro-social behavior. *Environment and Behavior*, *41*(1), 60–74. doi:10.1177/0013916507309996

Walsh, M., & Simpson, A. (2013). Touching, tapping…thinking? Examining the dynamic materiality of touch pad devices for literacy learning. *Australian Journal of Language and Literacy*, *36*, 148–157.

Ware, P. D. (2006). From sharing time to showtime! Valuing diverse venues for storytelling in technology-rich classrooms. *Language Arts*, *84*(1), 45–54.

Watzlawick, P., Bavelas, J. B., & Jackson, D. D. (1967). *Pragmatics of human communication: A study of interactional patterns, pathologies, and paradoxes*. New York, NY: Norton.

YouTube for Press. (n.d.). *YouTubeAbout*. Retrieved from www.youtube.com/about/press/

23

Development of a Joint Display as a Mixed Analysis

Michael D. Fetters and Timothy C. Guetterman

Acknowledgement

The empirical study presented here to depict joint display analysis is based on the Adaptive Designs Accelerating Promising Trials Into Treatments (ADAPT-IT) funded as U01NS073476 from the U.S. National Institutes of Health Common Fund.

1 Definition of Joint Display Development as Mixed Analysis

Fetters, Curry, and Creswell (2013) define a joint display as a way to, "integrate the data by bringing the data together through a visual means to draw out new insights beyond the information gained from the separate quantitative and qualitative results (p. 10)." Guetterman, Fetters, and Creswell (2015) have previously depicted various forms of joint displays based on a review of health-related joint displays by searching in the *Annals of Family Medicine,* the *Journal of Mixed Methods Research,* and the *International Journal of Multiple Research Approaches,* three journals known for a high impact factor and for publishing both empirical and methodological mixed methods articles, and Plano Clark and Sanders (2015) examined how joint displays were used to represent integration in published mixed methods research. Guetterman, Creswell, and Kuckartz (2015) took a further step by explaining steps for how to represent a joint display using software and linking joint displays to mixed methods designs. Johnson, Grove, and Clarke (2017) presented a four-step procedure for creating a joint display that they call the pillar integration process. Fetters developed detailed procedures to guide researchers through the steps involved in creating a joint display using mixed data analysis (2020, pp. 199–207). Johnson and Christensen (2020) have also addressed joint display analytical procedures and constructing a joint display for mixed data analysis (pp. 565–567).

The joint display is certainly recognized for its broad utility and flexibility in providing an interpretation of mixed methods findings (Bradt et al., 2015; Bustamante, 2017; Peroff, Morais, Seekamp, Sills & Wallace, 2019). Despite this previous literature on joint display structure and innovative presentations, little has been published that demonstrates in detail through the use of actual iterations of multiple draft versions how the creation of a joint display also represents a process of analysis.

Definition of Joint Display for Mixed Analysis

Fetters defined joint display analysis as, "the process of discovering linkages between the qualitative and quantitative constructs, organizing and reorganizing the findings into a matrix or figure to optimize the presentation as a finalized joint display" (2020, p. 194). For the purposes of this chapter, we define mixed methods joint display analysis as:

> the *process* of studying, examining, or investigating how to bring together or link qualitative and quantitative data in one or a series of visual representations with the intent of 1) identifying commonality between the two types of data, and 2) gaining a more robust understanding of what both types of data mean together by drawing conclusions or meta inferences based on combined findings.

In this definition, the emphasis is on the process of developing the visual display where both forms of data or results are presented and interpreted together, and not just an approach for presenting the results. Rather, joint display analysis is an interpretive process that leads to a better understanding of mixed data.

2 When Use of Joint Display Development as Mixed Analysis is Appropriate in Mixed Analysis

Researchers, evaluators, and practitioners who are using mixed methods research will virtually all find opportunities or occasions for creating joint displays as an approach to analysis of mixed data. A prerequisite is having both qualitative and quantitative data that are appropriate for merging in the analysis. At minimum, this requires that there be some commonality of one or more domains between the two types of data, or some level of linkages between the constructs from the quantitative findings and the themes from qualitative findings. Joint displays as mixed analysis can be used in a convergent mixed methods design for comparing the qualitative and quantitative data about a similar phenomenon. For example, Bradt et al. (2015) conducted a randomized crossover trial comparing music therapy and music medicine interventions to improve pain associated with cancer. They used a joint display to compare qualitative and quantitative results for differential benefits (e.g., improvement with both interventions, better with one but worse with the other, and worse with both). Similarly, the process can be used in an exploratory sequential mixed methods design when initial qualitative data are used to build or inform subsequent quantitative data collection, and then the results brought together using a joint display for mixed analysis. In an explanatory sequential mixed methods design involving initial quantitative data collection used to inform development of follow-up qualitative data collection, the process of combining the results of both can be achieved using joint display mixed analysis.

3 Technical Outline of Joint Display Development for Mixed Analysis

Fourteen considerations in the construction of a joint display for mixed methods data analysis are presented in Table 23.1.

These considerations are intended to help guide any researcher, evaluator, or practitioner who seeks to develop and potentially use a joint display as a final product.

1. Think creatively to build and expand upon other data combining strategies, such as merging. When creating a joint display there is an opportunity to creatively build upon good representation principles (e.g., think about what to communicate, avoid extraneous information, use space efficiently), but not be limited by notions about how tables and figures can be constructed. A key principle is to consider how the development approach is a process for better understanding the data. When building a display, it is helpful to consider some fundamental ideas for the audience. How can a joint display help convey what is intended? What type of organization would help the researcher, evaluator, practitioner, and ultimately the reader, better understand the data? How much detail is enough, but not too much? What type of information, such as text, statistical reporting, graphs, images would be most helpful?
2. Conduct rigorous intra-method analysis. This refers to analyzing independently the quantitative and qualitative data using rigorous procedures of the respective methodological approaches. While recognizing that intra-method analysis is critical, the iterative data collection and analysis of qualitative methods may help inform analysis of the quantitative data. When doing so, caution must be exercised to not let the knowledge of the emerging qualitative findings threaten the validity of the quantitative findings if knowledge of the qualitative findings by the investigator could threaten the validity when interpreting the quantitative findings. That is, in some circumstances, mixed methods researchers are required to meet criteria of intra-method analysis adherence. The only example of this to our knowledge is the requirement for strict adherence in a quantitative analysis where concern could arise relative to introduction of bias in the interpretation of quantitative data when the analysis calls for blinding of the investigators during the interpretation of the results.
3. Develop a data sources table. A data sources table is a deceivingly simple approach for beginning the process of identifying linkages. In workshops, we often recommend developing a section of the data sources table with quantitative data and a section with qualitative data. In its simplest form, one can include headings such as purpose, data source (e.g., focus groups or attitudinal survey), description (e.g., who, how many), and outcomes (product from the procedure). An example from the index study is provided below in Section 5, Table 23.2.
4. Become fully familiar with the results of both types of data. In the development of the joint display as analysis, the researcher, evaluator, or practitioner must become deeply aware and engaged with both types of findings: the qualitative and the quantitative. By re-considering the organization of each type of data, patterns for linkages may become more obvious.
5. Identify commonality of constructs and themes across the two types of data. Previous scholars have identified various metaphors and rubrics for guiding researchers, evaluators and practitioners to identify

TABLE 23.1

Checkbox of Considerations When Constructing a Joint Display for Mixed Data Analysis

---
1) Think creatively to build and expand upon other data combining strategies
2) Conduct rigorous intra-method analysis
3) Develop a data sources table
4) Become fully familiar with the results of both types of data
5) Identify commonality of constructs and themes across the two types of data
6) Identify a logical framework for organizing the two types together
7) Develop a preliminary display using the organizing framework chosen
8) Iteratively consider the most effective way of presenting each type of data together based on how the data appear together in the display
9) While building the display, consider not only the appearance but the implications of the findings
10) Consider adding color, grayscale, lines, overlap of symbols/shapes or some other mechanism to link information
11) Consider options for data transformation, including intra-method transformation and cross method data transformation
12) Consider if you have multiple joint displays whether you can could create an effective meta-joint display figure
13) Consider the extent the display will appeal to and be easily understood by the intended audience
14) Consider again the implications of the two types of data
---

commonality between constructs of the quantitative data and themes of the qualitative data. For example, Fetters and Molina-Azorin (2017) describe spiraling as a guide for identifying potential commonality between quantitative and qualitative data. The spiraling metaphor is useful for conveying the intellectual process characterized as a "widely circling spiral with progressively a smaller diameter until the apex at the bottom identifies a merged interpretation" (p. 301). In doing so, the researcher, evaluator, or practitioner considers both types of findings from intra-method analyses, seeking to iteratively identify related findings, and honing in on common topics, areas, or ideas for comparison. Moran-Ellis et al. (2006) describe following a thread back and forth between the qualitative and quantitative data. By doing so, one can find key themes or questions from both components. Bazeley and Kemp (2012) describe looking back and forth at the quantitative and qualitative data. By doing so, the researcher, evaluator, or practitioner can and iteratively relate the data and merge the data according to related findings.

6. Identify a logical framework for organizing the two types together. This consideration requires the researcher, evaluator, or practitioner to find a framework that can serve as an anchor for linking the data together. Starting with the data that were collected first is one logical way to start, especially when the project uses a sequential design. If using a particular scale or research instrument, the ordering of the scales or the items in the scale may provide a logical framework for considering *both* types of data. In contrast, a study theory and the elements of the theory might provide mutually related domains that can provide a structure (Bustamante, 2017). The major themes from a qualitative coding scheme may also provide an organizing framework for organizing the two types of data together.

7. Develop a preliminary joint display using the organizing framework chosen. For this step, the researcher, evaluator, or practitioner makes a first attempt to bring both forms of data together. We advise creating a table with sufficient columns and rows to create placeholders for both quantitative and qualitative data. Although we do not distinguish when to use rows versus columns, we suggest carefully thinking about what each will represent. One option is to have a column with quantitative results, a column with qualitative results, and a column devoted to metainferences or integrated results. Rows may consist of domains common to both forms of inquiry. Alternatively, rows could represent qualitative results, and columns quantitative results, or vice versa, with integrated results in each cell. We offer these uses of rows and columns merely as examples and suggest creativity while iteratively developing a joint display. In the process of seeing the data together for the first time, the process of analysis is further enhanced by thinking about the two types of data to be merged. One might consider Johnson, Grove, and Clarke's (2017) approach of using a "pillar integration process," four-stage technique for integrating and presenting qualitative and quantitative findings in a joint display. This procedure may help connect the constructs and themes (see step 6).

8. Iteratively consider the most effective way of presenting each type of data together based on how the data appear together in the display. This requires considering and assessing the effectiveness of the format for linking quantitative and qualitative data "pairings." More often than not, a researcher, evaluator, or practitioner will want to reconsider the structure of the joint display. See for example the process outlined in Section 5. Has the preliminary framework provided a robust structure for linking the quantitative and qualitative data together? Are the concepts most effectively organized for telling a mixed methods story? How can the data be reorganized to emphasize more findings previously not seen or not emphasized?

9. While building the display, consider not only the appearance but also the implications of the findings. One way to document implications is by writing memos. Memos are helpful in constructing interpretations and explanations of the data overtime to inform your mixed analysis. The analyst will want to iterate between the organizing framework and iterative development of the joint display. While building, deconstructing and reconstructing, consider the extent novel implications are possible?

10. Consider adding color, lines, overlap of symbols/ shapes, or some other mechanism to link information. Online publication makes it possible to add color into representations that may not be possible in print or may be expensive to reproduce. Animation could also be considered for showing changes or meanings. In static drawings, the additions of lines and arrows, visual figures, or emblems could be employed. For presentation in traditional print media without an option for color, consider how to use grayscale.

11. Consider options for data transformation, including intra-method transformation (e.g., quantitative scales represented as box plots) and cross-method data transformation (e.g., qualitative data transformed to quantitative format). There are many options for presenting data. Rather than presenting numerical values, one could transform quantitative data into an alternative format (e.g., using a scatter plot, bar graphs, box plots, etc.). Similarly, could the qualitative data be represented using a figure or conceptual model that would be compared to a quantitatively tested model? Howell Smith et al. (2019) included a joint display that showed how a grounded theory model evolved after quantitative testing.

12. Consider if multiple joint displays are needed, and whether a meta-joint display should be created. A meta-joint display is the linking of two or more joint

displays into a single figure. If a researcher has multiple joint displays, publishing can often be difficult due to restrictions on the number of tables and figures in article. For example, in many social science journals, tables and figures are part of the word count, and in health sciences journals the number is often restricted to five tables and figures total. If there is an option for creating a meta-joint display, efficiency may be possible (see Section 6, Figure 23.9).

13. Consider the extent to which the display will appeal to and be easily understood by the intended audience. Consider the whether the joint display stands on its own within the article. Can a reader completely understand how the quantitative and qualitative data are interrelated? Has adequate labeling been added? For example, rows and columns might be labeled as qualitative themes, quantitative results, or metainferences.

14. Consider again the implications of the two types of data. As a final step, consider the broader inferences and implications in order to develop an interpretation of the analysis. What conclusions can be drawn by considering the fit of both types of data together? That is, what are the metainferences resulting from the integration? Do the two types of related data confirm (tell the same story), complement (tell different, non-conflicting stories), expand (tell broader but overlapping stories), or conflict, discordance, or different perspectives (Fetters & Molina-Azorin, 2017)? Are additional analyses needed to provide clarifications?

Overview of the Study Used to Illustrate Joint Display Development as Mixed Data Analysis

The empirical demonstration of joint display analysis derives from the "Adaptive Designs Accelerating Promising Trials into Treatments (ADAPT-IT)" project. The U.S. National Institutes of Health Common Fund funded this project. This study relates to the recent development of adaptive clinical trials as innovative alternatives with potential benefits and efficiencies compared to traditional randomized controlled trials. The randomized controlled trial is considered by many trialists to be gold standard of evidence for health services research. Adaptive clinical trials use Bayesian and statistical simulation techniques to predict potential outcomes during a trial, and investigators can use that data to make adjustments, such as dropping an underperforming arm or reallocating target enrollment for each arm. An adaptive clinical trial has the potential to prevent continuing a lengthy and costly treatment arm that will most likely be ineffective, based on projections. Controversy about adaptive clinical trials among trialists regards their statistical and ethical assumptions, potential scientific benefits, and internal validity. The ADAPT-IT Project objective was to illustrate and explore how best to use adaptive clinical trial designs to improve the evaluation of drugs and medical devices, and to use mixed methods to characterize and understand the beliefs, opinions, and concerns of key stakeholders during and after the development process (Meurer et al., 2012).

Fundamentally, the research team was charged with two primary tasks. The first was the design of four clinical trials—due to significant interest, this was expanded to five trials. The topics addressed included these serious acute conditions: refractory status epilepticus, glycemic control in stroke, spinal cord trauma, post cardiac arrest treatment with hypothermia, and progesterone for ischemic and hemorrhagic stroke. Second, on the grant, the team was charged with evaluating the process of adaptive trial development. They conducted this evaluation of the process using surveys, focus groups, observations, and key stakeholder interviews through thematic analyses. The laboratory for these trials was the national Neurological Emergency Treatment Trials (NETT) group. NETT was funded by the National Institutes of Neurological Disorders and Stroke institute. All projects focused on high stakes diseases with the idea that treatment should start in the ambulance or emergency department. It was an open network, and the first trial in NETT finished early. Having assembled various researchers and stake holders in the ADAPT-IT process, the mixed methods evaluation aim of the project was to study the collaborative process using mixed methods. Figure 23.1 provides a procedural diagram of the convergent mixed methods design used for the mixed methods evaluation.

Participants

Four groups of stakeholders involved in adaptive clinical trials participated in the study. The groups were consultant statisticians, network statisticians, clinicians, and other key stakeholders. Consultant statisticians were specialists in adaptive designs. Network statisticians were traditional academic biostatisticians. Clinicians included individuals primarily involved in providing patient care. Finally, other stakeholders consisted of representatives of the Food and Drug Administration and National Institutes of Health, institutional review board members, and patient advocates.

Data Collection

As illustrated in Figure 23.2, the data were collected using a visual analog scale (only three questions represented) that resulted in quantitative data that we used to calculate a score of 0–100. Figure 23.2 further illustrates the open-ended questions that were used to supplement the mini-focus groups.

The data sources for this study are illustrated in Table 23.2. This table describes the pre-meeting survey with visual analog scales, qualitative short answer fields and demographics, as well as five mini-focus groups also conducted at the pre-meeting.

Intra-method Quantitative Data Analysis

The initial quantitative data analysis focused on descriptive statistics; hence, the calculation of mean scores and standard deviations on the visual analog scales, and comparisons of the four groups (consultant statisticians, network statisticians, clinicians, and other key stakeholders).

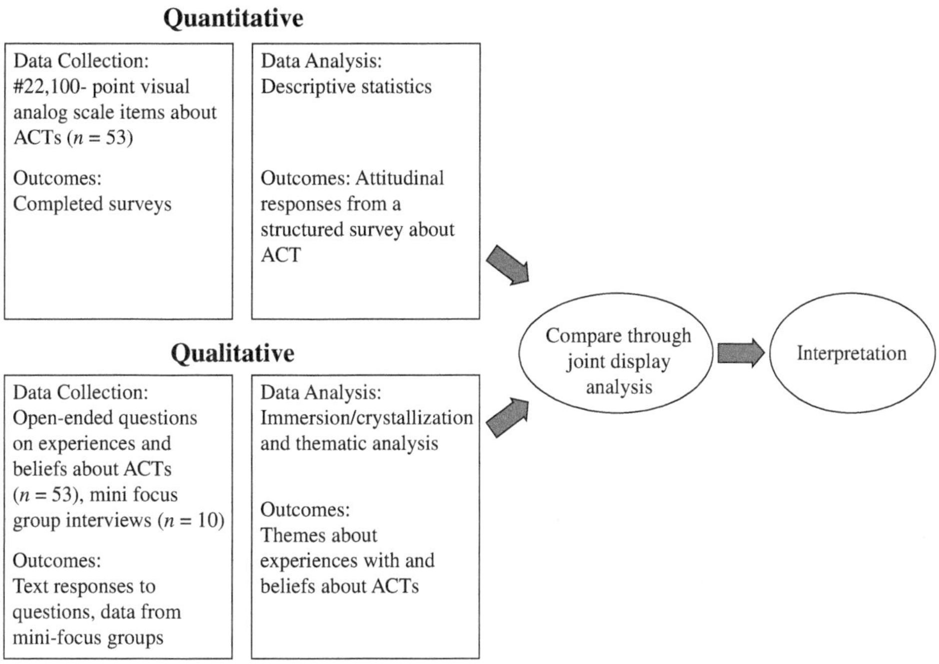

Development of a Joint Display as a Mixed Analysis

Quantitative

Data Collection:
#22,100- point visual analog scale items about ACTs (*n* = 53)

Outcomes:
Completed surveys

Data Analysis:
Descriptive statistics

Outcomes: Attitudinal responses from a structured survey about ACT

Qualitative

Data Collection:
Open-ended questions on experiences and beliefs about ACTs (*n* = 53), mini focus group interviews (*n* = 10)

Outcomes:
Text responses to questions, data from mini-focus groups

Data Analysis:
Immersion/crystallization and thematic analysis

Outcomes:
Themes about experiences with and beliefs about ACTs

→ Compare through joint display analysis → Interpretation

FIGURE 23.1 Procedural diagram of the convergent mixed methods design of the ADAPT-IT project.

---

14) Adaptive clinical trial designs pose ethical **disadvantages** from the **patient** perspective.

| Definitely Not | Probably Not | Possibly | Probably | Definitely |

Why?_____

_____

15) Adaptive clinical trial designs pose ethical **advantages** from the **researchers'** perspective.

| Definitely Not | Probably Not | Possibly | Probably | Definitely |

Why?_____

_____

16) Adaptive clinical trial designs pose ethical **disadvantages** from the **researchers'** perspective.

| Definitely Not | Probably Not | Possibly | Probably | Definitely |

Why?_____

_____

FIGURE 23.2 Excerpt from the ADAPT-IT project illustrating the visual analog scales and open-ended qualitative question prompts.

TABLE 23.2
Purpose, Data Sources, Description of the Source, and Outcome of Data Collection.

Purpose	Data Sources	Description	Outcomes
To understand concerns and strategies of personnel participating in face-to-face meetings, prior to design activities	Pre-meeting survey attitudes about traditional trials and adaptive clinical trials (*n* = 25)	• Survey instrument with 21 questions using quantitative visual analog scales • Qualitative short answer fields • Demographics questions	Assess attitudes about adaptive clinical trials and traditional clinical trials in a BASELINE assessment
	Mini-focus groups: Group 1 *n* = 4, Group 2 *n* = 4, Group 3 *n* = 6, Group 4 *n* = 4, Group 5 *n* = 4	• Transcripts of mini-focus groups • Observations by focus group facilitators	Details regarding experiences and beliefs about adaptive clinical trials and traditional designs

Table A. Design team assessments about ethical issues for patients in adaptive clinical trials

Theme N = 53	VAS Mean (SD)	NETT Statisticians n = 5	Consultant Statisticians n = 6	Clinicians n = 19	Other Participants n = 22 (FDA, NIH, etc.)
Patient perspectives-advantages (Q#13)	65.2 (24.9)	37.2 (18.0)	89.1 (10.6)	67.4 (24.1)	72.6 (15.3)
• When done well they treat patients in and out of the trial better • Faster, better, more efficient, less chance of going to worse group as trial goes on • It depends on the design, but for example response adaptive it may be more advantageous to have higher probability of being randomized to active arm. • It's really better for everybody if you're adaptively making decisions and it's leading you to the best treatment it's better for the patients in the trial. (Consult Stat MFG) • I think it's a false concern. When you do studies that people have consented for traditional clinical trials, they have-there was a tremendous rate of what's called the therapeutic misconception, which they think, contrary to the Belmont Report that actually the reason they're in the-the purpose of the trial is to improve their individual outcome, and the number who in any kind of quantitative way understand the randomization is very low. (Consult Stat MFG) • People (patients) would understand that we stacked this in their favor. We're trying to make this in your favor, so it's not a coin-tossing thing. So, you're right. It's how you – it's semantics, right? (Clin MFG) • Main ethical advantage is that you potentially reduce the number of patients who get the ineffective drug and that actually is a plus. (Clin MFG)					
Patient perspectives-disadvantages (Q#14)	37.3 (23.0)	71.6 (16.4)	18.1 (11.1)	39.2 (19.6)	40.7 (22.4)
• If enrolled in first part of trial, more likely to be randomized when little is known • Only if they reject treatments too early • I can only see it would the process unblended • It may be clear that one treatment group is looking to be more effective, but they don't have enough patients in one of the other cells, as many as they would like to have, and so some of the patients may get assigned to that other cell, because they need more patients in the cell, even though it doesn't look like that cell is the more effective cell. (Clin MFG)					

FIGURE 23.3 First draft of the ADAPT-IT joint display format comparing qualitative themes with quantitative attitudinal survey results by question.

Intra-method Qualitative Data Analysis

The initial qualitative analysis involved immersion in the data, development of a coding scheme, thematic analysis using a coding scheme matched to the major constructs in the attitudinal survey, identification of emerging themes, and thematic searches for related data. We then made comparisons across the four groups of participants (i.e., consultant statisticians, network statisticians, clinicians, and other key stakeholders) for similarities and differences. The initial analysis revealed similar comments across the groups with no clearly discerning features or trends among the different groups of participants.

Mixed Methods Analysis

With the intent to better understand how the data were related to each other, we then began a process of looking for linkages, including issues of commonality (Fetters, 2020). Because we intentionally matched, during the data collection phase, the open-ended qualitative responses, the mini-focus group interview guide, and the items the scales, it was logical to link scores from the visual analog scales with the qualitative data in a joint display (Fetters, 2020, p. 126).

As we developed the joint display drafts, and as will be illustrated by the figures, we initially focused on how to merge the quantitative and qualitative data together through juxtaposition of both types of findings in a meaningful way that would be conducive to ultimately drawing metainferences across both types of data. Metainferences represent interpretations or conclusions drawn about both the qualitative and the quantitative data. Mixed methods researchers will not be able to draw metainferences until reaching a certain level of sophistication in the organization and understanding of both types of data. Hence, in the earlier versions of the joint displays illustrated (Figures 23.3, 23.5–23.9), the reader should not expect or be surprised by the lack of metainferences in figures. None of the draft figures was ever considered final as we were exploring and analyzing how to merge both types of data together. Practically speaking, drawing metainferences before fully understanding the relevance of both types data for the constructs of interest might be premature. For each iteration of the draft joint displays, our intent is to illustrate how our thinking about the two types of data evolved. That is, we are striving to provide transparency about how we engaged in mixed methods joint display analysis. To suggest each draft was fully developed as a joint display would be disingenuous as the drafts illustrate how our thinking evolved.

4 Empirical Demonstration of Joint Display Development as Mixed Analysis

To illustrate these procedures, in the following, we present an empirical demonstration of how our research team built a joint display and used it as an analysis procedure. As will be seen, the drafts of each iteration of the joint display are imperfect. We present a critical reflection of what was missing or a needed refinement from each version and how the lessons learned informed the subsequent iteration.

The First Iteration of the ADAPT-IT Joint Display Format that Juxtaposed Related Mixed Data (Figure 23.3)

As illustrated in Figure 23.3, we first organized the four groups for which we were interested in a row across the top (i.e., NETT statisticians, consultant statisticians, clinicians, and other participants). We next identified a single question from the attitudinal survey that we truncated as the phrase "Patient perspectives–Advantages (Q#13)" in the first column and reported the mean and standard deviation aggregated across all participants (visual analog scale (VAS) Mean column) and for each of the four groups individually in the remaining columns. The order of the four groups followed the order in the data output. We next identified representations of typical quotes from the qualitative data sources that were related to advantages of adaptive trials from the patient's perspective. As noted in Figure 23.3, this was just a series of bullet points with the qualitative data unorganized. To contrast perspectives, we then chose the opposite question from the attitudinal survey that we truncated as the phrase "Patient perspectives-disadvantages (Q#14)" and reported means and standard deviations. We next identified representative quotes from the qualitative data sources that were related to disadvantages of adaptive trials from the patient's perspective. Figure 23.3 is an excerpt of the full joint display, which included four additional survey questions with related qualitative themes.

Critical Evaluation of the Figure 23.3 Joint Display Effectiveness

Having developed a first draft of the joint display, we critically considered the effectiveness of the display. From an *organizational* structure perspective, we found the two major categories being represented, e.g., "Patient perspectives–Advantages" and "Patient perspectives–Disadvantages" were not oriented well to correspond with the quantitative findings (i.e., the mean scores, *SD*, and the qualitative comments. From a *quantitative data representation* perspective, a primary concern with the first draft was that the joint display did not express well the range of scores within each group. We noted that the mean agreement on the visual analog scale did differ between the four groups, but we were perplexed about how to portray more effectively the within group variation. From a *qualitative data representation* perspective, we first were struck that the very truncated categories were too abstract to be understood without referring to the text. In addition, we remained uncertain whether it was most effective to compare the advantages and disadvantages to the patients in the same joint display, or if it might be better to portray advantages together from both the patient and the researcher perspectives. From a *quotes perspective*, we noted that some quotes had identifiers while others did not. For example, the first two bullets had no source of the quote in the parentheses, while the third bulleted point had

"(Consult Stat MFG)" signifying the source was from the consultant biostatistician mini focus groups. With these concerns, we sought a new iteration.

From a mixed methods perspective, the organization of the qualitative and quantitative results was not conducive to drawing metainferences as it was still unclear how the two types of data related to each other. As will be seen in subsequent iterations, it was necessary to achieve a successful juxtaposition of the two types of findings before we were prepared to draw metainferences.

Further Intra-method Quantitative Data Analytics (Figure 23.4)

Noting the means and the standard deviation, we brainstormed about how to portray the quantitative data differently. This led to the idea of developing box plots of the quantitative data as illustrated in Figure 23.4. While comprehensive, the output had a large range of numbers that was too overwhelming and required intense study to discern the overall meaning. A key methodological point is that we were not looking to compare all of the data. Rather, our intent was to explore the representation and visualization of the quantitative data. We were experimenting with ways to represent the quantitative results to include in a second iteration of a full joint display with qualitative results.

The Second Iteration of the ADAPT-IT Joint Display Format that Restructured the Data Presentation Using Box Plots (Figure 23.5)

The second version of the joint display is shown in Figure 23.5. From an *organizational structure* perspective, we added a column with a more descriptive name of the feature that we were trying to emphasize. As in the top left column, we inserted the full phrase from the actual survey, "Adaptive clinical trial designs pose ethical advantages from the patient's perspective." In the row below that question, we juxtaposed the mixed data relating to "Advantages from the researchers' perspectives." We kept the alternating row approach of quantitative findings, qualitative findings, quantitative findings, and then qualitative findings. From a *quantitative data representation* perspective, for this iteration, we inserted box plots from Figure 23.4 into the figure as a substitute for the mean and standard deviations. We were pleased with the effect of the box plots, and it clearly impacted our thinking about intra-group variation which had not been so obvious from the mean and standard deviation (*SD*) as initially used in Figure 23.3. As illustrated by Evergreen (2016), readers can process a boxplot more easily than the mean (*SD*) because people more easily process lengths.

From a *qualitative data representation* perspective, we added labels to each of the quotes relative to the source material. As illustrated by the first and second bullets, we distinguished between the comments from the open-ended question on visual analog scale surveys from the consultant statisticians (Consult Stat VAS) and the mini focus group comments from the consultant statisticians (abbreviated as Consult Stat MFG).

From a *mixed methods representation* perspective, each question heading provided an organizational structure to

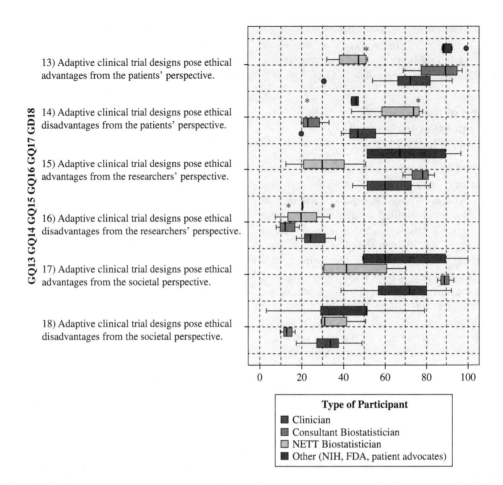

FIGURE 23.4 Box plots based on the responses using a visual analog scale format to six questions on ethical issues in the ADAPT-IT baseline survey.

compare the quantitative boxplot with the qualitative quotes immediately below the boxplot. Thus, it facilitated comparison on a common concept (e.g., ethical advantages from the patients' perspective), which showed promise for conducting a mixed methods analysis, and hence to identify metainferences.

Critical Evaluation of the Figure 23.5 Joint Display Effectiveness

With the second iteration, we felt that the box plots added significantly to the understanding of the quantitative scores on the visual analog scales of agreement. This also included the actually labeling of the visual analog scale from "Strongly Disagree" to "Strongly Agree." But the lateral orientation of the visual analog scales, even though this had been the orientation in the survey instrument, remained somewhat difficult to interpret. Moreover, this joint display was missing a legend to determine which stakeholder group was represented in each boxplot. From a qualitative perspective, there was a key theme regarding the process of obtaining informed consent that had emerged, and we were uncertain about whether to keep the comments general or to add subthemes. In addition, we noted need for better organization of the quotations by the four groups. As the structural juxtaposition of the qualitative and quantitative data were still sufficiently effective, but in our assessment not conducive to linking, we found it difficult to make metainferences, and deferred this until later in the development of the joint display structure.

The Third Iteration of the ADAPT-IT Joint Display Format (Figure 23.6) Featuring Intuitive Organizational Restructuring

The changes prompted by the critical evaluation of Figure 23.5 led to our development of Figure 23.6. From an *organizational structure* perspective, we trialed putting together the advantages from the patients' and researchers' perspectives rather the advantages and disadvantages from the patient's perspective as portrayed in Figure 23.6. From a *quantitative data representation* perspective, we felt that a vertical orientation, more like a thermometer from a "cold" level of enthusiasm to a "hot" level of enthusiasm, might yield a more visually appealing, intuitive, and more cognitively comprehensible presentation of responses of the four stakeholder groups for each question. From a *qualitative data representation* perspective, we trialed the addition of "consent" as category in addition to general comments. In addition, we sought better representation of all four groups, e.g., Consult Stat VAS (from survey open-ended comments after the visual analog scales), and Consult Stat MFG (from mini-focus group comments). From a *mixed data representation* perspective, this version

Development of a Joint Display as a Mixed Analysis 267

Table A. Stakeholder perspectives on ethical advantages to adaptive clinical trials

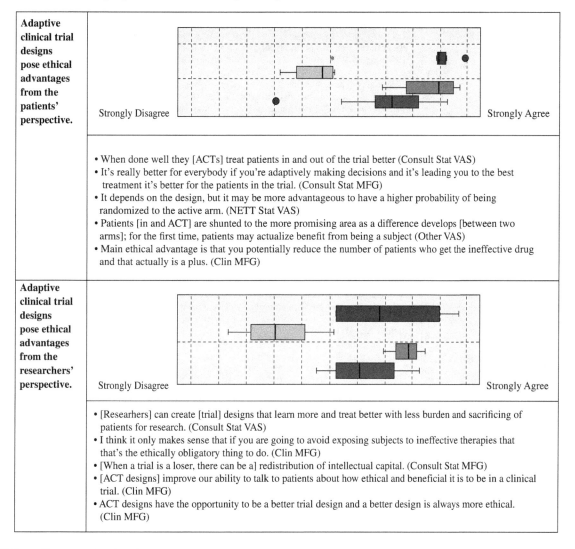

FIGURE 23.5 The second iteration of the ADAPT-IT joint display using box plots.

of the joint display facilitated a side-by-side comparison of quantitative survey data (means and variation for each group) with qualitative results for each question. For example, the reader can see each group's quantitative responses to the question of ethical advantages of adaptive clinical trials from the patients' perspective along with related qualitative quotes. Figure 23.6 is an excerpt that only includes two of six total questions.

Critical Evaluation of the Figure 23.6 Joint Display Effectiveness

From an *organizational structure* perspective, the order of the box plots by contributing group, did not follow the same order as quotes, i.e., black color (Figure 23.6, box plot 1 – for orientation purposes, the left most; originally lavender during the analysis) represented the consultant statisticians, light gray color (Figure 23.6, box plot 2; originally beige during the analysis) represented the network statisticians, the medium gray color represented the clinicians (Figure 23.6, box plot 3, originally green during the analysis), while the dark gray color (Figure 23.6, box plot 4; originally blue during analysis)[1] represented the group called other stakeholders, mostly regulators such as project officers and human subjects committee representatives, and others such as patient advocates. Also, the figure needed a legend to clearly label each group. From a *quantitative data representation* perspective, the labels of "Strongly Agree" and "Strongly Disagree" did not really convey the range of 0–100 that was an option on the visual analog scale continuum. As it was becoming clear that there were extremely different responses between the consultant statisticians and the network statisticians, we strategized on how to bring these together to highlight these differences. From a *mixed data representation* perspective, it remained difficult to discern the linkages of the qualitative text with the group representation of the box plots. Moreover, adding a sub-theme "Informed Consent" to the joint display figure proved to be more of a distraction than a helpful addition.

Table A. Stakeholder perspectives on ethical advantages to adaptive clinical trials

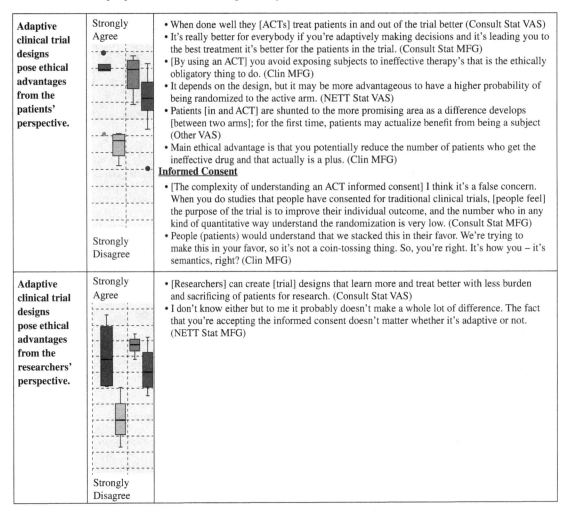

FIGURE 23.6 The third iteration of the ADAPT-IT joint display using intuitive restructuring.

The Fourth Iteration of the ADAPT-IT Joint Display Format (Figure 23.7) Using Color

Based on the concerns noted, we adjusted the joint display as illustrated in Figure 23.7. From an *organizationl structure* perspective, the most significant change was the addition of color during the analysis—depicted with gray scale for publication in this chapter— to the quotes to match the corre sponding group in the box plots in the figure. At this point, our primary concern was not publication of the joint display in color. Color is either not available, or expensive to use in many published formats. Rather, we noted the opportunity to *use color as an analytic tool* to better understand the quantitative and qualitative data. In addition, we moved the category type label on the y axis from the left side of the table into a header row. From a *quantitative data representation* perspective, we added 20-point gradation lines from 0–100 into the box plots. Moreover, we juxtaposed the extremely different quantitative responses on the visual analog scales between the consultant statisticians and the network statisticians. From a *qualitative data representation* perspective, we adjusted the order of the representative text, that is the qualitative text, to correspond with each of the four groups as reflected the ordering of the box plots.

Critical Evaluation of the Figure 23.7 Joint Display Effectiveness

Critically reflecting about the changes, from an *organizational structure* perspective, we felt that the color-coding (gray scale for the purposes of this chapter) by the stakeholder group during the analysis promoted better understanding of the relationship between the quantitative and qualitative data. Moreover, moving the category types into headers in a row effectively reduced the number of columns and brought greater emphasis to the box plots of the visual analog scales. While the juxtaposition of the two biostatistician groups—consultant and academic—brought greater emphasis to differences between the two biostatistician groups, it actually diminished the relative importance of the other two groups, clinicians and other stakeholders. In addition, for interpretation of the trends, it made it difficult to tell in a more continuous and progressive way how the groups differed. While the addition of color (now gray

Development of a Joint Display as a Mixed Analysis 269

Table A. Stakeholder perspectives on ethical advantages and disadvantages to adaptive clinical trials from the patients' perspective.

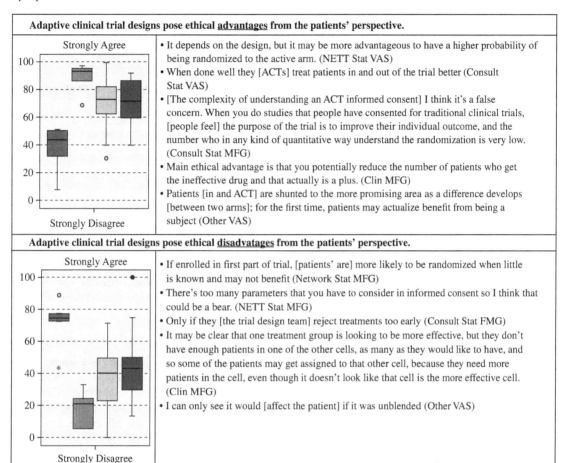

FIGURE 23.7 The fourth iteration of the ADAPT-IT joint display using color/shading.

scale for the purposes of this chapter) was helpful for better linking of the quantitative scores and the supporting qualitative comments, we felt that the source of the information for each data type was still not clear as the source of the qualitative comments was "buried" at the end of each quote in a parentheses (e.g., "NETT Stat VAS).

The Fifth Iteration of the Joint Display Format (Figure 23.8) Using Labelling

In light of the preceding considerations, we made a further iteration for publication of the joint display as an exemplar in *Health Services Research* (Fetters et al., 2013) as shown by the example in Figure 23.8, which is an excerpt of the larger joint display and shows just one question. For this iteration of the joint display figure, *organizationally*, we moved the content title to be represented below the box plots. In addition, a critical change was to add the group type, Consultant Biostatistician, Clinician, Other key stakeholder, and Academic biostatistician as sub-headers within the qualitative text. Moreover, we altered the order of the box plots to be arranged from the highest level of agreement to the lowest level of agreement in a left to right pattern. This format, while interposing the clinicians between the consultant biostatisticians and the network biostatisticians, actually functioned to further highlight the differences between the two biostatistician groups (the consultant biostatisticians and the network biostatisticians) illustrating their positions at opposite poles of each other. From a *mixed methods perspective*, seeing the distinction in the quantitative scores among the two biostatisticians groups revealed more subtle differences between groups in the qualitative findings.

Critical Evaluation of the Figure 23.8 Joint Display Effectiveness

The organizational structure in Figure 23.8 seemed the most effective of all the trialed formats for presenting the mixed data from the quantitative attitudinal survey and the interviews. Yet one problem remained, namely, how to present all six joint displays into a single paper when publication requirements were limited to only five figures and tables. At this point in time in the field of mixed methods research, the idea of adding metainferences, even though obvious now, was not a widely recognized component of building a joint display. Hence, the description of the meaning of the quantitative and

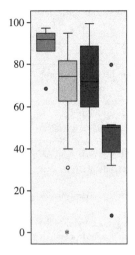

FIGURE 23.8 The fifth iteration of the ADAPT-IT joint display using labelling: Clinical trial expert opinions on the ethical advantages to adaptive clinical trials.

Source: Fetters, Curry, and Creswell (2013), and reproduced with permission of Wiley and Sons.

qualitative findings appeared in the text as it was not a part of this iteration of the joint display figure.

The Sixth Iteration of the ADAPT-IT Joint Display Format by Creating a Single Meta-figure (Figure 23.9) from Three Thematically Related Joint Displays

Prior to publication, the final iteration of the joint display involved the organization of three joint displays together as a single meta-figure that integrated three distinct concepts into a single display. We organized the three joint displays to represent the four stakeholder groups views of the perspectives of patients, researchers, and society about *ethical advantages* of adaptive clinical trials in a single combined meta-figure, and the three joint displays from the perspectives of patients, researchers, and society about *ethical disadvantages* of adaptive clinical trials as a second, single combined meta-figure. One of the two figures from the final publication is found as Figure 23.9.

Critical Evaluation of the Figure 23.9 Joint Display Effectiveness

The meta-figure joint display, that is, a series of three related joint displays illustrating the key stakeholders' views about *ethical advantages* from the perspectives of 1) patients, 2) researchers, and 3) society as a single meta-figure joint display, was included as a full page in the published article (Legocki, et al., 2015). This was accompanied by a second full page series of three related joint displays illustrating the key stakeholders' views about *ethical disadvantages* from the perspectives of 1) patients, 2) researchers, and 3) society as a second single meta-figure joint display. The choice to provide all three joint displays of ethical advantages as a single meta-joint display, and all three joint displays of ethical disadvantages as a single meta-joint display achieved an interesting outcome. The primary metainference, an interpretation across multiple joint displays, illustrated there was consistency across the groups with only relatively small changes relative to disagreement between the two biostatistician groups. A secondary metainference was that the three joint displays together highlighted how polarized the two biostatistician groups were across multiple domains: ethical advantages and disadvantages from the perspectives of patients, researchers, and society.

The Seventh Iteration of the Joint Display Format—Adding Metainferences (Figure 23.10)

Increasingly, mixed methods methodologists have advocated for the addition of a metainferences to joint displays. For example, Fetters, Guetterman, Scerbo, and Kron (2018) conducted a multiphase mixed methods project that involved developing and testing a computer simulation using a virtual human in a first phase. In the second phase they tested the virtual human in a single-blinded, multisite, mixed methods, randomized controlled trial to determine if medical students exposed to the virtual human intervention performed better in communicating with patients in a subsequent realistic clinical scenario than students exposed to a state-of-the-art computer-based learning module. The authors collected medical student quantitative attitudinal data and open-ended essay data about experiences with the systems during the trial (Kron et al., 2017). During their analysis, they created a joint display with the quantitative and qualitative findings. They went a step further by adding a final column with their metainferences or interpretation of the conclusions to be drawn by considering both types of data together.

Development of a Joint Display as a Mixed Analysis 271

Clinical trial expert opinions on ethical advantages to adaptive clinical trials

Opinions on potential ethical <u>advantages</u> of adaptive trials from patient perspectives
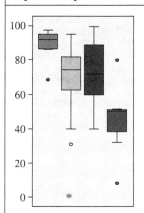 **Consultant Biostatistician:** • When done well they [ACTs] treat patients in and out of the trial better. (Survey) • [The complexity of understanding an ACT informed consent] I think it's a false concern. When you do studies that people have consented for traditional clinical trials, [people feel] the purpose of the trial is to improve their individual outcome, and the number who in any kind of quantitative way understand the randomization is very low. (MFG) **Clinician:** • I think it only makes sense that if you are going to avoid exposing subjects to ineffective therapies that that's the ethically obligatory thing to do. (MFG) • There is no problem explaining to patient that if we find one arm to be clearly interior we drop it, and one to be clearly superior we'll stop [the trial] early, (MFG) **Other Stakeholder:** • Whether or not an adaptive trial really offers ethical advantages (random) patients will perceive "a new and different" approach aimed at time issues and increased communication as progressive (Survey) **Academic Biostatistician:** • It depends on the design, but it may be more advantageous to have a higher probability of being randomized to the active arm. (Survey)
Opinions on potential ethical advantages of adaptive trials from the researchers' perspective
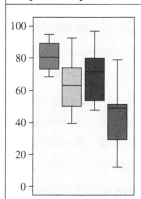 **Consultant Biostatistician:** • [Researchers] can create [trial] designs that learn more and treat better with less burden and sacrificing of patients for research, (Survey) • [When a trial is a loser, there can be a] redistribution of intellectual capital. (MFG) **Clinician:** • [ACT designs] improve our ability to talk to patients about how ethical and beneficial it is to be in a clincal trail. (MFG) • [ACT designs] conserve resources and protect patients exposed to the poor treatment (Survey) **Other Stakeholder:** • [Using an ACT] allows research to adapt to current trends (Survey) • Ethics of the trial is based on the soundness of the science of the trial design; if the trial is designed so that a valid result is obtained, there appear to be significant ethical advantages to adaptive designs, particularly in terms of reducing sample size and exposing subjects to inferior treatments for a shorter amount of time. (Survey) **Academic Biostatistician:** • We [as researchers] have an ethical obligation to design best possible trial. (MFG)
Opinions on potential ethical advantages of adaptive trials from a societal perspective
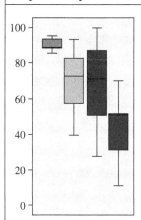 **Consultant Biostatistician:** • Fewer patients are "used" to identify ineffective therapies freeing them up for trials of potentially effective therapies. Also effective therapies can get to market faster. (Survey) • It's really better for everybody if you're adaptively making decisions and it's leading you to the best treatment it's better for the patients in the trial. (MFG) **Clinician:** • ACT designs have the opportunity to be a better trial design and a better design is always more ethical. (MFG) • If we end up with an ACT that reduces the overall number recruited, I think that the community would be more supportive; we changed the design so fewer people are going to be exposed to the less effective drug. (MFG) **Other Stakeholder:** • Consider the economic concerns of the health care industry. Again, there is a potential that adaptive designs could provide an advantage when used appropriately. (Survey) • If they're rigorous they can shorten trials, lead to success. (Survey) **Academic Biostatistician:** • If we use adaptive design, maybe we can save some time by adding or dropping a treatment arm. So, that way we can shorten the total time. That maybe a benefit to the entire society (MFG)

FIGURE 23.9 A meta-joint display figure of three joint displays about the ethical advantages of adaptive clinical trials from the perspectives of patients, researchers and society.

Source: Legocki et al. BMC Medical Ethics (2015) 16:27. doi 10.1186/s12910-015-0022-z

While the published versions of the ADAPT-IT empirical study did not actually include a final metainferences column, this could have been added with relative ease had the option been considered before publication. Figure 23.10 illustrates how we added metainferences to the joint display to illustrate how it can be done.

Critical Evaluation of the Figure 23.10 Joint Display Effectiveness

As illustrated by Figure 23.10, the addition of metainferences adds value because initial qualitative analysis revealed no substantive differences between the language of the consultant

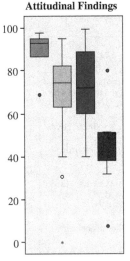

Attitudinal Findings	Illustrative Quotes	Metainferences
	Consultant biostatistician • When done well they [ACTs] treat patients in and out of the trial better. (Survey) • On participants' understanding the complexity of an ACT sufficiently to give informed consent: *I think it's a false concern. When you do studies that people have consented for traditional clinical trials, [people feel] the purpose of the trial is to improve their individual outcome, and the number who in any kind of quantitative way understand the randomization is very low.* (mini-focus group) **Clinician** • *I think it only makes sense that if you are going to avoid exposing subjects to ineffective therapies...that's the ethically obligatory thing to do.* (mini-focus group) • *There is no problem explaining to [the] patient that if we find one arm to be clearly inferior we drop...[that treatment], and one to be clearly superior we'll stop [the trial] early.* (mini-focus group) **Other key stakeholder** • *Whether or not an adaptive trial really offers ethical advantages patients will perceive "a new and different" approach aimed at time issues and increased communication as progressive.* (survey) **Academic biostatistician** • *It depends on the design, but it may be more advantageous to have a higher probability of being randomized to the active arm.* (survey)	Consultant biostatisticians and academic biostatisticians, two research team constituencies that needed to collaborate closely, had seemingly similar qualitative responses. But they had very different ratings about the ethical advantages of ACTs that had not been discerned in the initial qualitative findings interpretation. In light of the polarized attitudinal scores and means, reconsideration of the qualitative data revealed a *detailed and nuanced* argument by the consulting biostatisticians compared to generally suportive language by clinicians and other stakeholderst to *only an acknowledgement of potential advantages* by the network statisticians.

The adaptive clinical trial design poses ethical advnatages from the patient's perspective

FIGURE 23.10 A joint display figure of clinical trial expert opinions about the ethical advantages of adaptive clinical trials from the researchers that includes a metainferences column.

biostatisticians, clinicians, other stakeholders, and the network biostatisticians. The addition of the box plots for each of the four groups highlighted polarized views. This resulted in reconsideration of the qualitative data. This re-examination of the qualitative data revealed a seemingly "topographical difference" as qualitative differences between the four groups, especially, the consultant biostatisticians and network biostatisticians seemed to "pop out." The consultant biostatisticians provided detailed and nuanced arguments for ethical advantages while the network biostatisticians provided commentary that only acknowledged potential advantages. The understanding of the polarization of viewpoints actually led to an intervention that facilitated dialogue between the two biostatistician groups, an outcome of greatly enhanced collaboration and teamwork.

The Eighth Iteration of the Joint Display Format (Figure 23.11) Depicting Adaptation to Grayscale

For the purposes of many print materials, color is not an option. Hence, for the purposes of this book chapter (not featured in the original published version), we were tasked

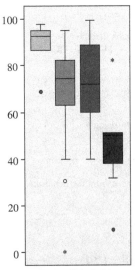

The adaptive clinical trial design poses ethical advantages from the patient's perspective

Consultant biostatistician
• When done well they [ACTs] treat patients in and out of the trial better. (Survey)
• On participants' understanding the complexity of an ACT sufficiently to give informed consent: *I think it's a false concern. When you do studies that people have consented for traditional clinical trials, [people feel] the purpose of the trial is to improve their individual outcome, and the number who in any kind of quantitative way understand the randomization is very low.* (Mini-focus group)

Clinician
• *I think it only makes sense that if you are going to avoid exposing subjects to ineffective therapies...that's the ethically obligatory thing to do.* (MFG)
• *There is no problem explaining to [the] patient that if we find one arm to be clearly inferior we drop* [that treatment], *and one to be clearly superior we'll stop* [the trial] *early.* (Mini-focus group)

Other key stakeholder
• *Whether or not an adaptive trial really offers ethical advantages patients will perceive "a new and different" approach aimed at time issues and increased communication as progressive.* (Survey)

Academic biostatistician
• *It depends on the design, but it may be more advantageous to have a higher probability of being randomized to the active arm.* (Survey)

Metainferences

Consultant biostatisticians and academic biostatisticians, two research team constituencies that needed to collaborate closely, had seemingly similar qualitative responses. But they had very different ratings about the ethical advantages of ACTs that had not been discerned in the initial qualitative findings interpretation. In light of the polarized attitudinal scores and means, reconsideration of the qualitative data revealed a *detailed and nuanced* argument by the consulting biostatisticians compared to generally supportive language by clinicians and other stakeholderst to *only an acknowledgement of potential advantages* by the network statisticians.

FIGURE 23.11 A joint display figure using progressive grayscale shading to show trends across groups about the ethical advantages of adaptive clinical trials from the perspectives of patients.

with changing the color assignment used during the analysis to grayscale. In doing so, we noted that the conversion of the color in the figures to gray scale was problematic but presented an opportunity. The order from left to right relative to the shades of gray in the figures appeared haphazard, and aesthetically were difficult for the eye to follow. Hence, we changed the gray scale shading to go from lighter to darker to highlight the progression of the box plots from left to right. Concomitantly, we changed the shading of the qualitative quotes to follow the same progression in gray scale shading of the boxplots (Figure 23.11).

Critical Evaluation of the Figure 23.11 Joint Display Effectiveness

By calibrating the progression of the trends with the progressively darker shading of the grayscale we assessed this format as more effective. Specifically, this iteration renders the trends and associations of box plots easier to discern through the eyes of the reader.

How the Constructing Process of the Joint Display Depicts Mixed Data Analysis

From a content perspective, while the textual qualitative data provided descriptive information on breadth of interests including mostly similarities in understanding of ethical issues of adaptive clinical trials, there were no apparent differences by group. Quantitative data from visual analog scales demonstrated a gap in views of two key stakeholder groups. Re-organization of the data provided more finely grained understanding of stakeholder baseline views. The visual analog scales clarified different anchor points regarding stakeholder views on relative importance of the ethical advantages and disadvantages. The interim analysis contributed to implementing an intervention to promote more dialogue between consultant biostatisticians and the network biostatisticians.

Methodological Conclusions

This joint display is called a side-by-side joint display as it provides the quantitative findings first, and then the qualitative findings. As a convergent design, a theme first, a statistics theme second, with vertical organization could have been considered, but the scoring provided an excellent organizational framework. This same ordering could have been created with an explanatory sequential design where survey data or other quantitative findings would be presented first with subsequent illustrative qualitative findings.

This project provides an example of integration in a convergent design that collected both qualitative and quantitative data. It illustrates organizing quantitative data in format conducive for comparison and integration. Intra-method data transformation occurred as mean scores and the standard deviation were transformed into box plots. The presentation of qualitative data was organized into a format conducive to comparison and integration. Based on a thematic analysis by stakeholders, we were able to maximize presentation of mixed results. The resulting joint display format was one of the earliest published using spatial organization and color integration. The joint display creation process provides a structured way to consider metainferences generated through a joint display mixed analysis.

5 Suggested Applications of Joint Display Development as Mixed Data Analysis

The potential for joint display development as a mixed methods analysis for mixed data should probably be considered for virtually any mixed methods project. If both quantitative and qualitative data have overlap in one or more domains based on the constructs and themes of the respective data collection procedures, there is potential to create a joint display. The juxtaposition of the two types of data together provides a visual opportunity to consider what the data about a common domain mean when reflected upon in the context of both types of data. As to whether a researcher, evaluator, or practitioner chooses to use the resulting joint displays as a step for further analyses, or as a finished product for presentation of findings in an article, report or dissertation will be left to the discretion of the investigator. Based on our own research across multiple mixed methods projects using joint displays, we recommend as a prequel to joint display analysis the consideration of joint display planning that greatly facilitates the collection of quantitative and qualitative data about key constructs of consideration in mixed methods research and evaluation projects (Fetters, 2020, pp. 195–99).

6 Strengths and Limitations of Joint Display Development as Mixed Data Analysis in Mixed Analysis

As in the other chapters in this book, a brief discussion about the strengths and limitations of joint display as mixed data analysis is warranted.

Strengths

Already, a joint display is considered a state-of-the art representation of mixed methods findings, but few researchers have discussed the mixed methods display as a powerful analytic tool as well. Using the approach to analysis can bring out linkages between the qualitative and quantitative data that might otherwise not have been obvious.

Limitations

Constructing a joint display requires time and careful thought, but usually the payoff will be an integrated analysis. When creating a joint display, there may be empty cells if relevant data were not collected with both quantitative and qualitative data collection, or if there were no data for a sub-group that is included in the joint display. Some journals or reviewers may be unfamiliar with a joint display, but usually most appreciate having an integrated figure. Finally, the drawing of metainferences does require interpretation, and there is no guarantee that different individuals would necessarily come to the same conclusions if presented the same joint display. We found using color, purely serendipitously initially, to be helpful for the analysis. Fortunately, the journal where we published the original joint displays was online only, and we knew the reader would be able to see the color distinction. Although journals often allow color for no charge in the electronic version, color is likely costly in a print version. Hence, there is a tension from what is helpful from an analytical perspective, and what can be used in joint display presentations.

7 Resources for Learning More About Joint Display Development as Mixed Data Analysis

Fetters, M. D. (2020). Developing a joint display. In M. D. Fetters, *The mixed methods research workbook—Activities for designing, implementing, and publishing projects*(pp. 193–210). Thousand Oaks, CA: Sage.

Guetterman, T. C., Creswell, J. W., & Kuckartz, U. (2015). Using joint displays and MAXQDA software to represent the results of mixed methods research. In M. McCrudden, G. Schraw, & C. Buckendahl (Eds.), *Use of visual displays in research and testing: Coding, interpreting, and reporting data* (pp. 145–176). Charlotte, NC: Information Age.

Guetterman, T. C., Fetters, M. D., & Creswell, J. W. (2015) Integrating quantitative and qualitative results in health science mixed methods research through joint displays. *Annals of Family Medicine*, *13*(6), 554–561. https://doi.org/10.1370/afm.1865

Johnson, R. E., Grove, A. L., & Clarke, A. (2017). Pillar integration process: A joint display technique to integrate data in mixed methods research. *Journal of Mixed Methods Research*, 1–20. https://doi.org/10.1177/1558689817743108

NOTE

1. Examples of the original coloring schemes can be seen in Legocki et al. *BMC Medical Ethics* (2015) 16:27. doi 10.1186/s12910-015-0022-z

REFERENCES

Bazeley, P., & Kemp, L. (2012). Mosaics, triangles, and DNA: Metaphors for integrated analysis in mixed methods research. *Journal of Mixed Methods Research*, *6*(1), 55–72. https://doi.org/10.1177/1558689811419514

Bradt, J., Potvin, N., Kesslick, A., Shim, M., Radl, D., Schriver, E., ... & Komarnicky-Kocher, L. T. (2015). The impact of music therapy versus music medicine on psychological outcomes and pain in cancer patients: A mixed methods study. *Supportive Care in Cancer*, *23*(5), 1261–1271. doi: 10.1007/s00520-014-2478-7

Bustamante, C. (2017). TPACK and teachers of Spanish: Development of a theory-based joint display in a mixed methods research case study. *Journal of Mixed Methods Research*, *13*(2), 163–178. https://doi.org/10.1177/1558689817712119

Evergreen, S. D. (2016). *Effective data visualization: The right chart for the right data*. Thousand Oaks, CA: SAGE.

Fetters, M. D. (2020). Developing a joint display. In M. D. Fetters (Ed.), *The mixed methods research workbook—Activities for designing, implementing, and publishing projects* (pp. 193–210). Thousand Oaks, CA: Sage.

Fetters, M. D., Curry, L. A., & Creswell, J. W. (2013). Achieving integration in mixed methods designs-principles and practices. *Health Services Research*, *48*(6 Pt 2), 2134–2156. https://doi.org/10.1111/1475-6773.12117

Fetters, M. D., Guetterman, T. C., Scerbo, M. W., & Kron, F. W. (2018) A two-phase mixed methods project illustrating development of a virtual human intervention to teach advanced communication skills and a subsequent blinded mixed methods trial to test the intervention for effectiveness. *International Journal of Multiple Research Approaches*, *10*, 296–316. https://doi.org/10.29034/ijmra.v10n1a19

Fetters, M. D., & Molina-Azorin, J. F. (2017). The journal of mixed methods research starts a new decade: The mixed methods research integration trilogy and its dimensions. *Journal of Mixed Methods Research*, *11*, 291–307. https://doi.org/10.1177/1558689817714066

Guetterman, T. C., Creswell, J. W., & Kuckartz, U. (2015). Using joint displays and MAXQDA software to represent the results of mixed methods research. In M. McCrudden, G. Schraw, & C. Buckendahl (Eds.), *Use of visual displays in research and testing: Coding, interpreting, and reporting data* (pp. 145–176). Charlotte, NC: Information Age.

Guetterman, T. C., Fetters, M. D., & Creswell, J. W. (2015) Integrating quantitative and qualitative results in health science mixed methods research through joint displays. *Annals of Family Medicine*, *13*(6), 554–561. https://doi.org/10.1370/afm.1865

Howell Smith, M. C., Babchuk, W. A., Stevens, J., Garrett, A. L., Wang, S. C., & Guetterman, T. C. (2019). Developing the Exploring Engineering Interest Inventory: Modeling the use of mixed methods-grounded theory. *Journal of Mixed Methods Research*. Advance online publication. https://doi.org/10.1177/1558689819872599

Johnson, R. B. & Christensen L. B. (2020) *Educational Research: Quantitative, Qualitative, and Mixed Approaches*. Thousand Oaks, Ca. Sage.

Johnson, R. E., Grove, A. L. & Clarke, A. (2017). Pillar integration process: A joint display technique to integrate data in mixed methods research. *Journal of Mixed Methods Research*, 1–20. https://doi.org/10.1177/1558689817743108

Kron, F. W., Fetters, M. D., Scerbo, M. W., White, C. B., Lypson, M. L., Padilla, M. A., ... & Becker, D. M. (2017). Using a computer simulation for teaching communication skills: A blinded multisite mixed methods randomized controlled trial. *Patient Education and Counseling*, *100*, 748–759. https://doi.org/10.1016/j.pec.2016.10.024

Legocki, L. J., Meurer, W. J., Frederiksen, S., Lewis, R. J., Durkalski, V. L., Berry, D. A., ... Fetters, M. D. (2015). Clinical trialists' perspectives on the ethics of adaptive clinical trials: A Mixed-Methods analysis. *BMC Medical Ethics*, *16*(27). https://doi.org/10.1186/s12910-015-0022-z

Meurer, W.J., Lewis, R.J., Tagle, D., Fetters, M.D., Legocki, L., Berry, S, ... Barsan, W.G. (2012). An overview of the Adaptive Designs Accelerating Promising Trials into

Treatments (ADAPT-IT) project. *Annals of Emergency Medicine*, 60, 451–457. https://doi.org/10.1016/j.annemergmed.2012.01.020

Moran-Ellis, J., Alexander, V.D., Dickinson, M., Fielding, J., Sleney, J., & Thomas, J. (2006) Triangulation and integration: Processes, claims, and implications. *Qualitative Research*, 6, 45–59. https://doi.org/10.1177%2F1468794106058870

Peroff, D.M., Morais, D.B., Seekamp, E., Sills E., & Wallace, T. (2019). Assessing residents' place attachment to the Guatemalan Maya landscape through mixed methods photo elicitation. *Journal of Mixed Methods Research, online*, 1–24. https://doi.org/10.1177/1558689819845800

Plano Clark, V. L., & Sanders, K. (2015). The use of visual displays in mixed methods research. In M. McCrudden, G. Schraw, & C. Buckendahl (Eds.), *Use of visual displays in research and testing* (pp. 177–206). Charlotte, NC: Information Age Publishing.

24

The Case Comparison Table

A Joint Display for Constructing and Sorting Simple Tables as Mixed Analysis

Judith Schoonenboom and R. Burke Johnson

1 Definition of a Case Comparison Table

This chapter introduces a specific type of joint display table called the case comparison table. Construction of a case comparison table is a form of data analysis in mixed methods research (henceforth: *mixed analysis*). We define a case comparison table as a simple table, in which each row contains information on one case of the research study (e.g., one student, one hospital, or one legal case), with part of the information coming from qualitative data sources, such as in-depth interview data, and another part coming from quantitative data sources, such as structured questionnaire data (see Table 24.1 and Table 24.2 in this chapter). In the first section of our chapter, we describe the case comparison table, and we clarify the five components of this chapter's title: *simple tables*, *analysis*, *mixed* analysis, *constructing*, and *sorting*.

Joint Displays as the Parent Category of Case Comparison Tables

Our case comparison table forms a subcategory of visualizations that are used in mixed methods research, commonly called *joint displays* (Guetterman, Creswell, & Kuckartz, 2015; Guetterman, Fetters, & Creswell, 2015). Joint display is an umbrella term for visualizations in which quantitative and qualitative data and/or results are presented together for comparative and integration purposes. Following Fetters, Curry, and Creswell (2013, p. 2143), we define a joint display as "a visual means to draw out new insights beyond the information gained from the separate quantitative and qualitative results." Joint displays need not be tables: Examples of joint displays other than tables are the mixed flowchart and the mixed concept map.

In mixed methods research, broadly defined, joint displays have various, partly overlapping, purposes. These purposes include, but are not limited to:

- Display meta-inferences from qualitative and quantitative findings
- Juxtapose quantitative results and qualitative findings (Plano Clark & Sanders, 2015, p. 183)
- Summarize links among theory, quantitative and qualitative data, and analysis (Bazeley, 2018)
- Show quantitative and qualitative findings (columns) for multiple research questions (rows) (Schoonenboom & Johnson, 2017)
- Show quantitative and qualitative findings (columns) for multiple independent/causal/predictor variables (rows) (Schoonenboom & Johnson, 2017)
- Show quantitative statistical information per qualitative theme (Guetterman, Fetters, et al., 2015)
- Interrelate specific quantitative results and qualitative findings (Guetterman, Fetters, et al., 2015)

2 When Use of Case Comparison Tables is Appropriate in Mixed Methods Research: The Use of Case Comparison Tables in the Stage of Analysis

Tables, of which the case comparison table is a subcategory, can be used in various stages of mono-method and mixed methods research (Bazeley, 2018; Miles & Huberman, 1994; Miles, Huberman, & Saldaña, 2020; Plano Clark & Sanders, 2015). Tables are most frequently used for presenting research results, for example, the results of statistical analysis. Tables also can be used for the research design to show the flow of the research process (Bazeley, 2018). They can be used in research planning, and to show when the researcher intends to do what. And they can be used in the development of the study's conceptual framework (Maxwell, 2013).

Tables that combine or integrate information from qualitative and quantitative sources are called *mixed tables*. Mixed tables can be used for many purposes, including:

- Show information from various qualitative and quantitative sources
- Note patterns, themes; make contrasts, comparisons; cluster; and count (early in the process). (Miles et al., 2020, p. 117)
- Follow up on surprises, triangulate, make if-then tests, and check out rival explanations (later in the analysis process; Miles et al., 2020, p. 117)

TABLE 24.1

Reconstructed Simple Case Comparison Table based on Lee and Greene (2007)

Descriptive data					Collected data		Analytic data			
ID	Discipline	S	R	C	GPA	Quotation	LP	PA	CS	EG
0607	Humanities	Q	S	4	4,00	I do *not have any language problems.*	0	0	0	1
0609	technology	Q	S	3	4,00	The professor is old so that *his pronunciation is not clear.* He *usually handed out important contents and I could understand it by reading the textbook.*	1	0	1	2
1315	business	I	S	3	4,00	*My biggest problem is related with speaking* in English. I will get a good grade because my mathematical background is strong.	1	0	1	2
2020	Technology	I	S	3	4,00	*I understand 80% of the lectures. Careful reading complements 20% of lack of understanding.*	1	0	1	2
0620	Science	Q	S	2	4,00	I understand only *60–70% of the lectures.* It has *made my scores less than my expectation.*	1	1	0	5
1310	business	Q	S	3	3,89	I want to participate and argue the subject. But I cannot find myself enough. *This does not affect my grade.*	1	0	0	3
0624	Technology	I	S	2	3,80	It is *easy to understand the lectures and participate in class discussions.* The instructor speaks slowly.	0	0	0	1
2036	Humanities	I	S	3	3,57	The major problem is *speaking.* I spoke *once or twice during the whole semester.*	1	0	0	4
0610	technology	I	S	3	3,53	*Listening is a problem.* Lack of cultural knowledge interferes with understanding the concept.	1	1	0	5
0605	humanities	I	S	2	3,50	Because of my poor listening, I am struggling with catching up with my content courses.	1	0	0	5
0603	Technology	Q	S	3	3,39	I still have some *problem in speaking.* This difficulty *doesn't affect my ability to do well* in all the courses I take.	1	0	0	3
2037	business	I	S	2	3,22	*Lack of knowledge about idiomatic expressions* prevents me from understanding questions on the homework assignment.	1	1	0	5
2025	technology	I	S	3	3,18	*I was not able to finish all the reading assignments every week.*	1	0	0	4
2031	humanities	Q	S	3	3,11	I have *problems with my hearing and how to speak correctly.*	1	0	0	4
0608	technology	I	S	4	2,89	I understand almost 100% of the lectures. I understand the professor completely. [...] *Grades are not important.* That is the least of my worries. After we graduate with a Ph.D., people are not going to ask "Did you get an A or a B in that class?" I might get a B in this course. As long as I am learning, it is OK with me.	0	0	0	1

Table notes:
Descriptive data
ID = Student ID; Discipline = Academic/course discipline; S = Quotation source (Q = questionnaire, I = interview); R = Quotation source role (S = student, F = faculty); note that we simplified Table 1 by removing quotations by faculty (there is no quotation with quotation source value 'F').
Collected data
C = CEEPT score ranging from 2 (worst) to 4 (best): (2=placement in the ESL One class, 3=placement in the ESL Two class, and 4=exempt from any ESL classes (Lee and Greene 2007, p. 371).
GPA = Student first-semester GPA (ranging from 0 (worst) to 4 (best)).
Quotation = Utterance about one student.
Analytic data created during analysis
LP = Student's Language Problems: student indicates having (1) or not having (0) language problems.
PA = Problems affect Achievement: student mentions (1) or does not mention (0) that language problems affect his or her achievement.
CS = Student's Compensation Strategies: student mentions (1) or does not mention (0) compensation strategies;
EG = Effect on student's Grade: how language problems affect a student's achievement: (1) student does not have language problems; (2) student mentions some ability or behavior that compensates for their language problems (3) language problems do not affect their achievement; (4) student indicates language problem, but not their effect on their achievement (5) language problems have a negative effect on achievement.
Sorting order Table sorted first descending by GPA (G), and then descending by CEEPT Score (C).
Highlighting Highlighted are students with CEEPT Score 3 and GPA 4 (see explanation in text).

TABLE 24.2

Reconstructed Simple Case Comparison Table from Shaw et al. (2013)

Descr. data	Collected data		Calculated data		Analytic data					
Practice	CRC-B (%)	CRC-12 (%)	Diff. (%)	High perf.	Team Structure	Leadership	Engagement	Psychological Safety	Intra-communication	Inter-communication
P22	47	71	24	Y	3. Strong	1. Weak	2. Moderate	2. Moderate	2. Moderate	1. Weak
P7	53	73	20	N	3. Strong	1. Weak	2. Moderate	1. Weak	2. Moderate	1. Weak
P21	38	56	18	N	–	–	–	–	–	–
P15	50	67	17	N	2. Moderate	1. Weak	2. Moderate	1. Weak	2. Moderate	1. Weak
P2	14	30	16	Y	3. Strong	2. Moderate	3. Strong	3. Strong	3. Strong	2. Moderate
P8	37	52	15	Y	3. Strong	2. Moderate	3. Strong	2. Moderate	2. Moderate	1. Weak
P11	54	66	12	N	1. Weak	1. Weak	2. Moderate	1. Weak	2. Moderate	NA
P16	43	48	5	Y	3. Strong	3. Strong	3. Strong	3. Strong	3. Strong	1. Weak
P23	93	86	–7	Y	3. Strong	2. Moderate	3. Strong	3. Strong	3. Strong	1. Weak
P19	52	44	–8	Y	3. Strong	3. Strong	3. Strong	3. Strong	3. Strong	NA
P17	41	10	–31	N	–	–	–	–	–	–
P10	71	33	–38	Y	3. Strong	2. Moderate	2. Moderate	2. Moderate	3. Strong	3. Strong

Table notes:
Descriptive data. Practice = ID of medical practice.
Collected data: CRC-B = Screening Rates Baseline (%); CRC-12 = Screening Rates 12-Month Follow-up (%)
Analytic data (summary of qualitative ordinal data) Team; Structure; Leadership; Engagement; Psychological Safety; Intracommunication; Intercommunication
Calculated data (analytic data calculated from other data within this table): High perf. = high performing practices (=overall judgment based on the analytic data); Diff. = difference between follow-up and baseline ratings
Grey cells: values crucial in our analysis.
Cases sorted on Diff.: difference between follow-up and baseline ratings.

- Compare qualitative and quantitative results to see whether they are congruent or not
- Present qualitative and quantitative information side by side, using different theoretical lenses (Guetterman, Fetters, et al., 2015)
- Embed qualitative information into quantitative findings (Guetterman, Fetters, et al., 2015)
- Display integration of qualitative and quantitative results (Guetterman, Creswell, et al., 2015; Johnson & Christensen, 2020)
- Indicate difference/similarity of quantitative and qualitative results (Guetterman, Creswell, et al., 2015; Johnson & Christensen, 2020)

In this chapter, we focus on the use of case comparison tables during analysis. This means that we exclude two other uses of mixed tables: (a) mixed tables that are not case comparison tables, in which the rows are not cases, but are, for example, the research questions or the themes; and (b) the use of mixed tables for purposes other than analysis—for example, for presenting final results. We use a broad definition of analysis, including not only analysis of the data, but also integration of findings (Guetterman, Fetters, et al., 2015) and drawing conclusions.

In addition, our focus is on modern, digital, sortable tables as we know them from word processors and spreadsheets. This focus on digital, sortable tables is not new. The use of such tables in qualitative data analysis has been discussed by Janesick (2016), La Pelle (2004), Meyer and Avery (2009), Miles and Huberman (1994), Miles et al. (2020), Ruona (2005), Ryan (2004), and in mixed analysis by Combs and Onwuegbuzie (2010). Our chapter builds on and extends these previous publications, while putting a larger emphasis on the process of sorting and resorting.

3 Technical Outline of Case Comparison Tables for Mixed Methods Research

Case Comparison Tables as Simple Tables

Our case comparison table belongs to the class of simple tables. We define a simple table as a two-dimensional grid of single rows and single columns, in which each cell contains information based on the combination or intersection of the rows and columns. This piece of information can be as diverse as one patient's weight, one student's score on a test, one quotation by an interviewed teacher, or a summary of one legal case. Note that *simple* does not necessarily mean *easy*. As we will see, a case comparison table can be very large, in which case, we need specific techniques to manage and understand our data.

Conversely, a table can be complex in three distinct ways: (a) it contains more than one piece of information per cell, such as a combination of height and weight; (b) it contains rows or columns that split (we could, for example, turn Table 24.2 into a complex table by creating one column "Screening rates," which splits into "Baseline" and "After 12 months"); and/or (c) it includes three or more dimensions, in which case it is called a multidimensional matrix. In this chapter, we will argue that, in the stage of analysis, a simple two-dimensional table is usually preferable to a table or matrix with a complex layout (La Pelle, 2004).

Constructing and Sorting Case Comparison Tables

Case comparison tables will change during analysis, not unlike other joint displays (Miles et al., 2020, p. 113): They are constructed and reconstructed. This analytical and iterative process is often best supported by using simple, sortable tables. Conversely, mixed tables used for presenting results in publications might need to be more complex. This applies to Miles et al.'s (2020, p. 111) meta-matrices and to almost all mixed tables in the literature on joint displays (Bazeley, 2018; Guetterman, Creswell, et al., 2015; Guetterman, Fetters, et al., 2015; Miles & Huberman, 1994; Miles et al., 2020; Plano Clark & Sanders, 2015). Different from Miles et al. (2020, p. 118), our claim is that the, often complex, mixed table that one needs for presenting results is typically not the same as the simple case comparison table that one needs for data analysis.

Throughout this chapter, *sorting* means that the table as a whole is sorted on the basis of the values of one or more sorting columns.

4 Empirical Demonstration of Case Comparison Tables for Mixed Methods Research: Two Real-Life Examples

Before we describe how to construct case comparison tables in detail, we present two case comparison tables that we constructed from two published mixed methods research studies: Lee and Greene (2007) and Shaw et al. (2013). We constructed our simple case comparison tables from complex tables and other information that was presented in the original publications.

Example 1: Lee and Greene (2007)

Lee and Greene's (2007) research purpose was to understand the predictive value of scores on an English as a Second Language (ESL) test—the CEEPT—of international graduate students at a large public university in the United States on their academic performance (measured as grade point average [GPA]) and their language difficulties in courses during their first semester. In addition, 100 students undertook a self-assessment, and 55 faculty evaluated their students. Interviews were conducted with 20 students and 10 faculty members.

We started our analysis from Lee and Greene's (2007, p. 378) observation that students' utterances contained the following two dimensions: the extent to which they found English demands for a particular course difficult and their perceived effect of English demands on their course performance. Similar to Lee and Greene (2007), our research question was whether we could establish a link between students' measured CEEPT and GPA and what students reported about the demands and the effect on their performance.

Our case comparison table included quotations and utterances by students and faculty members that were provided by Lee and Greene (2007); we used a subset of the quotations on which these authors based their analysis. Most of our information came from Table 5 in Lee and Greene (2007), an information-rich and highly complex table. We created a simple case comparison table, in which students are the cases (Table 24.1). We added two additional columns with analytic data, which we explain later.

We created the case comparison table in Table 24.1 by using one row for each person's quotation(s), and by providing the quantitative and any other qualitative information that we had about the case in which the quotation was embedded (i.e., the student to which the quotation referred). Table 24.1 is a case comparison table because each row in Table 24.1 contains information about one case only. Furthermore, it is a simple table because each cell contains only one piece of information and because it does not contain columns that split. For the purpose of demonstration, we removed utterances by faculty members from our case comparison table. As a result, Table 24.1 contains only quotations by students about themselves.

A case comparison table contains at least three types of data. *Descriptive data* provide descriptive characteristics of the case or the quotation of that row, in this case, student ID and discipline of the student (the case) and information on the source of the quotation, namely, its form (questionnaire or interview) and the type of person who uttered the quotation (student or faculty). *Collected data* provide data on something that the case or someone else did, which was relevant to the research question, in this case the student's CEEPT score, his or her GPA, and the quotation that was uttered. *Analytic data* provide values of analytic categories of the researcher that are used to classify and group the quotations and/or students. Analytic categories are developed during analysis.

Our analysis is an alternation between sorting and resorting the case comparison table using various columns as sorting columns, reflecting on the results, adding new analytic categories, and thus columns, which capture the differences resulting from the reflection, sorting, and resorting using various columns as sorting columns, and so forth (Figure 24.1). Next, in Figure 24.1 and the following text, we describe our analysis of Example 1 in more detail. Our analytical process is now described.

Phase 1 Analysis

- *We started by reflecting on a finding in Lee and Greene (2007)*: Lee and Greene (2007, p. 378) observed that one half of the students with CEEPT 2, the worst score, found the English demands difficult, nine of 11 with CEEPT 3 found the demands okay, and all of the students with CEEPT 4 found the English demands easy. Then, we performed the following analytical actions:
- *We added an analytic category that captured the reflection result*: We added a new analytic category: LP: mentioning language problems (1 = mentioned by the student, 0 = not mentioned);

The Case Comparison Table   281

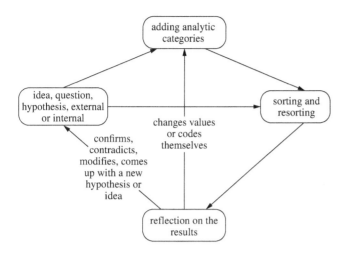

FIGURE 24.1 Heuristic for the analysis of case comparison tables.

- *We sorted and resorted*: We sorted our case comparison table various times, using various columns, including the new LP column, to determine whether new patterns would emerge.
- *We reflected on the results*: When we reflected on the quotations that were available to us (which are a subset of what Lee and Greene [2007] used), we noticed that, except for one outlier, students with a CEEPT 2 or 3 reported language problems, whereas none of the students with a CEEPT 4 reported language problems, a finding that differs slightly from Lee and Greene (2007). Thus, we found a discrepancy, which might later turn out to be relevant or might eventually be solved through further analysis.

Phase 2 Analysis

- *In a second round, we started by reflecting on another finding reported by Lee and Greene (2007)*: According to Lee and Greene (2007, p. 378), one half of the students with CEEPT 2 revealed that language problems did not affect their grade, whereas the other half reported a negative effect. None of the students with CEEPT 4 reported a negative effect, whereas 2/3 of the students with CEEPT 3 reported a negative effect.
- *We performed a second round of adding analytic categories that captured the reflection result*: We added an analytic category: PA: Language problems affect the student's grades: Student mentions (1) or does not mention (0) that language problems affect achievement.
- *We performed a second round of sorting and resorting*: We sorted our case comparison table several times, using different columns, including the new PA column, to see whether new patterns would emerge.
- *We reflected on our new results*: We discovered, that of those other students who had mentioned language problems, some mentioned that it affected their grade, whereas others did not, which is in line with Lee and Greene's findings.

Phase 3 Analysis

- *We performed a third round by sorting and resorting*: To search for links among measured CEEPT, GPA, and students' utterances, we first sorted our comparison table on GPA, CEEPT, and combinations of the two.
- *We reflected on the new results*: When we sorted the table first by GPA and then by CEEPT, which is the sorting order displayed in Table 24.1, we discovered an interesting pattern: All of the students with a moderately high CEEPT (3) and a high GPA (4) indicated some sort of compensation strategy for their language problems. These students are highlighted in Table 24.1. Student 0609 compensated his or her misunderstanding of the professor by reading the textbook, Student 1315 compensated problems with speaking English by a strong mathematical background, and Student 2020 compensated by careful reading.
- *We added one new analytic category that captured the reflection result*: We used the analytic category CS: mentioning compensation strategies: Student mentions (1) or does not mention (0) compensation strategies.

Phase 4 Analysis

- *We performed a fourth round of sorting and resorting*: We sorted our case comparison table various times, using various columns, including the new CS column, to determine whether new patterns would emerge.
- *We reflected on the new results*: From sorting and resorting, it became clear, that the three students with a CEEPT of 3 and a GPA of 4 were the only students mentioning compensation strategies: they are the only students with value 1 in the CS (compensation strategies) column. These finding might explain the lack of a unique effect of CEEPT on GPA: successful students have strategies to compensate for their language problems. This relevant observation is not discussed by Lee and Greene (2007).

Phase 5 Analysis

- *We performed another round of reflection on the results:* Using the columns LP, PA, and CS, we were able to divide the students into five non-overlapping categories: (a) students do not have language problems; (b) students mention some ability or behavior that compensates for their language problems (c) language problems do not affect their achievement;

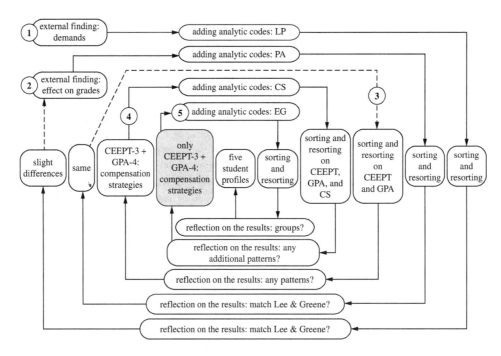

FIGURE 24.2 Heuristic for the analysis of case comparison tables, applied to Example 1. Most important finding in shaded box. Numbers indicate start of rounds.

(d) students indicate language problem, but not their effect on their achievement; and (e) language problems have a negative effect on achievement.

- *We added one new analytic category*: We used the five categories to create a new analytic category: EG = effect on students' grades.
- *We sorted and resorted*: We sorted our case comparison table various times, using various columns, including the new EG column, to see whether new patterns would emerge. This did not provide new insights.

Our iterative analysis process is visualized in Figure 24.2.

Based on the aforementioned analyses, we changed how we viewed the effect of CEEPT on GPA. We started with the idea of one simple effect, with one independent and one dependent variable. Through our analytic sorting, we discovered an important moderator: awareness of compensation strategies. This brought us one step closer to understanding under which circumstances, and for whom (Pawson & Tilley, 1997), language problems lead to obtaining a lower GPA.

Example 2: Shaw et al. (2013)

Shaw et al.'s (2013) research purpose was to evaluate an intervention aimed at improving colorectal cancer screening rates at 12 primary care practices in New Jersey (USA) through facilitated team meetings and learning collaboratives. Quantitative data on pre- and post-intervention screening rates were related to the qualitative characteristics of the practice teams, obtained by observations of meetings and collaboratives.

From Shaw et al.'s Table 5, we created our sortable simple Table 24.2 by restyling a few minor features that made their table complex. Furthermore, we added one column of analytic data: the difference between 12-month follow-up and baseline result and used this column to sort our case comparison table (see Table 24.2). For clarity, we made a distinction between analytic data, which are basically codes (like in Table 24.1), and calculated data, which are quantitative analytic data, obtained through calculation.

Our analysis proceeded as follows. We sorted and resorted Table 24.2 using all columns individually, except for practice, and reflected on the results. While sorting the practices (rows) on Diff., difference between follow-up and baseline ratings, we discovered an interesting pattern. It appears that, in general, the highest raise in screening rates are found in practices that have only weak or moderate leadership, psychological safety, engagement, and intra-communication. Those practices that are strong on these characteristics are mostly found in the bottom half of the table.

How can we explain this counterintuitive finding? One first idea, based upon reading Kegan and Lahey (2009) on organizational change, is that strong leadership and intra-communication might lead to strong habits in a team, making it more *difficult* to change. This is not an explanation yet, but a hypothesis for further exploration, which is not discussed in the original article. It is a hypothesis that becomes visible only after repeatedly sorting and resorting the columns of Table 24.2.

5 Suggested Applications of Case Comparison Tables in Mixed Methods Research

Purposes of Case Comparison Tables

Case comparison tables can be used for many purposes. Here, we discuss three purposes that rely specifically on continuously sorting and re-sorting. The main purpose in both real-life examples was *hypothesis and theory development*. Through a combination of adding analytic category columns and sorting and resorting the table, possible explanations for the main finding in the studies became visible: students' compensation strategies in Example 1 and a possible resistance to change of strong teams in Example 2. Note that these inductively developed hypotheses are not explanations yet, but tentative findings, and starting points for further inquiry.

Category development involves the use of one analytic category column (often a quantitative column) to categorize the contents of another column (often qualitative data: e.g., quotations). Continuously sorting columns by such an emergent analytic category makes visible the merits and flaws of the category-under-construction and leads to continuous updates of the category and its values (e.g., the development of the category Effect on student's Grade (EG) in Example 1 earlier).

Profile Development

Through continuously sorting and resorting of various columns, the researcher might discover that a specific value in one column often co-occurs with a specific value in one or more other columns. Cases with such a specific value combination are said to have a specific profile.

Causal analysis proceeds by putting columns in a chronological order. The researcher may then discover that a value in one column that describes something that happens to the case at an earlier stage ("left column") leads to, or *causes*, a value in another column that describes something that happens to the case at a later stage ("right column").

Case comparison tables are not meant as a device for identifying text fragments/*quotations* that are relevant for qualitative analysis. We assume that a researcher already has created quotations by assigning first, preliminary categories to the textual materials, which might eventually be revisited or revised later in the analysis process. Useful information on the process of coding texts, converting transcripts to tables, and importing files in spreadsheet software can be found in Janesick (2016), La Pelle (2004), Meyer and Avery (2009), and Ruona (2005). A second assumption is that for each case, the researcher has at least one column of quantitative data values (e.g., GPA for each student), and that part of the analysis consists of relating the quantitative data to either qualitative analytic categories and/or quotations.

How to Construct and Sort Case Comparison Tables

Preparing your Case Comparison Table

In this section, we discuss the two iterative key stages of constructing and using case comparison tables: preparing your table and performing the analysis. Depending on the size of your dataset and your needs, you can set up your case comparison table either in a sophisticated software program for qualitative or mixed analysis, or you can use a simple word processor or a spreadsheet. Whatever software you use initially, you can always easily export your case comparison table to one of the other programs. There are three key questions when preparing a case comparison table for analysis: What are your rows? What are your columns? What will go in the cells?

What are your rows, columns and cells? In case comparison tables, rows are used for the cases that you are studying. Cases can exist at various levels, for example, individuals, groups, locations, setting, events, and discussion utterances (Miles et al., 2020, p. 29). Each row contains information about one case only, such as one student (Example 1) or one practice (Example 2). Columns are typically used to describe characteristics of your cases: Each column describes one type of characteristic of your cases. As a result, each cell describes the quantitative or qualitative value of one characteristic of one case. Although swapping rows and columns is possible, our general advice is to use entities as rows and characteristics as columns throughout the data analysis phase, as you would in a statistical program (this advice differs from Miles et al., 2020, p. 113). This advice reflects the sorting unit in spreadsheets and word processors, which is the column, not the row.

In mixed methods research, cases occupy a special role. They are typically not examined in the quantitative strand of the research, where each respondent commonly contributes to establishing an effect at the group level, and are not examined as individual cases (Yin, 2018). Thus, in Example 1, CEEPT and GPA were used by Lee and Greene (2007) to calculate a mean effect. In a case comparison table, we take the quantitative information of each respondent, and put it side-by-side with qualitative information about this respondent, thereby turning the respondent from a point that contributes to establishing a mean effect, into a case that is investigated for its own sake, a process called "casing" by Ragin (1992, p. 217).

In Tables 24.1 and 24.2, each row provides information about one case only. There are occasions when cases require more than one row. First, your case may be at a higher level than your *unit of observation*. For example, a case comparison table with the interaction in dyads as its case would preferably have one row for each member of the dyad and identify the dyad to which individuals belong in a separate column. It is likely, that characteristics of the dyad interaction are influenced by characteristics of the individuals that make up the dyad, and sorting tables using characteristics of the individual members can bring this to the fore. This can only be undertaken, though, when each individual member has its own row.

Second, you might have similar information about each case from different sources, for example, judgments by students and by faculty members in Example 1. In this case, each judgment should have its own row, in order to be able to investigate differences between, for example, faculty and student judgments. Third, more than one quotation in a text may refer to the same aspect of the same case. In this case, one row should be used for each quotation, which makes it possible to investigate differences among quotations. In Example 1, it is thinkable that two or more quotations refer to the same individual student. As a result, each individual student could have one or more rows in the table, depending on the number of quotations for that student.

Often, you will have information about your cases at higher and lower levels. Pupils, for example, belong to a particular school class, school classes belong to a particular school, schools are located in a particular municipality, and so forth.

In case comparison table analysis, the higher level information is provided in separate columns (e.g., one column for class, one column for school, and one column for municipality). For most studies, this is more convenient than using relational databases to store the characteristics of the class in a separate table, making it impossible to do one sorting analysis on all characteristics of the cases at once (see also La Pelle, 2004, p. 87).

Our advice is this: Use only one table for all information, as long as you are focused on the same unit of analysis. Thus, as long as the student is our unit of analysis (Example 1), we can provide higher level information such as discipline, or information about the students coming from faculty member in the same table. Only when, in more complex case studies, the study contains multiple units of analysis, for example, cases at multiple levels, is it advised to create tables at the level of each case separately.

The information in the cells of a case comparison table will usually be a mix of what can be considered raw data, and data that are the result of qualitative or quantitative analysis. The following data types may be part of your case comparison table:

Static data types
  Descriptive data

- Name or ID
- Descriptive data of the unit of analysis or of higher level units, such as age and gender of a child, the teacher of its class, and the size of its school

  Collected data

- Scores obtained by direct measurement or self-reporting
- Quotations
- Qualitative observations

Analytic data

- Scores calculated from other scores (e.g., length x width; summative score)
- Scores derived from other scores other than by calculation (e.g., classification as high or low; overall score on the basis of qualitative observations)

Some data types are considered *static*, which means that they will not change after they have been collected, except for correcting errors. They are divided into *descriptive data*, characteristics of a case, and *collected data*, the result of something the case did during the study. *Analytic* data are obtained by some form of data analysis, some form of further processing the static data.

As our analysis of the cases proceeds, increasingly more data tend to be added to each case. In the case comparison table, these show up as additional columns. As a result, the tables tend to become larger during analysis, as an increasing number of columns are added (See Example 1). In our analysis, we often want to focus on a restricted number of characteristics of each case, and/or on a restricted number of cases, for example if the total number of cases is high. We recommend keeping the analysis manageable by focusing on a specific part of the table (see more details on this below). This advice differs from the advice given by La Pelle (2004, p. 87) and Miles et al. (2020, p. 113), who recommend the construction of several smaller tables. The disadvantage of splitting larger tables into smaller tables, however, is that this cannot easily be undone. In our solution, re-shuffling columns or re-sorting rows to change the focus of our analysis can easily be reverted.

Performing the Analysis.

What can we see? A case comparison table can be used for many purposes. Below are a few examples of the many kinds of connections that we can see and/or explore by adding analytic categories and sorting data columns:

- *Explanation.* The quantitative values can be explained by processes mentioned in the qualitative quotations (Example 1).
- *Multi-dimensionality.* A quotation that had been classified using one analytic category (e.g., high achievement) is shown to consist of two dimensions (high language achievement vs. high academic achievement, represented as two different columns in Example 1).
- *Profiles.* The values of several analytic categories are shown to hang together (demonstrated in Example 2).
- *Relationships among continuous, ordinal, or nominal variables.* A high value in one column tends to go together with either a high or a low value in the other column.
- *Interaction effects.* Values of interaction effects, in which there are different effects for different groups can be difficult to interpret. However, they are relatively easy to identify in a case comparison table if we order the results according to group.
- *Thresholds*—an effect of one variable on another occurs only if the independent variable has reached a specific level (e.g., only for more advanced pupils).
- *Ceiling/floor effects*—one variable does not affect the other, because the value of the other variable is already high/low for all or most participants.
- *Profiles*—values on various variables hang together in specific ways, thereby creating groups.
- *Exceptions (outliers)*—one case or individual has a value in one column that deviates from the remainder of the groups or one individual does not match the profiles that had been discovered.
- *Causation and prediction*—one value occurring earlier in a process, seems to be followed by a specific value of a column that describes an event or characteristic later in the process.

How Do We Perform the Analysis?

Our procedure of continuously sorting and resorting columns can be performed via standard word processing or spreadsheet software. In Microsoft Word, for example, it is possible to use up to three sorting columns simultaneously, and sort the data first on the basis of Column 1, sort within the entries that have the same value in Column 1 on the basis of Column 2, then on the basis of Column 3. If more than three sorting columns are needed, sorting can be undertaken in two or more steps. This advice differs from (La Pelle, 2004), who recommends combining cells, which would create a complex table. Although this might be sound advice in a situation in which much of analysis has been undertaken, our advice for case comparison tables is always to use only one type of information per cell, to keep the freedom of sorting and resorting data in different columns independently.

For qualitative values that have a natural order, it makes sense to add digits to enable meaningful sorting, for example 1. Weak, 2. Moderate, 3. Strong (see Table 24.2). This advice differs from the numerical codes of La Pelle (2004) and Ruona (2005), which are used in conjunction with a codebook, in which the numerical codes are described. Like Meyer and Avery (2009), we prefer to use meaningful qualitative labels in combination with digits for a meaningful sorting order.

Sorting and resorting is the foundation of a case comparison approach to mixed data analysis (Figure 24.1). By adding and using analytic, often qualitative, categories and descriptive, often quantitative, data to sort and compare quotations (as we did in Example 1), we can discover patterns. For example, we might discover links among the descriptive characteristics of participants, the qualitative quotations, and the analytic categories of the researcher (Combs & Onwuegbuzie, 2010; La Pelle, 2004). More importantly, we view sorting and comparing as a way to develop further the qualitative analytic categories themselves. This "thinking with your data" (Ruona, 2005, p. 259) includes questions such as: Do all quotations listed under a specific value of one analytic category really belong there? Does the analytic category and its assigned values provide an adequate description of what happens in the quotations? Do other quotations categorized under a different value of the analytic category really differ? These are the well-known questions for developing grounded theory (Glaser & Strauss, 1967). Using columns with analytic categories to sort cases and to determine whether there is some relationship between analytic categories and quotations is an excellent method to accomplish this because it brings the quotations related to one value of one analytic category next to each other. As we described in Example 2, we prefer meaningful codes (such as "low" or "high") to numerical codes because it better enables us to see whether the value assigned to the analytic category fits a specific quotation, or whether the quotation should be moved, or the analytic category adapted. In addition, different from Ruona (2005, p. 259), we consider sorting tables on the basis of various columns an excellent method to discover connections among analytic categories. If, for example, the analytic category "language problems (Table 24.1)" is displayed in one column, the analytic category "effect on grade" in another column, and if quantitative measures indicate the degree of presence or absence of what is described by the analytic category, we can discover various groups of students with different profiles.

Different from grounded theory, however, we emphasize the ideas and preconceptions that researchers bring to their studies (Figure 24.1). Theories do not just emerge from the data, but they arise through an interplay between the researcher's ideas/theories and the empirical world (Emmel, 2013).

In sorting, we use the values in one or more columns to sort or re-sort the cases—that is, to sort and re-sort the rows. In addition to re-sorting cases, re-shuffling columns, that is changing the order of columns, is a powerful tool for various reasons:

- Reshuffling the columns enables a researcher to focus on those columns that are relevant for that step of the analysis only, and leave other columns out of sight (but do not delete them!).
- Putting columns in the order of their appearance in a process can be used to reflect on process and causation.

As analytic categories change and new analytic categories are added during analysis, two issues are likely to emerge. The first is that one quotation relates to two (or more) values within one analytic category. There are three solutions to this problem: (a) split the quotation into two quotations and assign a different value to each split quotation; (b) duplicate the quotation and assign a different code to each of the two identical quotations; or (c) create a new analytic column and divide the two values over the two columns. Solution (a) and (b), described by Combs and Onwuegbuzie (2010), La Pelle (2004), and Ruona (2005), will lead to additional rows, whereas solution (c), described by Meyer and Avery (2009), will lead to additional columns. Our advice is to use additional columns instead of additional rows whenever possible. The reason for this is that every column that we add during analysis, enhances the possibilities for sorting the cases.

The second issue concerns the descriptions that we use to describe the values in our cells. Often, these descriptions change during analysis. In that case, we recommend changing old descriptions to new descriptions by means of sorting. Sorting can be used to list the cases with the same cell value underneath each other, so that a copy-paste, including all the cells that contain the code, can be undertaken easily, while it invites one to have one more look at the quotations that this code describes. Our advice differs from that of La Pelle (2004) and Ruona (2005), who recommend the use of Find and Replace. A well-known risk of Find and Replace, though, is that of unwanted changes being made in the text that one does not want to change.

What Do We Do with the Outcomes of these Sorting Exercises?

By performing these sorting exercises, we begin to see patterns that might otherwise remain hidden (see Examples 1 and 2 below). However, we know that humans are good at detecting patterns, including patterns that are actually random fluctuations. Therefore, it is important to put every pattern that we discover to the strongest possible test. Such tests include:

- Identify negative cases and attempt to explain these.
- Test whether and how an explanation of a negative case might apply to positive cases as well.
- Reflect on each of the new categories that have arisen as a result of sorting and ask whether these categories are the best possible ones.
- Use statistical tests.
- Attempt to formulate mechanisms that would explain the patterns found.
- Attempt to find alternative explanations.
- Determine how wildly/narrowly the pattern generalizes to the different participants in the study.
- Determine whether the pattern depends on or varies according to some other characteristic or variable.

By repeatedly applying these sorting exercises and tests, the researcher will arrive at a conclusion that is both well-fitting and nuanced.

6 Strengths and Limitations of Case Comparison Tables in Mixed Methods Research

We have shown that creating simple case comparison tables and sorting and resorting them enables researchers to identify patterns that might otherwise remain hidden. Through sorting and resorting, we discovered that students with the highest GPA, but a low CEEPT score, mentioned the use of compensation strategies (Example 1), and that the intervention to raise colorectal cancer screening rates appeared to be the least successful in practices with a strong team culture (Example 2). In addition to the increased knowledge based on additional analysis, both cases provide clear directions for future research to explain further these patterns.

Case comparison tables seem less suited for narrative analysis. By making sorting quotations a key feature of our analysis (Example 2), the connections among quotations, the story, can get lost. That makes sortable tables a perfect tool for finding themes across cases or individuals, but not for analyzing what happens within a case.

7 Resources for Learning More About Tables and Joint Displays in Mixed Analysis

Bustamante, C. (2019). TPACK and teachers of Spanish: Development of a theory-based joint display in a mixed methods research case study. *Journal of Mixed Methods Research, 13*, 163–178. doi:10.1177/1558689817712119

Guetterman, T. C. (2019, September 4). *Joint displays to facilitate integration of qualitative and quantitative research* [Video file]. *Mixed methods webinar series*. International Institute for Qualitative Methodology. Retrieved from www.youtube.com/watch?v=U6KvCN-7ZKM

Johnson, R. E., Grove, A. L., & Clarke, A. (2019). Pillar integration process: A joint display technique to integrate data in mixed methods research. *Journal of Mixed Methods Research, 13*, 301–320. doi:10.1177/1558689817743108

McCrudden, M. T., Schraw, G., & Buckendahl, C. W. (2015). *Use of visual displays in research and testing: Coding, interpreting, and reporting data*. Charlotte, NC: Information Age Publishing.

Younas, A., Pedersen, M., & Durante, A. (2020). Characteristics of joint displays illustrating data integration in mixed-methods nursing studies. *Journal of Advanced Nursing, 76*, 676–686. doi:10.1111/jan.14264

REFERENCES

Bazeley, P. (2018). *Integrating analyses in mixed methods research*. Los Angeles, CA: Sage.

Combs, J. P., & Onwuegbuzie, A. J. (2010). Describing and illustrating data analysis in mixed research. *International Journal of Education, 2*(2), E13. doi:10.5296/ije.v2i2.526

Emmel, N. (2013). *Sampling and choosing cases in qualitative research: A realist approach*. London, England: Sage.

Fetters, M. D., Curry, L. A., & Creswell, J. W. (2013). Achieving integration in mixed methods designs—principles and practices. *Health Services Research, 48*, 2134–2156. doi:10.1111/1475–6773.12117

Glaser, B. G., & Strauss, A. L. (1967). *The discovery of grounded theory: Strategies for qualitative research*. New York, NY: Aldine de Gruyter.

Guetterman, T., Creswell, J. W., & Kuckartz, U. (2015). Using joint displays and MAXQDA software to represent the results of mixed methods research. In M. T. McCrudden, G. Schraw, & C. W. Buckendahl (Eds.), *Use of visual displays in research and testing* (pp. 145–175). Charlotte, NC: Information Age Publishing.

Guetterman, T. C., Fetters, M. D., & Creswell, J. W. (2015). Integrating quantitative and qualitative results in health science mixed methods research through joint displays. *Annals of Family Medicine, 13*, 554–561. doi:10.1370/afm.1865

Janesick, V. J. (2016). *"Stretching" exercises for qualitative researchers*. Los Angeles, CA: Sage.

Johnson, R. B., & Christensen, L. B. (2020). *Educational research: Quantitative, qualitative, and mixed approaches* (7th ed.). Los Angeles, CA: Sage.

Kegan, R., & Lahey, L. L. (2009). *Immunity to change: How to overcome it and unlock the potential in yourself and your organization*. Boston, MA: Harvard Business Review Press.

La Pelle, N. (2004). Simplifying qualitative data analysis using general purpose software tools. *Field Methods, 16*, 85–108. doi:10.1177/1525822x03259227

Lee, Y.-J., & Greene, J. (2007). The predictive validity of an ESL placement test: A mixed methods approach. *Journal of Mixed Methods Research, 1*, 366–389. doi:10.1177/1558689807306148

Maxwell, J. A. (2013). *Qualitative research design: An interactive approach* (3rd ed.). Los Angeles, CA: Sage.

Meyer, D. Z., & Avery, L. M. (2009). Excel as a qualitative data analysis tool. *Field Methods, 21*, 91–112. doi:10.1177/1525822x08323985

Miles, M. B., & Huberman, A. M. (1994). *Qualitative data analysis: An expanded sourcebook* (2nd ed.). Thousand Oaks, CA: Sage.

Miles, M. B., Huberman, A. M., & Saldaña, J. (2020). *Qualitative data analysis: A methods sourcebook* (4th ed.). Los Angeles, CA: Sage.

Pawson, R., & Tilley, N. (1997). *Realistic evaluation.* London, England: Sage.

Plano Clark, V. L., & Sanders, K. (2015). The use of visual displays in mixed methods: Research strategies for effectively integrating the quantitative and qualitative components of a study. In M. T. McCrudden, G. Schraw, & C. W. Buckendahl (Eds.), *Use of visual displays in research and testing* (pp. 177–206). Charlotte, NC: Information Age Publishing.

Ragin, C. C. (1992). "Casing" and the process of social inquiry. In H. S. Becker & C. C. Ragin (Eds.), *What is a case? Exploring the foundations of social inquiry* (pp. 217–226). Cambridge, England: Cambridge University Press.

Ruona, W. E. A. (2005). Analyzing qualitative data. In R. A. Swanson & E. F. Holton, III (Eds.), *Research in organizations: Foundations and methods of inquiry* (pp. 233–263). San Francisco, CA: Berrett-Koehler Publishers.

Ryan, G. W. (2004). Using a word processor to tag and retrieve blocks of text. *Field Methods, 16,* 109–130. doi:10.1177/1525822x03261269

Schoonenboom, J., & Johnson, R. B. (2017). How to construct a mixed methods research design. *KZfSS Kölner Zeitschrift für Soziologie und Sozialpsychologie, 69*(2 Supplement), 107–131. doi:10.1007/s11577-017-0454-1

Shaw, E. K., Ohman-Strickland, P. A., Piasecki, A., Hudson, S. V., Ferrante, J. M., McDaniel, R. R., Jr., . . . Crabtree, B. F. (2013). Effects of facilitated team meetings and learning collaboratives on colorectal cancer screening rates in primary care practices: A cluster randomized trial. *Annals of Family Medicine, 11,* 220–228. doi:10.1370/afm.1505

Yin, R. K. (2018). *Case study research and applications* (6th ed.). Los Angeles, CA: Sage.

Part IV

Use of Software for Mixed Analysis

25

Mixing Beyond Mixed Methods

QDA Miner, SimStat, and WordStat

Normand Péladeau

1 Definition of Provalis Research's ProSuite

Provalis Research mixed method solution consists of a suite of three software. Released in 1989, SimStat is a general statistical software for the analysis of numerical and categorical data. It was created initially to deliver bootstrap resampling analysis, a statistical technique not available at that time in other statistical packages. In 1998, a content analysis and text mining module called WordStat was added, allowing the analysis of text data stored in SimStat data files using statistical methods and dictionary-based content analysis techniques. Over the years, additional supervised and unsupervised machine learning tools have been added. The last piece of software is QDA Miner. Published initially in 2004, it offers qualitative analysis features for the coding and analysis of qualitative text data and images such as coding-and-retrieval, memoing, reporting, and teamwork features.

2 When Use of ProSuite is Appropriate in MMR

Because all Provalis Research tools share the same file format, one can easily perform statistical analysis on numerical and categorical data using SimStat, perform qualitative coding on stored documents using QDA Miner, or apply the powerful content analysis and text mining features of WordStat on those same documents. Moreover, the coexistence of numerical, categorical, and textual data in the same data file gives a unique ability to explore relationships between numerical and textual variables or to compare qualitative codings or content categories among subgroups of individuals.

QDA Miner by itself is especially appropriate for small projects involving a mix of qualitative data, such as text and image and quantitative data. Its coding and annotation features are easy to learn and use and its integrated descriptive and comparative statistical features should satisfy the basic needs of most mixed methods researchers. QDA Miner is also fast and robust enough to handle large datasets that might be difficult for other qualitative software to handle. Specially designed search features relying on information retrieval and machine learning techniques provide advanced computer assistance either to speed up the qualitative coding of textual data or to increase its consistency. Such features were designed not to replace the human aspect of qualitative coding but, instead, to provide suggestions, thereby allowing the researcher to review those before any coding operation. In a sense, such forms of computer assistance provide a means for mixed methods researchers to analyze qualitative datasets that are too large for a purely qualitative approach, given the available resources, yet not big enough for more advanced text mining techniques.

WordStat involves a different approach to qualitative text data, allowing one to extract themes and trends inductively using unsupervised machine learning algorithms and statistical techniques or to categorize text data using content analysis dictionaries consisting of words, words patterns, phrases, and proximity rules. This approach, more appropriate to handle large amount of text data, gives the mixed methods researcher additional tools to handle new sources of data that have become more and more prevalent with the digitalization of information. We will see that such an approach does not take the human out of the equation, but simply moves the point at which the human judgment intervenes. The researcher still has the responsibility to scrutinize obtained results, to validate the extracted patterns, and to make the appropriate adjustments to improve the quality of the text analysis. WordStat may be used by itself but is also often combined with the qualitative features of QDA Miner.

3 Technical Outline of QDA Miner and WordStat

For many external observers, Provalis Research's venture into mixed methods started in 2004 with the release of QDA Miner 1.0. We will see later that this is not entirely accurate and does not reflect the whole picture. Introduced in an already competitive market, this new qualitative software offered features similar to other software available on the market at that time. It claimed, however, to differ from the others and present itself as being the only true mixed methods software on the market. Although this might no longer be the case today, we believe it is worth reviewing the three main reasons supporting such a bold claim.

Reason #1. Integrated Statistical Analysis

The very first release of QDA Miner 1.0 included many of the statistical analysis features suggested as being useful to qualitative researchers (Bazeley, 2003; Miles & Huberman, 1994) or those used by researchers who routinely *quantified the qual*. It offered hierarchical clustering on coding based on their co-occurrences, as well as clustering of cases based on their coding patterns. Coding co-occurrences and coding similarities could be analyzed using multidimensional scaling and proximity plots. QDA Miner 1.0 also allowed comparison analysis with a crosstabulation feature with association measures for assessing the association of coding with nominal, ordinal, or numerical variables, including statistical measures such as chi-square, likelihood ratios, F value, Pearson's r, and several nonparametric statistics. It also offered more advanced statistics and graphics, including correspondence analysis, heatmaps, and many other visualizations typical of quantitative research such as bar charts, line charts, and pie charts. In 2004, this was in sharp contrast to other qualitative software that did not even offer basic numerical transformation on code frequencies, such as the computation of percentages. Although many competing qualitative tools claimed to be offering support for mixed methods research, none of these could perform any of the analysis or display these kinds of graphs. Instead, they required the researcher to export the coding results to another software tool such as SPSS or Microsoft Excel to perform the quantitative analysis. In other words, at best, they allowed the mixing of qualitative and quantitative methods through the exportation to statistical tools. QDA Miner 1.0 was mixing qualitative and quantitative research tools in one software. But all this is history. Today, some of these quantitative analysis and visualization tools have become standard features in other qualitative analysis tools.

Reason #2. Cases-by-Variables Structure

One could say that the second element, still unique to QDA Miner, that justified the mixed methods label was that it shared the same file format as SimStat, the company's statistical software. In other words, when one creates a qualitative project in QDA Miner, one also creates a statistical database that could be directly opened by a statistical analysis software for the analysis of numerical data. However, whether a researcher uses SimStat or any other tools for statistical computing is irrelevant to the claim of offering better support for mixed methods. What is more crucial and represents the real basis for facilitating mixed methods research is the principle that qualitative data in QDA Miner must be stored and organized into a CASES-BY-VARIABLES structure (see the two top left window of Figure 25.1), a data layout quite familiar to quantitative

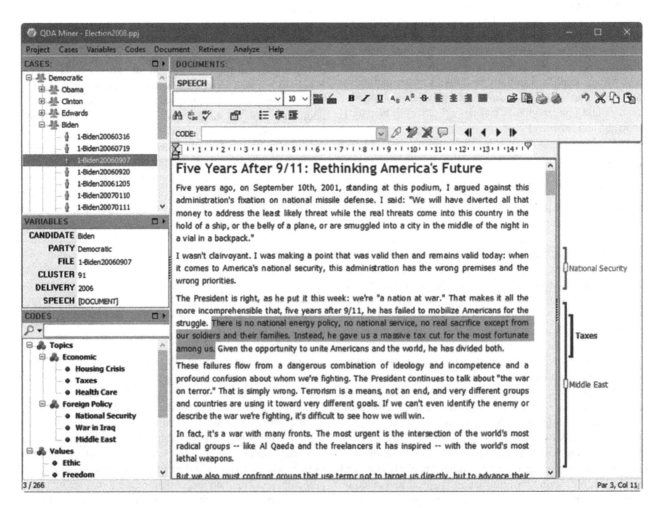

FIGURE 25.1 QDA Miner main interface.

researchers and common to statistical software. It is this structure that allows for the seamless integration of quantitative and qualitative data in a single project file. For example, one could easily attach to a qualitative research project consisting of interview transcripts and social demographic data, as well as responses of each interviewee to a questionnaire or any other kind of quantitative measurements. If a researcher performs a quantitative research study and collects survey responses from several hundred or thousands of respondents and wants to perform in-depth unstructured interviews with a small sample of them, he only needs to add a "document" variable to his existing data structure and store the full transcript of those interviews in the survey database in the corresponding case. The coexistence of the transcripts with all survey responses allows the seamless exploration of the relationship of coding occurrences or frequencies with any of those quantitative responses. It could be done within QDA Miner itself, using the CODING x VARIABLES feature, through the execution of SimStat, or like other qualitative software, through the transformation of qualitative coding into numerical variables and the exportation to an external file that could then be read by other statistical tools such as SPSS, SAS, or STATA. Qualitative data being treated as a variable, like any other quantitative or categorical variables, also allows the structuring of research projects where more than one qualitative data source could be associated with the same case, typical of panel and longitudinal data research projects. A typical example would be the combination of sociodemographic variables, responses to questionnaires and quantitative measuring instruments, along with a pre-intervention, a post-intervention, and a follow-up interview transcript. This capacity to associate many qualitative data sources to quantitative data from a single case is something that is either not possible in other software or can only be achieved by resorting to contrived structuring features.

Reason #3. Integration with a Quantitative Text Analysis Module

A third reason why QDA Miner 1.0 claimed to be a true mixed methods software was its close integration with WordStat, a content analysis and text mining software. Many people view mixed methods research as the combination of traditional qualitative research methods such as grounded theory, ethnography, and case studies, often involving interviews, observations, and other forms of naturalistic data collection and analysis, with traditional quantitative study methods, such as survey research, or any other form of quantitative measurements subjected, in the end, to statistical analysis. Text mining techniques and quantitative content analysis do not fit such a strict definition because they consist of the analysis of qualitative data, in the form of unstructured text, using quantitative techniques.

Although these techniques escape the strict definition of either qualitative research (qualitative data analyzed qualitatively) or quantitative studies (quantitative measures analyzed statistically), they remain single research methods if not combined with other ones. But the fact that WordStat presents itself as an add-on to QDA Miner or to SimStat greatly facilitates the combination of less common research methods to traditional ones which, by definition, could be considered as a different variety of mixed methods. For example, one can easily submit coded interviews stored in QDA Miner to an exploratory text mining analysis either to generate new insights or to achieve a form of triangulation by showing how the vocabulary used by interviewees illustrates some of the conclusions obtained through a qualitative analysis. An example somewhat close to this is provided by the study from Baumer, Mimno, Guha, Quan, and Gay (2017), wherein the same data were analyzed independently using a grounded theory approach and a topic modeling statistical technique. The comparison of the results shows that the two analyses produce some similar and some complementary insights about the phenomenon of interest. Another example would be the combination of social media data analysis using text mining techniques along with either surveys or focus group research, a combination that is now common practice in many market research firms.

One important defining aspect of mixed methods research is the integration of these methods at some stage of the research process. In the study previously mentioned (i.e., Baumer et al., 2017), data analyses were performed independently, and the integration came only at the very end, which would be considered by some more as an example of a multimethod, rather than a mixed methods, research project (Bazeley, 2018). We will see later that the possibility of combining text analysis techniques in WordStat and qualitative analysis in QDA Miner goes beyond the simple capacity of analyzing the same data sets independently using different methods.

Although it could be claimed that QDA Miner 1.0, which was released in 2004, was the only true mixed methods software on the market, with the growing popularity of mixed methods research in social sciences, and the foreseeable competition among software vendors, we have seen a convergence of functionalities in various qualitative software. Similar mixed methods features had been implemented in other qualitative tools such as NVivo, and more recently, in MaxQDA. We also witnessed the emergence of new tools like Dedoose that have been mixing qualitative and quantitative data and also claimed the status of a mixed methods tool.

At the time of this writing, QDA Miner was in its sixth major revision. Over the successive releases, additional features have been implemented, some of them designed to address qualitative researchers' needs and borrowed from other packages, and several other ones, unique to QDA Miner. Here are other noticeable features of QDA Miner, unique or not.

Intercoder Agreement

Although not specifically characteristic of mixed methods research, a unique feature of the first incarnation of the software was the computation of intercoder reliability statistics, a feature often requested by the more quantitatively inclined qualitative researchers, yet not available in other packages, with the exception of a free Nud*ist module developed and distributed by an independent researcher (Bourdon, 2000). The intercoder reliability feature in QDA Miner introduced four levels of agreements and several statistical corrections for chance, features partially adopted by other vendors several years later.

Data Importation and Exportation Features

Like many of its competitors, the current version of the software includes the ability to import from many different sources, including Word documents, Acrobat PDF, Rich Text, or HTML. It also added support for less popular document formats such as ePub, XPS, PowerPoint and OpenOffice document files. It can also import qualitative and quantitative data from many database formats, Excel spreadsheets, and text delimited files and do the same for SPSS and Stata files. When an Excel spreadsheet or a database is imported into QDA Miner, spreadsheet columns or database fields are automatically transformed into quantitative and qualitative variables, while all spreadsheet rows or database records become cases. Text fields become codable, while numerical ones, whether they are categorical, numerical, or dates, become available for filtering cases, performing comparisons, and so forth.

In 2015, QDA Miner introduced the importation from several survey platforms (SurveyMonkey, Qualtrics, SurveyGizmo, Voxco, and QuestionPro), three reference management tools (Endnote, Mendeley, Zotero), and various email servers and web services (Gmail, HotMail, Outlook, MBox, and EML), as well as data from social media like Twitter, Facebook, Reddit, YouTube, and RSS feeds. The latest version of QDA Miner, released in 2020, also supports the importation of Nexis UNI and Factiva news search output files, allowing the importation of newspapers, blog publications, and TV and radio news transcripts. One useful feature for researchers analyzing social media is the ability to monitor, after the initial search, those Internet platforms for new posts. This is achieved by the Web Collector, which consists of a small application running in the background and accessible via the Windows system tray. It can be scheduled to connect to the web at user-defined intervals and aggregate new posts to an existing project. For example, at the time of this writing the Twitter API limits the number of tweets one can collect at any given time to 18,000 per 15 minutes and is restricted to tweets no more than 10 days old. Although historical data can only be legally obtained by buying them through a social media aggregation service, the web collector provides a means to aggregate future tweets to those initially collected. One may collect this way more than a million tweets on a trending topic in a single day.

The Mixing of Geospatial and Time Data

Another form of mixed methods research involved the combination of qualitative data with geospatial information (Fielding & Cisneros-Puebla, 2010). Thanks to the unrelenting advocacy efforts of Cesar Cisneros-Puebla for this type of research, CAQDAS tools started to integrate geospatial features as early as 2008. QDA Miner introduced its own geotagging in version 4.0 released in 2011. It offers the ability to attach geographic coordinates to text segments, image areas, or qualitative tags and the capability to jump from a geotagged element to Google Earth for visualizing the geographic location associated with it. Although these types of features were not new in themselves, QDA Miner 4.0 went several steps further with the implementation of certain unique features. Probably the most distinctive one was the ability to attach to a coded segment a hyperlink with a time stamp or a time period along with geographic coordinates, allowing one to locate a specific event not only in space but in time as well. Those links could then be retrieved and filtered, allowing one to create dynamic visualization of the spatial distribution of a phenomenon over time on a single Google Earth map. Those visualizations could be exported as KMZ files storing a set of placemarks with customized icons and the associated text segment and source information (e.g., code, case id, coder's name). Time-tagged coded segments could also be displayed in chronological order using an interactive timeline (see Figure 25.2), allowing one to reconstruct a sequence of events and jump to the corresponding coded segment. Version 4.0 also introduced a date and location search tool that uses text patterns and gazetteers to identify and tag text segments containing either dates or geographic location information such as city, states, province, or country names.

The integration of GIS features did not stop there. In 2016, a new version, 5.0 of QDA Miner, was released with a mapping companion software: GISViewer. This tool uses web mapping services to display high resolution maps. It supports industry standards ArcGIS shapefiles, allowing the creation of multi-layered maps for interactive plots of data points and the production of choropleth maps and heatmaps. The new mapping tool allows filtering of data points on categorical, numerical, and date variables and the creation of custom animations to easily identify spatiotemporal trends, cyclical patterns, or relationships to numerical variables. Although not as powerful as full-featured GIS mapping tools such as ArcGIS or MapInfo, it was designed to be easy enough to allow researchers, without training in GIS, to create maps from qualitative data. This new version of QDA Miner also introduced a geocoding feature to transform various information such as city names, postal codes, or IP addresses into geographic coordinates. The information could later be used to map the spatial distribution of codes in a project.

Advance Text Searches and Autocoding Features

QDA Miner can be used to analyze text and still images, but, currently, it does not provide any support for the coding of audio or video files. It distinguishes itself, however, by an extensive support for the analysis of projects involving large quantities of text. Such computer assistance takes the form of many advance text search tools unique to the software.

For example, the Section Retrieval tool has been designed to extract and code sections of text in structured documents. It can leverage the boilerplates of structured interviews, report cards, or forms, or use the fixed string delimiters in interview or focus group transcripts to identify answers to specific questions or speech turns. A single search can retrieve all relevant sections across all documents in all cases and autocode them.

The keyword search is another unique feature that provides computer assistance to speed up the coding of qualitative projects. It blurs the distinction between qualitative and quantitative content analysis by offering a way to attach to any code in a qualitative codebook search terms, including words, word patterns, and phrases. One may then perform a search using those keywords and retrieve all documents, paragraphs, or sentences matching those terms and apply the appropriate code

Mixing Beyond Mixed Methods 295

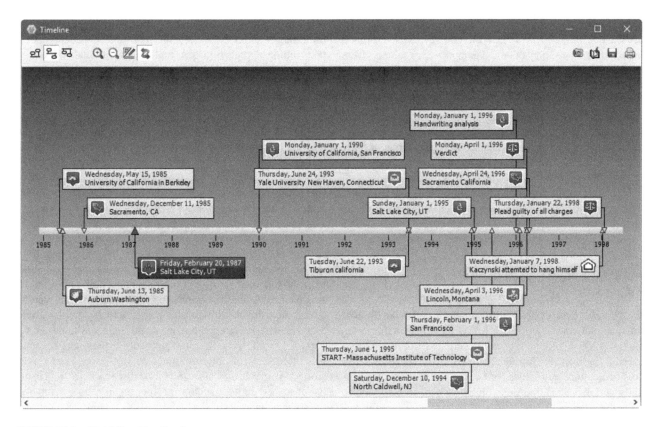

FIGURE 25.2 QDA Miner Timeline feature.

to the retrieved segments. Yet, the main distinction between a classical quantitative content analysis and this approach is that rather than providing a quantification of a concept by counting how many times entries are being mentioned, this feature merely retrieves the matching text segments, leaving the researcher the opportunity to review them and remove irrelevant ones before applying a code to the remaining text segments.

More advanced search tools rely on supervised and unsupervised machine learning to provide computer assistance for the coding of large projects. One example of supervised machine learning is the query-by-example feature that allows one to initialize a text search using a single sentence or paragraph and retrieve comparable text segments presented in descending order of similarity. By tagging a few of them as relevant or irrelevant and searching again, and by repeating this "search + relevance feedback" process, one can "train" the software to identify more relevant text segments and autocode them. On a new qualitative research project, this allows one to get a "sneak peek" at the remainder of the documents to see whether a peculiar idea is really atypical or can be found elsewhere. Rather than starting from a single text segment, one can also initiate a search by providing several examples and non-examples associated with specific qualitative codes either in the project itself or in another project file. This could greatly speed up the coding of partially coded projects. The query-by-example might also be useful for fully coded projects, allowing one to identify instances that might have been overlooked. A good example of the learning capability of the query-by-example is provided by Evans's (2009) work for his thesis in which he trained QDA Miner to identify metaphoric use of slavery terms in Alexander Hamilton's writings, a corpus of more than 10 million words. He started by retrieving all sentences containing words like "slaves" or "enslaved," and by coding them as either literal or metaphoric. He then performed a query-by-example, selecting all metaphoric coded segments as examples, and all literal ones as non-examples. After a few sequences of relevant feedback and searches, he was able to identify twice as many new examples of slavery metaphors in the entire text corpus, none of which containing the words with which he started.

Although supervised machine learning requires the provision of sample data corresponding to what one may be looking for, unsupervised machine learning relies instead on the identification of patterns within the documents themselves to extract information, with the expectation that such information could be relevant. The Cluster Extraction feature of QDA Miner is such a feature. It has been designed to speed up the coding of short text responses, such as brief comments, responses to open-ended questions, or short social media text like tweets. It can compare tens of thousands of responses and generate mutually exclusive sets of responses similar to each other. Such a similarity is established not solely on the words they contain, but also on parts of words, allowing the grouping of text segments using inflected or misspelled forms of the same words. Using simple drag-and-drop operations, the coder may then merge similar groupings of responses, split those containing more than one set of ideas, insert additional responses, or remove irrelevant ones before coding those groupings. The cluster coding feature typically speeds up the coding process of open-ended responses by a factor of 3 to 10 times. For very focused questions, it can reduce the coding time even more. For example, in a survey of online gamers where subjects were asked to identify their ethnicity, the cluster extraction tool was able to automatically group 5,754 out of the 6,048 responses into 110 clusters only, most of them consistent enough to be coded as is. This represents a 52 times speed improvement of the manual coding of each response.

Despite all the computer assistance to coding, none of these features will result in coding being applied automatically. The user will always be presented with the opportunity to review all retrieved text segments, to examine their context, and to remove those he/she believes are not appropriate before coding the remaining ones. This is in sharp contrast to WordStat, which attempts to achieve greater automation in text processing.

WordStat Content Analysis and Text Mining Software

WordStat was first released in 1998 as an add-on to the SimStat statistical software. This was a full 6 years before the initial release of QDA Miner. We could argue that its release represented, in itself, the introduction of a mixed methods set of tools of a nature quite different from the perception one normally gets from reading mixed methods research textbooks. It involves the analysis of both quantitative and qualitative data, the latter being potentially rich unstructured text. Yet, its quantitative approach to the analysis of qualitative data may be perceived by some researchers as a strange, and at worst, as treasonous by the more qualitatively inclined mixed methods researchers. These kinds of tools have often been described in a somewhat derogatory way as tools to count words, which is a blatant simplification of their full capabilities.

Initially designed to support the extraction of information from a large number of clinical records in program evaluation research, WordStat's approach to text data relies on the assumption that the semantic nature of words allows one to grasp specific phenomenon expressed in a limited number of ways. Much like a grounded theory expert who infers meaning from reading text, quantitative content analysis can find traces of the same realities by the extractions and processing of concepts using lexicons or statistical patterns in text data. It combines quantitative content analysis methods (Weber, 1990; Neuendorf, 2017), natural language processing, and data mining techniques.

Although it might have been perceived as marginally useful 20 or 30 years ago, the increased availability of information in digital formats, including journal articles, reports, news media, and the advent of the Internet, social media, blogs, and microblogging platforms such as Twitter, where people express their opinions, as well as electronic communications through emails, chat rooms, and mobile devices, have only accentuated the need for new tools capable of analyzing larger amounts of text. Traditional qualitative analysis tools are no longer up to the task, because of their inability to scale up. This new-found wealth of data requires new skills for researchers to tackle this new source of data.

WordStat can be complex for newcomers, offering a wide range of features to analyze text data. We can, however, bring down all these features to three broad strategies to extract information from large amounts of text: an exploratory text mining approach, a quantitative content analysis, and a machine learning approach.

Exploratory Text Mining

The exploratory text mining approach is an attempt to extract relevant information by letting the software identify patterns and trends in a text corpus in itself or in relationship to other variables or metadata. The most basic form of text exploration is the extraction of a list of the most frequent words presented in descending order of frequency. The application of a stop-word list to eliminate highly frequent, yet meaningless, words such as prepositions, conjunctions, pronouns, and some adverbs is essential to easily identify the most important topics. Stemming or lemmatization routines may also be applied to group inflected forms and morphological derivations into a single entry. A popular graphic representation of such type of data is the word cloud. WordStat provides such a graph as well as bar charts. A slightly more insightful frequency table can be obtained by the extraction of multiword expressions because it is often easier to interpret and less ambiguous than single words. WordStat can also automatically extract a frequency list of named entities, such as person, organization, company, or product names, as well as references to geographic locations and use of acronyms.

Although the extraction of any of these semantic elements provides some indication of what a text collection is about, it gives very little information about the context in which those elements appear. It is, however, possible in WordStat to reconstruct useful contextual information using two broad strategies: (a) by analyzing the co-occurrence of words and phrases or (b) by assessing the relationship of those elements to external metadata, often in the form of numerical or categorical variables. Knowing that a specific topic has been mentioned by 10% or maybe 20% of our participants might not be as useful as the demonstration that those mentions almost always occur in close proximity to positive or negative terms, or that they were expressed proportionally more often by women participants, by younger ones, or by those scoring high or low on a satisfaction scale. This recontextualization process of the decontextualized linguistic elements is what makes WordStat something more than just a word counting tool.

Co-occurrence Analysis

In its most basic form, the analysis of co-occurrences starts by the computation of a matrix that quantifies how often frequent words appear together either within the same sentence, the same paragraph, or the same document. The raw co-occurrence is then normalized using a measure of proximity, such as a Jaccard, a Dice, or a correlation coefficient, making them easier to compare. However, extracting information from such a matrix is very cumbersome due to its high dimensionality: A co-occurrence matrix of the 300 most frequent words would generate 44,700 distinct values. The upper limit in the number of words in WordStat being 7,000 words, this represents a matrix of 49 million cells, with almost 24.5 million distinct values. Several

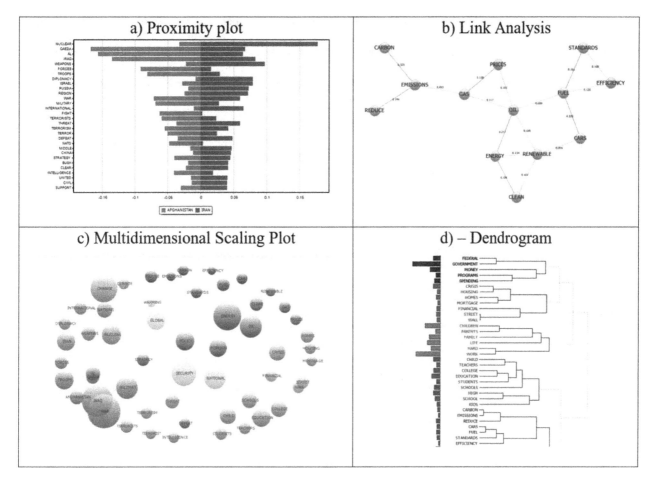

FIGURE 25.3 Graphic tools for co-occurrence analysis.

tools are available to extract useful information from such a matrix. They are represented in Figure 25.3.

The proximity plot (Figure 25.3a) is probably the simplest one, allowing one to focus on a single word to identify with which other words it is most often associated. It is equivalent to the extraction of all values in a single column of the matrix sorted in descending order. One can also select a few words to compare and contrast their association with other words. Such a graphic representation is often used in market research to characterize how people are talking about a specific product or service and by media experts or political scientists to identify how specific issues are being framed in the media and compare their representation in different media outlets.

By treating those co-occurrence measures as if they were proximity (the more often they co-occur, the closer they are), WordStat can also plot words in a 2D or 3D Euclidian space using multidimensional scaling (Figure 25.3c). In such a graph, words appearing often together will tend to be plotted next to each other, whereas words never appearing together will more likely be positioned far apart. Such a graphical representation might be useful to identify and to illustrate broad dimensions in the data. Its explanatory value, however, decreases when too many words are plotted or when the relative distances between words cannot be represented accurately, as expressed with a high stress value.

A more useful approach available in WordStat consists of applying a hierarchical cluster analysis to the full matrix to produce a dendrogram (Figure 25.3d). This dendrogram is built by successively grouping words that are the more closely associated. Although, at the initial stage of the clustering process, the small grouping of two or three words reveals common phrases and idioms, further grouping items into bigger clusters helps to reveal topics. For example, words like carbon and emission may be connected initially, but may later be associated with words like "reduce," "global," "warming," "energy," and "clean." An interesting property of hierarchical clustering when applied on words is that related topics also tend to be graphed close to each other, allowing the user to identify not only the range of topics being mentioned in a text collection but also suggesting a way to hierarchically organize those into broader categories. For example, after analyzing 243 political speeches from the 2008 U.S. presidential race, specific economic topics such a job creation and tax reduction were plotted next to each other, and in proximity to other domestic issues, such as health and education, while one could identify further down another grouping of topics related to the Middle East, such as a cluster of words related to the war in Iraq, and another one about al-Qaeda and Afghanistan, both of those plotted not far from another grouping of words about Iran and nuclear weapons.

Despite its usefulness, hierarchical clustering applied to word co-occurrence matrices has some limitations. Although it deals partly with synonymy by bringing many of the related words together, a word can only be associated with one cluster, and by doing so, clustering does not fully recognize the fact that words may have more than one meaning or be used in different contexts. By doing so, it may join together two unrelated sets of words. It also attempts to cluster all words, including some that may co-occur with few other words and would rather be ignored. Both inconveniences are dealt with more successfully by topic modeling techniques because a word may become associated with more than one topic while other words may be left out if not associated strongly enough. Another distinctive feature of topic modeling is that words will be weighted differently depending on their contribution to the extracted topic. WordStat implements two statistical methods for extracting topics from co-occurrence matrices: (a) factor analysis with Varimax rotation, and (b) non-negative matrix factorization (NNMF). Although the most popular topic modeling technique in computer sciences relies on Latent Dirichlet Allocation (LDA) for the topic extraction, we found that solutions obtained using factor analysis produced sets of words that were more distinct from each other and were generally perceived as being more coherent than were topics extracted using LDA (Péladeau & Davoodi, 2018). Another noteworthy difference with hierarchical cluster analysis is that topic modeling requires one to specify in advance the number of topics to extract, which might require one to perform several runs in order to identify an optimal solution. WordStat's implementation also includes a unique feature called "topic enrichment," which automatically adds associated phrases and suggests additional ones to be selected manually. It also identifies potential exception phrases that might help further disambiguate some words as well as misspellings that might prevent one from detecting the presence of a topic. Carefully selecting these suggestions allows one to obtain a set of items that can more accurately measure the prevalence of a topic. In information retrieval terms, it improves both precision and recall.

Comparison Analysis

Another way to quickly assess the context of words and phrases as well as topics, is through the assessment of the relationship of those text elements with associated numerical or categorical variables. WordStat's user interface includes panels to the right of the word frequency, phrases extraction, clustering, and topic modeling pages, allowing a constant comparison of the frequency of any of those elements with up to two variables using bar charts or line charts.

A dedicated crosstabulation page lets one further explore those relationships and apply various association statistics, such as chi-square, F test, Pearson's r, or other nonparametric associate measures. Besides creating highly customizable

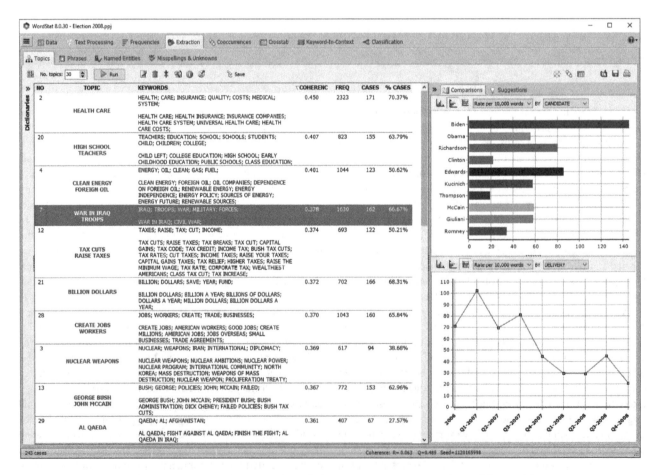

FIGURE 25.4 WordStat topic modeling feature wherein automatically extracted topics are compared by candidates and time.

Obama		Clinton		McCain		Romney	
More	Less	More	Less	More	Less	More	Less
Politics	Government	Information	Washington	Honor	Bush	Marriage	Care
Washington	Information	Privacy	War	Greater	College	Strength	Health
Change	Quality	Patients	Freedom	Nuclear	Working	Human	War
Lobbyists	Human	Science	Nuclear	Government	White	Governor	Senator
Black	Percent	Care	Taxes	Taxes	George	Healthcare	Workers
George	Healthcare	Nurses	Israel	Defeat	Dream	Court	Iraq
Moment	Defense	Health	Iraq	Forces	Young	Nations	Insurance
Afford	Patients	Research	Politics	Markets	Kids	Michigan	Jobs
Street	Greater	Percent	Military	VA	Start	Military	Election
War	Spending	Administration	Change	Reagan	Change	Strengthen	Companies
Term	Doctors	Medical	AL	Trust	Standing	Freedom	Afford
Dream	Federal	Women	Qaeda	Freedom	King	Iran	Women
Diplomacy	Marriage	Doctors	Weapons	Market	DR	Free	Pay
Election	Research	House	Iran	Security	Billion	Reagan	Start
Cities	Honor	Patient	Nations	Congress	Science	Spending	Administration

FIGURE 25.5 Deviation table for four candidates of the 2008 U.S. presidential election.

bar charts, line charts, polar plots, and bubble plots, the crosstab page offers more advanced visualizations tools such as a heatmap with dual clustering on rows and columns in which frequencies are represented using brightness of colors. It also offers 2D and 3D correspondence plots that are very useful for extracting information from large contingency tables. Another useful feature for comparison is the deviation table, which lists in a single table, words, phrases, or topics that are characteristic of each class of a categorical variable in descending order of specificity. The table can also include text elements that are negatively related to a specific class (see Figure 25.5).

Quantitative Content Analysis Features

Although text mining techniques can provide useful insights in matter of minutes or even seconds, the estimation of the prevalence of extracted information might lack precision and sensitivity. Also, because text mining relies on statistical patterns in text data, it might not work as well on small data sets. Another inconvenience of text mining techniques is their lack of sensitivity to low frequency events. The quantitative content analysis features of WordStat represents a solution to this by allowing the researcher to build a custom content analysis dictionary that will gather words, word patterns, and phrases into hierarchical tree of concepts. The software comes with several dictionaries allowing one to assess sentiments, psychological or sociological dimensions, political stances, personal values, brand images, and so on. Yet many research situations require the creation and validation of a custom dictionary or lexicon.

Building a custom content analysis dictionary and validating it can be time consuming. WordStat provides many tools to assist the researcher in such a task. Clustering or topic modeling solutions may be saved as content analysis dictionaries, potentially representing a useful starting point. Adding items to a custom dictionary can be achieved easily by dragging and dropping items from almost any output table. Another useful feature is provided by the "suggestions" panel that identifies, for a given word or content category, synonyms, antonyms, or semantically related terms (e.g., hypernyms, hyponyms) present in the text corpus being analyzed. It will also identify inflected and misspelled forms of the selected item. One can manually choose from this list, relevant ones and move them to the proper content category.

The keyword-in-context (KWIC) feature is an essential tool to assess how words are actually used and whether they are consistent with the construct one is attempting to measure. It can be used at any time during or after the dictionary construction process. By displaying the context in which a word appears, it allows one to assess whether the meaning of a particular word is dependent upon its use in certain phrases or idioms. The careful selection of these may then be used to disambiguate words with multiple meanings by treating those phrases and idioms as exceptions (false positives), or by replacing the ill-chosen word with those phrases and idioms that are appropriate (true positives). A more advanced way to perform disambiguation is through proximity rules. WordStat can associate a word to a content category in the presence or absence of other words or categories of words in its surroundings. One can specify, for any given word, multiple conditions related to surrounding context. An example of such a rule would be to associate a positive word like "satisfied" to a negative evaluation of a product if this word follows a negation such as "not", "never", or "don't" within up to three or four words and is in the same sentence as a reference to this product.

The careful combination of all those elements by a skillful researcher can engender a highly precise and sensitive measuring instrument in the form of a content analysis dictionary. A major benefit of such an approach is that not only can it allow the researcher to assess the desired constructs on its current text corpus, but it can be applied as well on new data sets, by him-herself or even by other researchers.

Automatic Document Classification

The third approach supported by WordStat consists of supervised machine learning techniques such as Naïve Bayes or k-Nearest Neighbor, allowing one to automatically assign documents to predefined categories. This is achieved by collecting a large set of documents that have been previously categorized and submitting the documents with their associated categorical value to one of the machine learning algorithms. WordStat will automatically identify the words associated with each category, weight them, and combine them to create a predictive model. The obtained classification model can then be stored on disk and applied to new documents in order to predict the appropriate category to which it belongs.

A common example of document classification is provided by the spam filtering feature of email clients or web services. Other possible applications could be the assessment of the political affiliation of candidates from their speeches or their writing, the automatic grading of essays, and the detection of positive and negative sentiments in social media posts. For qualitative researchers, machine learning may also be used to fully or partially automate the coding of large text collections by providing to the learning algorithms numerous text segments to which a qualitative code has been assigned along with other segments to which such a code does not apply. Once successfully developed and tested for its accuracy, this model can then be imported back into QDA Miner and used to retrieve text segments that should be coded the same way. It is important to consider that even if a model lacks precision and returns too many false positives, it may still have a good recall, allowing the qualitative researcher to save huge amounts of time by manually reviewing a much smaller amount of text segments.

WordStat's automatic document classification feature offers various cross-validation techniques (external dataset, leave-one-out, n-fold cross-validation) to assess the model's ability to make accurate predictions, as well as various feature selections and term weighting methods. The permutation of all these settings along with the selection of different word sample sizes can generate a massive number of predictive models each yielding different results. To assist in the identification of the best settings, WordStat includes an experiment module that can generate thousands of models from the permutation of settings. It will then batch process these models and aggregate results in a table and on a line plot, allowing one to easily identify the best performing classification model.

Mixing Qualitative and Quantitative Text Analysis

The possibility of quickly moving back and forth between QDA Miner and WordStat encourages the integration of various techniques from different methodological traditions into a single research project. For example, a cluster analysis of respondents to a survey based on their responses to open-ended questions could be used as a way to sample survey participants for an in-depth interview. One may also submit interview transcripts of a qualitative research project to WordStat in order to familiarize oneself with the range of topics being mentioned by all interviewees or to generate new insights that may then be explored qualitatively. Alternatively, a project involving a large quantity of documents and analyzed using either an exploratory text mining or a quantitative content analysis may necessitate the extraction of a small subset of documents to be reviewed, tagged, and annotated manually.

Although such integration is facilitated by the possibility to call WordStat directly from QDA Miner, several additional features, in both tools, further encourage the integration of qualitative and quantitative techniques for the analysis of textual data. For example, when one calls WordStat from QDA Miner, qualitative coding may be used to restrict text mining to specific coded segments or, on the contrary, to ignore text sections associated with specific codes. This is useful to remove from interview transcripts interventions by interviewers. It could also be used for the analysis of only specific sections of a collection of reports or journal articles, sections previously tagged in QDA Miner. It is even possible to compare text associated with different codes. For example, one could compare intervention by male and female participants in a series of focus group transcripts by attaching gender codes to the participant's speech turns and then instructing WordStat to compare text associated with these two codes. Such a feature may prove to be useful if one attempts to automate some of the coding tasks on a larger data set, by the identification of distinguishing key words and key phrases to be added to a content analysis dictionary, or through supervised machine learning.

Another form of integration is the possibility while still in WordStat to add new codes to the project codebook and autocode sentences or paragraphs extracted using the keyword retrieval feature, just like one would normally do in QDA Miner. This supplements the various text retrieval tools already available in QDA Miner with the possibility to search for relevant text segments using either hierarchical clustering, topic modeling, or a content analysis dictionary.

Finally, categorization dictionaries as well as automatic document classification models developed in WordStat may also be saved to disk and used within QDA Miner to retrieve relevant text segments or to perform automatic coding of text. These are just a few examples of how both tools interact with each other. The integration of qualitative and quantitative text analysis research methods clearly permeates through the design of both QDA Miner and WordStat and eliminates many of the barriers that one would encounter when attempting to combine qualitative data analysis with either quantitative content analysis, exploratory text mining, or automatic document classification.

4 Empirical Demonstration of QDA Miner and WordStat

The wide range of techniques offered by QDA Miner and WordStat can hardly be illustrated in a few empirical demonstrations. A more comprehensive picture would be better achieved by looking up the numerous academic papers published using these tools (see the resources section below). Although the typical coding-and-retrieval and memoing features of CAQDAS tools are familiar to most mixed methods researchers and need no presentation, it seems more appropriate to illustrate less well-known techniques and reveal how such techniques can improve the qualitative data analysis process. O'Kane, Smith and Lerman's (2019) article is, in our opinion, the most systematic presentation of how features found in some CAQDAS tools (namely QDA Miner and NVivo) could be used to enhance the transparency and trustworthiness of qualitative research. For example, they report that the query-by-example feature of QDA Miner was used on transcript of 11 in-depth interviews of award-winning plant managers to explore hunches about the importance of community involvement. After entering the phase "outreach to the community" in a query, performing an initial search, providing relevant feedback on the retrieved examples, and performing a second search, they were able to retrieve and code eight relevant text segments that confirmed their hunch. They later performed another query-by-example using the search term "walking around plant daily" in order to compare results with the list of text segments that were already coded and found two additional relevant examples that they had missed. The authors also show how coding cooccurrence analysis was used to identify a strong proximity of two codes related to emotions and actions in scientific activities and how a subsequent coding sequence analysis was used to illustrate how active engagements could be used as a coping mechanism to resolve negative emotions. According to O'Kane et al. (2019): "the code sequence analysis provided patterns to clarify relationships in the data and helped us construct a more robust story regarding how the process unfolds and how the different elements of the process relate to one another" (p. 18).

Their article demonstrates how many other techniques, including text searches, coding retrieval, word frequency, and code frequency analysis, as well as coding agreement, can enable the researchers in their efforts to explore hypothesis, review their coding, revise their codebook, and achieve more consistent, trustworthy qualitative results.

To illustrates how WordStat may be used to analyze large amounts of data in a timely manner, we will describe the process by which media coverage of an important historical event was performed and quickly published as a blog. On May 25, 2020, George Floyd was killed in Minneapolis, Minnesota by a White police officer. The release of a video of the incident triggered protests all over the United States and around the world for several weeks. On June 2, we decided to examine how major media organizations were covering these events. A search on Factiva allowed us to retrieve 927 news transcripts from eight major news outlets. The title and the body of each news transcript was extracted automatically in QDA Miner 6.0, resulting in a corpus of more than 1.8 million words. Because news transcripts could cover various topics, the text retrieval feature of QDA Miner was used to extract all paragraphs mentioning "Floyd"—resulting in the 6,362 paragraphs. These paragraphs, totaling 284,713 words, where then extracted to WordStat. The computation of a correspondence plot and a deviation table on words immediately revealed major differences in the vocabulary used by different media. For example, the words "black" and "white" were used less often by Fox News than by any other media outlet,

suggesting a lower emphasis on racial aspect of the crisis. The Wall Street Journal was the media outlet that seemed to focus the most on racial elements, with a high frequency of those two words, "black" occurring as the first word in the 20 topmost characteristic words, whereas "white" reached the fourth position. Words like "racism" and "racial" also showed up in this list (8th and 14th positions, respectively). Fox News also seemed to provide fewer details about the tragic event itself with less frequent use of words like "neck," "knee," "unharmed," or "Chauvin." When referring to the street protests, they also used the more negative term "riots," while the word "protests" was used less frequently than for any other media outlet.

Only a few seconds was needed by WordStat to produce the tables and graphics that allowed us to identify those patterns. However, looking at such differences in the top 300 most frequent words could be explained by the alternate use of other terms, such as "African-American" or "people of color" rather than "black" or "demonstration," "march," or "manifestations" as synonyms of protests. Some of those words may also be ambiguous or be used in a different context. To validate the first impression left by the exploratory text mining performed using single words only, we constructed a content analysis dictionary with categories such as race, law and order, police brutality, negative emotions, and so forth. Two of those categories attempted to differentiate how protests were characterized with words focusing on the negative elements like "riots," "chaos," looting," "rampage," "stealing," and "anarchy," and other less negative terms, including "protest," "demonstrators," and "march". WordStat's internal Thesaurus allows us to identify synonyms and related words used by journalists, while the keyword-in-context was used to validate each entry. For example, it allowed us to identify several references to the White House, forcing us to treat those as exceptions of the use of "white" as a reference to a racial element. It also allowed us to include the single word "color", because the keyword-in-context revealed that it was always part of expressions such as "people of color" or "communities of color." We ended up with a total of 207 words, categorized into 12 themes that were then used to either confirm or invalidate our first impressions. Figure 25.6 represents the proportion of time negative or more neutral or positive terms were used when talking about the protest movement.

And while the graphic reflects the fact that there were more peaceful protests than violent events, Fox news is almost twice as likely than other media to use negative terms when referring to those events. Analysis on the racial content category also confirms our first impression: racial references appear in only approximately 9% of the paragraphs mentioning George Floyd when the news originates from the Fox News network, but this percentage varies from 15% for CNN up to 35% for the Washington Post. A similar pattern was also found when looking at references to police brutality.

The development and application of a content analysis dictionary to measure more accurately and more comprehensively the various aspects we identified through a text mining approach allowed us to validate our first impressions and provide more robust evidence of disparities in media coverage of this tragic incident and its aftermath.

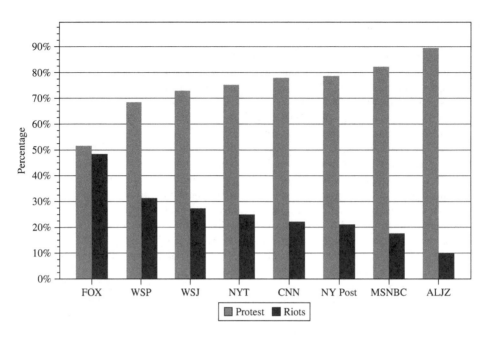

FIGURE 25.6 Use of "protest" words versus "riot" words by media.

5 Suggested Applications of QDA Miner and WordStat

QDA Miner qualitative data analysis software may be used to analyze interview or focus group transcripts, legal documents, journal articles, speeches, and even entire books, as well as drawings, photographs, paintings, and other types of visual documents. It can help one quickly analyze up to a few thousand open-ended responses, social media comments, or customer feedback. Although its advanced computer assistance features allow one to code and analyze documents more quickly and more reliably, one should seriously consider WordStat for larger datasets of unstructured text. This software can analyze from a few thousand comments to several million very quickly and has been applied on large datasets of customer feedback, social media, incident or maintenance reports, clinical records, news transcripts, legal documents, emails, financial reports, website content, speeches, insurance claims, employee interviews, resumes and job ads, and so forth. It has often been used for scientometric studies on a large number of journal abstracts as well as full articles in order to identify temporal trends and to compare research topics in different journals or different countries.

6 Strength and Limitations of QDA Miner and WordStat

The integration of machine learning and content analysis features makes this suite of software especially apt at dealing with projects involving large corpus of text as well as mixed methods research projects mixing, at the data collection stage, large quantitative studies with interviews or other forms of qualitative data.

Yet, these tools might not be appropriate for everybody. Mixed methods research projects in which the qualitative part is performed independently using more traditional qualitative approaches might not profit as much from such advanced features and close integration. Also, qualitative projects involving the coding of audio or video files or combining a variety of unrelated sources of data might very well be better served by using another, less structured, yet more flexible, qualitative software.

One must also recognize that the new possibilities offered by the integration of text analysis methods that are less familiar to social scientists might represent a challenge to researchers due to their lack of familiarity or formal training in the techniques borrowed from distant disciplines such as information science, computational linguistics, or artificial intelligence. Some researchers might also object to these techniques for theoretical or epistemological reasons or simply feel uncomfortable with this type of analysis. However, by doing so, they may deprive themselves of an opportunity to acquire new skills that could be useful to their existing research projects or help them tackle new sources of data. With the increase in the digitalization of our society, those skills will, without any doubt, become more and more relevant in the future.

This natural mixing of qualitative and quantitative data made possible by this cases-by-variables structure is also foreign to many qualitative researchers. This makes QDA Miner somewhat less intuitive to use for those not acquainted with the building of statistical data files. It also imposes some constraints on the nature of data that can be combined in a single project. For example, if a qualitative research project involves the collection of unrelated sources of data, such as interviews, news transcripts, social media data, field observations, images, and videos, it would be difficult to structure a single QDA Miner project in a way that could accommodate all of those. It would also be more difficult to structure qualitative data sources in cases if the quantity of sources per case varies greatly. An example of this would be attempting to store environmental policy documents from different countries where we might have just a few documents for most countries but several dozen from others and attempting to keep the country as the unit of analysis. An easy solution would be to use the documents rather than the countries as the unit of analysis, associate a country variable to each of them, and duplicate any other associated statistics to all cases. Another solution could be to simply merge all documents from a single country into a single document. This illustrates one important implication of such a structure: cases are the organizing elements that define the units of analysis.

With careful design and planning, QDA Miner may be able to handle projects with multiple sources of data, including, documents, spreadsheets, and images along with quantitative data, but it might be more appropriate in some situations to create multiple project files and perform analysis independently. This is something that could be done more easily in less structured, yet more flexible qualitative tools.

7 Resources for Learning More About QDA Miner and WordStat

The most useful resource to learn how to use QDA Miner and WordStat is undoubtedly the company web site (https://provalisresearch.com). The tutorial section contains more than 70 short video tutorials on various features of the software organized in thematic sections guiding users through all phases of the research, from the creation of a project to the analysis and reporting of results. Recorded webinars can also be viewed, offering more in-depth treatment of topics such as sentiment analysis, coding of open-ended responses, automatic document classification, or dictionary construction. The Company has a YouTube channel but there are also many users of the software who have posted YouTube videos highlighting the software and its features.

One can also find under the Studies section a list of more than 1,000 published studies that have involved the use of QDA Miner, WordStat, or both. Such a resource is invaluable not only to learn how other researchers have used these tools, but also how to present them in an academic work. However, for a more up-to-date and comprehensive search strategy, we recommend using the Google Scholar search engine because it allows one to identify published works on particular topics or those using specific techniques of the software. The software is also available for a 30-day trial. This gives one ample time to try it out and to test the full suite of the software's features and capabilities. The Company has an approved list of 20 plus trainers around the world who can give introductory or expert courses in the software in several different languages.

The Applications section on the website also illustrates a few of the many practical ways the software can be applied for analyzing open-ended questions, social media, customer feedback, human resources, scientific papers, and news transcripts, how one can measure sentiment or brand personality, perform media framing, assess corporate social responsibility or improve net promoter score surveys used by many companies, governments, and organizations.

REFERENCES

Baumer, E. P. S, Mimno, D., Guha, S., Quan, E., & Gay, G. K. (2017). Comparing grounded theory and topic modeling: Extreme divergence or unlikely convergence? *Journal of the Association for Information Science and Technology*, 68, 1397–1410. doi:10.1002/asi.23786

Bazeley, P. (2003). Computerized data analysis for mixed methods research. In A. Tashakkori & C. Teddlie (Eds.), *Handbook of mixed methods in social and behavioral research* (pp. 385–422). Thousand Oaks, CA: Sage.

Bazeley, P. (2018). *Integrating analysis in mixed methods research*. Thousand Oaks, CA: Sage.

Bourdon, S. (2000, September). *Inter-coder reliability verification using QSR NUD*IST'*. Paper presented at the Strategies in Qualitative Research Conference on Issues and Results from Analysis Using QSR NVivo and QSR NUD*IST, The Institute of Education, University of London, England.

Evans, M. (2009). *The republic and its problems: Alexander Hamilton and James Madison on the eighteenth-century critique of republics*. Doctoral Dissertation. University of Maryland.

Fielding, N., & Cisneros-Puebla, C. (2010). CAQDAS-GIS convergence: Toward a new integrated mixed method research practice? *Journal of Mixed Methods Research*, 3, 349–370. doi:10.1177/1558689809344973

Miles, M. B., & Huberman, A. M (1994). *Qualitative data analysis: An expanded sourcebook* (2nd ed.). Thousand Oaks, CA: Sage.

O'Kane, P., Smith, A., & Lerman, M. P. (2019). Building transparency and trustworthiness in inductive research through computer-aided qualitative data analysis software. *Organizational Research Methods*. Advance online publication. doi:10.1177/1094428119865016

Neuendorf, K. A. (2017). *The content analysis guidebook* (2nd ed.). Thousand Oaks, CA: Sage.

Péladeau, N., & Davoodi, E. (2018, January). Comparison of latent Dirichlet modeling and factor analysis for topic extraction: A lesson of history. In *Proceedings of the 51st Hawaii International Conference on System Sciences*. doi:10.24251/HICSS.2018.078. Retrieved from https://scholarspace.manoa.hawaii.edu/bitstream/10125/49965/paper0078.pdf

Weber, R. P. (1990). *Basic content analysis* (2nd ed.). Newbury Park, CA: Sage.

26

Using MAXQDA for Mixed Methods Research

Udo Kuckartz and Stefan Rädiker

1 About MAXQDA

MAXQDA is a software package for the analysis of qualitative and mixed data, which since its beginnings at the end of the 1980s has focused on the support of mixed methods research. Indeed, the very first version in 1989 was intended to assist the management of quantitative data in parallel to verbal data. At that time, when the use of multimedia data for social science analysis was still a long way off, the use of quantitative data in qualitative research was primarily designed for the management of profile data such as gender, age, education, or household income. In addition, support for surveys with both standardized and open-ended questions played an important role right from the start.

Over the past three decades, MAXQDA's functions for mixed methods research have been systematically expanded and developed. Moreover, in recent years great attention has been paid to the development and implementation of so-called "joint displays". Using joint displays, quantitative data or results (QUAN), and qualitative data or results (QUAL) are arranged to allow direct references and comparisons. The joint displays described by Guetterman, Creswell, and Kuckartz (2015) have now almost all been implemented in MAXQDA.

The area of mixed methods is still one of the focal points of MAXQDA's development today. In this chapter we give an overview of the mixed methods functions. MAXQDA belongs to the group of Qualitative Data Analysis Software (CAQDAS or QDAS) programs. MAXQDA's range of functions goes far beyond applications in mixed methods projects, and (almost) all types of qualitative research approaches are supported. The software also enables the analysis of audio and video data as well as data from social networks such as Twitter and YouTube. For a general introduction to the software and its functionality, please refer to the textbook by Kuckartz and Rädiker (2019).

2 Mixed Methods Designs and When Use of MAXQDA is Appropriate

In the history of the mixed methods movement, a variety of definitions have been proposed (Johnson, Onwuegbuzie, & Turner, 2007). The following considerations are based on the definition of mixed methods as a methodology, which contains qualitative and quantitative research strands. This is expressed in the definition recently provided by Creswell and Plano Clark:

> In mixed methods, the researcher collects and analyzes both qualitative and quantitative data rigorously in response to research questions and hypotheses, integrates (or mixes or combines) the two forms of data and their results, organizes these procedures into specific research designs that provide the logic and procedures for conducting the study, and frames these procedures within theory and philosophy. (Creswell & Plano Clark, 2018, p. 5)

According to this definition, we always have to deal with two types of data—quantitative and qualitative—when conducting analyses in mixed methods projects. When working with different types of data from the same research paradigm, such as narrative interviews and focus groups, this is not referred to as "mixed methods" but as "multiple methods". In this respect, we understand mixed methods research as a specific type of multimethod research, the latter being the more comprehensive term (Fetters & Molina-Azorin, 2017). MAXQDA also offers numerous possibilities for combining data and methods beyond mixed methods, but these are not the focus of this article.

The mixed methods community has long been discussing the naming, differentiation and grouping of mixed methods designs (Hesse-Biber & Johnson, 2015; Plano Clark & Ivankova, 2016; Tashakkori & Teddlie, 2010). In their latest book, Creswell and Plano Clark (2018) propose differentiating three basic designs:

- The *convergent design*, in which a qualitative and a quantitative study are carried out in parallel.
- The *exploratory design*, in which a qualitative study is carried out first and a quantitative study is carried out on the basis of the results; this corresponds, for example, to the classical qualitative preliminary study, in which knowledge of a previously largely unknown field of research is first collected with the aid of a qualitative study and then an instrument is developed which is used in a survey.
- The *explanatory design*, in which first a survey is carried out and then a qualitative study helps to examine individual questions in detail in a qualitative study or to clarify gaps and ambiguities in the results of the survey.

This terminology was also proposed by Fetters and Freshwater (2015a, p. 208), the editors of the *Journal of Mixed Methods Research (JMMR)*. Of course, in mixed methods research there exists many more diverse and complex forms of designs. Other scholars also continue to prefer other terminologies and design typologies (e.g., parallel or concurrent instead of convergent design). For this chapter, however, it is important to note that these three basic designs as well as the more complex designs are very well supported by MAXQDA. The real challenge in a mixed methods project is the *integrative data analysis*. The combination of methods is associated with the claim (or hope) that more than the sum of the individual parts, "QUAL" + "QUAN", can be achieved (Bazeley, 2010, p. 432; Bryman, 2007; Woolley, 2009). In short, it is about the hope of achieving a significant gain through integration or, as Fetters and Freshwater put it, "The 1 + 1 = 3 Integration Challenge" (2015b). This requires suitable strategies of integration and mixing. Thus, when talking about data analysis in the context of mixed methods research, one should first think about the determinants of such integrative analyses. What do integration strategies depend on? Which ones are available? There are primarily three factors that, in our opinion, determine what type of integration strategy can be chosen:

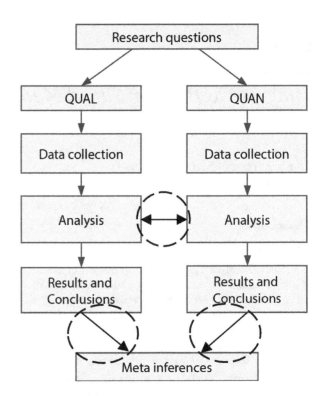

FIGURE 26.1 Points of integration in convergent design (highlighted with circles).

- First, the *motive and justification* for why the researchers chose a mixed methods approach. Bryman (2006) carried out an empirical study and analyzed 232 social science articles that appeared between 1994 and 2003 and in which qualitative and quantitative methods were combined. He showed that 82% of the examined articles in the quantitative strand used questionnaires and 71% in the qualitative strand used qualitative interviews. Bryman identified 16 different rationales, ranging from "greater validity", "completeness", "explanation" to "sampling", "unexpected results", "instrument development", "context" and "illustration" (Bryman, 2006, pp. 105–107). Different integration strategies have to be used if one wants to achieve greater validity than when it comes to completeness and illustration. In the first case (achieving greater validity), the analyses of qualitative and quantitative data are carried out separately. Otherwise, the studies would influence each other and the goal of increasing validity would be thwarted. The situation is different in the other two cases, where there is no reason why the two strands of methods should not be interlinked from the outset.
- The second determinant is the research design that has been constructed (Schoonenboom & Johnson, 2017). In the simplest case it is one of the basic designs described above, i.e., a convergent design, exploratory or explanatory design. Depending on the design, there are different possibilities for the points of integration. To identify the points of integration between QUAL and QUAN, we take a look at a convergent design (Figure 26.1). With such a design, integration can be based on the data or on the results; the former assumes that both data types come from all research participants: for example, people took part in narrative interviews and the same people also completed a standardized questionnaire.

  In the case of the two sequential design types, other points of integration arise—primarily at the junction of the two partial studies when, for example, the guidelines for subsequent problem-oriented interviews (Witzel & Reiter, 2012) are generated from the results of a survey. Additionally, there is another point of integration, namely the possibility of comparing the results of both studies, as with convergent designs.
- The third determinant of integration is the *sample*. How was the sample of the qualitative study determined and, likewise, how was the sample of the quantitative study determined? Are the two designs interlinked? Are both qualitative and quantitative data available for the same units (i.e., people, households, institutions, etc.)? How big are the samples? Which statistical calculations do the size and type of the sample allow, and what calculations are possible?

On the basis of these three determinants, we have developed ten different integration strategies (Kuckartz, 2017), whereby we consider it useful to distinguish between three principal types of integration strategies:

a. Results-based strategies;

b. Data-based strategies; and

c. Sequence-oriented strategies.

Joint displays, in which qualitative and quantitative data and/or results are presented together, play a special role within these strategies.

> Another important approach to data integration is the use of a joint display. Increasingly, methodologists have emphasized the use of joint displays in the form of figures, tables, and matrices to integrate data. (Greene, 2007; Fetters et al., 2013; Guetterman, Creswell, & Kuckartz, 2015) A joint display includes representations of the qualitative and quantitative data. Importantly, the development of a joint display facilitates not only analysis of the data during the interpretative stage but also presentation of data for dissemination and publication. (Fetters & Freshwater, 2015a, p. 211)

Very often joint displays are tables or matrices. However, there have been many developments and innovations in the field of joint displays in recent years, such that joint displays are now increasingly being designed as concept maps, graphics and diagrams (Guetterman, 2018; Haynes-Brown & Fetters, 2018). MAXQDA continuously picks up such new ideas for further development. For example, MAXQDA provides functions for interactive creation and operation of joint displays (Rädiker, 2018).

3 Technical Outline of MAXQDA

MAXQDA 2020 is the current version of MAXQDA. The interface and functionality are 100% identical on Windows and Mac. This has great advantages, especially for research teams, because Mac and Windows users can collaborate without any problems. Working with different systems is similar to working with Microsoft Office programs, i.e., the same project file can be opened on both systems and transferred between both systems without any reformatting or export procedures.

MAXQDA allows you to analyze both types of data, qualitative and quantitative, separately and integratively. Examples of qualitative data are interview and focus group transcripts, documents, images, videos, field notes, observation protocols, and social media data. Quantitative data usually consist (almost) exclusively of numbers; they are structured and require relatively little storage space. Qualitative data, on the other hand, are incredibly diverse, often very complex, and require considerably more storage space, especially video data. Figure 26.2 shows MAXQDA's Import ribbon tab and shows which qualitative data can be imported into MAXQDA.

The spectrum of importable data ranges from simple documents such as qualitative interviews to focus group transcripts with multiple speakers to survey data (with open-ended and closed-ended data), websites, data from social media and reference managers. For mixed methods analysis of research results, the ability to work with PDF documents is of great importance; for example, it allows you to compare research reports and articles from journals.

MAXQDA can—and this is particularly important for mixed methods research—analyze qualitative and quantitative data in separate forms. Thus, quantitative studies can only be statistically evaluated with MAXQDA. A special module called Stats is available for this purpose.

In mixed methods studies, the work with quantitative data can be done in different ways: variables can be defined in MAXQDA and entered in a special data editor. Alternatively, a complete data table can be imported as a rectangular data matrix, for example from Excel or SPSS. The connection between both data types is established in MAXQDA by the fact that the names of the document (i.e., the single data file) and the document group (i.e., the collection of data files) must correspond for each case. This means that a qualitative interview from the document group "Teachers" with the name "Ryan C." must have its values for the variables "document group" and "document name" in the quantitative data table. These two variables are therefore necessary in the quantitative data set in order to establish the link between the two types of data.

The MAXQDA module MAXDictio is also important for mixed methods analyses. MAXDictio enables the quantitative, word-based analysis of texts, which is particularly important for analyses with large numbers of cases, such as the analysis of Twitter data. This module enables researchers to facilitate a vast range of procedures for quantitative content analysis. Included are tools for visual text exploration, vocabulary analysis, dictionary-based analysis, and more.

In general, all steps of mixed methods data analysis are supported by MAXQDA. This starts with the preparation of the data (e.g., the transcription of interview recordings), extends to the management of the data in various document groups and temporary analytical document sets, to integrative analysis and the already mentioned joint displays.

4 Empirical Demonstration of MAXQDA in Mixed Methods Research and
5 Suggested Applications of MAXQDA in Mixed Methods Research

We will now describe some practical possibilities of mixed methods data analysis with MAXQDA. In doing so, we will orient ourselves according to the course of a research process and the differentiation of integration strategies into the three types described above: results-based, data-based, and sequence-oriented. The implementation with MAXQDA is demonstrated using our own research data; very often we

FIGURE 26.2 MAXQDA's Import ribbon tab.

use data from a research project on "Awareness of Climate Change" as an example. In this project, we conducted qualitative individual interviews and had the same research participants complete a standardized questionnaire on questions of climate awareness. A mixed methods approach was chosen for the project because previous research could not sufficiently explain the discrepancy between attitudes and personal behavior with regard to climate protection. All in all, the design followed the idea of an in-depth study or an explanatory design, i.e., previously only insufficiently explained connections were to be better explained through the use of a qualitative procedure, that is, through a new perspective. In the sense of Bryman's rationales (Bryman, 2006), it was "explanation", "completeness" and "enhancement" that motivated this study. Specifically, in relation to the course of the project, it followed the pattern of a convergent design, i.e., the two strands were carried out in parallel; the guideline of the open interview and the questionnaire instrument were developed simultaneously on the same theoretical background with overarching research questions and not as with a sequential design based on the results of the first study carried out. In the survey situation, the open interview was always conducted first and the questionnaire was then completed by the respondents.

The data management for the climate change project was such that the open interviews were first transcribed and then imported into MAXQDA. The questionnaire data were entered in Excel and then the Excel file was imported into MAXQDA using the Import Document Variables function.

Separate Analysis of Qualitative and Quantitative Data

In the first analysis step of this study, both types of data are analyzed separately.

Analysis of Qualitative Data

All qualitative data are managed in MAXQDA's "Document System" window. If different data types have been collected, e.g., open interviews, observations, focus groups, the corresponding data may be arranged in different folders (so-called Document Groups) of the "Document System", illustrated in Figure 26.3.

Which methods are used to analyze the qualitative data naturally depends on the approach chosen. For example, Creswell and Poth (2018) distinguish between narrative studies, phenomenological studies, grounded theory studies, ethnographic studies, and case studies. These and numerous other approaches are supported by MAXQDA. However, the scope of analysis options for the qualitative data is too large to be described here in full. We therefore concentrate on the most important points and, following the logic of a research process, show them in Table 26.1.

In the climate change project we followed the method of qualitative text analysis described by Kuckartz (2014b). This is a form of thematic analysis, the steps of which are similar to the method presented by Creswell (2016, pp. 152–165). From the research questions and the guidelines used in the interviews, a coding frame was developed, which was further developed and differentiated while working with the material. The coding took place in two coding phases: In the first step, the questions of the interview guide were coded along with "broad brush categories" and in a second step, subcategories were formed. In the second analytical step, MAXQDA's Creative Coding feature was used for visual organization and grouping during the formation of subcategories. The interview texts were thematically coded according to this coding frame. Subsequently, thematic summaries were written with the help of the MAXQDA's so-called Summary Grid function.

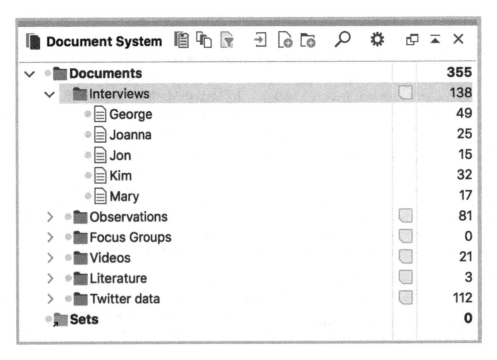

FIGURE 26.3 Different qualitative data types in MAXDQA's "Document System" window.

TABLE 26.1

MAXQDA's Tools for the Analysis of Qualitative Data.

Preparing the data	• Import of textual data (DOCX, RTF, ODT etc.), PDF documents, multimedia data (MP3, MP4, WAV etc.), surveys, social media data, images, webpages, bibliographical data. • Transcribe audio and video files, check the transcription with synchronous original. • Anonymize data.
Exploring the data	• Search for multiple search strings across documents or memos. Search for word combinations. • Code segments of data and identify themes. • Develop a coding frame. • Write memos and attach them to documents, codes or data segments or write free memos.
Analyzing and interpreting the data	• Paraphrase text segments and use an interactive table to build a coding frame. • Search in the coded data, e.g., in text passages that are coded with the same code. • Summarize coded data into researcher's words. Display summaries in user defined table views together with variable information. • Visually arrange and structure codes and themes on a blank canvas and transform the finalized structure into the coding frame. • Compare groups by displaying coded segments or code frequencies in synoptic table overviews. • Link text segments or image segments within a project to each other. Link to external sources like files, webpages, or geographical locations in Google Earth™ / Maps™.
Representing the data	• Show all codes and memos of single cases (for instance extreme cases). • Represent the coded segments in a single document by color (Document Portrait). • Display tables cases x codes that show if and how often codes and subcodes have been applied to selected cases. • Compare statements of selected groups. • Create word cloud display of most frequently used words in a single document or a document group. Limit display by adding words to a list of excluded words. • Visualize data and findings in concept maps, diagrams, or infographics. Add project data (documents, codes, memos, coded segments) as well as external data (images, links, geo-references) to a map. Add free objects and text fields. Freely arrange, group, or link elements with labeled arrows. Elements stay connected to original source data.
Interpreting the results and relating them to the current state of research	• Capture interpretations of results as memos and comments. • Perform literature reviews. • Compare and link the results of the study with the current state of research. • Use quotations from the original data to support the conclusions.

In all phases of the research process, memos were prepared in which the ideas and hypotheses emerging in the analysis process were recorded. The results of content comparisons and detailed analyses were also recorded as memos in the project.

Analysis of Quantitative Data

Quantitative data are handled by MAXQDA in the form of a "cases x variables" table. The data can be entered by the researchers or imported from statistical software, Excel or online survey tools such as LimeSurvey, and SurveyMonkey. Figure 26.4 shows MAXQDA's data editor. Each row of the table represents a case. Each column corresponds to one variable, so Figure 26.4 displays five variables: Document group, Document name, Gender, Age, and Awareness Index.

MAXQDA provides various options for the analysis of quantitative data:

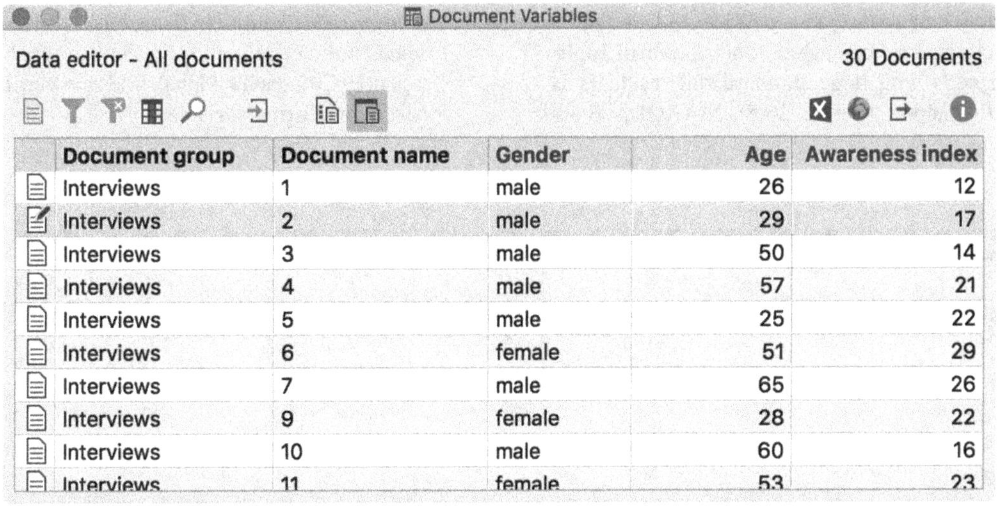

FIGURE 26.4 MAQDA's Data Editor for quantitative data.

Crosstabs

Employment Status * Region

Column percentages | Standardized residuals | Valid cases: 191; Missing cases: 0 (0,0%)

Employment Status	rural	urban	Total
employed	37,4 (-1,0)	51,0 (1,0)	44,5
part time	17,6 (0,7)	12,0 (-0,7)	14,7
retired	14,3 (-1,4)	27,0 (1,3)	20,9
self employed	26,4 (2,9)	4,0 (-2,8)	14,7
unemployed	4,4 (-0,4)	6,0 (0,3)	5,2
Total	100,0	100,0	100,0

FIGURE 26.5 Results table of crosstab "Employment Status * Region".

Frequencies: Tables and diagrams of frequencies and percentage distributions can be created. Unlike most statistics programs, the results views are interactive, i.e., variable values can be merged or deleted and all values are recalculated automatically.

Diagrams and visualizations: Pie and bar charts, histograms and box plots can be created to visualize the frequency distributions of variables. The relationships between two variables can be displayed as grouped bar charts or scatterplots.

Descriptive statistics: For metric (i.e., interval or ratio) variables, descriptive statistics can be computed, e.g., mean, standard deviation, variance, median, quartiles, range, standard error, and the 95% confidence interval for the mean. Moreover, z values can be computed and saved in a new variable.

Compare groups (categorical variables): The relationships between categorical variables can be displayed in a crosstab with column, row, cell percentages, and with expected frequencies and residuals. Also, Chi square with p value and measures of association are computed. The option of highlighting cells with large standardized residuals is especially helpful (Figure 26.5). MAXQDA Stats highlights all cells with a standardized residual (i.e., observed minus expected frequency divided by the root of the expected frequency) greater than 2 in blue and all cells with values smaller than 2 in red. If there are values the magnitude of which is greater than 2.6 the cells are additionally displayed in a darker color.

Compare groups (metric variables): Through a classical variance analysis, different groups can be compared for a dependent variable. The software computes F and p values and tests for the homogeneity of variances. A table with descriptive statistics contains information for each factor level and the total number of cases (Figure 26.6).

Correlation: Correlation analyses are used to examine relationships between variables, in particular the analysis of "the more, the more" and "the more, the less" correlations. Pearson's r can be computed for interval scale variables and Spearman's rho for ordinal scale variables. Scatterplots help to visually investigate such correlations.

Formation of scales and indices: It is possible to develop scales interactively and to calculate reliability coefficients (Cronbach's alpha). Indexes can be created based on existing variables.

Descriptive statistics

	N	Mean	Std.dev. (pop.)	Std.error	Mean lower b. (95%)	Mean upper b. (95%)	Minimum	Maximum
20-29	24	2,12	1,262	0,258	1,59	2,66	0,0	4,0
30-39	38	2,66	1,072	0,174	2,31	3,01	0,0	4,0
40-49	51	2,45	0,901	0,126	2,20	2,70	0,0	4,0
50-59	19	2,26	0,733	0,168	1,91	2,62	1,0	4,0
Total	132	2,42	1,012	0,088	2,25	2,60	0,0	4,0

Copy

FIGURE 26.6 Results table of anova "life satisfaction index * age group".

Integrative Analysis with MAXQDA

Integrative analyses are the big challenge when it comes to mixed methods projects. The general functions of MAXQDA can be used profitably for integrative analyses. Using the *link function*, that creates hyperlinks between two text parts, the results of qualitative and quantitative studies can be linked together in respective research reports. The *sorting functionality* in MAXQDA tables is also useful in this context. In this way, extreme cases can be identified in the quantitative data on the basis of selected variables (by sorting the table accordingly) and their qualitative data can then be analyzed in detail.

MAXQDA's special functions for integrative analysis are bundled in the Mixed Methods ribbon tab (Figure 26.7).

The following functions can be found in the Mixed Methods tab:

- *Activate by Document Variables*—Selection of qualitative data (QUAL) using the values of individual variables or variable combinations (QUAN).
- *Quote Matrix, Interactive Quote Matrix*—Grouped topic display. Statements on qualitative topics (QUAL) are broken down by variables from the quantitative study (e.g., test score for environmental awareness = low, medium, high) and presented in matrix form.
- *Crosstab*—The frequencies of qualitative topics (QUAL) are compared by variables from the quantitative study (e.g., test scores). Various calculation and percentage variants are available.
- *Quantitizing*—Data transformation QUAL -> QUAN: Qualitative data are transformed into quantitative data, e.g., existence of a code or frequency of a code per case.
- *Typology Table*—Descriptive statistical evaluation of quantitative data (QUAN) broken down by the types of typology formed in the qualitative study (QUAL). For metric (i.e., interval or ratio) variables, mean values and standard deviations are displayed; for categorical variables, percentages of selected variable values are displayed.
- *Similarity Analysis for Documents*—Creates a similarity matrix for documents based on their coded segments (QUAL) and variable values (QUAN).
- *Side-by-Side Display of Results (Coded Segments or Summaries)*—Tabular comparison of the results of the qualitative and quantitative study (basis: coded segments or thematic summaries).
- *Qualitative Themes for Quantitative Groups (Coded Segments or Summaries)*—Thematic analysis differentiated by groups: Groups are formed by variable values (QUAN). Coded segments or thematic summaries of the respective code for the documents of the respective group are compiled (QUAL).
- *Statistics for Qualitative Groups*—Like the Typology Table, but the groups to be compared are formed by subcategories of a code (QUAL).

These options can be used not only for one particular integration strategy, but also for many others and can be combined if necessary. How this happens exactly for the three types of integration strategies is described below.

Results-based Strategies of Integration with MAXQDA

One way of integrating qualitative and quantitative studies is to link the results of the two studies. This is a variant of integration when data from studies with two independent samples are analyzed in the context of a design, which is justified by an increase in validity.

Two options can be used and corresponding joint displays can be created for results-based integration strategies: firstly, the results of both strands can be connected with the help of hyperlinks, and secondly, results can be compared in a table. Connecting text passages via hyperlinks is the first choice when little time is available for the analysis phase. For both parts of the mixed study, written reports, or at least analytical outputs such as frequency counts or statistical tables, must be available. Technically this is done in MAXQDA in such a way that thematically corresponding text passages in the qualitative and quantitative report are linked using document links. These can be used as hyperlinks in Internet browsers for further analysis: a click on a link instantly jumps to its connected data segment.

The second option is a tabular comparison of coded segments or thematic summaries of the results of both studies. Before this variant is presented, we will explain the summary function of MAXQDA.

Working with Summaries

For the comparison of results from different strands, MAXQDA's option to work with summaries is of paramount importance. MAXQDA offers the Summary Grid and Summary Tables functions for this purpose. The basic idea of the Summary Grid is that it allows you to write thematic summaries, building on an already existing thematic coding of the data. The Summary Grid window (Figure 26.8) has three areas:

- In the left column, MAXQDA presents a thematic grid with codes (themes) in the rows and documents (cases) in the columns. A blue square indicates the presence of some coded segments in that document for that code. A green shading around it indicates that a summary of those segments has been created.

FIGURE 26.7 MAXQDA's Mixed Methods ribbon tab.

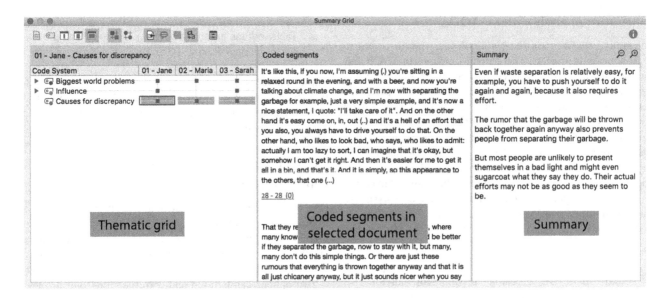

FIGURE 26.8 Writing thematic summaries for integrative analysis.

A red rectangle indicates for which document and which code in the thematic grid the coded segments are currently being displayed. In our example, one can switch between three themes ("Biggest world problems", "Influence" and "Causes for discrepancy"). The columns in Figure 26.7 are formed by the interviewed people ("01 - Jane, "02 - Maria" and "03 - Sarah"). Currently, Jane's statements about the causes of discrepancy are selected.

- The middle column displays the full content of the coded segments in Jane's interview. At the end of each segment, the paragraph from which it originates is indicated.
- The right column, which is initially empty, is where you can write your summary.

Side-by-Side Display of Results for Coded Segments or for Summaries

The technique of linking the results is immediately available, but the technique of contrasting the results of both studies in tabular form requires some preparatory work; both research reports or result materials must first be thematically coded (Creswell & Plano Clark, 2018, pp. 226 230; Kuckartz, 2014b, pp. 69–88), whereby the research questions determine the thematic codes. This means that not only the results report of the qualitative study but also the results report of the quantitative study is reviewed with regard to the occurrence of the topics of interest; the relevant text passages are selected and coded with the corresponding thematic code. The search functions of MAXQDA can also be used in this procedure to search for specific terms. It is also possible to automatically code the text passages found. If no written reports on the results of the two sub-studies are yet available, the existing preparatory work can be used instead. For example, the statistical tables can be coded for the quantitative results.

If the reports contain many pages, as is the case with larger studies such as the Eurobarometer studies, the tabular comparison of the coded segments of topics of interest may become very extensive. In the case of very important topics, it may also happen that many passages of text are coded throughout the report, but some of these may be quite redundant. In this case, it can be very useful to first write thematic summaries and then use these thematic summaries in place of the original text passages in the side-by-side displays. Another advantage of this method is that the tables created in this way already have a very high degree of compression, so that they can be easily transferred to the final integrative report without major changes.

Data-based Strategies of Integration with MAXQDA

The first option in the Mixed Methods ribbon tab, Activate by Document Variables, offers an easy way of integrating quantitative and qualitative data. In this way, the variables of the quantitative data set are used for targeted access to the qualitative data. This is done by formulating one or more logical conditions according to the "Variable Operator Value" pattern. The logical conditions can be simple, for example, if only a certain characteristic of a variable serves as a selection criterion ("membership in a NGO = yes"), but they can also combine two or more variables ("gender = female" and "membership in a NGO = yes") or be the result of a preceding statistical calculation ("value on the scale environmental attitudes > 1.96"). For integrative data analysis, it is particularly interesting that the selection of documents created by activating them via document variables can be saved in MAXQDA as "document sets" and are thus available for later analyses without the groups having to be formed again by formulating the selection conditions for each analysis.

Transformation of Qualitative Data into Quantitative Data

The conversion of coded qualitative data into numbers is called "quantitizing". This is a process that respondents already practice (unconsciously) when they convert their answer to a certain statement into a numerical value in a standardized survey and, for example, tick the value "7" on a scale from "(0) total rejection" to "(10) total approval". Quantifying coded qualitative data is a common strategy of integration. Kuckartz (2014a), Sandelowski, Voils, & Knafl (2009), and Vogl (2017) deal in great detail with the different possibilities of quantification.

How is quantification done in practice with MAXQDA? Whenever you code a segment, MAXQDA increases the count of how often the code is assigned to the document. This creates a matrix of "documents by codes" in the background without the user noticing. If a code is now to be transformed into a quantitative variable, a simple click on the Transform into Document Variable option is sufficient. A new variable is created, and the code name is selected as the name for the new variable. The frequencies of coding with this code are stored as values of the variables for each document and can then be statistically evaluated. MAXQDA's Stats module facilitates the combination of quantitative data with this quantified qualitative data and offers a variety of descriptive and inferential statistical methods. Now it's also easy to identify extreme cases even with large samples. You only have to click on the column heading of the desired variable (e.g. the environmental attitude scale) in the Data Editor and all rows (i.e. documents) are then sorted in ascending or descending order. In the first and last rows, after sorting, you will find the people with particularly high and particularly low values for the "environmental attitude" factor. The documents then are also highlighted in the "Document System" window and can be compared with each other – and you can compare their statements on specific topics using MAXQDA's Analyze > Compare Groups function.

Qualitative Exploration of Extreme Cases in a Quantitative Strand

This integration strategy of QUAL and QUAN identifies extreme cases, mostly on the basis of quantitative data. Then the qualitative data, focused on certain important topics, are analyzed in detail for these extreme cases, e.g. to examine how these cases differ from the others and what context factors may have relevant effects on the extreme values (Bazeley, 2012, p. 821; Creswell & Plano Clark, 2018, pp. 235–236).

The option to transform codes into document variables described above opens up the possibility of using the code frequencies to identify extreme cases to show who has high and low values on the code variable. After the transformation and sorting of the table, it is easy to identify the people who have talked about a specific topic extremely frequently during the interview.

Case Map: An Example for a Visual Joint Display

If you have qualitative and quantitative data for the same people, you can use the MAXQDA Maps module to create visual representations in which both data types are brought together. Figure 26.9 shows such a case map for the case of "James K". Here, the single display contains codes and subcodes; however, variable values could also be integrated.

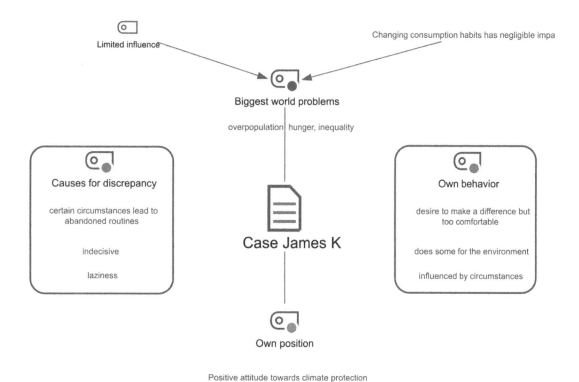

FIGURE 26.9 Case map as a joint display for "Case James K".

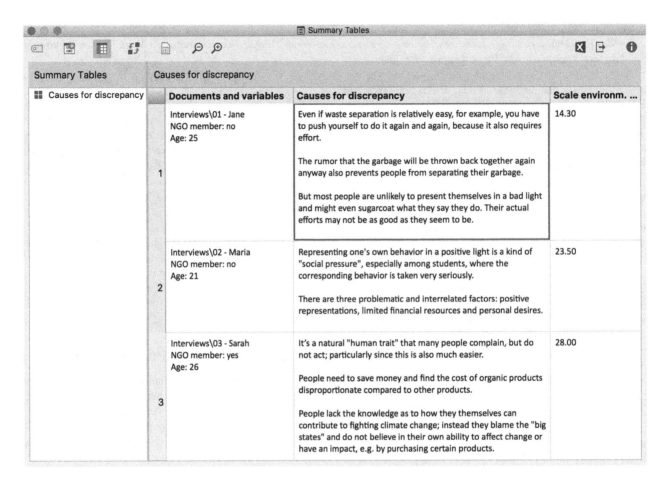

FIGURE 26.10 Joint display of summaries and variable values.

Case Overviews with Qualitative and Quantitative Data

The Summary Table function can be used to create case overviews containing both quantitative variable values and thematic summaries. Figure 26.10 shows such a joint display focusing on causes for discrepancy between environmental attitudes and behavior. The table starts with case #1, the interview "01 - Jane". Jane is 25 years old and not a member of an NGO (background information from the quantitative data). The following column contains the thematic summary written by the researchers on Jane's remarks in an interview about the causes for the discrepancy. The following column contains Jane's value on the quantitative scale "environmental attitudes". The table then continues with case #2 (Mary) and case #3 (Sarah).

Compare Statements on Qualitative Themes according to Quantitative Groups

In many cases, socio-demographic variables are included in the analysis as categorical variables, but they can also be scale or index values for which a categorization is previously carried out; corresponding examples can be found in Guetterman et al. (2015) and Creswell and Plano Clark (2018). Using this strategy and the corresponding joint displays, the quantitative data serve to group the qualitative data, e.g. thematic statements from qualitative interviews are ordered according to the level of "awareness of climate change" recorded by a questionnaire used at the same time (low, moderate, high). In principle, all variables of the quantitative strand can be used as grouping variables; for metric variables, a meaningful reduction to a manageable number of categories must first be made. This type of joint display can be generated in two different ways, using MAXQDA's QUAL Themes by QUAN Groups display or by using Quote Matrix function. A schematic representation of the result is shown in Figure 26.11.

Quantitative Analysis of Code Frequencies Broken Down by Groups

This strategy of integration and the joint display implementing this strategy has the same formal structure as the display described in Figure 26.11, but now the cells of the matrix do not contain text passages, but only information about the respective number of coded segments (Figure 26.12). How many people with a certain variable value (such as having a university degree) talk about a certain topic (qualitative data) and how many text passages are coded? Do more people with a university degree talk about the influence of global problems than people with no university degree and do they do this more often in the course of the interview? This aggregated numerical presentation corresponds to the logic of a statistical

	Variable: Awareness of climate change		
Code	Low (*N* = 5)	Moderate (*N* = 12)	High (*N* = 4)
Personal behavior	Text segments of this group coded with the code "Personal behavior"	Text segments of this group coded with the code "Personal behavior"	Text segments of this group coded with the code "Personal behavior"
Personal acceptance of responsibility	Text segments of this group coded with the code "Personal acceptance of responsibility"	Text segments of this group coded with the code "Personal acceptance of responsibility"	Text segments of this group coded with the code "Personal acceptance of responsibility"

FIGURE 26.11 Schematic structure of the "QUAL Themes by QUAN Groups" display.

	Variable: Awareness of climate change		
Code	Low (N=5)	Moderate (N=12)	High (N=4)
Personal behavior	Number of segments in this group coded with the code "Personal behavior"	Number of segments in this group coded with the code "Personal behavior"	Number of segments in this group coded with the code "Personal behavior"
Personal acceptance of responsibility	Number of segments in this group coded with the code "Personal acceptance of responsibility"	Number of segments in this group coded with the code "Personal acceptance of responsibility"	Number of segments in this group coded with the code "Personal acceptance of responsibility"
Documents	N (%)	N (%)	N (%)

FIGURE 26.12 Schematic structure of the "number of coded segments for quantitative groups" display (Crosstab).

crosstabulation. With the help of row and column percentages the respective comparative figures can be determined, and with the help of a chi-square test it can be checked against the probability that this distribution across the different categories could also occur randomly. An example from social science environmental research can be found in Kuckartz (2014a, pp. 140–142). To create such a crosstabulation, you need to choose the Crosstab option in the Mixed Methods ribbon tab. The codes that you want to include in the group comparison must be activated before the call. Once the Crosstab function has been opened, the groups that are to form the columns in the table are defined on the basis of variable values, e.g. "Awareness of climate change = low", "Awareness of climate change = moderate" and "Awareness of climate change = high".

The cells of this table display the code frequencies per group. You can choose whether the absolute or the percentage frequencies (related to columns or rows) are listed. To avoid a distortion of the results through people for whom a code has been coded very often, you can specify that coded segments are to be counted only once per document; now the frequency of a code in a particular group cannot be greater than its group size. The option of displaying the cells of the table in different colors depending on their code frequencies is particularly useful for large tables. In this way, the group-related differences can be identified at first glance.

Statistics by Qualitative Groups

This data-based integration strategy is particularly suitable if a typology has first been formed from the qualitative data or if the codes have been transformed into document variables. A well-known historical example of such an approach can be found in the study "The Unemployed of Marienthal" (Jahoda, Lazarsfeld, & Zeisel, 2002). In this study, attitude types were formed on the basis of various qualitative data relating to the experience of unemployment. A current example of such an analysis can be found in Creswell and Plano Clark (2018, p. 316).

This joint display integrates qualitative groups with quantitative data: the groups are compared with regard to statistical characteristics such as mean value, standard deviation, or their relative proportions. Figure 26.13 shows the selection dialog of the joint display "Statistics by Qualitative Groups". For a metric variable, the cells will show the mean and the standard deviation, and for categorical variables, the cells will show its absolute and relative frequencies.

Assuming that an evaluative, scaling content analysis was carried out, a code "Personal acceptance of responsibility" with the characteristics "low", "medium" and "high" as subcategories was formed and corresponding segments were coded by the researchers in each document. Then, this coding is used to form the groups in the joint display. In Figure 26.12, a comparison of these three groups is being generated: individuals with a low, medium, and high sense of responsibility for climate change; the respective group sizes are $N = 9$, $N = 12$ and $N = 9$. These qualitative groups are compared with respect to four variables: age, environmental awareness, gender, and member of a nature conservation organization.

The joint display "Statistics by QUAL Groups" can be used for multiple mixed methods designs. In principle, the results of this display correspond to the results of the joint display that you can create using the Typology Table option, but there the columns are formed by the values of a quantitative data-based variable instead of the presence of subcodes based on the qualitative data. In both cases the joint display is labeled

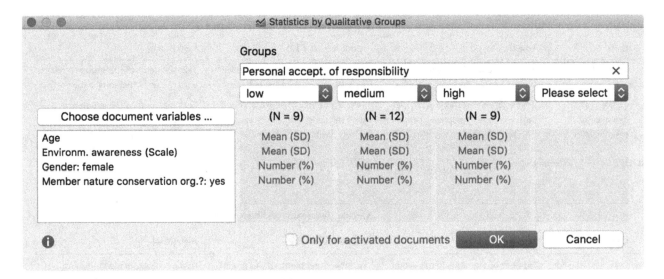

FIGURE 26.13 Selection dialog for the joint display "Statistics by Qualitative Groups".

	low (N=9)	medium (N=12)	high (N=9)
Age, Mean (SD)	36.1 (10.0)	36.6 (11.7)	40.6 (8.0)
Environm. awareness (Scale), Mean (SD)	2.0 (0.9)	2.3 (1.2)	3.0 (1.1)
Gender: female, Number (%)	1 (11.1)	4 (33.3)	7 (77.8)
Member nature conservation org.?: yes, Number (%)	2 (22.2)	2 (16.7)	2 (22.2)
N = Documents	9 (30.0%)	12 (40.0%)	9 (30.0%)

FIGURE 26.14 Joint display "Statistics by Qualitative Groups" (Typology Table).

a "Typology Table" and it is interactively linked to the data in MAXQDA: double-clicking on a result cell selects the documents with this categorical variable value – e.g. in Figure 26.14 with a corresponding click on the nine people of the "low acceptance" type.

Sequence-based Strategies of Integration in MAXQDA

For sequential mixed methods designs, the results of the first strand trigger the conception and sampling of the following strand. The decisive point of integration is precisely this transition between the two phases, and MAXQDA can provide valuable support here. Another point of integration occurs after the second phase, i.e., when the results of both phases are available. However, this kind of interaction corresponds to the situation in the case of a convergent design and is not described here again.

One case of an *exploratory sequential design* is a qualitative phase on the basis of which the instrument development for a subsequent survey takes place. In the first phase, thematic categories are developed from the qualitative data, the material is coded, and MAXQDA's Summary Grid is potentially used to produce thematic summaries. The items of a questionnaire can then be developed directly from the constructs identified and subcategories formed. The *Instrument Development Display* described by Guetterman et al. (2015, pp. 166–168) is also of interest in this context. In this display, quotes, codes, or summaries are compiled together with the items, response specifications, and scales developed from them. In MAXQDA, the Summary Grid, Summary Table, and the Interactive Quote Matrix can be used for this purpose.

In the case of an *explanatory sequential design*, the point of integration is similar to that of an exploratory sequential design: firstly, integration can take place during the planning of the follow-up phase, which is a qualitative strand and should contribute to clarifying the questions not already clarified by the quantitative phase. The second point of integration is localized after completion of the analysis phase of both phases. The decisive integration point, however, is the transition from the results of the quantitative phase to the planning of the qualitative phase. The template shown in Table 26.2, which can be created with the table functionality of MAXQDA, is suitable for this purpose. The questions of the resulting interview guide are always directly linked to the results and outstanding questions of the quantitative phase, such that it is transparent as to why the relevant topics should be addressed in the qualitative interview.

TABLE 26.2

Template for the Planning of a Qualitative Follow-up.

Quantitative Results	Qualitative Follow-up Questions
Results that require explanation, based on descriptive statistics, correlations, regression analysis, factor analysis etc.	Related questions for the interview guide
	Related questions for the interview guide
	Related questions for the interview guide
	...

The explanatory design also has a point of integration at the end of the follow-up qualitative phase, where the results of both phases can now be compiled in a joint display similar to a generalizing themes display. In this joint display, in a column entitled "Explanations", you can see which of the results of the quantitative study can now be explained and which remain open.

6 Strengths and Limitations of MAXQDA

A major strength of MAXQDA, unique in the field of QDA software, is that not only qualitative data, but also quantitative data can be analyzed using the specialized Stats module. Stats can also statistically analyze external files (e.g., in Excel's XLSX format), although it was originally designed for mixed methods analysis. Stats can also be used to carry out and analyze a quantitative project, from the definition of variables and the creation of frequency tables for each variable to descriptive (Johnson & Christensen, 2020, Ch. 19) and inferential statistics (Johnson & Christensen, 2020, Ch. 20).

Of particular note in this context is the close interlinking and interaction between quantitative and qualitative data. Subgroups of data can be formed on the basis of statistical analyses, which are then examined in detail with regard to their statements on qualitative topics. Such analysis options are of great benefit to mixed methods projects where the researcher intends to perform a integrated data analysis at various stages of the analysis process.

MAXQDA's greatest strength is undoubtedly its close connection to the research community and the implementation of methodological innovations, such as integration strategies and the joint displays described above. MAXQDA has few limitations in the actual sense and reaches these only in the case of big data analysis. The analysis of Twitter data often involves more than 50 thousand tweets. Such a large amount of data present great challenges for software originally designed for the analysis of qualitative data with small numbers of cases. However, with recent upgrades, significant improvements in performance have been achieved in this area, so that today even processing Twitter analyses with more than 20 thousand tweets is no longer a problem. Even though we cannot speak of limitations in the true sense of the word, the continued further development of mixed methods functions remains important. There are already plans, for example, to expand the analysis options for focus group data, a type of data very frequently used in mixed methods research. Furthermore, the implementation of further joint displays, as described in the article by Guetterman et al. (2015) and in the book by Miles, Huberman, and Saldaña (2013), is on the feature roadmap.

7 Resources for Learning More About MAXQDA

Kuckartz and Rädiker (2019) provide a comprehensive introduction to MAXQDA and the analysis capabilities it has to offer. In this textbook, the basic functions of MAXQDA are presented in the first main section on the logic of the research process. In the second main section, concrete analysis problems and cases are described, for example how focus group data can be analyzed and how literature reviews can be created. Chapter 13 is dedicated to the topic of mixed methods analysis.

Other publications on MAXQDA include Silver and Lewins (2014), who compare different QDA programs, and Woolf and Silver (2018) who present the features of MAXQDA in the context of their five-level approach. A practical description of the use of MAXQDA in mixed methods research can be found in Bazeley (2017). Numerous video tutorials are available on YouTube and on the website www.maxqda.com.

REFERENCES

Bazeley, P. (2010). Computer assisted integration of mixed methods data sources and analysis. In A. Tashakkori & C. Teddlie (Eds.), *SAGE Handbook of mixed methods in social and behavioral research* (2nd ed., pp. 431–467). Thousand Oaks, CA: Sage.

Bazeley, P. (2012). Integrative analysis strategies for mixed data sources. *American Behavioral Scientist*, *56*, 814–828. https://doi.org/10.1177/0002764211426330

Bazeley, P. (2017). *Integrating analyses for mixed methods research*. Thousand Oaks, CA: Sage.

Bryman, A. (2006). Integrating quantitative and qualitative research: How is it done? *Qualitative Inquiry*, *6*, 97–113. https://doi.org/10.1177/1468794106058877

Bryman, A. (2007). Barriers to integrating quantitative and qualitative research. *Journal of Mixed Methods Research*, *1*(1), 8–22. https://doi.org/10.1177/2345678906290531

Creswell, J. W. (2016). *30 essential skills for the qualitative researcher*. Thousand Oaks, CA: Sage.

Creswell, J. W., & Plano Clark, V. L. (2018). *Designing and conducting mixed methods research* (3rd ed.). Thousand Oaks, CA: Sage.

Creswell, J. W., & Poth, C. N. (2018). *Qualitative inquiry & research design: Choosing among five approaches* (4th ed.). Thousand Oaks, CA: Sage.

Fetters, M. D., & Freshwater, D. (2015a). Publishing a methodological mixed methods research article. *Journal of Mixed Methods Research*, *9*, 203–213. https://doi.org/10.1177/1558689815594687

Fetters, M. D., & Freshwater, D. (2015b). The 1 + 1 = 3 integration challenge. *Journal of Mixed Methods Research*, *9*, 115–117. https://doi.org/10.1177/1558689815581222

Fetters, M. D., & Molina-Azorin, J. F. (2017). The Journal of Mixed Methods Research starts a new decade: Principles for bringing in the new and divesting of the old language of the field. *Journal of Mixed Methods Research*, *11*(1), 3–10. https://doi.org/10.1177/1558689816682092

Guetterman, T. (2018, August). *Visual joint displays with graphs and images to represent mixed methods integration.* Paper presented at the MMIRA International Conference, Vienna, Austria.

Guetterman, T., Creswell, J. W., & Kuckartz, U. (2015). Using joint displays and MAXQDA software to represent the results of mixed methods research. In M. T. McCrudden, G. J. Schraw, & C. W. Buckendahl (Eds.), *Use of visual displays in research and testing: Coding, interpreting, and reporting data* (pp. 145–175). Charlotte, NC: Information Age Publishing.

Haynes-Brown, T., & Fetters, M. D. (2018, August). *The analytic process of developing a joint display in a mixed methods study: An example from the use of Information and Communication Technology (ICT) in secondary schools in Jamaica project.* Paper presented at the MMIRA International Conference, Vienna, Austria.

Hesse-Biber, S., & Johnson, B. (Eds.). (2015). *The Oxford handbook of multimethod and mixed methods research inquiry.* Oxford and New York: Oxford University Press.

Jahoda, M., Lazarsfeld, P. F., & Zeisel, H. (2002). *Marienthal: The sociography of an unemployed community.* New Brunswick, NJ: Transaction Publishers.

Johnson, B., & Christensen, L. (2020). *Educational research: Quantitative, qualitative, and mixed approaches* (7th ed.). Thousand Oaks, CA: Sage.

Johnson, R. B., Onwuegbuzie, A. J., & Turner, L. A. (2007). Toward a definition of mixed methods research. *Journal of Mixed Methods Research, 1*(2), 112–133. https://doi.org/10.1177/1558689806298224

Kuckartz, U. (2014a). *Mixed Methods: Methodologie, Forschungsdesigns und Analyseverfahren.* Wiesbaden, Germany: Springer VS.

Kuckartz, U. (2014b). *Qualitative text analysis: A guide to methods, practice & using software.* Thousand Oaks, CA: Sage.

Kuckartz, U. (2017). Datenanalyse in der Mixed-Methods-Forschung: Strategien der Integration von qualitativen und quantitativen Daten und Ergebnissen. *KZfSS Kölner Zeitschrift für Soziologie und Sozialpsychologie, 69*(S2), 157–183. https://doi.org/10.1007/S11577-017-0456-Z

Kuckartz, U., & Rädiker, S. (2019). *Analyzing qualitative data with MAXQDA. Text, audio, and video.* Cham, Switzerland: Springer.

Miles, M. B., Huberman, A. M., & Saldaña, J. (2013). *Qualitative data analysis: A methods sourcebook* (3rd ed.). Thousand Oaks, CA: Sage.

Plano Clark, V. L., & Ivankova, N. V. (2016). *Mixed methods research: A guide to the field.* Thousand Oaks, CA: Sage.

Rädiker, S. (2018, August). *Interactive joint displays in MAXQDA for mixed methods data analysis.* Paper presented at the MMIRA International Conference, Vienna, Austria.

Sandelowski, M., Voils, C., & Knafl, G. (2009). On quantitizing. *Journal of Mixed Methods Research, 3*, 208–222. https://doi.org/10.1177/1558689809334210

Schoonenboom, J., & Johnson, R. B. (2017). How to construct a mixed methods research design. *KZfSS Kölner Zeitschrift für Soziologie und Sozialpsychologie, 69*(S2), 107–131. https://doi.org/10.1007/s11577-017-0454-1

Silver, C., & Lewins, A. (2014). *Using software in qualitative research: A step-by-step guide* (2nd ed.). Thousand Oaks, CA: Sage.

Tashakkori, A. M., & Teddlie, C. B. (2010). *Sage handbook of mixed methods in social & behavioral research* (2nd ed.). Thousand Oaks, CA: Sage.

Vogl, S. (2017). Quantifizierung: Datentransformation von qualitativen Daten in quantitative Daten in Mixed-Methods-Studien. *KZfSS Kölner Zeitschrift für Soziologie und Sozialpsychologie, 69*(S2), 287–312. https://doi.org/10.1007/S11577-017-0461-2

Witzel, A., & Reiter, H. (2012). *The problem-centred interview: Principles and practice.* Thousand Oaks, CA: Sage.

Woolf, N. H., & Silver, C. (2018). *Qualitative analysis using MAXQDA: The five-level QDA method.* New York, NY: Routledge.

Woolley, C. M. (2009). Meeting the mixed methods challenge of integration in a sociological study of structure and agency. *Journal of Mixed Methods Research, 3*(1), 7–25. https://doi.org/10.1177/1558689808325774

27

Introduction to Dedoose for Mixed Analysis

Eli Lieber, Michelle Salmona, and Dan Kaczynski

As you will surely note from reading this volume, the concept and nature of mixed methods is many different things from many different perspectives. In our work conducting research incorporating different methods that entail collecting a variety of data types and our work advising others doing the same, we have come to appreciate the inherent complexity of mixed methods inquiry. At the same time, we have seen the tremendous value of what this work contributes to the expansion of knowledge in the many disciplines in which it is applied. From a historical perspective, mixed methods research has been constantly evolving. We have seen changes in techniques, the types of data available, an emergence of other platforms and tools for the collection of these data, the availability of increasingly powerful computing resources, and tools to serve the management, interaction with, and analysis of these data. Dedoose is one example of a platform and set of tools developed to serve this evolution. Key driving forces to the development of Dedoose include increasing the efficiencies and effectiveness in what can be done with data management, interaction with new forms of data, advances in analysis and, discovering new ways to present findings in compelling and informative ways. The primary goals of this chapter are to introduce the Dedoose platform, describe key features, and illustrate how these features have been capitalized upon in research projects using an exemplar research project.

1 Definition of Dedoose

Dedoose is a cloud-based Research and Evaluation Data Application (REDA) developed by SocioCultural Research Consultants. Cloud-based services and applications such as Skype, Google Docs, SurveyMonkey, SurveyGizmo, and GoToMeeting are becoming ubiquitous in research. Further, it is important to recognize that all of these tools are fundamentally information management systems. Therefore, the benefits of these tools are only as valuable as the thoughtfulness of those who use them. That is, these tools do not calculate some statistic and produce results. Rather, users import, manipulate, connect, explore, interpret, and present results based on the quality of the data and the thoughtfulness of the user.

Dedoose was designed by a multi-disciplinary social science team to support the qualitative and mixed methods work they were engaged in at the University of California, Los Angeles (UCLA). From this beginning, we have come to appreciate that in order to understand problems in the social sciences more comprehensively, a broad range of mixed data provides unique insights. Mixing data in the form of text, numbers, ratings, demographics, and other media (media is the term used in Dedoose for data) continue to enhance our understandings of complex social problems. Further, we encourage researchers and evaluators to work with others who can complement their expertise and perspectives as they design projects and analyze and interpret findings in their data. Beyond the data and methodological challenges, we also remain keenly aware of how contemporary research often involves teams made up of members with varying levels of substantive expertise and experience. These interdisciplinary teams benefit from tools where all can contribute to a larger project in effective and efficient ways. It was this set of challenges which prompted our UCLA team to create a collaborative, intuitive, welcoming, visual, and affordable research and evaluation data management platform (Lieber & Weisner, 2010).

Dedoose is designed to serve both traditional qualitative and mixed methods research. As such, Dedoose is fundamentally appropriate for use in any mixed methods project. Dedoose is, at its core, an information management system with additional features and functionality that allow individuals to manipulate and expand on the data in a project and navigate through project data toward the discovery, exploration, and presentation of meaningful patterns. Dedoose users can build connections and manipulate various forms of data within the application. Being an appropriate platform for both social science research and evaluation work, Dedoose is a research and evaluation data app (REDA) that provides researchers with multiple ways to conceptualize and visualize data. The use of methodological terminology is inherently complex. In this regard, in Dedoose all qualitative data files, be they text, video, audio, or images, are referred to as media. Dedoose is an appropriate platform for raw qualitative media file management, categorical, static or longitudinal (dynamic) demographic, survey, and other quantitative descriptor data, code weight/rating dimension data, and the integration of any or all aspects of the project data.

Being web-based, Dedoose enables collaborative work where members of a research or evaluation team can work together simultaneously in real time from any location. These flexible features of Dedoose offers tremendous value for teams and have intentionally been developed as a web-based application to serve the unique needs of those collaborating with others in their work. Basically, team members can share and contribute in real-time to building a database that all can benefit from in later analysis stages. Also, as a software as a service (SaaS) application, Dedoose uses a subscription-based business model where users pay low subscription fees, as opposed to purchasing, installing, maintaining, and upgrading a traditional software package. At any time, and from any Internet connected computer, individuals or multiple team members can contribute to the building and analysis of a project database.

In the Dedoose environment, aspects of a project database can be imported and exported in an appropriate format. For example, primary qualitative data can be imported as .doc, .docx, .txt, .rtf, .jpeg, .mp3, .mp4 file. Quantitative data can be imported from and exported to .csv, .xls, .xlsx format files. Data or the results of analytic activities can be exported as text, spreadsheets, tables, and/or graphs in a variety of formats depending on needs. Within the Dedoose environment, individuals or multiple members of a research or evaluation team can interact with and manipulate project data through developing and then applying codes in traditional code systems, as well as connecting the qualitative and quantitative data provided by research participants. In addition, a code weighting system allows researchers to introduce another dimension to the project based on the discovery and delineation of variation in qualitative content (see more on code weighting/rating below in Section 3). After creating connections between various aspects of a database and enriching the project data through coding and code weighting activity, the project data are ready for exploration and analysis (Salmona, Lieber, & Kaczynski, 2020).

2 When Use of Dedoose is Appropriate in MMR

When it comes to tools for data management and analysis where qualitative methods have been applied, as in MMR, we believe it important to keep in mind their purpose and how this differs from quantitative data analysis software. That is where, in contrast to the calculations that take place in quantitative analysis software where known computational formulas are drivers behind generating results, REDA users drive the process. When it comes to qualitative data, REDA are only as valuable as the theoretical frameworks that frame the understanding of a phenomenon, the code systems that operationalize these frameworks, and the consistency and reliability of those who apply these code systems. Within REDA, it is the user(s) who are responsible for creating the connections between aspects of the raw, transformed, and newly generated data and, hopefully, the REDA features and functionality provide an efficient way to conduct this work, visualize and explore results, and present findings.

As such, along with others, we have concerns regarding appropriate adoption of these tools, particularly when made available to those at risk of being seduced by the purported possibilities with less methodological experience and expertise. Salmona and Kaczynski (2016) identified two barriers to the appropriate adoption of REDA: perceived usefulness and ease of use, and a strong understanding of methodological transparency. Overcoming the first barrier is fairly straightforward, suggesting that to the extent one perceives a tool to be useful and easy to use one will more likely adopt the technology. The second raises more serious concerns about how one may inappropriately be influenced by a technology and led astray from one's methodological intentions. In short, who is driving, the user or the technology? Consumers and those training and/or guiding potential consumers of these tools need to reflect upon this issue before adoption.

3 Technical Outline of Dedoose for MMR

Dedoose was designed specifically for the analysis of both qualitative and mixed methods data (e.g., transcripts from interviews or focus groups, field notes, photos, audio, video, and spread sheets that can include open-ended, categorical, or continuous numerical variables). All system code, associated software, and project data reside entirely on secure commercial servers. From a security standpoint, the encryption standards and systems, along with the cloud platform features and protocols, assure that Dedoose is fully Health Insurance Portability and Accountability (HIPAA) compliant and meets the required security and ethics standards of institutional review boards across the globe. Projects are saved in the Dedoose database which is backed up on a nightly basis with encrypted copies stored in three georedundant locations. Further, individual project data can be downloaded at any time for local secure storage by project creators.

Projects can have any number of authorized users, and project administrators can assign these users to groups with various access privileges. All data in Dedoose are encrypted, yet team leaders may wish to impose restrictions on team member access. This is managed in a project's Security Center where groups with specific access privilege profiles can be added and users are assigned to those groups based on project responsibilities. This functionality assures maximum data security while allowing each team member to carry out their assigned tasks. Regardless of level of access, all team members can access a project simultaneously, in real time, via a native Dedoose executable or the Dedoose desktop app.

As a web-based platform, access to Dedoose is accomplished by connecting to Dedoose servers and logging into an account with individual username/password credentials. Once in the system, users can load any project(s) where they have authorized access.

Before describing Dedoose features and functionality in more detail, let's consider what REDA users are actually doing with these tools. Keeping in mind that these tools do not perform analysis for you, the researcher uses the tools to build a network of connections so that the features of the tools can be capitalized upon (see Figure 27.1). The tools in Dedoose allow researchers to move through, visualize, and filter their data efficiently. Users create the connections linking the different aspects of the database together.

Dedoose also allows for direct import of survey data where both descriptor data and open-ended narrative data are included. The survey importer automatically creates many of these connections, but, descriptor data are more commonly established on a manual basis.

Figure 27.1 illustrates the connections being established by REDA users within the environment. The key connections being made include the linking of qualitative media to

Introduction to Dedoose for Mixed Analysis

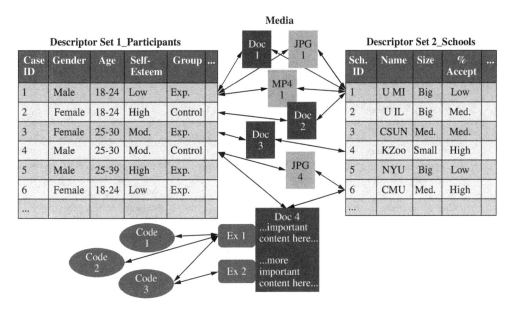

FIGURE 27.1 Building a web of connections.

descriptor data and the linking of codes and, where appropriate, codes weights/ratings to excerpts created within the qualitative media.

Note that Figure 27.1 includes two sets of descriptor data. Under most circumstances we recommend using only one descriptor set. However, if the focus of a study includes multiple levels distinguished by different descriptor fields (or variables), the use of multiple sets would be appropriate. In this example, the qualitative media are being gathered from individuals who vary across a set of descriptor fields (i.e., gender, age, self-esteem). These individuals attend different schools which vary across a separate set of fields (i.e., size and percentage acceptance rate). Thus, media files (e.g., .txt, .doc, .doc, .mp3, and .mp4) are connected to both the individual and the school which they attend. These multiple descriptor links allow for more vertical analysis inquiry. For example, do commonly coded data vary as a function of gender, self-esteem (at the individual level), and school size (at the school level)?

It is noteworthy that the most critical contribution to a project by individuals is the establishment and application of a code system. The code system is where individuals bring their understanding of meaning to the project which they have drawn from the qualitative media. For further information on the coding process please refer to the following texts: Charmaz (2014); Corbin & Strauss (2015); Kaczynski, Salmona, & Smith (2014); Patton (2015). Having a solid understanding of the code process is essential when conducting qualitative and mixed methods inquiry. The quality, thoughtfulness, and articulation of the code system, and their application to the media files, is fundamental to the ultimate credibility of a projects findings and recommendations.

Whether established automatically or manually, connections within the data allow Dedoose's analytic features to functionally support the investigative process. Connections are referred to as relationships in relational database terminology. Simply put, these connections help different aspects of the overall database find each other toward serving the creation of visualizations, filtering, and identifying and exploring patterns. Many of these connections are transparent to the user, but it can be valuable to have a clear understanding of the internal project architecture as one plans their building of the database and subsequent analytic activities. Fundamentally, such a database structure allows data to live in natural forms, while the connections allow for navigation throughout and an incorporation of any object in the database when engaged in exploration, filtering, and analysis.

Dedoose was designed to be transparent and simple to use. The fundamental tasks of data import, creating codes, tagging content, and the integration of qualitative and quantitative data are straightforward. There are more advanced features and functionality for filtering and data analysis which are available as needed.

The tasks to get started in Dedoose are listed in Table 27.1. These tasks will get the research set up in the application, guide on how to begin building their database, and how to conduct basic retrieval.

Table 27.2 lists more advanced features in Dedoose, allowing the researcher to expand the database, visualize the connections and relationships within the database that they have created, and collaboration with others.

Finally, Table 27.3 lists more advanced features in Dedoose allowing support for working in teams, filtering the data and more advanced coding.

The various aspects of a Dedoose project are illustrated in Figure 27.2 and include media, excerpts, codes, and descriptors.

- Media are your qualitative data and can be uploaded to the system in their natural forms as text, PDF, images, audio, and/or video.

- Descriptor data are all other types of data you may have collected from your study participants or dyads, settings, culture … (depending on the level of analysis at which you are working). These data can include

TABLE 27.1

The Basics

Feature	Description	Notes
System Requirements for Access to Dedoose	Dedoose Desktop App or a native Dedoose executable and other mechanisms as provided by the rapidly evolving technologies including WebAssembly, native executables, and complex tools that can compile the Dedoose App to HTML5, CSS, and JavaScript	
User Account	Established via Dedoose website and requires unique username/password credentials	
Subscription Fees	Ranging from $10.95 USD to $14.95 USD per user per month depending on number of users in group.	Student pricing available and no fees for individuals and small group users when inactive in any monthly cycle
Project Setup	Created via Dedoose Project Workspace	No limits on the number of projects a user may create or access
Qualitative Data Import to Media Workspace	*Documents*—docx, doc, txt, rtf, pdf, or manual creation; *Images*—jpeg, png, or bmp; *Audio*—mp3, wav, m4a, or wma; and *Video*—mp4	
Code System/Tree	Manually created, imported as xls, xlsx, or csv file, or automatically created upon *Survey Import* (see below)	
Excerpting and Coding	Define excerpt region in media and apply codes via code tree or quick code widget	
Excerpt Retrieval	Excerpts of interest based on coding activity activated via code tree, code cloud, associated tables, or excerpts workspace	Activating any subset of excerpts prompts presentation of those retrieved for review, modification, or export via *Chart Selection Reviewer*
Excerpt Export	Export to xls, xlsx, doc, or txt	Export options include selection of excerpt metadata—excerpt source characteristic, coding, and linked memos or descriptor data (see below)

demographics, ratings, test scores, experimental condition … data that can also be analyzed from a quantitative perspective, that live naturally within spreadsheets, and can be uploaded directly as an .xls or .csv file.

- Excerpts are those sections of text, clips on a stream, or portions of an image that contain content deemed relevant to addressing specific research questions, or for later recall in the interest of possible discovery, that are tagged with any number of codes from the code system.

The connections linking these different aspects, represented by the arrows in Figure 27.2, are how all objects in the database are connected. They are fundamental to all Dedoose data visualization, manipulation, exploration, filtering, analysis,

TABLE 27.2

Moving on with Dedoose

Feature	Description	Notes
Descriptor Data	Manually created, imported via csv, xls, or xlsx, or automatically generated upon *Survey Import*	Descriptors can include text, categorical, and/or numerical data
Descriptor-Media Linking	Relationships established manually or automatically via 'Title'-based association or upon *Survey Import* when both open and close-ended data are included	
Descriptor Export	Export to xls or xlsx	
Memos	Created and free-floating or linked to any number of objects in project and including title, content, and grouping capabilities	Memos are exportable to doc, docs, txt, rtf, pdf, or xml with options to include any associated data
Survey Import	Spreadsheet containing both open and close-ended content can be imported to automatically create a fully populated Dedoose project	
Analysis Workspace	Includes wide range of data visualizations—tables, charts, and plots—based on media, excerpts, descriptor data (including numbers), and/or user information to support qualitative, quantitative, and mixed methods exploration and data retrieval	Visualizations exportable to xls, xlsx, pdf, or image via screenshot
Collaboration	Multiple users with project access authorization can contribute to database creation and conduct analyses simultaneously and in real-time	Individual user access privileges controlled via Project Security Workspace

TABLE 27.3

Advanced Features

Feature	Description	Notes
Collaboration Supports	*Blind coding*—via data filtering or permission groups—to support independent user work without the distraction of content created by others; *Document Cloning* capabilities to duplicate documents with all excerpts and coding included to support exploration of team decision consistency; and; the *Dedoose Training Center* to create tests for interrater reliability focused on code application and code weight/rating decisions	
Code Weighting/Rating	Functionality to allow for associating continuous number schemata with coding activity to index excerpts across defined numerical range	
Upcoding	Automatically or retroactively apply super-ordinate codes to any excerpts where sub-ordinate codes are applied (or have been applied) when code tree is organized in a hierarchical form	
Data Filtering	Ability to filter database based upon media, descriptors, codes, excerpts, file metadata, case by case basis, users, or any combination	Filters can be created manually using any set of Boolean operators in Data Set or Excerpts Workspaces or via Analysis Workspace visualization features
Meta Project Features	Project merging, or export to xlsx or qdpx (in support of the Rotterdam Exchange Format Initiative: www.qdasoftware.org/)	The REFI-QDA Standard enables interoperability between different QDAS www.qdasoftware.org
Support	Provided via online resources—user guide, blog, and videos—phone, free regular introductory webinars, and privately arranged training	

and presentation of information critical to any successful research or evaluation endeavor.

Further considering Figure 27.2, there are two other features of Dedoose that are important to mention: dynamic descriptors and code weights/ratings. Descriptor data are typically understood within a project as remaining static. That is, they don't change during the duration of the project. However, in the context of a longitudinal study, the time points at which qualitative data are collected can be important to a complete analysis. As such, dynamic descriptors are characteristics of media that can be set on a file by file basis to represent differences, like 'time point' in a longitudinal study, beyond those captured by the static descriptor data. When linking qualitative media to static descriptor data, dynamic descriptors allow the researcher to also set the time point, phase, or any other changing characteristic that distinguish important differences in media files. In later analysis, dynamic descriptors can be drawn upon in identical ways as static descriptor data.

Code weights/ratings are another mixed methods feature of Dedoose. The basic idea is that often, not always, commonly coded qualitative content can be distributed along some numerical dimension. These dimensions can represent variation in quality, importance, sentiment, degree of preference … anything that can be represented across a numerical dimension. For example, one of the studies described below was focused on evaluation the home literacy environments of

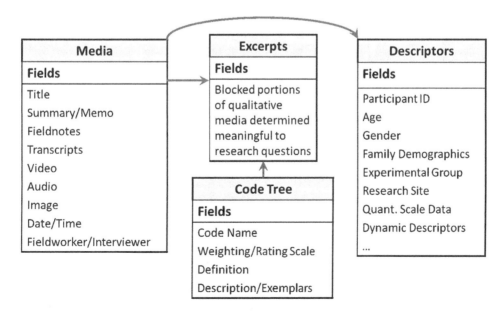

FIGURE 27.2 Primary aspects and connections in a Dedoose project database.

families with young children in the Head Start program (a program in the United States promoting school readiness for children under five years of age from low-income families). One of the codes used in the study was Reading by Mom. This code was used to tag all excerpts where mothers were talking about reading to their child. In looking at these excerpts across the participant population, there was clear variation in the quality of the reading episodes as the research team understood best practices in providing children with experiences which would improve school readiness. Accordingly, a 5-point rating scale was created as part of the Reading by Mom code to index the observed variation in reading quality. Subsequently, when the Reading by Mom code was applied to an excerpt a rating could also be applied. Note that, code weight or rating systems are typically not introduced until the research team has become very familiar with the range of variation in the database. These ratings are often applied during a second pass through the excerpts tagged with the code in question. After sufficient substantive coding has been completed and the inherent variation has become clear, the rating system can be defined, activated, and then applied to the existing excerpts. Code weights allow researchers to introduce a new dimension to the database and enable a range of powerful analytic possibilities. In creating and applying these scales, as opposed to self-report, researchers have the benefit of seeing the full range of variation in the participant sample and more reliably articulate the nuances observed and code different excerpts along the dimension.

Finally, as one of the fundamental drivers behind the development of Dedoose was to serve collaborative research, one final set of features focused on supporting team coordination and consistency is important to introduce and include here: coding blind, document cloning, and the Dedoose Training Center. As the details to engaging in each of these activities can be found elsewhere (see 'Resources for Learning More About Dedoose' below), only the basic mechanisms and rationale for each will be described here.

Coding Blind

First, keeping in mind that multiple users can be provided with access to a shared project, coding blind allows different members of a research team to interact with a media file without being distracted by the work of others. Using Dedoose filtering capabilities, any individual can essentially 'blind' themselves to any work in a project that they did not contribute. For example, User A might access a project, create excerpts, and apply codes to a particular document. User B can then filter out the work of User A and proceed with the same activities. Later, all work within the document can be revealed and examined. The primary goal here, particularly in early stages of a project, is to discover and explore differences in the ways different team members make decisions about where to create excerpts and which codes to apply. Through this exercise, the team can identify and discuss any differences and work together toward a shared vision on excerpt start and end points and how to make use of the existing code system.

Document Cloning

Document cloning is similar to coding blind but serves to focus the exercise explicitly on code selection decisions. Here, a designated team member takes responsibility for creating excerpts within a document without applying any codes. Copies, or clones, of this document are created for each team member with identical text and all excerpts in place. Each team member then accesses their assigned copy and applies the codes and, if desired, the code ratings/weights they believe appropriate for each excerpt. Subsequently, all coding and code rating/weighting decisions across team members can be compared, discussed, and notions of changes to the code system considered.

Training Center

Finally, Dedoose includes a Training Center intended to test for inter-rater reliability within the context of the actual study data. Tests comprised of specific sets of codes and excerpts selected from work carried out in the master project are created. Any number of trainees can then access and perform the tests. Code application tests present the selected excerpt content without indication of any codes that had been applied in the master project. Test takers are then responsible for assigning any codes they believe appropriate. Coding decisions between those initially determined and those assigned by the test taker are compared and results include a variety of information including Cohen's kappa coefficient. Similarly, code rating/weighting tests present the test taker with excerpt content and codes applied and are responsible for selecting the appropriate code rating/weight value. The primary test results here include Pearson's correlation coefficient.

Given our belief in the value of team consistency and transparency in how methods are applied, these Dedoose features provide both for team exercises in discovery, assessment, coordination, and documentation of their work, and the sharing of their findings to communicate methodological practices and achievement to research audiences.

4 Empirical Demonstration of Dedoose for MMR

Many problems in research and evaluation can benefit from integrating multiple research methods. These strategies can be appropriate for any area where quantitative and/or qualitative methods are employed. When mixed methods are effectively applied, we can explore and understand phenomena of interest in fuller and more natural and contextual ways (Johnson & Onwuegbuzie, 2004; Lieber, 2009; Onwuegbuzie & Leech, 2005; Tashakkori & Teddlie, 2003; Weisner, 1996; Yoshikawa, Weisner, Kalil, & Way, 2008). Mixed methods approaches help us to capitalize on the complementary strengths of what qualitative and quantitative methods can offer. The ultimate challenge is to select and implement the most appropriate and effective methods for a given set of circumstances toward generating results and findings that are meaningful and valuable to the consumers of our work. We now present, briefly in 4.1 and in more detail in 4.2, two projects which used Dedoose.

HIV Prevention

Historically, the study of STD/HIV transmission and prevention has been carried out by epidemiologists and medical service providers from predominantly quantitative perspectives. However, there is an increasing appreciation for the importance of considering the level of sociocultural fit in the design of prevention programs based on the belief that a better fit will lead to greater impacts and program sustainability. As such, more recent work in this area has added qualitative perspectives to complement the traditional quantitative perspective in intervention design, health message development, and evaluation. In one example, a large NIMH funded collaborative was formed to adapt, implement, and evaluate an existing STD/HIV transmission prevention program in several countries including China, Russia, India, and Peru. Findings from the application of ethnographic methods were relied upon to inform the identification of appropriate settings in which to implement the intervention programs and, subsequently, throughout the project to inform decisions about participant and fieldworker recruitment, data gathering settings and approaches, and dissemination of findings in the participant communities. The programs and impacts were assessed using both quantitative and qualitative data. Quantitative data analysis focused on biological markers collected from the research participants to assess rates of HIV, HSV-2, syphilis and other STIs. Concurrently, the qualitative data were analyzed toward adapting each program to the specific cultural context, thereby seeking to increase program effectiveness and sustainability. While these program adaptations took place in very different settings and took a variety of forms, the availability of both qualitative and quantitative data throughout the project allowed for project-wide coordination across countries and project-wide analyses. EthnoNotes was used by the China team to manage and analyze the qualitative data and then to prepare results to most clearly present study findings. Overall findings indicated that where the qualitative findings were put to use in design and implementation stages, the programs were more successful (Lieber, Li, Wu, Rotheram-Borus, Guan, & the NIMH Collaborative HIV Prevention Trial Group, 2006; NIMH Collaborative HIV/STD Prevention Trial Group, 2007a, 2007b, 2007c; Lieber, Chin, Li, Rotheram-Borus, Detels, Wu, Guan, & the NIMH Collaborative HIV Prevention Trial Group, 2009).

Emergent Literacy

Lieber (2016) capitalized many Dedoose features, including code weight/rating which was of particular value in this project. The overall study was focused on assessing the home literacy environments (HLE) of families with children in Head Start programs. The qualitative data for this study were gathered via an adaptation of the Ecocultural Family Interview (EFI). By design, the data generated by the EFI include both the rich qualitative data contained in stories provided by research participants about the focus of a study as well as numerical ratings related to many of the core themes developed to organize and communicate the findings from meanings extracted from the qualitative data (Weisner, Coots, Bernheimer, & Arzubiaga, 1997). The Dedoose platform offered an ideal feature set to manage, excerpt, and code the qualitative data, develop and apply code weights/ratings, integrate these data with parent responses to survey questions, and assess interrater reliability toward the establishment of team consistency. Basically, the EFI is a flexible approach to gathering rich and contextual information about the activities people engage in, the routines that organize these activities, the beliefs, values, and resources that influence these decisions, and to assess the strength or quality of how these activities vary across research participants. The Emergent Literacy Ecocultural Family Interview (EL EFI), developed for this study, was employed for all interviews. The EL EFI is a semi-structured, open-ended interview designed to assess the HLE through inquiring about of how and why a family seeks to organize their children's daily routines with respect to early literacy development.

The EL EFI interview protocol consists of questions focusing on aspects of activities, routines, beliefs, and values related to the child's literacy development and are designed to encourage interviewees to talk freely about these aspects of their lives. Main topics are first presented in general terms and the interviewer is encouraged to probe to elicit as much detail as possible about the various areas of daily life. For example, one topic focuses on the times when mothers are reading to their children. If not spontaneously provided, interviewers probe to encourage the sharing of more details on times when reading takes place, reading episode duration and frequency, whether reading takes place on a routine basis, and how both mothers and children experience the reading episode. Eighteen key themes/topics were identified based on qualitative data coding. Using Dedoose, each key topic was assigned a numerical rating along 5-point scale based on the researcher perceived quality of what was reported with respect to the range of what was reported across the range of families in this sample. For the four topics discussed further here, the average Cohens Kappa coefficient for interrater reliability was .78. Coefficients (calculated by Dedoose) for Pre-writing activities, Talking with Child, Letter Recognition, and Reading by Mother were .71, .78, .88, and .74, respectively. While the actual number of individuals, among six team members upon which these average coefficients were calculated, the values for each represent the average of all pairs of team members, on a code-by-code basis, responsible for associated active coding. All data were uploaded, tagged, and rated across the various dimensions and were linked to family descriptor data within Dedoose.

The primary purpose of section 4.2 is to illustrate how we moved from a set of rich and complex raw data and their integration with survey data and, following qualitative coding and code rating, to a comprehensive understanding of variation in the sample population. Subsequently, findings which resulted from both traditional quantitative analyses and then from the interplay between these numerical representations and the rich and integrated qualitative data allowed for more mixed methods perspectives. Beyond a range of other findings (see Lieber, 2016), we now describe how Dedoose was used to tag and

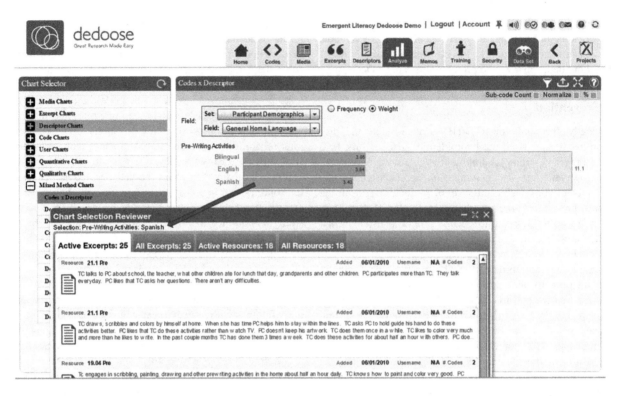

FIGURE 27.3 Illustration of navigation from visualization to underlying qualitative content.

rate HLE topics, explore across participant sub-groups, and, together, gain deeper and more multi-dimensional understandings of the data.

Excerpted content coded with key EL EFI topics were also rated along a 1 (low) to 5 (high) continuum defined by criteria representing 'quality' and specific for each content area were recorded via use of the Dedoose code weighting/rating system. Subsequent analysis focused on these ratings helped expose rich patterns as understood by variation in the quality of observed HLE practices. The criteria considered for determining quality ratings across the key topics analyzed here were as follows. 'Reading by mother' scores were based on variation in reading frequency, duration, level of pleasure expressed by both child and parent, and the degree to which reading took place on a routine basis. 'Pre-writing' scores—which represent demonstration of skills understood as common precursors to writing—were based on the child's painting, writing, coloring, or scribbling in the home with issues of frequency, level of pleasure and motivation, support, and spontaneity being considered. 'Letter Recognition' knowledge and activity scores were based on child's ability to recite, recognize, and write letters of the alphabet, read words, write their name, frequency of play with alphabet toys, parent efforts to teach the alphabet, and child's demonstrated curiosity about print. 'Parent-child talking' ratings were based on the frequency, content, and nature of parent-child conversation. Higher talking ratings were assigned to families that reported more frequent, varied, and balanced conversation (i.e., more equally shared dialogue as opposed to more unidirectional directive talk).

Quantitative analysis with reported primary home language as the grouping variable revealed several statistically significant differences in the quality of HLE activities. Statistically significant ANOVA results for each of these topics reveal a pattern of HLE differences across the three groups (primary reported speaking language being Bilingual, Spanish, or English). Overall, these findings revealed, across the three language groups, variation in the emphasis and quality of various HLE activities. Using charting features in Dedoose which allow for the visualization of the type of variation found here across language groups. Simply clicking on a bar in a Dedoose chart reveals the underlying qualitative content allowing for an exploration of the rich and contextual meanings beneath the patterns exposed by the quantitative analyses and Dedoose data visualization (see Figure 27.3).

Subsequent analyses focused on the degree to which different language group families engaged in higher or lower quality HLE activities across the various activities explored with 'high' quality defined as ratings of 4 or 5 for each topic. Dedoose filtering capabilities were used to identify, for each key topic, the percentage of families in each language group who was identified as providing high quality for reading practices, pre-writing activities, letter recognition, and parent-child communication (see Figure 27.4). This analysis revealed meaningful percentages of families in each language group, to varying degrees, engaged in high quality HLE activities. Optimal early literacy development is believed to occur where higher quality levels of experience related to each HLE activity takes places. While it was encouraging to find that many families engaged in what were considered high quality levels of activities in one area or another, an evaluation of overall HLEs quality required attention to the combinations of routines and activities that encourage early literacy development. Therefore, we turned our attention to families who demonstrated higher levels of

Introduction to Dedoose for Mixed Analysis

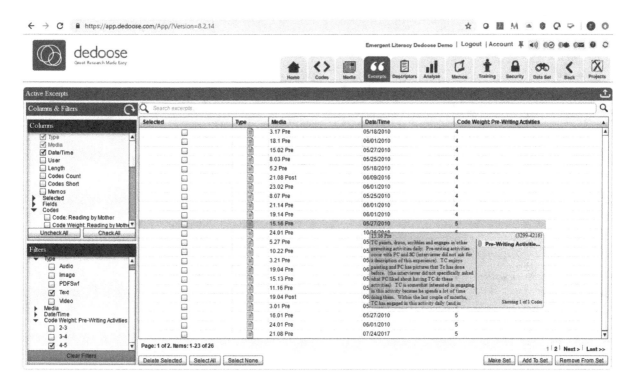

FIGURE 27.4 Example of excerpt filtering by code weight values.

HLE activity in multiple areas. Using the Dedoose filtering capabilities, we identified the families within each language group that showed high quality HLE activities across all topical sets of activities explored in the study. Results revealed that between 10 and 20 percent of families in each language group were combining high quality experiences and activities in all key areas of early literacy development.

The final analyses in this study involved returning to the qualitative data provided by the subset of families found to provide high quality experiences with their children for all HLE activities to better understand their characteristics and practices as a whole and any variation in activities across language groups (Lieber, 2016). In short, the most valuable findings from this study showed how and why this subset of families managed to provide more ideal early literacy development environments for their children. In turn, from an intervention perspective, we considered how more families of comparable backgrounds who showed lesser quality HLE activities could be supported and encouraged to engage in more frequent and higher quality HLE activities. These findings and the coding, code rating, and analytic journey were made possible through a combination of the EFI approach and the Dedoose features and functionality that facilitated data management and manipulation and the overall investigative process.

5 Suggested Applications of Dedoose in MMR

After importing multiple data sources to a project and the establishment of critical connections among the various aspects of the database, you are ready to take advantage of the Dedoose analytics and filtering capabilities. The Dedoose Analysis Workspace includes a folder structure organizing all pre-programmed and customizable analysis tools including construction of a variety of tables, charts, and plots (see Figure 27.5). An exhaustive list of Analysis Workspace features can be found in the Dedoose User Guide and would not be appropriate here. These features were developed in response to our understanding of how contemporary researchers and evaluators wish to view their data as well as recommendations we received from the Dedoose user community.

Dedoose visualizations (e.g., charts, tables, and plots) are intended to provide representations of the data in visual form to expose variation in code applications and/or code weighting on any media excerpts as a function of various characteristics of the study participants. For example, one may wish to query the database to learn, or inquire, for example:

- Is there variation in the frequency with which particular codes were applied to excerpts from groups differing in annual income and level of education?
- Are there differences in quality of reading experiences for children differing in their gender and mother's work status?
- How about as a function of father's work status?
- Across the sample participants in their responses to our interview questions, do we find that pairs of codes are frequently occurring together? That is, are certain themes being connected in the thoughts of participants as they think about our topics of interest?

These are just a few examples of the kinds of inquiry Dedoose analytic features are designed to address.

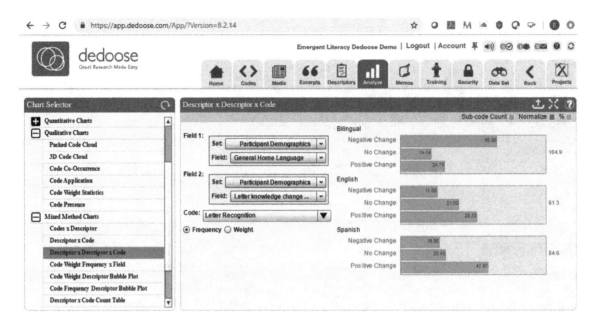

FIGURE 27.5 Snapshot of analysis workspace with descriptor by descriptor by code chart active.

Many Dedoose visualization tools can be quickly adjusted to explore multiple aspects of the database. For example, you can easily swap out mother's work status for father's work status to see what changes. All charts, tables, and plots are directly linked to the underlying qualitative content. Simply clicking a bar, bubble, or cell in a table will trigger the presentation of all associated excerpts and they can be further explored or exported. All visuals can be exported to Excel or PDF format. These features and functionality support the exploration of data visualization patterns, export for visual presentation or inclusion in manuscripts, and allow deeper investigation into the rich meanings contained in the excerpts that sit beneath the surface.

Finally, there are a number of ways to filter data in Dedoose to allow analytic focus on a subset of data meeting your filtering criteria. Especially in large databases, it is often the case that a line of inquiry will focus on subsets of participants and/or on excerpts that have been tagged with one of a subset of codes. It is important to keep in mind that Dedoose is both collaborative and dynamic. Any number of team members can be working on different parts of the project database with real-time updating for all team members active in the system. For example, if a researcher is generating and exporting charts for presentation at the same time a project assistant is engaged in coding excerpts, the researcher has immediate access to the new work that will be included when a new chart is created. Taken together, all Dedoose analytics, visuals, filtering and data navigation functionality are intended to increase the efficiency and effectiveness of individual and team-based qualitative and mixed methods analysis.

6 Strengths and Limitations of Dedoose in MMR

Perhaps the greatest strength of Dedoose is being web-based and the related benefits. As earlier discussed, Dedoose was developed to meet many specific challenges, many of which were very well served by a web application. Web apps are, by nature, collaborative, allowing multiple individuals the ability to work together simultaneously in real time regardless of the computer or computer platform from which they connect. Web apps offer two additional advantages: relief from any maintenance or upgrade demands and access by paying only low subscriptions fees as opposed to the high cost when purchasing a traditional desktop-based software license. With web apps being accessed through an Internet connection, and regardless of any new features or functions that may have been added, once logged in, users have full access to all available functionality without ever needing to upgrade, maintain, or patch.

When it comes to the Dedoose design and interface, users benefit from a range of benefits which distinguish web apps from traditional software. In Dedoose, workspaces are kept as clean and simple as possible, while allowing users to engage in activities that are appropriate at the time as intuitively as possible. This encourages an easy learning curve, and, as Dedoose evolves, the developers will keep a keen focus on user experiences to help ensure as much transparency without compromising the power of what can be accomplished in the environment. Dedoose was designed specifically to support mixed methods research based on a clear understanding of the systematic intermingling of qualitative and quantitative data and their subsequent manipulation, analysis, and presentation of findings.

Probably the most significant limitation of Dedoose is that, at least at the time this chapter was prepared, one must be connected to the Internet to use Dedoose. Further, Dedoose currently offers no support for Geographic Information System (GIS) data or direct import of social media streams. Although GIS and social media data can be exported, prepared, and then imported to Dedoose, there are more efficient tools for dealing with these types of data. Also, the current set of tables, charts, and plots in Dedoose cannot be customized beyond existing controls and options. That all said, Dedoose is constantly evolving and what is reported here is current at time of publication (see Salmona, Lieber, & Kaczynski, 2020).

7 Resources for Learning More About Dedoose

These resources will help researchers find their way through Dedoose by providing learning resources including video tutorials and step-by-step instructions for the various aspects of the application:

www.dedoose.com
www.dedoose.com/userguide
www.dedoose.com/blog
www.youtube.com/user/DedooseSCRC

Salmona, Lieber, & Kaczynski, (2020). *Qualitative and mixed methods data analysis using Dedoose: A practical approach for research across the social sciences.* Thousand Oaks, CA: Sage.

REFERENCES

Charmaz, K. (2014). *Constructing grounded theory* (2nd ed.). Thousand Oaks, CA: Sage.

Corbin, J., & Strauss, A. (2015). *Basics of qualitative research: Techniques and procedures for developing grounded theory* (4th ed.). Thousand Oaks, CA: Sage.

Johnson, R. B., & Onwuegbuzie, A. J. (2004). Mixed methods research: A research paradigm whose time has come. *Educational Researcher, 33*(7), 14–26, doi.org/10.3102/0013189X033007014

Kaczynski, D., Salmona, M., & Smith, T. (2014). Qualitative research in finance. *Australian Journal of Management, 39*(1), 127–135, doi.org/10.1177/0312896212469611

Lieber, E. (2009). Mixing qualitative and quantitative methods: Insights into design and analysis issues. *Journal of Ethnographic & Qualitative Research, 3*, 218–227.

Lieber, E. (2016). Collaborative research on emergent literacy: Capturing complex mixed methods data and tools for their integration and analysis. In M. Cameron Hay (Ed.), *Methods that matter: Integrating mixed methods for more effective social science research* (pp. 185–209). Chicago, IL: The University of Chicago Press.

Lieber, E., & Weisner, T. S. (2010). Meeting the practical challenges of mixed methods research. In A. Tashakkori & C. Teddlie (Eds.), *Sage handbook of mixed methods in social & behavioral research*, 2nd ed. (pp. 559–579). Thousand Oaks, CA: Sage.

Lieber, E., Nihira, K., & Mink, I. T. (2004). Filial piety, modernization, and the challenges of raising children for Chinese immigrants: Quantitative and qualitative evidence. *Ethos, 32*, 324–347, doi: 10.1525/eth.2004.32.3.324

Lieber, E., Li, L., Wu, Z., Rotheram-Borus, M. J., Guan, J., & the National Institute of Mental Health (NIMH) Collaborative HIV Prevention Trial Group (2006). HIV/AIDS Stigmatization fears as health seeking barriers in China. *AIDS and Behavior, 10*, 263–271, doi: 10.1007/s10461-005-9047-5

Lieber, E., Chin, D., Li, L., Rotheram-Borus, M. J., Detels, R., Wu, Z., Guan, J., and the National Institute of Mental Health (NIMH) Collaborative HIV Prevention Trial Group. (2009). Sociocultural contexts and communication about sex in China: Informing HIV/STD prevention programs. *AIDS Education and Prevention, 21*, 415–429, doi: 10.1521/aeap.2009.21.5.415

NIMH Collaborative HIV/STD Prevention Trial Group (Lieber, E., Ethnographic data collection team) (2007). Selection of populations represented in the NIMH Collaborative HIV/STD Prevention Trial. *AIDS, 21* (Suppl. 2) S19-S28, doi: 10.1097/01.aids.0000266454.26268.90

NIMH Collaborative HIV/STD Prevention Trial Group (Lieber, E., China-Ethnographic methods representative and secondary author) (2007). Design and integration of ethnography within an international behavior change HIV/sexually transmitted disease prevention trial. *AIDS, 21* (Suppl. 2): S37-S48, doi: 10.1097/01.aids.0000266456.03397.d3

NIMH Collaborative HIV/STD Prevention Trial Group (Lieber, E., China-Ethnographic methods representative and primary author) (2007). Formative study conducted in five countries to adapt the community popular opinion leader intervention. *AIDS, 21* (Suppl. 2): S91-S98, doi: 10.1097/01.aids.0000266461.33891.d0

Patton, M. Q. (2015). *Qualitative research & evaluation methods* (4th ed.). Thousand Oaks, CA: Sage.

Richards, L. (2015). *Handling qualitative data: A practical guide*, 3rd ed. Thousand Oaks, CA: Sage.

Salmona, M., & Kaczynski, D. (2016). Don't blame the software: Using qualitative data analysis software successfully in doctoral research. *Forum Qualitative Sozialforschung/ Forum: Qualitative Social Research, 17*(3), Art 11, http://nbn-resolving.de/urn:nbn:de:0114-fqs1603117

Salmona, M., Lieber, E. & Kaczynski, D. (2020). *Qualitative and mixed methods data analysis using Dedoose: A practical approach for research across the social sciences.* Thousand Oaks, CA: Sage.

Tashakkori, A., & Teddlie, C. (2003). The past and future of mixed methods research: From data triangulation to mixed model designs. In A. Tashakkori & C. Teddlie (Eds.), *Handbook of mixed methods in social & behavioral research* (pp. 671–702). Thousand Oaks, CA: Sage.

Weisner, T. S. (1996). Why ethnography should be the most important method in the study of human development. In R. Jessor, A. Colby, & R. Shweder (Eds.), *Ethnography and human development: Context and meaning in social inquiry* (pp. 305–324). Chicago. IL: University of Chicago Press.

Weisner, T. S., Coots, J. J., Bernheimer, L. P., & Arzubiaga, A. (1997). *The Ecocultural Family Interview Manual.* Unpublished manuscript. Los Angeles, CA: UCLA Center for Culture and Health.

Yoshikawa, H., Weisner, T. S., Kalil, A., & Way, N. (2008), Mixing qualitative and quantitative research in developmental science: Uses and methodological choices. *Developmental Psychology, 44*, 344–354, doi: 10.1037/0012–1649.44.2.344

28

Introduction to ATLAS.ti for Mixed Analysis

Brigitte Smit

> THE No.1 SOFTWARE—for Qualitative Data Analysis and Mixed Methods
>
> For those who want to see the big picture but appreciate details. Reveal meanings and relationships. ATLAS.ti makes it easy for you with a beautiful design. Gain rich insights with the most intuitive and powerful QDA software on the market.
>
> (www.atlasti.com)

1 Introduction and Definition: Computer-assisted Qualitative Data Analysis Software, ATLAS.ti: Language and Concepts

Not much has been written on the use of ATLAS.ti 8 in mixed methods research (MMR) and less so on mixed analysis. Therefore, the purpose of this chapter is to introduce the concept of computer-assisted qualitative data analysis software (CAQDAS), ATLAS.ti 8™ (referred to as ATLAS.ti here on), for use in mixed analysis, which includes qualitative and quantitative workings of empirical and theoretical data. ATLAS.ti is one of many software packages on the market, alongside QDA Miner and WordStat, MAXQDA, Dedoose, NVivo, and HyperRESEARCH (Johnson & Christensen, 2017). This chapter does not replace the manual for ATLAS.ti; instead, it offers a conceptual discussion of the functions that support mixed analysis, including data management functions, the literature review, qualitative analysis, quantitative content analysis and coding, inductive and deductive reasoning, survey data imports, and SPSS exports, as well as visual and textual reports.

ATLAS.ti was developed as a qualitative data analysis software package that allows the researcher to import, to sort, and to analyze rich texts, plain text documents, audio files, spreadsheets, databases, digital photos, documents, PDFs, biographical data, web pages, and social media. Although ATLAS.ti was initially developed for qualitative social research, and specifically qualitative data analysis, the power and the possibilities of ATLAS.ti has expanded hugely in the past few years. Previously, ATLAS.ti was considered an essential resource for researchers using qualitative research methods and approaches, including qualitative data analysis and tools, interviews, focus groups, and content analysis of unstructured data. More recently, a further feature of ATLAS.ti has been developed, which means that data such as open-ended and survey items, literature reviews, audio recordings, pictures, and web pages can be included in qualitative projects because these can now also be analyzed.

It is now widely accepted that new data types have become available in recent years and that computer-assisted qualitative data analysis software, including ATLAS.ti 8, has had to change to respond to this challenge (see Friese & Contreras, 2016). Besides the call in research for comprehensive data, the quest for meaning and the need for human interpretation still exists. Therefore, in addition to providing tools for the analysis of larger datasets, computer-assisted qualitative data analysis software also has a significant role to play in the analysis of small thick data. However, the data landscape has changed, and it may not even be necessary to go into the field to collect data for a research project, as the data are already available. These data can be downloaded and added to the software package for analysis. For example, this applies to social media data like Twitter or articles and contributions published online. Additionally, new features are available such as the direct import options for open-ended questions from online surveys. Data collected in and by reference managers and data stored in Evernote allow for the analysis of these type of data by software packages such as ATLAS.ti.

ATLAS.ti is a powerful workbench for the data analysis of large bodies of textual, graphical, audio, and video data. It offers a variety of tools for accomplishing the tasks associated with any systematic approach to unstructured data. Although, as stated previously, ATLAS.ti was initially targeted at qualitative analysis, some functionalities have been included in the software to offer mixed analysis robust tools to analyze data from a variety of sources, including theoretical texts and survey data. In the course of such an analysis, ATLAS.ti enables the researcher to explore complex phenomena hidden in the data. For coping with the inherent complexity of the tasks and the data, ATLAS.ti offers a formidable and intuitive environment that keeps the researcher focused on the analyzed data, assembling meaningful pieces from large amounts of data in creative, flexible, and yet systematic ways (Friese, 2012b, p. 9).

ATLAS.ti belongs to the field of CAQDAS programs (Braun & Clarke, 2014), which offer a means for supporting qualitative and quantitative data analysis (Friese, 2012a). The first version of ATLAS.ti was released in 1989, and the latest version, Version 8, in December 2016. Thomas Muhr at Technical University in Berlin developed a prototype of ATLAS.ti in the context of project ATLAS (1989–1992). The company Scientific Software Development, later ATLAS.ti Scientific Software Development GmbH (Muhr, 1991), released a first commercial version of ATLAS.ti in 1993. Although a rich history of computer software use exists, many researchers and postgraduate students remain unfamiliar with the concept of CAQDAS or with ATLAS.ti. The purpose of ATLAS.ti is to help researchers uncover and systematically analyze complex phenomena hidden in text and multimedia data. The program provides tools that allow the user to locate, to code, and to annotate findings in primary data material, to weigh and to evaluate their importance, and to visualize complex relations among them. ATLAS.ti consolidates large volumes of documents and keeps track of all notes, annotations, codes, and memos in all fields that require close study and analysis of primary material consisting of text, images, audio, video, and geodata (Friese, 2012b). It also provides analytical and visualization tools designed to open new interpretative views on the material. Accordingly, mixed analysis can be enhanced through the use of ATLAS.ti tapping into aspects of data analysis such as visualization, contextualization, and serendipity. The intent is to alert researchers that even though the software does not *do* the analysis for the researcher, it is a powerful tool for supporting and assisting the process of data analysis (Friese, 2012a). ATLAS.ti provides the tools that support the researcher to deal with the variety of data that have become available. A carefully conducted computer-assisted data analysis increases the validity and trustworthiness of the research findings, given the amount of empirical data and its easy access to search and to retrieve these data over an extended period.

2 Appropriate Use of ATLAS.ti in Mixed Analysis

One of the few articles that adresses bridging the qualitative/quantitative software divide was written by Annechino, Antin, and Lee (2010), who report that "although researchers frequently use separate software packages to store and analyze qualitative and quantitative data, combining these data on one software package can also be useful for exploring and analyzing data collected in mixed methods projects" (p. 115). Their research illustrates how, in a mixed methods research study, a relational database was developed to merge survey responses stored and analyzed in SPSS and semi-structured interview responses stored and analyzed in ATLAS.ti.

Given the voluminous and unorganized nature of qualitative data, a management tool that enables qualitative data analysis becomes attractive in that it permits instantaneous access to all the datasets once these have been added (imported) to the ATLAS.ti project for analysis. Management of data also refers to "storing of ideas, concepts, issues, questions, models and theories" (Lune & Berg, 2017, p. 198). This facilitates the researcher's closeness to the data. All project components, such as the datasets or documents, quotations, codes, memos, and networks, can be effortlessly accessed, and the movability among them is quick and comfortable. ATLAS.ti is easy to learn because the structure is logical, and working with it has an intuitive feel. Essentially, the interface emulates the traditional paper-and-pencil desktop style, where the data are displayed on the left-hand side of the screen (paper), whereas the marked segments of texts, codes, and notes about the data appear on the right-hand side—the margin area. The various tabs have a *Windows feel*, and their structure is based on the main aspects of analysis (entities) and thus easy to access.

If one considers the scenario for *data management and storing*, with data collected from interviews, 30 pages per one-hour interview, observation field texts, and focus group interviews, the researcher could end up with 1,000 pages of empirical data. Also, using articles and literature reviews for analysis, specifically scholarly literature that refers to scholarly theory and research (Loseke, 2017; Smit, Williamson, & Padayachee 2013), can amount to even more data in an ATLAS.ti project. A manual approach requires that these pages be copied into a second complete dataset to keep one dataset in context. The other dataset is cut, pasted, and colour-coded, manually or with a word processor—referred to as the manual-cum-word-processing method (Bong, 2002). However, ATLAS.ti facilitates easy use of software in comparison to non-use software for the control, management, and storing of data.

3 Technical Outline of ATLAS.ti

Paging manually through hundreds of pages of data is time-consuming but becomes swift and efficient in ATLAS.ti. Project data management is facilitated when using software, which offers "considerable benefits regarding time, efficiency and more thorough analysis" (Fielding & Lee, 1998, p. 57). ATLAS.ti supports any type of file format, including text, graphic, audio, and video format, as well as pdf documents. Even Google geodata are supported in ATLAS.ti and, as such, multimedia files can be played in sync with their transcriptions. These datasets are *parked* in a library for immediate and quick access, and at any point in time; data files are easily accessible without the concern of saving data files in a specific folder. By using ATLAS.ti, it becomes much easier to analyze data systematically and to ask questions that the researcher otherwise would not ask because the manual tasks involved are too time-consuming. Even large volumes of data and those of different media types can be structured and integrated very quickly with the aid of the software (Friese, 2012a, p. 1).

Furthermore, the software frees the researcher from all those tasks that a machine can do so much more efficiently, like modifying code words and coded segments, retrieving data based on various criteria, searching for words, integrating material in one place, attaching notes and finding them again, counting the numbers of coded incidences, and offering overviews at various stages of a project (Friese, 2012a, p. 1). When analyzing data manually, one often forgets over a period what specific codes meant at the time when they were created. ATLAS.ti offers an annotating system wherein codes can be defined and dated. Also, it is reasonable to assume that thinking about coding and analysis, based on reading and research, might change over time. Therefore, it is vital to have a traceable process given how much development has taken shape during the analysis. Learning the ATLAS.ti language is straightforward, and many concepts are taken from Grounded Theory (cf. Charmaz, 2006). Also, the language among various software packages is not consistent and, therefore, it is crucial that

ATLAS.ti language retains its integrity. The project explorer, similar to Windows Explorer, functions as a directory of an entire project. The project explorer displays all the entities and their related sub-entities, namely, datasets (documents), codes and selected segments of texts (quotations), memos, groups of codes (clusters of datasets or codes), and networks.

The *project* in ATLAS.ti refers to a single research project, which can be compared to an "electronic container" (Friese, 2012a, p. 10) that keeps track of all the data. This project holds the complete analysis together, which includes all the data (documents); segments of selected texts (quotations); all the codes that have been created; the comments and annotations, which were made about codes; memos; links; clusters of codes (groups of codes); and any queries that have been created, with the results presented in smart codes.

Friese (2017, p. 114) considers *hyperlinks* that directly relate data segments among quotations to express contradiction, support, and illustrations. Cross-references among text passages are very common even in conventional media like books and literature reviews. In conventional media, not much navigational support is provided for *traversing* among the pieces of data that reference each other. Computer-related hypertext applications include, for example, online help systems that display operational information in suitable small chunks (compared to lengthy printed information), but with a considerable amount of linkage to other pieces of information. A well-known hypermedia structure is the World Wide Web with its textual, all mark-up graphical, and other multimedia information distributed worldwide.

Evernote is primarily most useful for note-taking in the field given the import functionality of ATLAS.ti from Evernote. According to Munirah Mohamad (2017b), Evernote is one of the world's most preferred notetaking applications, which can be installed on a variety of devices such as iPad, iPhone, Android, and Windows and Mac-based machines. Evernote can hold notes in various formats, such as images, audio/video attachments, reminders, and typed texts as well as handwritten texts. Not only does Evernote support empirical field texts, but it can also save websites and PDF documents for a literature search, as well as MS Word documents as Evernote attachments. Even handwritten scribbles and photos can be saved in Evernote and later imported for analysis in ATLAS.ti (Munirah Mohamad, 2017b).

Twitter feeds are available from non-profit organizations, people, companies, and groups that tweet about real-time events and meetings (Paulus, Lester, & Dempster, 2014, p. 35). Twitter data can be used in research and can include keywords and hashtags, and authors can be searched, adding up-to-date information on the research topic. These tweets can be imported into ATLAS.ti for immediate analysis. If the researcher wants to use Twitter data as part of a project containing data from different sources (such as interview data, observational field notes, factor grants, or archival research data), then ATLAS.ti is very useful, allowing the researcher to analyze all in one single project. It also facilitates crystallization, sometimes referred to as triangulation of data. Twitter data also can be visualized in a network. When importing Twitter data, the researcher can choose to add codes, hashtags, authors, locations, and languages, which allows the researcher to gain a quick overview of the various hashtags used, by whom the messages were sent, from which geographical location, how many, and which tweets were retweeted. The code manager will give the researcher a quick overview of the types of topics, the frequencies, and the code co-occurrence Explorer. The table can show which topics were frequently mentioned together and how various topics are spread geographically and by language, and which issues are more specified and others. The network function in ATLAS.ti can visualize these data and, therefore, provide a quick overview of the Twitter topic.

Lastly, *geo documents* (e.g., Figure 28.1), which use Open Street Map as the data source, are also supported by ATLAS.ti. Even though there is only one data source, the researcher also can use more than one geo document in a project, for example, to create distinct sets of locations or to simulate tours (Fielding & Fielding, 2015; Friese, 2017). Although this geographical space may serve the researcher well, for instance, where data were collected and linked with specific geographic information systems (GPS) coordinates, a snapshot taken as a screenshot might compromise the anonymity of the data source (Paulus et al., 2014).

4 Empirical Demonstration of ATLAS.ti for Mixed Analysis

The next section demonstrates the use of ATLAS.ti for qualitative, quantitative, and mixed methods researchers conducting literature reviews.

Conducting a Literature Review using ATLAS.ti

Although literature reviews tend to be conducted manually, some researchers have found bibliographic management tools, such as Endnote, Mendeley, Zotero, and RefWorks, quite useful. These bibliographic management tools differ from qualitative data analysis software. Some researchers have taken advantage of tools such as ATLAS.ti to organize and to select in order to review and to analyze the literature. However, not many researchers have reported on the use of qualitative data analysis for literature reviews, which is puzzling, given that the review of literature is arguably the most utilized form of qualitative research, and the value of qualitative data analysis (QDA) as tools for this task has been acknowledged within the methodological literature and has been promoted by program developers.

Recent developments in software development facilitate the conduct of a literature review study using ATLAS.ti, wherein journal articles are imported using reference managers such as Mendeley and Endnote. Reference management software focuses on bibliographical data of the source, with CAQDAS tools focusing on the content of the articles, which are imported from the reference manager. ATLAS.ti supports multiple file formats, such as. pdf,. doc,. docx,. rtf,. txt, as well as. png and. jpg (Munirah Mohamad, 2017a). Conducting a MMR literature review involves understanding the current state of the field to join the scholarly conversation (Fink, 2010; Onwuegbuzie, Leech, & Collins, 2012; Paulus et al., 2014, p. 9). Onwuegbuzie

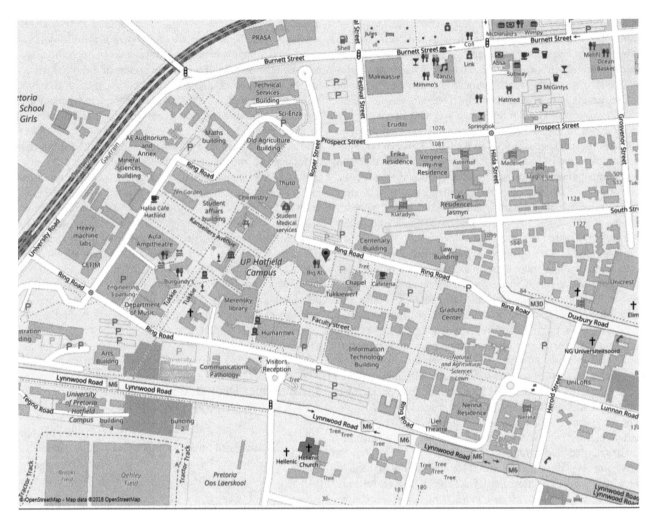

FIGURE 28.1 Geo document: University of Pretoria.

et al. (2012) have demonstrated how qualitative data analysis approaches could be used to analyze and to synthesize information extracted from a literature review, applying constant comparison analysis, domain analysis, taxonomic analysis, keywords-in-context (KWIC), classical content analysis, and theme analysis. Onwuegbuzie and Weinbaum (2017) have proposed a framework for yet another qualitative data analysis technique to analyze and to interpret literature review sources. They call this framework "qualitative comparative analysis-based research synthesis" (QCARS, p. 362). Whether the study is qualitative or quantitative or both, previous work needs to be understood to situate scholarly ideas in the broader context of the research domain or discipline.

Boote and Beile (2005) remind us that "a substantive, thorough, sophisticated literature review is a precondition for doing substantive, thorough, sophisticated research" (p. 3). Thus, the purpose of a literature review is to present the context and the background of a particular topic of interest for research. The researcher needs to examine the academic conversations surrounding the issue and link them to relevant literature. Gaps in the literature are identified, and future directions of research are also determined. Data sources for the literature review are indicated, and criteria for inclusion or exclusion of studies are delineated. International literature and cross-disciplinary research should provide conceptual and methodological details to interpret the findings, and also, the review should go beyond the description and include an understanding of theories and methods. The use of ATLAS.ti will assist the researcher in keeping track of search terms, keywords and databases sources, journals, and scholars, as well as management system programs. The literature review can be built into a project in ATLAS.ti, with the ability to add literature, and articles from the databases at any given time. The researcher can create a coding framework for the key question in the research, and then code specific sections of the articles, which allows a smooth and referenced way when writing the literature review. Short memos can be written and added to the literature review in ATLAS.ti to help the researcher keep track of the development of this review. Key ideas can be organized and captured as well as reflections on specific paragraphs or ideas in the literature. Onwuegbuzie and Frels (2016) call for a comprehensive literature review (CLR), which should include media, observations, documents, experts and secondary data (MODES), taking the traditional literature to the next level (Williams, 2018, p. 347) and, as such, geographic information systems (GIS) and Twitter feeds are considered valuable sources that can be included in the literature review. ATLAS.ti has excellent functionalities to include these data, and create an audit trail, which can be followed or accessed by other researchers (Williams, 2018, p. 348).

The rationale for using CAQDAS in conducting a literature review is relatively new. Although not many scholars have reported on the possibilities of using such software for analyzing theoretical work, certain scholars such as Paulus et al. (2014), Munirah Mohamad (2017a), Smit (2005, 2018), and Wright (2014) have written about using ATLAS.ti for the literature review, but mostly in the context of qualitative research. This chapter, therefore, wants to contribute to MMR by outlining the possibilities of using ATLAS.ti in conducting a literature review, including "method, theory, prior research, the social significance of the problem, philosophical underpinnings of the inquiry, implications for policy, and applications to practice" (Wolcott, 2009, p. 68). Essential reading to appreciate how qualitative data analysis can be assumed or adopted for the study of the literature was written by Onwuegbuzie et al. (2012), who, as noted previously, outlined thematic analysis, KWIC, word count, and constant comparative analysis. Qualitative data analysis strategies, appropriated in ATLAS.ti, have a great deal to offer mixed analysis.

Although ATLAS.ti is not classified as computer-assisted mixed methods data analysis software (CAMMDAS; Onwuegbuzie & Frels, 2016, p. 145), it can be used to import articles directly from reference managers, such as Mendeley, Endnote, Zotero, and RefWorks, to support the literature search and literature review, using XML format as the export. When importing documents from a reference manager, the researcher can use ATLAS.ti to gain a better in-depth understanding of those articles previously identified as being valuable for the literature review chapter. Put differently, the reference manager deals with bibliographic data, whereas ATLAS.ti focuses on the analysis and meaning-making of the content of the articles. Onwuegbuzie, Frels, and Hwang (2016) offer a helpful "typology for coding and analyzing information extracted from the literature based on Saldaña coding methods" (p. 130). The data, identified in the articles, are coded, using a variety of coding strategies, as discussed by Saldaña (2016). Coding the literature means highlighting text (quotations) and assigning codes that act as collecting devices, which means linking together various quotations that share a common feature. However, once identified, these codes also can be used to search and to retrieve information about the articles that the researcher has selected (Wright, 2014). The codes are then grouped or categorized to theme the data, to answer the research question(s) either empirically or theoretically or both. So, ATLAS.ti can assist in finding quotations that are related to a specific code, which the researcher would like to use in writing up the literature review.

In this context, O'Dwyer and Bernauer (2014) claim that unless one uses

> an appropriate means for making sense of data, one cannot adequately answer the research question or promote further understanding of a topic. If researchers analyze quantitative data that are descriptive, together with inferential statistics processes or analyze qualitative data that rely on some coding narrative, a combination of both of these methods is applicable for mixed methods research. The important point is that whether one is analyzing numbers or words, researchers need to use the appropriate processes and tools to make meaning of these data and this usually involves employing some data reduction using either statistics of the quantitative case or coding in the qualitative case. (p. 35)

Undoubtedly, ATLAS.ti can play a supportive role in the conduct of a comprehensive literature review, as proposed by Onwuegbuzie and Frels (2016).

The advantage of having a variety of resources grouped together in an ATLAS.ti project allows for quick searches of keywords to establish the relevance and the appropriateness of the resource. Useful functionalities in ATLAS.ti are word counts and word clouds (similar to Wordle: www.wordle.net; see Bernard, Wutich, & Ryan 2017, p. 462), which provide an overview of word frequencies in journal articles before deciding whether materials should be added to the review or selected for in-depth study. Word counts offer an overview of the most often-used concepts or keywords in a particular article or document. This functionality facilitates easy access to understanding the literature at a glance of the words used in a specific piece of text. This process is particularly helpful when deciding which articles to select and which ones to deselect.

Word frequency can be viewed in a word list (see Figure 28.2) or a word cloud (see Figure 28.3). The word cloud is another essential ATLAS.ti function, which assists with the selecting of research articles. Once the word cloud has been created, the frequency of words can be searched for in context using the *auto-coding* function. This search is similar to searching for KWIC (Leech & Onwuegbuzie 2011, pp. 75–76).

Data Analysis and Coding

Qualitative data analysis can be differentiated into three broad levels. These levels represent analytical approaches, analytical methods, and analytical techniques (Onwuegbuzie & Weinbaum, 2017, p. 364). ATLAS.ti users should be mindful of these different approaches and consider whether their analysis stance is an approach, a method, or a technique. Qualitative data analysis techniques refer specifically to data analysis (Leech & Onwuegbuzie, 2008) that represent a single step in the data analysis processes. Saldaña (2016) offers 33 coding strategies; for example, values coding, process coding, descriptive coding, and others, which are helpful for a software user in deciding how to design the code list. These codes can be clustered into categories to theme the data. Approaches, methods, and techniques interact with one another in a meaningful way. For example, Onwuegbuzie and Weinbaum (2017) claim that

> qualitative comparative analysis—representing a qualitative data analysis approach—is particularly useful for the literature review context because it can complement any of the other 33 qualitative data analysis approaches identified by Onwuegbuzie and Denham (2014), any of the qualitative data analysis

These cases can be comfortably included in the ATLAS.ti project and can be sorted into groups according to the type of information source. Comparative work or comparative analysis can be undertaken using and examining the findings or interpretations. The methodologies, the aims, and objectives can be compared in selected research articles, with each comparison being visualized in ATLAS.ti networks as well as in text format.

Coding in ATLAS.ti, as part of qualitative content analysis (Schreier, 2012), which involves selecting segments of text and attaching labels to them, is a vital task as researchers work with the data. Researchers working with ATLAS.ti should have a sound knowledge of the type of analysis they bring to the tool. Saldaña (2016) offers a range of coding strategies (see earlier), which are most helpful in discerning the type of codes that can be created. ATLAS.ti facilitates various ways of coding via the file menu, the toolbar, drag and drop, or from the code manager. Both inductive and deductive coding can be used, depending on the research question. A predetermined list of codes (deductive coding), which may be informed by the literature and accompanying theory, can be created in ATLAS.ti and used immediately. Codes, visible on the right-hand side of the screen, namely in the margin area, can also be structured using symbols or colors (Lewins & Silver, 2007; Woolf, 2007). There is no limit to the number of codes that can be created, and multiple codes may be linked or attached to one segment of text or quotation. Not only are the codes transparent, but they also each have a code name, as well as indicating the frequency of use and frequency of links to other codes that the author created, as well as the date on which it was created and when it was modified. Woolf and Silver (2018) explain that "the term code in ATLAS.ti refers to any named concept that represents what is identified in the data as meaningful about the project objectives" (p. 79). A further practical function in ATLAS.ti is the grouping or clustering function, wherein codes can be sorted into code groups for filtering purposes to facilitate further analysis. One more valuable function for coding in ATLAS.ti is auto-coding, which is associated with the text search function (find and select), which offers quick searches of large amounts of data for initial coding (Charmaz, 2006).

Annotating the ATLAS.ti project, that is, documents, quotations, codes, and memos, all types of groups, and network as well as links and relations, is a useful function, because most research projects extend over long periods, and researchers often lose track of, for instance, what and why specific codes were created. These annotations (comments) serve as personal reminders of what has been done. Memo writing in ATLAS.ti also serves as an effective mechanism to enhance the intellectual and theoretical development of an analysis (Smit, 2018). In this regard, Charmaz (2006) offers meaningful insight into the various types of *memos* that can be written, including personal, theoretical, and methodological ones. All the work in a project can be visually presented using *networks*, which are graphically displayed. Networks are not just pretty pictures, but show, for example, code groups, code–code links and their relations.

Word	Lenght	Count	Stakeholder Inte
absolutely	10	1	1
absorbed	8	1	1
academic	8	2	2
academics	9	1	1
accept	6	19	19
acceptability	13	1	1
acceptable	10	1	1
acceptance	10	25	25
accepted	8	3	3
accepting	9	3	3
access	6	12	12
accessibility	13	1	1
according	9	5	5
account	7	4	4
accountability	14	2	2
accountable	11	3	3
accountable"	12	1	1
accounting	10	1	1
accruing	8	1	1
accurate	8	1	1
accusations	11	1	1
accused	7	2	2
achievable	10	1	1
achieve	7	7	7
achieved	8	3	3
achieving	9	2	2
acknowledge	11	1	1
across	6	10	10
act	3	9	9
acting	6	1	1

FIGURE 28.2 An example of a word list from ATLAS.ti 8.

methods, (e.g., Miles & Huberman, 1994), or any of the qualitative data analysis techniques (e.g., Saldaña 2016) (p. 365).

They elaborate that

> by treating each relevant information source, for example, articles, book chapters, books, dissertation and thesis, monographs, encyclopedias, government documents, trade catalogues, legal and public records information as a case, qualitative comparative analysis can be undertaken even if the number of cases is relatively small, which lends itself to new topics that do not as yet have a large body of literature. (p. 365)

Introduction to ATLAS.ti for Mixed Analysis

FIGURE 28.3 An example of a word cloud from ATLAS.ti 8.

5 Suggested Applications: Inductive and Deductive Reasoning for Mixed Analysis

Elo and Kyngäs (2008) offer a clear description of inductive and deductive content analysis. They argue that content analysis is a method that may be used either with qualitative or quantitative data and in a deductive or in an inductive way. Inductive and deductive analysis processes can be presented in three main phases: preparation, organizing, and reporting. For example, concepts are derived from the data in inductive content analysis, and deductive content analysis is used when previous knowledge, experiences, or theories operationalize the structure of the analysis. Inductive content analysis is most often used when previous studies dealing with the research phenomena are scarce. A deductive approach is useful if the general aim was to test an earlier theory and to create theory-driven codes. The advantage of content analysis is that large volumes of textual data in different textual sources can be dealt with and used in corroborating evidence.

The inductive qualitative content analysis is used mostly when the data drive the analysis. When the codes are created from the data, they are inductively created codes driven by the data. Deductive thinking is most often associated with quantitative research and mixed methods research. However, given the repeat of inductive codes in the subsequent texts, a researcher can conduct an analysis using pre-existing categories derived from theory or previous research findings, and this then becomes an excellent example of deduction or deductive reasoning. The work by Armat, Assarroudi, Rad, Sharifi, and Heydari (2018) helps to understand the labels of inductive and deductive reasoning, proposing labels such as inductive dominant qualitative content analysis and deductive dominant quantitative analysis. For mixed methods research, these labels are helpful for both epistemologies and reasonings. The mixed analysis is also well described by Onwuegbuzie and Combs (2011, p. 2), who "provide an inclusive definition of mixed analysis that incorporates the definition and typologies that have been presented in major methodological works."

Qualitizing and Quantitizing Data

Another way of optimizing ATLAS.ti for mixed analysis is by qualitizing and quantizing data (Leavy, 2017, p. 182). One example is research conducted by Scherman, Zimmerman, and Smit (2018), in which the possibility of using qualitative and quantitative analysis of one data set was explored, and the relationships amongst factors were discussed. Earlier writings of Hesse-Biber (2010) report on how "computer-based technologies prompted an increased interest in combining a variety of methods. Computer-assisted software programs for analyzing qualitative data are beginning to seek ways to incorporate and integrate quantitative data into their programs" (p. 78). Hesse-Biber (2010) noted that "the introduction of CAQDAS has enabled researchers to begin to transform qualitative and quantitative data to suit their methodological purposes" (p. 78). To this end, ATLAS.ti is designed to allow the researcher to import quantitative data, such as survey data into the software, making it possible to work with both the qualitative and quantitative databases at the same time. According to Hesse-Biber (2010),

> CAQDAS programs allow researchers to group the qualitative textual data, such as interview material, into 'variable-like' categories. Quantizing[1] occurs when qualitative codes (labels are given to segments of data from texts that have been transcribed from interviews or other narrative sources, such as magazines or newspapers) are transformed into quantitative variables. Quantizing opens up the possibility of applying statistical techniques to material that once was qualitative. (p. 79)

Miles and Huberman (1994) were the first researchers to use the term quantitizing (see also Miles, Huberman, & Saldaña, 2014, pp. 42–44). In contrast, qualitizing refers to the transformation of quantitative data into qualitative data, a process first developed by Tashakkori and Teddlie (1998). (See also the chapter on qualitizing in this volume.) Qualitizing often involves the use of empirically grounded information provided by the qualitative component of the mixed methods research study as well as the research literature to decide how to determine the cut-off points that will be for each of the categories. Leavy (2017) in this regard, explains the processes of quantizing and qualitizing as the two forms of data transformation, as follows: "Quantizing is the process of transforming qualitative data into quantitative data (transforming qualitative codes into quantitative variables). ATLAS.ti can assist in the creation of variable data based on qualitative data, which can then be exported for statistical analysis" in SPSS (p. 182). In contrast, "qualitizing is the process of transforming quantitative data into qualitative data (transforming quantitative variable into qualitative codes) (Leavy, 2017, p. 182). Leavy (2017) illustrates that "a mixed data analysis design, involving the transformation of data from one form into another, can make it possible to discern complex relationships in the data and identify patterns" (p. 182). Hesse-Biber (2010) offers a cautionary note on using computer software programs to analyze mixed methods data. She warns that the growing use of computer software programs and tools for mixed methods analysis and qualitative analysis, in general, raises a concern about how data are analyzed and interpreted. Despite this concern, current researchers have found that value is added through the use of software such as ATLAS.ti for both qualitative and quantitative analysis.

Importing Survey Data and Exporting Data to SPSS

Survey data from Google Forms or Microsoft Excel can be imported for further analysis, using the coding, auto-coding, word clouds, or word lists. For mixed analysis, this is also useful for qualitizing quantitative data, and integrating the data analysis (Hesse-Biber, 2010). Open-ended questionnaire data can be imported into ATLAS.ti. Also, predetermined codebooks or code lists that were created from experiences or theory can be saved in a Microsoft Excel spreadsheet and imported into ATLAS.ti. Woods, Paulus, Atkins, and Macklin (2015) have found little evidence of researchers promoting QDA to analyze new forms of data or to adapt the research practices to motivating new program features. New features have been added to programs, enabling transcription of multimedia files and supporting the direct analysis of multimedia data, social media geodata, and survey data sets. They acknowledge that it takes time for researchers to adopt these programs, to incorporate them into the research practices, and then to publish their accounts of using the tools in the research, which might create a time lag in doing so. Woods et al. (2015) have found that researchers conducting mixed methods research studies have used ATLAS.ti, specifically responses to open-ended items in surveys. They report that ATLAS.ti was used in three phases of the research process, namely, data collection, data analysis and management, and data display and representation of findings, with data analysis and management being most frequently mentioned. However, no authors have reported using software to support literature reviews, with a few published articles including a report on using software for data display and representation of findings.

Data display and representation of findings using ATLAS.ti offer functions for visually displaying data and research findings. To visually present findings, screenshots can be used to illustrate coding processes or program outputs that depict the coding list or the conceptual schemes and relationships between data and codes. In ATLAS.ti, the co-occurrence table helps to generate tables and charts of code distributions. ATLAS.ti also offers networks to illustrate relationships among codes and categories and concepts and to help the researcher to theorize conceptual relationships (Woods et al., 2015, p. 12).

The entire ATLAS.ti project can be exported into SPSS (i.e., Statistical Package for Social Sciences) for further quantitative statistical analysis. Although ATLAS.ti is intended primarily (Friese, 2017) for supporting qualitative reasoning processes, quantitative and mixed data are supported by providing an export function to facilitate further data processing of the syntax file by SPSS. Codes are treated as variables and data segments or selected segments of text, namely quotations, are treated as cases (p. 211). For mixed analysis, this is useful for quantitizing qualitative data by integrating the data analysis (Hesse-Biber, 2010). ATLAS.ti can export the complete analysis of a project into an HTML file, which will be available in version 9. Such a file serves as a *trustworthiness* check because the complete analysis is transparent and up for scrutiny and critique, from the first interview question to the last query of the data. The methodological consideration of credibility and trustworthiness is vital in qualitative research and cannot be achieved with such accuracy without software for qualitative data analysis and the much-needed methodological rigour.

Quantitative research is predominantly used for statistical analysis. A useful statistical software tool can generate tabulated reports, charts, plots of distributions, and trends, as well as produce descriptive statistics and more sophisticated statistical analyses. Quantitative and qualitative research is commonly considered to differ fundamentally; yet, the objectors, as well as the applications, overlap in some ways. Quantitative research is deemed to have as its primary purpose, the quantification of data. This allows for generalizations of results from a sample to an entire population of interest. Quantitative research, on the one hand, is not infrequently followed by qualitative research, which can aim to explore selected findings a little further. Qualitative research, on the other hand, is considered to be particularly suitable for gaining an in-depth understanding of the underlying reasons and motivations. It provides insights into the setting of a problem. At the same time, it frequently generates ideas and hypotheses for later exploration, using quantitative research. This is typically a mixed methods research (MMR) design. The main differences between quantitative and qualitative research consist with respect to data sample, data collection, data analysis, and the outcomes of the study. As discussed earlier in this chapter, although undoubtedly formerly at home in purely qualitative research, a powerful and flexible program like ATLAS.

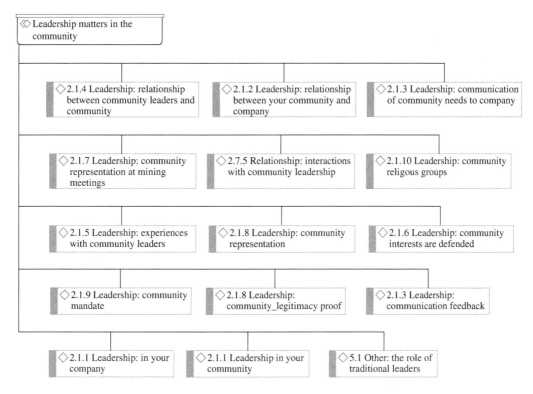

FIGURE 28.4 A network of a theme from the literature.

ti can also produce quantitative data. It features direct export to SPSS, and also, ATLAS.ti can export project results to the universal open XML data format. XML data can be quickly transformed and reshaped to be usable in a considerable number of applications. This makes ATLAS.ti uniquely suited for contemporary mixed methods research approaches.

Visual and Textual Report Writing

ATLAS.ti provides predefined reports and as well as configurable reports, which means that the researcher can decide what should be included in the report. Predefined reports are available in the Query Tool (Friese, 2017) under the report button. The user-configurable report is most useful for literature reviews, which serves as a textual output of the desired aspect of the review, for example, a theme discussion, such as in Figure 4.

6 Strengths and Limitations of ATLAS.ti

The strength of ATLAS.ti lies in the interface, which is user-friendly and allows for multiple codings to a segment of text, as well as hyperlinking of text segments, which trigger the creation of claims to build arguments about the data. The paper-pencil feel of the ATLAS.ti interface is particularly handy, especially for inductive reasoning. Assuming the researcher has an in-depth understanding of presenting theoretical and empirical data thematically, the software allows for an integration of the analysis and subsequent interpretation of the data. The networks allow for added visualisation of the data, which augment the conceptual engagement and exploration of the literature and the empirical data. The reporting functionality is beneficial because it allows for a variety of analyses, such as code lists, networks, and categorical descriptions, which can be used for the final write-up.

ATLAS.ti also has some limitations, and any software is only as good as its user. Most often, people stick with the software they learned first and seldom venture to learn another programme, unless it becomes their focus to learn another application. The reason for this relates to the fact that ATLAS.ti does not necessarily shorten the time for analysis. On the contrary, the learning curve might be steep, given the two-pronged approach of learning the technology as well as the methodology of qualitative data analysis. Also, the false expectation that ATLAS.ti *does* the analysis often leads to disappointment. But like any software, it cannot think for the researcher. Also, ATLAS.ti does not offer a fully-fledged statistical analysis functionality, although import and export functions from Excel and SPSS and frequency tables are available, together with an intercoder agreement analysis. Reflecting on limitations would be more accurate by systematically comparing ATLAS.ti with other programmes, such as MAXQDA, NVivo, and Transana, which is beyond the scope of this chapter.

7 Resources for Learning More About ATLAS.ti

Webinars

http://atlasti.com/learning-old/free-training/
http://atlasti.com/learning-old/free-training/#Free-Webinars

Videos

http://atlasti.com/video-tutorials/
www.youtube.com/user/ATLASti01

Blogs

http://atlasti.com/topic/blog/

Manuals

http://atlasti.com/manuals-docs/
http://downloads.atlasti.com/docs/manual/atlasti_v8_manual_en.pdf

"How to" Documents

ATLAS.ti 8 Windows
  Installation Instructions
  Project Exchange
  Team Work with ATLAS.ti 8 Windows
  Team Work with ATLAS.ti 8 Windows and ATLAS.ti Mac (mixed teams)
  Importing and Exporting Code Lists: ATLAS.ti 8 Windows
  Keyboard Shortcuts
  ATLAS.ti Mac
  Project Transfer Windows -> Mac
  ATLAS.ti for Mac – Admin Documentation
  Team Work with ATLAS.ti Mac
  Team Work with ATLAS.ti Mac and ATLAS.ti 8 Windows (mixed teams)
  Importing and Exporting Code Lists: ATLAS.ti 8 Mac
  Backing up ATLAS.ti Mac Projects

Latest Readings and Books

Onwuegbuzie, A. J., & Frels, R. K. (2016). *Seven steps to a comprehensive literature review: A multimodal and cultural approach.* London, England: Sage.

Smit, B. (2018). How can computer software add value to qualitative data analysis? A case for ATLAS.ti ™. In K. G. Tomaselli, *Making Sense of Research* (pp. 205–211). Pretoria, South Africa: Van Schaik.

Woolf, N. H., & Silver, C. (2018). *Qualitative analysis using ATLAS.ti. The five level QDA® methods.* New York, NY: Routledge, Taylor & Francis Group.

NOTE

1. The spelling differs:
   Hesse-Biber: quantizing
   Miles, Huberman & Saldaña: quantitizing

REFERENCES

Annechino, R., Antin, T. M. J., & Lee, J. P. (2010). Bridging the qualitative/quantitative software divide. *Field Methods, 22,* 115–124. doi:1177/1525822X09360760

Armat, M. R., Assarroudi, A., Rad, M., Sharifi, H., & Heydari, A. (2018). Inductive and Deductive: Ambiguous labels in qualitative content analysis. *The Qualitative Report, 23*(1), 219–221. Retrieved from http://nsuworks.nova.edu/tqr/vol23/iss1/16

Bernard, H. R., Wutich, A., & Ryan, G. W. (2017). *Analysing qualitative data. Systematic approaches* (2nd ed.). Thousand Oaks, CA: Sage.

Bong, S. A. (2002). Debunking myths in qualitative data analysis. *Forum Qualitative Sozialforschung, 3*(2) Art.10, Retrieved from https://www.qualitative-research.net/index.php/fqs/article/view/849

Boote, D. N., & Beile, P. (2005). Scholars before researchers: On the centrality of the dissertation literature review in research preparation. *Educational Researcher, 34*(6), 3–15. doi:10.3102/0013189X034006003

Braun, V., & Clarke, V. (2014). *Successful qualitative research. A practical guide for beginners.* Thousand Oaks, CA: Sage.

Charmaz, K. (2006). *Constructing grounded theory.* Thousand Oaks, CA: Sage.

Elo, S., & Kyngäs, H. (2008). The qualitative content analysis. *Journal of Advanced Nursing, 62,* 107–115, doi:10.1111/j.1365–2648.2007.04569.X

Fielding N. G., & Lee, R. M. (1998). *Computer analysis and qualitative research.* Thousand Oaks, CA: Sage.

Fielding, J. L., & Fielding, N. G. (2015). Emergent technologies in multimethod and mixed methods research: Incorporating GIS and CAQDAS. In S. Hesse-Biber & R. B. Johnson, *The Oxford handbook of multimethod and mixed methods research inquiry* (pp. 561–584). New York, NY: Oxford University Press

Fink, A. (2010). *Conducting research literature reviews. From the Internet to paper* (3rd ed.). Thousand Oaks, CA: Sage.

Friese, S. (2012a). *Qualitative data analysis with ATLAS.ti.* Thousand Oaks, CA: Sage.

Friese, S. (2012b). *ATLAS.ti 7 User manual.* Berlin, Germany: ATLAS.ti Scientific Software Development GmbH.

Friese, S. (2017). *ATLAS.ti 8 Windows – Full Manual.* Berlin, Germany: ATLAS.ti Scientific Software Development GmbH.

Friese, S., & Contreras, R. B. (2016). *CAQDAS and the new data challenge.* Retrieved from http://atlasti.com/2016/06/10/caqdas-new-data-challenge/

Hesse-Biber, S. N. (2010). *Mixed methods research. Merging theory with practice.* New York, NY: The Guilford Press.

Johnson, R. B., & Christensen, L. (2017). *Educational research. Quantitative, qualitative, and mixed approaches* (6th ed.). Thousand Oaks, CA: Sage.

Leavy, P. (2017). *Research design. Quantitative, qualitative, mixed methods, arts-based, and community-based participatory research approaches.* New York, NY: The Guilford Press.

Leech, N. L., & Onwuegbuzie, A. J. (2008). Qualitative data analysis: A compendium of techniques and a framework for selection for school psychology research and beyond. *School Psychology Quarterly, 23,* 587–604. doi:10.1037/1045–3830.23.4.587

Leech, N. L., & Onwuegbuzie, A. J. (2011). Beyond constant comparison data analysis: Using NVivo. *School Psychology Quarterly, 26,* 70–84. doi:10.1037/a0022711

Lewins, A., & Silver, C. (2007). *Using software in qualitative research.* Thousand Oaks, CA: Sage.

Loseke, D. R. (2017). *Methodological thinking: Basic principles of social research design* (2nd ed.). Thousand Oaks, CA: Sage.

Lune, H., & Berg, B. L. (2017). *Qualitative research methods for the social sciences* (9th ed.). New York, NY: Pearson.

Miles, M. B., Huberman, A. M. (1994). *An expanded sourcebook. Qualitative data analysis* (2nd ed.). Thousand Oaks, CA: Sage.

Miles, M. B., Huberman, A. M., & Saldaña, J. (2014). *Qualitative data analysis. A methods sourcebook* (3rd ed.). Thousand Oaks, CA: Sage.

Muhr, T. (1991). A prototype for the support of text interpretation. *Qualitative Sociology*, 14, 349–371. doi:10.1007/BF00989645

Munirah Mohamad, A. (2017a). *Using ATLAS.ti 8 Windows in Literature reviews*. Retrieved from http://atlasti.com/2017/02/09/lit-reviews/.

Munirah Mohamad, A. (2017b). *Bringing out the best in Evernote with ATLAS.ti 8 Windows*. Retrieved from http://atlasti.com/2017/05/30/evernote/

O'Dwyer, L. M., & Bernauer, J. A. (2014). *Quantitative research for the qualitative researcher*. Thousand Oaks, CA: Sage.

Onwuegbuzie, A. J., & Combs, J. P. (2011). Data analysis in mixed research: A primer. *International Journal of Education*, 3(1), E13. doi:10.5296/ije.v3i1.618

Onwuegbuzie, A. J., & Denham, M. (2014). Qualitative data analysis techniques. In L. H. Meyer (Ed.), *Oxford bibliographies in education*. Oxford, England: Oxford University Press. Retrieved from www.oxfordbibliographies.com/view/document/obo-9780199756810/obo-9780199756810–0078.xml

Onwuegbuzie, A. J., & Frels, R. K. (2016). *Seven steps to a comprehensive literature review: A multimodal and cultural approach*. Thousand Oaks, CA: Sage.

Onwuegbuzie, A. J., Frels, R. K., & Hwang, E. (2016). Mapping Saldaña's coding methods onto the literature review process. *Journal of Educational Issues*, 2, 130–149. doi:10.5296/jei.v2i1.8931

Onwuegbuzie, A. J., Leech, N. L., & Collins, K. M. T. (2012). Qualitative analysis techniques for the review of the literature. *The Qualitative Report*, 17 (Art. 56), 1–28. Retrieved from www.nova.edu/ssss/QR/QR17/onwuegbuzie.pdf

Onwuegbuzie, A. J., & Weinbaum, R. (2017). A framework for using qualitative comparative analysis for the review of the literature. *The Qualitative Report*, 22, 359–372. Retrieved from http://nsuworks.nova.edu/tqr/vol22/iss2/1

Paulus, T. M., Lester, J. N., & Dempster, P. G. (2014). *Digital tools for qualitative research*. Thousand Oaks, CA: Sage.

Saldaña, J. (2016). *The coding manual for qualitative researchers* (3rd ed.). Thousand Oaks, CA: Sage.

Scherman, V., Zimmerman, L., & Smit, B. (2018). Mixed method data analysis: An exploratory approach to strengthening inferences about relationships and affinities. *International Journal of Multiple Research Approaches*, 10, 57–76. doi:10.29034/ijmra.v10n1a4

Schreier, M. (2012). *Qualitative content analysis in practice*. Thousand Oaks, CA: Sage.

Smit, B. (2005). Computer-assisted qualitative data software: friend or foe. *South African Computer Journal*, 35, 107–111.

Smit, B. (2018). How can computer software add value to qualitative data analysis? A case for ATLAS.ti ™. In K. G. Tomaselli (Ed.), *Making sense of research* (pp. 205–211). Pretoria, South Africa: Van Schaik.

Smit, B., Williamson, C., & Padayachee, A. (2013). Ph.D. capacity building, from aid to innovation: The SANPAD-SANTRUST experience. *Studies in Higher Education*, 38, 441–455. doi:10.1080/03075079.2013.773218

Tashakkori, A., & Teddlie, C. (1998). *Mixed methodology: Combining qualitative and quantitative approaches*. Thousand Oaks, CA: Sage.

Williams, J. K. (2018). A comprehensive review of seven steps to a comprehensive literature review. *The Qualitative Report*, 23, 345–349.

Wolcott, H. F. (2009). *Writing up qualitative research* (3rd ed.). Thousand Oaks, CA: Sage.

Woods, M., Paulus, T., Atkins, D. P., & Macklin, R. (2015). Advancing qualitative research using qualitative data analysis software (QDAS)? Reviewing potential versus practice in published studies using ATLAS.ti and NVivo, 1994–2013. *Social Science Computer Review*, 1–21. doi:10.1177/0894439315596311.

Woolf, N. (2007). *A little structure in your codes will make your research a lot easier*. Berlin, Germany: ATLAS.ti library.

Woolf, N. H., & Silver, C. (2018). *Qualitative analysis using ATLAS.ti. The five level QDA® methods*. New York, NY: Routledge Taylor & Francis Group.

Wright, S. (2014). *Literature reviews on the move: Using the ATLAS.ti APP to support and enhance your literature reviews*. Retrieved from http://atlasti.com/2014/06/12/1722/

29

Using NVivo for Mixed Methods Research

Pat Bazeley

1 Definition of NVivo

NVivo is software designed to support analysis of qualitative and mixed methods data. It belongs to the "theory-building" class of qualitative data analysis programs (Tesch, 1990) as it goes beyond providing basic tools for data management, word searching, coding and retrieval: NVivo allows researchers to interrogate their data and associated coding systems through the application of logic-based queries that identify connections in their data and thus to develop (and test) higher-order concepts and theoretical propositions.

NVivo was originally developed by Lyn and Tom Richards, the founders of QSR International (www.qsrinternational.com), with the initial intention of meeting the needs of researchers working with non-numeric data in the social and behavioral sciences. Despite its primary focus on tools for analysis of qualitative data, since its very early days NVivo (or NUD*IST, as it was previously known) has also supported the work of mixed methods researchers looking for ways to combine demographic and numeric variables with their text data, or to convert qualitative coding to quantitative variables (Bazeley, 2002).

2 When Use of NVivo is Appropriate in MMR

Developments in technology over the past decade have combined with growth in the mixed methods movement to ensure that NVivo, like several other qualitative analysis programs, has continued to develop enhanced and new tools to meet the strategic analysis goals of a mixed methods researcher. These allow for inclusion of a greatly increased range of data types within a project, new ways of visualizing data and the relationships within data, versatile coding, searching, and query tools to support complementary and comparative analyses that combine text and numeric data, and improved methods for exporting qualitative coding information as variable data for further, statistical analysis. In this chapter I will introduce NVivo's tools within the context of the specific mixed methods analysis and integrative functions they serve.

Because the boundaries between major methodological approaches are unclear (Bazeley, 2018b), my definition of mixed methods research does not necessarily demand the combination of a quantitative with a qualitative method, although it typically happens that way. Rather it emphasises the role of integration of the approaches used: "In *mixed methods* research, varied approaches, sources of data, methods of data collection, and/or strategies for analysis are integrated during the process of achieving the purpose of the research" (Bazeley, 2018a, p. 10). More specifically, I see *integration* in mixed methods research as *purposeful interdependence* between data sources and/or the different methods used for analysis of those data (Bazeley, 2018a). The first of two primary ways in which integration occurs is through the iterative exchange between different elements in a project that takes place more or less incidentally during the design and development of the project, during data collection, and during the analysis process (e.g., Burch & Heinrich, 2016). In this process, ideas and understanding developed through one kind of data stimulate ideas, revised processes, and fresh perspectives in another, leading to deeper insights overall. The second primary way in which integration occurs is through a planned "point of interface" where different methods are deliberately brought together for a significant developmental or analytic purpose (Morse & Niehaus, 2009). This more deliberate approach to integration can be seen when the analytic gains from one method are used to inform the development or analysis of another, when data from different sources are brought together for complementary and/or comparative analyses, or when data are transformed to allow a second, different type of analysis that will complement or extend the initial analyses.

Mixed methods research might include any or all of the following tasks:

- Determining a purpose for a project;
- Design of a project, including:
  - deciding whether one or more sources of data are needed to answer the research questions;
  - ensuring that data to be generated can be analyzed in a way that will benefit the purpose of the research;
- Data gathering and management of those data;
- Preliminary preparation and analyses of data from different sources and of different types;
- Analysis of the combined data sets, including one or more of the following activities:
  - Combination of multiple and varied sources of data in a complementary analysis;

- Comparison of data from different sources or types;
- Comparative analyses based on the intersection of linked quantitative and qualitative sources;
- Transformative analyses in which qualitative coding is converted to variable data and analyzed statistically;
- Reporting from a project.

Capacities and tools provided within NVivo to support tasks involved in mixed methods analysis include:

- Mapping and visualization tools to assist with planning, exploring, thinking through, and communicating analyses.
- Capacity to import and manage data of multiple types (text, image, audiovisual, social media, survey) in a variety of formats.
- Data management tools that allow you to concurrently sort, cut, and recombine data in multiple ways, whilst also keeping track of source information for any segment of data.
- (Interactive) coding tools to bring together all that is known from across the full range of sources on any and all topics of interest for complementary analyses or as data for further comparative or transformative analyses.
- Auto coding tools to assist in theme identification (with potential for transformation) in large corpuses of text-based data.
- Linking and memoing tools to record reflections and connect these with evidence, and to connect items across the database.
- Searching tools to assist in exploring data and in locating specific items or combinations of items.
- Query tools that combine quantitative and qualitative data for complementary and comparative analyses.
- Query tools that identify patterns of association between data items.
- Capacity for transforming coded data to variable data for statistical analysis.

Effective use of software tools involves working out how best to apply them to the tasks that need to be undertaken. What follows is an outline of some strategies to achieve this, learned through long experience. For more detail, see also Bazeley (2018a), Jackson and Bazeley (2019), and Woolf and Silver (2018).

3 Technical Outline of NVivo for MMR and 4 Empirical Demonstration of NVivo for MMR

Tools available in NVivo to assist with the various stages of a mixed methods project will be illustrated with reference to an evolving mixed methods project. The *Wellbeing* project is designed to assess the health benefits to older women of participation in exercise and other community-based classes organized through the Older Women's Network of New South Wales. It began as, and primarily remains, an ongoing evaluation exercise to meet annual reporting requirements. At the same time, the data available are allowing for conceptual development in relation to what wellbeing means for older women, and for an exploration of the interrelationship between health and wellbeing for older women.

Determining Project Purpose and Design—Project Planning

Project planning typically involves reviewing relevant literature, and planning for obtaining the information needed to gain necessary understanding to meet the purposes of the research.

Literature providing a foundation for a mixed methods project is imported directly into NVivo from selected bibliographic databases (EndNote, RefWorks, Zotero, Mendeley). PDF articles are coded, and notes recorded in memos. 'See also links' directly link literature, data, and emerging ideas in a web of data to support theory development and reporting.

The complexity of mixed methods projects demands that planning be as thorough as possible, although flexibility is also necessary. Visual tools assist in the planning process, in mapping either a conceptual framework for a study or a theory of change model for an evaluative or explanatory (causal analysis) project. A (simplified) theory of change model for the Wellbeing project, developed from a focus group discussion using an NVivo concept map, is shown in Figure 29.1. This points to the varied kinds of information that will be required in order to determine the potential value of the activity programs for the wellbeing and health of older women. Concepts and categories identified in this process can, additionally, be explored and expanded using a mind map. A mind map translates to a starter coding system for data that will be gathered during the project.

A concept map can be used also to create a design diagram illustrating the type and sequencing of methods to be used in a project. This has dual benefits: it assists the researcher in planning the project by clarifying the steps needed to complete the project, and it assists in communicating the intent of the project to funding agencies or, eventually, to readers of reports from the project. As plans are likely to be modified during the course of the project, so visual diagrams can be duplicated and then modified, allowing for adaptation while the history of their development is preserved.

Data Management, Involving Multiple Data Types

Mixed data types and/or sources are an inherent component of a mixed methods project. As well as literature, the Wellbeing project makes use of annual questionnaires, interviews, cultural domain data (e.g., free listing), video, and observation. Records from these various data sources were imported as files into a single NVivo project, for both separate and joint

Using NVivo for Mixed Methods Research

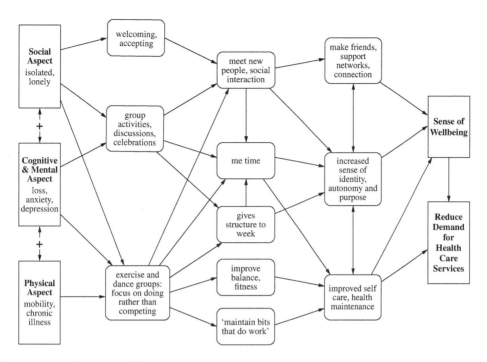

FIGURE 29.1 Concept map to show theory of change.

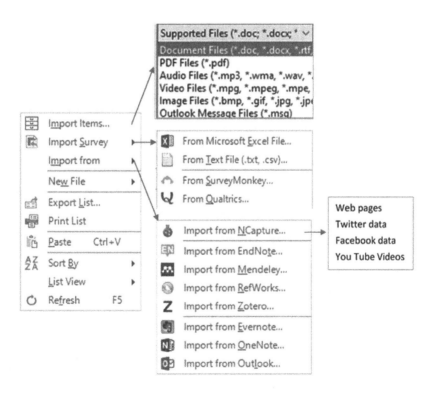

FIGURE 29.2 Import options, allowing mixed data types.

analyses (Figure 29.2 shows the range of data types that can be imported). Audio and video files can be transcribed within the software. Survey data that contains open-ended response fields is imported directly from an online source, or via MS Excel. Reports from statistical analyses are imported as text documents.

Management of these different files is facilitated by the use of folders, sets, and cases, to allow for retrieving, cutting, and splicing data in multiple ways, while never losing track of the source of any data segment. Imported files of different types are placed into different *folders* (those for the Wellbeing project are shown in Figure 29.3), serving both

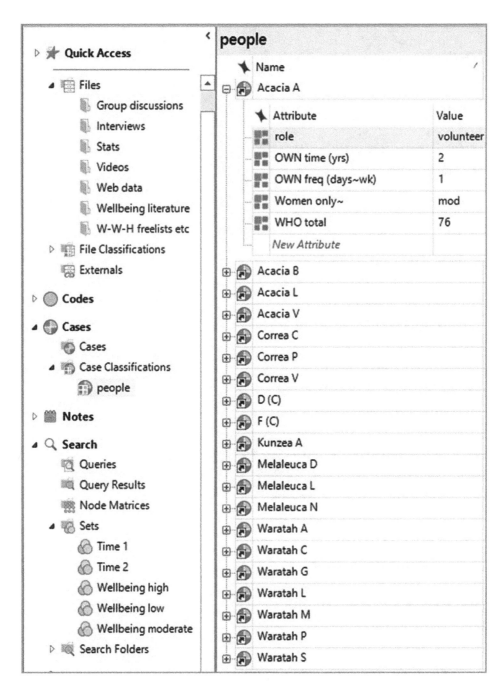

FIGURE 29.3 Navigation pane, showing data management tools.

visual clarity and searching within or interrogation of particular types of data. *Sets* comprise shortcuts to particular imported files; these might be collections of files from different phases of a project (e.g., Time 1 and Time 2 in the Wellbeing project), or perhaps a set of all files relating to older women with a low score for wellbeing. Files are placed in one folder only, but shortcuts to them can be placed in more than one set. These are used for comparative analyses or to restrict ("scope") other analyses to a particular set of the data. *Cases* are essentially a type of coding category used as an administrative tool to gather together everything that is known about a particular case—a unit of analysis—in a project, regardless of whether that information is found in multiple files, a single file, and/or just part of a file. Often cases represent people, but they might also represent sites, families, organizations, items in a collection, and so on. Importantly, for mixed methods work, demographic and variable data can be attached to cases as *attributes* of those cases, so that any qualitative data can be viewed in relation to associated quantitative data. These various management tools mean that selected folders or sets of qualitative data can be sorted, explored, and interrogated in relation to demographic or other variables. For example, interview or pictorial data about wellbeing gathered at different phases of a project can be compared for individuals or for women who have different scores on a wellbeing scale.

Preliminary Analyses

Although some integrative strategies can be employed using 'raw' data, in most projects preliminary (initial) analyses of data of different kinds from the separate sources will be necessary.

Text and Audio-visual Data

Once text, PDF sources, image and other multimedia sources are imported, reflective reviewing provides an initial overview of their content, giving context to later coding and providing seeds for questions and ideas that might become important as analysis proceeds. Reflections are recorded in linked memos or in a general research journal (within the software), potentially using see also links to connect thoughts with the source material that prompted them (Figure 29.4). These reflective journals will be extended throughout the project and become a vital resource during later analyses and when writing up; coding their content as you work helps with later retrieval of ideas, with the links pointing to supporting evidence.

Segments within imported sources are then coded to user-defined categories in one or more of several ways, with the first being most common:

- interactive coding in which the user selects a passage of text, a region of a picture, or a selection from an audio/video waveform, and uses drag-and-drop or context menus to apply one or more codes to represent the content and any other relevant aspects of that segment;
- auto coding based on the structure of the file (e.g., where there are different speakers) in order to identify and code sections (i.e., what those speakers said) to case codes that capture just what was contributed by each speaker;
- auto coding to 'themes', based on word/phrase analysis of the text; or
- predictive coding of uncoded text, based on existing patterns of coding;
- sentiment analysis, identifying positive or negative statements based on words used.

These last three should be used with great caution! NVivo provides results from these in codes, so that the content can be checked, merged and modified by the user.

Coding is designed to tag or index the content of the various sources for further interrogation, but the development and application of codes are, in themselves, an interpretive (i.e., analytic) activity as decisions are made about what has been said or written or otherwise shown in the files. Codes are initially created from a priori theorizing or freely as text is read, but then are progressively arranged in a hierarchical taxonomy of project concepts. This helps the user see "what have we got here" as well as with querying the data at later stages of the analysis. The coding system In the Wellbeing project went through several iterations as the project (and my thinking about it) developed. Currently it has code groups covering dimensions of wellbeing and health (e.g., physical, affect, relationships, personal resources), the focus of the conversation (ageing, challenges, wellbeing, health), and aspects of the social context (e.g., being female, widowhood); also groups of codes covering the more administrative aspects of running the Wellness Centers (system inputs, coordination, group activities).

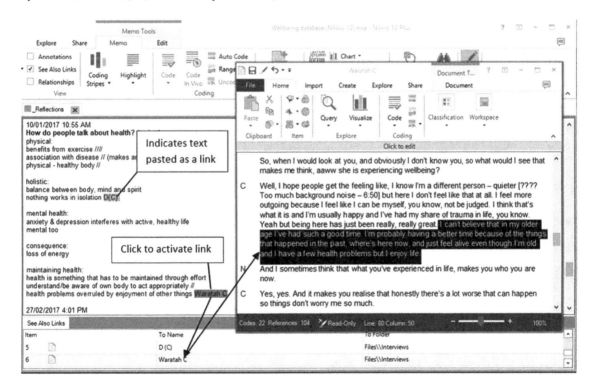

FIGURE 29.4 Using see also links to connect reflections with source material.

Survey and Social Media Data

When a survey dataset is imported into NVivo it retains its tabular format. A 'wizard' is used to automate the process of creating a case for each participant (i.e., one per row of data), with relevant open-ended responses coded to the case, and demographic, categorical and scaled responses recorded as attribute data for the case (similar to that shown in Figure 29.3). Open-ended responses are also auto coded to indicate the question being answered, and their content can be auto coded for themes and sentiment. Further searching or interactive coding of case data or responses to particular questions is, of course, also possible (and encouraged). Statistical analyses of closed-response data are conducted separately.

Social media datasets containing text and associated metadata (e.g., location, status of message, demographics of the sender) imported through NCapture are also imported in tabular format. Coding is less automated but data are quickly sorted, for example, by hashtags and usernames, with comments gathered into codes for further interactive coding.

Statistical Data

Preliminary coding and analysis of any statistical data such as from surveys or other databases that are part of a mixed methods project will normally be carried out using statistical software. This kind of information is then imported into a mixed methods NVivo project in one or both of two forms: (1) a report from the statistical data might be imported as a file, where it will be coded to capture relevant aspects of the content (including statistical results and tables) using the same coding system as was used for the qualitative data; (2) selected variables, for those cases where qualitative data are also available (e.g. from interviews), will be imported and recorded as attribute data for those cases, in MS Excel or IBM-SPSS format.

Integrative Analyses

Integrative analyses take many forms and shapes, as researchers construct methods for bringing together diverse forms of data, and for exploring and analyzing data in a variety of ways. Essentially, however, there are three core processes underpinning these different strategies for which the computer provides specific assistance. The '3 Cs' are to combine, to compare, and to convert.

Combining Data and Analyses in a Complementary Process

Data retrieved from different sources are integrated in a complementary way through using one source to supplement a finding from another by illustrating or expanding on it; through weaving the information from different sources together into a narrative, description, or explanation; or through merging the information into a composite understanding of the topic.

In many mixed methods projects, a great deal of complementary analysis occurs outside the computer environment as data and preliminary results from different sources are brought together by the researcher during an analytical writing process. There are, however, specific ways in which NVivo can facilitate this process, from early stages of a complementary analysis. (1) A simple process of retrieving coded segments for a particular code will bring together the data from all sources, regardless of type, on that topic or issue for complementary review and combination (Figure 29.5). Retrieved segments are ordered by folder, so that what is known about the topic can be

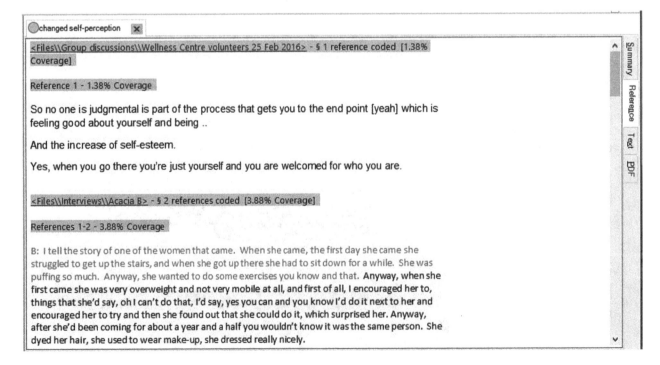

FIGURE 29.5 Code retrieval for complementary analysis.

Using NVivo for Mixed Methods Research

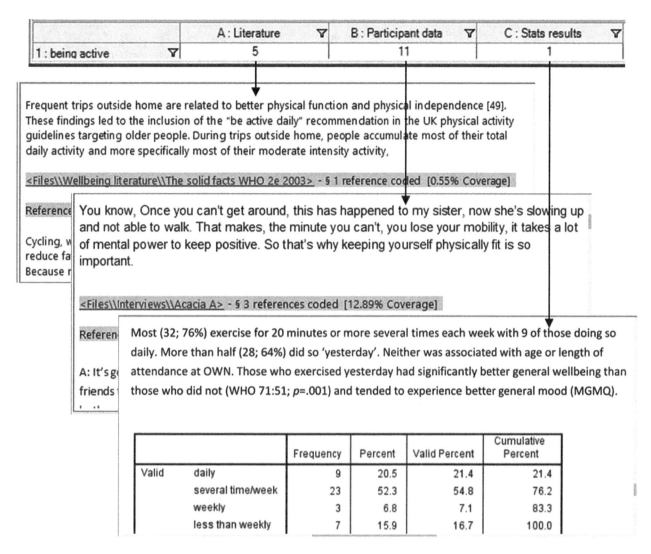

FIGURE 29.6 Matrix showing contribution of different sources on topic of physical activity.

reviewed as a whole, or for each type of source in sequence. (2) If there is a larger amount of data, a matrix coding query will separate the material relating to selected codes (in rows) as contributed by different source types (in columns). This will reveal what has been contributed by each type of data for each of the target codes, providing a range of counts and, critically, also access to the source content within each cell (Figure 29.6).

In the Wellbeing project, the process of sorting and refining codes, and of reviewing data from multiple sources together, in combination with mapping ideas, has contributed to developing a preliminary conceptual model of wellbeing for older women (Figure 29.7) that will be subject to refinement as the project progresses.

Comparative Processes

Comparative processes are an essential component for any kind of data analysis, and mixed methods is no exception. Constant comparison during coding to enrich category development is a well-known tool of theory development (Glaser & Strauss, 1967). Within-case and cross-case comparisons are a staple of both qualitative and mixed methods analysis (Bazeley, 2018, 2021; Miles, Huberman, & Saldaña, 2020). Such comparisons might be undertaken, for example, to compare responses given in different settings, in relation to different events, from different participant groups, or at different times. In NVivo, three tools are used for these types of analyses—framework analysis, the crosstab, and the matrix query.

For smaller projects, framework analysis is valuable for within-case and cross-case analyses. One or more cases define rows in the framework tool (these can be sorted by case attributes so that, for example, all females are listed before males), and codes reflecting topics discussed or categories identified in the data define columns. Coded data segments matching row and column specifications for a particular cell are displayed in a panel to the right of the matrix, allowing the user to review these and enter a summary in the relevant cell (Figure 29.8). Alternatively, cells can be auto-filled with all relevant coded data for each. The tabular layout helps the analyst to compare or perhaps see connections between responses coded differently for selected participants (working across a row). Reviewing summaries for different cases for the same code (reading down the columns) draws attention to key features and common patterns across the various cases. The resulting

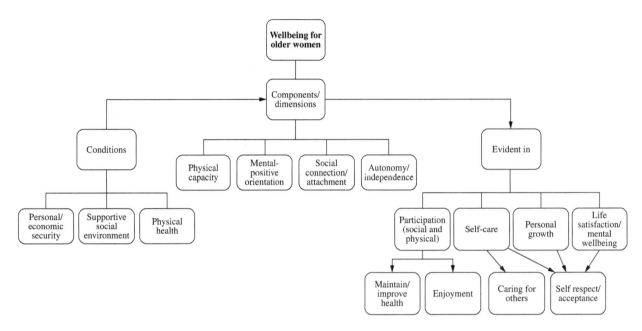

FIGURE 29.7 Wellbeing for older women—preliminary concept map.

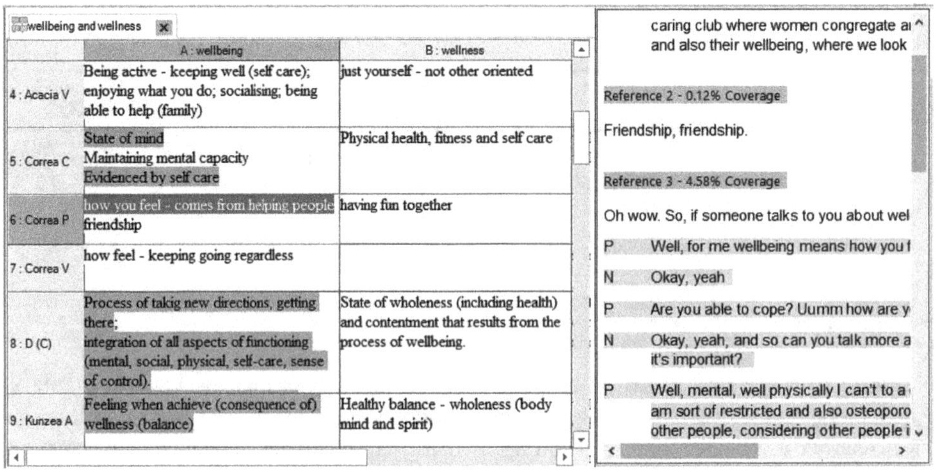

FIGURE 29.8 Cross-case analysis using a framework matrix.

matrix (summaries or coded data) can be exported for printing and further review.

These kinds of comparisons will occur in a mixed methods project also (where coded content in any cell potentially includes mixed data), but the particular contribution of software such as NVivo in a mixed methods context is to facilitate comparisons that combine quantitative and qualitative data. Thus, when projects involve more cases or a faster analytic process is desirable (e.g., viewing responses for all members of a numerically-defined group of cases together), or more freedom about what is used to define rows or columns in the analysis is needed, either a crosstab or a matrix coding query is used.

Cells in a crosstab or matrix will report on content found by intersecting items used to identify the rows and columns, providing both counts and qualitative content for each resulting cell. Content counted and shown can be limited (scoped) to that located in particular folders or items (e.g., codes or sets). These tools can serve a range of analytic purposes, answering questions such as:

- Do different (types of) sources agree?
- Is the way in which participants talk about the future differentially associated with their age (or other demographics), which classes they attend, for how long they have attended, whether they meet with other members at other times, or their score on the WHO wellbeing scale?
- If a score on a scale to assess depression is associated with a difference in verbal responses, do these differences validate the scaled measure?

- What does it mean experientially to be at a certain point as measured by, say, a visual analogue scale for pain?
- Do responses rating satisfaction with a service correspond with concurrently gathered verbal responses about the same service?
- Does examining differences across subgroups of a sample reveal variations in (or sub-dimensions of) a concept?

A crosstab is ideal for sorting qualitative data coded at one or more codes by values of demographic variables, categorical responses to survey questions, or scaled values—each of these having been stored as attribute data. The crosstab tool, used for this purpose, is illustrated in Figure 29.9, to show how a scaled score is reflected within the qualitative data—in this case, the ways in which (a small sample of) older women talk about some aspects of wellbeing sorted by their (grouped) scores on the WHO wellbeing scale. Numbers can be shown to represent cases, number of passages coded, or percentages (based on the available number of cases in the sample for either columns or rows). Double-clicking on any cell opens up original (text) data for that cell.

A matrix coding query works in a similar way, but is more versatile than the crosstab in the kinds of project items that can be used to define both the rows and the columns, and in the way in which these can be combined. As well as codes and attribute values, items entered might additionally include files or sets of files (as shown earlier in Figure 29.6), metaconcepts represented by sets of codes (entered as separate items or as a group), and results from previous queries. A greater range of counts are provided in the resulting matrix (including number of words, or files), although percentages, less usefully, are based on proportion of row or column content coded in a cell. Again, the qualitative content for each cell is available. Of interest in the Wellbeing project, for example, will be changes in understanding of health and wellbeing (codes) and in measures of wellbeing (attribute values), over time (sets, as more data are added), for women of different age groups (attribute values).

Transformative Processes, Directly Converting Data from One Form to Another

This third broad area of integration assisted by NVivo occurs during the analysis stage of a project, most often as codes used for qualitative data are counted or converted to variable data. This form of conversion is undertaken so that qualitatively derived variables can be used in a statistical analysis, so that data from different sources can be entered into a single database to aid complementary analysis, or in order to create a blended variable (a composite variable derived from both quantitative and qualitative sources) for use in further analyses. Alternatively, as demonstrated in the Wellbeing project, interpreted statistical data is included and coded with qualitative sources or perhaps is combined with qualitative data as summarized (qualitized) entries in a meta-analytic database.

people	WHO grouped = high (9)	WHO grouped = mod (8)	WHO grouped = low (3)	Total (20)
motivation	3	2	3	8
independence	4	0	1	5
self care	3	0	1	4
physical health	5	6	3	14
being active	4	7	2	13
social connection	8	8	3	19
Total (unique)	9	8	3	20

<Files\\Interviews\\Acacia L> - § 1 reference coded [4.73% Coverage]

Reference 1 - 4.73% Coverage

Women you know we really connect we can tell each other our problems and we don't hide. We become really friendly, like sisters. That's what, I'm really happy, this community.

<Files\\Interviews\\Acacia V> - § 2 references coded [9.55% Coverage]

Reference 1 - 0.53% Coverage

So I'm socialising, exercising, and out in the fresh air.

Reference 2 - 9.01% Coverage

: Well just getting amongst all the ladies of different nationalities and different ages, and joining in with them in doing things. I've always been like a people person and you know I like to help

FIGURE 29.9 Using the Crosstab tool to compare comments contributed by women experiencing different levels of wellbeing.

	forward orientation	at peace, relaxed	personal resources, self	being active	achievement, satisfaction, purpose	social connection
Acacia A	1	2	1	3	0	3
Acacia V	3	0	7	6	1	2
Correa C	4	0	7	0	0	5
Correa P	0	0	1	0	0	6
Correa V	2	1	3	0	1	5
Melaleuca D	2	2	3	4	1	5
Melaleuca L	8	5	0	1	0	5
Melaleuca N	2	4	3	2	0	5
Waratah A	3	0	0	3	0	4
Waratah C	0	0	0	2	1	3
Waratah G	0	1	0	2	1	4

FIGURE 29.10 A case by variable table derived from transformed qualitative coding.

Producing qualitatively derived variable data is aided, once more, by NVivo's crosstab or matrix coding query, either of which can be used to create and export a case by variable table in either xlsx, sav, or txt format, suitable for importing directly into a statistical program, or for adding to an existing statistical data set. Figure 29.10 shows coding counts (number of passages) for some cases for selected wellbeing dimensions; data can alternatively be exported as dichotomous (0/1) values to indicate coding presence. Careful thought (and justification) needs to be given by the user regarding which form most appropriately reflects the underlying qualitative data. These data are not appropriate for describing population parameters because of inherent sampling and response rate issues, but where sufficient cases exist in exported data, associations between code-derived variables can be assessed. If there is a dependent (outcome) variable, transformed data can be incorporated into predictive (regression-based) analyses; or latent class or cluster analysis can be applied to identify groups of either cases or variables based on the similarity of their patterns of distribution across variables or cases, respectively (Bazeley, 2018). Any conclusions drawn from these analyses should be interpreted cautiously, as being indicative more than conclusive, and always in association with analyses of the qualitative data on which they are based.

Exploratory Visualizations using Transformed Data

Exploratory multivariate statistical strategies—primarily cluster analysis, multidimensional scaling (MDS) and correspondence analysis—are often used with transformed qualitative data as they recognize the nominal nature of the variables and so do not have the same demands as regular inferential statistics with regard to sampling and normality of distribution for the variables used. These procedures result in graphic displays, supported by statistical output, that point to possible relationships between codes or other items. Cluster analysis (referred to earlier in connection with case by variable data) and multidimensional scaling can be applied to a similarity matrix of codes created in NVivo, and correspondence analysis to a matrix of codes by codes, or codes by attribute values.

In a reflected similarity matrix designed for cluster analysis or MDS, the same codes are entered in both rows and columns with cells indicating the frequency with which each pair of codes intersects (Figure 29.11). In using a matrix coding query to produce these matrices, NVivo offers a degree of precision not available in regular multivariate statistical analyses. Rather than simply identifying if pairs of codes are both present somewhere in the data for each case regardless of context, as usually occurs when analyzing variables from survey data in a statistical program, NVivo identifies and counts intersections of codes that occur on exactly the same segment of data, thus providing a greater warrant for assuming a meaningful connection between them. The resulting matrix is then exported to a statistical program for further analyses, where results are displayed graphically, with associated statistical data. Cluster analysis, as before, identifies coherent groups of codes (although the clusters will vary from those identified from a case by variable table); multidimensional scaling assists the researcher in identifying dimensions within the data from the way in which codes (as variables) are positioned in two- or three-dimensional space.

	relationships	forward orientati...	giving and recei...	personal resour...	mental wellbeing	physical health
relationships	174	11	11	10	7	14
forward orientation	11	61	0	5	3	11
giving and receiving care	11	0	45	10	4	2
personal resources, self	10	5	10	61	3	5
mental wellbeing	7	3	4	3	51	13
physical health	14	11	2	5	13	116
positive affect	15	5	2	4	0	4
at peace, relaxed	15	2	0	0	4	3

FIGURE 29.11 Part of a similarity matrix showing frequency with which pairs of codes intersect.

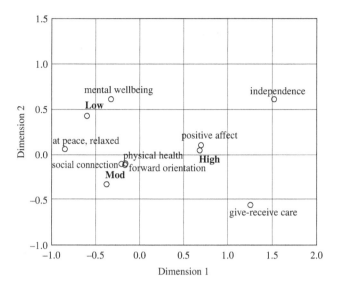

FIGURE 29.12 Correspondence analysis biplot*.

* Analysis of vectors for different levels of wellbeing suggests a particular focus on positive affect (primarily, sense of achievement), independence, and giving and receiving care by those with higher levels of wellbeing, and a focus on mental wellbeing and relaxation by those with a lower experience of wellbeing.

In matrices used for correspondence analysis, codes are intersected with other codes or attribute values. Again, the resulting matrix is exported, although its format needs to be changed to allow for analysis in software such as IBM-SPSS (Bazeley, 2018; see *My Easy Statistics* at www.youtube.com/watch?v=42Ts6JoG12A). The resulting biplot (e.g., Figure 29.12) suggests, for example, which inputs are most associated with each outcome variable, or which characteristics are associated with a particular attribute.

For those wishing to explore their qualitative data, NVivo will create multivariate displays (cluster, MDS) based on the similarity of either words or coding in selected files or selected codes, where similarity is statistically assessed based on the number of times the same (top 100) words appear in each item, or the same codes are used in coding each item. Figure 29.13 illustrates the output from a cluster analysis of the main wellbeing codes, based on word similarity—a cluster display of the sub-codes for these showed broad support for my interpretive grouping, although with some differences. MDS displays, in contrast to cluster, show each item as a point in three-dimensional space, with capacity to rotate the display in order to explore the different dimensional views. As for all transformative analyses, visual or statistical output should always be interpreted in the light of the qualitative content on which they are based.

5 Suggested Applications of NVivo in MMR

As shown for the Wellbeing project, NVivo is an appropriate tool to use for MMR in two critical respects:

- it is of assistance in the management and preliminary analysis of qualitative (e.g., text, image, multimedia, social media) data that will contribute to a mixed methods project;
- it provides tools that facilitate integrative analyses (combination, comparison, and conversion) of mixed methods data.

In so doing, NVivo supports mixed methods projects designed to satisfy a range of descriptive, conceptual, evaluative, and theory building purposes.

6 Strengths and Limitations Using NVivo in MMR

Use of software greatly facilitates a range of analyses that combine text, numeric, and visual elements—as illustrated in this chapter—that would otherwise be difficult or impossible. Integration, as a core element of mixed methods, is therefore greatly enhanced through the use of software such as NVivo. The particular strength offered to mixed methods researchers by NVivo is its capacity to flexibly manage very complex data sources and combinations through its use of codes, cases, sets, and matrix coding queries.

As with any software, NVivo's usefulness will be determined to an extent by user skill in working with the software, but more particularly by the capacity of the user to focus on and jointly interpret all available data at all stages of the project, from initial reflections and coding through to interpreting combined numeric and text displays generated from the data.

7 Resources for Learning More About Mixed Analysis Using NVivo

A fully-functioning 14-day demonstration version of NVivo can be downloaded from www.qsrinternational.com, where extensive information about the program is also available. NVivo provides a "getting started" tutorial for new users of the program whenever a new project is created in the software. Other tutorials covering main features are available through accessing Help in NVivo, under the File menu. Comprehensive, web-based Help files provide detailed instructions for all functions available in the software.

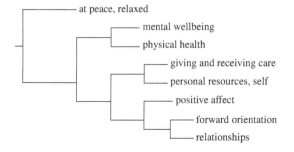

FIGURE 29.13 Wellbeing codes clustered, based on the similarity of words coded into those codes.

Those who are looking for a general introduction to NVivo in the context of strategies for analysis of qualitative data should turn to Jackson and Bazeley (2019), or Woolf and Silver (2018). Both of these texts are accompanied by companion web sites with additional videos, resources, and examples. Understanding of integration in mixed methods analysis and strategies for achieving it (with and without computer software) are comprehensively covered in Bazeley 2018(a).

REFERENCES

Bazeley, P. (2002). The evolution of a project involving an integrated analysis of structured qualitative and quantitative data: From N3 to NVivo. *International Journal of Social Research Methodology, 5*(3), 229–243. doi: 10.1080/13645570210146285

Bazeley, P. (2018a). *Integrating analyses in mixed methods research.* London: Sage.

Bazeley, P. (2018b). "Mixed methods in my bones": Transcending the qualitative-quantitative divide. *International Journal of Multiple Research Approaches, 10*(1), 334–341.

Bazeley, P. (2021). *Qualitative data analysis: Practical strategies* (2nd ed.). London: Sage.

Burch, P., & Heinrich, C. J. (2016). *Mixed methods for policy research and program evaluation.* Thousand Oaks, CA: Sage.

Jackson, K., & Bazeley, P. (2019). *Qualitative data analysis with NVivo* (3rd ed.). London: Sage.

Glaser, B. G., & Strauss, A. (1967). *The discovery of grounded theory: Strategies for qualitative research.* Chicago, IL: Aldine.

Miles, M. B., Huberman, A. M., & Saldaña, J. (2020). *Qualitative data analysis: A methods sourcebook* (4th ed.). Thousand Oaks, CA: Sage.

Morse, J. M., & Niehaus, L. (2009). *Mixed method design: Principles and procedures.* Walnut Creek, CA: Left Coast Press.

Tesch, R. (1990). *Qualitative research: analysis types and software tools.* London: Falmer.

Woolf, N. H., & Silver, C. (2018). *Qualitative analysis using NVivo: The five level QDA method.* New York, NY: Routledge.

30

Introduction to SPSS for Mixed Analysis

Nancy L. Leech

When conducting mixed analysis in a mixed methods research study, there are various sources to assist researchers in designing and planning the analysis (e.g., Combs & Onwuegbuzie, 2010; Onwuegbuzie & Combs, 2010; Onwuegbuzie & Hitchcock, 2015; Onwuegbuzie, Leech, & Collins, 2011; Onwuegbuzie, Slate, Leech, & Collins, 2007, 2009; Onwuegbuzie & Teddlie, 2003). These sources provide excellent explanations, with many providing step-by-step guidance for making decisions when conducting a mixed analysis. Yet, these sources fall short when the analyses require a computer program to assist in the computations. Unfortunately, there are scant resources available for explaining how to utilize computer programs when conducting mixed analysis, especially with respect to the use of computer-assisted quantitative data analysis (i.e., statistical) software programs. One program that can be very helpful when conducting mixed analysis is *SPSS* (IBM SPSS Software, n.d.). SPSS is a quantitative computer program that is widely used (Crossman, 2018) and can be very helpful when conducting mixed analysis in mixed methods research studies.

1 Definition of SPSS for Mixed Analysis

SPSS is "designed to solve business and research problems through ad hoc analysis, hypothesis testing, geospatial analysis and predictive analysis" (IBM SPSS Software, n.d.). SPSS is a computer program that can be useful when integrating qualitative and quantitative data in mixed methods research studies. Various analyses can be performed with SPSS; according to the IBM SPSS website, SPSS includes "machine learning algorithms, text analysis, open source extensibility, integration with big data and seamless deployment into applications" (IBM SPSS Software, n.d.). Used with datasets that are small or very large, users can conduct many different types of analysis.

SPSS is known for analyzing data that are numerical, also known as quantitative data. *Qualitative data*, which are non-numerical data, including words and pictures, can also be used with SPSS once it has been quantitized. *Mixed methods data* can include both qualitative and quantitative data, or just one type (i.e., either qualitative or quantitative) of data. Thus, as Onwuegbuzie and Combs (2010) state, there can be "quantitative data *or* qualitative data; or quantitative data *and* qualitative data" (p. 425). Finally, *mixed data analysis* is defined by Onwuegbuzie and Combs (2010) as:

> Mixed analysis involves the use of both quantitative and qualitative analytical techniques with the same framework, which is guided either a prior, a posteriori, or iteratively (representing analytical decisions that occur both prior to the study and during the study). It might be based on one of the existing mixed methods research paradigms (e.g., pragmatism, transformative-emancipatory) such that it meets one or more of the following rationales/purposes: triangulation, complementarity, development, initiation, and expansion. Mixed analyses involve the analyses of one or both data types (i.e., quantitative data *or* qualitative data; or quantitative data *and* qualitative data), which occur either concurrently (i.e., in no chronological order), or sequentially in two phases (in which the qualitative analysis phase precedes the quantitative analysis phase or vice versa, and findings from the initial analysis phase inform the subsequent phase), or more than two phases (i.e., iteratively). The analysis strands might not interact until the data interpretation stage, yielding a basic parallel mixed analysis, although more complex forms of parallel mixed analysis can be used, in which interaction takes place in a limited way before the data interpretation phase. The mixed analysis can be design based, wherein it is directly linked to the mixed methods design (e.g., sequential mixed analysis techniques used for sequential mixed methods). Alternatively, the mixed analysis can be phase based, in which the mixed analysis takes place in one or more phases (e.g., data transformation). In mixed analyses, either the qualitative or quantitative analysis strands might be given greater priority or approximately equal priority as a result of a priori decisions (i.e., determined at the research conceptualization phase) or decisions that emerge during the course of the study (i.e., a posteriori or iterative decisions). The mixed analysis could represent case-oriented, variable-oriented, and/or process/experience-oriented analyses. The mixed analysis is guided by an attempt to analyze data in a way that yields at least one of five types of generalizations (i.e., external statistical generalizations, internal statistical generalizations, analytical generalizations, case-to-case transfer, naturalistic generalization). At its most integrated form, the mixed analysis might involve some form of cross-over analysis, wherein one or more analysis types associated with one tradition (e.g., qualitative analysis) are used to analyze data associated with a different tradition (e.g., qualitative data). (pp. 425–426)

2 When Use of SPSS for Mixed Analysis is Appropriate in MMR

SPSS (IBM SPSS Software, n.d.) is appropriate to use in mixed methods research studies. Fortunately, there are many sources that describe when quantitative data will be available for analysis in a mixed methods research study (Combs & Onwuegbuzie, 2010; Onwuegbuzie & Combs, 2010; Onwuegbuzie & Hitchcock, 2015; Onwuegbuzie et al., 2011; Onwuegbuzie et al., 2007, 2009; Onwuegbuzie & Teddlie, 2003). In some mixed methods research studies, quantitative data are collected directly, for example, when asking how long a teacher has been working in the field of teaching, the response would be the number of years, which would represent quantitative data. Another way quantitative data can be found in mixed methods research studies is from qualitative data that have been quantized. *Quantitizing* is when qualitative data are transformed/converted to quantitative data that can be analyzed statistically (Miles & Huberman, 1994; Miles, Huberman, & Saldaña, 2020; Onwuegbuzie & Teddlie, 2003; Sandelowski, Voils, & Knafl, 2009; Tashakkori & Teddlie, 1998). Tashakkori and Teddlie (1998) describe quantitizing in the following way: "in most cases, QUAL data are converted into narrative categories, which are then converted into numeric codes (e.g., 0, 1 or 1, 2, 3), which can then be analyzed statistically" (p. 269). For example, open-ended responses could be coded as 0 or 1, with 0 representing open-ended responses that do not include pertinent information with regard to the research question and 1 representing open-ended responses that do include the information.

To assist in understanding mixed methods analyses, Onwuegbuzie and Combs (2010) present a "meta-framework for mixed analysis strategies" (p. 424). The meta-framework (Onwuegbuzie & Combs, 2010) is organized via the 13-step model of the mixed methods process developed by Collins, Onwuegbuzie, and Sutton (2006) with three research stages: (a) formulation, (b) planning, and (c) implementation. Onwuegbuzie and Combs's (2010) meta-framework suggests three types of mixed analyses: (a) cross-over mixed analysis, (b) non-cross-over mixed analysis, and (c) parallel analysis. Each of these analyses presents a different amount of interaction between the qualitative and quantitative analyses. According to Onwuegbuzie and Combs (2010), a *cross-over mixed analysis* is when analytical techniques from one tradition are used to analyze data from the other tradition. According to Onwuegbuzie and Hwang (2019a):

> Crossover mixed analyses involve using techniques from one tradition (e.g., quantitative) to analyze data associated with the other tradition (qualitative) (Hitchcock & Onwuegbuzie, 2019; Onwuegbuzie & Combs, 2010) in order to address the nine purposes of analysis described by Onwuegbuzie and Combs (2010): reduce, display, transform, correlate/associate, consolidate, compare, integrate, assert, and/ or import data. Crossover mixed analyses include methods such as *quantitizing*, which involves transforming qualitative data into numerical codes that can, in turn, be subjected to statistical analyses (Miles & Huberman, 1994; Onwuegbuzie & Teddlie, 2003; Sandelowski, et al., 2009; Tashakkori & Teddlie, 1998); and *qualitizing*, which involves transforming numerical data into narrative form, that, subsequently, can be subjected to qualitative analyses (Onwuegbuzie & Leech, 2019; Tashakkori & Teddlie, 1998). (p. ii)

For example, SPSS could be used to conduct a *t* test (i.e., quantitative technique) to analyze whether there are a different number of codes used in open-ended responses from interviewees who are male or female (i.e., qualitative data).

A *non-cross-over mixed analysis* is when analytical techniques from one tradition are only used with data from that tradition, with a time sequence (i.e., concurrent or sequential) and a phase-based analysis (i.e., data transformation, data correlation and comparison, analysis for inquiry conclusions and inferences; Onwuegbuzie & Combs, 2010). SPSS could be used in this type of analysis to run the analyses from the quantitative phase.

A *parallel analysis* is when separate quantitative and qualitative analyses are conducted with no time sequence (i.e., concurrent) and no phase-based analysis (i.e., data transformation, data correlation and comparison, analysis for inquiry conclusions and inferences; Onwuegbuzie & Combs, 2010). An example of a parallel analysis would be an article reporting the quantitative statistical analysis and then the qualitative statistical analysis, with mixing the analysis in the interpretation of the data in the discussion section. SPSS could be used in this type of analysis to conduct the quantitative statistical analysis.

3 Technical Outline of SPSS for Mixed Analysis for MMR

Regardless of the type of mixed analysis conducted (i.e., non-cross-over mixed analysis, cross-over mixed analysis, or parallel analysis; Onwuegbuzie & Combs, 2010), SPSS (SPSS Software, n.d.) can be used to compute the quantitative statistics. Table 30.1 presents a small sample of mixed analyses that can be conducted with SPSS.

4 Empirical Demonstration of SPSS for Mixed Analysis for MMR

This empirical demonstration presents how a small section of data from a mixed methods research study could be analyzed to demonstrate how SPSS can be used to conduct a mixed analysis. For many researchers, knowing how to move from quantitative and qualitative data to mixing the two types of data with SPSS can be daunting. It is important to consider "decisions mixed researchers make before, during, and/or after the conduct of their mixed analyses" (Onwuegbuzie & Combs, 2011, Mixed analysis defined section). According to Onwuegbuzie and Combs (2011), the five most common decisions include: the rationale/purpose for conducting the mixed analyses, how many data types to be analyzed, the time sequence of the

TABLE 30.1

A Sample of Mixed Analyses Available to Conduct with SPSS

1. Create a dichotomous variable from qualitative data and correlate with quantitative variables in SPSS
2. Create one or more nominal/categorical variables from qualitative data and conduct contingency table analysis in SPSS.
2a. Use contingency table analysis with two qualitative variables where SPSS gives row, column, and cell percentages.
2b. Use contingency table analysis with one qualitative /nominal variable and one quantitative variable with just a few levels or that has been categorized.
2c. Include qualitative variables from qualitative data in structural equation modeling with AMOS in SPSS.
3. Conduct an analysis of variance (ANOVA) where the categorical IV was constructed from the qual data.
4. Dichotomizing (i.e., binarizing) qualitative data (e.g., themes) would allow SPSS to conduct an independent samples t test on one or more quantitative dependent variables. That is, the independent samples t test would be used to compare two groups: for example, the group that endorsed the theme vs. the group that did not endorse the theme.
5. Construct interval-level quantitative data from open-ended questions (perhaps by rating the qualitative answers from 1 to 10) and then conduct an exploratory factor analysis to assess how the responses form into sub-factors.
6. Create multiple dichotomous quantitative variables (1 = yes, 0 = no) from the qualitative data assessing whether the qualitative data meets a specific criterion. Conduct correspondence analysis or multidimensional scaling to determine whether there are any patterns.
7. After quantitizing qualitative data, utilize one nominal variable to assess how participants fall into groups by conducting a cluster analysis.
8. Create a number of quantitative categorical/nominal variables from the qualitative data and then conduct a chi-square automatic interaction detection analysis to visualize the relationships.
9. Create dichotomous variables from the qualitative data to create a model to use to predict an interval/ratio quantitative variable using multiple regression analysis.
10. When data are nested (e.g., students are nested within classrooms, classrooms are nested within schools) quantitize the qualitative data at the student level and then conduct a hierarchical linear modeling analysis to assess whether there are differences.
11. Quantitize the qualitative data and then conduct a Bayesian Analysis to ask questions about predictions (e.g., how many students have taken algebra before applying for college?)
12. After collecting data with a quantitative measure that has 5 subfactors, quantitize (i.e., dichotomize) the qualitative data that came from questions to match the 5 quantitative subfactors then conduct canonical correlation analysis.
13. Quantitize the qualitative data and then conduct Item Response Theory (IRT).
14. When collecting qualitative data over time (e.g., journal entries from teachers each week for a semester), quantitize the qualitative data and conduct a diachronic analysis.

analyses, the priority of analytical components, and the number of analytical phases. These common decisions, along with other steps, are presented in Figure 30.1.

Walk Through of Empirical Study Using the 17 Steps in Figure 30.1

Using Figure 30.1, we will walk through a small portion of a study conducted by Leech, Haug, and Gold (2020). This concurrent, fully mixed, equal status mixed methods research study (Leech & Onwuegbuzie, 2009) involved an investigation of rural K-12 teachers' motivation to teach in a mid-western state in the United States. These authors had conducted other studies (Leech & Haug, 2015; Leech, Haug, Ridgewell, & Rubin, 2019) on K-12 teachers' motivation to teach. These past studies included only quantitative data. When the opportunity came available to survey teachers comparing teachers in rural and urban settings, the authors decided to add open-ended questions to increase their understanding of the teachers' motivation. For the complete study, there were many research questions, including qualitative, quantitative, and mixed methods research questions. To keep things simple and streamlined, for this example, we discuss one research question: Do teachers choose to teach in rural areas for different reasons than teachers who teach in urban areas?

From Figure 30.1, Step 1 is to determine the rationale/purpose for conducting the mixed analyses. The rationale/purpose of this study was complementarity—using results from one strand (e.g., qualitative) to seek elaboration, illustration, enhancement, and clarification of the other strand (e.g., quantitative).

Step 2 is to assess a priori statistical power for chosen analyses. We checked a priori power by using G*Power (Faul et al., 2009). Figure 30.2 presents the window for G*Power with our choices along with the calculations. This shows that for a chi-square/phi test we would need only 88 participants to find a medium effect size (w = .30) with power of .80. Therefore, with our sample size of 493 participants, we will have more than enough power: in fact, we may have so much power that we might find statistical significance for results that are not clinically important. For our analysis, we will compute phi, which can be interpreted as an effect size. Phi ranges from –1 to 1 and is interpreted the same as a correlation coefficient with values closer to 0 indicating less relationship.

Step 3 from Figure 30.1 is to collect data. A random selection of people with a teaching license was contacted via email in a western state and asked to participate in the online survey. A total of 490 teachers completed the survey instrument. Both qualitative and qualitative data were collected along with demographic information.

The Factors Influencing Teaching Choice (FIT Choice Scale; Watt & Richardson, 2007) provided the quantitative data. The FIT Choice scale has been found to provide valid and reliable data from pre-service teachers (Berger & D'Ascoli, 2012; Fokkens-Bruinsma & Canrinus, 2012; Lin, Shi, Wang, Zhang, & Hui, 2012; Watt & Richardson, 2007, 2008, 2012) and in-service teachers (Leech & Haug, 2015; Leech et al., 2019). The FIT Choice scale comprised 18 subfactors: (a) ability, (b) intrinsic career value, (c) work with children and adolescents, (d) enhance social equity, (e) make social contribution, (f) shape future of children/adolescents, (g) social status, (h) expertise, (i) difficulty, (j) social

Steps for Using SPSS with Data from a Mixed Methods Research Study

1. Determine the rationale/purpose for conducting the mixed analyses (Greene, Caracelli, & Graham, 1989):

> *Triangulation* – comparing results from the qualitative and quantitative analyses
>
> *Complementarity* – using results from one strand (e.g., qualitative) to seek elaboration, illustration, enhancement, and clarification of the other strand (e.g., quantitative)
>
> *Development* – using results from one strand (e.g., qualitative) to inform the other strand (e.g., quantitative)
>
> *Initiation* – comparing the results from two strands (i.e., qualitative and quantitative) to determine whether there are paradoxes and contradictions
>
> *Expansion* – using multiple analytical strands for each of the study phases to increase the range and breadth of the results

2. Assess a priori statistical power for chosen analyses. *A priori statistical power* is important to assess as it is

> how likely it is that the researcher will find a relationship or difference that really exists…having low power increases the probability of committing a Type II error. Moreover, having a small sample size, which is the most important controllable source of low power, may also increase the probability of committing a Type I error if the sample is a poor representation of the population. (Leech, Barrett, & Morgan, 2015, pp. 96-97).

FIGURE 30.1 Steps for using SPSS with data from a mixed methods research study.

dissuasion, (k) job security, (k) prior teaching and learning experiences, (l) social influences, (m) satisfied with choice to teach, (n) salary, (o) fallback career, (p) time for family, and (q) job transferability.

The qualitative data were collected at the same time using open-ended questions. There was a total of five open-ended questions. Responses from the qualitative question of "Why did you choose to teach in the area (rural, suburban, urban) you are currently teaching in?" is reported here.

Step 4 is to decide on the number of data types to be analyzed. For this study, the authors collected two data types. They collected qualitative data using open-ended questions and quantitative data using mostly closed-ended questions (mostly rating scale data). In addition to using within-method

Statistical power needs to be addressed before collecting the data to determine how many participants are needed to reach an acceptable level of power (.80 is often considered the minimal level). The easiest way to assess statistical power is through a free calculator, available on the Internet called G*Power (Faul, Erdfelder, Buchner, & Lang, 2009).

3. Collect data. This may be qualitative and quantitative data, or just qualitative data, or just quantitative data.

4. Decide on the data types to be analyzed. In mixed methods research studies, there are multiples ways of thinking through the number of data types. One method is for quantitative data to be analyzed with quantitative techniques and qualitative data to be analyzed with qualitative techniques; Fetters and Guetterman (current book, Onwuegbuzie & Johnson, in press) call this *within-method analysis*. A more mixed methods way of thinking about data types is through first analyzing the data using their natural approach (e.g., analyze qualitative data qualitatively and/or quantitative data quantitatively) and then use *data conversion* to transform the data to the other type and then analyze those "new" data to determine whether additional insights ensue (Tashakkori, Johnson, & Teddlie, 2020) this is also termed a *sequential mixed analysis*, where "data that are generated from the initial analysis then are converted into the other data type" (Onwuegbuzie & Combs, 2011, E13). Data can be converted in two ways—data can be quantitized and/or qualitized. *Quantitizing* is when qualitative data are transformed/converted to quantitative data that can be analyzed statistically (Miles & Huberman, 1994; Miles, Huberman, & Saldaña, 2020; Onwuegbuzie & Teddlie, 2003;

FIGURE 30.1 Continued.

analysis (Fetters & Guetterman, Chapter 23, this volume) they also used sequential analysis (Onwuegbuzie & Teddlie, 2003) or data conversion, wherein the qualitative data were quantitized (Tashakkori, Johnson, & Teddlie, 2021) and then used in quantitative analyses. In a basic conversion design (Tashakkori, Johnson, & Teddlie, 2021), only one data type is required but it is analyzed both quantitatively and qualitatively.

Step 5 is to decide on the time sequence of the mixed analysis. In this study, a sequential qualitative-quantitative analysis (Onwuegbuzie & Teddlie, 2003) was conducted: the qualitative

Sandelowski et al., 2009; Tashakkori & Teddlie, 1998). *Qualitizing* is when quantitative data are transformed/converted into narrative or qualitative data (Onwuegbuzie & Leech, 2019).

5. Decide on the time sequence of the mixed analysis. It is important to decide the order of the qualitative and quantitative strands in a mixed methods research study. The strands can be conducted sequentially, with one strand being conducted and then the other strand, or the strands can be conducted concurrently, or at the same time. With a sequential mixed methods research design, the first strand (e.g., qualitative strand) can inform the second strand (e.g., quantitative strand), which then leads to a sequential quantitative-qualitative analysis (Onwuegbuzie & Teddlie, 2003) or a sequential qualitative-quantitative analysis (Onwuegbuzie & Teddlie, 2003). Alternatively, there can be more than two phases, which would lead to an iterative sequential mixed analysis (Onwuegbuzie & Combs, 2010).

6. Decide on the priority of the analytical components (qualitative analysis components and quantitative analysis components). In a mixed methods study, priority can be given to the qualitative component, the quantitative component, or it can be equally distributed between the qualitative and quantitative components. Thus, the prioritized component is the *dominant component*. A dominant component is when one component of a mixed study is given more weight or importance, when the vast majority of the data are one type (qualitative or quantitative data), and/or when one primary epistemological approach is used to understand and interpret the analyses.

FIGURE 30.1 Continued.

data were analyzed, and then the results were quantitized to be analyzed quantitatively.

Step 6 is to decide on the priority of the analytical components (qualitative analysis components and quantitative analysis components). In this study, the quantitative strand had more weight, because it involved use of a quantitatively driven MM design. The reason for this statement about priority is because (a) more quantitative data were collected, and (b) the qualitative data were quantitized but the quantitative data were not qualitized.

SPSS for Mixed Analysis

7. Decide on the number of analytical phases. According to Greene (2007), in mixed methods research studies, there are typically four phases: data transformation, data correlation and comparison, analysis for inquiry conclusions and inferences, and using parts of one methodological tradition within the other tradition's analyses. Onwuegbuzie and Teddlie (2003) suggest seven analytical phases: (a) data reduction (i.e., reducing the dimensionality of the both the quantitative and qualitative data), (b) data display (i.e., providing displays of the data), (c) data transformation (i.e., qualitizing or quantitizing the data), (d) data correlation (i.e., correlating data from one tradition with data from the other tradition), (e) data consolidation (i.e., combining data from both traditions to create new variables or constructs), (f) data comparison (i.e., comparing quantitative and qualitative data), and (g) data integration (i.e., integrating quantitative and qualitative data).

8. Move or enter the quantitative data into SPSS. SPSS data are organized into nominal, ordinal, interval, or ratio variable. Be sure to use meaningful variable names and labels for the variables. Qualitative data are usually converted to nominal variables (which are also sometime know as qualitative variables) when used in SPSS.

9. Check the quality of the qualitative and quantitative data. For qualitative data, checking the quality of data includes conducting member checking, triangulating the results with multiple analyses, triangulating the results with multiple data sources, and so forth. For quantitative data, checking the quality of data includes assessing the reliability

FIGURE 30.1 Continued.

Step 7 is to decide on the number of analysis phases. Using Onwuegbuzie and Teddlie's (2003) typology, the following analytical phases were conducted in the study: data reduction, data display, data transformation, and data correlation. Not all of these phases are evident from the small example included here.

Step 8 is move or enter the quantitative data into SPSS; during this step, the authors moved the quantitative data into SPSS, which was collected with the FIT Choice Scale (Watt & Richardson, 2007). Variables and labels for the variables were created.

Step 9 is to check the quality of the qualitative and quantitative data. The trustworthiness of the qualitative data was checked by conducting multiple qualitative analyses and triangulating the results (Leech & Onwuegbuzie, 2007).

of data (e.g., internal consistency such as Cronbach's alpha, KR-20; test-retest reliability) and structural validity [e.g., exploratory factor analysis, confirmatory factor analysis, criterion-related validity, construct-related validity, content-related validity, (cf. Onwuegbuzie, Daniel, & Collins, 2009)]. For mixed methods data and research, Onwuegbuzie and Johnson (2006) and Johnson and Christensen (2020) outline 11 types of legitimation: (a) sample integration legitimation (i.e., the degree to which the researcher makes appropriate claims from the qualitative data [often complex, particular, and process claims based on small-n] and from the quantitative data [often claims about relationships among variables based on large-n] and combines these into meta-inferences, (b) emic-etic or inside-outside legitimation (i.e., the extent that the researcher adequately understands and presents the insider's viewpoint as well as the researcher/observer's viewpoint), (c) weakness minimization legitimation (i.e., the weakness of one method/strand is accounted for by the strength of another method/strand), (d) sequential legitimation (i.e., degree to which later strands in a sequential design build on knowledge/insights from prior strands; also assessing whether meta-inferences might have been different if the sequence had been reversed), (e) conversion legitimation (i.e., degree to which quantitizing or qualitizing was undertaken well and increases the quality of meta-inferences), (f) paradigmatic legitimation (i.e., when researchers successfully clarify their mixed philosophical and paradigmatic beliefs underlying their research), (g) pragmatic legitimation (degree to which mixed research questions are answered and actionable results are obtained (h) commensurability approximation legitimation (i.e., meta-inferences are based on mixed researchers deep understanding qualitative and quantitative research and make Gestalt shifts to produce mixed/integrated thinking), (i)

FIGURE 30.1 Continued.

Past data from research using the FIT Choice scale have shown validity and reliability and the current data were checked via confirmatory factor analysis and Cronbach's alpha. Legitimation (Onwuegbuzie & Johnson, 2006) of the mixed methods was assessed via weakness minimization (i.e., the weakness of one strand being increased by the other strand), conversion (i.e., quantitizing or qualitizing to increase meta-inferences), and multiple validities (i.e., the use of quantitative, qualitative, and mixed methods research validity types).

integration legitimation (degree to which qualitative-quantitative integration in data, analysis, and conclusions is present (j) multiple stakeholder (i.e., degree to which the research is justified according to different stakeholders, and always including the perspective of those with the least power, and most importantly, (k) multiple validities legitimation (i.e., the use of the pertinent subset of quantitative, qualitative, and mixed methods research validity types tailored for each research study).

10. Analyze the qualitative data by hand or with a computer program (e.g., Nvivo, MAXQDQ, QDA Miner, WordStat, Atlas-ti, Dedoose).

11. Add the information from the qualitative data analysis as nominal variables to SPSS. Construct new nominal and/or ordinal level variables in SPSS so that the qualitative data can be analyzed using SPSS that is designed to conduct analyses among and between nominal-, ordinal-, interval-, and ratio-level variables.

12. Select statistical analyses to help answer the research questions (e.g., correlation, regression, analysis of variance [ANOVA], contingency table). Keep in mind that nonparametric statistics are often needed for qualitative (nominal or categorical) outcome variables because of the violation of the normality assumption (and other assumptions such as equal intervals).

13. Check all data for assumptions of the planned statistical approaches to answer the research questions. For example, *assumptions* for many parametric statistics typically

FIGURE 30.1 Continued.

Step 10 is analyzing the qualitative data. For these data, the responses to the five open-ended questions were analyzed with multiple types of qualitative data analysis; for this example, we used constant comparative analysis (Glaser & Strauss, 1967) using a form of in vivo coding (Saldaña, 2013) and classical content analysis (Berelson, 1952). The following steps were followed to code with constant comparative analysis (Glaser & Strauss, 1967) with in vivo coding (Saldaña, 2013): (a) the researchers read through the data for each question, (b) the data were chunked into smaller meaningful segments, (c) each includes the assumption of normality, wherein the variables are not skewed. For an ANOVA, the assumptions include that observations are independent, homogeneity of variances (that the groups have similar variances), and the dependent variable is normally distributed (Leech et al., 2015). For analyses with more qualitative-type dependent variables, normal distributions are not possible; therefore, other types of analysis are needed. For example, a chi-square for contingency table analysis only has the assumptions of observations being independent and 80% of the expected frequencies being greater than 5 (Morgan, Barrett, Leech, & Gloeckner, 2020). The assumption of normal distributions is not part of these nonparametric statistics (such as chi square) that are often used with more qualitative or mixed methods types of analyses.

Utilizing *visual displays* during analysis and presentation can be very helpful. For example, many kinds of graphs are available to assess whether certain statistical assumptions have been met. More importantly, visual displays, usually called "joint displays" are used during analysis and in results presentation in mixed methods research (Fetters & Guetterman, in press in current book; Tufte, 2001; Schoonenboom & Johnson, in press in current book; Valsiner, 2000). In fact, the lack of the use of visual displays is one predictor of whether a manuscript will be rejected for publication (Onwuegbuzie & Hwang, 2019a) and quality of communication and readability of a manuscript (Onwuegbuzie & Hwang, 2019b). SPSS provides numerous options for visual displays.

14. Conduct the "statistical" analyses to help answer the research questions; these may include descriptive statistics, inferential statistics, and visual displays.

FIGURE 30.1 Continued.

segment was given a code or title that used the participants' words as much as possible and was descriptive, (d) each new chunk of data was compared to the previous codes and codes were reused if appropriate, (e) the codes were grouped by similarity, and (f) themes were written. Classical content analysis (Berelson, 1952) was conducted via the following procedures: (a) reading through the data set, (b) chunking the data into small, meaningful parts, (c) labeling each chunk with a code, and (d) counting the number of occurrences of the code. An Excel spreadsheet was used to track the coding. Each row in this spreadsheet represents data from one participant and columns A–C were identifying information (not included in this example), column D includes a chunk of data from the participants response and columns E through P are codes. For each

15. Assess post hoc statistical power for chosen analyses. *Post hoc power* is helpful to conduct especially when statistical significance has not been found. Onwuegbuzie and Leech (2004) state:

> Unfortunately, most researchers do not determine whether the statistically nonsignificant result is the result of insufficient statistical power. That is, without knowing the power of the statistical test, it is not possible to rule in or rule out low statistical power as a threat to internal validity (Onwuegbuzie, 2003). Nor can an a priori power analysis necessarily rule in/out this threat. This is because a priori power analyses involve the use of a priori estimates of effect sizes and standard deviations (Harris, 1997). As such, a priori power analyses do not represent the power to detect the observed effect of the ensuing study; rather, they represent the power to detect hypothesized effects. Before the study is conducted, researchers do not know what the observed effect size will be. All they can do is try to estimate it based on previous research and theory (Wilkinson & the Task Force on Statistical Inference, 1999). The observed effect size could end up being much smaller or much larger than the hypothesized effect size on which the power analysis is undertaken. (Indeed, this is a criticism of the power surveys highlighted previously; Mulaik, Raju, & Harshman, 1997.) In particular, if the observed effect size is smaller than what is proposed, the sample size yielded by the a priori power analysis might be smaller than is needed to detect it. In other words, a smaller effect size than anticipated increases the chances of Type II error. (p. 209)

FIGURE 30.1 Continued.

participant, their chunk was coded with a "1" in the column representing a code if that code was used for their chunk of data. A portion of the results from the classical content analysis are presented in Figure 30.3.

Step 11 from Figure 30.1 is to add the information from the qualitative data analysis as "numbers" to SPSS. For this analysis, we deleted the qualitative raw data (Column D in Figure 30.2) and have included the participant number in Column A. We needed to rename the codes because these would be made into the variable names in SPSS, and SPSS does not work with long variables or with variable names that include spaces. We chose very simple variable names (e.g., A1, A2) and made a key so that we would remember what code was tied to each variable. We imported the data from

For many statistical analyses, SPSS will conduct post hoc power which will provide the amount of power that was available for the test.

16. Compare separate qualitative and quantitative results and results from mixed analyses during the interpretation of results. Displays, both joint displays and *crossover displays*, can be useful to compare results from qualitative and quantitative strands. Onwuegbuzie and Hwang (2019a) state:

> With respect to mixed methods research studies, not only can they contain quantitative-based tables and figures and/or qualitative-based tables and figures, but also they can contain what Onwuegbuzie and Dickinson (2008) refer to as crossover displays that "summarize and integrate both qualitative and quantitative results within the same framework" (p. 205). More specifically, crossover displays of findings involve the display of findings that occur after some form of crossover mixed (methods) analysis has taken place. Crossover mixed analyses involve using techniques from one tradition (e.g., quantitative) to analyze data associated with the other tradition (qualitative) (Hitchcock & Onwuegbuzie, 2019; Onwuegbuzie & Combs, 2010) in order to address the nine purposes of analysis described by Onwuegbuzie and Combs (2010): reduce, display, transform, correlate/associate, consolidate, compare, integrate, assert, and/or import data. Crossover mixed analyses include methods such as quantitizing, which involves transforming qualitative data into numerical codes that can, in turn, be subjected to statistical analyses (Miles & Huberman, 1994; Onwuegbuzie & Teddlie, 2003; Sandelowski, Voils, Knafl, 2009; Tashakkori &Teddlie, 1998); and qualitizing,

FIGURE 30.1 Continued.

Excel into SPSS. See Figure 30.4 for the Excel spreadsheet before importing.

We needed to indicate to SPSS that the blank cells indicated not using that code (i.e., not a missing value); therefore, we used *Transform → Recode into same variable*, presented in Figure 30.5. Using the *Old and New Values* function ensured that SPSS kept the 1's but changed the empty cells to zeros. The 1's indicate the respondent had the code and a zero indicates they did not. Figure 30.6 presents the data after exporting it from Excel into SPSS. We which involves transforming numerical data into narrative form, that, subsequently, can be subjected to qualitative analyses (Onwuegbuzie & Leech, 2019; Tashakkori & Teddlie, 1998)...A special case of crossover mixed analyses are what are known as joint displays, which involve presenting both qualitative and quantitative findings (Fetters, Curry, & Creswell, 2015; Guetterman, Fetters, Curry, & Creswell, 2013), which involve "using tables or figures that combine and display both quantitative and qualitative data together" (Johnson, Grove, & Clarke, 2019, p. 301). Therefore, joint displays reflect Fetters and Freshwater's (2015) recent call for integration in mixed methods research in order to "produce a whole through integration that is greater than the sum of the individual qualitative and quantitative parts....Quantitatively, we express this as 1 + 1 = 3. That is, qualitative + quantitative = more than the individual components" (pp. 115-116). These authors expressed this synergy as the 1+1=3 integration challenge in mixed methods research (Fetters & Freshwater, 2015). However, Onwuegbuzie (2017a) and Onwuegbuzie and Hitchcock (2019) argue that this integration formula emphasizes a quantitative-qualitative separation that can prevent a more complete kind of integration. Instead, they posit a 1+1=1 integration formula that denotes a more comprehensive and dynamic characterization of integration and which involves the data collection, data analysis, and data interpretation phase. Therefore, contrastingly, crossover displays reflect this 1+1=1 integration formula, which allow researchers to be even more creative in developing their visual displays. Notwithstanding, regardless of the integration formula used to create visual displays, it is clear that

FIGURE 30.1 Continued.

mixed methods researchers have an even wider array of visual displays at their disposal than do both quantitative researchers and qualitative researchers. (p. ii)

17. Report results, including meta-inferences. Crossover displays and joint displays can be used both to enhance the readers' understanding of the data and to yield meta-inferences. Reporting the results from a mixed method study can be challenging. To better understand writing mixed methods reports, Leech (2015) investigated nine textbooks and chapters: Creswell and Plano Clark (2011); Dahlberg, Wittink, and Gallo (2010); Greene (2007); Hesse-Biber (2010); Johnson and Onwuegbuzie (2011); Morse and Niehaus (2009); O'Cathain (2009); Sandelowski (2003); and Teddlie and Tashakkori (2009). From a qualitative analysis, twelve themes were identified:

There are multiple ways to present a mixed research study

Start with and clearly state the research questions

Know and write for your audience

Work from an outline and allow for possible emergent changes

Know and state your epistemological assumptions

Respect both paradigms

Be aware of issues regarding social justice

Delineate why a mixed research study design was used

Discuss how the data are combined and integrated

Use displays (e.g., tables, quotes, etc.) when presenting the findings

Be sure to integrate your results and include meta-inferences

If you use a research team, be sure to communicate, especially about the

FIGURE 30.1 Continued.

added a variable from the quantitative data set for whether the respondent indicated they were in a rural or not rural school (see the first column in the data set). The second column is "record_id," which indicates the respondent's data that we have. This would assist us if we want to match the newly quantitized qualitative data with the quantitative data we collected.

Step 12 is to select statistical analyses. As stated previously, our research question for this example was: Do teachers choose to teach in rural areas for different reasons than teachers who

SPSS for Mixed Analysis

integration. (Leech, 2015, p. 870)

Furthermore, the most recent edition of the APA manual (2020) includes specifics on reporting results.

FIGURE 30.1 Continued.

teach in urban areas? From the constant comparison analysis and the classical content analysis, we identified 24 codes for not rural teachers and 20 codes for rural teachers. We decided to check whether there were statistically significant differences between rural and not rural teachers with respect to the frequency of each code. There were two variables of interest for each analysis. One variable was "rural or not," which represented a nominal variable with two levels (i.e., rural or not rural). The other variable was the code with each participant having a "1" for having that code or a "0" for not having the code, thereby making this variable nominal with two levels. Due to each variable being nominal with two levels, the nonparametric phi test is appropriate (Morgan et al., 2020).

Step 13 is to check all data for assumptions. The variables are nominal and hence are more qualitative-type variables; therefore, normality is not an assumption. There is the assumption

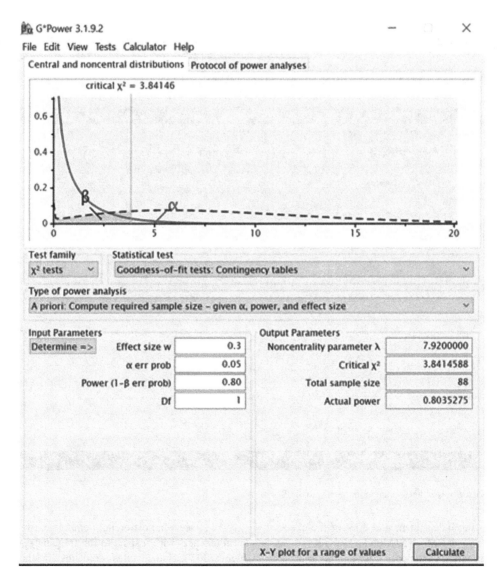

FIGURE 30.2 G*power calculation for Chi-square/Phi test.

370   N. L. Leech

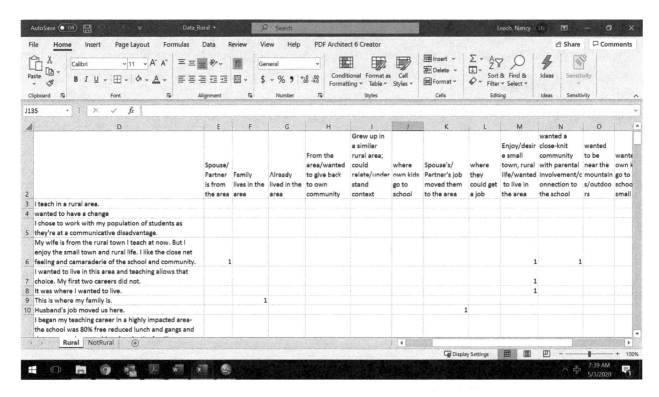

FIGURE 30.3 A section of the Excel spreadsheet used for classical content analysis.

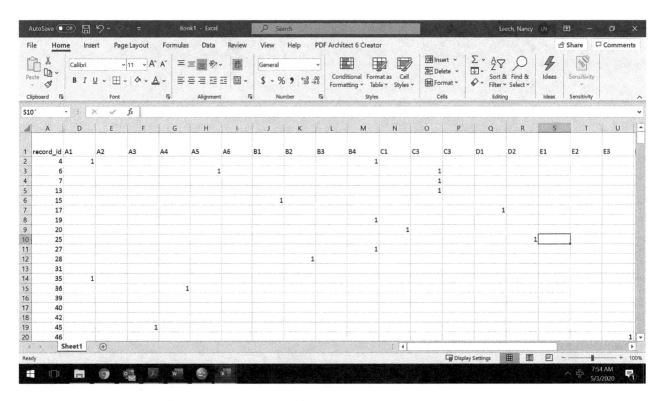

FIGURE 30.4 The Excel spreadsheet edited for importing to SPSS.

of observations being independent and 80% of the expected frequencies must be greater than 5 (Morgan et al., 2020). SPSS provides this information on the output for the phi tests.

Step 14 is conduct the "statistical" analyses. Based on these qualitative analyses, a simple bar graph was created as a visual display to see what differences emerge between rural and not rural teachers with respect to the frequency of each code (see Figure 30.7). Some codes were not similar across the two groups. Therefore, only a sample of the codes that were similar are compared in the figure.

SPSS for Mixed Analysis

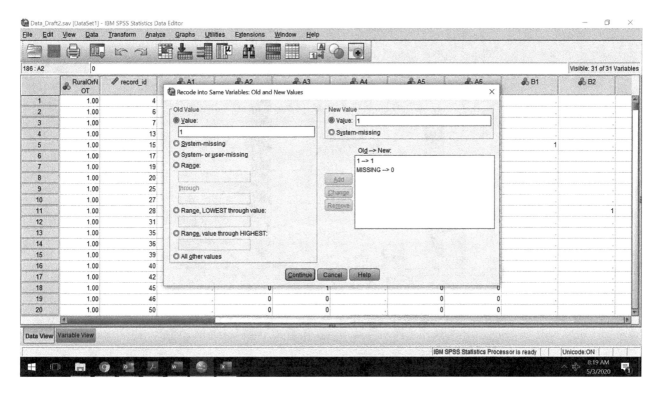

FIGURE 30.5 Recoding in SPSS.

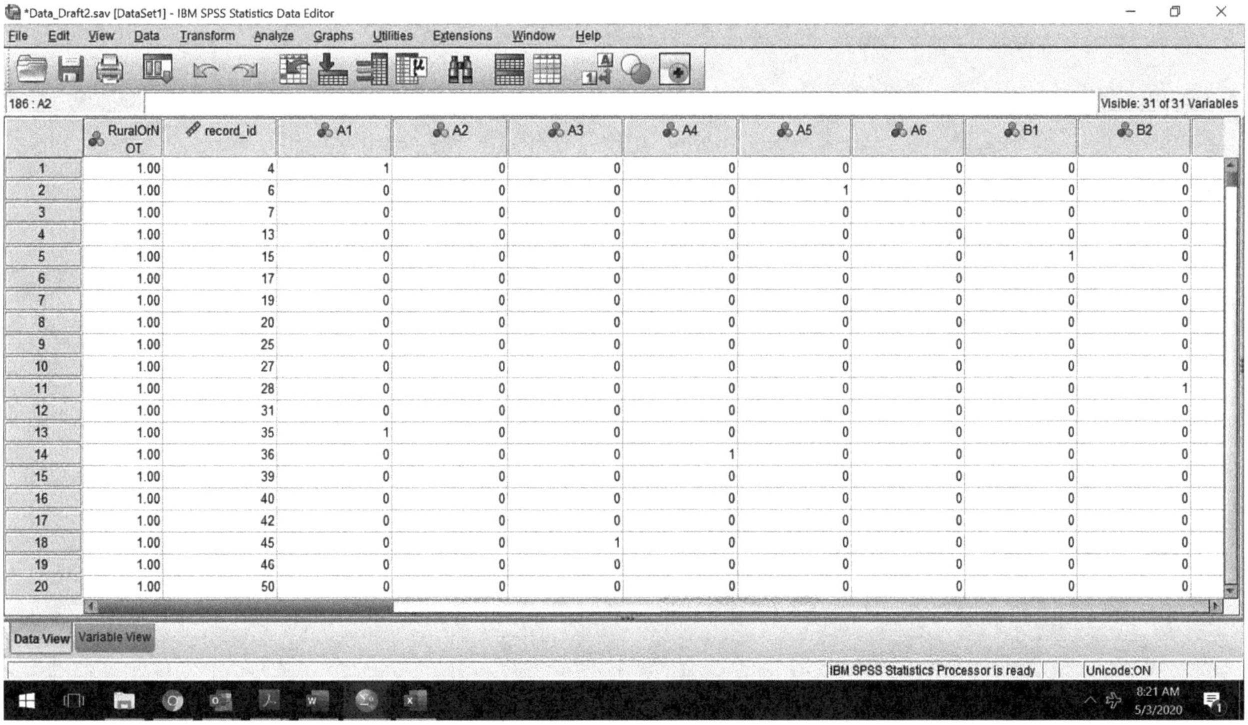

FIGURE 30.6 The data in SPSS.

Based on the visual display, we conducted seven phi tests to assess whether there were statistically significant differences between rural and not rural teachers with respect to the frequency of the similar codes that were used across the two groups. A phi test in SPSS is conducted by using the path Analyze→ Descriptive Statistics → Cross tabs. Output from one of the phi tests is shown in Figure 8.

The output shows that the phi analysis was statistically significant. Thus, there was a statistically significant difference between rural and not rural participants with respect to the

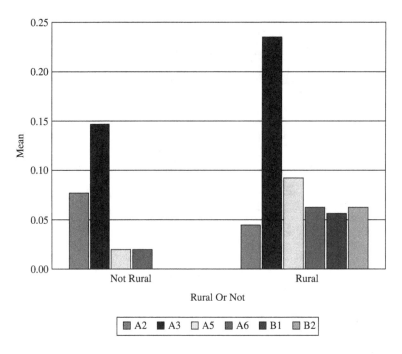

FIGURE 30.7 Visual display of a section of the data split by rural or not rural.

Crosstab

			RuralOrNOT		Total
			Not Rural	Rural	
A5	0	Count	154	305	459
		Expected Count	146.2	312.8	459.0
		% within RuralOrNOT	98.1%	90.8%	93.1%
	1	Count	3	31	34
		Expected Count	10.8	23.2	34.0
		% within RuralOrNOT	1.9%	9.2%	6.9%
Total		Count	157	336	493
		Expected Count	157.0	336.0	493.0
		% within RuralOrNOT	100.0%	100.0%	100.0%

Symmetric Measures

		Value	Approximate Significance
Nominal by Nominal	Phi	.134	.003
	Cramer's V	.134	.003
N of Valid Cases		493	

Note. The variable analyzed in this output (A5) is the code "Grew up in the area or similar one; could relate/understand context."

FIGURE 30.8 Phi output from SPSS.

Crossover Display of Results

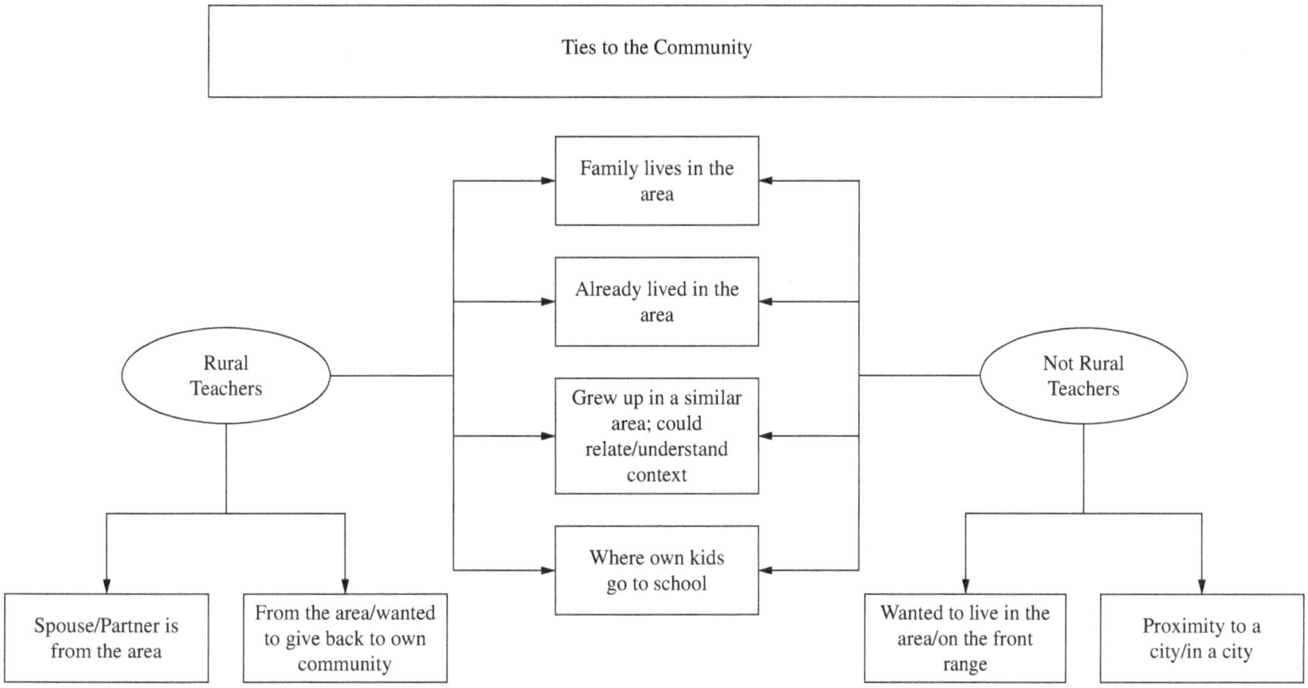

FIGURE 30.9 Crossover display of results.

number of participants who responded to the "family lives in the area" reason for choosing the area in which they taught. This is written as, phi = .13, p = .003. Phi can also be used as an effect size; for this example, a phi of .13 would indicate a small effect. Specifically, a statistically significantly greater proportion of rural teachers (9.2%) chose to teach in the area due to family living there than did non-rural teachers (1.9%).

Step 15 is to assess post-hoc statistical power for chosen analyses. This would have been an important step if the a priori power had been low or if the results of the analysis had not been statistically significant (Onwuegbuzie & Leech, 2004). Due to finding statistical significance, post-hoc power does not need to be calculated.

Step 16 is to compare separate qualitative and quantitative results and results from mixed analyses. Figure 30.9, a crossover display, was created to better understand the relationship among the codes. The lines and arrowheads indicate which themes are connected to each of the samples. The bolded arrows indicate a statistically significant difference between rural and not rural teacher groups.

Finally, Step 17, report results, including meta-inferences, will be accomplished via a journal article, wherein we will report the entirety of the results.

5 Suggested Applications of SPSS for Mixed Analysis in MMR

There are multiple mixed analyses to conduct with SPSS. Virtually all mixed analyses that involve a parametric member of the General Linear Model (GLM) can be facilitated by SPSS (Leech et al., 2015). Furthermore, an array of nonparametric mixed analyses can be conducted via SPSS (Leech & Onwuegbuzie, 2019). Finally, Bayesian statistics can now be conducted via SPSS. Table 30.2 presents how to use SPSS to conduct the mixed analyses that can be found in other chapters of this book.

6 Strengths and Limitations of SPSS for Mixed Analysis in MMR

SPSS has strengths and limitations for conducting mixed analysis. There are limitations to using SPSS for mixed analysis. One limitation is quantizing qualitative research (Tashakkori & Teddlie, 1998) or qualitizing quantitative data (Onwuegbuzie & Leech, 2019; Onwuegbuzie & Teddlie, 2003; Sandelowski, et al., 2009; Tashakkori & Teddlie, 1998) is not taught in most doctoral programs and, therefore, many researchers are unfamiliar with these techniques; consequently, it can be a difficult step to prepare mixed methods data for analysis with SPSS. When data are prepared for mixed methods analysis with SPSS, the qualitative data need to be quantitized and then entered into SPSS. This extra step can increase some researchers' motivation to choose to conduct a parallel analysis, or what some researchers term independent analysis (Schoonenboom & Johnson, 2017), wherein the qualitative data and quantitative data are analyzed separately. Another limitation is that SPSS is most efficient for conducting quantitative analysis. SPSS has an additional add-on package for traditional qualitative/text analysis, *SPSS Text Analytics for Surveys* (SPSS Text Analytics for Surveys, n.d.). Another

TABLE 30.2

SPSS Menus for Mixed Analyses

Mixed Analysis	SPSS icon/path/menu for conducting these analyses
Exploratory Factor Analysis and Principal Component Analysis of Qualitative Data (Jim Van Haneghan)	ANALYZE→DIMENSION REDUCTION→FACTOR
Correspondence Analysis of Qualitative Data (Wendy Dickinson)	ANALYZE→DIMENSION REDUCTION→CORRESPONDENCE ANALYSIS
Multidimensional Scaling of Qualitative Data (Ahmet Suerdem)	ANALYZE→SCALE
Cluster Analysis of Qualitative Data (Normand Peladeau)	ANALYZE→CLASSIFY
Chi-Square Automatic Interaction Detection Analysis of Qualitative Data (Kathleen Collins)	ANALYZE→CLASSIFY→TREE
Multiple Regression Analysis of Qualitative Data (John Hitchcock et al.)	ANALYZE→REGRESSION
Hierarchical Linear Modeling with Qualitative Data (John Hitchcock et al.)	ANALYZE→MIXED MODELS
Bayesian Analyses with Qualitative Data (Prathiba Natesan)	ANALYZE→BAYESIAN STATISTICS
Canonical Correlation Analysis of Qualitative Data (Tony Onwuegbuzie)	ANALYZE→GENERAL LINEAR MODEL→MULTIVARIATE
Item Response Theory with Qualitative Data (Vanessa Scherman)	Rasch extension for SPSS available for download from https://www.ibm.com/support/pages/item-response-theoryrasch-models-spss-statistics
Diachronic Analysis of Qualitative Data (M. Teresa Anguera)	Any quantitative techniques for categorical data

more practical limitation of SPSS is that it is very expensive to purchase (requiring payment each year) and, therefore, it is not available to many individuals over a period of time, especially people living in developing nations.

There are many strengths of using SPSS for mixed analysis. SPSS is well known across the world and a trusted computer program (Crossman, 2018). As shown in this chapter, SPSS can be used for many mixed analyses. Multiple mixed analyses are available to conduct with SPSS, AMOS, and other add-ons (IBM SPSS Software, n.d.).

7 Resources for Learning More About SPSS for Mixed Analysis

You can download a free trial of SPSS from www.ibm.com/products/spss-statistics

You can watch the following videos to learn more about SPSS:
www.youtube.com/watch?v=_zFBUfZEBWQ
www.youtube.com/watch?v=uCmC0LfB8Vs

Websites and slides on mixed analysis can be obtained from the following sources:

www.ualberta.ca/international-institute-for-qualitative-methodology/media-library/international-institute-of-qualitative-methods/webinars/pbazeleyint-mm-analysis.pdf

Onwuegbuzie, A. J., & Hitchcock, J. H. (2015). Advanced mixed analysis approaches. In S. N. Hesse-Biber & R. B. Johnson (Eds.), *Oxford handbook of multimethod and mixed methods research* (pp. 275–395). New York, NY: Oxford University Press.

REFERENCES

Berelson, B. (1952). *Content analysis in communicative research.* New York, NY: Free Press.

Berger, J.-L., & D'Ascoli, Y. (2012). Becoming a VET teacher as a second career: Investigating the determinants of career choice and their relation to perceptions and prior occupation. *Asia-Pacific Journal of Teacher Education, 40,* 317–341. doi:10.1080/1359866X.2012.700046

Collins, K. M. T., Onwuegbuzie, A. J., & Sutton, I. L. (2006). A model incorporating the rationale and purpose for conducting mixed methods research in special education and beyond. *Learning Disabilities: A Contemporary Journal, 4,* 67–100.

Combs, J. P., & Onwuegbuzie, A. J. (2010). Describing and illustrating data analysis in mixed research. *International Journal of Education, 2,* 1–23. Retrieved from www.macrothink.org/journal/index.php/ije/article/viewFile/526/392

Creswell, J. W., & Plano Clark, V. L. (2011). *Design and conducting mixed methods research* (2nd ed.). Thousand Oaks, CA: Sage.

Crossman, A. (2018, February). *A review of software tools for quantitative data analysis: How to get started with statistical analysis.* Retrieved from www.thoughtco.com/quantitative-analysis-software-review-3026539

Dahlberg, B., Wittink, M. N., & Gallo, J. J. (2010). Funding and publishing integrated studies: Writing effective mixed methods manuscripts and grant proposals. In A. Tashakkori & C. Teddlie (Eds.), *Handbook of mixed methods in social and behavioral science* (2nd ed.) (pp. 775–802). Thousand Oaks, CA: Sage.

Faul, F., Erdfelder, E., Buchner, A., & Lang, A. (2009). Statistical power analyses using G*Power 3.1: Tests for correlation and regression analyses. *Behavior Research Methods, 41,* 1149–1160. doi:10.3758/brm.41.4.1149

Fetters, M. D., Curry, L. A., & Creswell, J. W. (2013). Achieving integration in mixed methods designs. Principles and practice. *Health Services Research, 48,* 2134–2156. doi:10.1111/1475–6773.12117

Fetters, M. D., & Freshwater, D. (2015). The 1+1=3 integration challenge. *Journal of Mixed Methods Research, 9*, 115–117. doi:10.1177/1558689815581222

Fokkens-Bruinsma, M., & Canrinus, E. T. (2012). The factors influencing teaching (FIT)-Choice scale in a Dutch teacher education program. *Asia-Pacific Journal of Teacher Education, 40*, 249–269. doi:10.1080/1359866X.2012.700043

Glaser, B. G., & Strauss, A. L. (1967). *The discovery of grounded theory: Strategies for qualitative research*. New York, NY: Aldine de Gruyter.

Greene, J. C. (2007). *Mixed methods in social inquiry*. San Francisco, CA: Jossey-Bass.

Greene, J. C., Caracelli, V. J., & Graham, W. F. (1989). Toward a conceptual framework for mixed-method evaluation designs. *Educational Evaluation and Policy Analysis, 11*, 255–274. doi:10.2307/1163620

Guetterman, T. C., Fetters, M. D., & Creswell, J. W. (2015). Integrating quantitative and qualitative results in health science mixed methods research through joint displays. *Annals of Family Medicine, 13*, 554–561. doi:10.1370/afm.1865

Hesse-Biber, S. (2010). *Mixed methods research: Merging theory with practice*. New York, NY: Guilford.

Hitchcock, J. H., & Onwuegbuzie, A. J. (2019). Developing mixed methods crossover analysis approaches. *Journal of Mixed Methods Research*. Advance online publication. doi:10.1177/1558689819841782

IBM SPSS Software. (n.d.). Retrieved from www.ibm.com/analytics/spss-statistics-Software

Johnson, R. B., & Christensen, L. (2020). *Educational research: Quantitative, qualitative, and mixed approaches* (7th ed.). Thousand Oaks, CA: Sage.

Johnson, R. E., Grove, A. L., & Clarke, A. (2019). Pillar Integration Process: A joint display technique to integrate data in mixed methods research. *Journal of Mixed Methods Research, 13*, 301–320. doi:10.1177/1558689817743108

Johnson, R. B., & Onwuegbuzie, A. J. (2011). Mixed research. In R. B. Johnson & L. B. Christensen (Eds.), *Educational research: Quantitative, qualitative, and mixed approaches* (4th ed., pp. 439–459). Thousand Oaks, CA: Sage.

Leech, N. L., Barrett, K. C., & Morgan, G. A. (2015). *IBM SPSS for intermediate statistics: Use and interpretation* (5th ed.). New York, NY: Taylor and Francis.

Leech, N. L., Haug, C. A., & Gold, M. (2020). *Why do teachers remain teaching in rural districts?* [Manuscript in preparation.] School of Education and Human Development, University of Colorado Denver.

Leech, N. L., & Haug, C. A. (2015). Validating the FIT-Choice scale with in-service teachers in the United States. *Teacher Education & Practice, 28*, 548–560.

Leech, N. L., Haug, C. A., Ridgewell, N., & Rubin, W. (2019). Motivation to teach in the current climate: An examination of three school districts in transition. *Journal of Education, 200*(2), 75–88. doi:10.1177/0022057419875125

Leech, N. L., & Onwuegbuzie, A. J. (2007). An array of qualitative analysis tools: A call for data analysis triangulation. *School Psychology Quarterly, 22*, 557–584. https://doi.org/10.1037/1045-3830/22/4/557

Leech, N. L., & Onwuegbuzie, A. J. (2009). A typology of mixed methods research designs. *Quality and Quantity: International Journal of Methodology, 43*, 265–275. doi:10.1007/s11135-007-9105-3

Leech, N. L., & Onwuegbuzie, A. J. (2019). A call for greater use of nonparametric statistics. *Research in the Schools, 26*(2), xiii-xxvi.

Lin, E., Shi, Q., Wang, J., Zhang, S., & Hui, L. (2012). Initial motivation for teaching: Comparison between preservice teachers in the United States and China. *Asia-Pacific Journal of Teacher Education, 40*, 227–248. doi:10.1080/1359866X.2012.700047

Miles, M., & Huberman, A. M. (1994). *Qualitative data analysis: An expanded sourcebook* (2nd ed.). Thousand Oaks, CA: Sage.

Miles, M. B., Huberman, A. M., & Saldaña, J. (2020). *Qualitative data analysis: A methods sourcebook* (4th ed.). Thousand Oaks, CA: Sage.

Morgan, G. A., Barrett, K. C., Leech, N. L., & Gloeckner, G. W. (2020). *IBM SPSS for introductory statistics: Use and interpretation*. New York, NY: Routledge.

Morse, J. M., & Niehaus, L. (2009) *Mixed method design: Principles and procedures*. Walnut Creek, CA: Left Coast Press.

O'Cathain, A. (2009). Reporting mixed methods projects. In S. Andrew & E. J. Halcomb (Eds.), *Mixed methods research for nursing and the health sciences* (pp. 135–158). Oxford, UK: Wiley/Blackwell.

Onwuegbuzie, A. J. (2017a, March). *Mixed methods is dead! Long live mixed methods!* Invited keynote address presented at the Mixed Methods International Research Association Caribbean Conference at Montego Bay, Jamaica.

Onwuegbuzie, A. J., & Combs, J. P. (2010). Emergent data analysis techniques in mixed methods research: A synthesis. In A. Tashakkori & C. Teddlie (Eds.), *SAGE handbook of mixed methods in social and behavioral research* (2nd ed., pp. 397–430). Thousand Oaks, CA: Sage.

Onwuegbuzie, A. J., & Combs, J. P. (2011). Data analysis in mixed research: A primer. *International Journal of Education, 3*(1), E13. doi:10.5296/ije.v3i1.618

Onwuegbuzie, A. J., Daniel, L. G., & Collins, K. M. T. (2009). A meta-validation model for assessing the score-validity of student teacher evaluations. *Quality & Quantity: International Journal of Methodology, 43*, 197–209. doi:10.1007/s11135-007-9112-4

Onwuegbuzie, A. J., & Dickinson, W. B. (2008). Mixed methods analysis and information visualization: Graphical display for effective communication of research results. *The Qualitative Report, 13*, 204–225. Retrieved from www.nova.edu/ssss/QR/QR13-2/Onwuegbuzie.pdf

Onwuegbuzie, A. J., & Hitchcock, J. H. (2015). Advanced mixed analysis approaches. In S. N. Hesse-Biber & R. B. Johnson (Eds.), *Oxford handbook of multimethod and mixed methods research* (pp. 275–395). New York, NY: Oxford University Press.

Onwuegbuzie, A. J., & Hitchcock, J. H. (2019). Toward a fully integrated approach to mixed methods research via the 1 + 1 = 1 integration approach: Mixed Research 2.0. *International Journal of Multiple Research Approaches, 11*, 1–6. doi:10.29034/ijmra.v11n1editorial1

Onwuegbuzie, A. J., & Hwang, E. (2019a). Editorial: Frequency in the use of visual displays and its predictability of the editor's decision of manuscripts submitted to *Research in the Schools*. *Research in the Schools*, *26*(1), i–x.

Onwuegbuzie, A. J., & Hwang, E. (2019b). Writing style, readability, and communication vagueness as a predictor of the use of visual displays among manuscripts submitted to *Research in the Schools*. *Research in the Schools*, *26*(2), i–xiii.

Onwuegbuzie, A. J., & Johnson, R. B. (2006). The validity issue in mixed research. *Research in the Schools*, *13*(1), 48–63.

Onwuegbuzie, A. J., & Leech, N. L. (2004). Post-hoc power: A concept whose time has come. *Understanding Statistics*, *3*, 201–230. doi:10.1207/s15328031us0304_1

Onwuegbuzie, A. J., & Leech, N. L. (2019). On qualitizing. *International Journal of Multiple Research Approaches*, *11*, 98–128. doi:10.29034/ijmra.v11n2editorial2

Onwuegbuzie, A. J., Leech, N. L., & Collins, K. M. T. (2011). Toward a new era for conducting mixed analyses: The role of quantitative dominant and qualitative dominant crossover mixed analyses. In M. Williams & W. P. Vogt (Eds.), *The SAGE handbook of innovation in social research methods* (pp. 353–384). Thousand Oaks, CA: Sage.

Onwuegbuzie, A. J., Slate, J. R., Leech, N. L., & Collins, K. M. T. (2007). Conducting mixed analyses: A general typology. *International Journal of Multiple Research Approaches*, *1*, 4–17. doi:10.5172/mra.455.1.1.4

Onwuegbuzie, A. J., Slate, J. R., Leech, N. L., & Collins, K. M. T. (2009). Mixed data analysis: Advanced integration techniques. *International Journal of Multiple Research Approaches*, *3*, 13–33. doi:10.5172/mra.455.3.1.13

Onwuegbuzie, A. J., & Teddlie, C. (2003). A framework for analyzing data in mixed methods research. In A. Tashakkori & C. Teddlie (Eds.), *Handbook of mixed methods in social and behavioral research* (pp. 351–383). Thousand Oaks, CA: Sage.

Saldaña, J. (2013). *The coding manual for qualitative researchers* (2nd ed.). Thousand Oaks, CA: Sage.

Sandelowski, M. (2003). Tables or tableaux? The challenges of writing and reading mixed methods studies. In A. Tashakkori & C. Teddlie (Eds.), *Handbook of mixed methods in social and behavioral sciences*. Thousand Oaks, CA: Sage.

Sandelowski, M., Voils, C. I., & Knafl, G. (2009). On quantitizing. *Journal of Mixed Methods Research*, *3*, 208–222. doi:10.1177/1558689809334210

Schoonenboom, J., & Johnson, R. B. (2017). How to construct a mixed methods research design. *Kölner Zeitschrift für Soziologie und Sozialpsychologie (Cologne Journal for Sociology and Social Psychology)*, *69*(2), 107–131.

Tashakkori, A. M., Johnson, R. B., & Teddlie, C. B. (2021). *Foundations of mixed methods research: Integrating quantitative and qualitative approaches in the social and behavioral sciences* (2nd ed.). Los Angeles, CA: Sage.

Tashakkori, A., & Teddlie, C. (1998). Mixed methodology: Combining qualitative and quantitative approaches. *Applied Social Research Methods Series* (Vol. 46). Thousand Oaks, CA: Sage.

Teddlie, C., & Tashakkori, A. (2009). *Foundations of mixed methods research: Integrating quantitative and qualitative techniques in the social and behavioral sciences*. Thousand Oaks, CA: Sage.

Tufte, E. R. (2001). *The visual display of quantitative information* (2nd ed.). Cheshire, CT: Graphics Press.

Valsiner, J. (2000). Data as representations: Contextualizing qualitative and quantitative research strategies. *Social Science Information*, *39*, 99–113. doi:10.1177/053901800039001006

Watt, H. M. G., & Richardson, P. W. (2007). Motivational factors influencing teaching as a career choice: Development and validation of the FIT-Choice scale. *The Journal of Experimental Education*, *75*, 167–202. doi:10.3200/JEXE.75.3.167-202

Watt, H. M. G., & Richardson, P. W. (2008). Motivations, perceptions, and aspirations concerning teaching as a career for different types of beginning teachers. *Learning and Instruction*, *18*, 408–428. doi:10.1016/j.learninstruc.2008.06.002

Watt, H. M. G., & Richardson, P. W. (2012). Special issue on "Teaching motivations in different countries: Comparisons using the FIT-Choice scale." *Asia-Pacific Journal of Teacher Education*, *40*, 185–197. doi:10.1080/1359866X.2012.700049

Index

Note: bold page numbers indicate tables; italic page numbers indicate figures; numbers containing n refer to notes.

A

a posteriori decisions 2, 109
a priori decisions 2, 50, 80, *177*, 178, *358*, *365*
Abrams, K. 114
Abrams, S. S. 2, 223, 240, *241*, 243, 250–251
ADAPT-IT joint display study 262–273, *271*, *272*; box plots in 265–266, *266*, *267*, 267, 268, 269, 272, 273; color in 268–269, *269*; data analysis in 262; data collection using VAS in 262, *263*, 264, 265, 266, *266*, 267, 268; grayscale in 272–273, *272*; and intra-method analysis 260, 261, 262, 264, 265; and intuitive restructuring 266–267, *268*; iterations of 265–273; labelling in 269–270, *270*; meta-joint display in 270, *271*; meta-inferences in 270–272, *272*; and mixed methods analysis 264; overview 262–264, *263*, **263**, *264*; participants in 262; as side-by-side joint display 273
Agapito, D. 74–75
Aggarwal, P. 242
Agresti, A. 79, 85
agricultural research 173, 174–175
Aguiló, M. J. 74
AI (artificial intelligence) 52–54, *53*, 95, 252
Aiken, L. S. 85
Álamos-Concha, P. 192
Algina, J. 121
algorithms 11, 29, 31, 47, 48, 93, 95; and Bayesian analysis 109; and cluster analysis 57; decision tree *see* CHAID; machine learning 291, 300, 355; minimization 185; and social media analytics 219, 220, 223
Ali, M. 192
Allen, J. 57
Amaury, N. 93
AMOS 89, 96, **357**, 374
analysis phases 361, *361*; data analysis 142, 167, 283; data collection 117, 264; interpretation 2, *3*, *4*, 141, 142, 144, 355; mixed analysis phase 14–16; qualitative *see* qualitative phase; quantitative *see* qualitative phase; research design 2, 80, 355
analytic memos 155, 156–159, 160
analytical methods 4, 9, 193, 223, 335
Andendelfer, M. S. 66–67
Anderson, R. E. 17
Andrich, D. 120
Angrove, K. E. 248
Anguera, M. T. 135
animal behaviour research 135
Annechino, R. 332

ANOVA (analysis of variance) **6**, **357**, *363*, *364*
Antin, T. M. J. 332
API (application programming interface) 220, 221, 222, 294
Arab women, conceptualization in newspapers of 165
Arabie, P. 54
ArcGIS 231, 232, 235, 294
ArcMap 230
ArcView 234
Armat, M. R. 337
artificial intelligence (AI) 52–54, *53*, 95, 252
Assarroudi, A. 337
Atkins, D. P. 338
ATLAS.ti 13, 128, 167, 228, 231–232, 331–340, *363*; applications of 332, 337–339; and data analysis/coding 331, 332, 335–336; and data management 331, 332; definition/language/concepts of 331–332; empirical demonstration of 333–336, *334*; and Evernote 331, 333; and geodata 332, 333, *334*; and importing/exporting data 331, 333, 335, 338–339; and inductive/deductive reasoning 331, 337, 339; learning resources for 339–340; and literature reviews 331, 333–335; memo writing in 336; and qualitizing/quantitizing 337–338; strengths/limitations of 339; technical outline of 332–333; and visual/textual reports 339; and word counts/clouds 335, *336*, *337*
audio data 10, 89, 125, 128, 305, 320, 331, 347
autism research 110–113, 125, 132–133
Aversa, P. 192
Avery, L. M. 279, 283, 285
axiologies 141, 145, 220, 222–223, 243
Azzam, T. 37, 41

B

Baas, L. R. 206
Badiee, M. 143
Baguley, T. 81, 82, 85
Bakeman, R. 126, 130, 135
Balemba, S. 74
Ball, S. 230
Barcelona GIS case study 230–234, *232*, *233*; context 231; data collection/preparation 231; data handling/analysis 231–232; results 232–234, *233*
Bardot, A. 46
Barlow, E. A. 93

Barrett, K. C. *358*
Barroso, J. 159
Baumer, E. P. S. 293
Bauwens, J. 191–192
Bayesian analysis 1, **6**, 8, 9, 14, 15, 109–114, *373*, **374**; applications of 113; defined 109; and diachronic analysis 126–127; distributional information provided by 109, *110*, 111, **112**; empirical demonstration of 112–113; equation of 109, 126; learning resources for 114; meta- 10, 143; and Poisson distribution 111, 113; and posterior distribution 109, 110, 112, 113, 126; and rate ratio effect size 113, *113*; sample size for 110, 111, 113, 114; and SCED 111, 112, 113, 114; and SEM 91, 93, 96; strengths/limitations of 113–114; suitability for MMR of 2–3; technical outline of 111–112
Bazeley, P. 235, 261, 317, 343, 344, 354
Beach, D. 189
Beach, P. 252
Beauregard, E. 74
Beck, K. A. 174, 180
Beh, E. J. 37
behavioural sciences research 77, 89, 110–113, 125, 135
Beile, P. 334
Bell, B. A. 104
Bellis, M. A. 38
Bentler, P. M. 93
Benzécri, J. P. 38
Berg, B. L. 332
Berg-Schlosser, D. 192–193
Bernard, H. R. 25, 180
Bernauer, J. A. 335
big data 51, 91, 93, 317
biology 57, 61
bitmojios 15, 242
bivariate associations 16–17
bivariate regression 77, 79, 80–81
Black, W. C. 17
Blanco-Villaseñor, A. 35
Blashfield, R. K. 66–67
Blasius, J. 41
blogs 142, 243, 294, 296, 301
Blunch, N. J. 96
Boedeker, P. 114
Bond, T. G. 121
Bonferroni adjustment 9, 71, 72
Boolean logic 11, 28, 185
Boote, D. N. 334
Booth, Charles 228–229
Borg, I. 47, 55
Borgatti, S. P. 174, 214
Borja, J. 230

377

Borko, H. 25
Bosker, R. 100, 106
both-and logic 3, 7, 143
Bourke, Sid 168
box plots 265–266, *266*, 267, *267*, 268, 269, 272, 273
Bradt, J. 259–260
Breslin, F. C. 175
Brier, A. 52
Britain (UK) 52–54, *53*, 75, 228–229
Bronfenbrenner, U. 244
Brouwer, J. 213
Brown, I. 174
Brown, S. R. 200, 201, 207
Brown, T. A. 89
Bryk, A. S. 101, 106
Bryman, A. 306, 308
Buck, D. 45
Buckendahl, C. W. 286
Buckley, J. 114
Burnett, C. 240–241
Burton, L. 230
business/commercial research 73, 74–75, 173, 174
Bustamante, C. 286
Bustamante, R. M. 121
Byers, V. T. 246–247, 248, 249
Byrne, B. M. 96

C

CA (correspondence analysis) **6**, 15, 37–44, 144, 246, 292; conceptual demonstration of 38–39; and contingency tables 37, 38, 39, 40; and criminal justice 40–41, *40*, 44, **44**; defined 37; and display types 37; and drawings/visual art 37, 38; and epidemiology 39–40; interdisciplinary uses of 39; learning resources for 41, **41**; and mosaic displays 37, 38; and NVC analysis 246, 248, 249, *250*; and software 37, 38, 39, 40, **41**, 43–44, 352, 353, *353*, **357**, **374**; and spatial maps 37, 38, 39, 41; strengths/limitations of 41, **41**; suitability of MMR of 37–38; technical outline of 38; three-dimensional visualizations in 39; and visual/narrative clarity 38–39
Campbell, D. T. 253
cancer research 155–156, 159, 174, 259–260, 282, 286
canonical correlation analysis 4, 14, **374**
CAQDAS (Computer-Assisted Qualitative Data Analysis Software) 228, 232, 301, 305, 331, 332, 335, 337, *see also* ATLAS.ti; MAXQDA
Caracelli, V. J. 148, 240, *358*
Carbonell, K. B. 11
Carrington, P. J. 210
Carroll, J. D. 54
Casarrubea, M. 135
case comparison tables 12, 15, 277–286; analysis in, guidelines for 284–285; applications of 282–283; and category development 283; constructing/sorting, guidelines for 280, 283–286; defined 277; empirical demonstration of **278**, 280–282, *281*; heuristics for analysis of *281*, *282*; and hypothesis/theory development 283; learning resources for 286; and mixed tables 277–279, 280; and profile development 283; as simple tables 277, **278**, 279–280, **279**; strengths/limitations of 286; suitability for MMR of 277–279; technical outline of 279–280; testing outcomes in 286–287; three data types in 280
case-to-case transfer 2, 11, 355
causal networks **6**, 246
causation coding 5, **6**, 155
CDA (critical discourse analysis) 10, 162, **162**, 166, 168
central tendency 4, 7, 148, 245
centroids: and cluster analysis 60, 61; and Q methodology 200–201, 203, **203**, 204, **204**, 205–206, **205**
CFA (confirmatory factor analysis) 9, 89, 90–91, **90**, 92, 93, 362, *362*
CHAID (chi-square automatic interaction detection) **6**, 9–10, 15, 69–75, **357**, **374**; analysis process 70–71; applications in MMR of 73–75; as criterion-based model 71; and data mining process 69–70; defined 69; display of results 69, 70, 72; exhaustive 71, 74; learning resources for 75; predictive modeling in 69, 70, 71; and qualitative research process 70; sample size for 70, 71; strengths/limitations of 75; suitability for MMR of 71; technical outline of 71–72
Chakrabarti, P. 27, 33, 34
Chan, F. 74
Chan, W. S. 93
change, theory of 344, *345*
Charmaz, K. 321, 336
Chawla, P. 244
Chen, Y. 244
Cheung, F. M. 117
chi-square tests 15, 147, 292, 298, *364*, 369, *see also* CHAID
children 38, 173, 174, **178**, 250; autistic 110–113, 125, 132–133; and Internet safety 191–192; and kindergarten 82, 83–84, **83**, 101–102, 104, **105**, 107; of parents in prison 40–41, *40*, 44, **44**; and school readiness 324, 325–327, *see also* education research
Chile 166
China 52–54, *53*, 242, 252, 325
Christensen, L. 253, 259, *362*
Christensen, W. 85
Cisneros-Puebla, C. 234, 294
citizen research 234
Clark, P. 38
Clarke, A. 12, 259, 261, 274, 286, *367*
classical content analysis 173, 295, 334; and NVC analysis 243, 245, 248; and qualitizing data 144, 145; and SPSS 363, 364–365, 369
classification trees 69, 70, 72, 74, 75
climate change research 308, 314, 315
cloud-based applications 319, *see also* Dedoose
cluster analysis **6**, 28, 50, 53, 57–67, 144, 148, 352, 353, **357**, **374**; applications of 64–66; bag-of-words approach 66; and co-occurrence matrix 58–59, 60–61, 65, 66; defined 57; and dendrograms 59–61, *60*, 63, *64*; example, for identifying topics 63; example, for participant sampling 62–63, *63*; hierarchical methods *see* hierarchical clustering; and iterative partitioning 61; k-means method 9, 53, 61, 64, 66; learning resources for 66–67; and linkages 60, *60*; number of clusters in, choosing 61–62, 63; and Q-mode analysis 58, 62, 63, 64; and R-mode analysis 58, 62, 63, 64, 65; sample size for 57; and silhouette analysis 62, *62*, 63, *63*, 65; and similarity measurement 58–59; strengths/limitations of 66; suitability for MMR of 57–58; technical outline of 58–62; and text mining 58, 59, 61; twostep 9, 15, 147; Ward's method 60, 62, 66
Cmeciu, C. 65
co-occurrence analysis 9, 45, 58–59, 60–61, 65, 66, 296–298, *297*, 301
coding strategies *see* qualitative coding
Cohen, J./Cohen, P. 85
Coleman, J. S. 210
collaborative approach 17
Collins, K. M. T. 1, 17, 37–38, 41, 96, 136, 145, 243
ColorBrewer 235
Combs, J. P. 1–2, 3, 33, 77, 106, 117, 121, 141–142, 241, 279, 285, 337, *366–367*; and definition of mixed data analysis 355; and meta-framework 356; and sequential mixed analysis *359*
commensurability approximation legitimation 16, 17, 362
complementarity 2, 78, 84n1, 148, 344
computational linguistics 14, 252, 302
computer science 64
concept mapping 51–54, *53*, 63, 345
concurrent mixed analyses 4, **6**, 17, 71
conditioned behaviours 129, 130–131, *131*, 133, *133*, **133**
confirmatory factor analysis *see* CFA
Congdon, R. 104
constant comparison analysis 1, 4, 5, **6**, 144, 363–364
content analysis 25, 61, 151; classical *see* classical content analysis; evaluative/scaling 315; inductive/deductive 337; quantitative 117, 118, 163, 166, 293, 294–295, 299, 307, 331; software/dictionaries 291, 293, 296, 300, 301, 302, 336, *370*
content validity 11
contingency tables 37, 38, 39, 40, 83, 299, **357**, *363*

Index 379

Contractor, N. S. 214
conversion legitimation 16, *362*
Cook, T. D. 253
Cooper, B. 192
Cooper, M. C. 62
COPD (chronic obstructive pulmonary disease) 152
Cope, B. 251
Cope, M. 234
Corbin, J. 321
corporate websites 164–165, 168n6
correlation coefficients **6**, 14, 17, 58, 111, 204, 296, 324, 357
correspondence analysis *see* CA
Courcoux, P. 45
covariance matrix 10, **90**, 93, **94**
covariates 77, 83–84, **83**, **102**, 103, 104, 105, **105**, 106
COVID-19 pandemic 11, 13, 146, 147, 252–253
Cox, T. F./Cox, M. A. A. 54–55
Coxon, A. P. M. 54
Creamer, E. G. 151, 159, 160, 243
Creswell, J. W. 65–66, 117, 118, 121, 126, 259, 274, 277, 305, 314, 315, *368*
criminological research 40–41, *40*, 44, **44**, 227, 229–230
critical discourse analysis (CDA) 10, 162, **162**, 166, 168
Crocker, L. 121
cross-case analysis 1, 350
cross-tracks analysis 4
Crossley, N. 214
crossover displays 12, 147, **147**, 148, *366*, *373*
crossover mixed analyses 2, 3, 4, 5–12, **6**, 13, 16, 117; and active mixed analyses 18; applications of 16; dimensions of 5–6; inherently mixed 11–12; and non-crossover analyses 18; qualitizing in 10, 141–142, 143; quantitizing in *see* quantitizing; and SPSS 355, 356, *366–368*; strengths/limitations of 16–18
CTT (classical test theory) 119, 120
Curry, L. A. 259, 277
Curwood, J. C. 223

D

DA (discourse analysis) 161–162; corpus-based 168, 168n5; critical (CDA) 10, 162, **162**, 166, 168; mixed methodological *see* MMDA; three approaches 162, **162**, 168n3
Daigneault, P. M. 117
Daniel, L. G. 121
data condensation 70, 151
data correlation/comparison 155, 356, 361, *361*
data display 38–39, 70, 338, 361, *361*; categorical 37, 38; integrated 246
data mining 25, 26, 212, 296; and CHAID 69–70
data reduction 46, 54, 64, **90**, **205**, 335, 361, *361*
data transformation 2, 126, 159, 187, 261, 273, 311, 338; and SPSS 355, 356, 361, *361*
data visualization 37, 54, 186, 214, 220; and Dedoose 322, **322**, 326, 328

Davis, A. 209
Davoodi, E. 34
de Waal, C. 3
decision trees 9–10, 69, 173, 175, 176, 177–178, *177*, *see also* CHAID
Dedoose 12, 293, 319–329, 331, *363*; Analysis Workspace 327; applications of 327–328, *328*; and code process 321; and collaborative research 319–320, **323**, 324, 328; defined 319–320; and descriptor sets 321, *321*; empirical demonstration of 324–327, *326*, *327*; and importing/exporting files 320, 328; learning resources for 329; and security/ethics standards 320; strengths/limitations of 328; as subscription-based application 319–320; suitability for MMR of 320; technical outline of 320–324, **322**, *323*, **323**
deforestation 187–188
demographic information 13–16, 27, 34, 39, *73*, 293, 348
dendrograms 9, 59–61, *60*, 63, *64*, 297
Denham, M. A. 144, 239, 245
Denzin, N. K. 41, 70
dependence, statistical 100, 101, 119, 130
descriptive analyses 4, 7–8, 14, 70, 117, 148, 248; four measures used in 7; and NVC analysis 243, 244–245, 247, 248
descriptive coding 10, 152, 153, 158, 335
descriptive-based quantitizing 7–8, 14–15
Detwiler, J. 230
development 2, 78, 84n1, 148
Dey, I. 57
diachronic analysis **6**, 9, 10, 16, 125–136; applications of 135; and Bayesian analysis 126–127; and connecting technique 126, 129, 131, 136; defined 125–129; and design of observation instrument 127–128; and direct/indirect observation 125, 130; and diversification of quantitative analysis 129; empirical demonstration of 132–134; and focal/conditioned behaviours 129, 130, *131*, 132, *133*, **133**; and intersessional/intrasessional following 125–126; learning resources for 135–136; and multievent data 129, 135; and qualitative/quantitative data integration 1125–1126; and quantitizing 126; software for 127–128, 132–133, 135, **135**, **374**; strengths/limitations of 135; suitability for MMR of 129; technical outline of 130–132; transformation to code matrix in 126, 127–129, **127**, **128**, *see also* lag sequential analysis; polar coordinate analysis; TPA
dialectical pluralism 7
diaries 212, 227
Dice coefficient 59, 296
dichotomization 8, **357**
Dickinson, W. B. 37, 39, 147, 148, *366*

dictionary-based analysis 27, 28, 29, 30, *30*, 291, 299, 300, 301, 303, 307
digital/digitality 219, 220
Dillenbourg, P. 252
disability research 74
discourse analysis *see* DA and MMDA
discriminant analysis 9, 14
discursive psychology 10, 162, **162**, 167
distance matrixes 9, 193
distributional shape 7, 110
Dixon-Woods, M. 114
DL (deep learning) 93, 95, 96
DOLLY (Digital Online Life and You) 235, 236
Dominguez, S. 214
Doyle, S. 121
Drass, Kriss 185
drawings 10, 37
Driver, Janine 255
dummy coding 40, 80, 85, 168
Duncan, S. C./Duncan T. E. 93, 96
Durante, A. 286
DV (dependent variable) 14
Dymnicki, A. B. 57

E

Eco, U. 46
economic research 89, 210, 229
EDMs (ethnographic decision models) **6**, 11, 16, 173–181; applications of 180–181; and decision trees 173, 175, 176, *177*; defined 173; empirical demonstration of 175, 175–180; and errors in models 173, 180; and interviews/paired comparisons 174, 175, 176; learning resources for 181; recycling study *see* recycling decisions study; sample size for 173; and semi-structured interviews 173, 175; strengths/limitations of 181; suitability for MMR of 173–174; technical outline/six steps of 174–180
education research 26, 77, 80–81, 89, 125, 192, 206; and CA 38–39; and case comparison tables **278**, 280–282, *281*, 283–284; and CHAID 72–73, *72*, *73*; and coding strategies 156–159; and Dedoose 324, 325–327; and GIS 227, 229; and HLM 99, 100, 101–102, 101–105, 104, **105**, 107; and linear regression 80–81, 82, 83–84, **83**; and multiple linear regression analysis 77, 80–81, 82–84, **83**; and NVC analysis 246–251, **247**, **248**, *250*, 252; and qualitizing 146–147; and regression/quantitizing 78, 79; and SNA 210, 213; and SPSS 357–373, *358–369*
effect sizes 7, 8, 71, 80, 82, 106, 112, 357, *365*, 373; rate ratio 112, 113, *113*
EFA see exploratory factor analysis
EFI (Ecocultural Family Interview) 325
eigen equation/eigenvalues 25, 26, 47, 48
Eisner, E. W. 38
Ekman, P. 246, 247
Elo, S. 337

emojis 15, 242, 254–255
emotions 65, 74, 95, 301; and quantitizing 78
employment research 74, 125, 315
end-of-life research 175, 176–177
environmental research 165, 174, **176**, **178**, 180, 206; climate change awareness project 308, 314, 315
epidemiology 39–40, 211
epistemologies 18, 27, 145, 191, 193, 243, 337; and social media analytics 220, 221, 222, 223, 224, 225
equal-status crossover analyses 5–7, 11, 13
Escobar, M. R. 89
ESL (English as a Second Language) research **278**, 280–282, *281*
ethnicity 72, 73, *73*, 74, 175, 234, 249, 253, 296
ethnographic research 78, 193, 228, 231, 232, 325, *see also* EDMs
Euclidian space/distances 46, 47, 58, 63, 297
evaluation coding 10, 153, 154
Evans, M. 295
Everett, B. S. 67
Everett, M. G. 214
Evergreen, S. 37
Evernote 331, 333
exact tests *see* permutation tests
Excel **41**, 157, *157*, 221, 292, 294, 307, 308, 328, 338, 339, 348; and SPSS 366–368, *372*
expansion 2, 78, 85n1, 148
exploratory analyses 4, **6**, 82, 119, 316, *362*, **374**; and CHAID 69, 70; and cluster analysis 57, 61, 66
exploratory factor analysis (EFA) **6**, 9, 14, 16–17, 25–34; and CFA, compared 91; defined/goals of 25–26; and eigen equation/eigenvalues 25, 26; and factor analysis topic modeling *see* FATM; history/development of 25; and LDA 27–28; software for 25, 28; of themes **6**, 14, 25
exploratory-based quantitizing 7, 8–9, 14, 15
eye-tracking technology 252

F

Facebook 53, 95, 228, 243, 294
facial recognition technology 252
factor analysis 52, 54, 144; R 199, 200, 201, 202, *see also* CFA; exploratory factor analysis
factor loading 17, 25, 31, 201
factor rotation 89, 200, 201, 204
Fairclough, Norman 167
FAP (formative assessment process) 101–102, 105
FATM (factor analysis topic modeling) 9, 14, 26–34; and analysis 29; applications of 33; and case unit 9, 28, 30, 31; and data preparation 28–29; establishing meaningful topics 28, 29, 31–32; and generalizability of findings 26, 33; and LDA 27–28, 52; learning resources for 34; and NMF approach 28, 29; and QDA Miner 25, 26, 27, 29, 30, 33; and renaming topics 31, 32; and revision of topics 29; and RIS files

28; and sample integration validity 33; and sensibility of topics 29; and stemming/lemmatization 28, 29, 30; steps in 28–34; strengths/limitations of 34; suitability for MMR of 26–28; TBL example of 28, 29, 30–33, *32*, **32**, *33*; and transparency of data 27, 34; and use of topics 29–30; and varimax rotation 26, 28, 29, 31; and word frequency 26, 28, 29, 30, 34; and WordStat 25, 26, 27, 28, 29, 30–32, *30*, *31*, *33*, 34
Faust, K. 214
feminist standpoint theory 248
Ferron, J. M. 17, 104
Fetters, M. D. 39, 126, 141, 148, 259, 261, 274, 277, 306, *359*, *367*
Field, A. 85
Fielding, N. G. 234, 332
Filella, G. 74
FIQ (fully integrated qualitizing) **6**, 10, 145, 147
Fisher, G. A. 249
Fisher, R. A. 38
Fisher's design of experiments 200, 202
Fiss, P. C. 192
Fitzpatrick, R. 114
Floyd, George 301
fMRI (functional magnetic resonance imaging) 94–95
focal behaviour 129, 130, *131*, 132, *133*, **133**
focus groups 37, 39, 46, 51, 102, 105, 125, 293, 294, 305
formative assessment process (FAP) 101–102, 105
Formula One racing 192
Fort, J. D. 174
Foucault, Michel 254
Fox, C. M. 121
Fox, K. R. 66
Fox News 301, *302*
Franco, C. L. 254–255
Franzosi, R. 121
Freeman, L. C. 210, 214
Frels, R. K. 37–38, 334, 335
frequentist analysis 1, 5, **6**, **7**, 8, 10, 109, 113, 126
Frerichs, R. 40
Freshwater, D. 126, 141, 306, *367*
Friendly, M. 37, 39
Friese, S. 333
Froehlich, D. E. 122, 214
Frye, M. 27, 33, 34
fsQCA (fuzzy-set QCA) 186, 188, 191, 192, 193
Fugate, J. M. B. 254–255
fully integrated mixed analysis **6**, 141, *142*, 143, 144–145, 148, 149
fully integrated qualitizing (FIQ) **6**, 10, 145, 147
Furnari, S. 192
fuzzy sets 66, 186

G

G*Power 80, *359*, *369*
Gardner, B. B./Gardner, M. R. 209
Garro, L. C. 174

Gay, G. K. 293
Gee, James Paul 167, 242
Gelman, A. 81, 85
Geman, S./Geman, D. 109
gender 14, 15, 27, 33, 50, 85, 158, 305; and CHAID 72, 73, 74; and correspondence analysis 38, 40, *40*, 43, **44**
general linear model (GLM) 4, 16, 114, 126, 373, **374**
generalizations 8, 16; five types of 2, 355
geodata/geo documents 236n2, 332, 333, *334*, 338
Geographic information systems, *see* GIS
Gerber, H. R. 2, 223
Germany 165, 193
Germuth, A. A. 37
Giannakos, M. 252
Gibbs sampler 109, 112
Gill, R. 161, 162, 164, 168
GIS (geographic information systems) 6, 12, 16, 227–236, 294, 328, 334–335; applications of 234; case study for *see* Barcelona GIS case study; and citizen research 234; and context of time/space in MMR 227, 229; critical 228; defined 227–228; and geo-/referencing/-linking/-coding 228; and geo-visualization 230; and inaccuracies in maps 230; learning resources for 235–236; and social media 235; software for 228, 231–232; strengths/limitations of 235; suitability for MMR of 228–229; techniques/skills for 229–230
Github 112
Gladwin, Christina 173, 174, 177, 180
Glaesser, J. 192, 193
Glaze, L. 40
GLM (general linear model) 4, 16, 114, 126, 373, **374**
GMO (genetically modified organisms) research 65
Goffman, E. 52
Gold, M. 357
Goldstein, K. 95
goodness of fit 47, 81, 93, **94**
Google 53, *53*, 73–74, 95, 253, 303, 338
Google Earth 228, 231, 232, 294, **309**
Gower, J. C. 54, 59
Graham, W. F. 148, 240, *358*
Granovetter, M. S. 210, 211
Greenacre, M. 37, 39, 41
Greene, J. C. 148, 240, 280–282, 283, *358*, *361*, *368*
Greenhoff, K. 45
Groenen, P. J. F. 47, 55
grounded theory 1, 4, 70, 173, 261, 285, 308, 332; and coding techniques 152, 159; and QDA Miner/WordStat 293, 296
Grove, A. L. 12, 259, 261, 274, 286, *367*
GSEQ5 10, 128, 129, 132, 135
Guàrdia-Olmos, J. 94–95
Gudayol-Ferré, E. 94
Guest, G. 65
Guetterman, T. C. 259, 274, 286, 305, 316, *359*

Index

Guha, S. 293
Gun Violence Archive 154
Gutmann, M. 65–66

H

Haefliger, S. 192
Hair, J. F. J. 17
Hamer, R. 54
Hand, D. 69, 75
hand rotation 201, 203, 204, **204**, 205, **205**, 206
Hanson, W. 65–66
Hardy, M. A. 85
Harré, R. 246
Harway, N. I. 25
Hatch, J. A. 70
Haug, C. A. 357
Hawthorne effect 253
Headley, M. G. 107
health/medical research 77, 89, 91, *91*, *92*, 93–94, 136, 210, 253; and alternative therapies 174; and case comparison tables **279**, 282; and coding strategies 152, 155–156; and EDMs 173, 174, 175; and electronic health records (EHRs) 95; and end-of-life decisions 175, 176; epidemiology 39–40, 211; and GIS 229, 234; and HIV/AIDS 65, 234, 325; and HLM 99, 100, 101; and mothers/children 173, 174; *Wellbeing* project for older women 344–353, *see also* cancer research; public health
heatmaps 292, 294, 299
Henry, D. 57, 64
Herbert, M. 155
Hersperger, A. M. 92
Hesse-Biber, S. M. 337, 338, *368*
Heydari, A. 337
hierarchical clustering 9, 15, 59–61, 63, 65, 66, 297–298, 300
hierarchical linear modeling *see* HLM
Hildebrand, D. 3
Hill, C. E. 180
Hill, J. 81, 85
Hill, M. O. 40
Hiller, J. H. 249
Hines, A. 156–157
Hines, C. V. 17, 37
Hitchcock, J. H. 5, 7–8, 10, 16, 126, *367*; and crossover analysis 3, 4, 71, 210; and HLM 101, 107; and multi-mixed methods/meta-methods approaches 16; and NVC analysis 245; and qualitizing 141, 142, 143, 144; and quantitizing 77, 78
HIV/AIDS research 65, 234, 325
HLM (hierarchical linear modeling) **6**, 14, 15, 92, 99–107, **374**; analysis of results 104–105, **105**; applications of 99, 105–106; assessment of 105; and covariates 104; and data sources 102–103; defined 99–100; empirical demonstration of 99, 101–105, **105**; and ICC 100–101, 106; independent/dependent variables/statistical power 103–104; learning resources for 99, 106; model specification/research question/goal 103; and quantitized data 99–100, 101, **102**, 103, 105–106, 107; and research context 101–102; sample size for 101; single-/multi-level analyses 100; and statistical dependence 100, 101; strengths/limitations of 99, 101, 106; and study design 102–104, 105; suitability for MMR of 99, 101; technical outline of 99, 101, **102**; and qualitative data that have been quantitized 99
Hogan, N. S. 89
Hogarty, K. Y. 17
HOISAN 10, 128, 132–133, **135**
holistic approach **6**, 17, 41, 54, 144, 145, 156, 185
Hollbrook, Allyson 168
Hollstein, B. 210, 214
Holmes, L. 246
homophily 210, 211
Hong, S. 17
Hops, H. 93
horizontal mixed analysis *3*, 4
Hosmer, D. W. 85
Householder, A. S. 54
Howell Smith, M. C. 261
Hox, J. J. 104, 106
Huberman, A. M. 4, 57, 77, 144, 245, 246, **279**, 338
Hungary 164–165
Hunt, B. R. 66
hurricanes 173, 175
Hwang, E. 335, 356, *366–368*
hyperlinks 228, 244, 294, 311, 333, 339

I

ICC (intra-class correlation) 100–101, 104, 106
IJMRA (*International Journal of Multiple Research Approaches*) 16, 142
Iker, H. P. 25, 34
in vivo coding 5, **6**, 154–155, 363
independence assumption 80, 100
India 174–175, 325
inferential analyses 4, 5, 143, 144, 244; and quantitizing 7, 9–10, 14, 15, *see also* chi-square tests
INFIT/OUTFIT 120
initiation 2, 78, 84–85n1, 148
integration equations 126, 141–143, *142*, 144, *367–368*
inter-respondent matrix 7–8, **7**, 9, 10, 16; incident-based 8, **8**; intensity-based 8, **8**
interactive analysis *see* concurrent mixed analyses
intercoder reliability 52, 293, 339
International Society for the Scientific Study of Subjectivity (ISSSS) 202, 203, 206, 207
Internet 227, 296; hyperlinks 228, 244, 294, 311, 333, 339; safety 191–192, *see also* Dedoose; social media analytics
interpretation phase 2, *3*, 4, 141, 142, 355, *367*

interpretative phenomenological analysis (IPA) 4, 5, **6**
interrupted time-series models 93, 111
intersection 4, 11, 12, 130, 188, 279, 344, 352
intersessional/intrasessional following 125–126
interviews 38, 40, 78, 99, 344; coding 64; in-depth qualitative 33, 58, 62, 125, 174, 192; informal 174; post-sort 199, 201, 202, 203, 204, 205; repeated 101; semi-structured 11, 66, 173, 174, 175, 246, 325, 332; transcribed 28, 37, 320
intra-/inter-coder agreement/reliability 8, 118
intra-class correlation (ICC) 100–101, 104, 106
IPA (interpretative phenomenological analysis) 4, 5, **6**
IRT (item response theory) 1, **6**, 9, 14, 16, 117–122, **357**, **374**; applications of 121; and construct modeling 119; defined 117; and instrument development process 118–121; and item characteristics curve 119; and item-person map 120–121, *120*; learning resources for 121–122; and Rasch model 117, 119–120; strengths/limitations of 121; suitability for MMR of 117–118; technical outline of 118–121
ISSSS (International Society for the Scientific Study of Subjectivity) 202, 203, 206, 207
iterative partitioning 59, 61, 66
IV (independent variable) 14, 72, 75, **90**, 100, 111, 119, 211, 284; and multiple linear regression analysis 77, 79, 80, 81–82, 83, 85; and QCA 185, 191, 192
Ivankova, N. V. 151

J

Jaccard coefficient 46, 59, 63
Jackson, K. 344, 354
Jacob, S. 117
JAGS (just another Gibbs sampler) 112
Jahoda, M. 315
Janesick, V. J. 279, 283
Jang, E. E. 155
Jimarkon, P. 166
JMMR (*Journal of Mixed Methods Research*) 16, 148, 239, 259, 306
Johnson, G. K. 135
Johnson, J. C. 214
Johnson, R. B. 3, 7, 16, 17, 122, 243, 253, *362*, *368*; causation in MMR 155; dialectical pluralism 7; and qualitizing 142, 143, 145
Johnson, R. E. 12, 259, 261, 274, 286, *367*
joint displays **6**, 12, 15, 148, 259–274, *366*; applications of 273; color/animation in 261, 268–269, *269*; defined 259, 277; empirical demonstration of *see* ADAPT-IT joint display study; guidelines for developing 260–262, **260**; and intra-method analysis 260, 261, 262, 264, 265; learning resources for 274; and MAXQDA

305, 313, *313*, *314*, 315–316, 317; multiple/meta- 261–262, 270, *271*; and pillar integration process 259, 261; purposes of 277; strengths/limitations of 273–274; suitability for MMR of 259–260, *see also* case comparison tables

Jones, D. R. 114
Jöreskog, K. G. 89
Jorgenson, M. W. 167
Journal of Mixed Methods Research (JMMR) 16, 148, 239, 259, 306
journalism research 165, *see also* newspapers
Jung, J-K. 228

K

K-12 education 26, 357
k-means clustering 9, 53, 61, 64, 66
Kaczynski, D. 320, 321, 329
Kadushin, C. 211
Kaess, W. A. 249
Kafai, Y. 250
Kalantzis, M. 251
Kampen, J. K. 201
Karami, E. 174–175
Kaufman, L. 62
Kegan, R. 282
Kelly, J. G. 57
Kelly, Spencer 255
Kemp, L. 261
Kenny, David 96
Keshavarz, M. 174–175
keyword co-occurrence map 146, *146*
keywords-in-context (KWIC) 299, 334, 335
Kim, C. S. 242
King, J. 93
Kirner-Ludwig, M. 165
Kistler, S. J. 37
Klecka's tau 178
Kline, R. B. 89, 96
Knafl, G. 96, 106, 313
Knigge, L. 234
Kogan, L. R. 122
König, S. 107
Koskey, K. L. K. 121
Krauss, R. M. 244
Kress, G. 239
Kromrey, J. D. 17, 104
Kruskal, J. B. 47, 54
Kuckartz, U. 259, 274, 305, 313, 315, 317
KWIC (keywords-in-context) 299, 334, 335
Kyngäs, H. 337

L

La Pelle, N. 279, 283, 284, 285
lag sequential analysis 10, 129, 130, 132, *132*, **132**, 135, 136
Lahey, L. L. 282
Landau, S. 67
Larson, John Augustus 251–252
latent growth modeling (LGM) 89, **90**, 92–93, *92*, 95, 96
latent variable structural equation modeling *see* LVSEM
Laudien, S. M. 64
Lavega, P. 74

Lazarsfeld, P. F. 210, 211, 315
LDA (Latent Dirichlet Allocation) 27–28, 52, 298
leadership research 64, 66, 100, 155, 201, 282
Leal, I. 155–156, 159, 160
Leavy, P. 338
Lee, J. P. 332
Lee, R. M. 332
Lee, S. Y. 93
Lee, Y.-J 280–282, 283
Leech, N. L. 1, 16, 37–38, 96, 136, 162, 168n4; and NVC analysis 245, 246, 253; and qualitizing 10, 78, 143, 144–145, 147, 148, 149; and SPSS 357, *358*, *365*, *368–369*
Leese, M. 67
legitimation 16–17, 164, 165, 253, 362, *362–363*
Leong, F. T. L. 117
Lerman, M. P. 301
Levine-Donnerstein, D. 121
Lewins, A. 317
LGM (latent growth modeling) 89, **90**, 92–93, *92*, 95, 96
Li, S. 4
Lieber, E. 325, 329
Likert-format scale 8, 13, 110, 120, 142, 199–200
LINCE 10, 128
Lincoln, Y. S. 41, 70
linguistic approach 10, 14, 131, 224, 239, *see also* DA; NLP
LISREL 89, 96
literacy research 324, 325–327
literature reviews 11, 331, 333–335
Litts, B. 250
Liu, X.-f 104
LIWC (Linguistic Inquiry and Word Count) 27, 94
Lobe, B. 191–192
logistic regression 14, 77, 79, 85, 103, 173, 181, 192
longitudinal studies 92, 229, 293; and Dedoose 319, 323; and HLM 99, 101; and SNA 211, 213, 214, *see also* LGM
Losada, J. L. 135
Lui, D. 250
Lumify 225
Lune, H. 332
LVSEM (latent variable structural equation modeling) 89, **90**, 91, *92*
Lynch, T. L. 219

M

Maas, C. J. M. 104
McAlister-Shields, L. 248
McBride, D. E. 193
MacCallum, R. C. 17
McCammon, L. A. 156–158
McCarthy, John 251
McClelland, L. E. 121
McConnel, J. 252
McCrudden, M. T. 286
McDougall, D. E. 155
machine learning 11, 25, 295, 302; algorithms 291, 300, 355
Macia, L. 64–65

McKeown, Bruce 207
Macklin, R. 338
McLafferty, C. L. 2
Mclellan, E. 65
McMahon, B. T. 74
McNeill, D. 244, 246
macroanalyses 4, **6**
Magidson, J. 75
Magnifico, A. M. 223
magnitude coding 10, 153, 154, 155–156, 158, 159
Magnusson, M. S. 129, 131
Makszin, K. 192
management research 193, 230
Mannila, H. 75
maps/mapping 5, 15, 37, 51–52, 244, 246; concept 51–54, *53*, 63; inaccuracies in 230; item-person 120–121, *120*; keyword co-occurrence 146, *146*; and multidimensional scaling *see* MDS; and NVivo 344, 349, *350*, *see also* GIS; heatmaps
Mapshaper 235
March, J. 74
market/marketing research 57, 64, 89, 206, 242, 293, 297
Markov Chain Monte Carlo (MCMC) approach 93, 109
Marquart, J. M. 4
Martinez, A. 104
Martinez, H. 174, 180
Maruschak, L. 40
Masson, M. H. 46
Matthews, S. 230
maximum likelihood 17, 93, 109, 111
MAXQDA 12, 167, 192, 228, 293, 305–317, 331, 339, *363*; and analysis of code frequencies 314–315; and comparing thematic statements 314, *315*; data-based strategies in 312–316; empirical demonstration of 307–317; and Excel/SPSS 307, 308; and extreme cases 313; integration strategies with 306–307, 311–316, 317; and joint displays 305, 313, *313*, *314*, 315–316, 317; learning resources for 317; and mixed methods designs 305–307; and Mixed Methods tab 3, *311*, 315; and qualitative data analysis 308–309, 309–310, *309*, **309**, *310*; and quantitizing 312–313; results-based strategies in 311–312; sequence-based strategies in 316–317, *317*; and side-by-side displays 312; and statistics by qualitative groups 315–316, *316*; strengths/limitations of 317; and summaries 311–312, *312*, 314, *314*, 316; technical outline of 307, *307*
Mazur, A. G. 193
Mazzei, L. A. 243
MCMC (Markov Chain Monte Carlo) approach 93, 109
MDS (multidimensional scaling) **6**, 9, 15, 45–55, 63, 144, 352, 353, **374**; algorithms for 47, 48, 51, 52, 54; and anchor stimulus method 45, 51; applications of 51–54; with

asymmetric data 51; calculations for 47; and cognitive/frame mapping 51–52; data collection/preparation for 45–46; defined 45; empirical demonstration of 47–51; and Euclidian space 46, 47; initial parameters for 48–49, *48*; interpretation in 50–51, *50*; learning resources for 54–55; media analysis example of *see* media framing analysis using MDS; multi-way/multi-mode 51; and nonmetric data 54; and pattern detection 46, 52, 54; and permutation test *49*, *50*; primary/secondary approaches 48; and qualitative data 46–47; with rectangular data 51; and scree plot 47–48; and Shepard diagram 49, *49*; and SMACOF 47, *49*, 55; strengths/limitations of 54; and Stress decomposition chart 49, *49*; and Stress values 47–49, *48*, *50*; suitability for MMR of 45–47; and ties 48–49; and Torgeson method 47, *48*, *50*; transformation types in 48–49

mean, calculation of 5, **6**, 7

meaning making 16, 17, 18, 146, 160, 335; and DA 161, 162, 165, 167; miltimodal 239, 240, 241, 242, 250, 251

media analysis 301, *see also* newspapers

media framing analysis using MDS 52–54, *53*; and amount of data 52; and dimensional weighting model 53; and INDSCAL 52, 53, *53*, 54; and structured conceptualization 52, 53

median value 5, 7

medical research *see* health/medical research

Mendeley 294, 333, 335, 344

Mendes, J. 74–75

Merchant, G. 240–241, 244

Merton, R. K. 210, 211

mesoanalyses 4, **6**

Messick, S. 121

meta-analysis 10, 94, 114, 143, 149, 151, 159, 351

meta-inferences 3–4, 16, 17, 33, 71, 259, 277; and coding techniques 151, 159; learning resources for 149; and NVC analysis 246, 253; and qualitizing 141, *142*, 151; and SPSS 362, *362*, *368*, 373

meta-methods approach 13, 16, 143, 144–145, 148, 149

meta-synthesis 10, 151, 159

metathemes 37–38, 146, **147**

Mexico 174

Meyer, D. Z. 279, 283, 285

microanalyses 5, **6**

Mieczkowski, T. 74

Miles, J. 85

Miles, M. 4, 7, 57, 77, 144, 153, 160, 245, 246, 338; and case comparison tables 279, 280, 283

Milligan, G. W. 62

Mimno, D. 293

mixed analysis assumption legitimation 16–17

mixed analysis commensurability approximation legitimation 17

mixed analysis phase 14–16

mixed methodological discourse analysis *see* MMDA

mixed methods analysis/research (MMR), applications of 16

mixed methods analysis/research (MMR), appropriate use of 3–4; and when not to use 3

mixed methods analysis/research (MMR), defined 1–2, 186, 305, 343–344, 355

mixed methods analysis/research (MMR), four basic formulae/set theory notation for 2

mixed methods analysis/research (MMR), literature/online resources for 1, 16, 18

mixed methods analysis/research (MMR), strengths/limitations of 16–18

mixed methods analysis/research (MMR), technical outline of 4–5

mixed tables 277–279, 280

MMDA (mixed methodological discourse analysis) **6**, 10, 16, 161–168; advantages of 163; applications of 166–167; and Chilean press 166; and coding/data analysis 164, 165, 167; and conceptualization of Arab women in newspapers 165; and corporate websites 164–165, 168n6; and data collection 164, 167; and defining research question 163–164; empirical demonstration of 164–166; learning resources for 167–168; and meaning making 161, 162, 165, 167; and online political comments 166; and presentation of results 164; and researcher bias 163, 166; and social context 161–162, 163, 164, 165, 167, 168; and software 165, 167, 168n6; strengths/limitations of 167; suitability for MMR of 162–163; technical outline/four phases of 163–164

mode 5, 7

model building 81, 173, 181, 186, 187

Mohatt, N. 57

Molina-Azorin, J. F. 39, 261

Monge, P. R. 214

monoanalysis 1, 2, 4, 18

Moran-Ellis, J. 261

Morgan, G. A. *358*

Morgan, G. B. 104

mosaic displays 37, 38

Muhr, Thomas 331

multi-factor analysis 89

multi-mixed methods approach 13, 16, 142, 143, 145–146, 148

multi-qualitizing **6**, 10, 15, 143, 144, 145, 148

multi-quantitizing **6**

multidimensional scaling *see* MDS

multilevel analyses/modeling **6**, 82, 100, 103, 104

multimodalities 239–240, 250, 251, 253, 254

multiple analyses **6**, 14, 143, 144, 145, 147, 148

multiple correspondence analysis 9, *40*

multiple linear regression analysis **6**, 9, 10, 15, 16, 77–85; applications in MMR of 84–85; assessing models/variables in 81–82; and assessment of research context 82; and assumptions checks 80; and bivariate regression 79, 80–81; data sources/design in 82–83; empirical demonstration of 82–84; estimating equations in 81; and independent variables 77, 79, 80, 81–82, 83, 85; learning resources for 85; model specification/research question in 83; and multiple regression 79, 81, **374**; regression/quantitizing described 77–79; results/interpretation in 83–84, *83*; sample size for 80; strengths/limitations of 85; suitability for MMR of 79–80; technical outline of 80–82

multiple validities 253, 362, *363*

multivariate methods 40, **41**, 66, 352, 353, **374**; and Bayesian analysis 109, 112; and SEM 91, 93, *see also* CA; MDS; TPA

Mumford, K. R. 17

Munirah Mohammad, A. 333, 335

Murphy, E. 126

Mustafa-Awad, Z. 165

Mwangi, B. J. 174

Myers, N. 65

N

narrative profiles 15, 144, 145, 147, 148

Natesan Batley, P. 109, 110, 112, 114

Natesan, P. 10, 126, 141

National School Lunch Program, US (NSLP) 80–81, 83, 84

natural language processing (NLP) 11, 14, 225, 252, 296

natural linguistic programming (NLP) 93, 95, 96

Navarro, Joe 255

Nelson, J. A. 121

nesting 5, 93, *357*; and HLM 99, 100, 101, **102**, 103–104, 105, 106

networks *see* SNA

Newman, I. 10, 89, 126, 141

newspapers 52–53, 95, 125, 200, 294, 301, 337; and MMDA 161, 164, 165, 166

Nicholl, J. 126

Nigeria 13, 241

NLP (natural language processing) 11, 14, 225, 252, 296

NLP (natural linguistic programming) 93, 95, 96

NMF/NNMF (nonnegative matrix factorization) 28, 29, 52, 298

non-crossover mixed analysis 2, 3–4, *3*, 355

nonparametric analyses 1, 8, 9, 10, 146, 292, 298, 369, 373

Nordquist, Richard 168

Norris, S. 240

NPL 93–94

NSLP (National School Lunch Program, US) 80–81, 83, 84

NVC (nonverbal communication) analysis **6**, 12, 15, 239–255; applications of 251–253; and communication vagueness 249–250, *250*; and correspondence analysis 246, 248, 249; and cues 240, 243–244; and cultural context 241–242, 254; defined 239–242; and Discourses 242; and emotions 246–247, **247**; empirical demonstration of 246–251, *247*, **248**, *250*; how to conduct 244–246; and integrated data displays 246; learning resources for 254–255; literature gap for 239; and multimodalities 239–240, 250, 251, 253, 254; online 240–241, 242, 250–251, 254–255; reasons for conducting 243; strengths/limitations of 253–254; suitability for MMR of 242, 243; technical outline of 242–246; and text/literacies 239–240; three-dimensional model of 241, *241*; and videogames 240, 241, 244; what to analyze/frameworks of 243–244; when to conduct 243; where to conduct 243

NVivo 13, 228, 293, 301, 331, 339, 343–354, *363*; applications of 353; and cluster analysis/MDS 352, 353; coding system of 347; and combining data/analyses 348–349, *348*; and comparative processes 349–351, *349*, *350*, *351*; and correspondence analysis 352, 353, *353*; and DA 165, 167, 168n6; and data management 344–346, *345*, *346*; defined 343; and exploratory visualizations 352–353, *352*, *353*; and importing data 344–345, 347, 348; and integrative analyses 348–353; learning resources for 353–354; and preliminary analyses 347–348, *347*; and project planning 344, *345*; strengths/limitations of 353; suitability for MMR of 343–344; technical outline of 344–353; and transformative processes 351–352, *352*

Nzabonimpa, J. P. 149

O

observations 8, 10, 11, 46, 57, 69, 99, 174, 344; and correspondence analysis 37, 38, 39; and diachronic analysis 125, 126, 127, 128, 129, 135; and multiple linear regression analysis 77, 78, 80, 84

O'Cathain, A. 126, *368*
O'Dwyer, L. M. 335
Oh, H. S. 174
Ojo, E. O. 13, 16, 146, 147
O'Kane, P. 301
OLS (ordinary least squares) 81, 99, 100, 106, 109
Omasta, M. 154, 156–157
ontological imperative *see* social media analytics
ontologies 12, 27, 145, 243

Onwuegbuzie, A. J. 13, 39, 121, 162, 168n4, 337, *365*, 374; and analytical phases 2, *3*, 355, 361, *361*; and Bayesian analysis 10, 111, 113, 114; and case comparison tables 279, 285; and crossover mixed analysis 4, 5, 7, 16, 71, 117, 210, 356, *366–368*; and diachronic analysis 125, 126, 136; on factor analysis of text 33; and HLM 101, 106, 107; and inter-respondent matrix 7–8; and legitimation 16, 17, *362*; and literature reviews 333–334, 335, 335–336, 340; and mixed analysis defined 1–2, 355; and multi-mixed/ meta-methods approaches 16; and non-crossover mixed analysis 3–4; and NVC analysis 239, 240, 241, *241*, 243, 245, 246, 248, 253; and qualitizing 10, 141–142, 143, 144–145, 146, 147, 148, 149, *366–367*; and quantitizing 7, 11, 37–38, 77, 78, 96, 106, *359*, *366*; and radical middle 126, 223

open-ended survey questions 8, 11, 13, 14, 15, 75, 91, 106, 202; and ATLAS.ti 331, 338; and cluster analysis 62, 66; and coding techniques 152, 156, 157, 158; and Dedoose 320, 325; and FATM 26, 27, 28; and joint displays 262, *263*, 264, 265, 266, 270; and MAXQDA 305, 307; and MDS 51, 52; and NVivo 345, 348; and QDA Miner/WordStat 295, 296, 300, 302, 303; and qualitizing 144, 146, 147; and SNA 212, 213; and SPSS 356, 357, **357**, 358, 363

Optimal Design 106
organizational research 77, 100, 192, 206, 282
outcome of interest 79, 85, 187, 189, 190, 192, 193
OUTFIT/INFIT 120

P

p value 69, 71, *73*, 104, 157, 158, 310
PA (path analysis) 89, 90, **90**, 91, *91*
Pagliarin, S. 192
paired comparison technique 174, 175
paradigmatic corroboration 152, 155, 158
Paraguay 234
parallel mixed analysis 2, 3, **6**, 14, 356, 373
parametric analysis 54, 100, 373; frequentist 1, 8, 10
parenthetical elements 2
Park, H. A. 174
Parry, S. 93
participant-to-variable ratio 17
path analysis (PA) 89, 90, **90**, 91, *91*
pattern detection 46, 52, 54, 129, 135, 151
Patton, M. Q. 160, 321
Paulus, T. 338
Paulus, T. M. 335
PCA (principal components analysis) 9, 14, 16–17, **374**; and Q methodology 201, **203**, 204, **204**, 205–206, **205**, 206

Pearson's *r* 58, 159, 292, 298, 310, 324
Pedersen, M. 286
Pedersen, R. B. 189
Péladeau, N. 34
Penny, A. C. 38
permutation tests 1, *49*, 50, 53
Peró-Cebollero, M. 94
Petsimeris, P. 230
phenomenological analyses 4, **6**, 70, 152, 159, 246, 308; and IRT 117, 118, 121
phi test 357, 369, *369*, 370, 371–373, *372*
Phillips, L. J. 167
philosophical assumptions/stances 7
photographic data 10, 125, 221, 230, 232, 234, 320, 331
Picó, A. 255
pillar integration process 259, 261
Plano Clark, V. L. 107, 117, 121, 126, 143, 151, 314, 315, *368*; and cluster analysis 65–66; and mixed methods defined 305; and qualitizing 143, 151
Playfair, William 38
Plotly 225
poetry **6**, 148
Poisson distribution 111, 113
polar coordinate analysis 10, 129, 130–131, **130**, 132–133, *133*, **133**, 135, 136
political science research *60*, 166, 192–193, 206, 210, 297, *299*
Pollon, D. 155
polygraphs 251–252
Portell, M. 135
Portugal 74–75
post hoc power *365–366*, 373
posterior distribution 109, 110, 112, 113, 126
postpositivist stance 5, 145, 161, 202, 204–205, 227
Poth, C. N. 118, 121
Potter, J. 162, 164, 168
Potter, W. J. 121
poverty 14, 15, 83, **83**, 84, 104, 192, 228–229
PQMethod 200, 203
pragmatic approach 2, 25, 161, 163, 230, 234, 244, 355
Preacher, K. J. 17
predictive modeling 69, 70, 71, 105, 300
principle components analysis *see* PCA
prison/prisoners 40–41, *40*, 44, **44**
probability distribution 1, 109, 111
process coding 10, 152, 335
propinquity 210–211
Provalis Research tools *see* QDA Miner; SimStat; WordStat
psychoanalysis *see* therapy research
psychometric analyses 1, 8, 58, **90**, 91, 212, *see also* item response theory; MDS; Rasch analysis
public health 39–40
Pugh, K. J. 121
purposive sampling 52, 70, 118, 163, 175, 176
Putnam, R. D. 210
Putnam Rankin, C. 121
Python 214, 225

Q

Q methodology **6**, 11, 16, 144, 199–207; applications of 206; and centroids 200–201, 203, **203**, 204, **204**, 205–206, **205**; concourse of items in 199, 200; and consensus statements/tables 201, 205–206; defined 199; empirical demonstration of 202–206; and factor arrays 201, **203**, 204; and Fisher's design of experiments 200, 202; and hand rotation 201, 203, 204, **204**, 205, **205**, 206; and inherently mixed viewpoint 204; interpretation 199, 201, 204; and ISSSS 202, 203, 206, 207; learning resources for 207; and Likert-format scale, compared 199–200; mixed analysis in 199, 201–202, 204; and P-set 200, 203; and PCA 201, **203**, 204, **204**, 205–206, **205**, 206; and post-sort interviews 199, 201, 202, 203, 204, 205; Q analysis in 199, 200–201; Q-sample in 199, 200, 202, 203; Q-sort in 199–200, 203; sample size for 200; and skeptical novice viewpoint 205; software for 200, 201, 203; strengths/limitations of 199–200, 206–207; technical outline of 200–202; and utilitarian postpositive viewpoint 204–205; and varimax rotation 201, **203**, 204, **204**, 205, 206

Q-mode analysis 58, 62, 63, 64

QCA (qualitative comparative analysis) **6**, 11, 15, 144, 145, 185–194, 335–336; analytical steps 188; applications of 192–193; as case-/variable-oriented 185; case-informed 187, *187*; causal process tracing (CPT) strategy 189–190, *190*, 192, 194; and CCMs/STMs 185, and CNA/NCA 186; and conditions/outcome 185, 194n2; crisp-set (csQCA) 185, 186, 188, 192; defined 185–186; empirical demonstrations of 191–192; fuzzy-set (fsQCA) 186, 188, 191, 192, 193; in-depth case-informed strategy 189, *189*; learning resources for 194; mixed data-informed 187, *187*; and multiple conjunctural causation 185, 193, 194nn2,4; multivalue (mvQCA) 186, 188; and net effects thinking 185, 191, 193; and outcome of interest 187, 189, 190, 192, 193; post-QCA steps 188, 191, 192; pre-QCA steps 187–188, 191; and social network analysis 193; software for 185, 186, 192; statistical strategy 191, *191*, 192; steps in 187–188; strengths/limitations of 193–194; suitability for MMR/five strategies of 186–187, *186*; technical outline of 189–191; and truth tables 11, 185, 187, 188, 194n3; two-step 186

QDA Miner 2, 9, 12, **41**, 66, 167, 228, *292*, 331, *363*; and advanced text searches/autocoding features 294–296; applications of 302; and cases-by-variables structure 292–293; cluster Extraction feature 9, 66, 295, 295–296; and data importation/exportation 294; empirical demonstration of 300–301; and FATM 25, 26, 27, 29, 30, 33; and geospatial/time data 294, *295*; and integrated statistical analysis 292; and intercoder agreement 293; and keyword searching 294–295; learning resources for 303; and MDS 46, 52–53; Sections Retrieval tool 294; strengths/limitations of 302–303; suitability for MMR of 291; technical outline of 291–296; and WordStat, integration with 293, 300, 301

qualitative coding 1, 5, 16, 144, 151–160, 335–336; affective methods of 154–155; applications of 159; and causation coding 155; codes/themes compared 155; defined 151; and descriptive coding 152, 153, 154, 158; and emotion coding 154; empirical demonstration of 155–159; and evaluation coding 153, 154; learning resources for 160; and magnitude coding 153, 154, 155–156, 158, 159; and metaphor coding 154; and paradigmatic corroboration 152, 155, 158; and process coding 10, 152; strengths/limitations of 159–160; and structural coding 152–153, 154; suitability for MMR of 151–152; technical outline of 152–153; and values coding 154; and in vivo coding 154–155

qualitative comparative analysis *see* QCA

qualitative data analyses 1, 2, 3, 4, **6**, 11, 333–334; and Bayesian analysis 110; and chi-square automatic interaction detection *see* CHAID; and correspondence analysis *see* CA; and crossover analysis 13; and effect sizes 8; and exploratory factor analysis 25; and IRT 117, 118; and multidimensional scaling *see* MDS; and quantitative, combined 4, 33, 57–58

qualitative monoanalysis 1, 2, 4

qualitative phase 2, 11, 14–16, 17, 37, 84, 89, 117, 166, 316–317, 355

qualitative process coding 10, 152

qualitative-dominant crossover analyses 5, **6**, 7, 11, 13

qualitizing 15, 141–149, 337–338, *359–360*, *366–367*; applications of 148; and coding techniques 144, 151; and crossover mixed analyses/displays 10, 141–142, 143, 147, **147**, 148; defined 143; empirical demonstration of 145–147; five-point typology of 147; fully integrated (FIQ) **6**, 10, 145, 147; and integration equations 141–143, *142*, 144; learning resources for 149; multi- **6**, 10, 15, 143, 144, 145, 148; and multi-mixed methods approach 142, 143; and narrative profiles 144, 145, 147, 148; and sentiment analysis 146–147, *147*; single **6**, 10, 143, 144; strengths/limitations of 148–149; suitability for MMR of 143–144; technical outline of 144–145

Quan, E. 293

Quannari, E. M. 45

quantitative monoanalysis 1, 2, 4

quantitative phase 2, 11, 14, 15, 17, 84, 117, 148, 316, 355

quantitative-dominant crossover analyses 5, **6**, 7, 11, 13, 210

quantitizing 7–10, 18, 38, 62, 71, 77–79, 82, 84, 85n2, 337–338, *366*; and coding strategies 151, 152, 153, 157, 158, 159; descriptive-based 7–8, 14–15; and diachronic analysis 126; exploratory-based 7, 8–9, 14, 15; fully integrated **6**; and GIS 235; and HLM 99–100, 101, **102**, 103, 105–106, 107; inferential-based 7, 9–10, 15; learning resources for 85, 96; and MAXQDA 312–313; measurement-based 7, 9; and SEM 89; and SPSS 359–360, *359*

Quera, V. 135

questionnaires 11, 12, 74, 119, 120, 165, 293, 344, 358

R

R factor analysis 199, 200–201, 202

R language/program 47, 55, 89, 106–107, 112, 133, 167, 186, 214, 225; and Twitter 221–222

R-mode analysis 58, 63, 64, 65

race/racism 74, 84–85, **84**, 301, *302*

Rad, M. 337

Rädiker, S. 305, 317

Ragin, Charles 185, 192, 283

Ramlo, S. 201, 202, *202*, 207

randomization tests *see* permutation tests

randomized controlled trials (RCTs) 100, 106, 262, 270

Rasch analysis 1, 9, 117, 119–120, 121

rate ratio effect size 113, *113*

rating scales 8, **8**, 58, 119, 120, 142, 243, 324, *see also* Likert-format scale; Rasch analysis

Raudebush, S. W. 93, 101, 104, 106

RCTs (randomized controlled trials) 100, 106, 262, 270

reactive arrangements 253

recycling decisions study 174, 175, **176**, 177–179, **178**, *179*; decision tree in 176, 177–178, *177*; questions in 176, **178**; resolving errors in 180; validity of, testing 178–180, *180*

REDA (Research and Evaluation Data Application) 12, 319, 320, *see also* Dedoose

RefWorks 333, 335, 344
regression 77, 99, 100; bivariate linear 79, 80–81; independent/dependent variables in 77; logistic 14, 77, 79, 104; multiple linear 77, 79, 81, *see also* multiple linear regression analysis
Rehm, M. 214
Rencher, A. 85
research conceptualization phase 2, 355
researcher bias 163, 166, 253–254
retrospectivity 129
Richter, S. 39
Rientes, B. C. 214
Rihoux, B. 192
Roberts, E. 175, 176–177
Roberts, K. 114
Romney, A. K. 174
Rousseeuw, P. J. 62
Rubin, H. J./Rubin, I. S. 155
Runjags 112
Ruona, W. E. A. 279, 283, 285
Russell, P. 155
Ryan, G. W. 25, 174, 180, 279

S

Sackett, G. P. 126, 130
Saldaña, J. 1, 5, 106, 118, 144, 152, 154, 156–158, 160, 335, 336
Salmona, M. 320, 321, 329
sample integration validity 33
sample size 8, 17, 57, 70, 71, 80, 95–96, 101, 145, 173, 200, *358*; and Bayesian analysis 110, 111
Sandelowski, M. 77, 85, 96, 106, 159, 313, *368*
Sarstedt, M. 192
SAS 37, 38, 39, 40, **41**, 43–44, 89, 293
Satorra, A. 93
Sauer, H. 94
Sayago, S. 166, 168n7
SCED (single case experimental design) 111, 112, 113, 114
Scherman, V. 337
Schiffmann, S. S. 54
Schlösser, R. G. 94
Schmidt, L. A. 89
Schneider, C. Q. 192
Schneider, Florian 168
Schoeneberger, J. A. 104
Schoonenboom, J. 122
Schpecktor, A. 193
Schraw, G. 286
Schreiber, J. B. 93
Scott, J. 214
Scouvart, M. 187
Segers, K. 191–192
select perception subscale scores 14, 15
SEM (structural equation modeling) **6**, 9, 14, 15, 89–96; applications of 95; assumptions in 93; and CFA 9, 89, **90**, 91, *92*, 93; defined 89–90; empirical demonstration of 93–95; and goodness of fit 93, **94**; key terms in **90**; learning resources for 96; and LGM 89, **90**, 92–93, *92*, 95, 96; and LVSEM 89, **90**, 91, *92*;

and NLP/DL 93, 95, 96; and path analysis 89, 90, **90**, 91, *91*; sample size for 95–96; strengths/limitations of 95–96; suitability for MMR of 90–93, 93; symbols used in **91**; technical outline of 93; techniques 90–91, **91**
Sentencing Project 40
sentiment analysis 14, 27, 146–147, *147*, 220, 348
Seny Kan, K. A. 192
sequential analysis 4, **6**, 359, *359*, *360*, *see also* lag sequential analysis
sequential mixed analysis legitimation 17
set-theoretic methods (STMs) 2, 11, 185, 192, 193
Sharifi, H. 337
Sharma, K. 252
Shaw, E. K. 280, 282
Shaw, L. R. 74
Shevlin, M. 85
Shuk, E. 175
silhouette analysis 62, *62*, 63, *63*, 65
Silver, C. 317, 336, 340, 344, 354
similarity measuring 9, 15, 45, 52, *see also* cluster analysis
Simpson, A. 250
SimStat 12, 291, 292, 293
single case experimental design (SCED) 111, 112, 113, 114
single qualitizing **6**, 10, 143, 144
skewness/kurtosis coefficient 5, **6**, 7
Slate, J. R. 96, 136, 141
SMACOF 47, *49*, 55
Smit, B. 335, 337, 340
Smith, A. 301
Smith, R. N. 248
Smyth, P. 75
SNA (social network analysis) **6**, 11, 15, 193, 209–215; and contagion/diffusion 211; data analysis in 212–213; data collection in 212, *212*; defined 209–210; defining network (boundary-decision) in 211–212, 214; defining research questions in 211; empirical demonstration of 213; formal 210; and homophily/propinquity 210–211; learning resources for 214–215; and nodes/edges 209, 214; nominalist/realist approaches in 211; and one-/two-mode networks 209; roster/free recall methods in 212; and social capital 210; and sociocentric/egocentric networks 209, *210*, 211, 212; software for 212, 214–215; strengths/limitations of 213–214; suitability for MMR of 210–211; technical outline of 211–213
Snijders, T. 100, 106
Snow, John 39–40
social capital 210
social interaction 11
social media analytics **6**, 11–12, 93–94, 95, 219–225; and API 220, 221, 222, 294; applications of ontological imperative with 223; and data

analysis tools 225; and data visualisation 220; definition of ontological imperative with 219; empirical demonstration of ontological imperative with 221–223; and epistemologies 220, 221, 222, 223, 224, 225; and GIS 235; learning resources for ontological imperative with 225; and sentiment analysis 220, 225; and software 219–220, 293, 296, 300, 302, 331, 348; strengths/limitations of ontological imperative with 223–225; suitability for MMR of ontological imperative with 219–220; technical outline/five questions of ontological imperative with 220–221; *see also* Facebook; Twitter
social network analysis *see* SNA
social science research 12, 37, 45, 78, 89, 161; and HLM 100, 101, 105
socioeconomic status 40, 80, 85, 235, *see also* poverty
sociology 73, 74, 168n2
software 12, 227; space 219–220; *see also specific programs*
Soldevila, A. 74
Sondergeld, T. A. 121
Sorensen coefficient *see* Dice coefficient
South Africa 13–16, 146
Spain *see* Barcelona GIS case study
Spearman, C. 89
Spearman, Charles 201
Spillane, J. P. 66
sports/exercise research 73, 74, 125, 126, 135, 206
Spradley, J. 174
SPSS 13, **41**, 72, 200, 292, 293, 294, 307, 355–374; and 165, 167, 168n6; applications of 373, **374**; and ATLAS.ti 332, 338–339; defined 355; empirical demonstration/17 steps of 356–373, *358*–*369*; learning resources for 374; and NVivo 348, 353; strengths/limitations of 373–374; suitability for MMR of 356; technical outline of 356, **357**
Spybrook, J. 104
Stage, F. K. 93
Stahl, D. 67
Stainton-Rogers, R. 206
Stake, Robert 158
standard deviation 5, **6**, **7**, 84, 148, *365*; and Bayesian analysis 109, *110*, 111, 112, 113
STATA 89, 293, 294
statistical power 71, 80, 103–104, 106, 357, *365*–*366*, 373
Stefurak, T. 3
Steinberg, S. J./Steinberg, S. L. 230
Stelmack, J. 121
Stenner, P. 206
Stephenson, William 199, 201, 203, 204, 206, 207
Stevens, S. S. 110

Stewart, V. C. 121
STMs (set-theoretic methods) 2, 11, 185, 192, 193
Strauss, A. 321
structural coding 10, 152–153, 154
structural equation modeling *see* SEM
Strycker, L. A. 96
subjectivity 14; and cluster analysis 57, 61, 62; and MDS 45, 47, 51; measuring *see* Q methodology
Syes, Q. 38

T

t test 5, 100, 111, 148, 158, 356, **357**
T-pattern analysis *see* TPA
Tamás, P. 201
Tannen, Deborah 168
Tashakkori, A. 17, 77, 89, 142, 338, 356, *368*
Tatham, R. L. 17
Täuscher, K. 64
Taylor, Y. 45
TBL (team based learning) 28, 29, 30–33, *32*, **32**, *33*
Teddlie, C. 17, 38, 77, 126, 142, 338, 356, 361, *361*, *368*
tetrachoric correlation coefficients 14, 17
text mining 12, 14, 58, 59, 61, 146–147, **147**, 154, 167, 291, 293, 296, 299, 301
theme matrix 10
THEME/THEME Edu 10, 129, 133, 136
theory testing 89, 188, 189, 230
theory-building 151, 188, 189, 343, 353
therapy research 125, 126, **127**, 132, 200
thick data 12, 331
Thøgersen-Ntoumani, C. 66
Thomas, D. B. 206
Thomas, Dan 207
Thompson, B. 122
Thurstone, L. L. 89
time series analysis 69, 93, 111
Titscher, Stefan 167–168
Todd, R. W. 166
Tonkiss, F. 163, 164, 168
topic modeling 293, 298, *298*, 299, 300, *see also* FATM
Torgerson, W. S. 45, 47, 54
TOSMANA 186
total perception scale scores only 14, 15
tourism research 74–75
TPA (T-pattern analysis) 10, 127, **127**, 129, 131–132, *131*, *134*, 135–136
Tran, V. T. 119
transformative-emancipatory approach 2, 355
tree graph *see* dendrogram
Tres Turons, Parc dels *see* Barcelona GIS case study
triangulation 2, 78, 85n1, 148, 355, 361, *361*
Trimble, F. 159
Trochim, W. M. K. 52, 59
truth tables 11, 15, 185, 187, 188, 194n3
Tsaliki, L. 191–192
Tsogo, L. 46
Tudge, J. 117

Tufte, E. R. 39
Tukey, John W. 38
Tunisia 192
Twitter 95, 101, 106, 212, 228, 294, 296, 317; and ATLAS.ti 331, 333, 334–335; football fan demonstration of 220, 221–223; and GIS 235

U

UCINET 11, 214
United States (US) 39, 74, 154, 192; criminal justice system in 40–41, *40*, 44, **44**; education research in 13, 26, 66, 101–105, **278**, 280–282, *281*, 357–373, *372*, *373*; GIS research in 228, 234, 236; health/medical research in 65, 152–153, 173, 175, 176–177, **279**, 282; literacy research in 324, 325–327; and MDS media analysis 52–54, *53*; recycling study in *see* recycling decisions study
univariate analyses 5, **6**, 148
urban planning research 192, 206, 229, 234, *see also* Barcelona GIS case study

V

Vacha-Haase, T. 122
Valle, P. 74–75
values coding 5, **6**, 154, 335
Van de Bunt, G. G. 213
van de Vijver, F. J. R. 117
van Langenhove, L. 246
Van Thillo, M. 89
varimax rotation 9, 14, 201, **203**, 205, 298; and FATM 26, 28, 29, 31; and Q methodology 201, **203**, 204, **204**, 205, 206
VAS (visual analog scales) 262, *263*, 264, 265, 266, *266*, 267, 268, 273
vertical mixed analysis 3, 4
Vicari, S. 121
video data 13, 128, 305, 307, 320, 331, 344, 347
videogames 240, 241, 244
visual displays 9, 12, 38–39, 259, *364*, 370–371, *372*, *see also* crossover displays; joint displays
vocal behaviour 130
Vogt, W. P. 157–158, 160
Voils, C. I. 96, 106, 313
Volpato, R. 41
VOSviewer 146, **147**

W

Wagner, G. 94
Wainer, H. 38, 39, 40
Walker, J. 250
Walsh, M. 250
Wasserman, S. 214
Weick, K. E. 127
Weinbaum, R. 334, 335–336

Wellbeing project 344, 345–346, *345*, 347, 349, 350, *350*, 351, *351*, 352, *352*, 353, *353*
Weller, S. C. 174, 175, 180
Wertz, F. J. 122
West, S. G. 85
Wetherell, Margaret 164, 168, 168n3
Wheater, C. P. 38
whole systems approach 1, 4, 5, 10, 141
Widaman, K. F. 17
Widman, S. 250
Wilcox, R. 16
Wilson, M. 119, 121
Wish, M. 54
within-case analysis 1, **6**, 358–359, *359*
Wolcott, H. F. 335
Woodard, E. K. 159
Woods, M. 338
Woodside, A. G. 193
Woolf, N. H. 336, 340, 344, 354
WordStat 12, 167, 249, 331, *363*; applications of 302; and co-occurrence analysis 296–298, *297*; and comparison analysis 298–299, *299*; and document classification 300; empirical demonstration of 300–301, *302*; and exploratory text mining 296; extraction feature 9, 31, *31*; and FATM 25, 26, 27, 28, 29, 30–32, *30*, *31*, 33, 34; learning resources for 303; and MDS 46, 52; and mixed analysis 300; and QDA Miner, integration with 293, 300, 301; and quantitative content analysis 299; strengths/limitations of 302–303; suitability for MMR of 291; technical outline of 296–300; and topic modeling 298, *298*, 299
Wright, S. 89, 335

X

Xia, X. 193

Y

yoga research 155–156, 160
Younas, A. 286
Young, F. W. 54
Young, G. 54
Young, J. C. 174
YouTube 1, 18, 75, 128, 149, 255, 294, 303, 317
Yuan, K. H. 93

Z

Zeisel, H. 315
Zercher, C. 4
Zimmerman, L. 337
Zoran, A. G. 37, 245
Zotero 294, 333, 335, 344

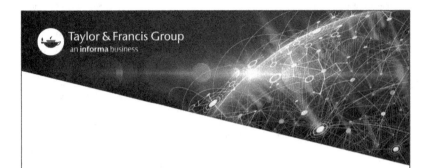